Data Structures and Program Design in C

Data Structures and Program Design in C

Robert L. Kruse
Saint Mary's University, Halifax, Nova Scotia

Bruce P. Leung
Center for Supercomputing Research and Development
University of Illinois at Urbana–Champaign

Clovis L. Tondo
International Business Machines Corporation
Center for Computer Science
Nova University, Ft. Lauderdale, Florida

Prentice Hall
Englewood Cliffs, New Jersey 07632

Library of Congress Cataloging-in-Publication Data

KRUSE, ROBERT LEROY
  Data Structures and Program Design in C /
  Robert L. Kruse, Bruce P. Leung, Clovis L. Tondo.
      p.   cm.
  Includes bibliographical references. Includes index.
  ISBN 0–13–725649–3
  1. C (Computer program language)   I. Leung, Bruce P.   II. Tondo, Clovis L.
  III. Title.
  QA76.73.C15K78 1991
  005.13'3—dc20   90–7161

Editorial production/supervision: *Kathleen Schiaparelli*
Interior design: *Kenny Beck*
Cover design: *Wanda Lubelska*
Manufacturing buyers: *Linda Behrens and Patrice Fraccio*
Page layout: *Rosemarie Paccione and Robert Kruse*

The typesetting for this book was done by the authors using PreTEX, a preprocessor and macro package for the TEX typesetting system and the POSTSCRIPT page-description language.
PreTEX is a trademark of Robert L. Kruse; TEX is a trademark of the American Mathematical Society; POSTSCRIPT is a registered trademark of Adobe Systems, Inc.

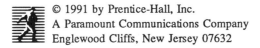

Printed in the United States of America

10

ISBN 0-13-725649-3

Prentice-Hall International (UK) Limited, *London*
Prentice-Hall of Australia Pty. Limited, *Sydney*
Prentice-Hall Canada Inc., *Toronto*
Prentice-Hall Hispanoamericana, S.A., *Mexico*
Prentice-Hall of India Private Limited, *New Delhi*
Prentice-Hall of Japan, Inc., *Tokyo*
Simon & Schuster Asia Pte. Ltd., *Singapore*
Editora Prentice-Hall do Brasil, Ltda., *Rio de Janeiro*

Contents

Preface

An apprentice carpenter may want only a hammer and a saw, but a master craftsman employs many precision tools. Computer programming likewise requires sophisticated tools to cope with the complexity of real applications, and only practice with these tools will build skill in their use. This book treats structured problem solving, the process of data abstraction and structuring, and the comparative study of algorithms as fundamental tools of program design. Several case studies of substantial size are worked out in detail, to show how all the tools are used together to build complete programs.

Many of the algorithms and data structures studied here possess an intrinsic elegance, a simplicity that cloaks the range and power of their applicability. Before long the student discovers that vast improvements can be made over the naive methods usually used in introductory courses. And yet this elegance of method is tempered with uncertainty. The student soon finds that it can be far from obvious which of several approaches will prove best in particular applications. Hence comes an early opportunity to introduce truly difficult problems of both intrinsic interest and practical importance and to exhibit the applicability of mathematical methods to algorithm verification and analysis.

The goal of programming is the construction of programs that are clear, complete, and functional. Many students, however, find difficulty in translating abstract ideas into practice. This book, therefore, takes special care in the formulation of ideas into algorithms and in the refinement of algorithms into concrete programs that can be applied to practical problems. The process of data specification and abstraction, similarly, comes before the selection of data structures and their implementations.

We believe in progressing from the concrete to the abstract, in the careful development of motivating examples, followed by the presentation of ideas in a more general form. At an early stage of their careers most students need reinforcement from seeing the immediate application of the ideas that they study, and they require the practice of writing and running programs to illustrate each important concept that they learn. This book therefore contains many sample programs, both short functions and complete programs of substantial length. The exercises and programming projects, moreover, constitute an indispensable part of this book. Many of these are immediate applications of the topic under study, often requesting that programs be written and run, so that algorithms may be tested and compared. Some are larger projects, and a few are suitable for use by a group of several students working together.

Synopsis

Programming Principles

By working through the first large project (Conway's game of Life), Chapter 1 expounds principles of top-down refinement, program design, review, and testing, principles that the student will see demonstrated and is expected to follow throughout the sequel. At the same time, this project provides an opportunity for the student to review the syntax of C, the programming language used throughout the book.

Introduction to Software Engineering

Chapter 2 introduces a few of the basic concerns of software engineering, including problem specification and analysis, prototyping, algorithm design, refinement, verification, and analysis. These topics are illustrated by the development of a second program for the Life game, one based on an algorithm that is sufficiently subtle as to show the need for precise specifications and verification, and one that shows why care must be taken in the choice of data structures.

Lists

The study of data structures begins in Chapter 3 with stacks, queues, and lists in contiguous implementation, always emphasizing the separation between the use of data structures and their implementation. Chapter 4 continues by studying the same data structures in linked implementations and culminates with a discussion of abstract data types. Compatible packages of C functions are developed for each implementation and are used in both large and small sample programs. The major goal of these chapters is to bring the student to appreciate data abstraction and to apply methods of top-down design to data as well as to algorithms.

Linked Lists

Searching

Tables and Information Retrieval

Sorting

Chapters 5, 6, and 7 present algorithms for searching, table access (including hashing), and sorting. These chapters illustrate the interplay between algorithms and the associated abstract data types, data structures, and implementations. The text introduces the "big Oh" notation for elementary algorithm analysis and highlights the crucial choices to be made regarding best use of space, time, and programming effort.

Mathematical Methods

These choices require that we find analytical methods to assess algorithms, and producing such analyses is a battle for which combinatorial mathematics must provide the arsenal. At an elementary level we can expect students neither to be well armed nor to possess the mathematical maturity needed to hone their skills to perfection. Our goal, therefore, is only to help students recognize the importance of such skills and be glad for later chances to study mathematics. Appendix A presents some necessary mathematics. Most of the topics in the appendix will be familiar to the well-prepared student, but are included to help with common deficiencies. The final two sections of Appendix A, on Fibonacci and Catalan numbers, are more advanced, are not needed for any vital purpose in the text, but are included to encourage combinatorial interest in the more mathematically inclined.

Recursion is a powerful tool, but one that is often misunderstood and sometimes used improperly. Some textbooks treat it as an afterthought, applying it only to trivial

Recursion

examples and apologizing for its alleged expense. Others give little regard to its pitfalls. We have therefore essayed to provide as balanced a treatment as possible. Whenever recursion is the natural approach it is used without hesitation. Its first use in this text is the second half of Chapter 7, where mergesort and quicksort are introduced. Chapter 8 (which may be read any time after stacks are defined) continues to study recursion in depth. It includes examples illustrating a broad range of applications, an exposition of the implementation of recursion, and guidelines for deciding whether recursion is or is not an appropriate method to employ.

Binary Trees

Binary trees are surely among the most elegant and useful of data structures. Their study, which occupies Chapter 9, ties together concepts from lists, searching, and sorting. At the same time, binary trees provide a natural example of recursively defined data structures, and therewith afford an excellent opportunity for the student to become more comfortable with recursion applied both to data structures and algorithms.

Trees and Graphs

Chapter 10 completes the study of data structures by collecting several important uses of multiway trees as data structures, including tries and B-trees, after which the chapter introduces graphs as more general structures useful for problem solving. The presentations in each major section of Chapter 10 are independent from each other.

Case Study: The Polish Notation

The case study in Chapter 11 examines the Polish notation in considerable detail, exploring the interplay of recursion, trees, and stacks as vehicles for problem solving and algorithm development. Some of the questions addressed can serve as an informal introduction to compiler design. Again, the algorithms are fully developed within a functioning C program. This program accepts as input an expression in ordinary (infix) form, translates the expression into postfix form, and evaluates the expression for specified values of the variable(s).

Removal of Recursion

Removal of recursion is a topic that, we hope, most programmers may soon no longer need to study. But at present much important work must be done in contexts (like FORTRAN or COBOL) disallowing recursion. Methods for manual recursion removal are therefore required, and are collected for reference as Appendix B. Some instructors will wish to include the study of threaded binary trees with Chapter 9; this section is therefore written so that it can be read independently of the remainder of Appendix B.

An Introduction to C

Appendix C, finally, is a brief introduction to the C programming language. This is not a thorough treatment of the language, but it is intended to serve as a review of C syntax and as a reference for the student.

Course Structure

prerequisite

The prerequisite for this book is a first course in programming, with experience using the elementary features of C. It is possible to introduce C concurrently if the students have had experience with a similar high level language such as Pascal. Chapter 2 includes a brief discussion of structures and Chapter 4 a study of pointers, in case students have not previously met these topics. A good knowledge of high school mathematics will suffice for almost all the algorithm analyses, but further (perhaps concurrent) preparation in discrete mathematics will prove valuable.

content

This book includes all the topics of the ACM Course CS 2 (*Program Design and Implementation*), with additional emphasis on data abstraction, data structures, algorithm analysis, and large case studies, so that it is also suitable for a version of Course CS 7

(*Data Structures and Algorithm Analysis*) that emphasizes program design along with implementations and applications of data structures. The book contains significantly more material than can usually be studied in a single term, and hence it allows flexibility in designing courses with different content and objectives.

CS 2   The core topics specified for ACM Course CS 2 occupy Chapters 1–8 and the first third of Chapter 9. A one-term course based closely on CS 2 will normally include almost all the content of these chapters, except for the more detailed algorithm analyses, verifications, and some of the sample programs. The later chapters include all the advanced optional topics suggested for possible inclusion in CS 2.

data structures   An elementary course on data structures and algorithms should consider Chapters 1 and 2 briefly (to look at the questions of data specification and time-space tradeoffs), emphasize Chapters 3–10, and select other topics if time permits.

CS 7   A more advanced course in Data Structures and Algorithm Analysis (ACM course CS 7) should begin with a brief review of the topics early in the book, placing special emphasis on data abstraction, algorithm analysis, and criteria for choosing data structures and algorithms under various conditions. The remaining chapters will then provide a solid core of material on data structures, algorithm design, and applications.

two-term course   A two-term course can cover the entire book, thereby attaining a satisfying integration of many of the topics from both of ACM courses CS 2 and CS 7. Students need time and practice to understand general methods. By combining the study of data abstraction, data structures, and algorithms with their implementation in projects of realistic size, an integrated course can build a solid foundation on which later, more theoretical courses can be built.

Even if it is not covered in its entirety, this book will provide enough depth to enable interested students to continue using it as a reference in later work. It is important in any case to assign major programming projects and to allow adequate time for their completion.

Further Features

- *Chapter Previews.*   Each chapter begins with an outline and a brief statement of goals and content to help the reader establish perspective.

- *Application Programs.*   The text includes several large, complete programs that illustrate principles of good software design and application of the methods developed in the text. Code reading is an important skill for a programmer, but one that is often neglected in textbooks.

- *Programming Precepts.*   Many principles of good programming are summarized with short, pithy statements that are well worth remembering.

- *Marginal Notes.*   Keywords and other important concepts are highlighted in the left margin, thereby allowing the reader to locate the principal ideas of a section without delay.

- *Pointers and Pitfalls.*   Each chapter of the book (except Chapter 11) contains a section giving helpful hints concerning problems of program design.

- *Exercises.*   Exercises appear not only at the ends of chapters but with almost every major section. These exercises help with the immediate reinforcement of the ideas of the section and develop further related ideas.

- *Projects.*   Programming projects also appear in most major sections. These include simple variations of programs appearing in the text, completion of projects begun in the text, and major new projects investigating questions posed in the text.

- *Review Questions.*   Each chapter (except Chapter 11) concludes with simple review questions to help the student collect and summarize the principal concepts of the chapter.

- *Instructor's Supplements.*   Instructors teaching from this book may obtain copies of the following materials:

  - The *Instructor's Resource Manual* contains teaching notes on each chapter, together with complete, detailed solutions to every exercise and programming project in the text. The manual also includes software disks with complete, running versions for every programming project in the text.

  - The *Transparency Masters* (several hundred in total) contain enlarged copies of almost all diagrams, program segments, and other important extracts from the text.

Acknowledgments

We are grateful to the many people—colleagues, students, friends, and family—who have contributed in numerous ways to the development of the Pascal version on which the current book is based. Some of these people are named in the preface to the Pascal Version. In addition, many more people have helped us produce the current C version.

BRIAN KERNIGHAN reviewed the entire manuscript with the greatest of care and provided us with many valuable comments and suggestions.

Further detailed reviews giving us much helpful information came from PHIL ADAMS (Nova University), ALAN J. FILIPSKI (Arizona State University), DAN HIRSCHBERG (University of California at Irvine), SAM HSU (Florida Atlantic University), GARY KNOTT (University of Maryland), DARREN MICLETTE (IBM), ANDREW NATHANSON (AGS Information Systems), TERRY SHORE (South Shore Enterprises), ED SIMCO (Nova University), MARTIN K. SOLOMON (Florida Atlantic University), CARLOS TONDO (South Shore Enterprises), and RED VISCUSO (IBM).

GERRY DIAZ, ROLLIE GUILD, ED SHOCKLEY, and EDEN YOUNT provided many helpful suggestions.

STEVEN MATHESON helped to develop the PreTEX typesetting system, including the software for typesetting C program listings.

We are grateful for the support of family and friends: ANNE ALDOUS, DAVE EGAN, CHRIS KING, ESTHER KRUSE, HOWARD and SHIRLEY LEUNG, JULIA MISTRELLO, DEEANNE SAFFORD, VICKI SHORE, and CAREN WEBSTER.

Finally, we owe much to our friends at Prentice Hall: our editor MARCIA HORTON (Editor in Chief for Computer Science and Engineering), JOHN WAIT, who suggested this project, supplements editor ALICE DWORKIN, marketing manager JENNIFER YOUNG, KATHLEEN SCHIAPARELLI and the production staff whose names appear on the copyright page, and all the others who have contributed to our work in many ways.

Data Structures and Program Design in C

C H A P T E R   1

Programming Principles

This chapter summarizes important principles of good programming, especially as applied to large projects, and illustrates methods for discovering effective algorithms. In the process we raise questions in program design that we shall address in later chapters, and review many of the special features of the language C by using them to write programs.

1.1 INTRODUCTION

The greatest difficulties of writing large computer programs are not in deciding what the goals of the program should be, nor even in finding methods that can be used to reach these goals. The president of a business might say, "Let's get a computer to keep track of all our inventory information, accounting records, and personnel files, and let it tell us when inventories need to be reordered and budget lines are overspent, and let it handle the payroll." With enough time and effort, a staff of systems analysts and programmers might be able to determine how various staff members are now doing these tasks and write programs to do the work in the same way.

problems of large programs

This approach, however, is almost certain to be a disastrous failure. While interviewing employees, the systems analysts will find some tasks that can be put on the computer easily and will proceed to do so. Then, as they move other work to the computer, they will find that it depends on the first tasks. The output from these, unfortunately, will not be quite in the proper form. Hence they need more programming to convert the data from the form given for one task to the form needed for another. The programming project begins to resemble a patchwork quilt. Some of the pieces are stronger, some weaker. Some of the pieces are carefully sewn onto the adjacent ones, some are barely tacked together. If the programmers are lucky, their creation may hold together well enough to do most of the routine work most of the time. But if any change must be made, it will have unpredictable consequences throughout the system. Later, a new request will come along, or an unexpected problem, perhaps even an emergency, and the programmers' efforts will prove as effective as using a patchwork quilt as a safety net for people jumping from a tall building.

purpose of book

The main purpose of this book is to describe programming methods and tools that will prove effective for projects of realistic size, programs much larger than those ordinarily used to illustrate features of elementary programming. Since a piecemeal approach to large problems is doomed to fail, we must first of all adopt a consistent, unified, and logical approach, and we must also be careful to observe important principles of program design, principles that are sometimes ignored in writing small programs, but whose neglect will prove disastrous for large projects.

problem specification

The first major hurdle in attacking a large problem is deciding exactly what the problem is. It is necessary to translate vague goals, contradictory requests, and perhaps unstated desires into a precisely formulated project that can be programmed. And the methods or divisions of work that people have previously used are not necessarily the best for use in a machine. Hence our approach must be to determine overall goals, but precise ones, and then slowly divide the work into smaller problems until they become of manageable size.

program design

The maxim that many programmers observe, "First make your program work, then make it pretty," may be effective for small programs, but not for large ones. Each part of a large program must be well organized, clearly written, and thoroughly understood, or else its structure will have been forgotten, and it can no longer be tied to the other parts of the project at some much later time, perhaps by another programmer. Hence we do not separate style from other parts of program design, but from the beginning we must be careful to form good habits.

Even with very large projects, difficulties usually arise not from the inability to find a solution but, rather, from the fact that there can be so many different methods *data structures*   and algorithms that might work that it can be hard to decide which is best, which may lead to programming difficulties, or which may be hopelessly inefficient. The greatest room for variability in algorithm design is generally in the way in which the data of the program are stored:

- How they are arranged in relation to each other.
- Which data are kept in memory.
- Which are calculated when needed.
- Which are kept in files, and how are the files arranged.

A second goal of this book, therefore, is to present several elegant, yet fundamentally simple ideas for the organization of data, and several powerful algorithms for important tasks within data processing, such as sorting and searching.

analysis   When there are several different ways to organize data and devise algorithms it becomes important to develop criteria to recommend a choice. Hence we devote attention to analyzing the behavior of algorithms under various conditions.

testing and verification   The difficulty of debugging a program increases much faster than its size. That is, if one program is twice the size of another, then it will likely not take twice as long to debug, but perhaps four times as long. Many very large programs (such as operating systems) are put into use still containing bugs that the programmers have despaired of finding, because the difficulties seem insurmountable. Sometimes projects that have consumed years of effort must be discarded because it is impossible to discover why they will not work. If we do not wish such a fate for our own projects, then we must use methods that will

program correctness
- Reduce the number of bugs, making it easier to spot those that remain.
- Enable us to verify in advance that our algorithms are correct.
- Provide us with ways to test our programs so that we can be reasonably confident that they will not misbehave.

Development of such methods is another of our goals, but one that cannot yet be fully within our grasp.

maintenance   Informal surveys show that, once a large and important program is fully debugged and in use, then less than half of the programming effort that will be invested altogether in the project will have been completed. *Maintenance* of programs, that is, modifications needed to meet new requests and new operating environments, takes, on average, more than half of the programming investment. For this reason, it is essential that a large project be written to make it as easy to understand and modify as possible.

1.2 THE GAME OF LIFE

If we may take the liberty to abuse an old proverb:

One concrete problem is worth a thousand unapplied abstractions.

case study   Throughout this chapter we shall concentrate on one case study that, while not large by realistic standards, illustrates both the methods of program design and the pitfalls that we should learn to avoid. Sometimes the example motivates general principles; sometimes the general discussion comes first; always it is with the view of discovering general methods that will prove their value in a range of practical applications. In later chapters we shall employ similar methods for much larger projects.

The example we shall use is the game called *Life*, which was introduced by the British mathematician J. H. CONWAY in 1970.

1.2.1 Rules for the Game of Life

definitions   Life is really a simulation, not a game with players. It takes place on an unbounded rectangular grid in which each cell can either be occupied by an organism or not. Occupied cells are called *alive*; unoccupied cells are called *dead*. Which cells are alive changes from generation to generation according to the number of neighboring cells that are alive, as follows:

transition rules   1. The neighbors of a given cell are the eight cells that touch it vertically, horizontally, or diagonally.

2. If a cell is alive but either has no neighboring cells alive or only one alive, then in the next generation the cell dies of loneliness.

3. If a cell is alive and has four or more neighboring cells also alive, then in the next generation the cell dies of overcrowding.

4. A living cell with either two or three living neighbors remains alive in the next generation.

5. If a cell is dead, then in the next generation it will become alive if it has exactly three neighboring cells, no more or fewer, that are already alive. All other dead cells remain dead in the next generation.

6. All births and deaths take place at exactly the same time, so that dying cells can help to give birth to another, but cannot prevent the death of others by reducing overcrowding, nor can cells being born either preserve or kill cells living in the previous generation.

1.2.2 Examples

As a first example, consider the community

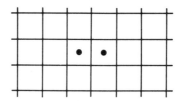

The counts of living neighbors for the cells are as follows:

moribund example

0	0	0	0	0	0
0	1	2	2	1	0
0	1	•1	•1	1	0
0	1	2	2	1	0
0	0	0	0	0	0

By rule 2 both the living cells will die in the coming generation, and rule 5 shows that no cells will become alive, so the community dies out.

On the other hand, the community

stability

0	0	0	0	0	0
0	1	2	2	1	0
0	2	•3	•3	2	0
0	2	•3	•3	2	0
0	1	2	2	1	0
0	0	0	0	0	0

has the neighbor counts as shown. Each of the living cells has a neighbor count of three, and hence remains alive, but the dead cells all have neighbor counts of two or less, and hence none of them becomes alive.

The two communities

alternation

0	0	0	0	0
1	2	3	2	1
1	•1	•2	•1	1
1	2	3	2	1
0	0	0	0	0

and

0	1	1	1	0
0	2	•1	2	0
0	3	•2	3	0
0	2	•1	2	0
0	1	1	1	0

continue to alternate from generation to generation, as indicated by the neighbor counts shown.

It is a surprising fact that, from very simple initial configurations, quite complicated progressions of Life communities can develop, lasting many generations, and it is usually *variety*   not obvious what changes will happen as generations progress. Some very small initial configurations will grow into large communities; others will slowly die out; many will reach a state where they do not change, or where they go through a repeating pattern every few generations.

popularity   Not long after its invention, MARTIN GARDNER discussed the Life game in his column in *Scientific American*, and, from that time on, it has fascinated many people, so that for several years there was even a quarterly newsletter devoted to related topics. It makes an ideal display for microcomputers.

Our first goal, of course, is to write a program that will show how an initial community will change from generation to generation.

1.2.3 The Solution

At most a few minutes' thought will show that the solution to the Life problem is so simple that it would be a good exercise for the members of a beginning programming class who had just learned about arrays. All we need to do is to set up a large rectangular *method*   array whose entries correspond to the Life cells and will be marked with the status of the cell, either alive or dead. To determine what happens from one generation to the next, we then need only count the number of living neighbors of each cell and apply the rules. Since, however, we shall be using loops to go through the array, we must be careful not to violate rule 6 by allowing changes made earlier to affect the count of neighbors for cells studied later. The easiest way to avoid this pitfall is to set up a second array that will represent the community at the next generation and, after it has been completely calculated, then make the generation change by copying it to the original array.

Next let us rewrite this method as the steps of an informal algorithm.

algorithm   Initialize an array called map to contain the initial configuration of living cells.

Repeat the following steps for as long as desired:

For each cell in the array do the following:

Count the number of living neighbors of the cell.

If the count is 0, 1, 4, 5, 6, 7, or 8, then set the corresponding cell in another array called newmap to be dead; if the count is 3, then set the corresponding cell to be alive; and if the count is 2, then set the corresponding cell to be the same as the cell in array map (since the status of a cell with count 2 does not change).

Copy the array newmap into the array map.

Print the array map for the user.

1.2.4 Life: The Main Program

The preceding outline of an algorithm for the game of Life translates into the following C program.

```
/* Simulation of Conway's game of Life on a bounded grid */
/* Version 1 */

#include "general.h"              /* common include files and definitions  */
#include "lifedef.h"              /* Life's defines and typedefs           */
#include "calls.h"                /* Life's function declarations          */

void main(void)
{
    int row, col;
    Grid_type map;                /* current generation                    */
    Grid_type newmap;             /* next generation                       */
```

initialization
```
    Initialize(map);
    WriteMap(map);
    do {
```
calculate changes
```
        for (row = 0; row < MAXROW; row++)
            for (col = 0; col < MAXCOL; col++)
                switch(NeighborCount(row, col, map)) {
                case 0:
                case 1:
                    newmap[row][col] = DEAD;
                    break;
                case 2:
                    newmap[row][col] = map[row][col];
                    break;
                case 3:
                    newmap[row][col] = ALIVE;
                    break;
                case 4:
                case 5:
                case 6:
                case 7:
                case 8:
                    newmap[row][col] = DEAD;
                    break;
                }
```
advance generation
```
        CopyMap(map, newmap);
        WriteMap(map);
    } while (Enquire());
}
```

Before we discuss the C program above we need to establish what is included with the
#include preprocessor command. There are three files: general.h, lifedef.h, and calls.h.

The file general.h contains the definitions and #include statements for the standard
files that appear in many programs and will be used throughout this book. The file
includes

```
#include <stdio.h>
#include <stdlib.h>
typedef enum boolean_tag { FALSE, TRUE } Boolean_type;

void Error(char *);
```

The function Error is a simple function we use throughout the book. Error displays an error message and terminates execution. Here is the function.

```
/* Error: print error message and terminate the program. */
void Error(char *s)
{
      fprintf(stderr, "%s\n", s);
      exit(1);
}
```

The file lifedef.h contains the definitions for the Life program:

```
#define MAXROW 50                    /* maximum number of rows       */
#define MAXCOL 80                    /* maximum number of columns    */
typedef enum status_tag { DEAD, ALIVE } Status_type;

typedef Status_type Grid_type[MAXROW][MAXCOL];
```

functions and calls.h contains the function prototypes for the Life program:

```
void CopyMap(Grid_type, Grid_type);
Boolean_type Enquire(void);
void Initialize(Grid_type);
int NeighborCount(int, int, Grid_type);
void WriteMap(Grid_type);
```

We create a new calls.h file with the function prototypes for each program we write. In this program we still must write the functions Initialize and WriteMap that will do the input and output, the function Enquire that will determine whether or not to go on to the next generation, the function CopyMap that will copy the updated grid, newmap, into map, and the function NeighborCount that will count the number of cells neighboring the one in row,col that are occupied in the array map. The program is entirely straightforward. First, we read in the initial situation to establish the first configuration of occupied cells. Then we commence a loop that makes one pass for each generation. Within this loop we first have a nested pair of loops on row and col that will run over all entries in the array map. The body of these nested loops consists of the one special statement

switch { ... },

which is a multiway selection statement. In the present application the function NeighborCount will return one of the values 0, 1, ..., 8, and for each of these cases we can take a separate action, or, as in our program, some of the cases may lead to the same action. You should check that the action prescribed in each case corresponds correctly to the rules 2, 3, 4, and 5 of Section 1.2.1. Finally, after using the nested loops and switch statement to set up the array newmap, the function CopyMap copies array newmap into array map, and the function WriteMap writes out the result.

Exercises
1.2

Determine by hand calculation what will happen to each of the communities shown in Figure 1.1 over the course of five generations. [*Suggestion*: Set up the Life configuration on a checkerboard. Use one color of checkers for living cells in the current generation and a second color to mark those that will be born or die in the next generation.]

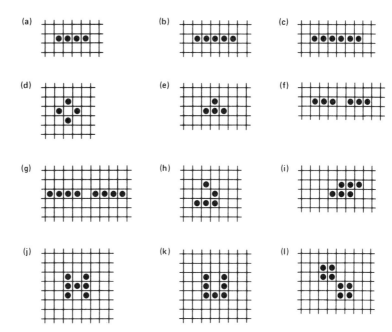

Figure 1.1. Life configurations

1.3 PROGRAMMING STYLE

Before we turn to writing the functions for the Life game, let us pause to consider several principles that we should be careful to employ in programming.

1.3.1 Names

In the story of creation (Genesis 2 : 19), God brought all the animals to ADAM to see what names he would give them. According to an old Jewish tradition, it was only when ADAM had named an animal that it sprang to life. This story brings an important moral to computer programming: Even if data and algorithms exist before, it is only when they are given meaningful names that their places in the program can be properly recognized and appreciated, that they first acquire a life of their own.

purpose of
careful naming

For a program to work properly it is of the utmost importance to know exactly what each variable represents, and to know exactly what each function does. Documentation explaining the variables and functions should therefore always be included. The names of variables and functions should be chosen with care so as to identify their meanings clearly and succinctly. Finding good names is not always an easy task, but is important enough to be singled out as our first programming precept:

Programming Precept

Always name your variables and functions
with the greatest care, and explain them thoroughly.

C requires declarations for local variables and arguments. Constants used in a program can be given names through enumerators or symbolic constants.

The careful choice of names can go a long way in clarifying a program and in helping to avoid misprints and common errors. Some guidelines are

guidelines
1. Give special care to the choice of names for functions, constants, symbolic constants, and all global variables and types used in different parts of the program. These names should be meaningful and should suggest clearly the purpose of the function, variable, and the like.

2. Keep the names simple for variables used only briefly and locally. A single letter is often a good choice for the variable controlling a for loop, but would be a poor choice for a function or for a variable used three or four times in widely separated parts of the program.

3. Use common prefixes or suffixes to associate names of the same general category. The files used in a program, for example, might be called

    InputFile   TransactionFile   TotalFile   OutFile   RejectFile

4. Avoid deliberate misspellings and meaningless suffixes to obtain different names. Of all the names

    index   indx   ndex   indexx   index2   index3

    only one (the first) should normally be used. When you are tempted to introduce multiple names of this sort, take it as a sign that you should think harder and devise names that better describe the intended use.

5. Avoid choosing cute names whose meaning has little or nothing to do with the problem. The statements

    ```
    while (tv == HOCK)
        Study( );
    if (!sleepy)
        Play( );
    else
        Nap( );
    ```

    may be funny but they are bad programming!

6. Avoid choosing names that are close to each other in spelling or otherwise easy to confuse.

7. Be careful in the use of the letter "l" (small ell), "O" (capital oh) and "0" (zero). Within words or numbers these usually can be recognized from the context, and cause no problem, but "l" and "O" should never be used alone as names. Consider the examples

$$l = 1; \qquad x = 1; \qquad x = l; \qquad x = O; \qquad O = 0;$$

1.3.2 Documentation and Format

Most students initially regard documentation as a chore that must be endured, after a program is finished, to ensure that the marker and instructor can read it, so that no credit will be lost for obscurity. The author of a small program indeed can keep all the details in his head, and so needs documentation only to explain the program to someone else. With large programs (and with small ones after some months have elapsed), it becomes impossible to remember how every detail relates to every other, and therefore to write large programs, it is essential that appropriate documentation be prepared along with each small part of the program. A good habit is to prepare documentation as the program is being written, and an even better one, as we shall see later, is to prepare part of the documentation before starting to write the program.

the purpose of documentation

Not all documentation is appropriate. Almost as common as programs with little documentation or only cryptic comments are programs with verbose documentation that adds little to understanding the program. Hence our second programming precept:

Programming Precept

Keep your documentation concise but descriptive.

The style of documentation, as with all writing styles, is highly personal, and many different styles can prove effective. There are, nonetheless, some commonly accepted guidelines that should be respected:

guidelines

1. Place a prologue at the beginning of each function including

   a. Identification (programmer's name, date, version number).
   b. Statement of the purpose of the function and method used.
   c. The changes the function makes and what data it uses.
   d. Reference to further documentation external to the program.

2. When each variable, constant, or type is declared, explain what it is and how it is used. Better still, make this information evident from the name.

3. Introduce each significant section of the program with a comment stating briefly its purpose or action.

4. Indicate the end of each significant section if it is not otherwise obvious.

5. Avoid comments that parrot what the code does, such as

count++;   /* *Increase counter by 1.* */

or that are meaningless jargon, such as

/* *horse string length into correctitude* */

(This example was taken directly from a systems program.)

6. Explain any statement that employs a trick or whose meaning is unclear. Better still, avoid such statements.

7. The code itself should explain *how* the program works. The documentation should explain *why* it works and *what* it does.

8. Whenever a program is modified, be sure that the documentation is correspondingly modified.

format   Spaces, blank lines, and indentation in a program are an important form of documentation. They make the program easy to read, allow you to tell at a glance which parts of the program relate to each other, where the major breaks occur, and precisely which statements are contained in each loop or each alternative of a conditional statement. There are many systems (some automated) for indentation and spacing, all with the goal of making it easier to determine the structure of the program.

A C beautifier, usually named cb, is a system utility that reads a C program moving the text between lines and adjusting the indentation so as to improve the appearance of the program and make its structure more obvious. The utility cb was originally available on UNIX. If a C beautifier is available on your system, you might experiment with it to see if it helps the appearance of your programs.

consistency   Because of the importance of good format for programs, you should settle on some reasonable rules for spacing and indentation and use your rules consistently in all the programs you write. Consistency is essential if the system is to be useful in reading programs. Many professional programming groups decide on a uniform system and insist that all the programs they write conform. Some classes or student programming teams do likewise. In this way, it becomes much easier for one programmer to read and understand the work of another.

Programming Precept

The reading time for programs is much more than the writing time.
Make reading easy to do.

1.3.3 Refinement and Modularity

problem solving   Computers do not solve problems; people do. Usually the most important part of the process is dividing the problem into smaller problems that can be understood in more detail. If these are still too difficult, then they are subdivided again, and so on. In *subdivision*

any large organization the top management cannot worry about every detail of every activity; the top managers must concentrate on general goals and problems and delegate specific responsibilities to their subordinates. Again, middle-level managers cannot do everything: They must subdivide the work and send it to other people. So it is with computer programming. Even when a project is small enough that one person can take it from start to finish, it is most important to divide the work, starting with an overall understanding of the problem, dividing it into subproblems, and attacking each of these in turn without worrying about the others.

Let us restate this principle with a classic proverb:

Programming Precept

Don't lose sight of the forest for its trees.

---

top-down refinement

This principle, called ***top-down refinement***, is the real key to writing large programs that work. The principle implies the postponement of detailed consideration, but not the postponement of precision and rigor. It does not mean that the main program becomes some vague entity whose task can hardly be described. On the contrary, the main program will send almost all the work out to various functions, and as we write the main program

specifications

(which we should do first), we decide *exactly* how the work will be divided among them. Then, as we later work on a particular function, we shall know before starting exactly what it is expected to do.

It is often not easy to decide exactly how to divide the work into functions, and sometimes a decision once made must later be modified. Even so, two guidelines can help in deciding how to divide the work:

Programming Precept

Each function should do only one task, but do it well.

That is, we should be able to describe the purpose of a function succinctly. If you find yourself writing a long paragraph to specify the task of a function, then either you are giving too much detail (that is, you are writing the function before it is time to do so) or you should rethink the division of work. The function itself will undoubtedly contain many details, but they should not appear until the next stage of refinement.

Programming Precept

Each function should hide something.

A middle-level manager in a large company does not pass on everything he receives from his departments to his superior; he summarizes, collates, and weeds out the information, handles many requests himself, and sends on only what is needed at the upper levels. Similarly, he does not transmit everything he learns from higher management to his subordinates. He transmits to each person only what he needs to do his job. The functions we write should do likewise.

One of the most important parts of the refinement process is deciding exactly what the task of each function is, specifying precisely what its input will be and what result it will produce. Errors in these specifications are among the most frequent program bugs and are among the hardest to find. First, the data used in the function must be precisely specified. These data are of five kinds:

parameters

- *Input parameters* are used by the function but are not changed by the function. In C, input parameters are usually passed by value; that is, a copy of the parameter is passed to the function. (Exception: Arrays are always passed by reference; that is, the address of the array is passed to the function.)

- *Output parameters* contain the results of the calculations from the function. In C, output parameters must be passed by reference.

- *Inout parameters* are used for both input and output; the initial value of the parameter is used and then modified by the function. In C, inout parameters must be passed by reference.

variables

- *Local variables* are declared in the function and exist only while the function is being executed. They are not initialized before the function begins and are discarded when the function ends.

- *Global variables* are used in the function but not defined in the function. It can be quite dangerous to use global variables in a function, since after the function is written its author may forget exactly what global variables were used and how. If the main program is later changed, then the function may mysteriously begin to misbehave. If a function alters the value of a global variable it is said to cause a *side*

side effects

effect. Side effects are even more dangerous than using global variables as input to the function because side effects may alter the performance of other functions, thereby misdirecting the programmer's debugging efforts to a part of the program that is already correct.

Programming Precept

Keep your connections simple. Avoid global variables whenever possible.

Programming Precept

Never cause side effects.
If you must use global variables as input, document them thoroughly.

In the case of a function that returns a non-void value, the definition of *side effect* is further expanded to include changes made to parameters as well as global variables. A function typically returns one result. When a function does not return a result the function should be of type void. When the function returns a result then the function should have a type qualifier that indicates the type of result being returned. If a function needs to produce more than one result, then some of the parameters should be passed by reference and the function should be of type void.

before and after
conditions
The second way in which the specifications of a function should be made precise is in describing the action of the function. The documentation should include a statement of exactly what conditions the function expects to find when it is started. These are called the **preconditions** for the function. The documentation should also indicate what changes the function will make, and therefore what conditions will hold after the function finishes. These are called the **postconditions** for the function.

While all these principles of top-down design may seem almost self-evident, the only way to learn them thoroughly is by practice. Hence throughout this book we shall be careful to apply them to the large programs that we write, and in a moment it will be appropriate to return to our first example project.

Exercises 1.3

E1. Rewrite the following function so that it accomplishes the same result in a less tricky way.

```
void DoesSomething (int *first, int *second)
{
        *first = *second − *first;
        *second = *second − *first;
        *first = *second + *first;
}
```

E2. Determine what each of the following functions does. Rewrite each function with meaningful variable names, with better format, and without unnecessary variables and statements.

mystery functions

a.
```
#define MAXINT 100
int Calculate (int apple, int orange)
{ int peach, lemon;
peach = 0; lemon = 0; if (apple < orange) {
peach = orange; } else if (orange <= apple) {
peach = apple; } else { peach = MAXINT; lemon = MAXINT;
} if (lemon != MAXINT) { return (peach); } }
```

b.
```
double Figure (double vector1 [ ], int n)
{ int loop1; double loop2; double loop3; int loop4;
loop1 = 0; loop2 = vector1 [loop1]; loop3 = 0.0;
loop4 = loop1; for (loop4 = 0; loop4 < n; loop4 = loop4 + 1)
{ loop1 = loop1 + 1; loop2 = vector1 [loop1 − 1];
loop3 = loop2 + loop3; } loop2 = loop1;
loop2 = loop3/loop2; return (loop2); }
```

c.
```
void Question (int *a17, int *stuff)
{ int another, yetanother, stillonemore;
another = yetanother; stillonemore = *a17;
yetanother = *stuff; another = stillonemore; *a17 = yetanother;
stillonemore = yetanother;
*stuff = another; another = yetanother; yetanother = *stuff; }
```

d. int Mystery (int apple, int orange, int peach)
   { if (apple > orange) if (apple > peach) if
   (peach > orange) return (peach); else if (apple < orange)
   return (apple); else return (orange); else return (apple); else
   if (peach > apple) if (peach > orange) return (orange); else
   return (peach); else return (apple); }

nested if statements

E3. The following statement is designed to check the relative sizes of three integers, which you may assume to be different from each other:

```
if (x < z) if (x < y) if (y < z) c = 1; else c = 2; else
if (y < z) c = 3; else c = 4; else if (x < y)
if (x < z) c = 5; else c = 6; else if (y < z) c = 7; else
if (z < x) if (z < y) c = 8; else c = 9; else c = 10;
```

   a. Rewrite this statement in a form that is easier to read.
   b. Since there are only six possible orderings for the three integers, only six of the ten cases can actually occur. Find those that can never occur, and eliminate the redundant checks.
   c. Write a simpler, shorter statement that accomplishes the same result.

cube roots

E4. The following C function calculates the cube root of a real number (by the NEWTON approximation), using the fact that, if y is one approximation to the cube root of x, then

$$z = \frac{2y + x/y^2}{3}$$

is a closer approximation.

```
double Fcn (double stuff)
{ double april, tim, tiny, shadow, tom, tam, square;
Boolean_type flag;
tim = stuff; tam = stuff; tiny = 0.00001;
if (stuff != 0) do { shadow = tim + tim;
square = tim * tim;
tom = (shadow + stuff/square);
april = tom/3;
if (april * april * april − tam > −tiny)
if (april * april * april − tam < tiny) flag = TRUE;
else flag = FALSE; else flag = FALSE;
if (flag == FALSE) tim = april; else tim = tam; }
while (flag == FALSE);
if (stuff == 0) return (stuff); else return (april); }
```

   a. Rewrite this function with meaningful variable names, without the extra variables that contribute nothing to the understanding, with a better layout, and without the redundant and useless statements.
   b. Write a function for calculating the cube root of x directly from the mathematical formula, by starting with the assignment y = x and then repeating

$$y = (2*y + x/(y*y))/3$$

until fabs(y*y*y − x) <= 0.00001.

c. Which of these tasks is easier?

statistics

E5. The **mean** of a sequence of real numbers is their sum divided by the count of numbers in the sequence. The (population) **variance** of the sequence is the mean of the squares of all numbers in the sequence, minus the square of the mean of the numbers in the sequence. The **standard deviation** is the square root of the variance. Write a well-structured C function to calculate the standard deviation of a sequence of n numbers, where n is a constant and the numbers are in an array indexed from 0 to $n − 1$, where n is a parameter to the function. Write, then use, subsidiary functions to calculate the mean and variance.

plotting

E6. Design a program that will plot a given set of points on a graph. The input to the program will be a text file, each line of which contains two numbers that are the x and y coordinates of a point to be plotted. The program will use a routine to plot one such pair of coordinates. The details of the routine involve the specific method of plotting and cannot be written since they depend on the requirements of the plotting equipment, which we do not know. Before plotting the points the program needs to know the maximum and minimum values of x and y that appear in its input file. The program should therefore use another routine Bounds that will read the whole file and determine these four maxima and minima. Afterward, another routine is used to draw and label the axes; then the file can be reset and the individual points plotted.

a. Write the main program, not including the routines.
b. Write the function Bounds.
c. Write the header lines for the remaining functions together with appropriate documentation showing their purposes and their requirements.

1.4 CODING, TESTING, AND FURTHER REFINEMENT

The three processes in the title above go hand-in-hand and must be done together. Yet it is important to keep them separate in our thinking, since each requires its own approach and method. **Coding**, of course, is the process of writing an algorithm in the correct syntax (grammar) of a computer language like C, and **testing** is the process of running the program on sample data chosen to find errors if they are present. For further refinement, we turn to the functions not yet written and repeat these steps.

1.4.1 Stubs

early debugging and testing

After coding the main program, most programmers will wish to complete the writing and coding of the functions as soon as possible, to see if the whole project will work. For a project as small as the Life game, this approach may work, but for larger projects, writing and coding all the functions will be such a large job that, by the time it is complete, many of the details of the main program and functions that were written early will have been forgotten. In fact, different people may be writing different functions, and some of those who started the project may have left it before all functions are written. It is much easier to understand and debug a program when it is fresh in your mind. Hence, for larger projects, it is much more efficient to debug and test each function as soon as it is written than it is to wait until the project has been completely coded.

Even for smaller projects, there are good reasons for debugging functions one at a time. We might, for example, be unsure of some point of C syntax that will appear in several places through the program. If we can compile each function separately, then we shall quickly learn to avoid errors in syntax in later functions. As a second example, suppose that we have decided that the major steps of the program should be done in a certain order. If we test the main program as soon as it is written, then we may find that sometimes the major steps are done in the wrong order, and we can quickly correct the problem, doing so more easily than if we waited until the major steps were perhaps obscured by the many details contained in each of them.

stubs   To compile the program correctly, there must be something in the place of each function that is used, and hence we must put in short, dummy functions, called **stubs**. The simplest stubs are those that do nothing at all:

```
/* Initialize: initialize grid map. */
void Initialize (Grid_type map)
{
}
/* WriteMap: write grid map. */
void WriteMap (Grid_type map)
{
}
/* NeighborCount: count neighbors of row,col. */
int NeighborCount (int row, int col, Grid_type map)
{
        return 1;
}
```

Even with these stubs we can at least compile the program and make sure that the declarations of types and variables are syntactically correct. Normally, however, each stub should print a message stating that the function was invoked. When we execute the program, we find that some variables are used without initialization, and hence, to avoid these errors, we can add code to function Initialize. Hence the stub can slowly grow and be refined into the final form of the function. For a small project like the Life game, we can simply write each function in turn, substitute it for its stub, and observe the effect on program execution.

1.4.2 Counting Neighbors

function   Let us now refine our program further. The function that counts neighbors of the cell
NeighborCount   in row, col requires that we look in the eight adjoining positions. We shall use a pair of for loops to do this, one running usually from row − 1 to row + 1 and the other usually from col − 1 to col + 1. We need to be careful, when row, col is on a boundary of the grid, that we look only at legitimate positions in the grid. To do so we introduce four

variables for the lower and upper limits of the loops, and make sure that they remain within range. Since the loops will incorrectly consider that the cell in position row, col is a neighbor of itself, we must make a correction after completing the loops.

```
/* NeighborCount: count neighbors of row,col. */
int NeighborCount(int row, int col, Grid_type map)
{
        int i, j;                        /* loop indices for row, column          */
        int rlow, rhigh;                 /* limits for row loop                   */
        int clow, chigh;                 /* limits for column loop                */
        int count;                       /* Count neighbors.                      */

        if (row <= 0)                    /* Determine the boundaries.             */
               rlow = 0;
        else
               rlow = row − 1;
        if (row >= MAXROW − 1)
               rhigh = MAXROW − 1;
        else
               rhigh = row + 1;
        if (col <= 0)
               clow = 0;
        else
               clow = col − 1;
        if (col >= MAXCOL − 1)
               chigh = MAXCOL − 1;
        else
               chigh = col + 1;
        count = 0;                       /* Nested loops count neighbors.         */
        for (i = rlow; i <= rhigh; i++)
               for (j = clow; j <= chigh; j++)
                      if (map [i] [j]  ==  ALIVE)
                             count++;
        if (map [row] [col]  ==  ALIVE)
               count−−;
        return count;
}
```

1.4.3 Input and Output

*careful input
and output*

It now remains only to write the functions Initialize, WriteMap, and Enquire that do the input and output. In computer programs designed to be used by many people, the functions performing input and output are often the longest. Input to the program must be fully checked to be certain that it is valid and consistent, and errors in input must be processed in ways to avoid catastrophic failure or production of ridiculous results.

The output must be carefully organized and formatted, with considerable thought to what should or should not be printed, and with provision of various alternatives to suit differing circumstances.

1. Initialization

The task that function Initialize must accomplish is to set the map to its initial configuration. To initialize the map, we could consider each possible coordinate pair separately *input method* and request the user to indicate whether the cell is to be occupied or not. This method would require the user to type in MAXROW ∗ MAXCOL = 50 ∗ 80 = 4000 entries, which is prohibitive. Hence, instead, we input only those coordinate pairs corresponding to initially occupied cells.

```
/* Initialize: initialize grid map. */
void Initialize (Grid_type map)
{
        int row, col;                           /* coordinates of a cell              */
        printf ("This program is a simulation of the game of Life.\n");
        for (row = 0; row < MAXROW; row++)
            for (col = 0; col < MAXCOL; col++)
                map [row] [col] = DEAD;
        printf ("On each line give a pair of coordinates for a living cell.\n");
        printf ("Terminate the list with the special pair −1 −1\n");
        scanf ("%d %d", &row, &col);
        while (row != −1 || col != −1) {
            if (row >= 0 && row < MAXROW && col >= 0 && col < MAXCOL)
                map [row] [col] = ALIVE;
            else
                printf ("Values are not within range.\n");
            scanf ("%d %d", &row, &col);
        }
}
```

output   For the output function WriteMap we adopt the simple method of writing out the entire array at each generation, with occupied cells denoted by ∗ and empty cells by dashes.

```
/* WriteMap: write grid map. */
void WriteMap (Grid_type map)
{
        int row, col;
        printf ("\n\n");
        for (row = 0; row < MAXROW; row++) {
            for (col = 0; col < MAXCOL; col++)
                if (map [row] [col] ==  ALIVE)
                        printf ("*");
                else
                        printf (" − ");
            printf ("\n");
        }
}
```

The function CopyMap copies newmap into map.

```
/* CopyMap: copy newmap into map. */
void CopyMap(Grid_type map, Grid_type newmap)
{
      int row, col;
      for (row = 0; row < MAXROW; row++)
            for (col = 0; col < MAXCOL; col++)
                  map[row][col] = newmap[row][col];
}
```

response from user   Finally comes the function Enquire that determines whether the user wishes to go on to calculate the next generation. The task of Enquire is to ask the user to respond yes or no; to make the program more tolerant of mistakes in input, this request is placed in a loop, and Enquire waits for a valid response.

```
/* Enquire: TRUE if the user wants to continue execution. */
Boolean_type Enquire(void)
{
    int c;
    do {
        printf("Continue (y,n)?\n");
        while ((c = getchar()) == '\n')
            ;                                  /* Ignore the new line character.        */
    } while (c != 'y' && c != 'Y' && c != 'n' && c != 'N');
    if (c == 'y' || c == 'Y')
        return TRUE;
    else
        return FALSE;
}
```

At this point, we have all functions for the Life simulation. It is time to pause and check that it works.

1.4.4 Drivers

separate debugging   For small projects, each function is usually inserted in its proper place as soon as it is written, and the resulting program can then be debugged and tested as far as possible. For large projects, however, compilation of the entire project can overwhelm that of a new function being debugged, and it can be difficult to tell, looking only at the way the whole program runs, whether a particular function is working correctly or not. Even in small projects the output of one function may be used by another in ways that do not immediately reveal whether the information transmitted is correct.

One way to debug and test a single function is to write a short auxiliary program whose purpose is to provide the necessary input for the function, call it, and evaluate the
driver program   result. Such an auxiliary program is called a ***driver*** for the function. By using drivers,

each function can be isolated and studied by itself, and thereby bugs can often be spotted quickly.

As an example, let us write drivers for the functions of the Life project. First, we consider the function NeighborCount. In the main program its output is used, but has not been directly displayed for our inspection, so we should have little confidence that it is correct. To test NeighborCount we shall supply it with the array map, call it for each entry of the array, and write out the results. The resulting driver hence uses function Initialize to set up the array and bears some resemblance to the original main program.

```
/* Driver: test NeighborCount( ). */
void main (void)
{
        Grid_type map;
        int i, j;

        Initialize (map);
        for (i = 0; i < MAXROW; i++) {
                for (j = 0; j < MAXCOL; j++)
                        printf ("%3d", NeighborCount (i, j, map));
                printf ("\n");
        }
}
```

Sometimes two functions can be used to check each other. The easiest way, for example, to check functions Initialize and WriteMap is to use a driver whose declarations are those of the main program, and whose action part is

```
Initialize (map);
WriteMap (map);
```

Both functions can be tested by running this driver and making sure that the configuration printed is the same as that given as input.

1.4.5 Program Tracing

group discussion

After the functions have been tested, it is time to check out the complete program. One of the most effective ways to uncover hidden defects is called a ***structured walkthrough***. In this the programmer shows the completed program to another programmer or a small group of programmers and explains exactly what happens, beginning with an explanation of the main program followed by the functions, one by one. Structured walkthroughs are helpful for three reasons. First, programmers who are not familiar with the actual code can often spot bugs or conceptual errors that the original programmer overlooked. Second, the questions that other people ask can help you to clarify your own thinking and discover your own mistakes. Third, the structured walkthrough often suggests tests that prove useful in later stages of software production.

It is unusual for a large program to run correctly the first time it is executed as a whole, and if it does not, it may not be easy to determine exactly where the errors are. On many systems sophisticated ***trace tools*** are available to keep track of function calls, changes of variables, and so on. A simple and effective debugging tool, however,

printf *statements*
for debugging

is to take **snapshots** of program execution by inserting printf statements surrounded by #ifdefs at key points in the program. A message can be printed each time a function is called, and the values of important variables can be printed before and after each function is called. Such snapshots can help the programmer converge quickly on the particular location where an error is occurring. **Scaffolding** is another term frequently used to describe code inserted into a program to help with debugging. Never hesitate to put scaffolding into your programs as you write them; it will be easy to recompile the code without the printf statements by not defining certain flags at compile time, and it may save you much grief during debugging.

For very large programs yet another tool is sometimes used. This is a **static analyzer**, a program that examines the source program (as written in C, for example) looking for uninitialized or unused variables, sections of the code that can never be reached, and other occurrences that are probably incorrect. One example is the UNIX utility lint. This utility finds portability problems, performs type checking more strictly than the compiler, and finds problems that are difficult to see. If a version of lint is available on your system you might want to run you code through it and check the warnings it may give.

1.4.6 Principles of Program Testing

choosing test data

So far we have said nothing about the choice of data to be used to test programs and functions. This choice, of course, depends intimately on the project under development, so we can make only some general remarks. First we should note:

Programming Precept

The quality of test data is more important than its quantity.

Many sample runs that do the same calculations in the same cases provide no more effective a test than one run.

Programming Precept

Program testing can be used to show the presence of bugs,
but never their absence.

It is possible that other cases remain that have never been tested even after many sample runs. For any program of substantial complexity, it is impossible to perform exhaustive tests, yet the careful choice of test data can provide substantial confidence in the program. Everyone, for example, has great confidence that the typical computer can add two floating-point numbers correctly, but this confidence is certainly not based on testing the computer by having it add all possible floating-point numbers and checking the results. If a double-precision floating-point number takes 64 bits, then there are 2^{128} distinct pairs of numbers that could be added. This number is astronomically large: All computers manufactured to date have performed altogether but a tiny fraction of this number of additions. Our confidence that computers add correctly is based on tests of each component separately, that is, by checking that each of the 64 digits is added correctly, and that carrying from one place to another is done correctly.

testing methods

　　　　There are at least three general philosophies that are used in the choice of test data.

1. The Black-Box Method

Most users of a large program are not interested in the details of its functioning; they only wish to obtain answers. That is, they wish to treat the program as a black box; hence the name of this method. Similarly, test data should be chosen according to the specifications of the problem, without regard to the internal details of the program, to check that the program operates correctly. At a minimum the test data should be selected in the following ways:

data selection

1. *Easy values*. The program should be debugged with data that are easy to check. More than one student who tried a program only for complicated data, and thought it worked properly, has been embarrassed when the instructor tried a trivial example.

2. *Typical, realistic values*. Always try a program on data chosen to represent how the program will be used. These data should be sufficiently simple so that the results can be checked by hand.

3. *Extreme values*. Many programs err at the limits of their range of applications. It is very easy for counters or array bounds to be off by one.

4. *Illegal values*. "Garbage in, garbage out" is an old saying that should not be respected in computer circles. When a good program has garbage coming in, then its output should at least be a sensible error message. It is preferable that the program should provide some indication of the likely errors in input and perform any calculations that remain possible after disregarding the erroneous input.

2. The Glass-Box Method

The second approach to choosing test data begins with the observation that a program can hardly be regarded as thoroughly tested if there are some parts of its code that, in fact, have never been executed. In the *glass-box* method of testing, the logical structure of the program is examined, and for each alternative that may occur, test data are devised that will lead to that alternative. Thus care is taken to choose data to check each possibility in every switch statement, each clause of every if statement, and the termination condition of each loop. If the program has several selection or iteration statements then it will require different combinations of test data to check all the paths that are possible. Figure 1.2 shows a short program segment with its possible execution paths.

path testing

For a large program the glass-box approach is clearly not practicable, but for a single small module, it is an excellent debugging and testing method. In a well-designed program, each module will involve few loops and alternatives. Hence only a few well-chosen test cases will suffice to test each module on its own.

modular testing

In glass-box testing, the advantages of modular program design become evident. Let us consider a typical example of a project involving 50 functions, each of which can involve 5 different cases or alternatives. If we were to test the whole program as one, we would need 5^{50} test cases to be sure that each alternative was tested. Each module separately requires only 5 (easier) test cases, for a total of $5 \times 50 = 250$. Hence a problem of impossible size has been reduced to one that, for a large program, is of quite modest size.

comparison

Before you conclude that glass-box testing is always the preferable method, we should comment that, in practice, black-box testing is usually more effective in uncovering errors. Perhaps one reason is that the most subtle programming errors often occur

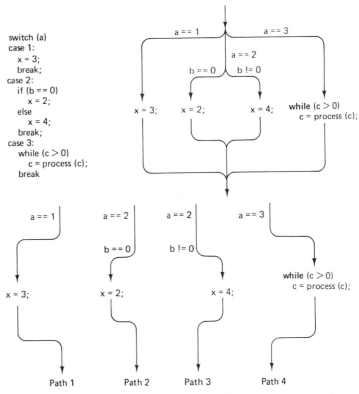

```
switch (a)
case 1:
  x = 3;
  break;
case 2:
  if (b == 0)
    x = 2;
  else
    x = 4;
  break;
case 3:
  while (c > 0)
    c = process (c);
  break
```

Figure 1.2. The execution paths through a program segment

interface errors not within a function but in the interface between functions, in misunderstanding of the exact conditions and standards of information interchange between functions. It would therefore appear that a reasonable testing philosophy for a large project would be to apply glass-box methods to each small module as it is written and use black-box test data to test larger sections of the program when they are complete.

3. The Ticking-Box Method

To conclude this section, let us mention one further philosophy of program testing, the philosophy that is, unfortunately, quite widely used. This might be called the *ticking-box* method. It consists of doing no testing at all after the project is fairly well debugged, but instead turning it over to the customer for trial and acceptance. The result, of course, is a time bomb.

Exercises **E1.** Find suitable black-box test data for each of the following:
1.4
    a. A function that returns the largest of its three parameters, which are real numbers.
    b. A function that returns the square root of a real number.

   c. A function that returns the least common multiple of its two parameters, which must be positive integers. (The *least common multiple* is the smallest integer that is a multiple of both parameters. Examples: The least common multiple of 4 and 6 is 12, of 3 and 9 is 9, and of 5 and 7 is 35.)

   d. A function that sorts three integers, given as its parameters, into ascending order.

   e. A function that sorts an array a of integers indexed from 0 to a variable n−1 into ascending order, where a and n are both parameters.

E2. Find suitable glass-box test data for each of the following:

   a. The statement

```
if (a < b) if (c > d) x = 1; else if (c == d) x = 2;
else x = 3; else if (a == b) x = 4; else if (c == d) x = 5;
else x = 6;
```

   b. The function NeighborCount(row, col, map).

Programming Projects 1.4

P1. Enter the Life program of this section on your computer and make sure that it works correctly.

P2. Test the Life program with the examples shown in Figure 1.1.

P3. Run the Life program with the initial configurations shown in Figure 1.3.

POINTERS AND PITFALLS

1. Be sure you understand your problem before you decide how to solve it.

2. Be sure you understand the algorithmic method before you start to program.

3. In case of difficulty, divide the problem into pieces and think of each part separately.

4. Keep your functions short and simple; rarely should a single function be more than a page long.

5. Use stubs and drivers, black-box and glass-box testing to simplify debugging.

6. Use plenty of scaffolding to help localize errors.

7. In programming with arrays, be wary of index values that are off by 1. Always use extreme-value testing to check programs that use arrays.

8. Keep your programs well-formatted as you write them—it will make debugging much easier.

9. Keep your documentation consistent with your code, and when reading a program make sure that you debug the code and not just the comments.

10. Explain your program to somebody else: Doing so will help you understand it better yourself.

11. Remember the Programming Precepts!

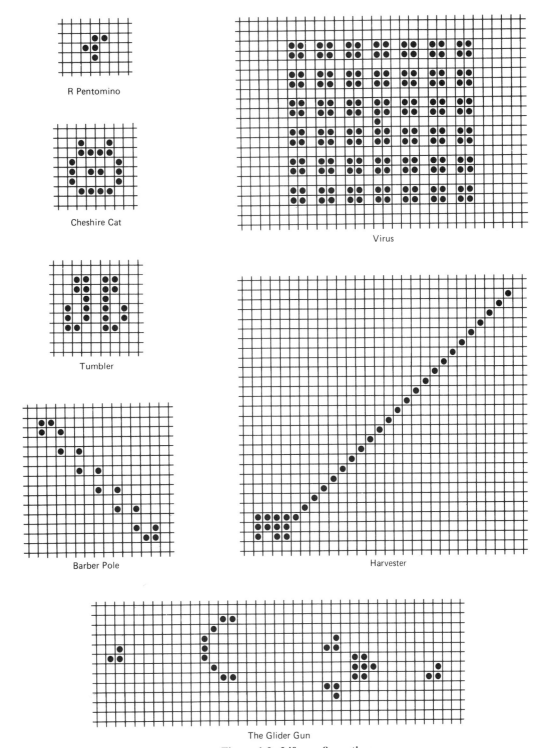

Figure 1.3. Life configurations

REVIEW QUESTIONS

Most chapters of this book conclude with a set of questions designed to help you review the main ideas of the chapter. These questions can all be answered directly from the discussion in the book; if you are unsure of any answer, refer to the appropriate section.

1.3   **1.** When is it appropriate to use one-letter variable names?

2. Name four kinds of information that should be included in program documentation.

3. Why should side effects of functions be avoided?

1.4   **4.** What is a program stub?

5. What is the difference between stubs and drivers, and when should each be used?

6. What is a structured walkthrough?

7. Name two methods for testing a program, and discuss when each should be used.

8. If you cannot immediately picture all details needed for solving a problem, what should you do with the problem?

REFERENCES FOR FURTHER STUDY

The C Language

The C programming language was devised by DENNIS M. RITCHIE. The standard reference is

> BRIAN W. KERNIGHAN and DENNIS M. RITCHIE, *The C Programming Language*, second edition, Prentice Hall, Englewood Cliffs, N.J., 1988, 272 pages.

This book contains many examples and exercises. For the solutions to the exercises in Kernighan and Ritchie, together with a chance to study C code, see

> CLOVIS L. TONDO and SCOTT E. GIMPEL, *The C Answer Book*, second edition, Prentice Hall, Englewood Cliffs, N.J., 1989, 208 pages.

Programming Principles

Two books that contain many helpful hints on programming style and correctness, as well as examples of good and bad practices, are

> BRIAN W. KERNIGHAN and P. J. PLAUGER, *The Elements of Programming Style*, second edition, McGraw–Hill, New York, 1978, 168 pages.

> DENNIE VAN TASSEL, *Program Style, Design, Efficiency, Debugging, and Testing*, second edition, Prentice Hall, Englewood Cliffs, N.J., 1978, 323 pages.

EDSGER W. DIJKSTRA pioneered the movement known as structured programming, which insists on taking a carefully organized top-down approach to the design and writing of programs, when in March 1968 he caused some consternation by publishing a letter entitled "Go To Statement Considered Harmful" in the *Communications of the ACM* (vol. 11, pages 147–148). DIJKSTRA has since published several papers and books that are most instructive in programming method. One book of special interest is

> E. W. DIJKSTRA, *A Discipline of Programming*, Prentice Hall, Englewood Cliffs, N.J., 1976, 217 pages.

The Game of Life

The prominent British mathematician J. H. CONWAY has made many original contributions to subjects as diverse as the theory of finite simple groups, logic, and combinatorics. He devised the game of Life by starting with previous, technical studies of cellular automata and devising reproduction rules that would make it difficult for a configuration to grow without bound, but for which many configurations would go through interesting progressions. CONWAY, however, did not publish his observations, but communicated them to MARTIN GARDNER. The popularity of the game skyrocketed when it was discussed in

> MARTIN GARDNER, "Mathematical Games" (regular column), *Scientific American* 223, no. 4 (October 1970), 120–123; 224, no. 2 (February 1971), 112–117.

The examples at the end of Sections 1.2 and 1.4 are taken from these columns. These columns have been reprinted with further results in

> MARTIN GARDNER, *Wheels, Life and Other Mathematical Amusements*, W. H. Freeman, New York, 1983, pp. 214–257.

This book also contains a bibliography of articles on Life. A quarterly newsletter, entitled *Lifeline*, was even published for some years to keep the real devotees up to date on current developments in Life and related topics.

Introduction to Software Engineering

This chapter continues to expound the principles of good program design, with special emphasis on techniques required for the production of large software systems. These techniques include problem specification, algorithm development, verification, and analysis, as well as program testing and maintenance. These general principles are introduced in the context of developing a second program for the Life game, one based on more sophisticated methods than those of the last chapter.

Software engineering is the discipline within computer science concerned with techniques needed for the production and maintenance of large software systems. Our goal in introducing some of these techniques is to demonstrate their importance in problems of practical size. Although much of the discussion in this chapter is motivated by the Life game and applied specifically to its program, the discussion is always intended to illustrate more general methods that can be applied to a much broader range of problems of practical importance.

2.1 PROGRAM MAINTENANCE

Small programs written as exercises or demonstrations are usually run a few times and then discarded, but the disposition of large practical programs is quite different. A program of practical value will be run many times, usually by many different people, and its writing and debugging mark only the beginning of its use. They also mark only the beginning of the work required to make and keep the program useful. It is necessary to *review* and *analyze* the program to ensure that it meets the requirements specified for it, *adapt* it to changing environments, and *modify* it to make it better meet the needs of its users.

Let us illustrate these activities by reconsidering the program for the Life game written and tested in Chapter 1.

1. Review of the Life Program

problems

If you have run the Life program on a small computer or on a busy time-sharing system, then you will likely have found two major problems. First, the method for input of the initial configuration is poor. It is unnatural for a person to calculate and type in the numerical coordinates of each living cell. The form of input should instead reflect the same visual imagery as the way the map is printed. Second, you may have found the program's speed somewhat disappointing. There can be a noticeable pause between printing one generation and starting to print the next.

Our goal is to improve the program so that it will run really efficiently on a microcomputer. The problem of improving the form of input is addressed as an exercise; the text discusses the problem of improving the speed.

2. Analysis of the Life Program

operation counts

We must first find out where the program is spending most of its computation time. If we examine the program, we can first note that the trouble cannot be in the function Initialize, since this is done only once, before the main loop is started. Within the loop that counts generations, we have a pair of nested loops that, together, will iterate

$$\text{MAXROW} \times \text{MAXCOL} = 50 \times 80 = 4000$$

times. Hence program lines within these loops will contribute substantially to the time used.

nested loops

The first thing done within the loops is to invoke the function NeighborCount. The function itself includes a pair of nested loops (note that we are now nested to a total depth of 5), which usually do their inner statement 9 times. The function also does 7 statements outside the loops, for a total (usually) of 16.

Within the nested loops of the main program there are, along with the call to the function, only the comparison to find which case to do and the appropriate assignment statement, that is, there are only 2 statements additional to the 16 in the function. Outside of the nested loops there is the function call CopyMap(map, newmap), which, in copying 4000 entries, is about equivalent to 1 more statement within the loops. There is also a call to the function WriteMap, some variation of which is needed in any case so that the user can see what the program is doing. Our primary concern is with the computation, however, so let us not worry about the time that WriteMap may need. We thus see that for each generation, the computation involves about

$$4000 \times 19 = 76,000$$

statements, of which about $4000 \times 16 = 64,000$ are done in the function.

On a small microcomputer or a tiny share of a busy time-sharing system, each statement can easily require 100 to 500 microseconds for execution, so the time to calculate a generation may easily range as high as 40 seconds, a delay that most users will find unacceptable.

Since by far the greatest amount of time is used in the function calculating the number of occupied neighbors of a cell, we should concentrate our attention on doing this job more efficiently. Before starting to develop some ideas, however, let us pause momentarily to pontificate:

Programming Precept

Most programs spend 90 percent of their time doing 10 percent of their instructions.
Find this 10 percent, and concentrate your efforts for efficiency there.

It takes much practice and experience to decide what is important and what may be neglected in analyzing algorithms for efficiency, but it is a skill that you should carefully develop to enable you to choose alternative methods or to concentrate your programming efforts where they will do the most good.

3. Problem-solving Alternatives

Once we know where a program is doing most of its work, we can begin to consider alternative methods in the hope of improving its efficiency. In the case of the Life game, let us ask ourselves how we can reduce the amount of work needed to keep track of the number of occupied neighbors of each Life cell. Is it necessary for us to calculate *use of array* the number of neighbors of every cell at every generation? Clearly not, if we use some way (such as an array) to remember the number of neighbors, and if this number does not change from one generation to the next. If you have spent some time experimenting with the Life program, then you will certainly have noticed that in many interesting configurations, the number of occupied cells at any time is far below the total number of positions available. Out of 4000 positions, typically fewer than 100 are occupied. Our program is spending much of its time laboriously calculating the obvious facts that cells isolated from the living cells indeed have no occupied neighbors and will not become occupied. If we can prevent or substantially reduce such useless calculation, we shall obtain a much better program.

As a first approach, let us consider trying to limit the calculations to cells in a limited area around those that are occupied. If this occupied area (which we would have to define precisely) is roughly rectangular, then we can implement this scheme easily by replacing the limits in the loops by other variables that would bound the occupied area. But this scheme would be very inefficient if the occupied area were shaped like a large ring, or, indeed, if there were only two small occupied areas in opposite corners of a very large rectangle. To try to carry out this plan for occupied areas not at all rectangular in shape would probably require us to do so many comparisons, as well as the loops, as to obviate any saving of time.

4. A Fresh Start and a New Method

Let us back up for a moment. If we can now decide to keep an array to remember the number of occupied neighbors of each cell, then the only counts in the array that will change from generation to generation will be those that correspond to immediate neighbors of cells that die or are born.

arrays and functions
We can substantially improve the running time of our program if we convert the function NeighborCount into an array and add appropriate statements to update the array while we are doing the changes from one generation to the next embodied in the switch statement, or, if we prefer (what is perhaps conceptually easier), while we are copying newmap into map we can note where the births and deaths have occurred and at that time update the array.

To emphasize that we are now using an array instead of the function NeighborCount, we shall change the name and write numbernbrs for the array.

algorithm development
The method we have now developed still involves scanning at least once through the full array map at every generation, which likely means much useless work. By being slightly more careful, we can avoid the need ever to look at unoccupied areas. As a cell is born or dies it changes the value of numbernbrs for each of its immediate neighbors. While making these changes we can note when we find a cell whose count becomes such that it will be born or die in the next generation. Thus we should set up two lists that will contain the cells that, so to speak, are moribund or are expecting in the coming generation. In this way, once we have finished making the changes of the current generation and printing the map, we will have waiting for us complete lists of all the births and deaths to occur in the coming generation. It should now be clear that we really need two lists for births and two for deaths, one each for the changes being made now (which are depleted as we proceed) and one list each (which are being added to) containing the changes for the next generation. When the changes on the current lists are complete, we print the map, copy the coming lists to the current ones, and go on to the next generation.

5. Algorithm Outline

Let us now summarize our decisions by writing down an informal outline of the program we shall develop.

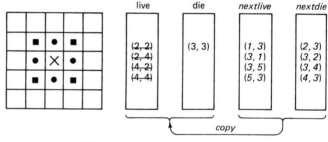

Figure 2.1. Life using lists

<table>
<tr><td>*initialization*</td><td>Get the initial configuration of living cells and use it to calculate an array holding the neighbor counts of all cells. Construct lists of the cells that will become alive and that will become dead in the first generation;</td></tr>
<tr><td>*main loop*</td><td>Repeat the following steps as long as desired:
    For each cell on the list of cells to become alive:
        Make the cell alive;
        Update the neighbor counts for each neighbor of the cell;
        If a neighbor count reaches the appropriate value, then add the cell to the list of cells to be made alive or dead in the next generation;
    For each cell on the list of cells to become dead:
        Make the cell dead; Update the neighbor counts for each neighbor of the cell; If a neighbor count reaches the appropriate value, then add the cell to the list of cells to be made alive or dead in the next generation;
    Write out the map for the user;</td></tr>
<tr><td>*prepare for next generation*</td><td>Copy the lists of cells to be changed in the next generation to the lists for the current generation.</td></tr>
</table>

Clearly a great many details remain to be specified in this outline, but before we consider these details, we need to develop some new tools.

**Exercises
2.1**

E1. Sometimes the user might wish to run the Life game on a grid smaller than 50×80. Determine how it is possible to make maxrow and maxcol into variables that the user can set when the program is run. Try to make as few changes in the program as possible.

E2. One idea for changing the program to save some of the if statements in the function NeighborCount is to add two extra rows and columns to the arrays map and newmap, by changing their dimensions to

$$[\text{MAXROW} + 2]\ [\text{MAXCOL} + 2].$$

(Note that this would also mean changing the cell coordinates to be 1 to MAXROW and 1 to MAXCOL rather than 0 to MAXROW$-$ 1 and 0 to MAXCOL $-$ 1.) Entries in the extra rows and columns would always be dead, so that the loops in NeighborCount could always run their full range from $i - 1$ to $i + 1$ and $j - 1$ to $j + 1$. How would this change affect the count of statements executed in NeighborCount?

**Programming
Projects
2.1**

P1. Rewrite the function Initialize so that it accepts the occupied positions in some symbolic form, such as a sequence of blanks and X's in appropriate rows, rather than requiring the occupied positions to be entered as numerical coordinate pairs.

P2. On a slow-speed terminal writing out the entire map at every generation will be quite slow. If you have access to a video terminal for which the cursor can be controlled by the program, rewrite the function WriteMap so that it updates the map instead of completely rewriting it at each generation.

2.2 LISTS IN C

As we develop the revised Life program that follows the scheme we have devised in the last section, we must make some decisions about what variables we shall need and the ways in which we shall implement the lists we have decided to use. (Lists will be covered in detail in Chapter 3.)

1. The Logical Structure of Lists

A list really has two distinct parts associated with it. First is a variable that gives the number of items in the list. Second is an array that contains the items on the list. In most languages the programmer must carry the counter variable and the array separately (and doing so is a frequent source of trouble for beginners). Sometimes tricks are used, such as using entry 0 of the array as the counter.

2. Definition and Examples

In our case, we may define a type called Listtype with declarations such as the following:

```
#define MAXLIST 200              /* maximum size of lists             */
```

declaration of list
```
typedef struct list_tag {
        int count;
        Entry_type entry [MAXLIST] ;     /* Entry_type is defined elsewhere.  */
} List_type;
```

The four lists that we wish to have are now variables of type List_type, declared as usual:

List_type die, live, nextdie, nextlive;

3. Hierarchical Structures: Data Abstraction

The entries in our lists will be coordinate pairs [x, y], and there is no reason why we should not think of these pairs as a single structure, by defining

```
typedef struct coord_tag {
    int row; /* x   */
    int col;  /* y   */
} Coord_type;
```

If we then define Entry_type in terms of Coord_type,

```
typedef Coord_type Entry_type;
```

we shall have put these coordinates into our lists, as we wish to do.

hierarchical
structures

Note that we now have an example of a structure (coord_tag) contained as entries in arrays that are members of another structure (list_tag). Such structures are called ***hierarchical***. By putting structures within structures, structures in arrays, and arrays in structures, we can build up complicated data structures that precisely describe the relationships in the data processed by a program.

top-down design of
data structures

When we work with structures, however, we should never think of them as having such a complicated form. Instead, we should use top-down design for data structures as well as for algorithms. When we process the large, outer structures, we need not be concerned about the exact nature of each component within the structure. When we write algorithms to manipulate the innermost components, we should treat them only in terms of their simple form and not be concerned as to whether they may later be embedded in larger structures or arrays. We can thus use structures to accomplish ***information hiding***, whereby we can design the upper levels both of algorithms and data structures without worrying about the details that will be specified later on lower levels of refinement.

As one further example of processing hierarchical structures, we can write a short function that will add an entry coordinate to the end of a list called list.

adding to a list

```
void Add (List_type *list, Coord_type coordinate)
{
    if (list->count >= MAXLIST)
        Error ("list overflow");
    else
        list->entry [list->count++] = coordinate;
}
```

The arrow (->) operator is used to access a structure member through a pointer to the structure. Thus, list->count dereferences the pointer list and accesses the structure member called count.

Exercises **E1.** Write a function that will delete the last coordinate from a list (as defined in the
2.2   text) or will invoke a function Error if the list was empty.

E2. Write functions that will copy one list to another list (as the structure type defined in the text). Use the following methods: **(a)** copy the entire structures; **(b)** use a loop to copy only the entries. Which version is easier to write? Which version will usually run faster, and why?

2.3 ALGORITHM DEVELOPMENT: A SECOND VERSION OF LIFE

After deciding on the basic method and the overall outline of the data structures needed for solving a problem, it is time to commence the process of algorithm development, beginning with an overall outline and slowly introducing refinements until all the details are specified and a program is formulated in a computer language.

2.3.1 The Main Program

In the case of the Life game, we can now combine our use of structures as the data structures for lists with the outline of the method given in part 5 of Section 2.1, thereby translating the outline into a main program written in C. With few exceptions, the declarations of constants, types, and variables follow the discussion in Sections 2.1 and 2.2 along with the corresponding declarations for the first version of the Life game. The include file lifedef.h contains:

```
#define MAXROW 50              /* maximum number of rows allowed     */
#define MAXCOL 80              /* maximum number of columns allowed  */
#define MAXLIST 100            /* maximum number of elements in a list */

typedef enum status_tag { DEAD, ALIVE } Status_type;   /* status of cell     */

typedef Status_type Grid_type[MAXROW][MAXCOL];   /* grid definition     */
typedef int Gridcount_type[MAXROW][MAXCOL];

typedef struct coord_tag {
    int row;
    int col;
} Coord_type;

typedef struct list_tag {
    int count;
    Coord_type entry[MAXLIST];
} List_type;
```

The include file calls.h contains the function prototypes:

```
void Copy(List_type *, List_type *);
int Enquire(void);
void Initialize(List_type *, List_type *, List_type *, List_type *,
                Grid_type, Gridcount_type);
void WriteMap(Grid_type);
void ReadMap(List_type *, Grid_type);
void Vivify(List_type *, Grid_type, Gridcount_type);
void Kill(List_type *, Grid_type, Gridcount_type);
void AddNeighbors(List_type *, List_type *, List_type *,
                Gridcount_type, Grid_type);
void SubtractNeighbors(List_type *, List_type *, List_type *,
                Gridcount_type, Grid_type);
void Add(List_type *, Coord_type);
```

The main program then is:

```
/* Simulation of Conway's game of Life on a bounded grid */
/* Version 2. */
#include "general.h"
#include "lifedef.h"              /* Life's defines and typedefs         */
#include "calls.h"                /* Life's function declarations        */
```

Life2, main program
```
void main(void)
{
        Grid_type map;              /* current generation                  */
        Gridcount_type numbernbrs;  /* number of neighbors                 */
        List_type live, nextlive;
        List_type die, nextdie;

        Initialize( &live, &die, &nextlive, &nextdie, map, numbernbrs);
        WriteMap(map);
        do {
                Vivify( &live, map, numbernbrs);
                Kill( &die, map, numbernbrs);
                WriteMap(map);
                AddNeighbors( &live, &nextlive, &nextdie, numbernbrs, map);
                SubtractNeighbors( &die, &nextlive, &nextdie, numbernbrs, map);
                Copy( &live, &nextlive);
                Copy( &die, &nextdie);
        } while (Enquire( ));
}
```

description   Most of the action of the program is postponed to various functions. After initializing all the lists and arrays, the program begins its main loop. At each generation we first go through the cells waiting in lists live and die in order to update the array map, which, as in the first version of Life, keeps track of which cells are alive. This work is done in the functions Vivify (which means *make alive*) and Kill. After writing the revised configuration, we update the count of neighbors for each cell that has been born or has died, using the functions AddNeighbors and SubtractNeighbors and the array numbernbrs. As part of the same functions, when the neighbor count reaches an appropriate value, a cell is added to the list nextlive or nextdie to indicate that it will be born or die in the coming generation. Finally, we must copy the lists for the coming generation into the current ones.

2.3.2 Refinement: Development of the Subprograms

After the solution to a problem has been outlined, it is time to turn to the various parts of the outline, to include more details and thereby specify the solution exactly. While making these refinements, however, the programmer often discovers that the task of each subprogram was not specified as carefully as necessary, that the interface between *specifications and* different subprograms must be reworked and spelled out in more detail, so that the *problem solving* different subprograms accomplish all necessary tasks, and so that they do so without duplication or contradictory requirements. In a real sense, therefore, the process of refinement requires going back to the problem-solving phase to find the best way to split the required tasks among the various subprograms. Ideally, this process of refinement and specification should be completed before any coding is done.

Let us illustrate this activity by working through the requirements for the various subprograms for the Life game.

1. The Task for AddNeighbors

Much of the work of our program will be done in the functions AddNeighbors and SubtractNeighbors. We shall develop the first of these, leaving the second as an exercise. The function AddNeighbors will go through the list live, and for each entry will find its immediate neighbors (as done in the original function NeighborCount), will increase the count in numbernbrs for each of these, and must put some of these on the lists nextlive and nextdie. To determine which, let us denote by n the updated count for one of the neighbors and consider cases.

cases for   1. It is impossible that $n = 0$, since we have just increased n by 1.
AddNeighbors
2. If $n = 1$ or $n = 2$, then the cell is already dead and it should remain dead in the next generation. We need do nothing.

3. If $n = 3$, then a previously live cell still lives; a previously dead cell must be added to the list nextlive.

4. If $n = 4$, then a previously live cell dies; add it to nextdie. If the cell is dead, it remains so.

5. If $n > 4$, then the cell is already dead (or is already on list nextdie) and stays there.

2. Problems

One subtle problem arises with this function. When the neighbor count for a dead cell reaches 3, we add it to the list nextlive, but it may well be that later in function *spurious entries* AddNeighbors, its neighbor count will again be increased (beyond 3) so that it should not be vivified in the next generation after all. Similarly when the neighbor count for a live cell reaches 4, we add it to nextdie, but the function SubtractNeighbors may well reduce its neighbor count below 4, so that it should be removed from nextdie. Thus the final determination of lists nextlive and nextdie cannot be made until the array numbernbrs has been fully updated, but yet, as we proceed, we must tentatively add entries to the lists.

postpone difficulty   It turns out that, if we postpone solution of this problem, it becomes much easier. In the functions AddNeighbors and SubtractNeighbors, let us add cells to nextlive and nextdie without worrying whether they will later be removed. Then when we copy nextlive and nextdie to lists live and die, we can check that the neighbor counts are correct (in live, for example, only dead cells with a neighbor count of exactly 3 should appear) and delete the erroneous entries with no difficulty.

duplicate entries   After doing this, however, an even more subtle error remains. It is possible that the same cell may appear in list nextlive (or nextdie) more than once. A dead cell, for example, may initially have a count of 2, which, when increased, adds the cell to nextlive. Its count may then be increased further, and in SubtractNeighbors decreased one or more times, perhaps ending at 3, so that SubtractNeighbors again adds it to nextlive. Then, when neighbor counts are updated in the next generation, this birth will incorrectly contribute 2 rather than 1 to the neighbor counts. We could solve this problem by searching the lists for duplicates before copying them, but to do so would be slow, and we can again solve the problem more easily by postponing it. When, in the next generation, we wish to vivify a cell, we shall first check whether it is already alive. If so, then we know that its entry is a duplicate of one earlier on list live. While we are postponing work, we might as well also postpone checking the neighbor counts, so that the copying function will now do nothing but copy lists, and all the checking is done in Vivify and Kill. Figure 2.2 shows the trace of Life2 for one small configuration and exhibits the appearance and deletion of spurious and duplicate entries in the various lists.

> **Programming Precept**
>
> Sometimes postponing problems simplifies their solution.

2.3.3 Coding the Functions

Now that we have spelled out completely and precisely the requirements for each function, it is time to code them into our programming language. In a large software project it is necessary to do the coding at the right time, not too soon and not too late. Most programmers err by starting to code too soon. If coding is begun before the requirements are made precise, then unwarranted assumptions about the specifications will inevitably be *specifications complete* made while coding, and these assumptions may render different subprograms incompatible with each other or make the programming task much more difficult than it need be.

> **Programming Precept**
>
> Never code until the specifications are precise and complete.

top-down coding   It is possible, on the other hand, to delay coding too long. Just as we design from the top down, we should code from the top down. Once the specifications at the top levels are complete and precise, we should code the subprograms at these levels and test them by including appropriate stubs. If we then find that our design is flawed, we can modify it without paying an exorbitant price in low-level functions that have been rendered useless.

Now that the specifications for several of the Life subprograms are complete, let us embody our decisions into functions coded in C.

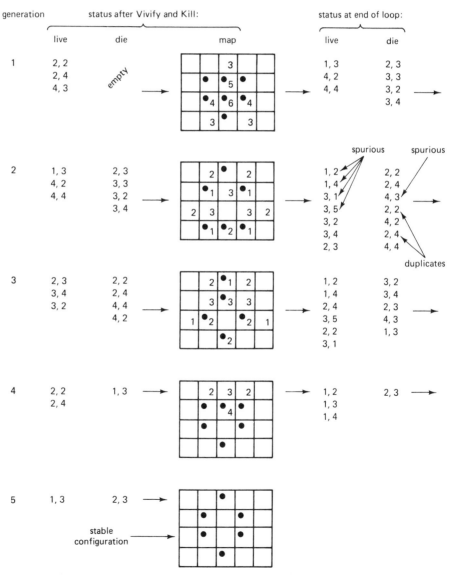

Figure 2.2. A trace of program Life2

1. Function Copy

Since we decided to postpone all the checking for spurious entries in the lists, the final version of the copying function is trivial. It need only copy one list to another and leave the first empty:

copy one list

```
/* Copy: copies the contents of one list to another. */
void Copy (List_type *to, List_type *from)
{
    int i;

    for (i = 0; i < from->count; i++)
        to->entry [i] = from->entry [i] ;
    to->count = from->count;
    from->count = 0;                        /* Clear the copied list.              */
}
```

2. Function Vivify

The function Vivify goes through the list live and vivifies each cell, provided that it was previously dead and had a neighbor count of exactly 3. Otherwise, the cell is one of the spurious entries, and Vivify deletes it from the list. Hence at the conclusion of the function, list live contains exactly those cells that were vivified and whose neighbor counts must therefore be updated by AddNeighbors.

make cells alive

```
/* Vivify: make cells alive and check for duplicates */
void Vivify (List_type *live, Grid_type map, Gridcount_type numbernbrs)
{
    int k, row, col;

    k = 0;
    while (k < live->count) {
        row = live->entry [k] .row;
        col = live->entry [k] .col;
        if (map [row] [col] == DEAD && numbernbrs [row] [col] == 3) {
            map [row] [col] = ALIVE;    /* Make the cell alive.              */
            k++;
        } else {                        /* Delete entry k from the list.     */
            live->count --;
            live->entry [k] = live->entry [live->count] ;
        }
    }
}
```

3. Function AddNeighbors

At the conclusion of function Vivify, the duplicate and spurious entries have all been removed from list live, and what remains are the cells that were actually vivified. Hence the function AddNeighbors can update all the related neighbor counts without problem. This function has the following form.

```
/* AddNeighbors: increase the neighbor count of vivified cells */
void AddNeighbors (List_type *live, List_type *nextlive, List_type *nextdie,
                   Gridcount_type numbernbrs, Grid_type map)
{
        int i, j;                       /* loop indices                    */
        int ilow, ihigh;                /* row loop limits                 */
        int jlow, jhigh;                /* column loop limits              */
        int k, row, col;                /* used to traverse list           */
        Coord_type nbr;                 /* structure form of a neighbor    */

        for (k = 0; k < live->count; k++) {  /* Loop through vivified cells.    */
                row = live->entry [k] .row;
                col = live->entry [k] .col;
                if (row <= 0)           /* Set the loop limits.            */
                        ilow = 0;
                else   ilow = row − 1;
                if (row >= MAXROW − 1)
                        ihigh = MAXROW − 1;
                else   ihigh = row + 1;
                if (col <= 0)
                        jlow = 0;
                else   jlow = col − 1;
                if (col >= MAXCOL − 1)
                        jhigh = MAXCOL − 1;
                else   jhigh = col + 1;

                for (i = ilow; i <= ihigh; i++)
                        for (j = jlow; j <= jhigh; j++)
                                if (i != row || j != col) {  /* Skip the cell itself.          */
                                        nbr.row = i;   /* Set up a coordinate structure.  */
                                        nbr.col = j;
                                        numbernbrs [i] [j] ++;
                                        switch (numbernbrs [i] [j] ) {
                                        case 0:
                                                printf ("Impossible case in AddNeighbors.\n");
                                                break;
                                        case 3:
                                                if (map [i] [j] ==  DEAD)
                                                Add (nextlive, nbr) ;
                                                break;
                                        case 4:
                                                if (map [i] [j] ==  ALIVE)
                                                Add (nextdie, nbr) ;
                                                break;
                                        }       /* switch statement                */
                                }
        }                                       /* k loop                          */
}
```

find a neighbor

put cells onto lists

4. Remaining Functions

The functions Kill and SubtractNeighbors are similar in form to Vivify and AddNeighbors; they will be left as exercises. The function WriteMap can be used without change from the first version, but a much more efficient version is possible that makes use of the lists live and die to update the screen rather than rewriting it at each generation. The function Add appears in Section 2.2. We shall postpone writing function Initialize to the end of the next section.

Programming   **P1.** Write the missing functions for the second version of Life: **(a)** Kill and **(b)** Sub-
Projects   tractNeighbors.
2.3   **P2.** Write driver programs for the functions **(a)** Kill and **(b)** SubtractNeighbors, and
                  devise appropriate test data to check the performance of these functions.

2.4 VERIFICATION OF ALGORITHMS

Another important aspect of the design of large programs is algorithm verification, that is, a *proof* that the algorithm accomplishes its task. This kind of proof is usually formulated by looking at the specifications for the subprograms and then arguing that these specifications combine properly to accomplish the task of the whole algorithm.

purpose   While constructing such a proof we may find that the specifications must be changed to enable us to infer the correctness of the algorithm, and, in doing so, the proof itself helps us formulate the specifications for each subprogram with greater precision. Hence algorithm verification and algorithm design can go hand-in-hand, and sometimes the verification can even lead the way. In any case, algorithm verification should precede coding.

2.4.1 Proving the Program

Let us again illustrate these concepts by turning to the Life program, first to be sure that its algorithm is correct and second to assist us in designing the remaining function, Initialize.

Indeed, the fact that there were subtle errors in our initial attempts to organize the work done in functions Vivify, Kill, AddNeighbors, SubtractNeighbors, and Copy should
caution   alert us to the possible presence of further errors, or at least to the necessity of exercising considerably more care to be sure that our algorithms are correct.

1. Possible Problems

By postponing the checking of neighbor counts, we were able to avoid difficulties both with the problems of duplicate and of erroneous entries. But, for example, how can we be sure that it is not still possible that the same cell might erroneously be included in both lists nextlive and nextdie? If so, then it might first be vivified and then killed immediately in the following generation (clearly an illegal happening). The answer to this particular question is *no*, since the main program calls both functions Vivify and Kill before either function AddNeighbors or SubtractNeighbors. Thus the cell keeps the same status (alive or dead) from the end of function Kill until the next generation, and the functions AddNeighbors and SubtractNeighbors check that only dead cells are added to nextlive and only living cells to nextdie.

How can we be sure that there are not more subtle questions of this sort, some of which might not be so easy to answer? The only way we can really be confident is to *prove* that our program does the right action in each case.

2. The Main Loop

The difficulty with our program is that what happens in one generation might affect the next generation in some unexpected way. Therefore we focus our attention on the large loop in the main program. At the beginning of the loop it is the contents of lists live and die that determine everything that happens later. Let us therefore summarize what we know about these lists from our previous study.

loop invariant

At the beginning of the main loop, list live *contains only dead cells, and list* die *contains only living cells, but the lists may contain duplicate entries, or spurious entries whose neighbor counts are wrong. The lists* nextlive *and* nextdie *are empty.*

At the very start of the program, it is one task of function Initialize to ensure that the lists live and die are set up properly, so that the preceding statements are correct at the start of the first generation. What we must prove, then, is that if the statements are true at the start of any one generation, then after the eight function calls within the loop, they will again be true for the next generation.

3. Proof by Mathematical Induction

At this point, you should note that what we are really doing is using the method of **mathematical induction** to establish that the program is correct. In this method of proof, we begin by establishing the result for an initial case. Next we prove the result for a later case, say case n, by using the result for earlier cases (those between the initial case and case $n - 1$). See Appendix A.1 for further discussion and examples of proof by mathematical induction.

initial case

induction step

For our program, verification of the initial case amounts to a verification that Initialize works properly. For the second part of the proof, let us examine the actions in the main loop, assuming that the statements are correct at its beginning. Function Vivify uses only list live and carefully checks each entry before it vivifies a cell, removing erroneous and duplicate entries from list live as it goes. Hence at the conclusion of Vivify, list live contains only those cells that were properly vivified, and no duplicates. Function Kill similarly cleans up list die. Since the two lists originally had no cells in common, and none has been added to either list, no cells have been improperly both vivified and killed. Next, function WriteMap is called, but does not change the lists. Function AddNeighbors works only from list live and puts only dead cells on list nextlive, and only living ones on list nextdie. Similarly, function SubtractNeighbors keeps the dead and living cells properly separated. Together these two functions add all the cells whose status should change in the next generation to the lists, but may add duplicate or spurious entries. Finally, the copying function sets up lists live and die and empties lists nextlive and nextdie, as required to show that all conditions in our statements are again true at the *end of proof* beginning of the next generation. The logic of our program is therefore correct.

2.4.2 Invariants and Assertions

Statements such as the one we established in the preceding proof are called *loop invari-ants*. In general, a loop invariant is a statement that is true at the beginning of every iteration of the loop. The statements we made about the status of various lists at dif-ferent points of the loop are called *assertions*, and assertions that hold at the beginning and end of each function (or, more generally, before and after any statement) are called *preconditions* and *postconditions*.

As an example, let us write down preconditions and postconditions for some of our functions:

Vivify:

precondition: List live contains only dead cells and contains all cells ready to be vivified.

postcondition: Array map has been updated with vivified cells, and list live contains only those cells that were vivified, with no duplicates or spurious entries.

AddNeighbors:

precondition: List live contains all vivified cells whose neighbor counts have not yet been updated.

postcondition: Array numbernbrs has increased counts for all cells neighboring cells in list live. If the increased neighbor count makes the cell a candidate to be vivified [*resp.* killed] then the cell has been added to list nextlive [*resp.* nextdie].

Initialize:

precondition: None.

postcondition: Array map contains the initial configuration of living and dead cells. Array numbernbrs contains counts of living neighbors correspond-ing to the configuration in array map. List live contains only dead cells and includes all candidates that may be vivified in the next generation. List die contains only living cells and contains all can-didates that may die in the next generation.

The purpose of loop invariants and assertions is to capture the essence of the dynamic process. It is not always easy to find loop invariants and assertions that will lead to *simplification* a proof that a program is correct, but it is a very useful exercise. Attempting to find invariants and assertions sometimes leads to simplifications in design of the algorithm, which make its correctness more obvious. Our goal should always be to make our algorithms so straightforward and clear that their logic is obviously correct, and the use of loop invariants can help in this process.

Programming Precept

Know your problem.
Give precise preconditions and postconditions for each function.

Algorithm verification is a subject under active research, in which many important questions remain to be answered. Correctness proofs have not yet been supplied for a large number of important algorithms that are in constant use. Sometimes exceptional cases appear that cause an algorithm to misbehave; correctness proofs would provide a consistent means to delineate these exceptions and provide for their processing.

2.4.3 Initialization

design of Initialize As we turn, finally, to the function Initialize, let us use the postconditions for the function to help in its composition. The first postcondition states that the array map is to be initialized with the starting configuration of living and dead cells. This task is similar to the initialization of the first version of the program, and we leave the resulting function ReadMap as an exercise. We shall, however, need the list of initially living cells for calculating the neighbor counts, so we shall also require ReadMap to put this list into list live. As one of its postconditions ReadMap will be required to make sure that there are no duplicates in this list. (This can be achieved easily if the reading is done properly.)

The second task is to initialize the neighbor counts in array numbernbrs. But we have required ReadMap to set up list live so that it contains exactly the information needed for function AddNeighbors to set the neighbor counts properly for all neighbors of living cells, provided that before calling AddNeighbors, we first set all entries in numbernbrs to 0. As well as initializing numbernbrs, function AddNeighbors will locate all dead cells that will become alive in the following generation and add them to list nextlive. Hence by setting nextlive to be empty before calling AddNeighbors and copying nextlive to live afterward, we accomplish another of the postconditions of Initialize.

The final postcondition is that list die contain all living cells that should die in the next generation. Some, but perhaps not all, of these may be found by AddNeighbors (in the main loop, the remainder would be found by SubtractNeighbors, which we have no way to use in Initialize). We can accomplish the postcondition more easily, however, by simply putting *all* the living cells into list die. Recall that function Kill allows spurious entries on its input list.

In this way the postconditions lead to the following function:

/ Initialize: set up the lists and grid. */*
```
void Initialize (List_type *live, List_type *die, List_type *nextlive,
            List_type *nextdie, Grid_type map, Gridcount_type numbernbrs)
```

initialization   `{`

```
    int row, col;                       /* used to set all entries in numbernbrs to 0 */

    ReadMap (live, map);                /* initializes map                          */
    for (row = 0; row < MAXROW; row++)
                                        /* Set all the entries in numbernbrs to 0.  */
        for (col = 0; col < MAXCOL; col++)
            numbernbrs [row] [col] = 0;
    nextlive->count = 0;                /* Initialize the lists used by AddNeighbors. */
    nextdie->count = 0;
    AddNeighbors (live, nextlive, nextdie, numbernbrs, map);
    /* Some of the cells just read in should die in the first generation. Kill will catch
      them. */
    Copy (die, live);
    Copy (live, nextlive);              /* Put output from AddNeighbors where needed. */
    nextdie->count = 0;
}
```

Exercises   **E1.** Write down preconditions and postconditions for each of the following functions.

2.4

    a. float SquareRoot (float x) returns the square root of x.

    b. float Meanx (List_type A) calculates the mean (average) x value in a list of coordinates (x, y) as declared in Section 2.2.

    c. void Copy (List_type *to, List_type *from).

    d. function Kill.

    e. function SubtractNeighbors.

    f. function WriteMap.

E2.   **a.** Write down the precondition and postcondition for the function ReadMap.

    b. Code the function ReadMap.

    c. Write a driver for ReadMap and test it.

2.5 PROGRAM ANALYSIS AND COMPARISON

In designing algorithms we need methods to separate bad algorithms from good ones, to help us decide, when we have several possible ways in which to proceed, which way will prove the most effective for our problem. For this reason the analysis of algorithms and the comparison of alternative methods constitute an important part of software engineering.

1. Statement Counts

Let us now see about how much more quickly the program Life2 should run than the previous version. As we did for the first version, let us ignore the time needed for input and output in the main program, and look only at the statements inside the principal loop counting generations. Since all the work of Life2 is done within functions, we must analyze each in turn. Each of the functions does most of its work within a loop that runs through the entries of one of the lists live, die, nextlive, or nextdie. Thus the key improvement of Life2 over the original program is that the amount of computation is no longer proportional to the size of the grid but to the number of changes being made. For a typical configuration, there might be about 100 occupied cells, with likely no more than 50 dying or being born in a single generation. With these assumptions, we see that each statement within the inner loops will be executed about 50 times. In Vivify there are 5 statements within the loop, in Copy only 1. Within the loop of AddNeighbors there are 2 assignment statements and 4 if statements, then 3 statements each done 9 times, and the switch statement done 8 times, for a total count of 41. The counts for Kill and

count for Life2   SubtractNeighbors are similar; thus we obtain for each generation about

$$50 \times (5 + 1 + 41 + 5 + 1 + 41) = 4700$$

statements. The number of statements executed outside the loops is insignificant (it is less than 10), so 4700 is a reasonable estimate of the statement count for each generation.

count for Life1   Our first version of the Life program had a count of 76,000 statements per generation. Thus our revised program should run as much as 16 times faster. This constitutes a substantial improvement, particularly in view of the fact that when program Life2 slows down, it is because many changes are being made, not because it is repeating the same predictable calculations.

2. Comparisons

programming effort   From other points of view, however, our second program is not as good as the first. The first of these is the point of view of programming effort. The first program was short and easy to write, simple to understand, and easy to debug. The second program is longer, entailed subtle problems, and required sophisticated reasoning to establish its correctness. Whether this additional work is worthwhile depends on the application and the number of times the program will be used. If a simple method works well enough, then we should not go out of our way to find a more sophisticated approach. Only when simple methods fail do we need to try further devices.

> ### Programming Precept
>
> Keep your algorithms as simple as you can.
> When in doubt, choose the simple way.

space requirements   The second point of view is that of storage requirements. Our first program used very little memory (apart from that for the instructions) except for the two arrays map and newmap. These arrays have entries that, in assuming only the two values alive and dead, can be packed so that each entry takes only a single bit. In a typical computer with word size of 32 or 16 bits, the two arrays need then occupy no more than 250 or 500 words, respectively. On the other hand, program Life2 requires, along with the space for its instructions, space for one such array, plus 4000 words for the array numbernbrs and 401 words for each of its four lists, giving a total of more than 5700 words.

3. Time and Space Trade-offs

We have just seen the first of many examples illustrating the substantial trade-offs that can occur between time and space in computer algorithms. Which to choose depends on available equipment. If the storage space is available and otherwise unused, it is obviously preferable to use the algorithm requiring more space and less time. If not, then time may have to be sacrificed. Finally, for an important problem, by far the best approach may be to sit back and rethink the whole problem: you will have learned much from your first efforts and may very well be able to find another approach that will save both time and space.

> **Programming Precept**
>
> Consider time and space trade-offs in deciding on your algorithm.

> **Programming Precept**
>
> Never be afraid to start over.
> Next time it may be both shorter and easier.

Exercises 2.5

E1. We could save the time needed to copy lists if we did two generations instead of one inside the main loop. We would pass the names of which of the lists to use to all the functions, and in writing the instructions for the second generation, we would simply swap the pairs of lists. How many statements, approximately, would be saved per generation? Do you think this change is worth implementing? If so, do it.

E2. We could save the space needed for the array map by making a slight modification in how we keep information in the array numbernbrs. We could use positive entries in numbernbrs to denote living cells and negative entries to denote dead cells. However, we could then not tell whether an entry of 0 meant a dead cell or a living cell with no living neighbors. We could easily overcome that problem by changing the definition of neighbor so that a cell is considered its own neighbor (so the neighbor count for a dead cell would range from 0 to 8, stored in numbernbrs as 0 to −8, and that for a living cell from 1 to 9).

   a. With this change of definition, write down the revised rules (from Section 1.2.1) for the game of Life.

   b. Do you think that implementing the changes to eliminate array map is worth the effort? Why or why not?

   c. If you answered the last question positively, describe exactly what changes are needed in the program.

E3. Note that there is some inefficiency in the program Life2 in having functions AddNeighbors and SubtractNeighbors called once from the main program, since these functions must loop through the lists live and die just as Vivify and Kill already do. It would be faster if these functions were written to update the neighbors of only one cell and were called from Vivify and Kill whenever a cell was vivified or killed.

a. Will the program work correctly if these changes are made?

b. If not, what further changes will make it work?

c. With your revised program, find the proper loop invariants and verify that your algorithm is correct.

Programming Projects 2.5

P1. If you use a video terminal with direct cursor addressing, write a version of the function WriteMap that takes advantage of the lists live and die to update the map rather than completely rewriting it at each generation.

P2. Run the complete program Life2 and compare timings with those of Life1.

2.6 CONCLUSIONS AND PREVIEW

This chapter has surveyed a great deal of ground, but mainly from a bird's-eye view. Some themes we shall treat in much greater depth in later chapters; others must be postponed to more advanced courses; still others are best learned by practice.

2.6.1 The Game of Life

1. Future Directions

We are not yet finished with the game of Life, although we next shall turn to other topics. When we return to the Life game (at the end of Chapter 6), we shall find an algorithm that does not require us to keep a large rectangular grid in memory.

2. Problem specification

For the moment, however, let us make only one observation, one that you may well have already made and, if so, one that has likely been bothering you. What we have done throughout this chapter and the previous one has been, in fact, incorrect, in that we have not been solving the Life game as it was originally described in Section 1.2. The rules make no mention of the boundaries of the grid containing the cells. In our programs, when a moving colony gets sufficiently close to a boundary, then room for neighbors disappears, and the colony will be distorted by the very presence of the boundary. That is not supposed to be.

It is of course true that in any computer simulation there are absolute bounds on the values that may appear, but certainly our use of a 50 by 80 grid is highly restrictive and arbitrary. Writing a more realistic program must be one of our goals when we return to this problem. But on a first try, restrictions are often reasonable. Nevertheless,

---

Programming Precept

Be sure you understand your problem completely.
If you must change its terms, explain exactly what you have done.

When we started in Section 1.4, we did nothing of the sort, but plunged right in with an approach leaving much to be desired. Almost every programmer learns this experience the hard way and can sympathize with the following:

Programming Precept

Act in haste and repent at leisure.
Program in haste and debug forever.

The same thought can be expressed somewhat more positively:

Programming Precept

Starting afresh is usually easier than patching an old program.

A good rule of thumb is that, if more than ten percent of a program must be modified, then it is time to rewrite the program completely. With repeated patches to a large program, the number of bugs tends to remain constant. That is, the patches become so complicated that each new patch tends to introduce as many new errors as it corrects.

3. Prototyping

An excellent way to avoid having to rewrite a large project from scratch is to plan from the beginning to write two versions. Before a program is running it is often impossible to know what parts of the design will cause difficulty or what features need to be changed to meet the needs of the users. Engineers have known for many years that it is not possible to build a large project directly from the drawing board. For large projects engineers always build **prototypes**, that is, scaled-down models that can be studied, tested, and sometimes even used for limited purposes. Models of bridges are built and tested in wind tunnels; pilot plants are constructed before attempting to use new technology on the assembly line.

software prototypes   Prototyping is especially helpful for computer software, since it eases communication between users and designers early in the project, thereby reducing misunderstandings and helping to settle the design to everyone's satisfaction. In building a software prototype the designer can use programs that are already written for input-output, for sorting, or for other common requirements. The building blocks can be assembled with as little new programming as possible to make a working model that can do some of the intended tasks. Even though the prototype may not function efficiently or do everything that the final system will, it provides an excellent laboratory for the user and designer to experiment with alternative ideas for the final design. The following precept is due to FRED BROOKS.

Programming Precept

Always plan to build a prototype and throw it away.
You'll do so whether you plan to or not.

2.6.2 Program Design

1. Criteria for Programs

A major goal of this book is to evaluate algorithms and data structures that purport to solve a problem. Amongst the many criteria by which we can judge a program, the following are some of the most important:

1. Does it solve the problem that is requested, according to the given specifications?
2. Does it work correctly under all conditions?
3. Does it include clear and sufficient information for its user, in the form of instructions and documentation?
4. Is it logically and clearly written, with short modules and subprograms as appropriate to do logical tasks?
5. Does it make efficient use of time and of space?

Some of these criteria will be closely studied for the programs we write. Others will not be mentioned explicitly, but not because of any lack of importance. These criteria, rather, can be met automatically if sufficient thought and effort are invested in every stage of program design. We hope that the examples we study will reveal such care.

2. Software Engineering

Software engineering is the study and practice of methods helpful for the construction and maintenance of large software systems. Although small by realistic standards, the program we have studied in this chapter illustrates many aspects of software engineering.

Software engineering begins with the realization that it is a very long process to obtain good software. It begins before any programs are coded and continues maintenance for years after the programs are put into use. This continuing process is known as the *life cycle* of software. This life cycle can be divided into phases as follows:

phases of life cycle

1. *Analyze* the problem precisely and completely. Be sure to *specify* all necessary user interface with care.
2. *Build* a prototype and *experiment* with it until all specifications can be finalized.
3. *Design* the algorithm, using the tools of data structures and of other algorithms whose function is already known.
4. *Verify* that the algorithm is correct, or make it so simple that its correctness is self-evident.
5. *Analyze* the algorithm to determine its requirements and make sure that it meets the specifications.
6. *Code* the algorithm into the appropriate programming language.
7. *Test* and *evaluate* the program on carefully chosen test data.
8. *Refine* and *repeat* the foregoing steps as needed for additional subprograms until the software is complete and fully functional.
9. *Optimize* the code to improve performance, but only if necessary.
10. *Maintain* the program so that it will meet the changing needs of its users.

Most of these topics have been discussed and illustrated in various sections of this and the preceding chapter, but a few further remarks on the first phase, problem analysis and specification, are in order.

3. Problem Analysis

Analysis of the problem is often the most difficult phase of the software life cycle. This is not because practical problems are conceptually more difficult than are computing science exercises—the reverse is often the case—but because users and programmers tend to speak different languages. Here are some questions on which the analyst and user must reach an understanding:

specifications

1. What form will the input and output data take? How much data will there be?
2. Are there any special requirements for the processing? What special occurrences will require separate treatment?
3. Will these requirements change? How? How fast will the demands on the system grow?
4. What parts of the system are the most important? Which must run most efficiently?
5. How should erroneous data be treated? What other error processing is needed?
6. What kinds of people will use the software? What kind of training will they have? What kind of user interface will be best?
7. How portable must the software be, to move to new kinds of equipment? With what other software and hardware systems must the project be compatible?
8. What extensions or other maintenance are anticipated? What is the history of previous changes to software and hardware?

4. Requirements Specification

The problem analysis and experimentation for a large project finally lead to a formal statement of the requirements for the project. This statement becomes the primary way in which the user and the software engineer attempt to understand each other and establishes the standard by which the final project will be judged. Among the contents of this specification will be the following:

1. *Functional requirements* for the system: what it will do and what commands will be available to the user.
2. *Assumptions* and *limitations* on the system: what hardware will be used for the system, what form the input must take, the maximum size of input, the largest number of users, and so on.
3. *Maintenance requirements*: anticipated extensions or growth of the system, changes in hardware, changes in user interface.
4. *Documentation requirements*: what kind of explanatory material is required for what kinds of users.

The requirements specifications state *what* the software will do, not *how* it will be done. These specifications should be understandable both to the user and to the programmer. If carefully prepared, they will form the basis for the subsequent phases of design, coding, testing, and maintenance.

2.6.3 The C Language

In this chapter and the previous one, we have had a whirlwind tour of many features of C. No attempt has been made to present an orderly or complete description of C features. A concise summary of C appears in Appendix C, to which you should refer with questions of C syntax. For further examples and discussion, consult a C textbook.

Programming Projects 2.6

P1. A *magic square* is a square array of integers such that the sum of every row, the sum of every column, and sum of each of the two diagonals are all equal. Two magic squares are shown in Figure 2.3.[1]

17	24	1	8	15
23	5	7	14	16
4	6	13	20	22
10	12	19	21	3
11	18	25	2	9

sum = 34   sum = 65

Figure 2.3. Two magic squares

a. Write a program that reads a square array of integers and determines whether or not it is a magic square.

b. Write a program that generates a magic square by the following method. This method works only when the size of the square is an odd number. Start by placing 1 in the middle of the top row. Write down successive integers 2, 3, ... along a diagonal going upward and to the right. When you reach the top row (as you do immediately since 1 is in the top row), continue to the bottom row as though the bottom row were immediately above the top row. When you reach the rightmost column, continue to the leftmost column as though it were immediately to the right of the rightmost one. When you reach a position that is already occupied, instead drop straight down one position from the previous number to insert the new one. The 5×5 magic square constructed by this method is shown in Figure 2.3.

P2. *One-dimensional Life* takes place on a straight line instead of a rectangular grid. Each cell has four neighboring positions: those at distance one or two from it on each side. The rules are similar to those of two-dimensional Life except (1) a dead cell with either two or three living neighbors will become alive in the next generation, and (2) a living cell dies if it has zero, one, or three living neighbors. (Hence a dead cell with zero, one, or four living neighbors stays dead; a living cell with two or four living neighbors stays alive.) The progress of sample communities is shown in Figure 2.4. Design, write, and test a program for one-dimensional Life.

---

[1] The magic square on the left appears as shown here in the etching *Melancolia* by ALBRECHT DÜRER. Note the inclusion of the date of the etching, 1514.

Figure 2.4. One-dimensional Life configurations

P3.   **a.** Write a program that will print the calendar of the current year.

b. Modify the program so that it will read a year number and print the calendar for that year. A year is a leap year (that is, February has 29 instead of 28 days) if it is a multiple of 4, except that century years (multiple of 100) are leap years only when the year is divisible by 400. Hence the year 1900 is not a leap year, but the year 2000 is a leap year.

c. Modify the program so that it will accept any date (day, month, year) and print the day of the week for that date.

d. Modify the program so that it will read two dates and print the number of days from one to the other.

e. Using the rules on leap years, show that the sequence of calendars repeats exactly every 400 years.

f. What is the probability (over a 400 year period) that the 13th of a month is a Friday? Why is the 13th of the month more likely to be a Friday than any other day of the week? Write a program to calculate how many Friday the 13ths occur in this century.

POINTERS AND PITFALLS

1. To improve your program, review the logic. Don't optimize code based on a poor algorithm.

2. Never optimize a program until it is correct and working.

3. Don't optimize code unless it is absolutely necessary.

4. Keep your functions short; rarely should any function be more than a page long.

5. Be sure your algorithm is correct before starting to code.

6. Verify the intricate parts of your algorithm.

7. Keep your logic simple.

8. Review the Programming Precepts!

REVIEW QUESTIONS

2.1   **1.** What is program maintenance?

2.2   **2.** What are hierarchical structures, and how should they be processed?

2.3   **3.** When should allocation of tasks among functions be made?

         4. How long should coding be delayed?

2.4   **5.** What is mathematical induction?

         6. What is a loop invariant?

         7. What are preconditions and postconditions of a subprogram?

2.5   **8.** What is a time-space tradeoff?

2.6   **9.** What is a prototype?

         10. Name at least six phases of the software life cycle and state what each is.

         11. Define software engineering.

         12. What are requirements specifications for a program?

REFERENCES FOR FURTHER STUDY

software engineering   A thorough discussion of many aspects of structured programming is:

> EDWARD YOURDON, *Techniques of Program Structure and Design*, Prentice Hall, Englewood Cliffs, N. J., 1975, 364 pages.

A perceptive discussion (in a book that is also enjoyable reading) of the many problems that arise in the construction of large software systems is:

> FREDERICK P. BROOKS, JR., *The Mythical Man–Month: Essays on Software Engineering*, Addison-Wesley, Reading, Mass., 1975, 195 pages.

A good textbook on software engineering is:

> IAN SOMMERVILLE, *Software Engineering*, Addison-Wesley, Wokingham, England, 1985, 334 pages.

Program testing has been developed to the point where its methods can fill a large book:

> WILLIAM E. PERRY, *A Structured Approach to Systems Testing*, Prentice Hall, Englewood Cliffs, N. J., 1983, 451 pages.

algorithm verification   Two books concerned with proving programs and using assertions and invariants to develop algorithms are

> DAVID GRIES, *The Science of Programming*, Springer-Verlag, New York, 1981, 366 pages.

> SUAD ALAGIĆ and MICHAEL A. ARBIB, *The Design of Well–Structured and Correct Programs*, Springer-Verlag, New York, 1978, 292 pages.

Keeping programs so simple in design that they can be proved to be correct is not easy, but is very important. C. A. R. HOARE (who invented the quicksort algorithm that we shall study in Chapter 7) writes: "There are two ways of constructing a software design: One way is to make it so simple that there are obviously no deficiencies, and the other way is to make it so complicated that there are no obvious deficiencies. The first method is far more difficult." This quotation is from the 1980 Turing Award Lecture, "The emperor's old clothes," *Communications of the ACM* 24 (1981), 75–83.

Two books concerned with methods of problem solving are

problem solving
> GEORGE PÓLYA, *How to Solve It*, second edition, Doubleday, Garden City, N.Y., 1957, 253 pages.

> WAYNE A. WICKELGREN, *How to Solve Problems*, W. H. Freeman, San Francisco, 1974, 262 pages.

The programming project on one-dimensional life is taken from

> JONATHAN K. MILLER, "One-dimensional Life," *Byte* 3 (December, 1978), 68–74.

C H A P T E R 3

Lists

This chapter introduces the study of data structures by studying various kinds of lists, including stacks and queues, together with their implementations in computer storage and C functions. The separation between the use of data structures and their implementation is emphasized. Several examples are developed, including a simulation problem.

3.1 STATIC AND DYNAMIC STRUCTURES

Soon after the introduction of loops and arrays, every elementary programming class attempts some programming exercise like the following:

> *Read an integer n, which will be at most 25, then read a list of n numbers, and print the list in reverse order.*

This little exercise will probably cause difficulty for some students. Most will realize that they need to use an array, but some will attempt to set up the array to have n entries and will be confused by the error message resulting from attempting to use a variable rather than a constant to declare the size of the array. Other students will say, "I could solve the problem if I knew that there were 25 numbers, but I don't see how to handle fewer." Or "Tell me before I write the program how large n is, and then I can do it."

lists and arrays   The difficulties of these students come not from stupidity, but from thinking logically. In a beginning course, there is sometimes not enough distinction drawn between two quite different concepts. First is the concept of a ***list*** of n numbers, a list whose size is variable, that is, a list for which numbers can be inserted or deleted, so that, if $n = 3$, then the list contains only 3 numbers, and if $n = 19$, then it contains 19 numbers. Second is the programming feature called an ***array*** or a vector, which contains a constant number of positions, that is, whose size is fixed when the program is compiled.

implementation   The two concepts are, of course, related in that a list of variable size can be implemented in a computer as occupying part of an array of fixed size, with some of the entries in the array remaining unused.

In this chapter we shall see that sometimes there are several different ways to implement a list within computer memory, and therefore the careful programmer needs *choice of* to make a conscious decision about which of these to choose. The need for careful *data structures* decision making about how to store data, in fact, extends back even further in the process of program design. We shall soon see that there is more than one kind of list (*stacks* and *queues* are the first two kinds we study), and therefore the programmer must first decide what kind of list (or what other conceptual structure) is needed for the data *choice of* and then must decide how the conceptual structure will be implemented in computer *implementations* memory. By keeping these decisions separate, we shall be able both to simplify the programming process and avoid some of the pitfalls that attend premature decisions.

Already in Section 2.2 we have discussed the implementation of lists inside C arrays. We set up a structure type, so that we could keep track both of the array and of the variable that counts entries in the list, tied together as one logical structure. In this chapter we shall continue with similar methods.

3.2 STACKS

3.2.1 Definition and Operations

stacks   The easiest kind of list to use is called a ***stack*** and is defined formally as a list in which all insertions and deletions are made at one end, called the ***top*** of the stack. A helpful analogy (see Figure 3.1) is to think of a stack of trays or of plates sitting on the counter

Figure 3.1. Stacks

in a busy cafeteria. Throughout the lunch hour, customers take trays off the top of the stack, and employees place returned trays back on top of the stack. The tray most recently put on the stack is the first one taken off. The bottom tray is the first one put on, and the last one to be used.

Sometimes this picture is described with plates or trays on a spring-loaded device so that the top of the stack stays near the same height. This imagery is poor and should be avoided. If we were to implement a computer stack in this way, it would mean moving every item in the stack whenever one item was inserted or deleted. This would be costly. It is far better to think of the stack as resting on a firm counter or floor, so that only the top item is moved when it is added or deleted. The spring-loaded imagery, however, has contributed a pair of colorful words that are firmly embedded in computer jargon, and which we shall use. When we add an item to a stack, we say that we ***push*** it onto the

push and pop   stack, and when we remove an item, we say that we ***pop*** it from the stack. From the same analogy, the term ***push-down list*** is used synonymously with stack, but we shall not employ this term. See Figure 3.2.

3.2.2 Examples

1. Stack Frames for Subprograms

As one important application of stacks, consider what happens within the computer system when subprograms are called. The system (or the program) must remember the place where the call was made, so that it can return there after the subprogram is

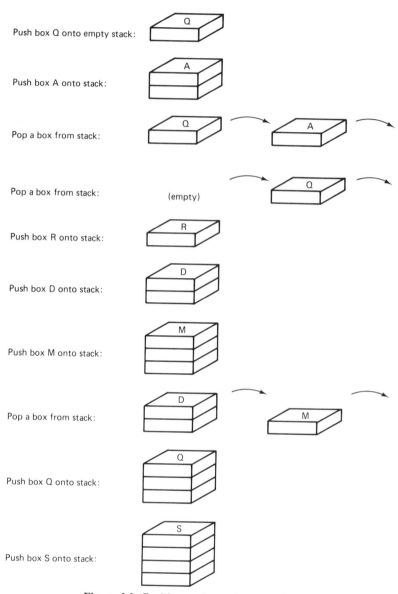

Push box Q onto empty stack:

Push box A onto stack:

Pop a box from stack:

Pop a box from stack: (empty)

Push box R onto stack:

Push box D onto stack:

Push box M onto stack:

Pop a box from stack:

Push box Q onto stack:

Push box S onto stack:

Figure 3.2. Pushing and popping a stack

complete. It must also remember all the local variables, CPU registers, and the like, so that information will not be lost while the subprogram is working. We can think of all this information as one large structure, a temporary storage area for each subprogram.

subprogram data storage

Suppose now that we have three subprograms called A, B, and C, and suppose that A invokes B and B invokes C. Then B will not have finished its work until C has finished and returned. Similarly A is the first to start work, but it is the last to be finished, not until sometime after B has finished and returned. Thus the sequence by which subprogram activity proceeds is summed up as the property *last in, first out*. If we

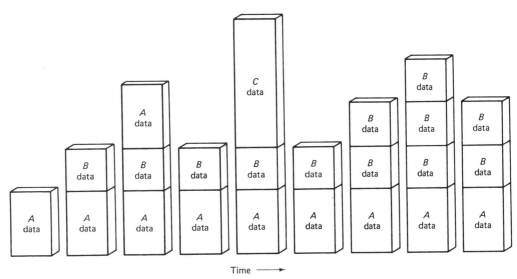

Time ⟶

Figure 3.3. Stack frames for subprogram calls

consider the machine's task of assigning temporary storage areas for use by subprograms, then these areas would be allocated in a list with this same property, that is, in a stack (see Figure 3.3). Hence yet one more name sometimes used for stacks is *LIFO lists*, based on the acronym for this property.

2. Reversing a Line

As a simple example of using stacks, let us suppose that we wish to make a function that will read a line of input and will then write it out backward. We can accomplish this task by pushing each character onto a stack as it is read. When the line is finished, we then pop characters off the stack, and they will come off in the reverse order. Hence our function takes the following form:

```
/* ReverseRead: read one line of input and write it backward. */
void ReverseRead(void)
{
        Item_type item;
        Item_type *item_ptr = &item;
        Stack_type stack;
        Stack_type *stack_ptr = &stack;
        Initialize(stack_ptr);              /* Initialize the stack to be empty.     */
        while (!Full(stack_ptr) && (item = getchar()) != '\n')
                Push(item, stack_ptr);      /* Push each item onto the stack.        */
        while (!Empty(stack_ptr)) {
                Pop(item_ptr, stack_ptr);   /* Pop an item from the stack.           */
                putchar(item);
        }
        putchar('\n');
}
```

In this function we have used not only Push and Pop but also a function Initialize that initializes the stack to be empty and Boolean-valued functions Empty that checks whether the stack is empty or not and Full that checks if it is completely full. The declarations for a stack appear in Section 3.2.3.

3. Information Hiding

use of functions

Notice that we have been able to write our function before we consider how the stack will actually be implemented in storage and before we write the details of the various functions. In this way we have an example of ***information hiding***: If someone else had already written the functions for handling stacks, then we could use them without needing to know the details of how stacks are kept in memory or of how the stack operations are actually done.

3.2.3 Array Implementation of Stacks

1. Declarations

To implement a stack in a computer we shall set up an array that will hold the items in the stack and a counter to indicate how many items there are. In C we can make declarations such as the following, where MAXSTACK is a symbolic constant giving the maximum size allowed for stacks and Item_type is the type describing the data that will be put into the stack. Type Item_type depends on the application and can range from a single character or number to a large structure with many elements. Our stack.h contains:

```
#define MAXSTACK 10

typedef char Item_type;

typedef struct stack_tag {
      int top;
      Item_type entry [MAXSTACK] ;
} Stack_type;

Boolean_type Empty (Stack_type *) ;
Boolean_type Full (Stack_type *) ;
void Initialize (Stack_type *) ;
void Push (Item_type, Stack_type *) ;
void Pop (Item_type *, Stack_type *) ;
```

2. Pushing and Popping

Pushing and popping the stack are then implemented as follows. We must be careful of the extreme cases: We might attempt to pop an item from an empty stack or to push an item onto a full stack. We shall regard such attempts as errors fatal to the execution of the program, and therefore we must also write Boolean-valued functions so that by checking emptiness or fullness the program can guard against these errors ever occurring.

```
/* Push: push an item onto the stack. */
void Push (Item_type item, Stack_type *stack_ptr)
{
        if (stack_ptr->top >= MAXSTACK)
                Error ("Stack is full");
        else
                stack_ptr->entry [stack_ptr->top++] = item;
}
/* Pop: pop an item from the stack. */
void Pop (Item_type *item_ptr, Stack_type *stack_ptr)
{
        if (stack_ptr->top <= 0)
                Error ("Stack is empty");
        else
                *item_ptr = stack_ptr->entry [--stack_ptr->top];
}
```

Error is a function that receives a pointer to a character string, prints the string, and then invokes the standard function exit to terminate the execution of the program.

```
/* Error: print error message and terminate the program. */
void Error (char *s)
{
        fprintf (stderr, "%s\n", s);
        exit (1);
}
```

In normal circumstances Error is not executed because, as in ReverseRead, we check whether the stack is full before we push an item and we check if the stack is empty before we pop an item.

3. Other Operations

```
/* Empty: returns non-zero if the stack is empty. */
Boolean_type Empty (Stack_type *stack_ptr)
{
        return stack_ptr->top <= 0;
}
/* Full: returns non-zero if the stack is full. */
Boolean_type Full (Stack_type *stack_ptr)
{
        return stack_ptr->top >= MAXSTACK;
}
```

The next function initializes a stack to be empty before it is first used in a program:

```
/* Initialize: initialize the stack to be empty. */
void Initialize (Stack_type *stack_ptr)
{
        stack_ptr->top = 0;
}
```

4. Advantages of the Operational Approach

flexibility of implementation

If you think that we are belaboring the obvious by introducing all these functions, then in one sense you are right, since their substance is so simple that they could easily be written out wherever they are needed in a program, rather than keeping them as separate functions. For large programs there is one important advantage, however, to using a structure to implement stacks and separate functions to process them. It may well happen that, after we start work on a large project, we realize that another way of implementing our stacks in storage would prove better than the method we had used. If the instructions have been written out every time a stack is pushed or popped, then every occurrence will need to be changed. If we have used structures and functions, then only the definition of the structure type and the declarations of the functions must be altered.

clarity of program

top-down design

A second advantage, of course, is that the very appearance of the words *Push* and *Pop* will immediately alert a person reading the program to what is being done, whereas the instructions themselves might be more obscure. A third advantage we shall find is that separating the use of data structures from their implementation will help us improve the top-down design of both our data structures and our programs.

Exercises 3.2

E1. Draw a sequence of stack frames showing the progress of each of the following segments of code. (stack_ptr is a pointer to a stack of characters and x, y, z are character variables.)

a. Initialize(stack_ptr);
   Push('a', stack_ptr);
   Push('b', stack_ptr);
   Push('c', stack_ptr);
   Pop(&x, stack_ptr);
   Pop(&y, stack_ptr);
   Pop(&z, stack_ptr);

b. Initialize(stack_ptr);
   Push('a', stack_ptr);
   Push('b', stack_ptr);
   Initialize(stack_ptr);
   Push('c', stack_ptr);
   Pop(&x, stack_ptr);
   Push('a', stack_ptr);
   Pop(&y, stack_ptr);
   Push('b', stack_ptr);
   Pop(&z, stack_ptr);

c. Initialize(stack_ptr);
   Push('a', stack_ptr);
   Push('b', stack_ptr);
   Push('c', stack_ptr);
   while (!Empty(stack_ptr))
      Pop(&x, stack_ptr);

d. Initialize(stack_ptr);
   Push('a', stack_ptr);
   Push('b', stack_ptr);
   Push('c', stack_ptr);
   Pop(&x, stack_ptr);
   Pop(&y, stack_ptr);
   Push(x, stack_ptr);
   Push(y, stack_ptr);
   Pop(&z, stack_ptr);

E2. Let stack_ptr be a pointer to a stack stack of integers and item be an integer variable. Use the functions Push, Pop, Initialize, Empty, and Full to write functions doing each of the following tasks. [You may declare additional variables in your functions if needed.]

a. Return the top element of the stack and leave the top element unchanged. If the stack is empty, return INT_MAX.

    b. Return the third element from the top of the stack, provided that the stack contains at least three integers. If not, return INT_MAX. Leave the stack unchanged.

    c. Return the bottom element of stack (or INT_MAX if stack is empty), and leave the stack unchanged. [*Hint*: Use a second stack.]

    d. Delete all occurrences of x from the stack, leaving the other elements of the stack in the same order.

E3. Sometimes a program requires two stacks containing the same type of items. If the two stacks are stored in separate arrays, then one stack might overflow while there was considerable unused space in the other. A neat way to avoid this problem is to put all the space in one array and let one stack grow from one end of the array and the other stack start at the other end and grow in the opposite direction, toward the first stack. In this way, if one stack turns out to be large and the other small, then they will still both fit, and there will be no overflow until all the space is actually used. Declare a new structure type DoubleStack that includes the array and the two indices topA and topB, and write functions PushA, PushB, PopA, and PopB to handle the two stacks within one DoubleStack.

E4. Write a program that uses a stack to read an integer and print all its prime divisors in descending order. For example, with the integer 2100 the output should be

$$7 \quad 5 \quad 5 \quad 3 \quad 2 \quad 2.$$

[*Hint*: The smallest divisor greater than 1 of any integer is guaranteed to be a prime.]

E5. A stack may be regarded as a railway switching network like the one in Figure 3.4.

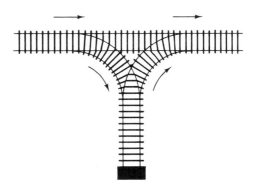

Figure 3.4. Switching network for stack permutations

    Cars numbered 1, 2, ..., n are on the line at the left, and it is desired to rearrange (permute) the cars as they leave on the right hand track. A car that is on the spur (stack) can be left there or sent on its way down the right track, but it can never be sent back to the incoming track. For example, if $n = 3$, and we have the cars 1, 2, 3 on the left track, then 3 first goes to the spur. We could then send 2 to the spur, then on its way to the right, then send 3 on the way, then 1, obtaining the new order 1, 3, 2.

a. For $n = 3$, find all possible permutations that can be obtained.

b. Same, for $n = 4$.

c. [Challenging] For general n, find how many permutations can be obtained by using this stack.

3.3 QUEUES

3.3.1 Definitions

In ordinary English a queue is defined as a waiting line, like a line of people waiting to purchase tickets, where the first person in line is the first person served. For computer applications we similarly define a *queue* to be a list in which all additions to the list are made at one end, and all deletions from the list are made at the other end. Queues are also called *first-in, first-out lists*, or *FIFO* for short. See Figure 3.5.

Figure 3.5. A queue

applications Applications of queues are, if anything, even more common than are applications of stacks, since in performing tasks by computer, as in all parts of life, it is so often necessary to wait one's turn before having access to something. Within a computer system there may be queues of tasks waiting for the line printer, for access to disk storage, or even, in a time-sharing system, for use of the CPU. Within a single program, there may be multiple requests to be kept in a queue, or one task may create other tasks, which must be done in turn by keeping them in a queue.

front and rear The item in a queue ready to be served, that is, the first item that will be removed from the queue, we call the *front* of the queue (or, sometimes, the *head* of the queue). Similarly, the last item in the queue, that is, the one most recently added, we call the *rear* (or the *tail*) of the queue.

3.3.2 Implementations of Queues

1. The Physical Model

As we did for stacks, we can create a queue in computer storage easily by setting up an ordinary array to hold the items. Now, however, we must keep track of both the front and the rear of the queue. One method would be to keep the front of the queue always in the first location of the array. Then an item could be added to the queue simply by increasing the counter showing the rear, in exactly the same way as we added an item to a stack. To delete an item from the queue, however, would be very expensive indeed, since after the first item was removed, all the remaining items would need to be moved one position up the queue to fill in the vacancy. With a long queue, this process would be prohibitively slow. Although this method of storage closely models a queue of people waiting to be served, it is a poor choice for use in computers.

2. Linear Implementation

For efficient processing of queues, we shall therefore need two indices so that we can keep track of both the front and the rear of the queue without moving any items. To add an item to the queue, we simply increase the rear by one and put the item in that position. To remove an item, we take it from the position at the front and then increase the front by one. This method, however, still has a major defect. Both the front and

defect rear indices are increased but never decreased. Even if there are never more than two items in the queue, an unbounded amount of storage will be needed for the queue if the sequence of operations is

Add, Add, Delete, Add, Delete, Add, Delete, ...

The problem, of course, is that, as the queue moves down the array, the storage space at the beginning of the array is discarded and never used again. Perhaps the queue can be likened to a snake crawling through storage. Sometimes the snake is longer, sometimes shorter, but if it always keeps crawling in a straight line, then it will soon reach the end of the storage space.

Note, however, that for applications where the queue is regularly emptied (such as

advantage when a series of requests is allowed to build up to a certain point, and then a task is initiated that clears all the requests before returning), at a time when the queue is empty, the front and rear can both be reset to the beginning of the array, and the simple scheme of using two indices and straight-line storage becomes a very efficient storage method.

3. Circular Arrays

In concept we can overcome the inefficient use of space simply by thinking of the array as a circle rather than a straight line. See Figure 3.6. In this way as items are added and removed from the queue, the head will continually chase the tail around the array, so that the snake can keep crawling indefinitely but stay in a confined circuit. At different times the queue will occupy different parts of the array, but we never need worry about running out of space unless the array is fully occupied, in which case we truly have overflow.

Figure 3.6. Queue in a circular array

4. Implementation of Circular Arrays

Our next problem is to implement a circular array as an ordinary linear (that is, straight-line) array. To do so, we think of the positions around the circle as numbered from 0 to MAX−1, where MAX is the total number of entries in the circular array, and to implement the circular array, we use the same-numbered entries of a linear array. Then moving the

modular arithmetic   indices is just the same as doing modular arithmetic: When we increase an index past MAX−1 we start over again at 0. This is like doing arithmetic on a circular clock face; the hours are numbered from 1 to 12, and if we add four hours to ten o'clock, we obtain two o'clock.

Perhaps a good human analogy of this linear representation is that of a priest serving communion to people kneeling at the front of a church. The communicants do not move until the priest comes by and serves them. When the priest reaches the end of the row, he returns to the beginning and starts again, since by this time a new row of people have come forward.

5. Circular Arrays in C

In C we can increase an index i by 1 in a circular array by writing

$$\text{if } (i >= \text{MAX} - 1)$$
$$i = 0;$$
$$\text{else}$$
$$i++;$$

or even more easily (but perhaps less efficiently at run time) by using the % operator:

$$i = (i + 1) \% \text{MAX};$$

6. Boundary Conditions

Before writing formal algorithms to add to and delete from a queue, let us consider the boundary conditions, that is, the indicators that a queue is empty or full. If there is exactly one entry in the queue, then the front index will equal the rear index. When this one entry is removed, then the front will be increased by 1, so that an empty queue is indicated when the rear is one position before the front. Now suppose that the queue is nearly full. Then the rear will have moved well away from the front, all the way around the circle, and when the array is full the rear will be exactly one position behind the front. Thus we have another difficulty: The front and rear indices are in exactly the same relative positions for an empty queue and for a full queue! There is no way, by looking at the indices alone, to tell a full queue from an empty one. This situation is illustrated in Figure 3.7.

empty or full?

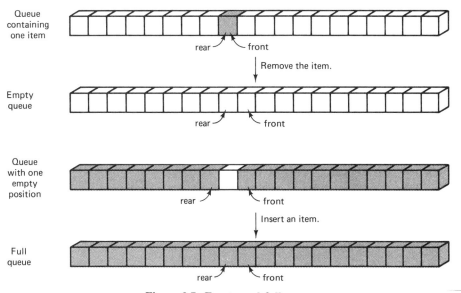

Figure 3.7. Empty and full queues

7. Possible Solutions

1. empty position

2. flag

There are at least three essentially different ways to resolve this problem. One is to insist on leaving one empty position in the array so that the queue is considered full when the rear index has moved within two positions of the front. A second method is to introduce

3. special values

a new variable. This can be a Boolean variable that will be used when the rear comes just before the front to indicate whether the queue is full or not (a Boolean variable to check emptiness would be just as good) or an integer variable that counts the number of items in the queue. The third method is to set one or both of the indices to some value(s) that would otherwise never occur in order to indicate an empty (or full) queue. If, for example, the array entries are indexed from 0 to MAX-1, then an empty queue could be indicated by setting the rear index to -1.

8. Summary of Implementations

To summarize the discussion of queues, let us list all the methods we have discussed for implementing queues.

1. The physical model: a linear array with the front always in the first position and all entries moved up the array whenever the front is deleted (this is generally a poor method for use in computers).

2. A linear array with two indices always increasing (this is a good method if the queue can be emptied all at once).

3. A circular array with front and rear indices and one position left vacant.

4. A circular array with front and rear indices and a Boolean variable to indicate fullness (or emptiness).

5. A circular array with front and rear indices and an integer variable counting entries.

6. A circular array with front and rear indices taking special values to indicate emptiness.

postpone implementation decisions

In the next chapter we shall find still other ways to implement queues. The most important thing to remember from this list is that, with so many variations in implementation, we should always keep questions concerning the use of data structures like queues separate from questions concerning their implementation, and in programming we should always consider only one of these categories of questions at a time. After we have considered how queues will be used in our application, and after we have written the functions employing queues, we will have more information to help us choose the best implementation of queues suited to our application.

3.3.3 Circular Queues in C

Next let us write formal C functions for some of the possible implementations of a queue. We shall choose the last two implementations and leave the others as exercises. In all cases, however, we take the queue as stored in an array indexed with the range

0 to MAXQUEUE-1

and containing entries of a type called Item_type. The variables front and rear will point to appropriate positions in the array.

1. Implementation with a Counter

First, we take the method in which a variable count is used to keep track of the number of items in the queue. The queue.h file contains the structure declaration for a queue and the function prototypes associated with queues:

```
#define MAXQUEUE 3                          /* small value for testing              */

typedef char Item_type;

typedef struct queue_tag {
        int count;
        int front;
        int rear;
        Item_type entry [MAXQUEUE] ;
} Queue_type;

void AddQueue (Item_type, Queue_type *);
void DeleteQueue (Item_type *, Queue_type *);
void Initialize (Queue_type *);
int Size (Queue_type *);
Boolean_type Empty (Queue_type *);
Boolean_type Full (Queue_type *);
```

type queue

The first function we need will initialize the queue to be empty.

```
/* Initialize: initialize queue. */
void Initialize (Queue_type *queue_ptr)
{
        queue_ptr->count = 0;
        queue_ptr->front = 0;
        queue_ptr->rear = -1;
}
```

initialize

The key functions for adding to and deleting from a queue follow our preceding discussion closely. We use a function Error (included in general.h) to keep track of error conditions.

```
/* AddQueue: add item to the queue. */
void AddQueue (Item_type item, Queue_type *queue_ptr)
{
        if (queue_ptr->count >= MAXQUEUE)
            Error ("Queue is full");
        else {
            queue_ptr->count++;
            queue_ptr->rear = (queue_ptr->rear + 1) % MAXQUEUE;
            queue_ptr->entry [queue_ptr->rear] = item;
        }
}
```

insertion

/* *DeleteQueue: delete and return item in front of queue.* */

deletion   void DeleteQueue (Item_type *item, Queue_type *queue_ptr)
{
       if (queue_ptr->count <= 0)
              Error("Queue is empty");
       else {
              queue_ptr->count--;
              *item = queue_ptr->entry [queue_ptr->front];
              queue_ptr->front = (queue_ptr->front + 1) % MAXQUEUE;
       }
}

We shall also find use for three functions concerning the size of the queue, all of which are easy to write with this implementation.

/* *Size: return current number of items in the queue.* */

size   int Size (Queue_type *queue_ptr)
{
       return queue_ptr->count;
}

/* *Empty: returns non-zero if the queue is empty.* */

empty?   Boolean_type Empty (Queue_type *queue_ptr)
{
       return queue_ptr->count <= 0;
}

/* *Full: returns non-zero if the queue is full.* */

full?   Boolean_type Full (Queue_type *queue_ptr)
{
       return queue_ptr->count >= MAXQUEUE;
}

2. Implementation with Special Index Values

Next let us turn to the method that relies on special values for the indices. Most of the necessary changes in declarations are clear. The modified queue.h then becomes

#define MAXQUEUE 3

typedef char Item_type;

typedef struct queue_tag {

type queue   int front;
       int rear;
       Item_type entry [MAXQUEUE];
} Queue_type;

void AddQueue (Item_type, Queue_type *);
void DeleteQueue (Item_type *, Queue_type *);
void Initialize (Queue_type *);
int Size (Queue_type *);
Boolean_type Empty (Queue_type *);
Boolean_type Full (Queue_type *);

We shall use the conditions rear == −1 and front == 0 to indicate an empty queue. The initialization function is

initialize

```
/* Initialize: initialize queue. */
void Initialize (Queue_type *queue_ptr)
{
       queue_ptr->front = 0;
       queue_ptr->rear = −1;
}
```

To write the function for adding to the queue, we must first (for error checking) find a condition indicating whether the queue is full or not. Fullness is typically indicated by rear == front − 1 together with rear > −1, but it is also possible that front == 0 and rear >= MAXQUEUE − 1. Building these conditions into the function, we obtain

insertion

```
/* AddQueue: add item to the queue. */
void AddQueue (Item_type item, Queue_type *queue_ptr)
{
       if ((queue_ptr->rear == queue_ptr->front − 1 &&
             queue_ptr->rear > −1) ||
             (queue_ptr->rear == MAXQUEUE − 1 &&
             queue_ptr->front == 0))
             Error ("Queue is full");
       else {
             queue_ptr->rear = (queue_ptr->rear + 1) % MAXQUEUE;
             queue_ptr->entry [queue_ptr->rear] = item;
       }
}
```

Since emptiness is indicated by rear == −1, the deletion function closely resembles the previous version.

deletion

```
/* DeleteQueue: delete and return item in front of queue. */
void DeleteQueue (Item_type *item_ptr, Queue_type *queue_ptr)
{
       if (queue_ptr->rear <= −1)
             Error ("Queue is empty");
       else {
             *item_ptr = queue_ptr->entry [queue_ptr->front];
             if (queue_ptr->front != queue_ptr->rear)
                   queue_ptr->front = (queue_ptr->front + 1) % MAXQUEUE;
             else {                          /* The queue is now empty.          */
                   queue_ptr->front = 0;
                   queue_ptr->rear = −1;
             }
       }
}
```

The three functions Size, Empty, and Full will be left as exercises.

Exercises 3.3

E1. Suppose that queue_ptr is a pointer to a queue that holds characters and that x, y, z are character variables. Show the contents of the queue at each step of the following code segments.

a. Initialize(queue_ptr);
    AddQueue('a', queue_ptr);
    AddQueue('b', queue_ptr);
    DeleteQueue(&x, queue_ptr);
    AddQueue(x, queue_ptr);
    DeleteQueue(&y, queue_ptr);
    DeleteQueue(&z, queue_ptr);

b. Initialize(queue_ptr);
    AddQueue('a', queue_ptr);
    x = 'b';
    AddQueue('x', queue_ptr);
    DeleteQueue(&y, queue_ptr);
    AddQueue(x, queue_ptr);
    DeleteQueue(&z, queue_ptr);
    AddQueue(y, queue_ptr);

E2. Suppose that you are a financier and purchase 100 shares of stock in Company X in each of January, April, and September and sell 100 shares in each of June and November. The prices per share in these months were

accounting

Jan	Apr	Jun	Sep	Nov
$10	$30	$20	$50	$30

Determine the total amount of your capital gain or loss using **(a)** FIFO (first-in, first-out) accounting and **(b)** LIFO (last-in, first-out) accounting (that is, assuming that you keep your stock certificates in (a) a queue or (b) a stack). The 100 shares you still own at the end of the year do not enter the calculation.

E3. Use the functions developed in the text to write other functions that will

    a. Empty one stack onto the top of another stack.

    b. Move all the items from a queue onto a stack.

    c. Start with a queue and an empty stack, and use the stack to reverse the order of all the items in the queue.

E4. Implement the simple representation of queues in a linear array when it can be assumed that the queue can be emptied when necessary. Write a function AddQueue that will add an item if there is room and, if not, will call another function that will empty the queue. While writing this second function, you may assume the existence of an auxiliary function Service(Item_type item) that will process a single item that you have just removed from the queue.

E5. Write C functions to implement queues by the simple but slow method of keeping the head of the queue always in the first position of a linear array.

E6. Write C functions to implement queues in a linear array with two indices front and rear, such that when rear reaches the end of the array all the items are moved to the front of the array.

E7. Write the three functions Size, Empty, and Full for the implementation of a queue in a circular array with special index values to indicate emptiness.

E8. Rewrite the first set of C functions for queue processing from the text, using a Boolean variable full instead of a counter of items in the queue.

E9. Write C functions to implement queues in a circular array with one unused entry in the array. That is, we consider that the array is full when the rear is two positions before the front; when the rear is one position before, it will always indicate an empty queue.

Programming Project 3.3

P1. Write a function that will read one line of input from the terminal. The input is supposed to consist of two parts separated by a colon ':'. As its result your function should produce a single character as follows:

N	No colon on the line.
L	The left part (before the colon) is longer than the right.
R	The right part (after the colon) is longer than the left.
D	The left and right parts have the same length but are different.
S	The left and right parts are exactly the same.

	Input	Output
Examples:	*Input*	*Output*
	Sample Sample	N
	Short:Long	L
	Sample:Sample	S

Use a queue to keep track of the left part of the line while reading the right part.

3.4 APPLICATION OF QUEUES: SIMULATION

3.4.1 Introduction

Simulation is the use of one system to imitate the behavior of another system. Simulations are often used when it would be too expensive or dangerous to experiment with the real system. There are physical simulations, such as wind tunnels used to experiment with designs for car bodies and flight simulators used to train airline pilots. Mathematical simulations are systems of equations used to describe some system, and computer simulations use the steps of a program to imitate the behavior of the system under study.

computer models   In a computer simulation, the objects being studied are usually represented as data, often as data structures like structures or arrays whose entries describe the properties of the objects. Actions in the system being studied are represented as operations on the data, and the rules describing these actions are translated into computer algorithms. By changing the values of the data or by modifying these algorithms, we can observe the changes in the computer simulation, and then, we hope, we can draw worthwhile inferences concerning the behavior of the actual system in which we are interested.

While one object in a system is involved in some action, other objects and actions will often need to be kept waiting. Hence queues are important data structures for use in computer simulations. We shall study one of the most common and useful kinds of computer simulations, one that concentrates on queues as its basic data structure. These simulations imitate the behavior of systems (often, in fact, called **queueing systems**) in which there are queues of objects waiting to be served by various processes.

3.4.2 Simulation of an Airport

As a specific example, let us consider a small but busy airport with only one runway (see Figure 3.8). In each unit of time one plane can land or one plane can take off, but not both. Planes arrive ready to land or to take off at random times, so at any given unit of time, the runway may be idle or a plane may be landing or taking off, and there may be several planes waiting either to land or take off. We therefore need two queues,
rules which we shall call landing and takeoff, to hold these planes. It is better to keep a plane waiting on the ground than in the air, so a small airport allows a plane to take off only if there are no planes waiting to land. Hence, after receiving requests from new planes to land or take off, our simulation will first service the head of the queue of planes waiting to land, and only if the landing queue is empty will it allow a plane to take off. We shall wish to run the simulation through many units of time, and therefore we embed the main action of the program in a loop that runs for curtime (denoting *current time*) from 1 to a variable endtime. With this notation we can write an outline of the main program.

Landing queue

Plane landing

Runway

Takeoff queue

Figure 3.8. An airport

```
                    /* simulation of an airport */
                    /* This is an outline only; not ready to compile. */
   first outline    void main(void)
                    {
                            Queue_type landing, takeoff;
                            Queue_type *pl = &landing;
                            Queue_type *pt = &takeoff;
                            Plane_type plane;
                            int curtime;              /* current time unit                        */
                            int endtime;              /* total number of time units to run        */
                            int i;                    /* loop control variable                    */
                            Initialize(pl);           /* Initialize landing queue.                */
                            Initialize(pt);           /* Initialize takeoff queue.                */
                            for (curtime = 1; curtime <= endtime; curtime++) {
                                    for (i = 1; i <= RandomNumber(); i++) {   /* landing queue     */
   new plane                               NewPlane(&plane);
   ready to land                          if (Full(pl))
                                                Refuse(plane);   /* Refuse plane if full.         */
                                        else
                                                AddQueue(plane, pl);   /* Add to landing queue.   */
                                    }
                                    for (i = 1; i <= RandomNumber(); i++) {   /* takeoff queue     */
   new plane                               NewPlane(&plane);
   ready to take off                      if (Full(pt))
                                                Refuse(plane);
                                        else
                                                AddQueue(plane, pt);
                                    }
   plane landing                       if (!Empty(pl)) {            /* Bring plane to land.        */
                                            plane = DeleteQueue(pl);
                                            Land(plane);
   plane taking off                     } else if (!Empty(pt)) {    /* Allow plane to take off.    */
                                            plane = DeleteQueue(pt);
                                            Fly(plane);
                                    } else
   idle runway                                  Idle();
                            }
                            Conclude();
                    }
```

Some of the declarations we are going to use are

```
typedef enum action_tag { ARRIVE, DEPART } Action_type;
typedef struct plane_tag {
    int id;                              /* identification number of airplane       */
    int tm;                              /* time of arrival in queue                */
} Plane_type;
```

3.4.3 The Main Program

Although this outline clearly shows the use of queues in this simulation, more detail is needed to keep track of all the interesting statistics concerning the problem, such as the number of planes processed, the average time spent waiting, and the number of planes (if any) refused service. These details are reflected in the declarations of constants, types, and variables to be inserted into the main program. We shall then need to write the subprograms to specify how this information is processed. The declaration of type Queue_type is deliberately omitted from the following program, in order that we can postpone until later the decision concerning which method will be used to implement the queues. Most of the remaining declarations are self-explanatory, except for the last two variables, which are concerned with generating random numbers, and will be explained when we consider the use of random numbers.

The version of the main program in runnable C differs little from the preceding outline except for the inclusion of the many parameters used to update all the variables.

```
void main (void)                        /* simulation of an airport           */
{
        Queue_type landing, takeoff;
        Queue_type *pl = &landing;
        Queue_type *pt = &takeoff;
        Plane_type plane;
        int curtime;          /* current time; one unit = time for take off or landing */
        int endtime;                    /* total number of time units to run    */
        double expectarrive;            /* number of planes arriving in one unit */
        double expectdepart;        /* number of planes newly ready to take off */
        int i;                          /* loop control variable                */
        int idletime;                   /* number of units when runway is idle  */
        int landwait;                   /* total waiting time for planes landed  */
        int nland;                      /* number of planes landed              */
        int nplanes;                    /* number of planes processed so far    */
        int nrefuse;                    /* number of planes refused of airport  */
        int ntakeoff;                   /* number of planes taken off           */
        int pri;                        /* pseudo-random integer                */
        int takeoffwait;                /* total waiting time for take off      */
```
initialize
```
        Initialize (pl); Initialize (pt);
        nplanes = nland = ntakeoff = nrefuse = 0;
        landwait = takeoffwait = idletime = 0;
        Start ( &endtime, &expectarrive, &expectdepart);
        for (curtime = 1; curtime <= endtime; curtime++) {
```
new plane(s)
ready to land
```
                pri = RandomNumber (expectarrive);
                for (i = 1; i <= pri; i++) { /* Add to landing queue.        */
                        NewPlane ( &plane, &nplanes, curtime, ARRIVE);
                        if (Full (pl))
                                Refuse (plane, &nrefuse, ARRIVE);
                        else   AddQueue (plane, pl);
                }
```

<table>
<tr><td>new plane(s)
ready to take off</td><td>

```
pri = RandomNumber(expectdepart);
for (i = 1; i <= pri; i++) {  /* Add to takeoff queue.             */
        NewPlane(&plane, &nplanes, curtime, DEPART);
        if (Full(pt))
                Refuse(plane, &nrefuse, DEPART);
        else
                AddQueue(plane, pt);
}
```
</td></tr>
<tr><td>plane landing</td><td>

```
if (!Empty(pl)) {             /* Bring plane to land.             */
        DeleteQueue(&plane, pl);
        Land(plane, curtime, &nland, &landwait);
```
</td></tr>
<tr><td>plane taking off</td><td>

```
} else if (!Empty(pt)) {   /* Allow plane to take off.           */
        DeleteQueue(&plane, pt);
        Fly(plane, curtime, &ntakeoff, &takeoffwait);
```
</td></tr>
<tr><td>runway idle</td><td>

```
} else
        Idle(curtime, &idletime);
}
```
</td></tr>
<tr><td>finish simulation</td><td>

```
Conclude(nplanes, nland, ntakeoff, nrefuse, landwait,
                takeoffwait, idletime, endtime, pt, pl);
}
```
</td></tr>
</table>

3.4.4 Steps of the Simulation

The actions of the functions for doing the steps of the simulation are generally straightforward, so we proceed to write each in turn, with comments only as needed for clarity.

1. Initialization

<table>
<tr><td></td><td>

```
/* start: print messages and initialize the parameters. */
void Start(int *endtime, double *expectarrive, double *expectdepart)
{
        Boolean_type ok;
```
</td></tr>
<tr><td>instruct user</td><td>

```
        printf("This program simulates an airport with only one runway.\n");
        printf("One plane can land or depart in each unit of time.\n");
        printf("Up to %d planes can ", MAXQUEUE);
        printf("be waiting to land or take off at any time.\n");
```
</td></tr>
<tr><td>input parameter</td><td>

```
        printf("How many units of time will the simulation run? ");
        scanf("%d", endtime);
        Randomize();                  /* Initialize random number generation.  */
        do {
                printf("Expected number of arrivals per unit time "
                        "(real number)? ");
                scanf("%lf", expectarrive);
                printf("Expected number of departures per unit time? ");
                scanf("%lf", expectdepart);
```
</td></tr>
</table>

error checking

```
                          if (*expectarrive < 0.0 || *expectdepart < 0.0) {
                                  printf("These numbers must be nonnegative.\n");
                                  ok = FALSE;
                          } else if (*expectarrive + *expectdepart > 1.0) {
                                  printf("The airport will become saturated. "
                                          "Read new numbers?\n");
                                  ok = !Enquire();      /* If user says yes, repeat loop.          */
                          } else
                                  ok = TRUE;
                  } while (ok == FALSE);
          }
```

2. Accepting a New Plane

```
                  /* NewPlane: make a new record for a plane, update nplanes. */
                  void NewPlane(Plane_type *p, int *nplanes, int curtime,
                                  Action_type kind)
          {
                  (*nplanes)++;
                  p->id = *nplanes;
                  p->tm = curtime;
                  switch(kind) {
                  case ARRIVE:
                          printf("      Plane %3d ready to land.\n", *nplanes);
                          break;
                  case DEPART:
                          printf("      Plane %3d ready to take off.\n", *nplanes);
                          break;
                  }
          }
```

3. Handling a Full Queue

```
                  /* Refuse: processes a plane when the queue is full. */
                  void Refuse(Plane_type p, int *nrefuse, Action_type kind)
          {
                  switch(kind) {
                  case ARRIVE:
                          printf("      Plane %3d directed to another airport.\n", p.id);
                          break;
                  case DEPART:
                          printf("      Plane %3d told to try later.\n", p.id);
                          break;
                  }
                  (*nrefuse)++;
          }
```

4. Processing an Arriving Plane

```
/* Land: process a plane p that is actually landing. */
void Land(Plane_type p, int curtime, int *nland, int *landwait)
{
        int wait;

        wait = curtime − p.tm;
        printf("%3d : Plane %3d landed; in queue %d units.\n",
                    curtime, p.id, wait);
        (*nland)++;
        *landwait += wait;
}
```

5. Processing a Departing Plane

```
/* Fly: process a plane p that is actually taking off. */
void Fly(Plane_type p, int curtime, int *ntakeoff, int *takeoffwait)
{
        int wait;

        wait = curtime − p.tm;
        printf("%3d : Plane %3d took off; in queue %d units.\n",
                    curtime, p.id, wait);
        (*ntakeoff)++;
        *takeoffwait += wait;
}
```

6. Marking an Idle Time Unit

```
/* Idle: updates variables for idle runway. */
void Idle(int curtime, int *idletime)
{
        printf("%3d : Runway is idle.\n", curtime);
        (*idletime)++;
}
```

7. Finishing the Simulation

```
/* Conclude: write out statistics and conclude simulation. */
void Conclude(int nplanes, int nland, int ntakeoff,
                int nrefuse, int landwait, int takeoffwait,
                int idletime, int endtime,
                Queue_type *pt, Queue_type *pl)
```

```
{
        printf("Simulation has concluded after %d units.\n", endtime);
        printf("Total number of planes processed:   %3d\n", nplanes);
        printf("   Number of planes landed:          %3d\n", nland);
        printf("   Number of planes taken off:       %3d\n", ntakeoff);
        printf("   Number of planes refused use:     %3d\n", nrefuse);
        printf("   Number left ready to land:        %3d\n", Size(pl));
        printf("   Number left ready to take off:    %3d\n", Size(pt));
        if (endtime > 0)
                printf("   Percentage of time runway idle:  %6.2f\n",
                        ((double) idletime/endtime) * 100.0);
        if (nland > 0)
                printf("   Average wait time to land:        %6.2f\n",
                        (double) landwait/nland);
        if (ntakeoff > 0)
                printf("   Average wait time to take off:    %6.2f\n",
                        (double) takeoffwait/ntakeoff);
}
```

3.4.5 Random Numbers

A key step in our simulation is to decide, at each time unit, how many new planes become ready to land or take off. Although there are many ways in which these decisions can be made, one of the most interesting and useful is to make a random decision. When the program is run repeatedly with random decisions, the results will differ from run to run, and with sufficient experimentation, the simulation may display a range of behavior not unlike that of the actual system being studied.

system random number generator

Many computer systems include random number generators, and if one is available on your system, it can be used in place of the one developed here.

The idea is to start with one number and apply a series of arithmetic operations that will produce another number with no obvious connection to the first. Hence the numbers we produce are not truly random at all, as each one depends in a definite way on its predecessor, and we should more properly speak of **pseudorandom** numbers. If we begin the simulation with the same value each time the program is run, then the whole sequence of pseudorandom numbers will be exactly the same, so we normally begin by setting the starting point for the pseudorandom integers to some random value, for example, the time of day:

seed for pseudorandom numbers

```
/* Randomize: set starting point for pseudorandom integers. */
void Randomize(void)
{
        srand((unsigned int) (time(NULL) % 10000));
}
```

The function time returns the number of seconds elapsed since 00:00:00 GMT, January 1, 1970. The expression time(NULL) % 10000 produces an integer between 0 and 9999—

the number of seconds elapsed modulus 10000. This number provides a different starting point for srand each time it is run.

uniform distribution

We can then use the standard system function rand for producing each pseudorandom number from its predecessor. The function rand produces as its result an integer number between 0 and INT_MAX. (Consult the file limits.h to determine the value of INT_MAX on your system.) For our simulation we wish to obtain an integer giving the number of planes arriving ready to land (or take off) in a given time unit. We can assume that the time when one plane enters the system is independent of that of any other plane.

Poisson distribution

The number of planes arriving in one unit of time then follows what is called a **Poisson distribution** in statistics. To calculate the numbers, we need to know the **expected value**, that is, the average number of planes arriving in one unit of time. If, for example, on average one plane arrives in each of four time units, then the expected value is 0.25. Sometimes several planes may arrive in the same time unit, but often no planes arrive, so that taking the average over many units gives 0.25.

The following function determines the number of planes by generating pseudorandom integers according to a Poisson distribution:

Poisson generator

```
/* RandomNumber: generate a pseudorandom integer according to the Poisson distri-
     bution. */
int RandomNumber(double expectedvalue)
{
      int n = 0;                       /* counter of iterations                      */
      double em;                       /* e^{-v}, where v is the expected value      */
      double x;                        /* pseudorandom number                        */

      em = exp(-expectedvalue);
      x = rand()/(double) INT_MAX;
      while (x > em) {
            n++;
            x *= rand()/(double) INT_MAX;
      }
      return n;
}
```

3.4.6 Sample Results

We conclude this section with the output from a sample run of the airport simulation. You should note that there are periods when the runway is idle and others when the queues are completely full, so that some planes must be turned away.

This program simulates an airport with only one runway.
One plane can land or depart in each unit of time.
Up to 5 planes can be waiting to land or take off at any time.
How many units of time will the simulation run ? 30
Expected number of arrivals per unit time (real number) ? 0.47
Expected number of departures per unit time ? 0.47

Plane 1 ready to land.

1: Plane 1 landed; in queue 0 units.

2: Runway is idle.

both queues are
empty

Plane 2 ready to land.

Plane 3 ready to land.

3: Plane 2 landed; in queue 0 units.

4: Plane 3 landed; in queue 1 units.
Plane 4 ready to land.
Plane 5 ready to land.
Plane 6 ready to take off.
Plane 7 ready to take off.

5: Plane 4 landed; in queue 0 units.
Plane 8 ready to take off.

6: Plane 5 landed; in queue 1 units.
Plane 9 ready to take off.
Plane 10 ready to take off.

7: Plane 6 took off; in queue 2 units.

8: Plane 7 took off; in queue 3 units.

9: Plane 8 took off; in queue 3 units.
Plane 11 ready to land.

10: Plane 11 landed; in queue 0 units.

landing queue is
empty

Plane 12 ready to take off.

11: Plane 9 took off; in queue 4 units.
Plane 13 ready to land.
Plane 14 ready to land.

12: Plane 13 landed; in queue 0 units.

13: Plane 14 landed; in queue 1 units.

14: Plane 10 took off; in queue 7 units.
Plane 15 ready to land.
Plane 16 ready to take off.
Plane 17 ready to take off.

15: Plane 15 landed; in queue 0 units.
Plane 18 ready to land.
Plane 19 ready to land.
Plane 20 ready to take off.
Plane 21 ready to take off.

16: Plane 18 landed; in queue 0 units.
Plane 22 ready to land.

17: Plane 19 landed; in queue 1 units.

takeoff queue is full

Plane 23 ready to take off.
Plane 23 told to try later.

18: Plane 22 landed; in queue 1 units.
Plane 24 ready to land.
Plane 25 ready to land.
Plane 26 ready to land.

Plane 27 ready to take off.
Plane 27 told to try later.
19: Plane 24 landed; in queue 0 units.
Plane 28 ready to land.
Plane 29 ready to land.
Plane 30 ready to land.
Plane 31 ready to land.

landing queue is full   Plane 31 directed to another airport.
20: Plane 25 landed; in queue 1 units.
Plane 32 ready to land.
Plane 33 ready to take off.
Plane 33 told to try later.
21: Plane 26 landed; in queue 2 units.
22: Plane 28 landed; in queue 2 units.
23: Plane 29 landed; in queue 3 units.
Plane 34 ready to take off.
Plane 34 told to try later.
24: Plane 30 landed; in queue 4 units.
Plane 35 ready to take off.
Plane 35 told to try later.
Plane 36 ready to take off.
Plane 36 told to try later.
25: Plane 32 landed; in queue 4 units.
Plane 37 ready to take off.
Plane 37 told to try later.
26: Plane 12 took off; in queue 15 units.
27: Plane 16 took off; in queue 12 units.
28: Plane 17 took off; in queue 13 units.
29: Plane 20 took off; in queue 13 units.
Plane 38 ready to take off.
30: Plane 21 took off; in queue 14 units.

Summary   Simulation has concluded after 30 units.
Total number of planes processed: 38
 Number of planes landed: 19
 Number of planes taken off: 10
 Number of planes refused use: 8
 Number left ready to land: 0
 Number left ready to take off: 1
Percentage of time runway idle: 3.33
Average wait time to land: 1.11
Average wait time to take off: 8.60

**Exercise
3.4**

E1. In the airport simulation we did not specify which implementation of queues to use. Which of the implementations would be best to use, and why? If the choice of implementation does not make much difference, explain why.

Programming Projects 3.4

P1. Experiment with several sample runs of the airport simulation, adjusting the values for the expected numbers of planes ready to land and take off. Find approximate values for these expected numbers that are as large as possible subject to the condition that it is very unlikely that a plane must be refused service. What happens to these values if the maximum size of the queues is increased or decreased?

P2. Modify the simulation to give the airport two runways, one always used for landings and one always used for takeoffs. Compare the total number of planes that can be served with the number for the one-runway airport. Does it more than double?

P3. Modify the simulation to give the airport two runways, one usually used for landings and one usually used for takeoffs. If one of the queues is empty, then both runways can be used for the other queue. Also, if the landing queue is full and another plane arrives to land, then takeoffs will be stopped and both runways used to clear the backlog of landing planes.

P4. Modify the simulation to have three runways, one always reserved for each of landing and takeoff and the third used for landings unless the landing queue is empty, in which case it can be used for takeoffs.

P5. Modify the original (one-runway) simulation so that when each plane arrives to land, it will (as part of its structure) have a (randomly generated) fuel level, measured in units of time remaining. If the plane does not have enough fuel to wait in the queue, it is allowed to land immediately. Hence the planes in the landing queue may be kept waiting additional units, and so may run out of fuel themselves. Check this out as part of the landing function, and find about how busy the airport can get before planes start to crash from running out of fuel.

random numbers **P6.** Write a stub to take the place of the random number function. The stub can be used both to debug the program and to allow the user to control exactly the number of planes arriving for each queue at each time unit.

P7. Write a driver program for function RandomNumber; use it to check that the function produces random integers whose average over the number of iterations performed is the specified expected value.

scissors-paper-rock **P8.** In a certain children's game each of two players simultaneously puts out a hand held in a fashion to denote one of scissors, paper, or rock. The rules are that scissors beats paper (since scissors cut paper), paper beats rock (since paper covers rock), and rock beats scissors (since rock breaks scissors). Write a program to simulate playing this game with a person who types in S, P, or R at each turn.

P9. After leaving a pub a drunk tries to walk home. The streets between the pub and *random walk* the home form a rectangular grid. Each time the drunk reaches a corner he decides at random what direction to walk next. He never, however, wanders outside the grid.

    a. Write a program to simulate this random walk. The number of rows and columns in the grid should be variable. Your program should calculate, over many random walks on the same grid, how long it takes the drunk to get home on average. Investigate how this number depends on the shape and size of the grid.

    b. To improve his chances, the drunk moves closer to the pub—to a room on the

Figure 3.9. A random walk

upper left corner of the grid. Modify the simulation to see how much faster he can now get home.

c. Modify the original simulation so that, if the drunk happens to arrive back at the pub, then he goes in and the walk ends. Find out (depending on the size and shape of the grid) what percentage of the time the drunk makes it home successfully.

d. Modify the original simulation so as to give the drunk some memory to help him, as follows. Each time he arrives at a corner, if he has been there before on the current walk, he remembers what streets he has already taken and tries a new one. If he has already tried all the streets from the corner, he decides at random which to take now. How much more quickly does he get home? The main program and the remaining functions are the same as in the previous version.

3.5 OTHER LISTS AND THEIR IMPLEMENTATION

1. General Lists

Stacks are the easiest kind of list to use because all additions and deletions are made at one end of the list. In queues changes are made at both ends, but only at the ends, so queues are still relatively easy to use. For many applications, however, it is necessary to access all the elements of the list and to be able to make insertions or deletions at any point in the list. It might be necessary, for example, to insert a new name into the middle of a list that is kept in alphabetical order.

2. Two Implementations

1. counter   The usual way of implementing a list, the one we would probably first think of, is to keep the entries of the list in an array and to use an index that counts the number of entries in

2. special value
the list and allows us to locate its end. Variations of this implementation are often useful, however. Instead of using a counter of elements, for example, we can sometimes mark entries of the array that do not contain list elements with some special symbol denoting emptiness. In a list of words, we might mark all unused positions by setting them to blanks. In a list of numbers, we might use some number guaranteed never to appear in the list.

relative advantages
If it is frequently necessary to make insertions and deletions in the middle of the list, then this second implementation will prove advantageous. If we wish to delete an element from the middle of a list where the elements are kept next to each other, then we must move many of the remaining elements to fill in the vacant position, while with the second implementation, we need only mark the deleted position as empty by putting the special symbol there. See Figure 3.10. If, later, we wish to insert a new element into a list in the first implementation, we must again move many elements. With the second implementation, we need only move elements until we encounter a position marked empty. With the first implementation, on the other hand, other operations are easier. We can tell immediately the number of elements in the list, but with the second implementation, we may need to step through the entire array counting entries not marked empty. With the first implementation, we can move to the next entry of the list simply by increasing an index by one; with the second, we must search for an entry not marked empty.

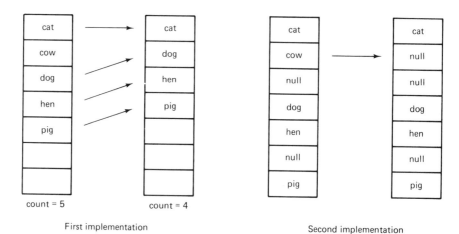

Figure 3.10. Deletion from a list

3. Operations on Lists

Because variations in implementation are possible, it is wise in designing programs to separate decisions concerning the use of data structures from decisions concerning their implementation. To help in delineating these decisions, let us enumerate some of the operations we would like to do with lists.

First, there are three functions whose purposes are clear from their names:

status operation   Boolean_type Empty (List_type *list);
Boolean_type Full (List_type *list);
int Size (List_type *list);

For most other operations we must specify the place in the list to use. At any instant we are only looking at one entry of the list, and we shall refer to this entry as the ***window***

window into a list   into the list. Hence, for a stack the window is always at the same end of the list; for a queue, it is at the front for deletions and at the rear for additions. For an arbitrary list we can move the window through the list one entry at a time, or position it to any desired entry. The following are some of the operations we wish to be able to do with windows and lists:

/* *Initialize: initialize the list to be empty.* */
void Initialize (List_type *list);

/* *IsFirst: non-zero if w is the first element of the list.* */
Boolean_type IsFirst (List_type *list, int w);

/* *IsLast: non-zero if w is the last element of the list.* */
Boolean_type IsLast (List_type *list, int w);

window positioning   /* *Start: position the window at the first entry of list.* */
void Start (List_type *list, int *w);

/* *Next: position window on the next entry, if there is one.* */
void Next (List_type *list, int *w);

/* *Preceding: position window on the preceding entry, if there is one.* */
void Preceding (List_type *list, int *w);

/* *Finish: position window to the last entry of the list.* */
void Finish (List_type *list, int *w);

list changes   /* *Delete: delete entry at window and update window.* */
void Delete (List_type *list, int *w);

/* *InsertAfter: insert item after the window.* */
void InsertAfter (List_type *list, int *w, Item_type item);

/* *InsertBefore: insert item before current window.* */
void InsertBefore (List_type *list, int *w, Item_type item);

/* *Replace: replace the item at the window w.* */
void Replace (List_type *list, int w, Item_type item);

/* *Retrieve: retrieve an item at the window w.* */
void Retrieve (List_type list, int w, Item_type *item);

4. List Traversal

One more action is commonly done with lists—***traversal*** of the list—which means to start at the beginning of the list and do some action for each item in the list in turn,

traverse and visit   finishing with the last item in the list. What action is done for each item depends on the application, for generality we say that we ***visit*** each item in the list. Hence we have the final function for list processing:

/* *Traverse: traverse list and invoke* Visit *for each item.* */
void Traverse (List_type *list, void (*Visit) (Item_type x));

function as an   (Yes, this declaration is standard C; pointers to functions are allowed as formal parameters
argument   for other functions, although this feature is not often used in elementary programming.)
When function Traverse finishes, the window has not been changed. To be sure of
proper functioning, it is necessary to assume that function Visit makes no insertions or
deletions in the list list.

5. C Programs

Let us now finally turn to the C details of the two implementations of lists introduced
earlier. Both methods will require the declaration of a constant MAXLIST giving the
maximum number of items allowed in a list and typedefs used. The first method then
requires the following structure and typedefs:

```
#define MAXLIST 10

typedef char Item_type;
```

type list
```
typedef struct list_tag {
              int count;
              Item_type entry [MAXLIST];
} List_type;
```

The second method replaces the last declaration with

```
typedef struct list_tag {
              Item_type entry [MAXLIST];
} List_type;
```

To show the relative advantages of the two implementations, let us write the functions
Size and Delete for each implementation.

```
/* Size: return the size of a list. */
```
size, version 1
```
int Size (List_type *list)
{
       return list->count;
}
```

```
/* Size: return the size of a list. */
```
size, version 2
```
int Size (List_type *list_ptr)
{
    int i;
    int count = 0;
    for (i = 0; i < MAXLIST; i++)
       if (list_ptr->entry [i] != '\0')
           count++;
    return count;
}
```

As you can see, the first version is somewhat simpler. On the other hand, for the Delete
function, the second version is simpler.

/ Delete: delete entry at window and update window. */*

deletion, version 1

```
void Delete(List_type *list_ptr, int *w)
{
      int i;

      for (i = *w + 1; i < list_ptr->count; i++)
            list_ptr->entry[i - 1] = list_ptr->entry[i];
      list_ptr->count--;
      if (Empty(list_ptr))
            Start(list_ptr, w);
      else if (*w > Size(list_ptr))
            Finish(list_ptr, w);
}
```

/ Delete: delete entry at window and update window. */*

deletion, version 2

```
void Delete(List_type *list_ptr, int *w)
{
    Boolean_type flag;

    flag = IsLast(list_ptr, w);
    list_ptr->entry[*w] = (Item_type) NULL;
    if (flag)
        Start(list_ptr, w);
    else
        Next(list_ptr, w);
}
```

Although there remain a good many functions to write in order to implement these list
structures fully in C, most of the details are simple and can safely be left as exercises. It
is, of course, permissible to use functions already written as part of later functions. To
illustrate this, let us conclude this section with a version of function Traverse that will
work with either implementation.

/ Traverse: traverse the list and invoke Visit for each item. */*

```
void Traverse(List_type *list_ptr, void (*Visit)(Item_type))
{
      int w;
      Item_type item;

      if (!Empty(list_ptr)) {              /* only if not empty              */
            Start(list_ptr, &w);
            while (!IsLast(list_ptr, &w)) {
                  Retrieve(list_ptr, &w, &item);
                  (*Visit)(item);
                  Next(list_ptr, &w);      /* next position in the list      */
            }
            Retrieve(list_ptr, &w, &item);  /* Get last item.                */
            (*Visit)(item);
      }
}
```

As an example, let us write a simple version of the function Visit. We shall assume that the items are characters, and we simply print the character.

```
/* Visit: print the item retrieved from the list. */
void Visit(Item_type item)
{
    printf("item is %c\n", item);
}
```

Exercises
3.5

E1. Write C functions to implement the following operations on a list implemented with **(a)** a structure type including an array of items and a counter of items in the list and **(b)** an array with NULL entries denoting an empty position.

  a. Boolean_type Empty(List_type *list_ptr);
  b. Boolean_type Full(List_type *list_ptr);
  c. Boolean_type IsFirst(List_type *list_ptr, int w);
  d. Boolean_type IsLast(List_type *list_ptr, int w);
  e. void Initialize(List_type *list_ptr);
  f. void Start(List_type *list_ptr, int *w);
  g. void Finish(List_type *list_ptr, int *w);
  h. void Next(List_type *list_ptr, int *w);
  i. void Preceding(List_type *list_ptr, int *w);
  j. void InsertAfter(List_type *list_ptr, int *w, Item_type item);
  k. void InsertBefore(List_type *list_ptr, int *w, Item_type item);
  l. void Replace(List_type *list_ptr, int w, Item_type item);
  m. void Retrieve(List_type *list_ptr, int w);

E2. Given the functions for operating with lists developed in this section, do the following tasks.

  a. Write a function that deletes the last entry of a list.
  b. Write a function that deletes the first entry of a list.
  c. Write a function that reverses the order of the entries in a list.
  d. Write a function that splits a list into two other lists, so that the entries that were in odd-numbered positions are now in one list (in the same relative order as before) and those from even-numbered positions are in the other new list.

The word **deque** (pronounced either "deck" or "DQ") is a shortened form of **double-ended queue** and denotes a list in which items can be added or deleted from either the first or the last position of the list, but no changes can be made elsewhere in the list. Thus a deque is a generalization of both a stack and a queue.

E3. Is it more appropriate to think of a deque as implemented in a linear array or in a circular array? Why?

E4. Write the four algorithms needed to add an item to each end of a deque and to delete an item from each end of the deque.

E5. Note from Figure 3.4 that a stack can be represented pictorially as a spur track on a straight railway line. A queue can, of course, be represented simply as a straight track. Devise and draw a railway switching network that will represent a deque. The network should have only one entrance and one exit.

E6. Suppose that data items numbered 1, 2, 3, 4, 5, 6 come in the input stream in this order. By using (1) a queue and (2) a deque, which of the following rearrangements can be obtained in the output order?

(a) 1 2 3 4 5 6   (b) 2 4 3 6 5 1   (c) 1 5 2 4 3 6
(d) 4 2 1 3 5 6   (e) 1 2 6 4 5 3   (f) 5 2 6 3 4 1

scroll   **E7.** A *scroll* is a data structure intermediate to a deque and a queue. In a scroll all additions to the list are at its end, but deletions can be made either at the end or at the beginning. Answer the preceding questions in the case of a scroll rather than a deque.

a. Is it more appropriate to think of a scroll as implemented in a linear array or a circular array? Why?

b. Write the four algorithms needed to add an item to each end of a scroll and to delete an item from each end of a scroll.

c. Devise and draw a railway switching network that will represent a scroll. The network should have only one entrance and one exit.

d. Suppose that data items numbered 1, 2, 3, 4, 5, 6 come in the input stream in this order. By using a scroll, which of the following rearrangements can be obtained in the output order?

(a) 1 2 3 4 5 6   (b) 2 4 3 6 5 1   (c) 1 5 2 4 3 6
(d) 4 2 1 3 5 6   (e) 1 2 6 4 5 3   (f) 5 2 6 3 4 1

E8. Suppose that we think of dividing a deque in half by fixing some position in the middle of it. Then the left and right halves of the deque are each a stack. Thus a deque can be implemented with two stacks. Write algorithms that will add to and delete from each end of the deque considered in this way. When one of the two stacks is empty and the other one not, and an attempt is made to pop the empty stack, you will need to move items (equivalent to changing the place where the deque was broken in half) before the request can be satisfied. Compare your algorithms with those of Exercise E4 in regard to

a. clarity;

b. ease of composition;

c. storage use;

d. time used for typical accesses;

e. time used when items must be moved.

unordered list   **E9.** In this section we have implicitly assumed that all operations on a list were required to preserve the order of the items in the list. In some applications, however, the order of the items is of no importance. In the lists live and die that we set up for the Life game in Chapter 2, for example, it made no difference in what order the entries were in the lists, and so when we needed to delete an item from the list, we could fill its hole simply by moving the last item from the list into the vacant position and reducing the count of items on the list by 1. Function Vivify thus had the form

```
/* Vivify: vivify a dead cell provided it meets the required conditions. */
void Vivify (void)
{
    i = 1;
    while (i <= count)
        if (entry [i] is OK) {
            process entry [i];
            i++;
        } else {
            entry [i] = entry [count];
            count −−;
        }
}
```

Determine which of the operations on lists from this section will be simplified if the order of entries in the lists can be changed as desired. Rewrite the associated functions for these operations.

POINTERS AND PITFALLS

1. Don't confuse lists with arrays.

2. Choose your data structures as you design your algorithms, and avoid making premature decisions.

3. Practice information hiding: Use functions to access your data structures.

4. Postpone decisions on the details of implementing your data structures as long as you can.

5. Stacks are the simplest kind of lists; use stacks when possible.

6. Avoid tricky ways of storing your data; tricks usually will not generalize to new situations.

7. Be sure to initialize your data structures.

8. Always be careful about the extreme cases and handle them gracefully. Trace through your algorithm to determine what happens when a data structure is empty or full.

9. Don't optimize your code until it works perfectly, and then only optimize it if improvement in efficiency is definitely required. First try a simple implementation of your data structures. Change to a more sophisticated implementation only if the simple one proves too inefficient.

10. When working with general lists, first decide exactly what operations are needed, then choose the implementation that enables those operations to be done most easily.

REVIEW QUESTIONS

1. What is the difference between an array and a list?

2. What are the operations that can be done on a stack?

3. What are stack frames for subprograms? What do they show?

4. What are the advantages of writing the operations on a data structure as functions?

5. Define the term *queue*. What operations can be done on a queue?

6. How is a circular array implemented in a linear array?

7. List three different implementations of queues.

8. Define the term *simulation*.

9. Why are random numbers used in computer programs usually not really random?

10. What is a *deque*?

11. Which of the operations possible for general lists are also possible for queues? for stacks?

12. List three operations possible for general lists that are not allowed for either stacks or queues.

REFERENCES FOR FURTHER STUDY

data abstraction

The separation of properties of data structures and their operations from the implementation of the data structures in memory and functions is called ***data abstraction.*** The following book takes this point of view consistently and develops further properties of lists:

> JIM WELSH, JOHN ELDER, and DAVID BUSTARD, *Sequential Program Structures*, Prentice Hall International, London, 1984, 385 pages.

For many topics concerning data structures, the best source for additional information, historical notes, and mathematical analysis is the following series of books, which can be regarded almost like an encyclopædia for the aspects of computing science that they discuss:

encyclopædic reference: KNUTH

> DONALD E. KNUTH, *The Art of Computer Programming* published by Addison-Wesley, Reading, Mass.

Three volumes have appeared to date:

1. *Fundamental Algorithms*, second edition, 1973, 634 pages.

2. *Seminumerical Algorithms*, second edition, 1980, 700 pages.

3. *Sorting and Searching*, 1973, 722 pages.

From now on we shall often give references to this series of books, and for convenience we shall do so by specifying only the name KNUTH together with the volume and page numbers. In particular, stacks, queues, and deques are studied in KNUTH, Volume 1, pp. 234–251, with the inclusion of many interesting extensions and exercises. The algorithms are written both in English and in an assembler language, where KNUTH calculates detailed counts of operations to compare various algorithms.

In Volume 2, pp. 1–177, KNUTH studies the construction and testing of pseudorandom number generators in great depth.

An elementary survey of computer simulations appears in *Byte* 10 (October 1985), pp. 149–251. A simulation of the National Airport in Washington, D.C., appears on pp. 186–190.

Linked Lists

This chapter studies the implementation of lists by the use of links. Several examples are developed, and the chapter closes with a discussion of the general principles of abstract data types and data structures.

4.1 DYNAMIC MEMORY ALLOCATION AND POINTERS

4.1.1 The Problem of Overflow

fixed bounds

In the examples we have studied in the previous chapters we have assumed that all items of data are kept within arrays, arrays that must be declared to have some size that is fixed when the program is written, and that can therefore not be changed while the program is running. When writing a program, we have had to decide on the maximum amount of memory that would be needed for our arrays and set this aside in the declarations. If we run the program on a small sample, then much of this space will never be used. If we decide to run the program on a large set of data, then we may exhaust the space set aside and encounter overflow, even when the computer memory itself is not fully used, simply because our original bounds on the array were too small.

problem of overflow

Even if we are careful to declare our arrays large enough to use up all the available memory, we can still encounter overflow, since one array may reach its limit while a great deal of unused space remains in others. Since different runs of the same program may cause different lists to grow or shrink, it may be impossible to tell before the program actually executes which lists will overflow.

We now exhibit a way to keep lists and other data structures in memory without using arrays, whereby we can avoid these difficulties.

4.1.2 Pointers

The idea we use is that of a pointer. A **pointer**, also called a **link** or a **reference**, is defined to be a variable that gives the location of some other variable, typically of a structure containing data that we wish to use. If we use pointers to locate all the structures in which we are interested, then we need not be concerned about where the structures themselves are actually stored, since by using a pointer, we can let the computer system itself locate the structure when required.

Figure 4.1 shows pointers to several structures. Pointers are generally depicted as arrows and structures as rectangular boxes. In the diagrams, variables containing pointers

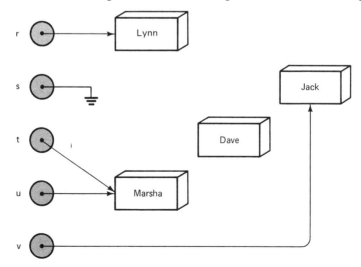

Figure 4.1. Pointers to structures

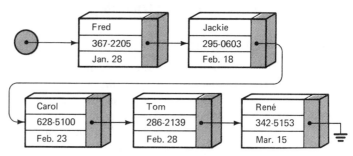

Figure 4.2. A linked list

are generally shown in shaded boxes. Hence in the diagram r is a pointer to the structure "Lynn" and v is a pointer to the structure "Jack." As you can see, the use of pointers is quite flexible: two pointers can refer to the same structure, as t and u do in Figure 4.1, or a pointer can refer to no structure at all. We denote this latter situation within diagrams by the electrical ***ground symbol***, as shown for pointer s. Care must be exercised when using pointers, moreover, to be sure that, when they are moved, no structure is lost. In the diagram, the structure "Dave" is lost, with no pointer referring to it, and therefore there is no way to find it.

pointers referring nowhere

linked list

The idea of a ***linked list*** is, for every structure in the list, to put a pointer into the structure giving the location of the next structure in the list. This idea is illustrated in Figure 4.2.

As you can see from the illustration, a linked list is simple in concept. It uses the same idea as a children's treasure hunt, where each clue that is found tells where to find the next one. Or consider friends passing a popular cassette around. Fred has it, and has promised to give it to Jackie. Carol asks Jackie if she can borrow it, and then will next share it with Tom. And so it goes. A linked list may be considered analogous to following instructions where each instruction is given out only upon completion of the previous task. There is then no inherent limit on the number of tasks to be done, since each task may specify a new instruction, and there is no way to tell in advance how many instructions there are. The list implementations studied in Chapter 3, on the other hand, are analogous to a list of instructions written on a single sheet of paper. It is then possible to see all the instructions in advance, but there is a limit to the number of instructions that can be written on the single sheet of paper.

With some practice in their use, you will find that linked lists are as easy to work with as lists implemented within arrays. The methods differ substantially, however, so we must spend some time developing new programming skills. Before we turn to this work, let us consider a few more general observations.

4.1.3 Further Remarks

1. Contiguous and Linked Lists

The word ***contiguous*** means *in contact, touching, adjoining*. The entries in an array are contiguous, and from now on we shall speak of a list kept in an array as a ***contiguous list***. We can then distinguish as desired between contiguous lists and linked lists, and we shall use the unqualified word *list* only to include both.

2. Pointers for Contiguous Lists

A pointer is simply a variable giving the location of some item, and for contiguous lists, we have in fact been using pointers informally throughout the last chapter. The variable *top* is a pointer giving the location of the item on the top of a stack, and the variables *front* and *rear* give the locations of the front and rear of a queue. To avoid possible confusion, however, we shall generally reserve the word *pointer* for use with linked lists and continue to use the word *index* (and, later in this chapter, the word *cursor*) to refer to a location within an array.

4.1.4 Dynamic Memory Allocation

As well as preventing unnecessary overflow problems caused by running out of room in arrays, the use of pointers has advantages in a multitasking or time-sharing environment.

time sharing   If we use arrays to reserve in advance the maximum amount of memory that our program might need, then this memory is assigned to us and will be unavailable for other tasks. If it is necessary to page our job out of memory, then there may be time lost as unused memory is copied to and from a disk. Instead of using arrays to hold all our items, we can begin very small, with space only for the program instructions and simple variables, and whenever we need space for an additional item, we can request the system for the needed memory. Similarly, when an item is no longer needed, its space can be returned to the system, which can then assign it to another user. In this way a program can start small and grow only as necessary, so that when it is small, it can run more efficiently, and when necessary it can grow to the limits of the computer system.

Even with only one user this dynamic control of memory can prove useful. During one part of a task a large amount of memory may be needed for some purpose, which can later be released and then allocated again for another purpose, perhaps now containing data of a completely different type than before.

4.1.5 Pointers and Dynamic Memory in C

C provides powerful facilities for processing pointers and standard functions for requesting additional memory and for releasing memory during program execution.

1. Static and Dynamic Variables

Variables that can be used during execution of a C program come in two varieties. ***Static variables*** are those that are declared and named, as usual, while writing the program. Space for them exists as long as the program in which they are declared is running. (There is a storage class for variables in C called static; the variables are known only in the function where they are declared and their space exists for the duration of the main program. We are using the term ***static variable*** here to denote any variable that is declared while writing the program.) ***Dynamic variables*** are created (and perhaps destroyed) during program execution. Since dynamic variables do not exist while the program is compiled, but only when it is run, they cannot be assigned names while it is being written.

The only way to access dynamic variables is by using pointers. Once it is created, however, a dynamic variable does contain data and must have a type like any other variable. Thus we can talk about creating a new dynamic variable of type x and setting a pointer to point to it, or of moving a pointer from one dynamic variable of type x to another, or of returning a dynamic variable of type x to the system.

Static variables, on the other hand, cannot be created or destroyed during execution of the program in which they are declared, although pointer variables can be used to point to static variables. For example,

```
void f(void)
{
    char c;
    . . .
}
```

The function f has a local variable c of type character. There will be space allocated for c when the function f executes. The function itself cannot destroy the space reserved for c or ask for more space for c. When f terminates, however, c is destroyed. The variable c is a static variable as opposed to a dynamic variable, for which the program controls the allocation and disposal of the space. If a dynamic variable is created in a function, then it can continue to exist even after the function terminates.

2. C Notation

C uses a star ∗ to denote a pointer. If p is a pointer to a character, we declare it by

$$\text{char } *p;$$

If Node_type denotes the type of items in which we are interested, then we declare a pointer type that is bound to type Node_type with the declaration

```
typedef struct node_tag {
        . . .
} Node_type;

Node_type *q;
```

The type Node_type to which a pointer refers can be arbitrary, but in most applications it will be a structure. The words link and reference are also frequently used to designate pointer types.

3. Type Binding

C sets stringent rules for the use of pointers. Each pointer is **bound** to the type of variable to which it points, and the same pointer should not be used to point (at different times) to variables of different types. Variables of two different pointer types cannot be mixed with each other; C will allow assignments between two pointer variables of the same type, but it will produce a warning when you assign pointers of different types. If we have declarations

```
char *a, *b;
Node_type *x, *y;
```

then the assignments x = y;   and a = b;   are legal, but the assignment x = a;   is illegal.

4. NULL **Pointers**

Sometimes a pointer variable p has no dynamic variable to which it currently refers. This situation can be established by the assignment

p = NULL;

and it can subsequently be checked by a condition such as

if (p != NULL) ....

In diagrams we use the electrical ground symbol

for a NULL pointer.

NULL is a symbolic constant defined in the include file stdio.h, and, in fact, the value of NULL is the constant zero. This means that the constant NULL is generic in that it can be assigned to a variable of any pointer type. It also means that the statements

if (p != NULL) ...   and   if (p) ...

equivalent forms   do exactly the same thing. Both forms are commonly used in C programs. The first form shows more clearly that a pointer is being checked to see if it points to a dynamic variable. The second form, being more compact, is often easier to read when it appears inside a complicated expression. We shall use both forms interchangeably in the programs we write.

undefined pointers   Note carefully the distinction between a pointer variable whose value is undefined
versus NULL *pointers*   and a pointer variable whose value is NULL. The assertion p == NULL means that p currently points to no dynamic variable. If the value of p is undefined, then p might point to any random location in memory. As with all variables, when the program begins execution, the values of pointer variables are undefined. Before we can use the value of a pointer variable p, therefore, we must either assign p = NULL or create a dynamic variable to which it points, as follows.

5. **Creating and Destroying Dynamic Variables**

The creation and destruction of dynamic variables is done with standard functions in C. If p has been declared as a pointer to type Node_type, then the statement

p = (Node_type *) malloc(sizeof(Node_type));

malloc   creates a new dynamic variable of type Node_type and assigns its location to the pointer p. The library function malloc allocates a block of memory and returns a pointer to that block of memory, or it returns NULL if there is not enough remaining memory to satisfy the request. The argument to malloc indicates, in bytes, the size of the block of
sizeof   memory that is requested. For our application, we determine this size by using the unary

compile-time operator sizeof, which computes the size in bytes of any object or type. Hence,

$$\text{sizeof}(\text{Node\_type})$$

calculates the number of bytes occupied by a variable of Node_type. The placement of *type cast* (Node_type *) before the call to malloc is a *type cast*: The value returned by malloc is a generic pointer; the type cast forces it to become Node_type.

If there is insufficient memory to create the new dynamic variable, malloc will fail and will return NULL. Your program should always check for a NULL pointer returned by malloc.

free   When a dynamic variable is no longer needed, the function call

$$\text{free}(p);$$

returns the space used by the dynamic variable to which p points to the system. After the function free(p) is called, the pointer variable p is undefined, and so cannot be used until it is assigned a new value. These actions are illustrated in Figure 4.3.

Either a call p = malloc(...) or an assignment such as p = q or p = NULL is required before p can be used. After a call free(p), the value of p is undefined, so it is wise to set p = NULL immediately, to be sure that p is not used with an undefined value.

6. Following the Pointers

The star * that appears in the declaration of a C pointer can also be used in a statement that uses the pointer. For example, the declaration

$$\text{char } *p;$$

dereferencing is read "p is a pointer to char" and when we use *p in an expression we read "what p points to." Again, the words *link* and *reference* are often used in this connection. The action of taking *p is sometimes called "dereferencing the pointer p."

7. Restrictions on Pointer Variables

The only use of variables of type Item_type * is to find the location of variables of type Item_type. Thus pointer variables can participate in assignment statements, can be

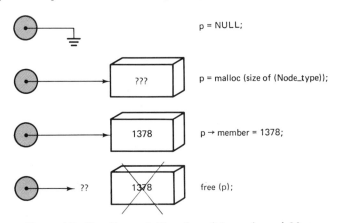

Figure 4.3. Creating and disposing of dynamic variables

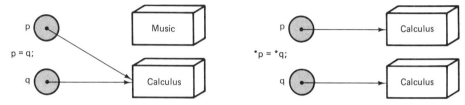

Figure 4.4. Assignment of pointer variables

pointer operations   checked for equality, can appear in calls to functions, and the programmer is allowed to do
some limited arithmetic with pointers. Appendix C gives more information on pointers.

assignment   In regard to assignment statements, it is important to remember the difference between p = q and *p = *q, both of which are legal (provided that p and q are bound to
the same type), but which have quite different effects. The first statement makes p point
to the same object to which q points, but does not change the value of either that object,
or of the other object that p was pointing to. The latter object will be lost unless there is
some other pointer variable that still refers to it. The second statement, *p = *q, on the
contrary, copies the value of the object *q into the object *p, so that we now have two
objects with the same value, with p and q pointing to the two separate copies. Finally, the
two assignment statements p = *q and *p = q have mixed types and are illegal (except
in the case that both p and q point to pointers of their same type!). Figure 4.4 illustrates
these assignments.

Exercises
4.1

These exercises are based on the following declarations, where the type Node_type is
declared as follows.

```
typedef struct node_tag {
        char c;
        struct node_tag *next;
} Node_type;
Node_type *p, *q, *r;
Node_type x, y, z;
```

E1. For each of the following statements, either describe its effect, or state why it is
illegal.

    a. p = (Node_type *) malloc(sizeof(Node_type));
    b. *q = (Node_type *) malloc(sizeof(Node_type));
    c. x = (Node_type *) malloc(sizeof(Node_type));
    d. p = r;

e.	q = y;	**j.**	free(*p);
f.	r = NULL;	**k.**	free(r);
g.	z = *p;	**l.**	*q = NULL;
h.	p = *x;	**m.**	*p = *x;
i.	free(y);	**n.**	z = NULL;

swap **E2.** Write a C function to interchange pointers p and q, so that after the function is performed, p will point to the node to which q formerly pointed, and vice versa.

E3. Write a C function to interchange the values in the dynamic variables to which p and q point, so that after the function is performed *p will have the value formerly in *q and vice versa.

E4. Write a C function that makes p point to the same node to which q points, and disposes of the item to which p formerly pointed.

E5. Write a C function that creates a new variable with p pointing to it, and with contents the same as those of the node to which q points.

4.2 LINKED STACKS AND QUEUES

With these tools of pointers we can now begin to consider the implementation of linked lists into C. Since stacks and queues are among the easiest lists to process, we begin with them.

4.2.1 Declarations

1. Nodes and Type Declarations

Recall from Figure 4.2 that each entry of a linked list will be a structure containing not only the items of information but also a pointer to the next structure in the list. Translating this requirement into C declarations yields

```
typedef struct node_tag {
        Item_type info;
        struct node_tag *next;
} Node_type;
```

use before declaration   Note that we have a problem of circularity in this declaration. struct node_tag * appears in the declaration of the structure node. This is called a ***self-referential structure***. It means that the pointer next may point to a structure of the same type as the structure Node_type.

2. Beginning of the List

In our linked list we shall use the pointer next to move from any one node in the linked list to the next one, and thereby we can work our way through the list, once we have started. We must now, however, address a small problem that never arises with contiguous lists or other static variables and arrays: How do we find the beginning of the list?

Perhaps an analogy with reading a magazine article will help. If we are in the middle of reading an article, then upon reaching the bottom of a page we often find the instruction "Continued on page ...," and by following such instructions we can continue reading until we reach the end of the article. But how do we find the beginning? We look in the table of contents, which we expect to find in a fixed location near the beginning of the magazine.

static head

For linked lists also we must refer to some fixed location to find the beginning; that is, we shall use a static variable to locate the first node of the list. One method of doing this is to make the first node in the list a static variable, even though all the remaining nodes are dynamically allocated. In this way the first node will have a unique name to which we can refer. Although we shall sometimes use this method, it has the disadvantage that the first node of the list is treated differently from all the others, a fact that can sometimes complicate the algorithms.

3. Headers

For linked stacks and queues and sometimes for other kinds of linked lists, we shall employ another method that avoids these problems. The **header** for a linked list is a pointer variable that locates the beginning of the list. The header will usually be a static variable, and by using its value we can arrive at the first (dynamic) node of the list. The header is also sometimes called the **base** or the **anchor** of the list. These terms are quite descriptive of providing a variable that ties down the beginning of the list, but since they are not so widely used, we shall generally employ the term *header*.

initialization

When execution of the program starts we shall wish to initialize the linked list to be empty; with a header pointer, this is now easy. The header is a static pointer; so it exists when the program begins, and to set its value to indicate that its list is empty, we need only the assignment

header = NULL;

4. The End of the List

Finding the end of a linked list is a much easier task than is finding its beginning. Since each node contains a pointer to the next, the pointer field of the last node of the list has nowhere to point, so we give it the special value NULL. In this way we know that we are at the end of the list if and only if the node we are using has a NULL pointer to the next. Here we have one small advantage of linked lists over a contiguous implementation: There is no need to keep an explicit counter of the number of nodes in the list.

4.2.2 Linked Stacks

Let us now turn to writing functions for processing linked stacks. As with the items of contiguous stacks, we shall *push* and *pop* nodes from one end of a linked stack, called its *top*. We now face a small problem of inconsistency with the implementation of stacks in the last chapter: The entries of contiguous stacks were declared to have type Item_type,

items and nodes

whereas the entries of linked stacks will have type Node_type, which we have already declared to consist of an Item_type together with a pointer. For some applications of linked stacks we wish to process nodes, but for other applications we wish to be able to process items directly, so that we can substitute a linked implementation of stacks for a contiguous implementation without having to make any changes in the rest of the program.

For this reason we introduce two new functions, PushNode and PopNode, which will process nodes in a linked stack. We can then use these functions to write linked versions of the functions Push and Pop, which, as in the last chapter, will process items directly. If we have an item item that we wish to push onto a linked stack, we must first make a new node and put item into the node, and then push the node onto the stack. Hence we obtain:

item processing

```
/* Push: make a new node with item and push it onto stack. */
void Push (Item_type item, Stack_type *stack_ptr)
{
        PushNode (MakeNode (item), stack_ptr);
}
```

The function Push uses a function MakeNode that allocates enough space for a new node and initializes it. This sequence of instructions is used often, so it is kept as a function for general use.

```
/* MakeNode: make a new node and insert item. */
Node_type *MakeNode (Item_type item)
{
        Node_type *p;

        if ((p = (Node_type *) malloc (sizeof (Node_type))) == NULL)
                Error ("Exhausted memory.");
        else {
                p->info = item;
                p->next = NULL;
        }
        return p;
}
```

The connection between the two functions for popping a node or an item from the stack is just as close.

```
/* Pop: pop a node from the stack and return its item. */
void Pop (Item_type *item, Stack_type *stack_ptr)
{
        Node_type *node_ptr;

        PopNode ( &node_ptr, stack_ptr);
        *item = node_ptr->info;
        free (node_ptr);
}
```

Node *processing*   Next let us turn to the processing of nodes in a linked stack. The first question to settle is to determine whether the beginning or the end of the linked list will be the top of the stack. At first glance it may appear that (as for contiguous lists) it might be easier to add a node at the end of the list, but this method makes popping the stack difficult: There is no quick way to find the node immediately before a given one in a linked list, since the pointers stored in the list give only one-way directions. Thus, after we remove the last element, to find the new element at the end of the list it might be necessary to trace all the way from the head of the list. To pop our linked stack it is better to make all additions and deletions at the beginning of the list. Each linked list has a header variable that points to its first node; for a linked stack we shall call this header variable top, and it will always point to the top of the stack. Since each node of a linked list points to the next one, the only information needed to keep track of a linked stack is the location of its top. For consistency with other data structures, we shall put this information in a simple structure, and hence we obtain the following declaration of a linked stack:

```
typedef struct stack_tag {
      Node_type *top;
} Stack_type;
```

Then we can declare the stack and a pointer to it:

```
Stack_type stack;
Stack_type *stack_ptr = &stack;
```

and a pointer node_ptr to a structure of the type Node_type

```
Node_type *node_ptr;
```

Let us start with an empty stack, which now means

```
stack_ptr->top = NULL;
```

and add the first node. We shall assume that this node has already been made somewhere in dynamic memory, and we shall locate this node by using a pointer node_ptr. Pushing node_ptr onto the stack consists of the instructions

```
stack_ptr->top = node_ptr;
node_ptr->next = NULL;
```

As we continue, let us suppose that we already have the stack and that we wish to push a node node_ptr onto it. The required adjustments of pointers are shown in Figure 4.5. First, we must set the pointer coming from the new node node_ptr to the old top of the stack, and then we must change the top to become the new node. The order of these two assignments is important: If we attempted to do them in the reverse order, the change of top from its previous value would mean that we would lose track of the old part of the list. We thus obtain the following function.

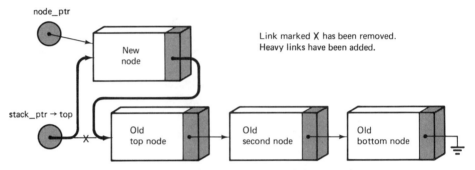

Figure 4.5. Pushing a node onto a linked stack

/* *PushNode: push node onto the linked stack.* */

push node
```
void PushNode(Node_type *node_ptr, Stack_type *stack_ptr)
{
    if (node_ptr == NULL)
        Error("Attempted to push a nonexistent node");
    else {
        node_ptr->next = stack_ptr->top;
        stack_ptr->top = node_ptr;
    }
}
```

In all our functions it is important to include error checking and to consider extreme cases. Hence we consider it an error to attempt to push a nonexistent node onto the stack. One extreme case for the function is that of an empty stack, which means top == NULL. Note that in this case the function works just as well to add the first node to an empty stack as to add another node to a nonempty stack.

It is equally simple to pop a node from a linked stack. This process is illustrated in Figure 4.6 and is implemented in the following function.

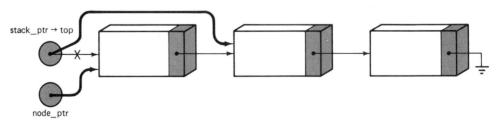

Figure 4.6. Popping a node from a linked stack

pop node
```
/* PopNode: pop node from the linked stack. */
void PopNode(Node_type **node_ptr, Stack_type *stack_ptr)
{
    if (stack_ptr->top == NULL)
        Error("Empty stack");
    else {
        *node_ptr = stack_ptr->top;
        stack_ptr->top = (*node_ptr)->next;
    }
}
```

In the function PushNode the first parameter is

$$\text{Node\_type } *\text{node\_ptr}$$

It indicates that node_ptr is a pointer to a variable of type Node_type. In PopNode the first parameter is

$$\text{Node\_type } **\text{node\_ptr}$$

It indicates that node_ptr is a pointer to a pointer to a variable of type Node_type. Remember that in a call by reference we pass the address of the variable. When we need to make a call by reference and the variable involved is a pointer, we pass the address of the pointer. The parameter to the function is then a pointer to a pointer to a variable.

Note that the principal instructions for popping the linked stack are exactly the reverse of those for pushing a node onto the stack. In popping the stack, it is necessary to check the stack for emptiness, but in pushing it, there is no need to check for overflow, since the function itself does not call for any additional memory. The extra memory for the new node is already assigned to the node to which node_ptr points.

4.2.3 Linked Queues

In contiguous storage, queues were significantly harder to manipulate than were stacks, because it was necessary to treat straight-line storage as though it were arranged in a circle, and the extreme cases of full queues and empty queues caused difficulties. It is for queues that linked storage really comes into its own. Linked queues are just as easy to handle as are linked stacks. We need only keep two pointers, front and rear, that will point, respectively, to the beginning and the end of the queue. The operations of insertion and deletion are both illustrated in Figure 4.7.

type queue
To show the logical connection between the head and tail pointers of a linked queue, we shall introduce a structure type:

```
typedef struct queue_tag {
    Node_type *front;
    Node_type *rear;
} Queue_type;
```

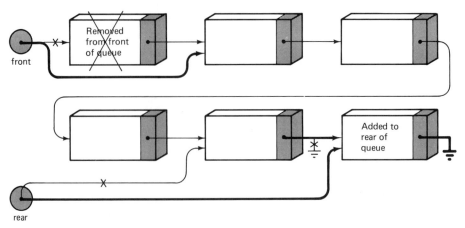

Figure 4.7. Operations on a linked queue

A queue should be initialized to be empty with the function:

```
/* Initialize: initialize the queue to be empty. */
void Initialize(Queue_type *queue_ptr)
{
    queue_ptr->front = queue_ptr->rear = NULL;
}
```
initialize

To add a node to the rear of a queue, we then write

```
/* AddNode: add a node to the rear of the queue. */
void AddNode(Node_type *node_ptr, Queue_type *queue_ptr)
{
    if (node_ptr == NULL)
        Error("Attempted to push a nonexistent node");
    else if (queue_ptr->front == NULL) {
        queue_ptr->front = node_ptr;
        queue_ptr->rear = node_ptr;
    } else {
        queue_ptr->rear->next = node_ptr;
        queue_ptr->rear = node_ptr;
    }
}
```
insert node

Note that this function includes error checking to prevent the insertion of a nonexistent
node into the queue. The cases when the queue is empty or not must be treated separately,
since the addition of a node to an empty queue requires setting both the front and the
rear to the new node, while addition to a nonempty queue requires changing only the
rear.

To remove a node from the front of a queue, we use the following function:

delete node

```
/* DeleteNode: delete a node from the front of the queue. */
void DeleteNode(Node_type **node_ptr, Queue_type *queue_ptr)
{
        if (queue_ptr->front == NULL)
                Error("Empty queue");
        else {
                *node_ptr = queue_ptr->front;
                queue_ptr->front = (*node_ptr)->next;
                if (queue_ptr->front == NULL)
                        queue_ptr->rear = NULL;
        }
}
```

Again the possibility of an empty queue must be considered separately. It is an error to attempt deletion from an empty queue. It is, however, not an error for the queue to become empty after a deletion, but then the rear and front should both become NULL to indicate clearly that the queue is empty.

simplicity

If you compare these algorithms for linked queues with those for contiguous queues, you will see that the linked versions are both conceptually easier and easier to program.

implementations

The functions we have developed process nodes; to enable us to change easily between contiguous and linked implementations of queues, we also need versions of functions AddQueue and DeleteQueue that will process items directly for linked queues. We leave writing these functions as exercises.

**Exercises
4.2**

E1. When deleting an item from a linked stack or queue, we checked for emptiness, but when adding an item, we did not check for overflow. Why?

E2. Write a C function to initialize a linked stack to be empty.

E3. For contiguous stacks and queues we wrote Boolean-valued functions Empty and Full along with the various functions. Write analogous functions in C for **(a)** linked stacks and **(b)** linked queues.

E4. By allocating and freeing new nodes, write functions **(a)** AddQueue and **(b)** Delete-Queue that will process items directly for linked queues and that can be substituted directly for their contiguous counterparts.

circularly linked list

A ***circularly linked list***, illustrated in Figure 4.8, is a linked list in which the node at the tail of the list, instead of having a NULL pointer, points back to the node at the head of the list. We then need only one pointer tail to access both ends of the list, since we know that tail->next points back to the head of the list.

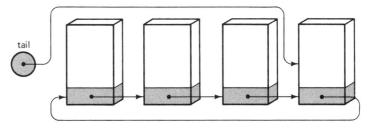

Figure 4.8. A circularly linked list with tail pointer

E5. If we implement a queue as a circularly linked list then we need only one pointer rear (or tail) to locate both the front and the rear. Write C functions to process a queue stored in this way:

   a. Initialize.

   b. AddNode.

   c. DeleteNode.

deque **E6.** Recall (Section 3.5, Exercise 3) that a ***deque*** is a list in which additions or deletions can be made at either the head or the tail, but not elsewhere in the list. With a deque stored as a circularly linked list, three of the four algorithms to add a node to either end of the deque and to delete a node from either end become easy to write, but the fourth does not.

   a. Which of the four operations is difficult? Why?

   b. Write a C function to initialize a circularly linked deque to be empty.

   c. Write C functions for the three easy operations on a linked deque.

   d. Write a C function for the fourth operation.

4.3 FURTHER OPERATIONS ON LINKED LISTS

For stacks and queues all the operations are performed at one of the ends of the list, but for more general linked lists, changes, insertions, or deletions may be made at any point. In fact, all the operations listed in Section 3.5 apply equally well to linked lists as to contiguous lists.

4.3.1 Algorithms for Simply Linked Lists

To illustrate the kind of actions we can perform with linked lists, let us consider for a moment the problem of editing text, and suppose that each node holds one word as well as the link to the next node. The sentence "Stacks are lists" appears as in (a) of Figure 4.9. If we *insert* the word "simple" we obtain the list in (b). Next we decide to *replace* "lists" by "structures" and *insert* the three nodes "but important data" to obtain (c). Afterward, we decide to *delete* "simple but" and so arrive at list (d). Finally, we *traverse* the list to print its contents.

1. List Traversal

As a first example let us write a function to perform ***list traversal***, which means to move through the list, visiting each node in turn. What we mean by *visiting* each node depends entirely on the application; it might mean printing out some information, or doing some task that depends on the data in the node. Thus we leave the task unspecified and, as in Section 3.5, use a call to a function named Visit. To traverse the list, we shall need a local pointer p that will start at the first node on the list and move from node to node. We need a loop to accomplish this movement, and since we wish to allow the possibility

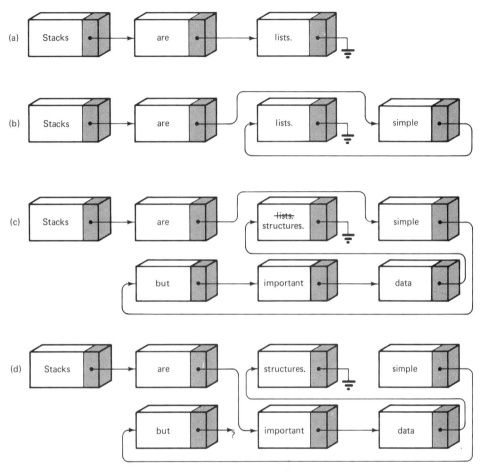

Figure 4.9. Actions on a linked list

of an empty list (for which the loop will not iterate at all), the correct form could be a
for loop. Termination occurs when p points off the end of the list, whereupon we have
p = NULL. The function then becomes

linked traversal

```
/* Traverse: traverse the list visiting one node at a time. */
void Traverse(Node_type *head, void (*Visit)(Node_type *))
{
      Node_type *p;
      for (p = head; p; p = p->next)
            (*Visit)(p);
}
```

Notice the close analogy between traversal of a linked list and traversal of a contiguous
list. If head and tail are indices marking the start and finish of a contiguous list inside
an array list of items, then traversal of the contiguous list is performed by the following
function:

contiguous traversal

```
/* Traverse: traverse the list visiting one node at a time. */
void Traverse (int head, int tail, Node_type list [ ] ,
                    void (*Visit) (Node_type *) )
{
        int p;
        for (p = head; p <= tail; p++)
            (*Visit) ( &list [p] ) ;
}
```

Comparing these versions of traversal, we see that the initialization is the same, the general structure is the same, and the instruction p = p->next replaces p++ as the way to advance one node through the list. Figure 4.10 illustrates this process.

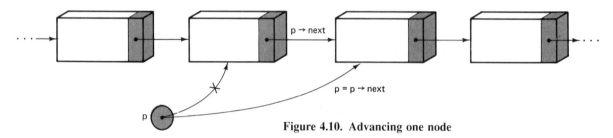

p → next

p = p → next

p

Figure 4.10. Advancing one node

The function Visit normally performs the necessary actions when we visit a node. As an example, we display the contents of the node.

```
/* Visit: visit node p: print its information. */
void Visit (Node_type *p)
{
        printf ("p->info: %c\n", p->info) ;
}
```

2. Insertion After a Node

Next let us consider the problem of inserting a new node into an arbitrary position in our list. If p is a pointer to some node in the list, and we wish to insert the new node *after* the node that p points to, then the method used for inserting a new node at the rear of a queue works with little change:

```
/* InsertNode: insert node q after node p. */
void InsertNode (Node_type *p, Node_type *q)
{
        if (p == NULL || q == NULL)
                Error ("At least one of nodes p and q is nonexistent") ;
        else {
                q->next = p->next;
                p->next = q;
        }
}
```

The action of this function is illustrated in Figure 4.11.

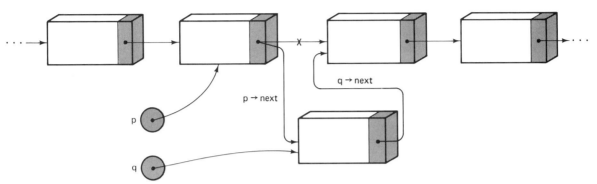

Figure 4.11. Insertion after a node

3. Insertion Before a Node

Suppose now that p points to some node in the list, and we wish to insert a new node *before* the node that p points to. We now have a difficulty, since the link that must be changed is the one coming into p, and there is no way to find this link directly from p and q, since we have no way to move backward through the list.

tracing the list   One way we could use to find the link entering p is to start at the head of the list and traverse it to the desired point, but this is usually not a good method, since its running time is proportional to the length of the list up to p, a length that we do not know in advance and that might be prohibitively large.

swap fields   A second method, the details of which are left as an exercise, is to use a small trick. First, insert the node q after p instead of before p. Then, by copying appropriate information fields between the structures, swap the information in p and q so that the information in q comes before that in p. This method, while it often runs faster than the first one, may become very slow if the information fields are large and will be dangerous if not fatal if there are other variables elsewhere in the program that point to either of the two nodes that were swapped.

two pointers   Hence we shall consider yet a third method to solve the problem of inserting q before p, a method requiring slightly more bookkeeping, but one that moves only pointers, never the information in the nodes, and whose running time does not depend on the length of the list. What we do is to propose keeping a second pointer variable throughout all our processing of the list. This second pointer r will move in lock step with p, with r always kept exactly one node closer to the head of the list than p. Inserting the new node q before p is now easy, since it is only inserting q after r, and then updating r by setting r = q. Inserting the new node before the first node of the list (in which case the trailing pointer r is undefined) is now a special case, but an easy one, similar to adding a node to a linked stack. This process is illustrated in Figure 4.12, which leads to the following function.

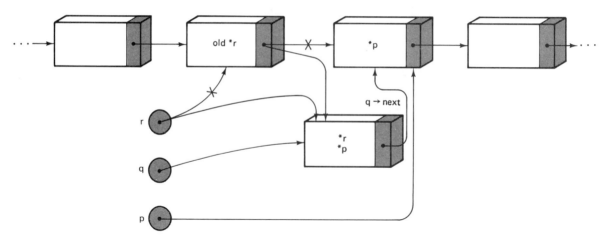

Figure 4.12. Insertion into a linked list with two pointers

insertion between
pointers

```
/* InsertBetween: insert q between the nodes r and p. */
void InsertBetween (Node_type *q, Node_type **head,
                    Node_type **r, Node_type *p)
{
    if (p == *head) {
        q->next = p;
        *r = *head = q;                /* q is at the head of the list.          */
    } else {
        q->next = p;
        (*r)->next = q;                /* q is after r and before p.            */
        *r = q;
    }
}
```

4. The Two-Pointer Implementation

new implementation

In writing the function just finished we have introduced a subtle change in the structure of our linked list, a change that really amounts to a new implementation of the list, one that requires keeping pointers to two adjacent nodes of the list at all times. In this implementation, some operations (like insertion) become easier, but others may become harder. In list traversal, for example, we must be more careful to get the process started correctly. When p points to the head of the list, then r is necessarily undefined. Thus the first step of traversal must be considered separately. The details are left as an exercise. Similarly, insertion of a new node before the current head of the list is a special case, but an easy one already considered in studying linked stacks.

5. Deletion

Deletion of a node from a linked list is another operation in which the implementation makes a significant difference. From our study of linked stacks and queues, we know that it is never difficult to delete the first node on a linked list. If we wish to delete a node p that is not the first one, however, then to adjust the links, we must locate the link coming into p. In a simply linked list with only one pointer, this task is difficult, but with a second pointer r one step behind p, it is easy. After including appropriate error checking, we obtain the following function:

two-pointer deletion

```
/* Delete: delete node p from the list; r is in front of p. */
void Delete(Node_type *r, Node_type *p)
{
        if (r == NULL || p == NULL)
                Error("At least one of nodes r and p is nonexistent");
        else if (r->next != p)
                Error("Nodes r and p not in sequence");
        else
                r->next = p->next;
}
```

This function as written keeps no pointer to the node being deleted, but does not dispose of it either. Instead, the function assumes that the deleted node is to be used by the calling program and the calling program will keep some pointer other than p with which to find the deleted node.

6. Other Implementations

Many variations are possible in the implementation of linked lists, some of which provide advantages in certain situations. In addition to the one-pointer and two-pointer simply linked lists, we might, for example, consider circularly linked lists in which the last node, rather than containing a NULL link, has a link to the first node of the list (see Figure 4.8 and Exercise E6 of Section 4.2).

circularly linked list

doubly linked list

Another form of data structure is a ***doubly linked list*** (like the one shown in Figure 4.13) in which each node contains two links, one to the next node in the list and one to the preceding node. It is thus possible to move either direction through the list while keeping only one pointer. With a doubly linked list, traversals in either direction, insertions, and deletions from arbitrary positions in the list can be programmed without difficulty. The cost of a doubly linked list, of course, is the extra space required in each node for a second link.

dummy node

Yet one more variation in implementation is to include a ***dummy node*** at the beginning (or, less commonly, at the end) of a linked list. This dummy node contains no information and is used only to provide a link to the first true node of the list. It is never

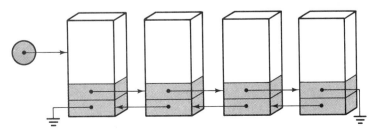

Figure 4.13. Doubly linked list with header

deleted and, if desired, can even be a static variable (that is, one declared as the program is written). Use of a dummy node at the head of the list simplifies the form of some functions. Since the list is never empty, the special case of an empty list does not need to be considered, and neither does the special case of inserting or deleting at the head of the list.

Some of the exercises at the end of this section request functions for manipulating doubly linked lists. We shall study linked lists with dummy header nodes in the application in the next section.

4.3.2 Comparison of Implementations

Now that we have seen several algorithms for manipulating linked lists and several variations in their implementation, let us pause to assess some relative advantages of linked and of contiguous implementation of lists.

advantages The foremost advantage of dynamic storage for linked lists is flexibility. Overflow *overflow* is no problem until the computer memory is actually exhausted. Especially when the individual structures are quite large, it may be difficult to determine the amount of contiguous static storage that might be needed for the required arrays, while keeping enough free for other needs. With dynamic allocation, there is no need to attempt to make such decisions in advance.

changes Changes, especially insertions and deletions, can be made in the middle of a linked list more easily than in the middle of a contiguous list. Even queues are easier to handle in linked storage. If the structures are large, then it is much quicker to change the values of a few pointers than to copy the structures themselves from one location to another.

disadvantages The first drawback of linked lists is that the links themselves take space, space that might otherwise be needed for additional data. In most systems, a pointer requires the same amount of storage (one word) as does an integer. Thus a list of integers will require double the space in linked storage that it would require in contiguous storage. On the other hand, in many practical applications the nodes in the list are quite large, with data fields taking hundreds of words altogether. If each node contains 100 words of data, *space use* then using linked storage will increase the memory requirement by only one percent, an insignificant amount. In fact, if extra space is allocated to arrays holding contiguous lists to allow for additional insertions, then linked storage will probably require less space altogether. If each item takes 100 words, then contiguous storage will save space only if all the arrays can be filled to more than 99 percent of capacity.

random access The major drawback of linked lists is that they are not suited to random access. With contiguous storage, the program can refer to any position within a list as quickly as to any other position. With a linked list, it may be necessary to traverse a long path to reach the desired node.

Finally, access to a node in linked storage may take slightly more computer time, since it is necessary, first, to obtain the pointer and then go to the address. This consideration, however, is usually of no importance. Similarly, you may find at first that *programming* writing functions to manipulate linked lists takes a bit more programming effort, but, with practice, this discrepancy will decrease.

In summary, therefore, we can conclude that contiguous storage is generally preferable when the structures are individually very small, when few insertions or deletions need to be made in the middle of a list, and when random access is important. Linked storage proves superior when the structures are large and flexibility is needed in inserting, deleting, and rearranging the nodes.

4.3.3 Programming Hints

To close this section we include several suggestions for programming with linked lists, as well as some pitfalls to avoid.

pointers and pitfalls   1. Draw "before" and "after" diagrams of the appropriate part of the linked list, showing the relevant pointers and the way in which they should be changed.

2. To determine in what order values should be placed in the pointer fields to implement the various changes, it is usually better first to assign the values to previously undefined pointers, then to those with value NULL, and finally to the remaining pointers. After one pointer variable has been copied to another, the first is free to be reassigned to its new location.

undefined links   3. Be sure that no links are left undefined at the conclusion of your algorithm, either as links in new nodes that have never been assigned, or links in old nodes that have become dangling, that is, that point to nodes that no longer are used. Such links should either be reassigned to nodes still in use or set to the value NULL.

extreme cases   4. Always verify that your algorithm works correctly for an empty list and for a list with only one node.

multiple dereferencing   5. Try to avoid constructions such as p->next->next, even though they are syntactically correct. A single variable should involve only a single pointer reference. Constructions with repeated references usually indicate that the algorithm can be improved by rethinking what pointer variables should be declared in the algorithm, introducing new ones if necessary, so that no variable includes more than one pointer reference (->).

alias variable   6. It is possible that two (or more) different pointer variables can point to the same node. Since this node can thereby be accessed under two different names, it is called an ***alias variable***. The node can be changed using one name and later used with the other name, perhaps without the realization that it has been changed. One pointer can be changed to another node, and the second left dangling. Alias variables are therefore dangerous and should be avoided as much as possible. Be sure you clearly understand whenever you must have two pointers that refer to the same node, and remember that changing one reference requires changing the other.

Exercises   **E1.** Write a C function that counts the number of nodes in a linked list.

4.3   **E2.** Draw a before-and-after diagram describing the main action of the Delete function presented in the text.

E3. Write a function that will concatenate two linked lists. The function should have two parameters, pointers to the beginning of the lists, and the function should link the end of the first list to the beginning of the second.

E4. Write a function that will split a list in two. The function will use two pointers as parameters; p will point to the beginning of the list, and q to the node at which it should be split, so that all nodes before q are in the first list and all nodes after q are in the second list. You may decide whether the node q itself will go into the first list or the second. State a reason for your decision.

E5. Write a function that will insert a node before the node p of a linked list by the following method. First, insert the new node after p, then copy the information fields that p points to the new node, and then put the new information fields into what p points to. Do you need to make a special case when p is the first node of the list?

E6. Write a function to delete the node p from a linked list when you are given only the pointer p without a second pointer in lock step.

   a. Use the device of copying information fields from one node to another in designing your algorithm.

   b. Will your function work when p is the first or the last node in the list? If not, either describe the changes needed or state why it cannot be done without providing additional information to your function.

   c. Suppose that you are also given a pointer head to the first node of the list. Write a deletion algorithm that does not copy information fields from node to node.

E7. Modify the function to traverse a linked list so that it will keep two pointers p and r in lock step, with r always moving one node behind p (that is, r is one node closer to the head of the list). Explain how your function gets started and how it handles the special cases of an empty list and a list with only one node.

E8. Write a function that will reverse a linked list while traversing it only once. At the conclusion, each node should point to the node that was previously its predecessor; the head should point to the node that was formerly at the end, and the node that was formerly first should have a NULL link.

E9. Write an algorithm that will split a linked list into two linked lists, so that successive nodes go to different lists. (The first, third, and all odd-numbered nodes go to the first list, and the second, fourth, and all even-numbered nodes go to the second.)

The following exercises concern circularly linked lists. See Exercise 6 of Section 4.2. For each of these exercises, assume that the circularly linked list is specified by a pointer rear to its last node, and ensure that on conclusion your algorithm leaves the appropriate pointer(s) pointing to the rear of the appropriate list(s).

E10. Write a function to traverse a circularly linked list, visiting each node. First, do the case where only a single pointer moves through the list, and then describe the changes necessary to traverse the list with two pointers moving in lock step, one immediately behind the other.

E11. Write a function to delete a node from a circularly linked list.

E12. Write a function that will concatenate two circularly linked lists, producing a circularly linked list.

E13. Write a function that will split a circularly linked list into two circularly linked lists.

E14. Write functions for manipulating a doubly linked list as follows:

    a. Add a node after p.

    b. Add a node before p.

    c. Delete node p.

    d. Traverse the list.

E15. A doubly linked list can be made circular by setting the values of links in the first and last nodes appropriately. Discuss the advantages and disadvantages of a circular doubly linked list in doing the various list operations.

E16. Make a chart that will compare the difficulties of doing various operations on different implementations of lists. The rows should correspond to all the operations on lists specified in Section 3.5.3 and the columns to (a) contiguous lists, (b) simply linked lists, and (c) doubly linked lists. Fill in the entries to show the relative difficulty of each operation for each implementation. Take into account both programming difficulty and expected running time.

4.4 APPLICATION: POLYNOMIAL ARITHMETIC

4.4.1 Purpose of the Project

calculator for polynomials

As an application of linked lists, this section outlines a program for manipulating polynomials. Our program will imitate the behavior of a simple calculator that does addition, subtraction, multiplication, division, and perhaps some other operations, but one that performs these operations for polynomials.

reverse Polish calculations

There are many kinds of calculators available, and we could model our program after any of them. To provide a further illustration of the use of stacks, however, let us choose to model what is often called a ***reverse Polish*** calculator. In such a calculator, the operands (numbers usually, polynomials for us) are entered *before* the operation is specified. The operands are pushed onto a stack. When an operation is performed, it pops its operands from the stack and pushes its result back onto the stack. If ? denotes pushing an operand onto the stack, $+$, $-$, $*$, $/$ represent arithmetic operations, and $=$ means printing the top of the stack (but not popping it off), then ? ? $+$ $=$ means reading two operands, then calculating and printing their sum. The instruction ? ? $+$? ? $+$ $*$ $=$ requests four operands. If these are a, b, c, d, then the result printed is $(a + b) * (c + d)$. Similarly, ? ? ? ? $-$ $=$ $*$? $+$ $=$ pushes a, b, c onto the stack, replaces b, c by $b - c$ and prints its value, calculates $a * (b - c)$, pushes d on the stack, and finally calculates and prints $(a * (b - c)) + d$. The advantage of a reverse Polish calculator is that any expression, no matter how complicated, can be specified without the use of parentheses.

This Polish notation is useful for compilers as well as for calculators. For the present, however, a few minutes' practice with a reverse Polish calculator will make you quite comfortable with its use.

4.4.2 The Main Program

1. Outline

The task of the calculator program is quite simple in principle. It need only accept new commands and perform them as long as desired. In preliminary outline, the main program takes the form

first outline

```
/* Preliminary outline: program for manupulating polynomials */
void main(void)
{
    Initialize(stack);
    while (there are more commands) {
        GetCommand(cmd);                /* command to execute           */
        DoCommand(cmd);
    }
}
```

2. Performing Commands

To turn this outline into a C program, we must specify what it means to obtain commands and how this will be done. Before doing so, let us make the decision to represent the commands by the characters ?, =, +, −, *, /. Given this decision, we can immediately write the function DoCommand in C, thereby specifying exactly what each command does:

stack operations

```
#include "poly.h"
#include "node.h"
#include "stack.h"
#include "calls.h"
/* DoCommand: do command cmd for polynomials. */
void DoCommand(char cmd, Stack_type *sp)
{
    Item_type item;
    Polynomial_type *p, *q;

    switch(cmd) {
```

input
```
    case '?':                       /* Read polynomial and push it onto stack.    */
        Push(ReadPolynomial( ), sp);
        break;
```
output
```
    case '=':                       /* Write polynomial on the top of the stack.  */
        TopStack( &item, sp);
        WritePolynomial(item);
        break;
```
addition
```
    case '+':                       /* Add top two polynomials and push answer.   */
        Pop( &p, sp);
        Pop( &q, sp);
        Add(p, q, sp);       /* p + q                                      */
        break;
```

subtraction

```
case ' − ':                    /* Subtract two polynomials and push answer.   */
        Pop( &p, sp);
        Pop( &q, sp);
        Subtract(p, q, sp);    /* q − p                                        */
        break;
```

multiplication

```
case '*':                      /* Multiply two polynomials and push answer.   */
        Pop( &p, sp);
        Pop( &q, sp);
        Multiply(p, q, sp);    /* p * q                                        */
        break;
```

division

```
case '/':                      /* Divide two polynomials and push answer.     */
        Pop( &p, sp);
        Pop( &q, sp);
        Divide(p, q, sp);      /* q/p                                          */
        break;
    }
}
```

We use three include files that contain the typedefs we need to build and evaluate the polynomials.

poly.h:

type polynomial

```
typedef struct polynomial_tag {
        double coef;
        int exp;
        struct polynomial_tag *next;
} Polynomial_type;
```

node.h:

```
typedef struct polynomial_tag *Item_type;
```

type node

```
typedef struct node_tag {
        Item_type info;
        struct node_tag *next;
} Node_type;
```

stack.h:

type stack

```
typedef struct stack_tag {
        Node_type *top;
} Stack_type;
```

3. Reading Commands: The Main Program

Now that we have decided that the commands are to be denoted as single characters, we could easily program function GetCommand to read one command at a time from the terminal. It is often convenient, however, to read a string of several commands at once, such as ? ? + ? ? + * = , and then perform them all before reading more. To allow for this possibility, let us read a whole line of commands at once and set up an array to hold them. With this decision we can now write the main program in its final form, except for the additional declarations that we shall insert after choosing our data structures. We shall use a function ReadCommand to read the string of commands; this function will also be responsible for error checking.

```
#define MAXCOMMAND 10
```

main program
```
/* Implement calculator for polynomials. */
void main (void)
{
     int i, n;
     Stack_type stack;
     char command [MAXCOMMAND] ;

     Initialize ( &stack) ;
     do {
          n = ReadCommand (command) ;
          for (i = 0; i < n; i++)
               DoCommand (command [i], &stack) ;
     } while (Enquire ( )) ;
}
```

4. Input Functions

Before we turn to our principal task (deciding how to represent polynomials and writing functions to manipulate them), let us complete the preliminaries by giving details for the input functions. The prompting function need only write one line, but note that this line gives the user the opportunity to request further instructions if desired.

prompting user
```
/* Prompt: prompt the user for command line. */
void Prompt (void)
{
     int c;

     printf ("Enter a string of commands or ! for help.\n") ;
     while ( (c = getchar ( )) == '\n')
          /* empty */ ;                    /* Discard leftover newlines, if any.        */
     ungetc (c, stdin) ;
}
```

Function ReadCommand must check that the symbols typed in represent legitimate operations and must provide instructions if desired, along with doing its main task. If there is an error or the user requests instructions, then the command string must be re-entered from the start.

read commands

```
/* ReadCommand: read a command line and save it in command. */
int ReadCommand(char command[ ])
{
      int c, n;

            do {                             /* Read a valid command line.         */
                  n = 0;                     /* number of characters read          */
                  Prompt( );
                  while ((c = getchar( )) != '\n')
                        if (strchr(" ,\t", c) != NULL)
                                    /* empty */ ;   /* Skip white-space characters.  */
                        else if (strchr("?+-*/=", c) == NULL)
                              break;          /* non-command character               */
                        else
                              command[n++] = c;
                  if (c ==  '!')
                        Help( );
                  Geteol(c);                 /* Skip characters until new line.      */
            } while (c != '\n');
            command[n] = '\0';               /* Add end of string marker.            */
            return n;
}
```

error checking

instructions

The next function is a utility that skips all characters until the end of a line.

```
/* Geteol: get characters until the end of the line. */
void Geteol(int c)
{
      while (c != '\n')
            c = getchar( );
}
```

The following function provides help to the user when requested.

instructions

```
/* Help: provide instructions for the user. */
void Help(void)
{
      printf("Enter a string of commands in reverse Polish form.\n");
      printf("The valid instructions are:\n");
      printf(" ?  Read a polynomial onto stack\n");
      printf(" +  Add top two polynomials on stack\n");
      printf(" -  Subtract top two polynomials on stack\n");
      printf(" *  Multiply top two polynomials on stack\n");
      printf(" /  Divide top two polynomials on stack\n");
      printf(" =  Print polynomial on top of the stack\n");
}
```

5. Stubs and Testing

At this point we have written quite enough of our program that we should pause to compile it, debug it, and test it to make sure that what has been done so far is correct. If we were to wait until all remaining functions had been written, the program would become so long and complicated that debugging would be much more difficult.

For the task of compiling the program, we must, of course, supply stubs for all the missing functions. At present, however, we have not even completed the type declarations: the most important one, that of a Polynomial, remains unspecified. We could make this type declaration almost arbitrarily and still be able to compile the program, *temporary type* but for testing, it is much better to make the temporary type declaration
declaration

typedef double Polynomial_type;

and test the program by running it as an ordinary reverse Polish calculator. The following is then typical of the stubs that are needed:

```
double Add (Polynomial_type x, Polynomial_type y)
{
        return x + y;
}
```
stub

In addition to stubs of the functions for doing arithmetic and the function Erase (which *stack package* need do nothing), we need a package of functions to manipulate the stack. If you wish, you may use the package for linked stacks developed in this chapter, but with the items in the stack only real numbers, it is probably easier to use the contiguous stack algorithms developed in Section 3.2. The functions Initialize and TopStack do not appear there, but are trivial to write. With these tools we can fully debug and test the part of the program now written, after which we can turn to the remainder of the project.

4.4.3 Data Structures and Their Implementation

If we carefully consider a polynomial such as

$$3x^5 - 2x^3 + x^2 + 4$$

we see that the important information about the polynomial is contained in the coefficients *essence of a* and exponents of x; the variable x itself is really just a place holder (a dummy variable). *polynomial* Hence, for purposes of calculation, we may think of a polynomial as a sum of terms, each of which consists of a coefficient and an exponent. In a computer we can similarly implement a polynomial as a list of pairs of coefficients and exponents. Each of these pairs will constitute a structure, so a polynomial will be represented as a list of structures. We must then build into our functions rules for performing arithmetic on two such lists.

implementation of a polynomial   Should we use contiguous or linked lists? If, in advance, we know a bound on the degree of the polynomials that can occur and if the polynomials that occur have nonzero coefficients in almost all their possible terms, then we should probably do better with contiguous lists. But if we do not know a bound on the degree, or if polynomials with only a few nonzero terms are likely to appear, then we shall find linked storage preferable. To illustrate the use of linked lists, we adopt the latter implementation, as illustrated in Figure 4.14.

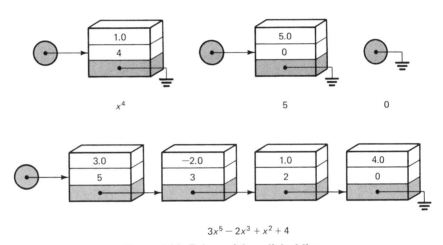

$$3x^5 - 2x^3 + x^2 + 4$$

Figure 4.14. Polynomials as linked lists

assumptions   We shall consider that each node represents one term of a polynomial, and we shall keep only nonzero terms in the list. The polynomial that is identically 0 will be represented by an empty list. Hence each node will be a structure containing a nonzero coefficient, an exponent, and, as usual for linked lists, a pointer to the next term of the polynomial. To refer to polynomials, we shall always use header variables for the lists; hence, it is sensible to make pointers of type Polynomial_type and use it for the headers. Moreover, the remaining terms after any given one are again a (smaller) polynomial, so the field next again naturally has type Polynomial_type. Refer to the include files in Section 4.4.2.

We have not yet indicated the order of storing the terms of the polynomial. If we allow them to be stored in any order, then it might be difficult to recognize that

$$x^5 + x^2 - 3 \text{ and } -3 + x^5 + x^2 \text{ and } x^2 - 3 + x^5$$

restriction   all represent the same polynomial. Hence we adopt the usual convention that the terms of every polynomial are stored in the order of decreasing exponent within the linked list, and we further assume that no two terms have the same exponent and that no term has a zero coefficient.

4.4.4 Reading and Writing Polynomials

With polynomials implemented as linked lists, writing out a polynomial becomes simply a traversal of the list, as follows.

writing

```
/* WritePolynomial: write a polynomial to standard output. */
void WritePolynomial(Polynomial_type *p)
{
    if (!p)                              /* Polynomial is an empty list.          */
        printf("zero polynomial\n");
    else while (p) {
        printf("%5.2lfx^%1d", p->coef, p->exp);
        p = p->next;
        if (p)
            printf("+");
        else
            printf("\n");
    }
}
```

As we read in a new polynomial, we shall be constructing a new linked list, adding a node to the list for each term (coefficient-exponent pair) that we read. The process of creating a new node, attaching it to the tail of a list, putting in the coefficient and exponent, and updating the tail pointer to point to the new term will reappear in almost every function for manipulating polynomials. We therefore write it as a separate utility.

making one term

```
/* InsertTerm: insert a new term at the end of polynomial. */
Polynomial_type *InsertTerm(double coef, int exp, Polynomial_type *tail)
{
    if ((tail->next = MakeTerm(coef, exp)) == NULL)
        Error("Cannot allocate polynomial term");
    return tail->next;
}
```

dummy first node

We can now use this function to insert new terms as we read coefficient-exponent pairs. InsertTerm, however, expects to insert the new term *after* the term to which tail currently points, so how do we make the first term of the list? One way is to write a separate section of code. It is easier, however, to use a ***dummy header***, as follows. Before starting to read, we make a new node at the head of the list, and we put dummy information into it. We then insert all the actual terms, each one inserted after the preceding one. When the function concludes the head pointer is advanced one position to the first actual term, and the dummy node is freed. This process is illustrated in Figure 4.15 and is implemented in the following function:

reading

```
/* ReadPolynomial: read a polynomial and return its pointer. */
Polynomial_type *ReadPolynomial(void)
{
        double coef;
        int exp, lastexp;
        Polynomial_type *result, *tail;
```

instructions

```
        printf("Enter coefficients and exponents for the polynomial.\n"
                "Exponents must be in descending order.\n"
                "Enter coefficient or exponent 0 to terminate.\n");
```

initialize

```
        lastexp = INT_MAX;
        tail = result = MakeTerm(0.0, 0);   /* dummy head                      */
```

read one term

```
        while(1) {
                printf("coefficient? ");
                scanf("%lf", &coef);
                if (coef == 0.0)
                        break;
                printf("exponent? ");
                scanf("%d", &exp);
```

error checking

```
                if (exp >= lastexp || exp < 0) {
                        printf("Bad exponent. Polynomial is terminated "
                                "without its last term.\n");
                        break;
                }
```

make one term

```
                tail = InsertTerm(coef, exp, tail);
                if (exp == 0)
                        break;
                lastexp = exp;
        }
```

conclude

```
        tail->next = NULL;          /* Terminate the polynomial.          */
        tail = result;              /* Prepare to dispose of the head.    */
        result = result->next;      /* Advance to first term.             */
        free(tail);                 /* Free dummy head.                   */
        return result;
}
```

4.4.5 Addition of Polynomials

The requirement that the terms of a polynomial appear with descending exponents in the list simplifies their addition. To add two polynomials we need only scan through them once each. If we find terms with the same exponent in the two polynomials, then we add the coefficients; otherwise, we copy the term of larger exponent into the sum and go on. When we reach the end of one of the polynomials, then any remaining part of the other is copied to the sum. We must also be careful not to include terms with zero coefficient in the sum.

```
/* Add: add two polynomials and push the answer onto stack. */
void Add(Polynomial_type *p, Polynomial_type *q, Stack_type *sp)
{
       double sum;
       Polynomial_type *ptmp = p;
       Polynomial_type *qtmp = q;
       Polynomial_type *result, *tail;
```

initialize
```
       tail = result = MakeTerm(0.0, 0);
       while (p && q)
```

equal-exponent
terms
```
              if (p->exp == q->exp) {   /* Add coefficients.                          */
                     if ((sum = p->coef + q->coef) != 0.0)
                            tail = InsertTerm(sum, p->exp, tail);
                     p = p->next;
                     q = q->next;
```

unequal exponents
```
              } else if (p->exp > q->exp) {  /* Copy p to result.                     */
                     tail = InsertTerm(p->coef, p->exp, tail);
                     p = p->next;
              } else {                         /* Copy q to result.                    */
                     tail = InsertTerm(q->coef, q->exp, tail);
                     q = q->next;
              }
```

remaining terms
```
       /* One or both of the summands has been exhausted. */
       /* At most one of the following loops will be executed. */
       for (; p; p = p->next)
              tail = InsertTerm(p->coef, p->exp, tail);
       for (; q; q = q->next)
              tail = InsertTerm(q->coef, q->exp, tail);
```

conclude
```
       tail->next = NULL;                      /* Terminate polynomial.                */
       Push(result->next, sp);
       free(result);                           /* Free dummy head.                     */
       Erase(ptmp);                            /* Erase summand.                       */
       Erase(qtmp);
}
```

4.4.6 Completing the Project

1. The Missing Functions

At this point the remaining functions for the calculator project are sufficiently similar to those already written that they can be left as exercises. The function Erase need only traverse the list (as done in WritePolynomial) disposing of the nodes as it goes. Functions for the remaining arithmetical operations have the same general form as our function for addition. Some of these are easy: Subtraction is almost identical with addition. For multiplication we can first write (a simple) function that multiplies a polynomial by a monomial, where **monomial** means a polynomial with only one term. Then we combine use of this function with the addition function to do a general multiplication. Division is a little more complicated.

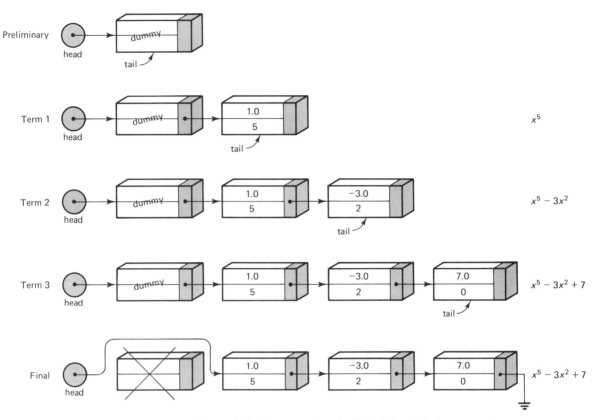

Figure 4.15. Construction of a linked list with dummy node

2. Group Project

Production of a coherent package of algorithms for manipulating polynomials makes an interesting group project. Different members of the group can write functions for different operations. Some of these are indicated as projects at the end of this section, but you may wish to include additional features as well. Any additional features should be planned carefully to be sure that they can be implemented in a reasonable time, without disrupting other parts of the program.

specifications   After deciding on the division of work among its members, the most important decisions of the group relate to the exact ways in which the functions should communicate with each other, and especially with the calling program. If you wish to make any changes in the organization of the program, be certain that the precise details are spelled out clearly and completely for all members of the group.

cooperation   Next, you will find that it is too much to hope that all members of the group will complete their work at the same time, or that all parts of the project can be combined and debugged together. You will therefore need to use program stubs and drivers (see Sections 1.4.1 and 1.4.4) to debug and test the various parts of the project. One member of the group might take special responsibility for these. In any case, you will find it very effective for different members to read, help debug, and test each other's subprograms.

coordination   Finally, there are the responsibilities of making sure that all members of the group complete their work on time, of keeping track of the progress of various aspects of the project, of making sure that no subprograms are integrated into the project before they are thoroughly debugged and tested, and of combining all the work into the finished product.

Exercises 4.4

E1. Decide whether the stack for the calculator should be contiguous or linked. Justify your decision. Incorporate the necessary functions to implement the stack in the way you decide.

E2. If polynomials are stored as circularly linked lists instead of simply linked lists, then a polynomial can be erased more quickly. What changes are needed to the addition function (and other subprograms) to implement circularly linked lists?

E3. Consider generalizing the project of this section to polynomials in several variables.

Programming Projects 4.4

P1. Write function Erase.

P2. Write function Subtract.

P3. Write a function that will multiply a polynomial by a monomial (that is, by a polynomial consisting of a single term).

P4. Use the function of the preceding problem, together with the function that adds polynomials, to write the function Multiply.

P5. Write function Divide.

P6. The function ReadCommand, as written, will accept any sequence of commands, but some sequences are illegal. If the stack begins empty, for example, then the sequence + ? ? is illegal, because it is impossible to add two polynomials before reading them in. Modify function ReadCommand as follows so that it will accept only legal sequences of commands. The function should set up a counter and initialize it to the number of polynomials on the stack. Whenever the command ? appears in the stream the counter is increased by one (since the read command ? will push an additional polynomial onto the stack), and whenever one of + , − , *, / appears, it is decreased by one (since these commands will pop two polynomials and push one onto the stack). If the counter ever becomes zero or negative then the sequence is illegal.

P7. Many reverse Polish calculators use not only a stack but also provide memory locations where operands can be stored. Extend the project to provide for memory locations for polynomials, and provide additional commands to store the top of the stack into a memory location and to push the polynomial in a memory location onto the stack.

P8. Write a function that will discard the top polynomial on the stack, and include this capability as a new command.

P9. Write a function that will interchange the top two polynomials on the stack, and include this capability as a new command.

P10. Write a function that will add all the polynomials on the stack together, and include this capability as a new command.

P11. Write a function that will compute the derivative of a polynomial, and include this capability as a new command.

P12. Write a function that, given a polynomial and a real number, evaluates the polynomial at that number, and include this capability as a new command.

4.5 LINKED LISTS IN ARRAYS

old languages

Several of the older but widely-used computer languages, such as FORTRAN, COBOL, and BASIC, do not provide facilities for dynamic storage allocation or pointers. Even when implemented in these languages, however, there are many problems where the methods of linked lists are preferable to those of contiguous lists, where, for example, the ease of changing a pointer rather than copying a large structure proves advantageous. This section shows how to implement linked lists using only simple integer variables and arrays.

The idea is to begin with a large array (or several arrays to hold different parts of a structure) and regard the array as our allocation of unused space. We then set up our own functions to keep track of which parts of the array are unused and to link entries of the array together in the desired order.

dynamic memory

The one feature of linked lists that we must invariably lose in this implementation method is the dynamic allocation of storage, since we must decide in advance how much space to allocate to each array. All the remaining advantages of linked lists, such as flexibility in rearranging large structures or ease in making insertions or deletions anywhere in the list, will still apply, and linked lists still prove a valuable method.

advantages

The implementation of linked lists within arrays even proves valuable in languages like C that do provide pointer types and dynamic memory allocation. The applications where arrays may prove preferable are those where the number of items in a list is known in advance, where the links are frequently rearranged, but relatively few additions or deletions are made, or applications where the same data are sometimes best treated as a linked list and other times as a contiguous list. An example of such an application is illustrated in Figure 4.16, which shows a small part of a student record system. Identification numbers are assigned to students first-come, first-served, so neither the names nor the marks in any particular course are in any special order. Given an

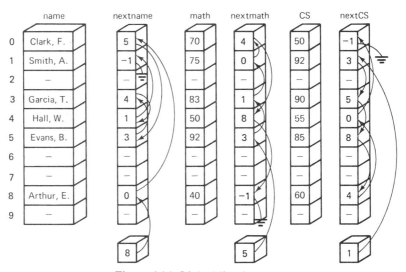

Figure 4.16. Linked lists in arrays

multiple linkages

identification number, a student's records may be found immediately by using the identification number as an index to look in the arrays. Sometimes, however, it is desired to print out the student records alphabetically by name, and this can be done by following the links stored in the array nextname. Similarly, student records can be ordered by marks in any course by following the links in the appropriate array.

cursors

In the implementation of linked lists in arrays, pointers become indices relative to the start of arrays, and the links of a list are stored in an array, each entry of which gives the index where, within the array, the next entry of the list is stored. To distinguish these indices from the pointers of a linked list in dynamic storage, we shall refer to links within arrays as **cursors** and reserve the word *pointer* for links in dynamic storage.

For the sake of writing programs we shall use two arrays for each linked list, info [ ] to hold the information in the nodes and next [ ] to give the cursor to the next node. These arrays will be indexed from 0 to MAX−1, where MAX is a symbolic constant. Since we begin the indices with 0, we can use the cursor value −1 to indicate the end of the list, just as the pointer value NULL is used in dynamic storage. This choice is also illustrated in Figure 4.16.

You should take a moment to trace through Figure 4.16, checking that the cursor values as shown correspond to the arrows shown from each entry to its successor.

To obtain the flavor of implementing linked lists in arrays, let us rewrite several of the algorithms of this chapter with this implementation.

malloc and free

Our first task is to set up a list of available space and write functions to obtain a new node and to return a node to available space. We shall set up a stack to keep track of available space, but now this stack will be linked by means of cursors in the array next. To keep track of the stack of available space, we need an integer variable avail that will give the index of its top. If this stack is empty (which will be represented by avail = −1) then we will need to obtain a new node, that is, a position within the array that has not yet been used for any node. Thus we shall keep another integer variable lastnode that will count the total number of positions within our array that have been used to hold list entries. When lastnode exceeds MAX−1 (the bound we have assumed for array size) then we will have overflow and the program can proceed no further. When the main program starts, both variables avail and lastnode should be initialized to −1, avail to indicate that the stack of space previously used but now available is empty, and lastnode to indicate that no space from the array has yet been assigned. This available-space list is illustrated in Figure 4.17. This figure, by the way, also illustrates how two linked lists can coexist in the same array.

The decisions we have made translate into the following declarations:

```
int avail, lastnode;
int next [MAX];
```

We put MAX in an include file and call the file list.h:

```
#define MAX 5
```

We take this small value for testing the program. In a typical application, MAX would be as large as available memory permits. With these declarations we can now rewrite the functions for keeping track of unused space. At the start of the program, the lists should be initialized by invoking the following:

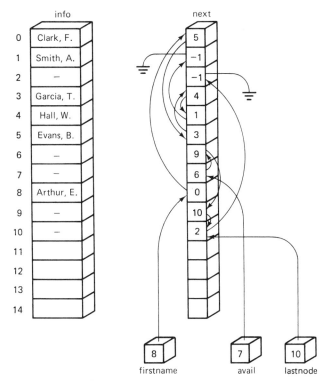

Figure 4.17. The available-space list

```
                      /* Initialize: initialize head and indices avail and lastnode. */
initialization        void Initialize(int *head, int *avail, int *lastnode)
                      {
                          *head = −1;              /* The list is empty.                */  */
                          *avail = −1;             /* Stack of available nodes is empty. */  */
                          *lastnode = −1;          /* None of the positions has been used. */  */
                      }
```

The following function NewNode allocates a new node from available space:

```
                      /* NewNode: select the index of first available position. */
allocate              int NewNode(int *avail, int *lastnode, int next[])
                      {
                          int n = −1;
                          if (*avail != −1) {
                              n = *avail;
                              *avail = next[*avail];
                          } else if (*lastnode < MAX) {
                              (*lastnode)++;
                              n = *lastnode;
                          } else  Error("No available position left");
                          return n;
                      }
```

The purpose of the next function, called FreeNode, is to return a node that in no longer needed to the list of available space. This function now takes the form:

/* FreeNode: return node at position n to available space. */

free
```
void FreeNode(int *head, int *avail, int next[], int n)
{
     int i;

     if (n <= −1)
          Error("Invalid node to return to available space");
     else {
          if (*head == n)
               *head = next[*head];
          else
               for (i = *head; i < MAX; i++) {
                    if (next[i] == n) {
                         next[i] = next[n];
                         break;
                    }
               }
          next[n] = *avail;
          *avail = n;
     }
}
```

The translation of other functions so as to manipulate linked lists implemented within arrays proceeds in much the same way as the functions already developed, and most of these functions will be left as exercises. To provide further models, however, let us write a translation of the function to traverse a list.

/* Traverse: traverse a linked list starting at head with links in the table next[]. */

traverse
```
void Traverse(int head, int next[], void (*Visit)(int))
{
     int i;

     for (i = head; i != −1; i = next[i])
          (*Visit)(i);
}
```

The function Visit has the same purpose and is similar in form to the function Visit developed in Section 4.3.1.

Exercises 4.5

E1. Draw arrows showing how the list entries are linked together in each of the following next tables. Some tables contain more than one list.

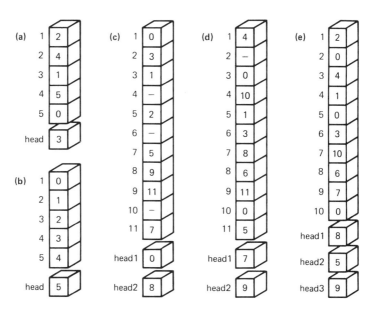

E2. Construct next tables showing how each of the following lists is linked into alphabetical order. Also give the value of the variable head that starts the list.

(a)
1 array
2 stack
3 queue
4 list
5 deque
6 scroll

(b)
1 push
2 pop
3 add
4 delete
5 insert

(c)
1 the
2 of
3 and
4 to
5 a
6 in
7 that
8 is
9 I
10 it
11 for
12 as

(d)
1 London
2 England
3 Rome
4 Italy
5 Madrid
6 Spain
7 Oslo
8 Norway
9 Paris
10 France
11 Warsaw
12 Poland

E3. For the list of cities and countries in part (d) of the previous question construct a next table that produces two linked lists, one containing all the cities in alphabetical order and the other all the countries in alphabetical order. Also give values to the two header variables.

E4. Write a function that counts the number of nodes in a linked list implemented in an array.

E5. Write a function that will concatenate two linked lists implemented in one next table. The function should have two parameters, cursors to the beginning of the lists, and the function should link the end of the first list to the beginning of the second.

E6. Write a function that will split a list in two. The function will use two parameters; n will point to the node at which it should be split and next contains the indices. Is it easier to require that n initially point to the node that will be last in the first list after splitting or to the node that will be first in the second list?

E7. Write a function that will reverse a linked list within an array while traversing it only once. At the conclusion, each node should point to the node that was previously its predecessor; the header should point to the node that was formerly at the end, and the node that was formerly first should have a -1 cursor.

4.6 ABSTRACT DATA TYPES AND THEIR IMPLEMENTATIONS

4.6.1 Introduction

Suppose that in deciphering a long and poorly documented program you found the following sets of instructions:

```
xxt->xlnk = w;      w->xlnk = NULL;      xxt = w;
```

reading programs   and

```
if ((xxh == xxt + 1 && xxt >= 0) || (xxt == mxx && xxh == 0))
    tryagain();
else {
    xxt++;
    if (xxt > mxx)
        xxt = 0;
    xx[xxt] = wi;
}
```

In isolation it may not be clear what either of these sections of code is intended to do, and without further explanation, it would probably take a few minutes to realize that in fact they have essentially the same function! Both segments are intended to add an item to the end of a queue, the first queue in a linked implementation and the second queue in contiguous storage.

Researchers working in different subjects frequently have ideas that are fundamentally similar but are developed for different purposes and expressed in different language. Often years will pass before anyone realizes the similarity of the work, but when the observation is made, insight from one subject can help with the other. In computer science, even so, the same basic idea often appears in quite different disguises that obscure the similarity. But if we can discover and emphasize the similarities, then we may be able to generalize the ideas and obtain easier ways to meet the requirements of many applications.

analogies

When we first introduced stacks and queues in Chapter 3, we considered them only as they are implemented in contiguous storage, and yet upon introduction of linked stacks and queues in this chapter, we had no difficulty in recognizing the same underlying logical structure. The obscurity of the code at the beginning of this section reflects the programmer's failure to recognize the general concept of a queue and to distinguish between this general concept and the particular implementation needed for each application.

similarity

implementation   The way in which an underlying structure is implemented can have substantial effects on program development, and on the capabilities and usefulness of the result. Sometimes these effects can be subtle. The underlying mathematical concept of a real number, for example, is usually (but not always) implemented by computer as a floating-point number with a certain degree of precision, and the inherent limitations in this implementation often produce difficulties with round-off error. Drawing a clear separation between the logical structure of our data and its implementation in computer memory will help us in designing programs. Our first step is to recognize the logical connections among the data and embody these connections in a logical data structure. Later we can consider our data structures and decide what is the best way to implement them for efficiency of programming and execution. By separating these decisions they both become easier, and we avoid pitfalls that attend premature commitment.

To help us clarify this distinction and achieve greater generality let us now reconsider some of the data structures we have studied from as general a perspective as we can.

4.6.2 General Definitions

1. Mathematical Concepts

Mathematics is the quintessence of generalization and therefore provides the language we need for our definitions. The place to start is the definition of a type:

DEFINITION   A *type* is a set, and the elements of the set are called the *values* of the type.

We may therefore speak of the type int, meaning the set of all integers, the type double, meaning the set of all real numbers, or the type char, meaning the set of symbols (characters) that we wish to manipulate in our algorithms.

Notice that we can already draw a distinction between an abstract type and its implementation: The C type int, for example, is not the set of all integers; it consists only of the set of those integers directly represented in a particular computer, the largest of which is INT_MAX (see the system file limits.h for your C compiler).

Similarly, the C type double generally means a certain set of floating-point numbers (separate mantissa and exponent) that is only a small subset of the set of all real numbers. The C type char also varies from computer to computer; sometimes it is the ASCII character set; sometimes it is the EBCDIC character set; sometimes it is some other set of symbols. Even so, all these types, both abstract types and implementations, are sets and hence fit the definition of a type.

2. Atomic and Structured Types

Types such as int, double, and char are called *atomic* types because we think of their values as single entities only, not something we wish to subdivide. Computer languages like C, however, provide tools such as arrays, structures, and pointers with which we can build new types, called *structured* types. A single value of a structured type (that is, a single element of its set) is an array or file or linked list. A value of a structured type has two ingredients: It is made up of *component* elements, and there is a *structure*, a set of rules for putting the components together.

building types
For our general point of view we shall use mathematical tools to provide the rules for building up structured types. Among these tools are sets, sequences, and functions. For the study of lists the one that we need is the ***finite sequence***, and for its definition we use mathematical induction. A definition by induction (like a proof by induction) has two parts: First is an initial case, and second is the definition of the general case in terms of preceding cases.

DEFINITION

> A ***sequence of length*** 0 is empty. A ***sequence of length*** $n \geq 1$ of elements from a set T is an ordered pair (S_{n-1}, t) where S_{n-1} is a sequence of length $n - 1$ of elements from T, and t is an element of T.

From this definition we can build up longer and longer sequences, starting with the empty sequence and adding on new elements from T, one at a time.

sequential versus contiguous
From now on we shall draw a careful distinction between the word ***sequential***, meaning that the elements form a sequence, and the word ***contiguous***, which we take to mean that the nodes have adjacent addresses in memory. Hence we shall be able to speak of a *sequential* list in either a *linked* or *contiguous* implementation.

3. Abstract Data Types

The definition of a finite sequence immediately makes it possible for us to attempt a definition of a list: a ***list*** of items of a type T is simply a finite sequence of elements of the set T. Next we would like to define stacks and queues, but if you consider the definitions, you will realize that there will be nothing regarding the sequence of items to distinguish these structures from a list. The only difference among stacks, queues, and more general lists is in the *operations* by which changes or accesses can be made to the list. Hence, before turning to these other structures we should complete the definition of a list by specifying what operations can be done with a list. Including a statement of these operations with the structural rules defining a finite sequence, we obtain

DEFINITION

> A ***list*** of elements of type T is a finite sequence of elements of T together with the operations
>
> 1. Initialize the list to be empty.
> 2. Determine whether the list is empty or not.
> 3. Determine whether the list is full or not.
> 4. Find the length of the list.
> 5. Retrieve any node from the list, provided that the list is not empty.
> 6. Store a new node replacing the node at any position in the list, provided that the list is not empty.
> 7. Insert a new node into the list at any position, provided that the list is not full.
> 8. Delete any node from the list, provided that the list is not empty.

It is now easy to see what changes are needed to define stacks and queues.

DEFINITION

A **stack** of elements of type T is a finite sequence of elements of T together with the operations

1. Initialize the stack to be empty.

2. Determine if the stack is empty or not.

3. Determine if the stack is full or not.

4. If the stack is not full, then insert a new node at one end of the stack, called its **top**.

5. If the stack is not empty, then retrieve the node at its top.

6. If the stack is not empty, then delete the node at its top.

DEFINITION

A **queue** of elements of type T is a finite sequence of elements of T together with the operations

1. Initialize the queue to be empty.

2. Determine if the queue is empty or not.

3. Determine if the queue is full or not.

4. Insert a new node after the last node in the queue, if it is not full.

5. Retrieve the first node in the queue, if it is not empty.

6. Delete the first node in the queue, if it is not empty.

Note that these definitions make no mention of the way in which the abstract data type (list, stack, or queue) is to be implemented. In the past two chapters we have studied different implementations of each of these types, and these new definitions fit any of these implementations equally well. These definitions produce what is called an ***abstract***

abstract data type   ***data type***, often abbreviated as ***ADT***. The important principle is that the definition of any abstract data type involves two parts: First is a description of the way in which the components are related to each other, and second is a statement of the operations that can be performed on elements of the abstract data type.

4.6.3 Refinement of Data Specification

Now that we have obtained such general definitions of abstract data types, it is time to begin specifying more detail, since the objective of all this work is to find general principles that will help with designing programs, and we need more detail to accomplish this objective. There is, in fact, a close analogy between the process of top-down refinement of algorithms and the process of top-down specification of data structures that

top-down   we have now begun. In algorithm design we begin with a general but precise statement
specification   of the problem and slowly specify more detail until we have developed a complete program. In data specification we begin with the selection of the mathematical concepts and abstract data types required for our problem and slowly specify more detail until finally we can describe our data structures in terms of a programming language.

stages of refinement   The number of stages required in this specification process depends on the application. The design of a large software system will require many more decisions than will the design of a single small program, and these decisions should be taken in several stages of refinement. Although different problems will require different numbers of stages of refinement, and the boundaries between these stages sometimes blur, we can pick out four levels of the refinement process.

conceptual   1. On the *abstract* level we decide how the data are related to each other and what operations are needed, but we decide nothing concerning how the data will actually be stored or how the operations will actually be done.

algorithmic   2. On the *data structures* level we specify enough detail so that we can analyze the behavior of the operations and make appropriate choices as dictated by our problem. This is the level, for example, at which we choose between contiguous lists and linked lists. Some operations are easier for contiguous lists and others for linked lists: finding the length of the list and retrieving the kth element are easier for contiguous lists; inserting and deleting are easier for linked lists. Some applications require many insertions or deletions at arbitrary positions in a list, so we prefer linked lists. For other problems contiguous lists prove better.

programming   3. On the *implementation* level we decide the details of how the data structures will be represented in computer memory. Here, for example, we decide whether a linked list will be implemented with pointers and dynamic memory or with cursors in an array.

4. On the *application* level we settle all details required for our particular application, such as names for variables or special requirements for the operations imposed by the application.

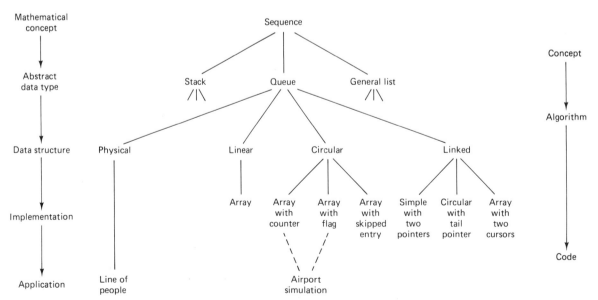

Figure 4.18. Refinement of a queue

The first two levels are often called ***conceptual*** because at these levels we are more concerned with problem solving than with programming. The middle two levels can be called ***algorithmic*** because they concern precise methods for representing data and operating with it. The last two levels are specifically concerned with ***programming***.

Figure 4.18 illustrates these stages of refinement in the case of a queue. We begin with the mathematical concept of a sequence and then the queue considered as an abstract data type. At the next level, we choose from the various data structures shown in the diagram, ranging from the physical model (in which all items move forward as each one leaves the head of the queue) to the linear model (in which the queue is emptied all at once) to circular arrays and finally linked lists. Some of these data structures allow further variation in their implementation, as shown on the next level. At the final stage, the queue is coded for a specific application.

Let us conclude this section by restating its most important principles as programming precepts:

> ### Programming Precept
>
> Let your data structure your program.
> Refine your algorithms and data structures at the same time.

> ### Programming Precept
>
> Once your data are fully structured,
> your algorithms should almost write themselves.

Exercises 4.6

E1. Draw a diagram similar to that of Figure 4.18 showing levels of refinement for **(a)** a stack and **(b)** a list.

E2. Give formal definitions of the terms **(a)** *deque* and **(b)** *scroll*, using the definitions given for stack and queue as models.

POINTERS AND PITFALLS

1. For general advice on the use of lists, see the Pointers and Pitfalls at the end of Chapter 3.

2. Before choosing implementations, be sure that all the data structures and their associated operations are fully specified on the abstract level.

3. In choosing between linked and contiguous implementations of lists, consider the necessary operations on the lists. Linked lists are more flexible in regard to insertions, deletions, and rearrangement; contiguous lists allow random access.

4. Contiguous lists usually require less computer memory, computer time, and programming effort when the items in the list are small and the algorithms are simple. When the list holds large structures, linked lists usually save space, time, and often programming effort.

5. Dynamic memory and pointers allow a program to adapt automatically to a wide range of application sizes and provide flexibility in space allocation among different data structures. Static memory (arrays and cursors) is sometimes more efficient for applications whose size can be completely specified in advance.

6. For advice on programming with linked lists in dynamic memory, see the guidelines at the end of Section 4.3.

REVIEW QUESTIONS

4.1   **1.** Give two reasons why dynamic memory allocation is a valuable device.

2. Define the terms *pointer, contiguous, static variable*, and *dynamic variable*.

3. What is the difference between "p = NULL" and "p is undefined"?

4. Is the header for a linked list usually a static variable or a dynamic variable?

4.2   **5.** In popping a linked stack we first checked that the stack was not empty, but in pushing it we did not first check that it was not full. Why not?

4.3   **6.** Is it easier to insert a new node before or after a specified node in a linked list? Why?

7. Write a C function that counts the nodes of a linked list.

8. If the items in a list are integers (one word each) compare the amount of space required altogether if (a) the list is kept contiguously in an array 90% full, (b) the list is kept contiguously in an array 40% full, and (c) the list is kept as a linked list (where the pointers take one word each).

9. Repeat the comparisons of the previous exercise when the items in the list are structures taking 200 words each.

10. What is an *alias* variable, and why is it dangerous?

11. What is the major disadvantage of linked lists in comparison with contiguous lists?

4.4   **12.** Discuss some problems that occur in group programming projects that do not occur in individual programming projects. What advantages does a group project have over individual projects?

4.5   **13.** What are some reasons for implementing linked lists in arrays with cursors instead of in dynamic memory with pointers?

4.6   **14.** What two parts must be in the definition of any abstract data type?

15. In an abstract data type how much is specified about implementation?

16. Name (in order from abstract to concrete) four levels of refinement of data specification.

REFERENCES FOR FURTHER STUDY

The references given at the end of Chapter 3 continue to be appropriate for the current chapter. In particular, linked lists are studied in depth in KNUTH, Volume 1, pp. 251–272, and an algorithm for polynomial addition appears in pp. 272–276. Abstract data types are treated extensively in the book by WELSH, ELDER, and BUSTARD (reference in Chapter 3).

Searching

This chapter studies two important methods for retrieving information from a list: sequential search and binary search. One of our major purposes is to compare various algorithms, to see which are preferable under different conditions. To do this we shall develop sophisticated tools, such as comparison trees, which help to analyze the performance of algorithms. The chapter concludes by showing how algorithm analysis is simplified by using a new mathematical tool, the big Oh notation.

5.1 SEARCHING: INTRODUCTION AND NOTATION

keys and records

Information retrieval is one of the most important applications of computers. We are given a name and are asked for an associated telephone listing. We are given an account number and are asked for the transactions occurring in that account. We are given an employee name or number and are asked for the personnel records of the employee. In these examples and a host of others, we are given one piece of information, which we shall call a ***key***, and we are asked to find a record that contains other information associated with the key. A rule that, for simplicity, we adopt throughout this chapter is that, given a key, there should be at most one record with that key. On the other hand, it is quite possible that, given a key, there is no record at all that has that key.

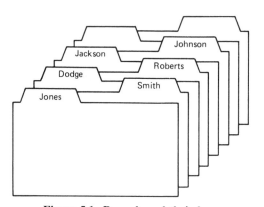

Figure 5.1. Records and their keys

external and internal searching

Searching for keys to locate records is often the most time-consuming action in a program, and therefore the way the records are arranged and the choice of method used for searching can make a substantial difference in the program's performance. The searching problem falls naturally into two cases. If there are many records, perhaps each one quite large, then it will be necessary to store the records in files on disk or tape, external to the computer memory. This case is called ***external*** searching. In the other case the records to be searched are stored entirely within the computer memory. This case is called ***internal*** searching. In this chapter we consider only internal searching. Although many of the methods we shall develop in this and later chapters are useful for external searching, a comprehensive study of methods for external searching lies beyond the scope of this book.

C conventions

To write our programs in C, we establish some notation. What we have called records will be C structures, and the C type that these records have we shall name as Item_type. One of the members (or components) of each item will be denoted key and have a type called Key_type. We thus assume that the program will have declarations of the form

```
typedef ... Key_type;

typedef struct item_tag {
        ...                              /* various components              */
        Key_type key;
        ...                              /* more components                 */
} Item_type;
```

Typical declarations for the key type are

```
typedef float Key_type;
typedef int Key_type;
typedef char *Key_type;
```

We begin with a *list* of the items to be searched. If we have a linked list (implemented with pointers in dynamic memory) we shall assume the type declaration

```
typedef struct node_tag {
        Item_type info;
        struct node_tag *next;
} Node_type;

typedef struct list_tag {
        Node_type *head;
} List_type;
```

In the case of a contiguous list we use the following declarations, where the constant MAX is declared elsewhere.

```
typedef struct list_tag {
        int count;                       /* count of items                  */
        Item_type entry [MAX] ;          /* entries in the list             */
} List_type;
```

target

parameters

These declarations will be defined in the files list.h and array.h, respectively. The key for which we are searching is always called the ***target*** of the search, and in programs is denoted target. Hence our goal is to find an item in the list whose key is equal to the target.

Any searching function that we write will hence have two input parameters, the target and the list being searched. Its return value will be the location of the target. Since we have assumed that each key appears at most once in the list, this location will be uniquely determined. If the search is unsuccessful, then the function will return NULL or −1 for a linked list or contiguous list, respectively.

We shall often need to compare two keys to determine which comes first or whether or not they are equal. If the keys are numbers, we can, of course, compare them by using such operations as ' < ' and ' == '. If the keys are character strings, however, we shall need to use the standard C function strcmp instead. This function takes two strings as its arguments; it returns a value < 0 if the first string precedes the second, 0 if they are equal, and a value > 0 if the second string precedes the first.

We would like to code our algorithms in a way that will cover all the possibilities at once, so that we can change the code from processing numbers to processing strings as easily and quickly as we can. One method for doing this is to introduce new functions such as

Boolean_type EQ (Key_type key1, Key_type key2);
Boolean_type LT (Key_type key1, Key_type key2);

function calls: execution expense

We would then use these functions in our routines whenever we need to compare keys. This method, however, induces a function call every time a pair of keys is compared. Since the time needed to compare keys is often the most critical part of our algorithms, the extra overhead associated with a function call is a high price to pay at execution time for every comparison of keys.

special operators: programming expense

If, on the other hand, we code our algorithms either specifically for numerical keys or for character strings, then we lose generality. When we later wish to apply our algorithms to keys other than those for which they were coded, we must pay a high price in programming time to rewrite them for the new keys.

macros

The C language, fortunately, provides a feature that allows us to code our algorithms in as general a form as by using function calls and, at the same time, to achieve the same execution efficiency as using operators designed for a specific kind of key. This feature is the provision of **macros**. When a function call appears in a program, the compiler generates instructions that temporarily suspend the execution of the calling program and go to the function to begin executing its instructions. When the function terminates it then executes instructions to return to the calling program and communicate the function result. Macros, on the other hand, are handled by a preprocessor, not the C compiler itself. When a macro is used, its instructions are copied into the program itself before it is compiled. Hence, at execution time, these instructions are done without the extra overhead of calling and returning from a function.

Macros are declared by using the #define direction to the preprocessor. Macros may use parameters just as functions can, but since macros are expanded before the compiler starts work, the formal parameters are not assigned types. When types are checked by the compiler, these formal parameters will already have been replaced by the actual arguments with which the macro was used.

For our applications, we shall need only simple macros. For numerical keys, the macros are:

#define EQ(a, b) ((a) == (b))
#define LT (a, b) ((a) < (b))

If we wish to apply our algorithms to character strings, we simply replace these macro definitions with the following versions:

#define EQ(a, b) (!strcmp((a), (b)))
#define LT (a, b) (strcmp((a), (b)) < 0)

Exercises 5.1

E1. Complete a package of macros for comparing (1) numbers and (2) character strings, by writing the following macros in each case:

a. GT (greater than),   **c.** LE (less than or equal),
b. NE (not equal),   **d.** GE (greater than or equal).

E2. Write the macros EQ and LT for the case when each key is a structure consisting of two components, first an integer and then a character string. If the integer component of the first key is less than (greater than) the integer component of the second key, then the first key is less than (*resp.* greater than) the second. If two keys have equal integer components, then they are compared by comparing their character-string components.

5.2 SEQUENTIAL SEARCH

Beyond doubt, the simplest way to do a search is to begin at one end of the list and scan down it until the desired key is found or the other end is reached. This is our first method.

1. Contiguous Version

In the case when the list list is contiguous we obtain the following function.

```
/* SequentialSearch: contiguous version */
int SequentialSearch(List_type list, Key_type target)
{
    int location;

    for (location = 0; location < list.count; location++)
        if (EQ(list.entry[location].key, target))
            return location;
    return -1;
}
```

The while loop in this function keeps moving through the list as long as the target key target has not been found but terminates as soon as the target is found. If the search is unsuccessful, then found remains false, and at the conclusion location has moved to a position beyond the end of the list (recall that for an unsuccessful search the return value will be −1).

2. Linked Version

A version of sequential search for linked lists is equally easy.

```
/* SequentialSearch: linked list version */
Node_type *SequentialSearch(List_type list, Key_type target)
{
    Node_type *location;

    for (location = list.head; location != NULL; location = location->next)
        if (EQ(location->info.key, target))
            return location;
    return NULL;
}
```

3. Comparison of Keys Versus Running Time

importance of comparison count

As you can see, the basic method of sequential search is exactly the same for both the contiguous and linked versions, even though the implementation details differ. In fact, the target is compared to exactly the same keys in the items of the list in either version. Although the running times of the two versions may differ a little because of the different implementations, in both of them all the actions go in lock step with comparison of keys. Hence if we wish to estimate how much computer time sequential search is likely to require, or if we wish to compare it with some other method, then knowing the number of comparisons of keys that it makes will give us the most useful information, information actually more useful than the total running time, which is too much dependent on whether we have the contiguous or linked version, or what particular machine is being used.

4. Analysis of Sequential Search

Short as sequential search is, when we start to count comparisons of keys, we run into difficulties because we do not know how many times the loop will be iterated. We have no way to know in advance whether or not the search will be successful. If it is, we do not know if the target will be the first key on the list, the last, or somewhere between. Thus to obtain useful information, we must do several analyses.

unsuccessful search

Fortunately, these are all easy. If the search is unsuccessful, then the target will have been compared to all items in the list, for a total of n comparisons of keys, where n is the length of the list. For a successful search, if the target is in position k, then it will have been compared with the first k keys in the list, for a total of exactly k comparisons. Thus the best time for a successful search is 1 comparison, and the worst is n comparisons.

successful search

We have obtained very detailed information about the timing of sequential search, information that is really too detailed for most uses, in that we generally will not know exactly where in a list a particular key may appear. Instead, it will generally be much more helpful if we can determine the *average* behavior of an algorithm. But what do we mean by average? One reasonable assumption, the one that we shall always make, is to take each possibility once and average the results.

average behavior

Note, however, that this assumption may be very far from the actual situation. Not all English words, for example, appear equally often in a typical essay. The telephone operator receives far more requests for the number of a large business than for that of an average family. The C compiler encounters the keywords if, int and for more often than the keywords auto and register.

provisos

There are a great many interesting, but exceedingly difficult, problems associated with analyzing algorithms where the input is chosen according to some statistical distribution. These problems, however, would take us too far afield to be considered here.

Under the assumption of equal likelihood we can find the average number of key comparisons done in a successful sequential search. We simply add the number needed for all the successful searches, and divide by n, the number of items in the list. The result is

$$\frac{1 + 2 + 3 + \cdots + n}{n}.$$

The first formula established in Appendix A.1 is

$$1 + 2 + 3 + \cdots + n = \tfrac{1}{2}n(n+1).$$

average number of key comparisons Hence the average number of key comparisons done by sequential search in the successful case is

$$\frac{n(n+1)}{2n} = \tfrac{1}{2}(n+1).$$

Exercises 5.2

E1. One good check for any algorithm is to see what it does in extreme cases. Determine what both versions of sequential search do when

    a. There is only one item in the list.
    b. The list is empty.
    c. The list is full (contiguous version only).

E2. Trace the contiguous version of sequential search as it searches for each of the keys present in a list containing three items. Determine how many comparisons are made, and thereby check the formula for the average number of comparisons for a successful search.

E3. If we can assume that the keys in the list have been arranged in order (for example, numerical or alphabetical order), then we can terminate unsuccessful searches more quickly. If the smallest keys come first, then we can terminate the search as soon as a key greater than or equal to the target key has been found. If we assume that it is equally likely that a target key not in the list is in any one of the $n+1$ intervals (before the first key, between a pair of keys, or after the last key), then what is the average number of comparisons for unsuccessful search in this version?

At each iteration, sequential search checks two inequalities, one a comparison of keys to see if the target has been found, and the other a comparison of indices to see if the end of the list been reached. A good way to speed up the algorithm by eliminating the second comparison is to make sure that eventually key target will be found, by increasing the size of the list, and inserting an extra item at the end with key target. Such an item *sentinel* placed in a list to ensure that a process terminates is called a ***sentinel***. When the loop terminates, the search will have been successful if target was found before the last item in the list and unsuccessful if the final sentinel item was the one found.

E4. Write a C function that embodies the idea of a sentinel in the contiguous version of sequential search.

E5. Find the number of comparisons of keys done by the function written in Exercise E4 for

    a. Unsuccessful search.
    b. Best successful search.
    c. Worst successful search.
    d. Average successful search.

E6. In the linked version of sequential search suppose that (as we have assumed) we are given a pointer only to the start of the list. Explain why adding a sentinel to the list is not a particularly helpful idea. What extra information would make it worthwhile?

Programming
Projects
5.2

P1. Write a program to test the contiguous version of sequential search. You should make the appropriate declarations required to set up the list and put keys into it. A good choice for the keys would be the integers from 1 to n. Modify the sequential search function so that it keeps a counter of the number of key comparisons that it makes. Find out how many comparisons are done in an unsuccessful search (for some key that you know is not in the list). Also call the function to search once for each key that is in the list, and thereby calculate the average number of comparisons made for a successful search. Run your program for representative values of n, such as $n = 10$, $n = 100$, $n = 1000$.

P2. Do project P1 for a linked list instead of a contiguous list.

P3. Take the driver program written in project P1 to test the contiguous version of sequential search, and insert the version that uses a sentinel (see Exercises E4–E6). Also insert instructions (system dependent) for obtaining the CPU time used. For various values of n, determine whether the version with or without sentinel is faster. Find the cross-over point between the two versions, if there is one. That is, at what point is the extra time needed to insert a sentinel at the end of the list the same as the time needed for extra comparisons of indices in the version without a sentinel?

5.3 BINARY SEARCH

method

Sequential search is easy to write and efficient for short lists, but a disaster for long ones. Imagine trying to find the name "Thomas Z. Smith" in a large telephone book by reading one name at a time starting at the front of the book! To find any item in a long, sorted list, there are far more efficient methods. One of the best is first to compare the item with one in the center of the list and then restrict our attention to only the first or second half of the list, depending on whether the item comes before or after the central one. In this way, at each step we reduce the length of the list to be searched by half. In only twenty comparisons this method will locate any requested name in a list of a million names.

restrictions

The method we are discussing is called ***binary search***. This approach requires that the items in the list be of a scalar or other type that can be regarded as having an order and that the list already be completely in order. As in the previous section, we shall use the macros LT and EQ to compare keys.

We should also note that the standard C library contains the function bsearch, declared in stdlib.h, for performing searches.

random access

Binary search is not good for linked lists, since it requires jumping back and forth from one end of the list to the middle, an action easy within an array, but slow for a linked list. Hence this section studies only contiguous lists.

dangers

Simple though the idea of binary search is, it is exceedingly easy to program it incorrectly. The method dates back at least to 1946, but the first version free of errors and unnecessary restrictions seems to have appeared only in 1962. One study (reference at the end of the chapter) showed that about 90 percent of professional programmers fail to code binary search correctly, even after working on it for a full hour. Let us therefore take special care to make sure that we make no mistakes. To do this, we must state exactly what our variables designate; we must state precisely what conditions must be true before and after each iteration of the loop contained in the program; and we must make sure that the loop will terminate properly.

Our binary search algorithm will use two indices, top and bottom, to enclose the part of the list in which we are looking for the target key target. At each iteration we shall reduce the size of this part of the list by about half. More formally, we can state the

loop invariant loop invariant that must hold before and after each iteration of the loop in the function:

> *The target key, provided it is present, will be found between the indices* bottom *and* top, *inclusive.*

We establish the initial correctness of this statement by setting bottom to 0 and top to list.count -1, where list.count is the number of items in the list.

termination Next, we note that the loop should terminate when top $\leq$ bottom, that is, when the remaining part of the list contains at most one item, providing that we have not terminated the loop earlier by finding the target. Finally, we must make progress toward termination by ensuring that the number of items remaining to be searched, top $-$ bottom $+1$, strictly decreases at each iteration of the loop.

Several slightly different algorithms for binary search can be written.

5.3.1 The Forgetful Version

Perhaps the simplest variation is to forget the possibility that the target key target might be found quickly and continue, whether target has been found or not, to subdivide the list until what remains has length 1. Our first function proceeds in this way. We shall use three indices in the program: top and bottom will bracket the part of the list that may contain target, and middle will be the midpoint of this reduced list.

```
/* Binary1: forgetful version of binary search */
int Binary1 (List_type list, Key_type target)
{
        int top, bottom, middle;

        top = list.count − 1;            /* Initialize bounds to encompass entire list. */
        bottom = 0;
        while (top > bottom) {           /* Check terminating condition.              */
              middle = (top + bottom)/2;
              if (LT(list.entry[middle].key, target))
                    bottom = middle + 1;  /* Reduce to the top half of the list.       */
              else
                    top = middle;         /* Reduce to the bottom half of the list.    */
        }
        if (top == −1)
              return −1;                  /* Search of an empty list always fails.     */
        if (EQ(list.entry[top].key, target))
              return top;
        else
              return −1;
}
```

loop termination   Note that the if statement that divides the list in half is not symmetrical, since the condition tested puts the midpoint into the lower of the two intervals at each iteration. On the other hand, integer division of nonnegative integers always truncates downward. It is only these two facts together that ensure that the loop always terminates. Let us determine what occurs toward the end of the search. The loop will iterate only as long as top > bottom. But this condition implies that when middle is calculated we always have

$$\text{bottom} <= \text{middle} < \text{top}$$

since integer division truncates downward. Next, the if statement reduces the size of the interval from top − bottom either to top − (middle + 1) or to middle − bottom, both of which, by the inequality, are strictly less than top − bottom. Thus at each iteration the size of the interval strictly decreases, so the loop will eventually terminate.

After the loop terminates we must finally check to see if the target key has been found, since all previous comparisons have tested only inequalities.

5.3.2 Recognizing Equality

Although Binary1 is a simple form of binary search, it will often make unnecessary iterations because it fails to recognize that it has found the target before continuing to iterate. Thus we may save computer time with the following variation, which checks at each stage to see if it has found the target.

improved version
```
/* Binary2: version that recognizes discovery of the target */
int Binary2 (List_type list, Key_type target)
{
        int top, bottom, middle;         /* middle will be index of target if found.   */

        top = list.count − 1;            /* Initialize variables.                      */
        bottom = 0;

        while (top >= bottom) {          /* Check terminating conditions.              */
                middle = (top + bottom)/2;
                if (EQ(list.entry[middle].key, target))  /* Successful search.          */
                        return middle;
                else if (LT(list.entry[middle].key, target))
                        bottom = middle + 1;  /* Reduce to top half of the list.        */
                else
                        top = middle − 1;     /* Reduce to bottom half of list.         */
        }
        return −1;
}
```

loop termination   Proving that the loop in Binary2 terminates is easier than the proof for Binary1. In Binary2 the form of the if statement within the loop guarantees that the length of the interval is reduced by more than half at each iteration. Note that when top = bottom, we allow the loop to iterate one more time. In this way the target can be compared to the final candidate from list without having to write an extra comparison outside the loop.

comparison of methods
Which of these two versions of binary search will do fewer comparisons of keys? Clearly Binary2 will, if we happen to find the target near the beginning of the search. But each iteration of Binary2 requires two comparisons of keys, whereas Binary1 requires only one. Is it possible that if many iterations are needed, then Binary1 may do fewer comparisons? To answer this question we shall develop a new method in the next section.

Exercises 5.3

E1. Suppose that the list list contains the integers 1, 2, ..., 8. Trace through the steps of Binary1 to determine what comparisons of keys are done in searching for each of the following targets: **(a)** 3, **(b)** 5, **(c)** 1, **(d)** 9, **(e)** 4.5.

E2. Repeat Exercise E1 using Binary2.

E3. Suppose that L_1 and L_2 are lists containing n_1 and n_2 integers, respectively, and both lists are already sorted into numerical order.

    a. Use the idea of binary search to describe how to find the median of the $n_1 + n_2$ integers in the combined lists.

    b. Write a function that implements your method.

Programming Projects 5.3

P1. Adapt the driver program outlined in project P1 of Section 5.2 so that it can be used to test Binary1. You should check both successful and unsuccessful searches for selected values of n. If your system can provide a measure of elapsed CPU time, you should also obtain timings for average successful and unsuccessful searches for your function.

P2. Adapt the program to test Binary2, as in the previous project.

P3. Accessing an array element requires additional operations to calculate the actual position at run-time. This can involve multiplications for multidimensional arrays. Modify Binary1 to take advantage of pointers in C and eliminate the indexing operations by making top, middle and bottom pointers to Item. Compare the time for this version and the one in the text.

P4. Do Project P3 for Binary2.

P5. On most computers addition is faster than division. Use the following idea to make a new version of binary search that does no division. First use addition to construct an auxiliary table of the powers of 2 that are less than the length of the list list.count, and then by adding and subtracting appropriate entries from this table reduce the bounds of the interval being searched. Compare the time required by this version to the time required by Binary 1 and Binary 2.

5.4 COMPARISON TREES

definitions
The ***comparison tree*** (also called ***decision tree*** or ***search tree***) of an algorithm is obtained by tracing through the action of the algorithm, representing each comparison of keys by a ***vertex*** of the tree (which we draw as a circle). Inside the circle we put the index of the key against which we are comparing the target key. ***Branches*** (lines) drawn down from the circle represent the possible outcomes of the comparison and are labeled accordingly. When the algorithm terminates, we put either F (for failure) or the

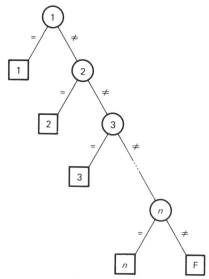

Figure 5.2. Comparison tree for sequential search

location where the target is found at the end of the appropriate branch, which we call a *leaf*, and draw as a square. Leaves are also sometimes called *end vertices* or *external vertices* of the tree. The remaining vertices are called the *internal vertices* of the tree.

The comparison tree for sequential search is especially simple; it is drawn in Figure 5.2.

The number of comparisons done by an algorithm in a particular search is the number of internal (circular) vertices traversed in going from the top of the tree (which is called its *root*) down the appropriate path to a leaf. The number of branches traversed to reach a vertex from the root is called the *level* of the vertex. Thus the root itself has level 0, the vertices immediately below it have level 1, and so on. The largest level that occurs is called the *height* of the tree. Hence a tree with only one vertex has height 0. In future chapters we shall sometimes allow trees to be empty, that is, to consist of no vertices at all, and we adopt the convention that an empty tree has height -1.

To complete the terminology we use for trees we shall now, as is traditional, mix our metaphors by thinking of family trees as well as botanical trees: We call the vertices immediately below a vertex v the *children* of v and the vertex immediately above v the *parent* of v.

5.4.1 Analysis for $n = 10$

1. Shape of Trees

That sequential search on average does far more comparisons than binary search is obvious from comparing its tree with the trees for Binary1 and Binary2, which for $n = 10$ are drawn in Figure 5.3 and Figure 5.4, respectively. Sequential search has a long, narrow tree, which means many comparisons, whereas the trees for binary search are much wider and shorter.

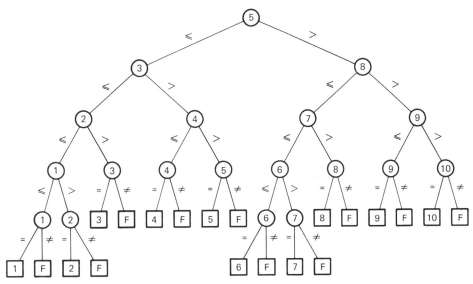

Figure 5.3. Comparison tree for Binary1, $n = 10$

2. Three-Way Comparisons and Compact Drawings

two versions

In the tree drawn for Binary2 we have shown the algorithm structure more clearly (and reduced the space needed) by combining two comparisons to obtain one three-way comparison for each pass through the loop. Drawing the tree this way means that every vertex that is not a leaf terminates some successful search and the leaves correspond to unsuccessful searches. Thus the drawing in Figure 5.4 is more compact, but remember that two comparisons are really done for each of the vertices shown, except that only one comparison is done at the vertex at which the search succeeds in finding the target.

It is this compact way of drawing comparison trees that will become our standard method in future chapters.

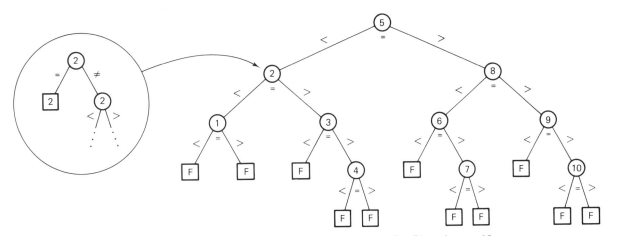

Figure 5.4. Comparison tree for Binary2, $n = 10$

From the trees it is easy to read off how many comparisons will be done when $n = 10$. In the worst case, it is simply one more than the height of the tree; in fact, in every case it is the number of interior vertices lying between the root and the vertex that terminates the search.

3. Binary1 **Comparison Count**

external path length

In Binary1, every search terminates at a leaf; to obtain the average number of comparisons for both successful and unsuccessful searches, we need what is called the ***external path length*** of the tree: the sum of the number of branches traversed in going from the root once to every leaf in the tree. For the tree in Figure 5.3 the external path length is

$$4 \times 5 + 6 \times 4 + 4 \times 5 + 6 \times 4 = 88.$$

Half the leaves correspond to successful searches, and half to unsuccessful. Hence the average number of comparisons needed for either a successful or unsuccessful search by Binary1 is $44/10 = 4.4$ when $n = 10$.

4. Binary2 **Comparison Count**

internal path length

In the tree as it is drawn for Binary2, all the leaves correspond to unsuccessful searches; hence the external path length leads to the number of comparisons for an unsuccessful search. For successful searches, we need the ***internal path length***, which is defined to be the sum, over all vertices that are not leaves, of the number of branches from the root to the vertex. For the tree in Figure 5.4 the internal path length is

$$0 + 1 + 2 + 2 + 3 + 1 + 2 + 3 + 2 + 3 = 19.$$

Recall that Binary2 does two comparisons for each non-leaf except for the vertex that finds the target, and note that the number of these internal vertices traversed is one more than the number of branches (for each of the $n = 10$ internal vertices), so we obtain the average number of comparisons for a successful search to be

average successful count

$$2 \times \left(\frac{19}{10} + 1 \right) - 1 = 4.8.$$

The subtraction of 1 corresponds to the fact that one fewer comparison is made when the target is found.

For an unsuccessful search by Binary2, we need the external path length of the tree in Figure 5.4. This is

$$5 \times 3 + 6 \times 4 = 39.$$

We shall assume for unsuccessful searches that the $n + 1$ intervals (less than the first key, between a pair of successive keys, or greater than the largest) are all equally likely; for the diagram we therefore assume that any of the 11 failure leaves are equally likely.

average unsuccessful count

Thus the average number of comparisons for an unsuccessful search is

$$\frac{2 \times 39}{11} \approx 7.1.$$

5. Comparison of Algorithms

For $n = 10$, Binary1 does slightly fewer comparisons both for successful and for unsuccessful searches. To be fair, however, we should note that the two comparisons done by Binary2 at each internal vertex are closely related (the same keys are being compared), so that an optimizing compiler may not do as much work as two full comparisons, in which case, in fact, Binary2 may be a slightly better choice than Binary1 for successful searches when $n = 10$.

5.4.2 Generalization

What happens when n is larger than 10? For longer lists, it may be impossible to draw the complete comparison tree, but from the examples with $n = 10$, we can make some observations that will always be true.

1. 2-trees

Let us define a **2-tree** as a tree in which every vertex except the leaves has exactly two children. Both versions of comparison trees that we have drawn fit this definition, and are 2-trees. We can make several observations about 2-trees that will provide information about the behavior of binary search methods for all values of n.

terminology   Other terms for 2-tree are **strictly binary tree** and **extended binary tree**, but we shall not use these terms, because they are too easily confused with the term *binary tree*, which (when introduced in Chapter 9) has a somewhat different meaning.

number of vertices   In a 2-tree, the number of vertices on any level can be no more than twice the
in a 2-tree   number on the level above, since each vertex has either 0 or 2 children (depending on whether it is a leaf or not). Since there is one vertex on level 0 (the root), the number of vertices on level t is at most 2^t for all $t \geq 0$. We thus have the facts:

LEMMA 5.1   *The number of vertices on each level of a 2-tree is at most twice the number on the level immediately above.*

LEMMA 5.2   *In a 2-tree, the number of vertices on level t is at most 2^t for $t \geq 0$.*

2. Analysis of Binary1

For Binary1 both successful and unsuccessful searches terminate at leaves; there are thus $2n$ leaves. All these leaves, furthermore, must be on the same level or on two adjacent levels. (This observation can be proved by mathematical induction: It is true for a list of size 1, and when Binary1 divides a larger list in half, the sizes of the two halves differ by at most 1, and the induction hypothesis shows that their leaves are on the same or adjacent levels.) The height (number of levels below root) of the tree is the maximum number of key comparisons that an algorithm does, and for Binary1 is at most one more than the average number, since all leaves are on the same or adjacent levels. By Lemma 5.2 the height is also the smallest integer t such that $2^t \geq 2n$. Take logarithms with base 2. (For a review of properties of logarithms, see Appendix A.2.) We obtain that the number of comparisons of keys done by Binary1 in searching a list of n items is approximately

comparison count,
Binary1

$$\lg n + 1.$$

As can be seen from the tree, the number of comparisons is essentially independent of whether the search is successful or not.

3. Notation

The notation for base 2 logarithms just used will be our standard notation. In analyzing algorithms we shall also sometimes need natural logarithms (taken with base $e = 2.71828\ldots$). We shall denote a natural logarithm by ln. We shall rarely need

logarithms

logarithms to any other base. We thus summarize,

> ### Convention
>
> Unless stated otherwise, all logarithms will be taken with base 2.
> The symbol lg denotes a logarithm with base 2,
> and the symbol ln denotes a natural logarithm.
> When the base for logarithms is not specified (or is not important),
> then the symbol log will be used.

floor and ceiling

After we take logarithms, we frequently need to move either up or down to the next integer. To specify this action, we define the **floor** of a real number x to be the largest integer less than or equal to x, and the **ceiling** of x to be the smallest integer greater than or equal to x. We denote the floor of x by $\lfloor x \rfloor$ and the ceiling of x by $\lceil x \rceil$.

4. Analysis of Binary2, Unsuccessful Search

To count the comparisons made by Binary2 for a general value of n for an unsuccessful search, we shall examine its comparison tree. For reasons similar to those given for Binary1, this tree is again full at the top, with all its leaves on at most two adjacent levels at the bottom. For Binary 2, all the leaves correspond to unsuccessful searches, so there are exactly $n + 1$ leaves, corresponding to the $n + 1$ unsuccessful outcomes: less than the smallest key, between a pair of keys, and greater than the largest key. Since these leaves are all at the bottom of the tree, Lemma 5.2 implies that the number of leaves

comparison count
for Binary2,
unsuccessful case

is approximately 2^h, where h is the height of the tree. Taking (base 2) logarithms, we obtain that $h \approx \lg(n + 1)$. This value is the approximate distance from the root to one of the leaves. Since two comparisons of keys are performed for each internal vertex, the number of comparisons done in an unsuccessful search is approximately $2\lg(n + 1)$.

5. The Path Length Theorem

To calculate the average number of comparisons for a successful search, we first obtain an interesting and important relationship that holds for any 2-tree.

THEOREM 5.3   *Denote the external path length of a 2-tree by E, the internal path length by I, and let q be the number of vertices that are not leaves. Then*

$$E = I + 2q.$$

proof   To prove the theorem we use the method of mathematical induction. If the tree contains only its root, and no other vertices, then $E = I = q = 0$, and the first case of the theorem is trivially correct. Now take a larger tree, and let v be some vertex that is not a leaf, but for which both the children of v are leaves. Let k be the number of branches on the path from the root to v. Now let us delete the two children of v from the 2-tree. Since v is not a leaf but its children are, the number of non-leaves goes down from q to $q - 1$. The internal path length I is reduced by the distance to v, that is, to $I - k$. The distance to each child of v is $k + 1$, so the external path length is reduced from E to $E - 2(k + 1)$, but v is now a leaf, so its distance, k, must be added, giving a new external path length of

$$E - 2(k + 1) + k = E - k - 2.$$

Since the new tree has fewer vertices than the old one, by the induction hypothesis we know that

$$E - k - 2 = (I - k) + 2(q - 1).$$

end of proof   Rearrangement of this equation gives the desired result.

6. Binary2, **Successful Search**

In the comparison tree of Binary2, the distance to the leaves is $\lg(n + 1)$, as we have seen. The number of leaves is $n + 1$, so the external path length is about

$$(n + 1) \lg(n + 1).$$

Theorem 5.3 then shows that the internal path length is about

$$(n + 1) \lg(n + 1) - 2n.$$

To obtain the average number of comparisons done in a successful search, we must first divide by n (the number of non-leaves) and then add 1 and double, since two comparisons were done at each internal node. Finally, we subtract 1, since only one comparison is done at the node where the target is found. The result is approximately

$$\frac{2(n + 1)}{n} \lg(n + 1) - 3$$

comparisons of keys.

5.4.3 Comparison of Methods

simplified counts

Note the similarities and differences in the formulae for the two versions of binary search. Recall, first, that we have already made some approximations in our calculations, and hence our formulae are only approximate. For large values of n the difference between $\lg n$ and $\lg(n + 1)$ is insignificant, and $(n + 1)/n$ is very nearly 1. Hence we can simplify our results as follows:

	Successful search	*Unsuccessful search*
Binary1	$\lg n + 1$	$\lg n + 1$
Binary2	$2 \lg n - 3$	$2 \lg n$

assessment

In all four cases the times are proportional to $\lg n$, except for small constant terms, and the coefficients of $\lg n$ are, in all cases, the number of comparisons inside the loop. The fact that the loop in Binary2 can terminate early contributes disappointingly little to improving its speed for a successful search; it does not reduce the coefficient of $\lg n$ at all, but only reduces the constant term from $+1$ to -3. A moment's examination of the comparison trees will show why. More than half of the vertices occur at the bottom level, and so their loops cannot terminate early. More than half the remaining ones could terminate only one iteration early. Thus, for large n, the number of vertices relatively high in the tree, say, in the top half of the levels, is negligible in comparison with the number at the bottom level. It is only for this negligible proportion of the vertices that Binary2 can achieve better results than Binary1, but it is at the cost of nearly doubling the number of comparisons for all searches, both successful and unsuccessful ones.

conclusions

With the smaller coefficient of $\lg n$, Binary1 will do fewer comparisons when n is sufficiently large, but with the smaller constant term, Binary2 may do fewer comparisons when n is small. But for such a small value of n, the overhead in setting up binary search and the extra programming effort probably make it a more expensive method to use than sequential search. Thus we arrive at the conclusion, quite contrary to what we would intuitively conclude, that Binary2 is probably not worth the effort, since for large problems Binary1 is better, and for small problems, SequentialSearch is better. To be fair, however, with some computers and optimizing compilers, the two comparisons needed in Binary2 will not take double the time of the one in Binary1, so in such a situation Binary2 might prove the better choice.

Our object in doing analysis of algorithms is to help us decide which may be better under appropriate circumstances. Disregarding the foregoing provisos, we have now been able to make such a decision, and have available to us information that might otherwise not be obvious.

logarithmic graphs

The number of comparisons of keys done in the average successful case by SequentialSearch, Binary1, and Binary2 are graphed in Figure 5.5. The numbers shown in the graphs are from test runs of the functions; they are not approximations. The first graph in Figure 5.5 compares the three functions for small values of n, the number of items in the list. In the second graph we compare the numbers over a much larger range by employing a ***log-log graph*** in which each unit along an axis represents doubling the corresponding coordinate. In the third graph we wish to compare the two versions of binary search; a ***semilog graph*** is appropriate here, so that the vertical axis maintains linear units while the horizontal axis is logarithmic.

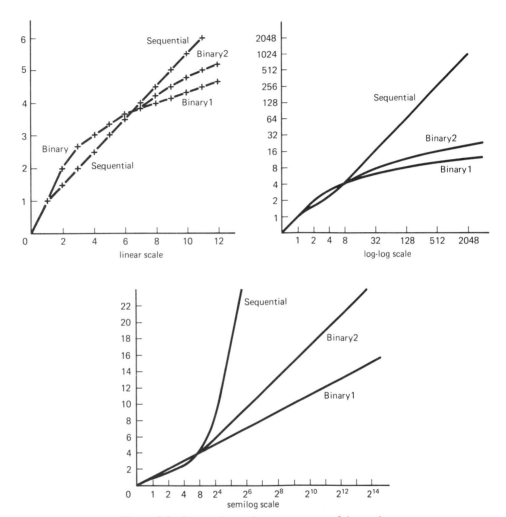

Figure 5.5. Comparison of average successful searches

5.4.4 A General Relationship

hypotheses

Before leaving this section, let us use Theorem 5.3 to obtain a relationship between the average number of key comparisons for successful and for unsuccessful searches, a relationship that holds for any searching method for which the comparison tree can be drawn as we did for Binary2. That is, we shall assume that the leaves of the comparison tree correspond to unsuccessful searches, that the internal vertices correspond to successful searches, and that two comparisons of keys are made for each internal vertex, except that only one is made at the vertex where the target is found. If I and E are the internal and external path lengths of the tree, respectively, and n is the number of items in the list, so that n is also the number of internal vertices in the tree, then, as in the analysis of Binary2, we know that the average number of comparisons in a successful search is

$$S = 2\left(\frac{I}{n} + 1\right) - 1 = \frac{2I}{n} + 1$$

and the average number for an unsuccessful search is $U = 2E/(n + 1)$. By Theorem 5.3, $E = I + 2n$. Combining these expressions, we can therefore conclude that

THEOREM 5.4

Under the specified conditions, the average numbers of key comparisons done in successful and unsuccessful searches are related by

$$S = \left(1 + \frac{1}{n}\right) U - 3.$$

*successful and
unsuccessful
searches*

In other words, the average number of comparisons for a successful search is almost exactly the same as that for an unsuccessful search. Knowing that an item is in the list is very little help in finding it, if you are searching by means of comparisons of keys.

Exercises 5.4

E1. Draw the comparison trees for Binary1 and Binary2 when **(a)** $n = 5$, **(b)** $n = 7$, **(c)** $n = 8$, **(d)** $n = 13$. Calculate the external and internal path lengths for each of these trees, and verify that the conclusion of Theorem 5.3 holds.

E2. Sequential search has less overhead than binary search, and so may run faster for small n. Find the break-even point where SequentialSearch and Binary1 make the same number of comparisons of keys, in terms of the formulae for the number of comparisons done in the average successful search.

E3. Suppose that you have a list of 10,000 names in alphabetical order in an array and you must frequently look for various names. It turns out that 20 percent of the names account for 80 percent of the retrievals. Instead of doing a binary search over all 10,000 names every time, consider the possibility of splitting the list into two, a high-frequency list of 2000 names, and a low-frequency list of the remaining 8000 names. To look up a name, you will first use binary search on the high-frequency list, and 80 percent of the time you will not need to go on to the second stage, where you use binary search on the low-frequency list. Is this scheme worth the effort? Justify your answer by finding the number of comparisons done for the average successful search, both in the new scheme and in a binary search of a single list of 10,000 names.

E4. If you modified binary search so that it divided the list not essentially in half at each pass, but instead into two pieces of sizes about one-third and two-thirds of the remaining list, then what would be the approximate effect on its average count of comparisons?

E5. Write a "ternary" search function analogous to Binary2 that examines the key one-third of the way through the list, and if the target key x is greater, then examines the key two-thirds of the way through, and thus in any case at each pass reduces the length of the list by a factor of three. Compare the count of comparisons of your algorithm with binary search.

Programming Projects 5.4

P1. We have ignored the time needed to initialize the search functions and to complete index calculations. For this reason, sequential search will be the better method for values of n somewhat larger than your answer to Exercise E2. Modify the test programs written for sequential search and binary search (both versions) in previous sections, so that the programs will record the CPU time used, and determine the break-even point for running time on your computer.

P2. Use the program of Project P1 to compare running times for an average successful search for Binary1 and Binary2. Use values of n about equal to **(a)** 10, **(b)** 300, **(c)** 1000.

P3. Write a program that will do a "hybrid" search, using binary search (your choice of the two algorithms or some variation) for large lists and switching to sequential search when the list is sufficiently reduced. (Because of different overhead, the best switch-over point is not necessarily the same as your answer to Exercise E2 or Project P1.)

5.5 LOWER BOUNDS

We know that for an ordered contiguous list, binary search is much faster than sequential search. It is only natural to ask if we can find another method that is much faster than binary search.

1. Polishing Programs

One approach is to attempt to polish and refine our programs to make them run faster. By being clever we may be able to reduce the work done in each iteration by a bit and thereby speed up the algorithm. One method, called *Fibonacci search*, even manages to replace the division inside the loop by certain subtractions (with no auxiliary table needed), which on some computers will speed up the function.

basic algorithms and small variations

Fine tuning of a program may be able to cut its running time in half, or perhaps reduce it even more, but limits will soon be reached if the underlying algorithm remains the same. The reason why binary search is so much faster than sequential search is not that there are fewer steps within its loop (there are actually more) or that the code is optimized, but that the loop is iterated fewer times, about $\lg n$ times instead of n times, and as the number n increases, the value of $\lg n$ grows much more slowly than does the value of n.

In the context of comparing underlying methods, the differences between Binary1 and Binary2 become insignificant. For large lists Binary2 may require nearly double the time of Binary1, but the difference between $2 \lg n$ and $\lg n$ is negligible compared to the difference between n and $2 \lg n$.

2. Arbitrary Searching Algorithms

Let us now ask whether it is possible for any search algorithm to exist that will, in the worst and the average cases, be able to find its target using significantly fewer comparisons of keys than binary search. We shall see that the answer is *no*, providing that we stay within the class of algorithms that rely only on comparisons of keys to determine where to look within an ordered list.

general algorithms and comparison trees

Let us start with an arbitrary algorithm that searches an ordered list by making comparisons of keys, and imagine drawing its comparison tree in the same way as we drew the tree for Binary1. That is, each internal node of the tree will correspond to some comparison of keys and each leaf to one of the possible outcomes. (If the algorithm is formulated as three-way comparisons like those of Binary2, then we expand each internal vertex into two, as shown for one vertex in Figure 5.4.) The possible outcomes to which the leaves correspond include not only the successful discovery of the target but also the different kinds of failure that the algorithm may distinguish. Binary search of a list of length n produces $k = 2n + 1$ outcomes, consisting of n successful outcomes and $n + 1$ different kinds of failure (less than the smallest key, between each pair of keys, or larger than the largest key). On the other hand, our sequential search function produced only $k = n + 1$ possible outcomes, since it distinguished only one kind of failure.

height and external path length

As with all search algorithms that compare keys, the height of our tree will equal the number of comparisons that the algorithm does in its worst case, and (since all outcomes correspond to leaves) the external path length of the tree divided by the number of possible outcomes will equal the average number of comparisons done by the algorithm. We therefore wish to obtain lower bounds on the height and the external path length in terms of k, the number of leaves.

3. Observations on 2-trees

Here is the result on 2-trees that we shall need:

LEMMA 5.5

Let T be a 2-tree with k leaves. Then the height h of T satisfies $h \geq \lceil \lg k \rceil$ and the external path length $E(T)$ satisfies $E(T) \geq k \lg k$. The minimum values for h and $E(T)$ occur when all the leaves of T are on the same level or on two adjacent levels.

proof of last assertion

We begin the proof by establishing the assertion in the last sentence. Suppose that some leaves of T are on level r and some are on level s, where $r > s + 1$. Now take two leaves on level r that are both children of the same vertex v, detach them from v, and attach them as children of some (former) leaf on level s. Then we have changed T into a new 2-tree T' that still has k leaves, the height of T' is certainly no more than that of T, and the external path length of T' satisfies

$$E(T') = E(T) - 2r + (r - 1) - s + 2(s + 1) = E(T) - r + s + 1 < E(T)$$

since $r > s + 1$. The terms in this expression are obtained as follows. Since two leaves at level r are removed, $E(T)$ is reduced by $2r$. Since vertex v has become a leaf, $E(T)$ is increased by $r - 1$. Since the vertex on level s is no longer a leaf, $E(T)$ is reduced by s. Since the two leaves formerly on level r are now on level $s + 1$, the term $2(s + 1)$ is added to $E(T)$. This process is illustrated in Figure 5.6.

We can continue in this way to move leaves higher up the tree, reducing the external path length and possibly the height each time, until finally all the leaves are on the same

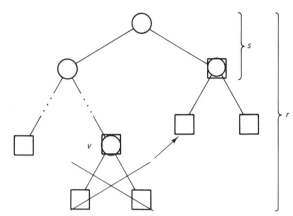

Figure 5.6. Moving leaves higher in a 2-tree

or adjacent levels, and then the height and the external path length will be minimal amongst all 2-trees with k leaves.

proof of $h \geq \lceil \lg k \rceil$ To prove the remaining assertions in Lemma 5.5, let us from now on assume that T has minimum height and path length amongst the 2-trees with k leaves, so all leaves of T occur on levels h and (possibly) $h - 1$, where h is the height of T. By Lemma 5.2 the number of vertices on level h (which are necessarily leaves) is at most 2^h. If all the leaves are on level h, then $k \leq 2^h$. If some of the leaves are on level $h - 1$, then each of these (since it has no children) reduces the number of possible vertices on level h by 2, so the bound $k \leq 2^h$ continues to hold. We take logarithms to obtain $h \geq \lg k$ and, since the height is always an integer, we move up to the ceiling $h \geq \lceil \lg k \rceil$.

proof of
$E(T) \geq k \lg k$ For the bound on the external path length, let x denote the number of leaves of T on level $h - 1$, so that $k - x$ leaves are on level h. These vertices are children of exactly $\frac{1}{2}(k - x)$ vertices on level $h - 1$, which, with the x leaves, comprise all vertices on level $h - 1$. Hence, by Lemma 5.2,

$$\tfrac{1}{2}(k - x) + x \leq 2^{h-1},$$

which becomes $x \leq 2^h - k$. We now have

$$
\begin{aligned}
E(T) &= (h - 1)x + h(k - x) \\
&= kh - x \\
&\geq kh - (2^h - k) \\
&= k(h + 1) - 2^h.
\end{aligned}
$$

From the bound on the height, we already know that $2^{h-1} < k \leq 2^h$. If we set $h = \lg k + \epsilon$, then ϵ satisfies $0 \leq \epsilon < 1$, and substituting ϵ into the bound for $E(T)$ we obtain

$$E(T) \geq k(\lg k + 1 + \epsilon - 2^\epsilon).$$

It turns out that, for $0 \leq \epsilon < 1$, the quantity $1 + \epsilon - 2^\epsilon$ is between 0 and 0.0861. Thus the minimum path length is quite close to $k \lg k$ and, in any case, is at least this large, *end of proof*   as was to be shown. With this, the proof of Lemma 5.5 is complete.

4. Lower Bounds for Searching

Finally, we return to the study of our arbitrary searching algorithm. Its comparison tree may not have all leaves on two adjacent levels, but, even if not, the bounds in Lemma 5.5 will still hold. Hence we may translate these bounds into the language of comparisons, as follows.

THEOREM 5.6   *Suppose that an algorithm uses comparisons of keys to search for a target in a list. If there are k possible outcomes, then in its worst case the algorithm must make at least $\lceil \lg k \rceil$ comparisons of keys, and in its average case, it must make at least $\lg k$ comparisons of keys.*

Observe that there is very little difference between the worst-case bound and the average-case bound. By Theorem 5.4, moreover, for many algorithms it does not much matter whether the search is successful or not, in determining the bound in the above theorems. When we apply Theorem 5.6 to algorithms like binary search for which, on an ordered list of length n, there are n successful and $n + 1$ unsuccessful outcomes, we obtain a worst-case bound of

$$\lceil \lg(2n + 1) \rceil \geq \lceil \lg(2n) \rceil = \lceil \lg n \rceil + 1$$

and an average-case bound of $\lg n + 1$ comparisons of keys. When we compare these numbers with those obtained in the analysis of Binary1, we obtain

COROLLARY 5.7   **Binary1** *is optimal in the class of all algorithms that search an ordered list by making comparisons of keys. In both the average and worst cases,* **Binary1** *achieves the optimal bound.*

5. Other Ways to Search

Just because we have found the bounds in Theorem 5.6, it does not imply that no algorithm can run faster than binary search, only those that rely only on comparisons of keys. To take a simple example, suppose that the keys are the integers from 1 to n themselves. If we know that the target key x is an integer in this range, then we would never perform a search algorithm to locate its item; we would simply store the items in an array indexed from 1 to n and immediately look in index x to find the desired item.

interpolation search   This idea can be extended to obtain another method called ***interpolation search***. We assume that the keys are either numerical or are information, such as words, that can be readily encoded as numbers. The method also assumes that the keys in the list are uniformly distributed, that is, that the probability of a key being in a particular range equals its probability of being in any other range of the same length. To find the target key target, interpolation search then estimates, according to the magnitude of the number target relative to the first and last entries of the list, about where target would be in the list and looks there. It then reduces the size of the list according as target is less than or greater than the key examined. It can be shown that on average, with uniformly distributed keys, interpolation search will take about $\lg \lg n$ comparisons of keys, which, for large n, is somewhat fewer than binary search requires. If, for example, $n = 1,000,000$, then Binary1 will require about $\lg 10^6 + 1 \approx 21$ comparisons, while interpolation search may need only about $\lg \lg 10^6 \approx 4.32$ comparisons.

Finally, we should repeat that, even for search by comparisons, our assumption that requests for all keys are equally likely may be far from correct. If one or two keys are much more likely than the others, then even sequential search, if it looks for those keys first, may be faster than any other method.

The importance of search, or more generally, information retrieval, is so fundamental that much of data structures is devoted to its methods, and in later chapters we shall return to these problems again and again.

Exercise 5.5

E1. Suppose that a search algorithm makes three-way comparisons like Binary2. Let each internal node of its comparison tree correspond to a successful search and each leaf to an unsuccessful search.

   a. Use Lemma 5.5 to obtain a theorem like Theorem 5.6 giving lower bounds for worst and average case behavior for an unsuccessful search by such an algorithm.

   b. Use Theorem 5.4 to obtain a similar result for successful searches.

   c. Compare the bounds you obtain with the analysis of Binary2.

Programming Project 5.5

P1. Write a program to do interpolation search; verify its correctness (especially termination); and run it on the same sets of data used to test the binary search programs. See the references at the end of the chapter for suggestions and program analysis.

5.6 ASYMPTOTICS

1. Introduction

The time has come to distill important generalizations from our analyses of searching algorithms. As we have progressed we have been able to see more clearly which aspects of algorithm analysis are of great importance and which parts can safely be neglected. It is, for example, certainly true that sections of a program that are performed only once outside loops can contribute but negligibly little to the running time. We have studied two different versions of binary search and found that the most significant difference between them was a single comparison of keys in the innermost loop, which might make one slightly preferable to the other sometimes, but that both versions would run far faster than sequential search for lists of moderate or large size.

designing algorithms for small problems

The design of efficient methods to work on small problems is an important subject to study, since a large program may need to do the same or similar small tasks many times during its execution. As we have discovered, however, for small problems, the large overhead of a sophisticated method may make it inferior to a simpler method. For a list of two or three items, sequential search is certainly superior to binary search. To improve efficiency in the algorithm for a small problem, the programmer must necessarily devote attention to details specific to the computer system and programming language, and there are few general observations that will help with this task.

choice of method for
large problems

The design of efficient algorithms for large problems is an entirely different matter. In studying binary search, we have seen that the overhead becomes relatively unimportant; it is the basic idea that will make all the difference between success and a problem too large to be attacked.

asymptotics

The word ***asymptotics*** that titles this section means the study of functions of a parameter n, as n becomes larger and larger without bound. In comparing searching algorithms, we have seen that a count of the number of comparisons of keys accurately reflects the total running time for large problems, since it has generally been true that all the other operations (such as incrementing and comparing indices) have gone in lock step with comparison of keys.

basic actions

In fact, the frequency of such basic actions is much more important than is a total count of all operations including the housekeeping. The total including housekeeping is too dependent on the choice of programming language and on the programmer's particular style, so dependent that it tends to obscure the general methods. Variations in housekeeping details or programming technique can easily triple the running time of a program, but such a change probably will not make the difference between whether the computation is feasible or not. A change in fundamental method, on the other hand, can make a vital difference. If the number of basic actions is proportional to the size n of the input, then doubling n will about double the running time, no matter how the housekeeping is done. If the number of basic actions is proportional to $\lg n$, then doubling n will hardly change the running time. If the number of basic actions is proportional to n^2, then the time will quadruple, and the computation may still be feasible, but may be uncomfortably long. If the number of basic operations is proportional to 2^n, then doubling n will square this number. A computation that took 1 second might involve a million (10^6) basic operations, and doubling the input might require 10^{12} basic operations, moving the time from 1 second to $11\frac{1}{2}$ days.

goal

Our desire in formulating general principles that will apply to the analysis of many classes of algorithms, then, is to have a notation that will accurately reflect the way in which the computation time will increase with the size, but that will ignore superfluous details with little effect on the total. We wish to concentrate on one or two basic operations within the algorithm, without too much concern for all the housekeeping operations that will accompany them. If an algorithm does $f(n)$ basic operations when the size of its input is n, then its total running time will be at most $cf(n)$, where c is a constant that depends on the algorithm, on the way it is programmed, and on the computer used, but c does not depend on the size n of the input (at least when n is past a few initial cases).

2. The Big Oh Notation

These ideas are embodied in the following notation:

DEFINITION   If $f(n)$ and $g(n)$ are functions defined for positive integers, then to write

$$f(n) \text{ is } O(g(n))$$

[read $f(n)$ is ***big Oh*** of $g(n)$] means that there exists a constant c such that $|f(n)| \leq c|g(n)|$ for all sufficiently large positive integers n.

Under these conditions we also say that "$f(n)$ has **order** at most $g(n)$" or "$f(n)$ grows no more rapidly than $g(n)$".

common orders   When we apply this notation, $f(n)$ will normally be the operation count or time for some algorithm, and we wish to choose the form of $g(n)$ to be as simple as possible. We thus write $O(1)$ to mean computing time that is bounded by a constant (not dependent on n); $O(n)$ means that the time is directly proportional to n, and is called **linear time.** We call $O(n^2)$ **quadratic time**, $O(n^3)$ **cubic**, $O(2^n)$ **exponential**. These five orders, together with **logarithmic time** $O(\log n)$ and $O(n \log n)$, are the ones most commonly used in analyzing algorithms.

Figure 5.7 shows how these seven functions (with constant 1) grow with n. Notice especially how much slower $\lg n$ grows than n; this is essentially the reason why binary search is superior to sequential search for large lists. In the next chapter we shall study algorithms whose time is $O(1)$; notice that both the function 1 and the function $\lg n$ become farther and farther below all the others for large n. Notice also how much more rapidly 2^n grows than any of the other functions. An algorithm for which the time grows exponentially with n will prove usable only for very small values of n.

We can now express the conclusions of our algorithm analyses very simply:

- On a list of length n sequential search has time $O(n)$.

- On a list of length n binary search has time $O(\log n)$.

3. Imprecision of the Big Oh Notation

Note that the constant c in the definition of the big Oh notation depends on which functions $f(n)$ and $g(n)$ are under discussion. Thus we can write that $17n^3 - 5$ is $O(n^3)$ (here $c = 17$ will do, as will any larger c), and also $35n^3 + 100$ is $O(n^3)$ (here

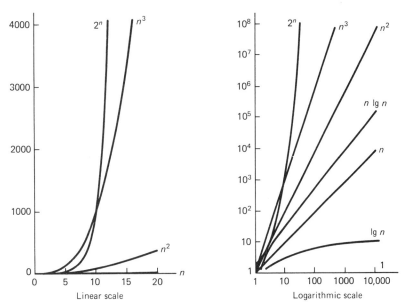

Figure 5.7. Growth rates of common functions

$c \geq 35$). Hence, with the big Oh notation, we have lost the distinction in time required by Binary1 and Binary2.

poor uses   Note also that it is equally correct to write that $35n^3$ is $O(n^7)$ as that $35n^3$ is $O(n^3)$. It is correct but uninformative to write that both binary and sequential search have time that is $O(n^5)$. If $h(n)$ is any function that grows faster than $g(n)$, then a function that is $O(g(n))$ must also be $O(h(n))$. Hence the big Oh notation can be used imprecisely, but we shall always refrain from doing so, instead using the smallest possible of the seven functions shown in Figure 5.7.

4. Keeping the Dominant Term

We would often like to have a more precise measure of the amount of work done by an algorithm, and we can obtain one by using the big Oh notation within an expression, as follows. We define

$$f(n) = g(n) + O(h(n))$$

to mean that $f(n) - g(n)$ is $O(h(n))$. Instead of thinking of $O(h(n))$ as the class of all functions growing no faster than $ch(n)$ for some constant c, we think of $O(h(n))$ as a single but arbitrary such function. We then use this function to represent all the terms of our calculation in which we are not interested, generally all the terms except the one that grows the most quickly. The number of comparisons in the average successful *search comparisons*   search by one of our functions can now be summarized as:

SequentialSearch	$\frac{1}{2}n + O(1)$
Binary1	$\lg n + O(1)$
Binary2	$2\lg n + O(1)$

danger   In using the big Oh notation in expressions, it is necessary always to remember that $O(h(n))$ does not stand for a well-defined function but for an arbitrary function from a large class. Hence ordinary algebra cannot be done with $O(h(n))$. For example, we might have two expressions

$$n^2 + 4n - 5 = n^2 + O(n)$$

and

$$n^2 - 9n + 7 = n^2 + O(n)$$

but $O(n)$ represents different functions in the two expressions, so we cannot equate the right sides or conclude that the left sides are equal.

5. Ordering of Common Functions

Although the seven functions graphed in Figure 5.7 are the only ones we shall usually need for algorithm analysis, a few simple rules will enable you to determine the order of many other kinds of functions.

powers   1. The powers of n are ordered according to the exponent: n^a is $O(n^b)$ if and only if $a \leq b$.

logarithms   2. The order of $\log n$ is independent of the base taken for the logarithms; that is, $\log_a n$ is $O(\log_b n)$ for all $a, b > 1$.

3. A logarithm grows more slowly than any positive power of n: $\log n$ is $O(n^a)$ for any $a > 0$, but n^a is never $O(\log n)$ for $a > 0$.

exponentials

4. Any power n^a is $O(b^n)$ for all a and all $b > 1$, but b^n is never $O(n^a)$ for $b > 1$.

5. If $a < b$, then a^n is $O(b^n)$, but b^n is not $O(a^n)$.

products

6. If $f(n)$ is $O(g(n))$ and $h(n)$ is any nonzero function, then the function $f(n)h(n)$ is $O(g(n)h(n))$.

chain rule

7. The preceding rules may be applied recursively (a chain rule) by substituting a function of n for n. (Example: $\log\log n$ is $O\left((\log n)^{\frac{1}{2}}\right)$.)

Exercises 5.6

E1. For each of the following pairs of functions, find the smallest integer value of n for which the first becomes larger than the second.

    a. n^2, $15n + 5$.
    b. 2^n, $8n^4$.
    c. $0.1n$, $10 \lg n$,   when $n > 1$.
    d. $0.1n^2$, $100n \lg n$,   when $n > 1$.

E2. Arrange the following functions into increasing order; that is, $f(n)$ should come before $g(n)$ in your list if and only if $f(n)$ is $O(g(n))$.

$$
\begin{array}{lll}
1000000 & (\lg n)^3 & 2^n \\
n \lg n & n^3 - 100n^2 & n + \lg n \\
\lg \lg n & n^{0.1} & n^2
\end{array}
$$

E3. Let x and y be real numbers with $0 < x < y$. Prove that n^x is $O(n^y)$ but that n^y is not $O(n^x)$.

E4. Show that logarithmic time does not depend on the base a chosen for the logarithms. That is, prove that

$$\log_a n \text{ is } O(\log_b n)$$

for any real numbers $a > 1$ and $b > 1$.

Programming Project 5.6

P1. Write a program to test on your computer how long it takes to do $n \lg n$, n^2, 2^n, n^5, and $n!$ additions for $n = 5, 10, 15, 20$.

POINTERS AND PITFALLS

1. In designing algorithms be very careful of the extreme cases, such as empty lists, lists with only one item, or full lists (in the contiguous case).

2. Be sure that all your variables are properly initialized.

3. Double check the termination conditions for your loops, and make sure that progress toward termination always occurs.

4. In case of difficulty, formulate statements that will be correct both before and after each iteration of a loop, and verify that they hold.

5. Avoid sophistication for sophistication's sake. If a simple method is adequate for your application, use it.

6. Don't reinvent the wheel. If a ready-made function is adequate for your application, use it.

7. Sequential search is slow but robust. Use it for short lists or if there is any doubt that the keys in the list are properly ordered.

8. Be extremely careful if you must reprogram binary search. Verify that your algorithm is correct and test it on all the extreme cases.

9. Drawing trees is an excellent way both to trace the action of an algorithm and to analyze its behavior.

10. Rely on the Big Oh analysis of algorithms for large applications but not for small applications.

REVIEW QUESTIONS

5.3   **1.** Name three conditions under which sequential search of a list is preferable to binary search.

5.4   **2.** In searching a list of n items how many comparisons does sequential search do? binary search, first version?

3. Why was binary search implemented only for contiguous lists, not for simply linked lists?

4. Draw the comparison tree for Binary1 for searching a list of length **(a)** 1, **(b)** 2, **(c)** 3.

5. Draw the comparison tree for Binary2 for searching a list of length **(a)** 1, **(b)** 2, **(c)** 3.

6. If the height of a 2-tree is 3, what are **(a)** the largest and **(b)** the smallest number of vertices that can be in the tree?

7. Define the terms *internal* and *external path length* of a 2-tree. State the path length theorem.

5.5   **8.** What is the smallest number of comparisons that any method relying on comparisons of keys must make, on average, in searching a list of n items?

9. If Binary2 does 20 comparisons for the average successful search, then about how many will it do for the average unsuccessful search, assuming that the possibilities of the target less than the smallest key, between any pair of keys, or larger than the largest key are all equally likely?

5.6   **10.** What is the purpose of the big Oh notation?

REFERENCES FOR FURTHER STUDY

The primary reference for this chapter is KNUTH, Volume 3. (See the end of Chapter 3 for bibliographic details). Sequential search occupies pp. 389–405; binary search covers pp. 406–414; then comes Fibonacci search, and a section on history. KNUTH studies every method we have touched, and many others besides. He does algorithm analysis in considerably more detail than we have, writing his algorithms in a pseudo-assembly language and counting operations in detail there.

Proving the correctness of the binary search algorithm is the topic of

> JON BENTLEY, "Programming pearls: Writing correct programs," *Communications of the ACM* 26 (1983), 1040–1045.

In this column, BENTLEY shows how to formulate a binary search algorithm from its requirements, points out that about ninety percent of professional programmers whom he has taught were unable to write the program correctly in one hour, and gives a formal verification of correctness.

"Programming Pearls" is a regular column that contains many elegant algorithms and helpful suggestions for programming. These columns have been collected in the following two books:

> JON BENTLEY, *Programming Pearls*, Addison–Wesley, Reading, Mass., 1986, 195 pages.

> JON BENTLEY, *More Programming Pearls: Confessions of a Coder*, Addison–Wesley, Reading, Mass., 1988, 207 pages.

The following paper studies 26 published versions of binary search, pointing out correct and erroneous reasoning and drawing conclusions applicable to other algorithms:

> R. LESUISSE, "Some lessons drawn from the history of the binary search algorithm," *The Computer Journal* 26 (1983), 154–163.

Theorem 5.4 (successful and unsuccessful searches take almost the same time on average) is due to

> T. N. HIBBARD, *Journal of the ACM* 9 (1962), 16–17.

Interpolation search is presented in

> C. C. GOTLIEB and L. R. GOTLIEB, *Data Types and Structures*, Prentice Hall, Englewood Cliffs, N. J., 1978, pp. 133–135.

Tables and Information Retrieval

This chapter continues the study of information retrieval begun in the last chapter, but now concentrating on tables instead of lists. We begin with ordinary rectangular arrays, then other kinds of arrays, and then we generalize to the study of hash tables. One of our major purposes again is to analyze and compare various algorithms, to see which are preferable under different conditions. The chapter concludes by applying the methods of hash tables to the Life game.

6.1 INTRODUCTION: BREAKING THE lg n BARRIER

In the last chapter we showed that, by use of key comparisons alone, it is impossible to complete a search of n items in fewer than $\lg n$ comparisons, on average. But this result speaks only of searching by key comparisons. If we can use some other method, then we may be able to arrange our data so that we can locate a given item even more quickly.

In fact, we commonly do so. If we have 500 different records, with an index between 1 and 500 assigned to each, then we would never think of using sequential or binary search to locate a record. We would simply store the records in an array of size 500, and use the index n to locate the record of item n by ordinary table lookup.

table lookup

functions for information retrieval

Both table lookup and searching share the same essential purpose, that of *informa-tion retrieval*. We begin with a key (which may be complicated or simply an index) and wish to find the location of the item (if any) with that key. In other words, both table lookup and our searching algorithms provide *functions* from the set of keys to locations in a list or array. The functions are in fact one-to-one from the set of keys that actually occur to the set of locations that actually occur, since we assume that each item has only one key, and there is only one item with a given key.

tables

In this chapter we study ways to implement and access arrays in contiguous storage, beginning with ordinary rectangular arrays, and then considering tables with restricted location of nonzero entries, such as triangular tables. We turn afterward to more general problems, with the purpose of introducing and motivating the use first of access tables and then hash tables for information retrieval.

We shall see that, depending on the shape of the table, several steps may be needed to retrieve an entry, but, even so, the time required remains $O(1)$—that is, it is bounded by a constant that does not depend on the size of the table—and thus table lookup can be more efficient than any searching method.

conventions

Before beginning our discussion we should establish some conventions. In C, all arrays are indexed starting from 0 and are referenced using individually bracketed index expressions like somearray[i*2][j + 1][k]. We will, however, sometimes talk about arrays with arbitrary upper and lower bounds, which are not directly available in C. So, for general discussions of arrays, we will use parenthesized index expressions like $(i_0, i_1, \ldots, i_n)$. When referring to a specific C implementation we will use proper C syntax, namely $[i_0][i_1] \ldots [i_n]$.

6.2 RECTANGULAR ARRAYS

Because of the importance of rectangular arrays, almost all high-level languages provide convenient and efficient means to store and access them, so that generally the programmer need not worry about the implementation details. Nonetheless, computer storage is fundamentally arranged in a contiguous sequence (that is, in a straight line with each entry next to another), so for every access to a rectangular array, the machine must do some work to convert the location within a rectangle to a position along a line. Let us take a slightly closer look at this process.

1. Row- and Column-Major Ordering

Perhaps the most natural way to read a rectangular array is to read the entries of the first row from left to right, then the entries of the second row, and so on until the last row has been read. This is also the order in which most compilers store a rectangular array, and is called *row-major ordering*. For example, if the rows of an array are numbered from 1 to 2 and the columns are numbered from 1 to 3, then the order of indices with which the entries are stored in row-major ordering is

$$(1, 1) \quad (1, 2) \quad (1, 3) \quad (2, 1) \quad (2, 2) \quad (2, 3).$$

FORTRAN   Standard FORTRAN instead uses *column-major ordering*, in which the entries of the first column come first, and so on. This example in column-major ordering is

$$(1, 1) \quad (2, 1) \quad (1, 2) \quad (2, 2) \quad (1, 3) \quad (2, 3).$$

Figure 6.1 further illustrates row- and column-major orderings for an array with three rows and four columns.

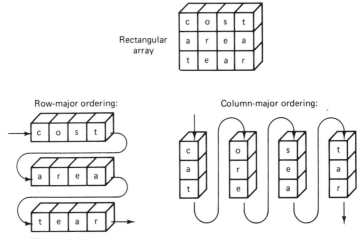

Figure 6.1. Sequential representation of a rectangular array

2. Indexing Rectangular Arrays

In the general problem, the compiler must be able to start with an index (i, j) and calculate where the corresponding entry of the array will be stored. We shall derive a formula for this calculation. For simplicity we shall use only row-major ordering and suppose that the rows are numbered from 0 to $m - 1$ and the columns from 0 to $n - 1$. This conforms exactly to the way C defines and handles arrays. The general case is treated as an exercise. Altogether, the array will have mn entries, as must its sequential implementation. We number the entries in the array from 0 to $mn - 1$. To obtain the formula calculating the position where (i, j) goes, we first consider some special cases. Clearly $(0, 0)$ goes to position 0, and, in fact, the entire first row is easy: $(0, j)$ goes to position j. The first entry of the second row, $(1, 0)$, comes after $(0, n - 1)$, and thus goes into position n. Continuing, we see that $(1, j)$ goes to position $n + j$. Entries of the next row will have two full rows, that is, $2n$ entries, preceding them. Hence entry

index function,
rectangular array

$(2, j)$ goes to position $2n + j$. In general, the entries of row i are preceded by ni earlier entries, so the desired formula is

$$\text{Entry } (i, j) \text{ goes to position } ni + j.$$

A formula of this kind, which gives the sequential location of an array entry, is called an ***index function***.

3. Variation: An Access Table

The index function for rectangular arrays is certainly not difficult to calculate, and the compilers of most high-level languages will simply write into the machine-language program the necessary steps for its calculation every time a reference is made to a rectangular array. On small machines, however, multiplication can be quite slow, so a slightly different method can be used to eliminate the multiplications.

access table,
rectangular array

This method is to keep an auxiliary array, a part of the multiplication table for n. The array will contain the values

$$0, \quad n, \quad 2n, \quad 3n, \quad \ldots, \quad (m-1)n.$$

Note that this array is much smaller (usually) than the rectangular array, so that it can be kept permanently in memory without losing too much space. Its entries then need be calculated only once (and note that they can be calculated using only addition). For all later references to the rectangular array, the compiler can find the position for (i, j) by taking the entry in position i of the auxiliary table, adding j, and going to the resulting position.

This auxiliary table provides our first example of an ***access table*** (see Figure 6.2). In general, an access table is an auxiliary array used to find data stored elsewhere. The terms ***access vector*** and ***dope vector*** (the latter especially when additional information is included) are also used.

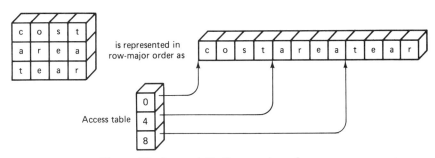

Figure 6.2. Access table for a rectangular array

Exercises
6.2

E1. What is the index function for a two-dimensional rectangular array with bounds

$$(0 \ldots m - 1, 0 \ldots n - 1)$$

under column-major ordering?

E2. Give the index function, with row-major ordering, for a two dimensional array with arbitrary bounds

$$(r \ldots s, t \ldots u).$$

E3. Find the index function, with the generalization of row-major ordering, for an array with d dimensions and arbitrary bounds for each dimension.

6.3 TABLES OF VARIOUS SHAPES

matrix

Information that is usually stored in a rectangular array may not require every position in the rectangle for its representation. If we define a ***matrix*** to be an array of numbers, then often some of the positions within the matrix will be required to be 0. Several such examples are shown in Figure 6.3. Even when the entries in a table are not numbers, the positions actually used may not be all of those in a rectangle, and there may be better implementations than using a rectangular array and leaving some positions vacant. In this section, we examine ways to implement tables of various shapes, ways that will not require setting aside unused space in a rectangular array.

6.3.1 Triangular Tables

Let us consider the representation of a lower triangular table shown in Figure 6.3. Such a table can be defined formally as a table in which all indices (i, j) are required to satisfy

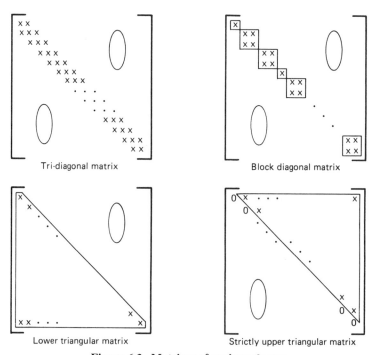

Tri-diagonal matrix

Block diagonal matrix

Lower triangular matrix

Strictly upper triangular matrix

Figure 6.3. Matrices of various shapes

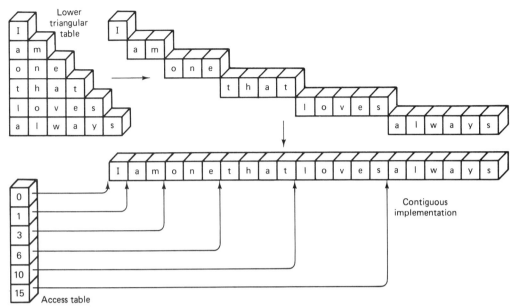

Figure 6.4. Contiguous implementation of a triangular table

$i \geq j$. We can implement a triangular table in a sequential array by sliding each row out after the one above it, as shown in Figure 6.4.

To construct the index function that describes this mapping, we again make the slight simplification of assuming that the rows and the columns are numbered starting with 0. To find the position where (i, j) goes, we now need to find where row number i starts, and then to locate column j we need only add j to the starting point of row i. If the entries of the contiguous array are also numbered starting with 0, then the index of the starting point will be the same as the number of entries that precede row i. Clearly there are 0 entries before row 0, and only the one entry of row 0 precedes row 1. For row 2 there are $1 + 2 = 3$ preceding entries, and in general we see that preceding row i there are exactly

$$1 + 2 + \cdots + i = \tfrac{1}{2}i(i + 1)$$

entries. Hence the desired function is that entry (i, j) of the triangular table corresponds to entry

index function,
rectangular table

$$\tfrac{1}{2}i(i + 1) + j$$

of the contiguous array.

As we did for rectangular arrays, we can again avoid all multiplications and divisions by setting up an access table whose entries correspond to the row indices of the triangular table. Position i of the access table will permanently contain the value $\tfrac{1}{2}i(i + 1)$. The access table will be calculated only once at the start of the program, and then used repeatedly at each reference to the triangular table. Note that even the initial calculation of this access table requires no multiplication or division, but only addition to calculate its entries in the order

access table,
triangular table

$$0, \quad 1, \quad 1 + 2, \quad (1 + 2) + 3, \quad \cdots .$$

6.3.2 Jagged Tables

In both of the foregoing examples we have considered a rectangular table as made up from its rows. In ordinary rectangular arrays all the rows have the same length; in triangular tables, the length of each row can be found from a simple formula. We now consider the case of jagged tables such as the one in Figure 6.5, where there is no predictable relation between the position of a row and its length.

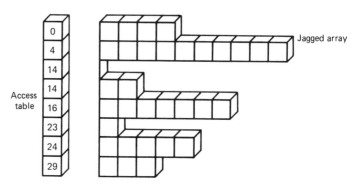

Figure 6.5. Access table for jagged table

It is clear from the diagram that, even though we are not able to give an *a priori* function to map the jagged table into contiguous storage, the use of an access table remains as easy as in the previous examples, and elements of the jagged table can be referenced just as quickly. To set up the access table, we must construct the jagged table in its natural order, beginning with its first row. Entry 0 of the access table is, as before, the start of the contiguous array. After each row of the jagged table has been constructed, the index of the first unused position of the contiguous storage should then be entered as the next entry in the access table and used to start constructing the next row of the jagged table.

6.3.3 Inverted Tables

Next let us consider an example illustrating multiple access tables, by which we can refer to a single table of records by several different keys at once.

Consider the problem faced by the telephone company in accessing the records of its customers. To publish the telephone book, the records must be sorted alphabetically by the name of the subscriber. But to process long-distance charges, the accounts must be sorted by telephone number. To do routine maintenance, the company also needs to have its subscribers sorted by their address, so that a repairman may be able to work *multiple records* on several lines with one trip. Conceivably the telephone company could keep three (or more) sets of its records, one sorted by name, one by number, and one by address. This way, however, would not only be very wasteful of storage space, but would introduce endless headaches if one set of records were updated but another was not, and erroneous and unpredictable information might be used.

multiple access By using access tables we can avoid the multiple sets of records, and we can still *tables* find the records by any of the three keys almost as quickly as if the records were fully sorted by that key. For the names we set up one access table. The first entry in this table is the position where the records of the subscriber whose name is first in alphabetical order are stored, the second entry gives the location of the second (in alphabetical order) subscriber's records, and so on. In a second access table, the first entry is the location of the subscriber's records whose telephone number happens to be smallest in numerical order. In yet a third access table the entries give the locations of the records sorted lexicographically by address. Notice that in this method all the fields that are treated as keys are processed in the same way. There is no particular reason why the records themselves *unordered records* need to be sorted according to one key rather than another, or, in fact, why they need to *for ordered access* be sorted at all. The records themselves can be kept in an arbitrary order—say, the order *tables* in which they were first entered into the system. It also makes no difference whether the records are in an array, with entries in the access tables being indices of the array, or whether the records are in dynamic storage, with the access tables holding pointers to individual records. In any case, it is the access tables that are used for information retrieval, and, as ordinary contiguous arrays, they may be used for table lookup, or binary search, or any other purpose for which a contiguous implementation is appropriate.

An example of this scheme for a small number of accounts is shown in Figure 6.6.

Index	Name	Address	Phone
1	Hill, Thomas M.	High Towers #317	2829478
2	Baker, John S.	17 King Street	2884285
3	Roberts, L. B.	53 Ash Street	4372296
4	King, Barbara	High Towers #802	2863386
5	Hill, Thomas M.	39 King Street	2495723
6	Byers, Carolyn	118 Maple Street	4394231
7	Moody, C. L.	High Towers #210	2822214

Access Tables		
Name	Address	Phone
2	3	5
6	7	7
1	1	1
5	4	4
4	2	2
7	5	3
3	6	6

Figure 6.6. Multikey access tables: an inverted table

Exercises 6.3

E1. The **main diagonal** of a square matrix consists of the entries for which the row and column indices are equal. A **diagonal matrix** is a square matrix in which all entries not on the main diagonal are 0. Describe a way to store a diagonal matrix without using space for entries that are necessarily 0, and give the corresponding index function.

E2. A *tri-diagonal matrix* is a square matrix in which all entries are 0 except possibly those on the main diagonal and on the diagonals immediately above and below it. That is, T is a tri-diagonal matrix means that $T[i][j] = 0$ unless $|i - j| \leq 1$.

   a. Devise a space-efficient storage scheme for tri-diagonal matrices, and give the corresponding index function.

   b. The *transpose* of a matrix is the matrix obtained by interchanging its rows with the corresponding columns. That is, matrix B is the transpose of matrix A means that $B[j][i] = A[i][j]$ for all indices i and j corresponding to positions in the matrix. Write a function that transposes a tri-diagonal matrix using the storage scheme devised in the previous exercise.

E3. An *upper triangular matrix* is a square array in which all entries below the main diagonal are 0.

   a. Describe the modifications necessary to use the access table method to store an upper triangular matrix.

   b. The transpose of a lower triangular matrix will be an upper triangular matrix. Write a function that will transpose a lower triangular matrix, using access tables to refer to both matrices.

E4. Consider a table of the triangular shape shown in Figure 6.7, where the columns are indexed from $-n$ to n and the rows from 0 to n.

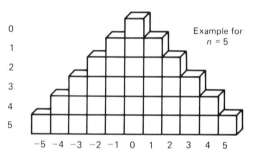

0
1
2
3
4
5

Example for
n = 5

−5 −4 −3 −2 −1 0 1 2 3 4 5

Figure 6.7. A table symmetrically triangular around 0

   a. Devise an index function that maps a table of this shape into a sequential array.

   b. Write a function that will generate an access table for finding the first entry of each row of a table of this shape within the contiguous array.

   c. Write a function that will reflect the table from left to right. The entries in column 0 (the central column) remain unchanged, those in columns −1 and 1 are swapped, and so on.

Programming Projects 6.3

Implement the method described in the text that uses an access table to store a lower triangular table, as applied in the following projects.

   P1. Write a function that will read the entries of a lower triangular table from the terminal.

   P2. Write a function that will print a lower triangular table at the terminal.

   P3. Suppose that a lower triangular table is a table of distances between cities, as often appears on a road map. Write a function that will check the triangle rule: The distance from city A to city C is never more than the distance from A to city B, plus the distance from B to C.

6.4 TABLES: A NEW ABSTRACT DATA TYPE

At the beginning of this chapter we studied several *index functions* used to locate entries in tables, and then we turned to *access tables*, which were arrays used for the same purpose as index functions. The analogy between functions and table lookup is indeed very close: With a function, we start with an argument and calculate a corresponding value; with a table, we start with an index and look up a corresponding value. Let us now use this analogy to produce a formal definition of the term *table*, a definition that will, in turn, motivate new ideas that come to fruition in the following section.

1. Functions

domain, codomain, and range

In mathematics a **function** is defined in terms of two sets and a correspondence from elements of the first set to elements of the second. If f is a function from a set A to a set B, then f assigns to each element of A a unique element of B. The set A is called the **domain** of f, and the set B is called the **codomain** of f. The subset of B containing just those elements that occur as values of f is called the **range** of f. This definition is illustrated in Figure 6.8.

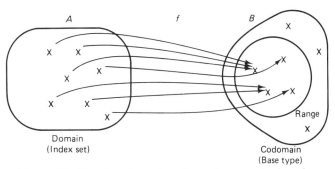

Figure 6.8. The domain, codomain, and range of a function

index set, value type

Table access begins with an index and uses the table to look up a corresponding value. Hence for a table we call the domain the **index set**, and we call the codomain the **base type** or **value type**. (Recall that in Section 4.6.2 a *type* was defined as a set of values.) If, for example, we have the array declaration

$$\text{float somearray [n]}$$

then the index set is the set of integers between 0 and $n-1$, and the base type is the set of all real numbers. As a second example, consider a triangular table with m rows whose entries have type Item. The base type is then simply type Item and the index type is the set of ordered pairs of integers

$$\{(i,j)\,|\,0 \le j \le i \le m-1\}.$$

2. An Abstract Data Type

We are now well on the way toward defining *table* as a new abstract data type, but recall from Section 4.6.2 that to complete the definition, we must also specify the operations that can be performed. Before doing so, let us summarize what we know.

DEFINITION

the ADT table

A *table* with index set I and base type T is a function from I into T together with the following operations.

1. *Table access*: Evaluate the function at any index in I.

2. *Table assignment*: Modify the function by changing its value at a specified index in I to the new value specified in the assignment.

These two operations are all that are provided by C and some other languages, but that is no reason why we cannot allow the possibility of further operations. If we compare the definition of a list, we find that we allowed insertion and deletion as well as access and assignment. We can do the same with tables.

3. *Insertion*: Adjoin a new element x to the index set I and define a corresponding value of the function at x.

4. *Deletion*: Delete an element x from the index set I and restrict the function to the resulting smaller domain.

Even though these last two operations are not available directly in C, they remain very useful for many applications, and we shall study them further in the next section. In some other languages, such as APL and SNOBOL, tables that change size while the program is running are an important feature. In any case, we should always be careful to program *into* a language and never allow our thinking to be limited by the restrictions of a particular language.

3. Implementation

index functions and access tables

divide and conquer

The definition just given is that of an abstract data type and in itself says nothing about implementation, nor does it speak of the index functions or access tables studied earlier. Index functions and access tables are, in fact, implementation methods for more general tables. An index function or access table starts with a general index set of some specified form and produces as its result an index in some subscript range, such as a subrange of the integers. This range can then be used (possibly normalized) as subscripts for arrays provided by the programming language. In this way, the implementation of a table is divided into two smaller problems: finding an access table or index function and programming an array. You should note that both of these are special cases of tables, and hence we have an example of solving a problem by dividing it into two smaller problems of the same nature. This process is illustrated in Figure 6.9.

4. Comparisons

Let us compare the abstract data types *list* and *table*. The underlying mathematical construction for a list is the sequence, and for a table, it is the set and the function.

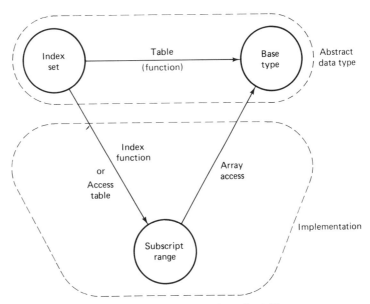

Figure 6.9. Implementation of a table

lists and tables   Sequences have an implicit order; a first element, a second, and so on, but sets and functions have no such order. (If the index set has some natural order, then sometimes this order is reflected in the table, but this is not a necessary aspect of using tables.) Hence information retrieval from a list naturally involves a search like the ones studied in the previous chapter, but information retrieval from a table requires different methods, *retrieval*   access methods that go directly to the desired entry. The time required for searching a list generally depends on the number n of items in the list and is at least $\lg n$, but the time for accessing a table does not usually depend on the number of items in the table; that is, it is usually $O(1)$. For this reason, in many applications table access is significantly faster than list searching.

traversal   On the other hand, traversal is a natural operation for a list but not for a table. It is generally easy to move through a list performing some operation with every item in the list. In general, it may not be nearly so easy to perform an operation on every item in a table, particularly if some special order for the items is specified in advance.

tables and arrays   Finally, we should clarify the distinction between the terms *table* and *array*. In general, we shall use *table* as we have defined it in this section and restrict the term *array* to mean the programming feature available in C and most high-level languages and used for implementing both tables and contiguous lists.

6.5 HASHING

6.5.1 Sparse Tables

1. Index Functions

We can continue to exploit table lookup even in situations where the key is no longer an index that can be used directly as in array indexing. What we can do is to set up a one-to-one correspondence between the keys by which we wish to retrieve information and indices that we can use to access an array. The index function that we produce will be somewhat more complicated than those of previous sections, since it may need to convert the key from, say, alphabetic information to an integer, but in principle it can still be done.

The only difficulty arises when the number of possible keys exceeds the amount of space available for our table. If, for example, our keys are alphabetical words of eight letters, then there are $26^8 \approx 2 \times 10^{11}$ possible keys, a number much greater than the number of positions that will be available in high-speed memory. In practice, however, only a small fraction of these keys will actually occur. That is, the table is *sparse*. Conceptually, we can regard it as indexed by a very large set, but with relatively few positions actually occupied.

2. Hash Tables

The idea of a ***hash table*** (such as the one shown in Figure 6.10) is to allow many of the different possible keys that might occur to be mapped to the same location in an array

index function not one to one

under the action of the index function. Then there will be a possibility that two records will want to be in the same place, but if the number of records that actually occur is small relative to the size of the array, then this possibility will cause little loss of time. Even when most entries in the array are occupied, hash methods can be an effective means of

hash function

information retrieval. We begin with a ***hash function*** that takes a key and maps it to some index in the array. This function will generally map several different keys to the same index. If the desired record is in the location given by the index, then our problem

collision

is solved; otherwise we must use some method to resolve the ***collision*** that may have occurred between two records wanting to go to the same location. There are thus two questions we must answer to use hashing. First, we must find good hash functions, and, second, we must determine how to resolve collisions.

Before approaching these questions, let us pause to outline informally the steps needed to implement hashing.

3. Algorithm Outlines

First, an array must be declared that will hold the hash table. With ordinary arrays the keys used to locate entries are usually the indices, so there is no need to keep them within the array itself, but for a hash table, several possible keys will correspond to the

keys in table

same index, so one field within each record in the array must be reserved for the key itself.

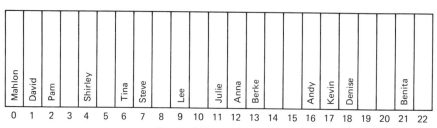

Figure 6.10. A hash table

initialization   Next, all locations in the array must be initialized to show that they are empty. How this is done depends on the application; often it is accomplished by setting the key fields to some value that is guaranteed never to occur as an actual key. In C, it is common to use a NULL pointer to represent an empty position.

insertion   To insert a record into the hash table, the hash function for the key is first calculated. If the corresponding location is empty, then the record can be inserted, else if the keys are equal, then insertion of the new record would not be allowed, and in the remaining case (a record with a different key is in the location), it becomes necessary to resolve the collision.

retrieval   To retrieve the record with a given key is entirely similar. First, the hash function for the key is computed. If the desired record is in the corresponding location, then the retrieval has succeeded; otherwise, while the location is nonempty and not all locations have been examined, follow the same steps used for collision resolution. If an empty position is found, or all locations have been considered, then no record with the given key is in the table, and the search is unsuccessful.

6.5.2 Choosing a Hash Function

The two principal criteria in selecting a hash function are that it should be easy and quick to compute and that it should achieve an even distribution of the keys that actually occur across the range of indices. If we know in advance exactly what keys will occur, then it is possible to construct hash functions that will be very efficient, but generally we do not know in advance what keys will occur. Therefore, the usual way is for the *method*   hash function to take the key, chop it up, mix the pieces together in various ways, and thereby obtain an index that (like the pseudorandom numbers generated by computer) will be uniformly distributed over the range of indices.

It is from this process that the word *hash* comes, since the process converts the key into something that bears little resemblance. At the same time, it is hoped that any patterns or regularities that may occur in the keys will be destroyed, so that the results will be randomly distributed.

Even though the term *hash* is very descriptive, in some books the more technical terms *scatter-storage* or *key-transformation* are used in its place.

We shall consider three methods that can be put together in various ways to build a hash function.

1. Truncation

Ignore part of the key, and use the remaining part directly as the index (considering non-numeric fields as their numerical codes). If the keys, for example, are eight-digit integers and the hash table has 1000 locations, then the first, second, and fifth digits from the right might make the hash function, so that 62538194 maps to 394. Truncation is a very fast method, but it often fails to distribute the keys evenly through the table.

2. Folding

Partition the key into several parts and combine the parts in a convenient way (often using addition or multiplication) to obtain the index. For example, an eight-digit integer can be divided into groups of three, three, and two digits, the groups added together, and truncated if necessary to be in the proper range of indices. Hence 62538194 maps to $625 + 381 + 94 = 1100$, which is truncated to 100. Since all information in the key can affect the value of the function, folding often achieves a better spread of indices than does truncation by itself.

3. Modular Arithmetic

Convert the key to an integer (using the above devices as desired), divide by the size of the index range, and take the remainder as the result. This amounts to using the C modulus operator % . The spread achieved by taking a remainder depends very much on the modulus (in this case, the size of the hash array). If the modulus is a power of a small integer like 2 or 10, then many keys tend to map to the same index, while other indices remain unused. The best choice for modulus is a prime number, which usually *prime modulus* has the effect of spreading the keys quite uniformly. (We shall see later that a prime modulus also improves an important method for collision resolution.) Hence, rather than choosing a hash table size of 1000, it is better to choose either 997 or 1009; $1024 = 2^{10}$ would usually be a poor choice. Taking the remainder is usually the best way to conclude calculating the hash function, since it can achieve a good spread at the same time that it ensures that the result is in the proper range. About the only reservation is that, on a tiny machine with no hardware division, the calculation can be slow, so other methods should be considered.

4. C Example

As a simple example, let us write a hash function in C for transforming a key consisting of alphanumeric characters into an integer in the range

$$0 .. \text{HASHSIZE} - 1.$$

That is, we shall begin with the type

```
typedef char *Key_type;
```

We can then write a simple hash function as follows:

```
#include <stdlib.h>
#include "hash.h"
```
simple hash function
```
/* Hash: calculate the hash value of s. */
int Hash(Key_type s)
{
    int h = 0;
    while (*s)                        /* Loop through all the characters in s.  */
        h += *s++;                    /* Add the value of each to h.            */
    return abs(h % HASHSIZE);
}
```

The file hash.h contains

```
/* declarations for a chained hash table */
#define HASHSIZE 997
typedef char *Key_type;

typedef struct item_tag {
      Key_type key;
} Item_type;

typedef struct node_tag {
      Item_type info;              /* information to store in table        */
      struct node_tag *next;       /* next item in the linked list         */
} Node_type;

typedef Node_type *List_type;
typedef List_type Hashtable_type [HASHSIZE];
```

We have simply added the integer codes corresponding to each of the characters in the string. In general, this method will be no better (or worse) than any number of others. We could, for example, subtract some of the codes, multiply them in pairs, or ignore every other character. Sometimes an application will suggest that one hash function is better than another; sometimes it requires experimentation to settle on a good one.

6.5.3 Collision Resolution with Open Addressing

1. Linear Probing

The simplest method to resolve a collision is to start with the hash address (the location where the collision occurred) and do a sequential search for the desired key or an empty location. Hence this method searches in a straight line, and it is therefore called **linear probing**. The array should be considered circular, so that when the last location is reached, the search proceeds to the first location of the array.

2. Clustering

example of clustering

The major drawback of linear probing is that, as the table becomes about half full, there is a tendency toward **clustering**; that is, records start to appear in long strings of adjacent positions with gaps between the strings. Thus the sequential searches needed to find an empty position become longer and longer. Consider the example in Figure 6.11, where the occupied positions are shown in color. Suppose that there are n locations in the array and that the hash function chooses any of them with equal probability $1/n$. Begin with a fairly uniform spread, as shown in the top diagram. If a new insertion hashes to location b, then it will go there, but if it hashes to location a (which is full), then it will also go into b. Thus the probability that b will be filled has doubled to $2/n$. At the next stage, an attempted insertion into any of locations a, b, c, or d will end up in d, so the probability of filling d is $4/n$. After this, e has probability $5/n$ of being filled, and so as additional insertions are made the most likely effect is to make the string of full positions beginning at location a longer and longer, and hence the performance of the hash table starts to degenerate toward that of sequential search.

instability

The problem of clustering is essentially one of instability; if a few keys happen randomly to be near each other, then it becomes more and more likely that other keys will join them, and the distribution will become progressively more unbalanced.

Figure 6.11. Clustering in a hash table

3. Increment Functions

rehashing

If we are to avoid the problem of clustering, then we must use some more sophisticated way to select the sequence of locations to check when a collision occurs. There are many ways to do so. One, called ***rehashing***, uses a second hash function to obtain the second position to consider. If this position is filled, then some other method is needed to get the third position, and so on. But if we have a fairly good spread from the first hash function, then little is to be gained by an independent second hash function. We will do just as well to find a more sophisticated way of determining the distance to move from the first hash position and apply this method, whatever the first hash location is. Hence we wish to design an increment function that can depend on the key or on the number of probes already made and that will avoid clustering.

4. Quadratic Probing

If there is a collision at hash address h, this method probes the table at locations $h + 1$, $h + 4$, $h + 9$, ..., that is, at locations $h + i^2$ (% HASHSIZE) for $i = 1, 2, \ldots$. That is, the increment function is i^2.

This method substantially reduces clustering, but it is not obvious that it will probe all locations in the table, and in fact it does not. If HASHSIZE is a power of 2, then relatively few positions are probed. Suppose that HASHSIZE is a prime. If we reach the same location at probe i and at probe j, then

$$h + i^2 \equiv h + j^2 \ (\% \text{ HASHSIZE})$$

so that

$$(i - j)(i + j) \equiv 0 \ (\% \text{ HASHSIZE}).$$

Since HASHSIZE is a prime, it must divide one factor. It divides $i - j$ only when j differs from i by a multiple of HASHSIZE, so at least HASHSIZE probes have been made. HASHSIZE divides $i + j$, however, when j = HASHSIZE $- i$, so the total number of distinct positions that will be probed is exactly

$$(\text{HASHSIZE} + 1)/2.$$

It is customary to take overflow as occurring when this number of positions has been probed, and the results are quite satisfactory.

calculation Note that quadratic probing can be accomplished without doing multiplications: After the first probe at position x, the increment is set to 1. At each successive probe, the increment is increased by 2 after it has been added to the previous location. Since

$$1 + 3 + 5 + \cdots + (2i - 1) = i^2$$

for all $i \geq 1$ (you can prove this fact by mathematical induction), probe i will look in position

$$x + 1 + 3 + \cdots + (2i - 1) = x + i^2,$$

as desired.

5. Key-Dependent Increments

Rather than having the increment depend on the number of probes already made, we can let it be some simple function of the key itself. For example, we could truncate the key to a single character and use its code as the increment. In C, we might write

increment = *key;

A good approach, when the remainder after division is taken as the hash function, is to let the increment depend on the quotient of the same division. An optimizing compiler should specify the division only once, so the calculation will be fast, and the results generally satisfactory.

In this method, the increment, once determined, remains constant. If HASHSIZE is a prime, it follows that the probes will step through all the entries of the array before any repetitions. Hence overflow will not be indicated until the array is completely full.

6. Random Probing

A final method is to use a pseudorandom number generator to obtain the increment. The generator used should be one that always generates the same sequence provided it starts with the same seed. The seed, then, can be specified as some function of the key. This method is excellent in avoiding clustering, but is likely to be slower than the others.

7. C Algorithms

To conclude the discussion of open addressing, we continue to study the C example already introduced, which used alphanumeric keys of the type

typedef char *Key_type;

We set up the hash table with the declarations

#define HASHSIZE 997   /* a prime number of appropriate size   */

typedef Item_type Hashtable_type [HASHSIZE] ;

Hashtable_type H;

initialization The hash table must be initialized by setting the key field of each item in H to NULL.

We shall use the hash function already written in Section 6.5.2, part 4, together with quadratic probing for collision resolution. We have shown that the maximum number of probes that can be made this way is $(HASHSIZE + 1)/2$, and we keep a counter c to check this upper bound.

With these conventions, let us write a function to insert a record r, with key r.key, into the hash table H.

```
#include "hashopen.h"
```

```
/* Insert: insert an item into a hash table using open addressing. */
void Insert(Hashtable_type H, Item_type r)
{
    int c = 0;                     /* count to be sure that table is not full   */
    int i = 1;                     /* increment used for quadratic probing      */
    int p;                         /* position currently probed in H            */
    p = Hash(r.key);
    while (H[p].key != NULL&&       /* Is the location empty?                   */
            strcmp(r.key, H[p].key) && /* Has target key been found?            */
            c <= HASHSIZE/2) {      /* Has overflow occurred?                   */
        c++;
        p += i;
        i += 2;                    /* Prepare increment for the next iteration. */
        if (p >= HASHSIZE)
            p %= HASHSIZE;
    }
    if (H[p].key == NULL)
        H[p] = r;                  /* Insert the new item.                     */
    else if (strcmp(r.key, H[p].key) == 0)
        Error("duplicate key");    /* The same key cannot appear twice.        */
    else
        Error("table overflow");   /* Counter has reached its limit.           */
}
```

insertion appears beside the function definition; *quadratic probing* appears beside the increment line.

The include file hashopen.h contains

```
/* declarations for a hash table with open addressing */
#define HASHSIZE 997
typedef char *Key_type;
typedef struct item_tag {
    Key_type key;
} Item_type;
typedef Item_type Hashtable_type[HASHSIZE];
```

A function to retrieve the record (if any) with a given key will have a similar form and is left as an exercise.

8. Deletions

Up to now we have said nothing about deleting items from a hash table. At first glance, it may appear to be an easy task, requiring only marking the deleted location with the special key indicating that it is empty. This method will not work. The reason is that an empty location is used as the signal to stop the search for a target key. Suppose that, before the deletion, there had been a collision or two and that some item whose hash address is the now-deleted position is actually stored elsewhere in the table. If we now try to retrieve that item, then the now-empty position will stop the search, and it is impossible to find the item, even though it is still in the table.

special key   One method to remedy this difficulty is to invent another special key, to be placed in any deleted position. This special key would indicate that this position is free to receive an insertion when desired but that it should not be used to terminate the search for some other item in the table. Using this second special key will, however, make the algorithms somewhat more complicated and a bit slower. With the methods we have so far studied for hash tables, deletions are indeed awkward and should be avoided as much as possible.

6.5.4 Collision Resolution by Chaining

Up to now we have implicitly assumed that we are using only contiguous storage while working with hash tables. Contiguous storage for the hash table itself is, in fact, the natural choice, since we wish to be able to refer quickly to random positions in the table, *linked storage* and linked storage is not suited to random access. There is, however, no reason why linked storage should not be used for the records themselves. We can take the hash table itself as an array of pointers to the records, that is, as an array of list headers. An example appears in Figure 6.12.

It is traditional to refer to the linked lists from the hash table as **chains** and call this method collision resolution by **chaining**.

1. Advantages of Linked Storage

There are several advantages to this point of view. The first, and the most important when the records themselves are quite large, is that considerable space may be saved. *space saving* Since the hash table is a contiguous array, enough space must be set aside at compilation time to avoid overflow. If the records themselves are in the hash table, then if there are many empty positions (as is desirable to help avoid the cost of collisions), these will consume considerable space that might be needed elsewhere. If, on the other hand, the hash table contains only pointers to the records, pointers that require only one word each, then the size of the hash table may be reduced by a large factor (essentially by a factor equal to the size of the records), and will become small relative to the space available for the records, or for other uses.

The second major advantage of keeping only pointers in the hash table is that it *collision resolution* allows simple and efficient collision handling. We need only add a link field to each record, and organize all the records with a single hash address as a linked list. With a good hash function, few keys will give the same hash address, so the linked lists will be short and can be searched quickly. Clustering is no problem at all, because keys with distinct hash addresses always go to distinct lists.

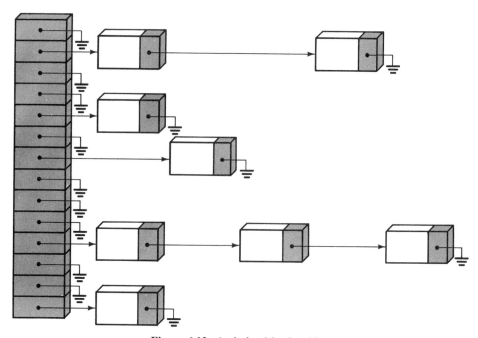

Figure 6.12. A chained hash table

overflow   A third advantage is that it is no longer necessary that the size of the hash table exceed the number of records. If there are more records than entries in the table, it means only that some of the linked lists are now sure to contain more than one record. Even if there are several times more records than the size of the table, the average length of the linked lists will remain small and sequential search on the appropriate list will remain efficient.

deletion   Finally, deletion becomes a quick and easy task in a chained hash table. Deletion proceeds in exactly the same way as deletion from a simple linked list.

2. Disadvantage of Linked Storage

These advantages of chained hash tables are indeed powerful. Lest you believe that chaining is always superior to open addressing, however, let us point out one important *use of space*   disadvantage: All the links require space. If the records are large, then this space is negligible in comparison with that needed for the records themselves; but if the records are small, then it is not.

Suppose, for example, that the links take one word each and that the items themselves take only one word (which is the key alone). Such applications are quite common, *small records* where we use the hash table only to answer some yes-no question about the key. Suppose that we use chaining and make the hash table itself quite small, with the same number n of entries as the number of items. Then we shall use $3n$ words of storage altogether: n for the hash table, n for the keys, and n for the links to find the next node (if any) on each chain. Since the hash table will be nearly full, there will be many collisions, and some of the chains will have several items. Hence searching will be a bit slow. Suppose, on the other hand, that we use open addressing. The same $3n$ words of storage put entirely into the hash table will mean that it will be only one third full, and therefore there will be relatively few collisions and the search for any given item will be faster.

3. C Algorithms

A chained hash table in C takes declarations like

declarations

```
typedef struct node_tag {
        Item_type info;                 /* information to store in table    */
        struct node_tag *next;          /* next item in the linked list     */
} Node_type;

typedef Node_type *Hashtable_type[HASHSIZE];
```

The structure node_tag consists of an Item_type, called info, and an additional member, called next, that points to the next node in a linked list
    The code needed to initialize the hash table is

```
for (i = 0; i < HASHSIZE; i++)
    H[i] = NULL;
```

initialization

We can even use previously written functions to access the hash table. The hash function itself is no different from that used with open addressing; for data retrieval we can simply use the function SequentialSearch (linked version) from Section 5.2, as follows:

retrieval

```
/* Retrieve: retrieve an item from a hash table using chaining. */
Node_type *Retrieve(Hashtable_type H, Key_type target)
{
        return SequentialSearch(H[Hash(target)], target);
}
```

Our function for inserting a new entry will assume that the key does not appear already; otherwise, only the most recent insertion with a given key will be retrievable.

insertion

```
/* Insert: insert an item into a hash table using chaining. */
void Insert(Hashtable_type H, Node_type *node)
{
        int h;                          /* index in hash table              */

        h = Hash(node->info.key);       /* Find the index.                  */
        node->next = H[h];              /* Insert node at the head of the list. */
        H[h] = node;                    /* Set the hash table to point to node. */
}
```

As you can see, both of these functions are significantly simpler than the versions for open addressing, since collision resolution is not a problem.

Exercises
6.5

E1. Write a C function to insert an item into a hash table with open addressing and linear probing.

E2. Write a C function to retrieve an item from a hash table with open addressing and **(a)** linear probing; **(b)** quadratic probing.

E3. Devise a simple, easy to calculate hash function for mapping three-letter words to integers between 0 and $n - 1$, inclusive. Find the values of your function on the words

PAL LAP PAM MAP PAT PET SET SAT TAT BAT

for $n = 11, 13, 17, 19$. Try for as few collisions as possible.

E4. Suppose that a hash table contains HASHSIZE = 13 entries indexed from 0 through 12 and that the following keys are to be mapped into the table:

10   100   32   45   58   126   3   29   200   400   0

a. Determine the hash addresses and find how many collisions occur when these keys are reduced % HASHSIZE.

b. Determine the hash addresses and find how many collisions occur when these keys are first folded by adding their digits together (in ordinary decimal representation) and then reducing % HASHSIZE.

perfect hash
functions

c. Find a hash function that will produce no collisions for these keys. (A hash function that has no collisions for a fixed set of keys is called ***perfect***.)

d. Repeat the previous parts of this exercise for HASHSIZE = 11. (A hash function that produces no collision for a fixed set of keys that completely fill the hash table is called ***minimal perfect***.)

E5. Another method for resolving collisions with open addressing is to keep a separate array called the ***overflow table***, into which all items that collide with an occupied location are put. They can either be inserted with another hash function or simply inserted in order, with sequential search used for retrieval. Discuss the advantages and disadvantages of this method.

E6. Write an algorithm for deleting an item from a chained hash table.

E7. Write a deletion algorithm for a hash table with open addressing, using a second special key to indicate a deleted item (see part 8 of Section 6.5.3). Change the retrieval and insertion algorithms accordingly.

E8. With linear probing, it is possible to delete an item without using a second special key, as follows. Mark the deleted entry empty. Search until another empty position is found. If the search finds a key whose hash address is at or before the first empty position, then move it back there, make its previous position empty, and continue from the new empty position. Write an algorithm to implement this method. Do the retrieval and insertion algorithms need modification?

Programming   **P1.** Consider the following 32 C reserved words.
Project 6.5

auto	break	case	char	const
continue	default	do	double	else
enum	extern	float	for	goto
if	int	long	register	return
short	signed	sizeof	static	struct
switch	typedef	union	unsigned	void
volatile	while			

    a. Devise an integer-valued function that will produce different values when applied to all 32 reserved words. [You may find it helpful to write a short program to assist. Your program could read the words from a file, apply the function you devise, and determine what collisions occur.]

    b. Find the smallest integer HASHSIZE such that, when the values of your function are reduced % HASHSIZE, all 32 values remain distinct.

6.6 ANALYSIS OF HASHING

1. The Birthday Surprise

The likelihood of collisions in hashing relates to the well-known mathematical diversion: How many randomly chosen people need to be in a room before it becomes likely that two people will have the same birthday (month and day)? Since (apart from leap years) there are 365 possible birthdays, most people guess that the answer will be in the hundreds, but in fact, the answer is only 24 people.

    We can determine the probabilities for this question by answering its opposite: With m randomly chosen people in a room, what is the probability that no two have the same birthday? Start with any person, and check his birthday off on a calendar. The probability that a second person has a different birthday is 364/365. Check it off. The probability that a third person has a different birthday is now 363/365. Continuing this way, we see that if the first $m - 1$ people have different birthdays, then the probability that person m has a different birthday is $(365 - m + 1)/365$. Since the birthdays of different people are independent, the probabilities multiply, and we obtain that the probability that m people all have different birthdays is

probability
$$\frac{364}{365} \times \frac{363}{365} \times \frac{362}{365} \times \cdots \times \frac{365 - m + 1}{365}.$$

This expression becomes less than 0.5 whenever $m \geq 24$.

collisions likely   In regard to hashing, the birthday surprise tells us that with any problem of reasonable size, we are almost certain to have some collisions. Our approach, therefore, should not be only to try to minimize the number of collisions, but also to handle those that occur as expeditiously as possible.

2. Counting Probes

As with other methods of information retrieval, we would like to know how many comparisons of keys occur on average during both successful and unsuccessful attempts to locate a given target key. We shall use the word **probe** for looking at one item and comparing its key with the target.

The number of probes we need clearly depends on how full the table is. Therefore (as for searching methods), we let n be the number of items in the table, and we let t (which is the same as HASHSIZE) be the number of positions in the array. The **load**

load factor   **factor** of the table is $\lambda = n/t$. Thus $\lambda = 0$ signifies an empty table; $\lambda = 0.5$ a table that is half full. For open addressing, λ can never exceed 1, but for chaining there is no limit on the size of λ. We consider chaining and open addressing separately.

3. Analysis of Chaining

With a chained hash table we go directly to one of the linked lists before doing any probes. Suppose that the chain that will contain the target (if it is present) has k items.

unsuccessful   If the search is unsuccessful, then the target will be compared with all k of the
retrieval   corresponding keys. Since the items are distributed uniformly over all t lists (equal probability of appearing on any list), the expected number of items on the one being searched is $\lambda = n/t$. Hence the average number of probes for an unsuccessful search is λ.

successful retrieval   Now suppose that the search is successful. From the analysis of sequential search, we know that the average number of comparisons is $\frac{1}{2}(k + 1)$, where k is the length of the chain containing the target. But the expected length of this chain is no longer λ, since we know in advance that it must contain at least one node (the target). The $n - 1$ nodes other than the target are distributed uniformly over all t chains; hence the expected number on the chain with the target is $1 + (n - 1)/t$. Except for tables of trivially small size, we may approximate $(n - 1)/t$ by $n/t = \lambda$. Hence the average number of probes for a successful search is very nearly

$$\tfrac{1}{2}(k + 1) \approx \tfrac{1}{2}(1 + \lambda + 1) = 1 + \tfrac{1}{2}\lambda.$$

4. Analysis of Open Addressing

For our analysis of the number of probes done in open addressing, let us first ignore the problem of clustering, by assuming that not only are the first probes random, but after a collision, the next probe will be random over all remaining positions of the table. In fact,

random probes   let us assume that the table is so large that all the probes can be regarded as independent events.

Let us first study an unsuccessful search. The probability that the first probe hits an occupied cell is λ, the load factor. The probability that a probe hits an empty cell is $1 - \lambda$. The probability that the unsuccessful search terminates in exactly two probes is therefore $\lambda(1 - \lambda)$, and, similarly, the probability that exactly k probes are made in an unsuccessful search is $\lambda^{k-1}(1 - \lambda)$. The expected number $U(\lambda)$ of probes in an unsuccessful search is therefore

$$U(\lambda) = \sum_{k=1}^{\infty} k\lambda^{k-1}(1 - \lambda).$$

This sum is evaluated in Appendix A.1; we obtain thereby

unsuccessful retrieval

$$U(\lambda) = \frac{1}{(1-\lambda)^2}(1-\lambda) = \frac{1}{1-\lambda}.$$

To count the probes needed for a successful search, we note that the number needed will be exactly one more than the number of probes in the unsuccessful search made before inserting the item. Now let us consider the table as beginning empty, with each item inserted one at a time. As these items are inserted, the load factor grows slowly from 0 to its final value, λ. It is reasonable for us to approximate this step-by-step growth by continuous growth and replace a sum with an integral. We conclude that the average number of probes in a successful search is approximately

successful retrieval

$$S(\lambda) = \frac{1}{\lambda}\int_0^\lambda U(\mu)d\mu = \frac{1}{\lambda}\ln\frac{1}{1-\lambda}.$$

linear probing

Similar calculations may be done for open addressing with linear probing, where it is no longer reasonable to assume that successive probes are independent. The details, however, are rather more complicated, so we present only the results. For the complete derivation, consult the references at the end of the chapter. For linear probing the average number of probes for an unsuccessful search increases to

$$\frac{1}{2}\left(1 + \frac{1}{(1-\lambda)^2}\right)$$

and for a successful search the number becomes

$$\frac{1}{2}\left(1 + \frac{1}{1-\lambda}\right).$$

Load factor	0.10	0.50	0.80	0.90	0.99	2.00
Successful search, expected number of probes:						
Chaining	1.05	1.25	1.40	1.45	1.50	2.00
Open, Random probes	1.05	1.4	2.0	2.6	4.6	—
Open, Linear probes	1.06	1.5	3.0	5.5	50.5	—
Unsuccessful search, expected number of probes:						
Chaining	0.10	0.50	0.80	0.90	0.99	2.00
Open, Random probes	1.1	2.0	5.0	10.0	100.	—
Open, Linear probes	1.12	2.5	13.	50.	5000.	—

Figure 6.13. Theoretical comparison of hashing methods

5. Theoretical Comparisons

Figure 6.13 gives the values of the above expressions for different values of the load factor.

We can draw several conclusions from this table. First, it is clear that chaining consistently requires fewer probes than does open addressing. On the other hand, traversal of the linked lists is usually slower than array access, which can reduce the advantage, especially if key comparisons can be done quickly. Chaining comes into its own when the records are large, and comparison of keys takes significant time. Chaining is also especially advantageous when unsuccessful searches are common, since with chaining, an empty list or very short list may be found, so that often no key comparisons at all need be done to show that a search is unsuccessful.

With open addressing and successful searches, the simpler method of linear probing is not significantly slower than more sophisticated methods, at least until the table is almost completely full. For unsuccessful searches, however, clustering quickly causes linear probing to degenerate into a long sequential search. We might conclude, therefore, that if searches are quite likely to be successful, and the load factor is moderate, then linear probing is quite satisfactory, but in other circumstances another method should be used.

6. Empirical Comparisons

It is important to remember that the computations giving Figure 6.13 are only approximate, and also that in practice nothing is completely random, so that we can always expect some differences between the theoretical results and actual computations. For sake of comparison, therefore, Figure 6.14 gives the results of one empirical study, using 900 keys that are pseudorandom numbers between 0 and 1.

Load factor	0.1	0.5	0.8	0.9	0.99	2.0
Successful search, average number of probes:						
Chaining	1.04	1.2	1.4	1.4	1.5	2.0
Open, Quadratic probes	1.04	1.5	2.1	2.7	5.2	—
Open, Linear probes	1.05	1.6	3.4	6.2	21.3	—
Unsuccessful search, average number of probes:						
Chaining	0.10	0.50	0.80	0.90	0.99	2.00
Open, Quadratic probes	1.13	2.2	5.2	11.9	126.	—
Open, Linear probes	1.13	2.7	15.4	59.8	430.	—

Figure 6.14. Empirical comparison of hashing methods

conclusions In comparison with other methods of information retrieval, the important thing to note about all these numbers is that they depend only on the load factor, not on the absolute number of items in the table. Retrieval from a hash table with 20,000 items in 40,000 possible positions is no slower, on average, than is retrieval from a table with 20 items in 40 possible positions. With sequential search, a list 1000 times the size will take 1000 times as long to search. With binary search, this ratio is reduced to 10 (more precisely, to lg 1000), but still the time needed increases with the size, which it does not with hashing.

Finally, we should emphasize the importance of devising a good hash function, one that executes quickly and maximizes the spread of keys. If the hash function is poor, the performance of hashing can degenerate to that of sequential search.

**Exercises
6.6**

E1. Suppose that each item (record) in a hash table occupies s words of storage (exclusive of the pointer field needed if chaining is used), and suppose that there are n items in the hash table.

    a. If the load factor is λ and open addressing is used, determine how many words of storage will be required for the hash table.

    b. If chaining is used, then each node will require $s + 1$ words, including the pointer field. How many words will be used altogether for the n nodes?

    c. If the load factor is λ and chaining is used, how many words will be used for the hash table itself? (Recall that with chaining the hash table itself contains only pointers requiring one word each.)

    d. Add your answers to the two previous parts to find the total storage requirement for load factor λ and chaining.

    e. If s is small, then open addressing requires less total memory for a given λ, but for large s, chaining requires less space altogether. Find the break-even value for s, at which both methods use the same total storage. Your answer will depend on the load factor λ.

E2. Figures 6.13 and 6.14 are somewhat distorted in favor of chaining, because no account is taken of the space needed for links (see part 2 of Section 6.5.4). Produce tables like Figure 6.13, where the load factors are calculated for the case of chaining, and for open addressing the space required by links is added to the hash table, thereby reducing the load factor.

    a. Given n nodes in linked storage connected to a chained hash table, with s words per item (plus 1 more for the link), and with load factor λ, find the total amount of storage that will be used, including links.

    b. If this same amount of storage is used in a hash table with open addressing and n items of s words each, find the resulting load factor. This is the load factor to use for open addressing in computing the revised tables.

    c. Produce a table for the case $s = 1$.

    d. Produce another table for the case $s = 5$.

    e. What will the table look like when each item takes 100 words?

E3. One reason why the answer to the birthday problem is surprising is that it differs from the answers to apparently related questions. For the following, suppose that there are n people in the room, and disregard leap years.

    a. What is the probability that someone in the room will have a birthday on a random date drawn from a hat?

    b. What is the probability that at least two people in the room will have that same random birthday?

    c. If we choose one person and find his birthday, what is the probability that someone else in the room will share the birthday?

E4. In a chained hash table, suppose that it makes sense to speak of an order for the keys, and suppose that the nodes in each chain are kept in order by key. Then a search can be terminated as soon as it passes the place where the key should be, if present. How many fewer probes will be done, on average, in an unsuccessful search? In a successful search? How many probes are needed, on average, to insert a new node in the right place? Compare your answers with the corresponding numbers derived in the text for the case of unordered chains.

E5. In our discussion of chaining, the hash table itself contained only pointers, list headers for each of the chains. One variant method is to place the first actual item of each chain in the hash table itself. (An empty position is indicated by an impossible key, as with open addressing.) With a given load factor, calculate the effect on space of this method, as a function of the number of words (except links) in each item. (A link takes one word.)

Programming Project 6.6

P1. Produce a table like Figure 6.14 for your computer, by writing and running test programs to implement the various kinds of hash tables and load factors.

6.7 CONCLUSIONS: COMPARISON OF METHODS

This chapter and the previous one have together explored four quite different methods of information retrieval: sequential search, binary search, table lookup, and hashing. If we are to ask which of these is best, we must first select the criteria by which to answer, and these criteria will include both the requirements imposed by the application and other considerations that affect our choice of data structures, since the first two methods are *choice of data* applicable only to lists and the second two to tables. In many applications, however, we *structures* are free to choose either lists or tables for our data structures.

In regard both to speed and convenience, ordinary lookup in contiguous tables is *table lookup* certainly superior, but there are many applications to which it is inapplicable, such as when a list is preferred or the set of keys is sparse. It is also inappropriate whenever insertions or deletions are frequent, since such actions in contiguous storage may require moving large amounts of information.

Which of the other three methods is best depends on other criteria, such as the form of the data.

other methods Sequential search is certainly the most flexible of our methods. The data may be stored in any order, with either contiguous or linked representation. Binary search is much more demanding. The keys must be in order, and the data must be in random-access representation (contiguous storage). Hashing requires even more, a peculiar ordering of the keys well suited to retrieval from the hash table, but generally useless for any other purpose. If the data are to be available immediately for human inspection, then some kind of order is essential, and a hash table is inappropriate.

Finally, there is the question of the unsuccessful search. Sequential search and *near miss* hashing, by themselves, say nothing except that the search was unsuccessful. Binary search can determine which data have keys closest to the target, and perhaps thereby can provide useful information.

6.8 APPLICATION: THE LIFE GAME REVISITED

At the end of Chapter 2 we noted that the bounds we used for the arrays in CONWAY's game of Life were highly restrictive and artificial. The Life cells are supposed to be on an unbounded grid. In other words, we would really like to have the C declaration

typedef Cell_type Grid_type [int] [int] ;

sparse table

which is, of course, illegal. Since only a limited number of these cells will actually be occupied at any one time, we should really regard the grid for the Life game as a sparse table, and therefore a hash table proves an attractive way to represent the grid.

6.8.1 Choice of Algorithm

Before we specify our data structures more precisely, let us consider the basic algorithm that we might use. We already have two versions of the Life simulation, and we should not introduce a third unless we know that it will prove a significant improvement. The first version scanned the entire grid at each generation, an action that is not suitable for a sparse array (where it would be impossibly slow). The second version, on the other hand, was designed essentially to treat the grid as a sparse array. It never explicitly scans through cells that are dead, but uses four lists to locate all cells that need attention. Rather than writing a complete new program from scratch, let us therefore see how far we can go to use the overall structure of the second program Life2 in conjunction with

modify Life2

a hash table to represent the sparse array.

6.8.2 Specification of Data Structures

We have already decided to represent our sparse array of cells as a hash table, but we have not yet decided between open addressing and chaining. For each cell we must keep the status of the cell (alive or dead), the number of living neighbors, and (since the key itself must be explicitly kept when using a hash table) the row and column of the cell.

use of space

With these four entries in each record, there are few space considerations to advise our decision. With chaining, the size of each record will increase 25 percent to accommodate the necessary pointer, but the hash table itself will be smaller and can take a higher load factor than with open addressing. With open addressing, the records will be smaller, but more room must be left vacant in the hash table to avoid long searches and possible overflow.

flexibility

After space considerations, the second question we should ask concerns flexibility. Do we need to make deletions, and, if so, when? We could keep track of all cells until the memory is full, and then delete those that are not needed. But this would require rehashing the full array, which would be slow and painful. With chaining we can easily dispose of cells as soon as they are not needed, and thereby reduce the number of cells in the hash table as much as possible.

access

Finally, we should review the requirements for accessing the cells. As we work with a given cell, we need to locate its eight neighbors, and we can use the hash table to do so. Some of these neighbors may be inserted into the four lists live, die, nextlive, and nextdie. When we later retrieve a cell from one of these lists, we could again use the hash table to find it, but doing so would be repeating work. If we use chaining, then we can add a cell to a list either by inserting the cell itself or a pointer to it, rather than by inserting its coordinates as before. In this way we can locate the cell directly with no need for any search. At the same time, linked lists can help to avoid problems with unnecessary overflow.

specification

For reasons both of flexibility and time saving, therefore, let us decide to use dynamic memory allocation, a chained hash table, and linked lists.

list implementation

The most obvious way to implement the four lists is by connecting the cells into one of the lists by means of a pointer field. This would need to be a second pointer field in the structure for a cell, since the first pointer field is used for chains from the hash table. A subtle problem arises, however. We have no guarantee that the same cell may not simultaneously be on two of the lists, and with only one available pointer field, the entries of the two lists will become mixed up. The obvious way to cure this problem is to keep a total of five pointer fields for each cell, one for the hash-table chain and four for possible use in the four lists. This solution wastes a great deal of space, since many of the cells will not be on any of the four lists, and very few (if any) will be on more than one.

indirect linked list

A much better way is to put pointers to cells into the four lists, not the cells themselves. The result is illustrated in Figure 6.15. Each node of the list thus contains two pointers, one to a cell and one to the next node of the list.

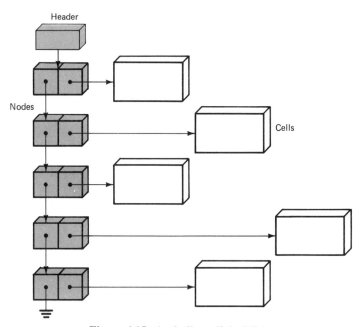

Figure 6.15. An indirect linked list

6.8.3 The Main Program

With these decisions made, we can now tie down the representation and notation for our data structures by writing the main program. Since we are following the method of Life2, the action part is almost identical with that of Life2. The necessary declarations are in lifedef.h, as follows:

```
/* declarations for Life3 */

#define HASHSIZE 997

typedef enum status_tag { ALIVE, DEAD } Status_type;
```

cell information

```
typedef struct cell_tag {              /* description of one position in the grid   */
        Status_type state;
        int nbrs;
        int row, col;
        struct cell_tag *next;
} Cell_type;
```

list specification

```
typedef struct node_tag {              /* Construct indirect linked lists of cells.   */
        Cell_type *entry;
        struct node_tag *next;
} Node_type;

typedef Cell_type *Hashtable_type [HASHSIZE];
```

The main program contains the definitions of the global variables for the hash table and the four lists.

```
#include "lifedef.h"

Hashtable_type H;        /* holds all living cells and dead cells with living neighbors */
Node_type *live, *nextlive;             /* headers for the four                    */
Node_type *die, *nextdie;               /* indirect linked lists                   */

void main(void)
{
        Initialize();
```

main loop

```
        do {
                Vivify(live);
                Kill(die);
                WriteMap();
                AddNeighbors();
                SubtractNeighbors();
                live = nextlive;
                die = nextdie;
                nextlive = NULL;
                nextdie = NULL;
        } while (Enquire());
}
```

6.8.4 Functions

Let us now write several of the functions, so as to show how processing of the cells and of the lists transpires. The remaining functions will be left as exercises.

1. Function Vivify

The task of the function Vivify is to traverse the list live, determine whether each cell on it satisfies the conditions to become alive, and vivify it if so, else delete it from the list. The usual way to facilitate deletion from a linked list is to keep two pointers in lock step, one position apart, while traversing the list. This method appears as an exercise, but here we use another, one that gives a simpler program at the expense of a little time and (temporarily) space.

deletion method   Let us take advantage of the indirect linkage of our lists, and when we wish to delete an entry from the list, let us leave the node in place, but set its entry field to NULL. In this way, the node will be flagged as empty when it is again encountered in the function AddNeighbors.

```
/* Vivify: vivify cells that satisfy conditions to become alive. */
void Vivify (Node_type *live)
{
      Cell_type *c;

      while (live != NULL) {
            c = live->entry;
            if (c->state ==  DEAD && c->nbrs ==  3)
                  c->state = ALIVE;
            else
                  live->entry = NULL;
            live = live->next;
      }
}
```

2. Function AddNeighbors

The task of this function to increase the neighbor count by 1 for each neighbor of all the cells that remain on list live and to add cells to lists nextlive and nextdie when *insertion and* appropriate. The ordering of the cells on these lists is unimportant; hence we shall treat *deletion* them as stacks, since stacks are the easiest lists to process. We shall use an auxiliary function

Node_type *Insert (Node_type *list, Cell_type *p)

to create a new node pointing to the given cell and push it onto the given list.

Finding the neighbors of a given cell will require using the hash table; we shall postpone this task by referring to

Cell_type *GetCell (int x, int y) ;

hash table retrieval   which will return a pointer to the cell being sought, creating the cell if it was not previously in the hash table.

```
/* AddNeighbors: increase neighbor count by 1. */
void AddNeighbors(void)
{
    int x, y;                            /* row and column of a neighbor          */
    Node_type *p, *q;
    Cell_type *neighbor;                 /* cell with coordinates (x, y)          */
    Cell_type *c;

    while (live != NULL) {
        if (live->entry != NULL) {
            c = live->entry;
            for (x = c->row − 1; x <= c->row + 1; x++)
                for (y = c->col − 1; y <= c->col + 1; y++)
                    if (x != c->row || y != c->col) {
                        neighbor = GetCell(x, y);
                        neighbor->nbrs++;
                        switch (neighbor->nbrs) {
                        case 3:
                            if (neighbor->state ==  DEAD)
                                nextlive = Insert(nextlive, neighbor);
                            break;
                        case 4:
                            if (neighbor->state ==  ALIVE)
                                nextdie = Insert(nextdie, neighbor);
                            break;
                        }
                    }
        }
        p = live;
        live = live->next;
        free(p);
    }
}
```

find a neighbor

get the neighbor
update count and
lists

continue traversal

3. Processing the Hash Table

If you compare the two foregoing functions with the corresponding functions for program Life2 in Chapter 2, you will find that they are almost a direct translation from contiguous storage to linked storage. We now turn to the first basic difference, the function that explicitly references the hash table. The task of the function

$$\text{Cell\_type } *\text{GetCell(int x, int y)};$$

task   is first to look in the hash table for the cell with the given coordinates. If the search is successful, then the function returns a pointer to the cell; otherwise, it must create a new cell, assign it the given coordinates, initialize its other fields to the default values, and put it in the hash table as well as return a pointer to it.

This outline translates into the following C function.

```
/* GetCell: return the cell with coordinates (x, y) if it is present; otherwise, create it. */
Cell_type *GetCell(int x, int y)
{
        int location;                           /* location returned by the hash function  */
        Cell_type *p;

        location = Hash(x, y);
        p = H[location];
                        /* p now points to the start of the chain containing the cell at i, j. */
        while (p != NULL)                 /* Search the chain for the desired cell.   */
            if (p->row == x && p->col == y)
                    return p;
            else
                    p = p->next;
/* If the cell was not found we must create a new cell, initialize it, and insert it into the
   hash table. */
        p = (Cell_type *)malloc(sizeof(Cell_type));
        p->row = x;
        p->col = y;
        p->state = DEAD;
        p->nbrs = 0;
        p->next = H[location];
        H[location] = p;

        return p;
}
```

look in hash table — marginal note beside `p = H[location];`

make a new cell — marginal note beside `p = (Cell_type *)malloc(...)`

4. The Hash Function

Our hash function will differ slightly from those earlier in the chapter, in that its argument already comes in two parts (row and column), so that some kind of folding can be done easily. Before deciding how, let us for a moment consider the special case of a small array, where the function is one-to-one and is exactly the index function. When there are exactly maxrow entries in each row, the index i, j maps to

$$i + \text{maxrow} * j$$

to place the rectangular array into contiguous storage, one row after the next.

It should prove effective to use a similar mapping for our hash function, where we replace maxrow by some convenient number (like a prime) that will maximize the spread and reduce collisions. Hence we obtain

```
#define FACTOR 101                      /* Choose a convenient prime.          */

/* Hash: hash function for Life3 */
int Hash(int i, int j)
{
        return (i + FACTOR * j) % HASHSIZE;
}
```

5. Other Subprograms

The remaining subprograms all bear considerable resemblance either to one of the preceding functions or to the corresponding function in Life2, and these subprograms can therefore safely be left as projects.

Programming Projects 6.8

P1. Write the function Kill.

P2. Write the function SubtractNeighbors. You will need to remove a cell from the hash table and dispose of it when it reaches the default case: the cell is dead and has a neighbor count of 0.

P3. Write the function Insert.

P4. Rewrite the function Vivify to use two pointers in traversing the list live, and dispose of redundant nodes when they are encountered. Also make the accompanying simplifications in the functions AddNeighbors and SubtractNeighbors.

P5. The program as we have written it contains a bug, that of dangling pointers. When function SubtractNeighbors disposes of a cell, it may still be on one of the lists nextlive or nextdie, since these are allowed to contain redundant entries. Vivify and Kill may then err in the next generation. Correct the bug as follows.

　　a. Implement the plan of keeping space-available stacks, as discussed in Section 3.2.3. You will need to keep two stacks, one for available cells and one for available nodes. You will need to write four functions for obtaining and disposing of cells and nodes.

　　b. Suppose that there are some (dangling) pointers to cells that have been placed on the available stack. Show that, when the next generation starts, the functions Vivify and Kill will safely remove all such dangling pointers, before the available cells are reused.

P6. Run the complete program Life3. Use the same configurations tested on Life2, and compare the time and space requirements.

POINTERS AND PITFALLS

1. Use top-down design for your data structures, just as you do for your algorithms. First determine the logical structure of the data, then slowly specify more detail, and delay implementation decisions as long as possible.

2. Before considering detailed structures, decide what operations on the data will be required, and use this information to decide whether the data belong in a *list* or a *table*. Traversal of the data structure or access to all the data in a prespecified order generally implies choosing a list. Access to any item in time $O(1)$ generally implies choosing a table.

3. For the design and programming of lists, see Chapters 3–5.

4. Use the logical structure of the data to decide what kind of table to use: an ordinary array, a table of some special shape, a system of inverted tables, or a hash table.

5. Choose the simplest structure that allows the required operations and that meets the space requirements of the problem. Don't write complicated functions to save space that will then remain unused.

6. Let the structure of the data help you decide whether an index function or an access table is better for accessing a table of data. Use the features built into your programming language whenever possible.

7. In using a hash table, let the nature of the data and the required operations help you decide between chaining and open addressing. Chaining is generally preferable if deletions are required, if the records are relatively large, or if overflow might be a problem. Open addressing is usually preferable when the individual records are small and there is no danger of overflowing the hash table.

8. Hash functions must usually be custom-designed for the kind of keys used for accessing the hash table. In designing a hash function, keep the computations as simple and as few as possible while maintaining a relatively even spread of the keys over the hash table. There is no obligation to use every part of the key in the calculation. For important applications, experiment by computer with several variations of your hash function, and look for rapid calculation and even distribution of the keys.

9. Recall from the analysis of hashing that some collisions will almost inevitably occur, so don't worry about the existence of collisions if the keys are spread nearly uniformly through the table.

10. For open addressing, clustering is unlikely to be a problem until the hash table is more than half full. If the table can be made several times larger than the space required for the records, then linear probing should be adequate; otherwise more sophisticated collision resolution may be required. On the other hand, if the table is many times larger than needed, then initialization of all the unused space may require inordinate time.

REVIEW QUESTIONS

6.1 **1.** In terms of the big Oh notation, compare the difference in time required for table lookup and for list searching.

6.2 **2.** What are row- and column-major ordering?

6.3 **3.** Why do jagged tables require access tables instead of index functions?

4. For what purpose are inverted tables used?

5. What is the difference in purpose, if any, between an index function and an access table?

6.4 **6.** What operations are available for an abstract table?

7. What operations are usually easier for a list than for a table?

6.5 **8.** What is the difference in purpose, if any, between an index function and a hash function?

9. What objectives should be sought in the design of a hash function?

10. Name three techniques often built into hash functions.

11. What is *clustering* in a hash table?

12. Describe two methods for minimizing clustering.

13. Name four advantages of a chained hash table over open addressing.

14. Name one advantage of open addressing over chaining.

6.6 15. If a hash function assigns 30 keys to random positions in a hash table of size 300, about how likely is it that there will be no collisions?

REFERENCES FOR FURTHER STUDY

The primary reference for this chapter is KNUTH, Volume 3. (See the end of Chapter 3 for bibliographic details.) Hashing is the subject of Volume 3, pp. 506–549. KNUTH studies every method we have touched, and many others besides. He does algorithm analysis in considerably more detail than we have, writing his algorithms in a pseudoassembly language, and counting operations in detail there.

An alternative treatment that includes careful analysis of algorithms for searching, hashing, as well as other topics, is

LYDIA I. KRONSJO, *Algorithms: Their Complexity and Efficiency*, John Wiley, New York, 1979.

The following book (pp. 156–185) considers arrays of various kinds, index functions, and access tables in considerable detail:

C. C. GOTLIEB and L. R. GOTLIEB, *Data Types and Structures*, Prentice Hall, Englewood Cliffs, N.J., 1978.

Extensions of the birthday surprise are considered in

M. S. KLAMKIN and D. J. NEWMAN, *Journal of Combinatorial Theory* 3 (1967), 279–282.

Sorting

This chapter studies several important methods for sorting lists, both contiguous and linked. At the same time, we shall develop further tools that help with the analysis of algorithms.

7.1 INTRODUCTION AND NOTATION

We live in a world obsessed with keeping information, and to find it, we must keep it in some sensible order. Librarians make sure that no one misplaces a book; income tax authorities trace down every dollar we earn; credit bureaus keep track of almost every detail of our actions. We once saw a cartoon in which a keen filing clerk, anxious to impress the boss, said frenetically, "Let me make sure these files are in alphabetical order before we throw them out." If we are to be the masters of this explosion instead of its victims, we had best learn how to keep track of it all!

practical importance   A few years ago, it was estimated, more than half the time on many commercial computers was spent in sorting. This is perhaps no longer true, since sophisticated methods have been devised for organizing data, methods that do not require that it be kept in any special order. Eventually, nonetheless, the information does go out to people, and then it must be sorted in some way. Because sorting is so important, a great many algorithms have been devised for doing it. In fact, so many good ideas appear in sorting methods that an entire course could easily be built around this one theme. Amongst the differing environments that require different methods, the most important is the distinction

external and   between **external** and **internal**, that is, whether there are so many structures to be sorted
internal sorting   that they must be kept in external files on disks, tapes, or the like, or whether they can all be kept internally in high-speed memory. In this chapter we consider only internal sorting.

reference   It is not our intention to present anything close to a comprehensive treatment of internal sorting methods. For such a treatment, see Volume 3 of the monumental work of D. E. KNUTH (reference given at end of Chapter 3). KNUTH expounds about twenty-five sorting methods and claims that they are "only a fraction of the algorithms that have been devised so far." We shall study only five methods in detail, chosen, first, because they are good—each one can be the best choice under some circumstances; second, because they illustrate much of the variety appearing in the full range of methods; and third, because they are easy to write and understand, without too many details to complicate their presentation. Several variations of these methods will also appear as exercises.

notation   Throughout this chapter we use the same notation as in previous chapters, so that list will be a list of items to be sorted. Each item x will have a key x.key by which the items are to be sorted. To compare keys we shall use macros, as described in Chapter 6, so that our routines can easily be transformed from sorting one kind of keys to another. The macros that we shall need are taken from EQ (equal), LT (less than), GT (greater than), LE (less than or equal), and GE (greater than or equal). If we have a contiguous list list declared in a program, then it will be a structure containing an array entry indexed from 0 to count − 1, where the counter count is also a field in list, and the list pointer lp will be the parameter for the functions we write. The definitions for the types we use are in list.h:

```
#define MAXKEY 10
#define MAXLIST 20                    /* small sizes for testing          */
typedef struct item_tag {
        Key_type key [MAXKEY];
} Item_type;
typedef struct list_tag {
        int count;
        Item_type entry [MAXLIST];
} List_type;
```

If we have a linked list, then each node will consist of a field called info of type Item_type and a field called next that will contain a pointer to the next node. The list is specified by a pointer called head that points to the first item in the list. Our functions return a pointer to the beginning of the sorted list. When the list is contiguous the function returns the same pointer it received because in a contiguous list we rearrange the elements in a fixed contiguous area. When the list is a linked list the function returns a pointer to the head of the list because in a linked list we rearrange the elements by relinking the list.

basic operations In studying searching algorithms, it soon became clear that the total amount of work done was closely related to the number of comparisons of keys. The same observation is true for sorting algorithms, but sorting algorithms must also either change pointers or move items around within the list, and therefore time spent this way is also important, especially in the case of large items kept in a contiguous list. Our analyses will therefore concentrate on these two basic actions.

analysis As for searching algorithms, both the worst-case performance and the average performance of a sorting algorithm are of interest. To find the average, we shall consider what would happen if the algorithm were run on all possible orderings of the list (with n items, there are $n!$ such orderings altogether) and take the average of the results.

7.2 INSERTION SORT

example Every avid player of a card game learns to sort a hand of cards almost automatically. One of the most common approaches is to look at the cards one at a time, and when each new card is seen, to insert it in the proper place in the (partial) hand of cards. This approach leads easily to an algorithm for computer sorting that is so natural that it should be in every programmer's repertoire.

To develop the algorithm, it is better to think of the cards not as held in one's hand, but as being placed face up in a row on a table one at a time as they are being sorted. As each new card is seen, then, it is compared with the row of cards, and some of them are pushed one position to the right to make room to insert the new one. An example is shown in Figure 7.1.

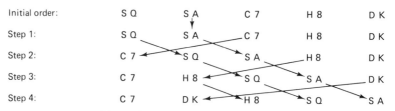

Figure 7.1. Example of insertion sort

The *insertion sort* algorithm thus proceeds on the idea of keeping the first part of the list, when once examined, in the correct order. An initial list with only one item is automatically in order. If we suppose that we have already sorted the first $i-1$ items, then we take item i and search through this sorted list of length $i-1$ to see where to insert item i.

7.2.1 Contiguous Version

For a contiguous list, we could use either sequential or binary search to find the place to insert item i. Binary search produces a slightly more complicated algorithm, and this will be pursued in the exercises. To make our algorithm even simpler, however, we shall here choose sequential search instead. A small trick will simplify the algorithm: If we do the search from the last toward the first item in the sorted list, then at the same time as we search, we can move the items to make room to insert list.entry [i] when we find the proper place. Let us now write the algorithm.

contiguous insertion sort

```
/* InsertSort: sort a list with count elements by the insertion sort method. */
List_type *InsertSort(List_type *lp)
{
    int i, j;
    Item_type tmp;

    for (i = 1; i < lp->count; i++) {
        if (LT(lp->entry[i].key, lp->entry[i-1].key)) {
            tmp = lp->entry[i];         /* Copy unsorted entry from the list.     */
            for (j = i - 1; j >= 0; j--) {  /* Shift previous entries.            */
                lp->entry[j + 1] = lp->entry[j];
                if (j == 0 || LE(lp->entry[j-1].key, tmp.key))
                    break;      /* Found the position for tmp.                   */
            }
            lp->entry[j] = tmp;     /* Copy unsorted entry to correct location. */
        }
    }
    return lp;
}
```

The action of the program is nearly self-explanatory. Since a list with only one item is automatically sorted, the loop on i starts with the second item. If it is in the correct place, nothing needs to be done. Otherwise, the new item is pulled out of the list into the variable tmp, and the for loop pushes items one position down the list until the correct position is found, and finally tmp is inserted there before proceeding to the next unsorted item. The case when tmp belongs in the first position of the list must be treated specially, since in this case there is no item with a smaller key that would terminate the search. We treat this special case by using an if statement to determine if j is at the beginning of the list. The function returns the same pointer it received. We did that to maintain the interface required by the linked version of InsertSort.

7.2.2 Linked Version

algorithm

For a linked version of insertion sort, we shall traverse the original list, taking one item at a time and inserting it in the proper place in the sorted list. The pointer variable tail will give the end of the sorted part of the list, and tail->next will give the first item that has not yet been inserted into the sorted sublist. We shall let q also point to this item, and use a pointer p to search the sorted part of the list to find where to insert what q points to. If q belongs before the current head of the list, then we insert it there. Otherwise, we move p down the list until p->info.key >= q->info.key and then insert q before p. To enable insertion before p (see Section 4.3.1, part 3), we keep a second pointer r in lock step one position closer to the head than p.

stopping the loop

A **sentinel** is an extra item added to one end of a list to ensure that a loop will terminate without having to include a separate check. Since we have tail->next = q, the node q is already in place to serve as a sentinel for the search, and the loop moving p is simplified.

Finally, let us note that a list with 0 or 1 item is already sorted, so that we can check these cases separately and thereby avoid trivialities elsewhere. The details appear in the following function, and are illustrated in Figure 7.2.

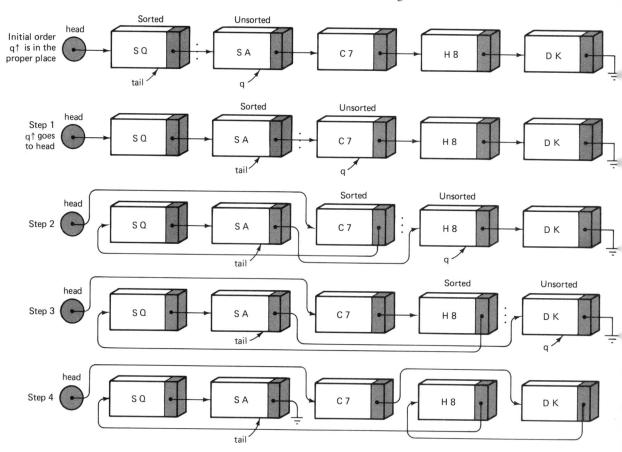

Figure 7.2. Trace of linked insertion sort

linked insertion sort

```
/* InsertSort: sort a linked list of elements by the insertion sort method. */
List_type *InsertSort(List_type *head)
{
        List_type *p, *q, *r, *tail = head;
        if (head)                            /* Proceed only for nonempty list.       */
            while (tail->next) {
                q = tail->next;
                if (LT(q->info.key, head->info.key)) {
                    tail->next = q->next;
                    q->next = head;
                    head = q;       /* new head of the list                  */
                } else {            /* Search sublist.                       */
                    r = head;
                    p = head->next;
                    while (GT(q->info.key, p->info.key)) {
                        r = p;
                        p = p->next;
                    }
                    if (q == p)     /* q is already in place.                */
                        tail = q;
                    else {          /* q goes between r, p.                  */
                        tail->next = q->next;
                        q->next = p;
                        r->next = q;
                    }
                }
            }
        return head;
}
```

The definition for List_type changes accordingly:

```
#define MAXKEY 10

typedef struct item_tag {
      Key_type key[MAXKEY];
} Item_type;

typedef struct list_tag {
      Item_type info;
      struct list_tag *next;
} List_type;
```

Even though the mechanics of the linked version are quite different from those of the contiguous version, you should be able to see that the basic method is the same. The only real difference is that the contiguous version searches the sorted sublist in reverse order, while the linked version searches it in increasing order of position within the list.

7.2.3 Analysis

Since the basic ideas are the same, let us analyze only the performance of the contiguous version of the program. We also restrict our attention to the case when the list list is initially in random order (meaning that all possible orderings of the keys are equally likely). When we deal with item i, how far back must we go to insert it? There are i possible positions: not moving it at all, moving it one position, up to moving it $i - 1$ positions to the front of the list. Given randomness, these are equally likely. The probability that it need not be moved is thus $1/i$, in which case only one comparison of keys is done, with no moving of items.

inserting one item   The contrary case, when item i must be moved, occurs with probability $(i - 1)/i$. Let us begin by counting the average number of iterations of the second for loop. Since all of the $i - 1$ possible positions are equally likely, the average number of iterations is

$$\frac{1 + 2 + \cdots + (i - 1)}{i - 1} = \frac{(i - 1)i}{2(i - 1)} = \frac{i}{2}.$$

One key comparison and one assignment are done for each of these iterations, with one more key comparison done outside the loop, along with two assignments of items. Hence, in this second case, item i requires, on average, $\frac{1}{2}i + 1$ comparisons and $\frac{1}{2}i + 2$ assignments.

When we combine the two cases with their respective probabilities, we have

$$\frac{1}{i} \times 1 + \frac{i - 1}{i} \times \left(\frac{i}{2} + 1\right) = \frac{i + 1}{2}$$

comparisons and

$$\frac{1}{i} \times 0 + \frac{i - 1}{i} \times \left(\frac{i}{2} + 2\right) = \frac{i + 3}{2} - \frac{2}{i}$$

assignments.

inserting all items   We wish to add these numbers from $i = 2$ to $i = n$, but to avoid complications in the arithmetic, we first use the Big Oh notation (see Section 5.6) to approximate each of these expressions by suppressing the terms bounded by a constant. We thereby obtain $\frac{1}{2}i + O(1)$ for both the number of comparisons and the number of assignments of items. In making this approximation, we are really concentrating on the actions within the main loop and suppressing any concern about operations done outside the loop or variations in the algorithm that change the amount of work only by some bounded amount.

To add $\frac{1}{2}i + O(1)$ from $i = 2$ to $i = n$, we apply Theorem A.1 (the sum of the integers from 1 to n), obtaining:

$$\sum_{i=2}^{n} \left(\tfrac{1}{2}i + O(1)\right) = \tfrac{1}{2} \sum_{i=2}^{n} i + O(n) = \tfrac{1}{4}n^2 + O(n).$$

for both the number of comparisons of keys and the number of assignments of items.

So far we have nothing with which to compare this number, but we can note that as n becomes larger, the contributions from the term involving n^2 become much larger

than the remaining terms collected as $O(n)$. Hence as the size of the list grows, the
time needed by insertion sort grows like the square of this size.

best and worst cases   The worst-case analysis of insertion sort will be left as an exercise. We can observe
quickly that the best case for insertion sort occurs when the list is already in order, when
insertion sort will do nothing except $n-1$ comparisons of keys. We can now show that
there is no sorting method that can possibly do better in its best case.

THEOREM 7.1.   *Verifying that a list of n items is in the correct order requires at least $n-1$
comparisons of keys.*

Proof   Consider an arbitrary program that checks whether a list of n items is in order or not
(and perhaps sorts it if it is not). The program will first do some comparison of keys,
and this comparison will involve some two items from the list. Sometime later, at least
one of these two items must be compared with a third, or else there would be no way
to decide where these two should be in the list relative to the third. Thus this second
comparison involves only one new item not previously in a comparison. Continuing in
this way, we see that there must be another comparison involving some one of the first
three items and one new item. Note that we are not necessarily selecting the comparisons
in the order in which the algorithm does them. Thus, except for the first comparison,
each one that we select involves only one new item not previously compared. All n of
the items must enter some comparison, for there is no way to decide whether an item is
in the right place unless it is compared to at least one other item. Thus to involve all n
end of proof   items requires at least $n-1$ comparisons, and the proof is complete.

With this theorem we find one of the advantages of insertion sort: it verifies that a
list is correctly sorted as quickly as can be done. Furthermore, insertion sort remains an
excellent method whenever a list is nearly in the correct order and few items are many
positions removed from their correct locations.

**Exercises
7.2**

E1. By hand, trace through the steps insertion sort will use on each of the following
lists. In each case, count the number of comparisons that will be made and the
number of times an item will be moved.

a. the following three words to be sorted alphabetically:

triangle   square   pentagon.

b. the three words in part (a) to be sorted according to the number of sides of the
corresponding polygon, in increasing order.

c. the three words in part (a) to be sorted according to the number of sides of the
corresponding polygon, in decreasing order.

d. the following seven numbers to be sorted into increasing order:

26 33 35 29 19 12 22

e. the following list of 14 names to be sorted into alphabetical order:

Tim Dot Eva Roy Tom Kim Guy Amy Jon Ann Jim Kay Ron Jan

E2. What initial order for a list of keys will produce the worst case for insertion sort in the contiguous version? In the linked version?

E3. How many key comparisons and item assignments does contiguous insertion sort make in its worst case?

E4. Modify the linked version of insertion sort so that a list that is already sorted, or nearly so, will be processed rapidly.

Programming Projects 7.2

test program for sorting

P1. Write a program that can be used to test and evaluate the performance of insertion sort (and, later, other methods). The following outline may be used.

a. Write the main program for the case of contiguous lists. The main program should use functions to set up the list of items to be sorted, print out the unsorted list if the user wishes, sort the list, and print the sorted list if the user wishes. The program should also determine the amount of CPU time required in the sorting phase, and it should establish counters (which will be updated by inserting code into the sorting function) to keep track of the number of comparisons of keys and assignments of items.

b. Use a random number generator to construct lists of integer numbers to be sorted. Suitable sizes of the lists would be $n = 10, 20, 100,$ and 500. It would be best to keep the lists in permanent files, so that the same lists can be used to evaluate different sorting methods.

c. Write a function to put the random numbers into the keys of items to be sorted. Do at least two cases: First, the structures (of type Item_type) should consist of the key alone, and, second, the structures should be larger, with about 100 words of storage in each structure. The fields other than the key need not be initialized.

d. Run the program to test the performance of contiguous insertion sort for short lists and long ones, and for small structures and large ones.

e. Rewrite the main program for the case of linked lists instead of contiguous ones.

f. Rewrite the function so that it sets up the structures as the nodes of a linked list. Either incorporate the possibility of both small and large structures, or explain why there is no need to do so.

g. Run the program to test the performance of linked insertion sort.

binary insertion sort

P2. Rewrite the contiguous version of function InsertSort so that it uses binary search to locate where to insert the next item. Compare the time needed to sort a list with that of the original function InsertSort. Is it reasonable to use binary search in the linked version of InsertSort? Why or why not?

scan sort

P3. There is an even easier sorting method, which instead of using two pointers to move through the list, uses only one. We can call it *scan sort*, and it proceeds by starting at one end and moving forward, comparing adjacent pairs of keys, until it finds a pair out of order. It then swaps this pair of items, and starts moving the other way, continuing to swap pairs until it finds a pair in the correct order. At this point it knows that it has moved the one item as far back as necessary, so that the first part of the list is sorted, but, unlike insertion sort, it has forgotten how far forward has been sorted, so it simply reverses direction and sorts forward again, looking for a pair out of order. When it reaches the far end of the list, then it is finished.

    a. Write a C program to implement scan sort for contiguous lists. Your program should use only one index variable (other than lp->count), one variable of type Item_type to be used in making swaps, and no other local variables.

    b. Compare the timings for your program with those of InsertSort.

bubble sort **P4.** A well-known algorithm called ***bubble sort*** proceeds by scanning the list from left to right, and whenever a pair of adjacent keys is found to be out of order, then those items are swapped. In this first pass, the largest key in the list will have "bubbled" to the end, but the earlier keys may still be out of order. Thus the pass scanning for pairs out of order is put in a loop that first makes the scanning pass go all the way to lp->count, and at each iteration stops it one position sooner. **(a)** Write a C function for bubble sort. **(b)** Find the number of key comparisons and swaps it makes on average, and compare the results with those for insertion sort.

7.3 SELECTION SORT

Insertion sort has one major disadvantage. Even after most items have been sorted properly into the first part of the list, the insertion of a later item may require that many of them be moved. All the moves made by insertion sort are moves of only one position at a time. Thus to move an item 20 positions up the list requires 20 separate moves. If the items are small, perhaps a key alone, or if the items are in linked storage, then the many moves may not require excessive time. But if the items are very large, structures containing hundreds of components like personnel files or student transcripts, and the structures must be kept in contiguous storage, then it would be far more efficient if, when it is necessary to move an item, it could be moved immediately to its final position. Our next method accomplishes this goal.

1. The Algorithm

This method is also modeled on sorting a hand of cards, but this time the hand is held by a player who likes to look at all his cards at once. As he looks over his cards, he selects the highest one and puts it where it belongs, selects the second highest and puts it in its place, and continues in this way until all the cards are sorted.

    This method (applied to the same hand used to illustrate insertion sort) is demonstrated in Figure 7.3.

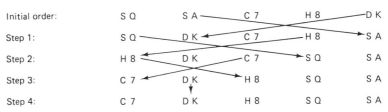

Figure 7.3. Example of selection sort

This method translates into the following algorithm, called selection sort. Since its objective is to minimize data movement, selection sort is primarily useful with contiguous lists, and we therefore give only a contiguous version. The algorithm uses a function called MaxKey, which finds the maximum key on the part of the pointer to list given as the parameter. The function Swap simply swaps the two items with the given indices. For convenience in the discussion to follow, we write these two as separate subprograms.

contiguous selection sort

```
/* SelectSort: sort a list of contiguous elements. */
List_type *SelectSort(List_type *lp)
{
        int i, j;
        for (i = lp->count−1; i > 0; i−−) {
                j = MaxKey(0, i, lp);
                Swap(j, i, lp);
        }
        return lp;
}
```

Note that when all items in a list but one are in the correct place, then the remaining one must be also. Thus the for loop stops at 1.

largest key in list

```
/* MaxKey: find and return index of largest key. */
int MaxKey(int low, int high, List_type *lp)
{
        int i, max = low;
        for (i = low + 1; i <= high; i++)
                if (LT(lp->entry[max].key, lp->entry[i].key))
                        max = i;
        return max;
}
```

interchange items

```
/* Swap: swap two items in a contiguous list. */
void Swap(int i, int j, List_type *lp)
{
        Item_type tmp;
        tmp = lp->entry[i];
        lp->entry[i] = lp->entry[j];
        lp->entry[j] = tmp;
}
```

2. Analysis

ordering unimportant

À *propos* of algorithm analysis, the most remarkable fact about this algorithm is that we can calculate in advance exactly how many times each for loop will iterate. In the number of comparisons it makes, selection sort pays no attention to the original ordering of the list. Hence for a list that is nearly correct to begin with, selection sort is likely to be much slower than insertion sort. On the other hand, selection sort does have the advantage of predictability: its worst-case time will differ little from its best.

advantage of selection sort   The primary advantage of selection sort regards data movement. If an item is in its correct final position, then it will never be moved. Every time any pair of items is swapped, then at least one of them moves into its final position, and therefore at most $n - 1$ swaps are done altogether in sorting a list of n items. This is the very best that we can expect from any method that relies entirely on swaps to move its items.

We can analyze the performance of function SelectSort in the same way that it is programmed. The main function does nothing except some bookkeeping and calling the subprograms. Function Swap is called $n - 1$ times, and each call does 3 assignments of items, for a total count of $3(n - 1)$. The function MaxKey is called $n - 1$ times, with the length of the sublist ranging from n down to 2. If t is the number of items on the part of the list for which it is called, then MaxKey does exactly $t - 1$ comparisons

comparison count for selection sort   of keys to determine the maximum. Hence, altogether, there are

$$(n - 1) + (n - 2) + \cdots + 1 = \tfrac{1}{2}n(n - 1)$$

comparisons of keys, which we approximate to $\tfrac{1}{2}n^2 + O(n)$.

3. Comparisons

Let us pause for a moment to compare the counts for selection sort with those for insertion sort. The results are

	Selection	*Insertion (average)*
Assignments of items	$3.0n + O(1)$	$0.25n^2 + O(n)$
Comparisons of keys	$0.5n^2 + O(n)$	$0.25n^2 + O(n)$

The relative advantages of the two methods appear in these numbers. When n becomes large, $0.25n^2$ becomes much larger than $3n$, and if moving items is a slow process, then insertion sort will take far longer than will selection sort. But the amount of time taken for comparisons is, on average, only about half as much for insertion sort as for selection sort. Under other conditions, then, insertion sort will be better.

Exercises 7.3   **E1.** By hand, trace through the steps selection sort will use on each of the following lists. In each case, count the number of comparisons that will be made and the number of times an item will be moved.

 a. The following three words to be sorted alphabetically:

 triangle   square   pentagon.

 b. The three words in part (a) to be sorted according to the number of sides of the corresponding polygon, in increasing order.

 c. The three words in part (a) to be sorted according to the number of sides of the corresponding polygon, in decreasing order.

 d. The following seven numbers to be sorted into increasing order:

 26 33 35 29 19 12 22.

 e. The following list of 14 names to be sorted into alphabetical order:

 Tim Dot Eva Roy Tom Kim Guy Amy Jon Ann Jim Kay Ron Jan.

E2. There is a simple algorithm called **count sort** that will construct a new, sorted list from a List in a new array, provided we are guaranteed that all the keys in the list are different from each other. Count sort goes through the list once, and for each key lp->entry[i].key scans the list to count how many keys are less than lp->entry[i].key. If c is this count, then the proper position in the sorted list for this key is $c + 1$. Determine how many comparisons of keys will be done by count sort. Is it a better algorithm than selection sort?

Programming Projects 7.3

P1. Run the test program written as a project in the previous section to compare selection sort with insertion sort (contiguous version). Run at least four cases: with small lists (about 20 entries) and large (about 500), and with small items (key only) and large (about 100 words per item). The keys should be placed in random order.

P2. Write and test a linked version of selection sort.

7.4 SHELL SORT

As we have seen, in some ways insertion sort and selection sort behave in opposite ways. Selection sort moves the items very efficiently but does many redundant comparisons. In its best case, insertion sort does the minimum number of comparisons, but is inefficient in moving items only one place at a time. Our goal now is to derive another method avoiding as much as possible the problems with both of these. Let us start with insertion sort and ask how we can reduce the number of times it moves an item.

diminishing increments

The reason why insertion sort can move items only one position is that it compares only adjacent keys. If we were to modify it so that it first compares keys far apart, then it could sort the items far apart. Afterward, the items closer together would be sorted, and finally the increment between keys being compared would be reduced to 1, to ensure that the list is completely in order. This is the idea implemented in 1959 by D. L. SHELL in the sorting method bearing his name. This method is also sometimes called **diminishing increment sort**. Before describing the algorithm formally, let us work through a simple example of sorting names.

example

Figure 7.4 shows what will happen when we first sort all names that are at distance 5 from each other (so there will be only two or three names on each such list), then re-sort the names using increment 3, and finally perform an ordinary insertion sort (increment 1).

You can see that, even though we make three passes through all the names, the early passes move the names close to their final positions, so that at the final pass (which does an ordinary insertion sort), all the items are very close to their final positions so the sort goes rapidly.

choice of increments

There is no magic about the choice of 5, 3, and 1 as increments. Many other choices might work as well or better. It would, however, probably be wasteful to choose powers of 2, such as 8, 4, 2, and 1, since then the same keys compared on one pass would be compared again at the next, whereas by choosing numbers that are not multiples of each other, there is a better chance of obtaining new information from more of the comparisons. Although several studies have been made of Shell sort, no one has been able to prove that one choice of the increments is greatly superior to all others. Various

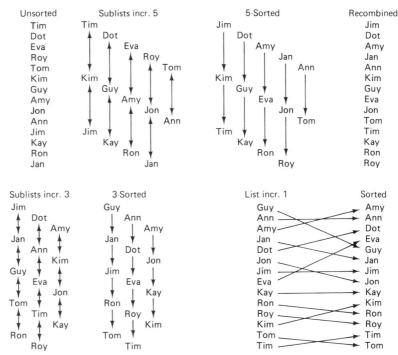

Figure 7.4. Example of Shell sort

suggestions have been made. If the increments are chosen close together, as we have done, then it will be necessary to make more passes, but each one will likely be quicker. If the increments decrease rapidly, then fewer but longer passes will occur. The only essential feature is that the final increment be 1, so that at the conclusion of the process, the list will be checked to be completely in order. For simplicity in the following algorithm, we start with increment = lp->count and at each pass reduce the increment by

$$increment = increment/3 + 1$$

We can now outline the algorithm for contiguous lists.

Shell sort

```
/* ShellSort: sort a contiguous list using Shell Sort. */
List_type *ShellSort(List_type *lp)
{
    int i, increment = lp->count;

    do {
        increment = increment/3 + 1;
        for (i = 0; i < increment; i++)
            InsertSort(i, increment, lp);
    } while (increment > 1);
    return lp;
}
```

analysis

The function InsertSort(i, increment, lp) is exactly the contiguous version of function InsertSort developed in Section 7.2, except that the list starts at the variable i instead of 1 and the increment between successive values is increment instead of 1. The details of modifying InsertSort are left as an exercise.

The analysis of ShellSort turns out to be exceedingly difficult, and to date, good estimates on the number of comparisons and moves have been obtained only under special conditions. It would be very interesting to know how these numbers depend on the choice of increments, so that the best choice might be made. But even without a complete mathematical analysis, running a few large examples on a computer will convince you that ShellSort is quite good. Very large empirical studies have been made of ShellSort, and it appears that the number of moves, when n is large, is in the range of $n^{1.25}$ to $1.6n^{1.25}$. This constitutes a substantial improvement over insertion sort.

Exercises 7.4

E1. By hand, sort the list of 14 names at the beginning of this section using Shell sort with increments of **(a)** 8, 4, 2, 1 and **(b)** 7, 3, 1. Count the number of comparisons and moves that are made in each case.

E2. Explain why Shell sort is ill suited for use with linked lists.

Programming Projects 7.4

P1. Rewrite the function InsertSort to serve as the function Sort embedded in ShellSort.

P2. Run Shell sort on the same data used to compare sorting algorithms in the previous sections, and check its performance against that of insertion sort and selection sort.

7.5 LOWER BOUNDS

Now that we have seen a method that performs much better than our first attempts, it is appropriate to ask,

How fast is it possible to sort?

To answer, we shall limit our attention (as we did when answering the same question for searching) to sorting methods that rely entirely on comparisons between pairs of keys to do the sorting.

comparison tree

Let us take an arbitrary sorting algorithm of this class and consider how it sorts a list of n items. Imagine drawing its comparison tree. Sample comparison trees for insertion sort and selection sort applied to three numbers a, b, c are shown in Figure 7.5. As each comparison of keys is made, it corresponds to an interior vertex (drawn as a circle). The leaves (square nodes) show the order that the numbers have after sorting.

Note that the diagrams show clearly that, on average, selection sort makes more comparisons of keys than insertion sort. In fact, selection sort makes redundant comparisons, repeating comparisons that have already been made.

comparison trees: height and path length

The comparison tree of an arbitrary sorting algorithm displays several features of the algorithm. Its height is the largest number of comparisons that will be made, and hence gives the worst-case behavior of the algorithm. The external path length, after division by the number of leaves, gives the average number of comparisons that the algorithm will do. The comparison tree displays all the possible sequences of comparisons that can be made as all the different paths from the root to the leaves. Since these comparisons

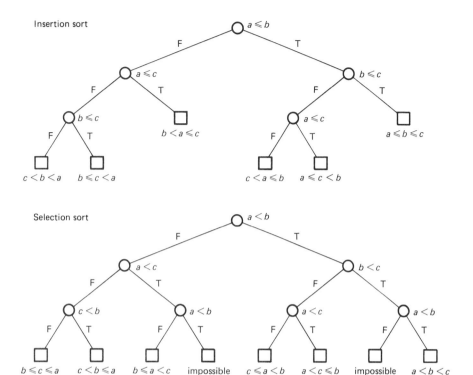

Figure 7.5. Comparison trees, insertion and selection sort, $n = 3$

control how the items are rearranged during sorting, any two different orderings of the list must result in some different decisions, hence different paths through the tree, which must then end in different leaves. The number of ways that the list containing n items could originally have been ordered is $n!$ (see Appendix A.3.1), and thus the number of leaves in the tree must be at least $n!$. Lemma 5.5 now implies that the height of the tree is at least $\lceil \lg n! \rceil$ and its external path length is at least $n! \lg n!$. Translating these results into the number of comparisons, we obtain

THEOREM 7.2.

Any algorithm that sorts a list of n items by use of key comparisons must, in its worst case, perform at least $\lceil \lg n! \rceil$ comparisons of keys, and, in the average case, it must perform at least $\lg n!$ comparisons of keys.

Stirling's formula from Appendix A.3.3 gives an approximation to the factorial of an integer, which, after taking the base 2 logarithm, gives

$$\lg n! \approx (n + \tfrac{1}{2}) \lg n - (\lg e)n + \lg \sqrt{2\pi} + \frac{\lg e}{12n}.$$

approximating $\lg n!$ The constants in this expression have the approximate values

$$\lg e \approx 1.442695041$$

$$\lg \sqrt{2\pi} \approx 1.325748069.$$

This approximation to $\lg n!$ is very close indeed, much closer than we shall ever need for analyzing algorithms. For almost all purposes, the following rough approximation will prove quite satisfactory:

$$\lg n! \approx (n + \tfrac{1}{2})(\lg n - 1\tfrac{1}{2}) + 2$$

and often we use only the approximation $\lg n! = n \lg n + O(n)$.

other methods

Before ending this section we should note that there are sometimes methods for sorting that do not use comparisons and can be faster. For example, if you know in advance that you have 100 items and that their keys are exactly the integers between 1 and 100 in some order, with no duplicates, then the best way to sort them is not to do any comparisons, but simply, if a particular item has key i, then place it in location i. With this method we are (at least temporarily) regarding the items to be sorted as being in a table rather than a list, and then we can use the key as an index to find the proper place in the table for each item. Project P1 suggests an extension of this idea to an algorithm.

Exercises 7.5

E1. Draw the comparison trees for (a) insertion sort and (b) selection sort applied to four objects.

E2. (a) Find a sorting method for four keys that is optimal in the sense of doing the smallest possible number of key comparisons in its worst case. (b) Find how many comparisons your algorithm does in the average case (applied to four keys). Modify your algorithm to make it come as close as possible to achieving the lower bound of $\lg 4! \approx 4.585$ key comparisons. Why is it impossible to achieve this lower bound?

E3. Suppose that you have a shuffled deck of 52 cards, 13 cards in each of 4 suits, and you wish to sort the deck so that the 4 suits are in order and the 13 cards within each suit are also in order. Which of the following methods is fastest?

   a. Go through the deck and remove all the clubs; then sort them separately. Proceed to do the same for the diamonds, the hearts, and the spades.

   b. Deal the cards into 13 piles according to the rank of the card. Stack these 13 piles back together and deal into 4 piles according to suit. Stack these back together.

   c. Make only one pass through the cards, by placing each card in its proper position relative to the previously sorted cards.

Programming Projects 7.5

P1. Construct a list of n (pseudo-)random numbers between 0 and 1. Suitable values for n are 10 (for debugging) and 500 (for comparing the program with other methods). Write a program to sort these numbers into a table via the following "interpolation sort." First, clear the table (to all -1). For each number from the old list, multiply it by n, take the integer part, and look in that position of the table. If that position is -1, put the number there. If not, move left or right (according to the relative size of the current number and the one in its place) to find the place to insert the

interpolation sort

new number, moving the entries in the table over if necessary to make room (as in the fashion of insertion sort). Show that your algorithm will really sort the numbers correctly. Compare its running time with that of the other sorting methods applied to the same unsorted list.

linked distribution sort

P2. [suggested by B. LEE] Write a program to perform a linked distribution sort, as follows. Take the keys to be numbers, as in the previous project; set up an array of linked lists; and distribute the keys into the linked lists according to their magnitude. The linked lists can either be kept sorted as the numbers are inserted or sorted during a second pass, during which the lists are all connected together into one sorted list. Experiment to determine the optimum number of lists to use. (It seems that it works well to have enough lists so that the average length of each list is about 3.)

7.6 DIVIDE AND CONQUER

If you compare the lower bounds derived in the last section with the expected performance of insertion sort and selection sort, then you will see that there is a considerable gap. If $n = 1000$, for example, then insertion sort does about 250,000 comparisons, and selection sort does about 500,000, whereas the lower bound is about 8,500. An optimal method, therefore, should run almost 30 times faster than insertion sort when $n = 1000$. In this section we shall derive more sophisticated sorting algorithms that come close to providing the best performance that the lower bounds will allow.

7.6.1 The Main Ideas

shorter is easier

Making a fresh start is often a good idea, and we shall do so by forgetting (temporarily) almost everything that we know about sorting. Let us try to apply only one important principle that has shown up in every method we have done and that we know from common experience: It is much easier to sort short lists than long ones. If the number of items to be sorted doubles, then the work more than doubles (with insertion or selection sort it quadruples, roughly). Hence if we can find a way to divide the list into two roughly equal-sized lists and sort them separately, then we will save work. If you were working in a library and were given a thousand index cards to put in alphabetical order, then a good way would be to distribute them into piles according to the first letter and sort the piles separately.

divide and conquer

The idea of dividing a problem into smaller but similar subproblems is called ***divide and conquer***. First, we note that comparisons by computer are usually two-way branches, so we shall divide the items to sort into two lists at each stage of the process.

What method, you may ask, should we use to sort the reduced lists? Since we have (temporarily) forgotten all the other methods we know, let us simply use the same method, divide and conquer, again, repeatedly subdividing the list. But we won't keep going forever: Sorting a list with only one item doesn't take any work, even if we know no formal sorting methods.

In summary, let us informally outline divide-and-conquer sorting:

divide-and-conquer
sorting

```
void Sort(list)
{
    if (list has length greater than 1) {
        Partition the list into lowlist, highlist;
        Sort(lowlist);
        Sort(highlist);
        Combine(lowlist, highlist);
    }
}
```

We still must decide how we are going to partition the list into two sublists and, after they are sorted, how we are going to combine the sublists into a single list. There are two methods, each of which works very well in different circumstances.

1. *Mergesort*: In the first method we simply chop the list into two sublists of sizes as nearly equal as possible and then sort them separately. Afterward, we carefully merge the two sorted sublists into a single sorted list. Hence this method is called **mergesort**.

2. *Quicksort*: The second method does more work in the first step of partitioning the list into two sublists, and the final step of combining the sublists then becomes trivial. This method was invented and christened **quicksort** by C. A. R. HOARE. To partition the list, we first choose some key from the list for which, we hope, about half the keys will come before and half after. Call this key the **pivot**. Then we *pivot* partition the items so that all those with keys less than the pivot come in one sublist, and all those with greater keys come in another. Then we sort the two reduced lists separately, put the sublists together, and the whole list will be in order.

7.6.2 An Example

Before we refine our methods into detailed functions, let us work through a specific example. We take the following seven numbers to sort:

$$26 \quad 33 \quad 35 \quad 29 \quad 19 \quad 12 \quad 22.$$

1. Mergesort Example

The first step of mergesort is to chop the list into two. When (as in this example) the list has odd length, let us establish the convention of making the left sublist one entry larger than the right sublist. Thus we divide the list into

$$26 \quad 33 \quad 35 \quad 29 \qquad \text{and} \qquad 19 \quad 12 \quad 22$$

first half and first consider the left sublist. It is again chopped in half as

$$26 \quad 33 \qquad \text{and} \qquad 35 \quad 29.$$

For each of these sublists, we again apply the same method, chopping each of them into sublists of one number each. Sublists of length one, of course, require no sorting. Finally, then, we can start to merge the sublists to obtain a sorted list. The sublists 26 and 33 merge to give the sorted list 26 33, and the sublists 35 and 29 merge to give

29 35. At the next step we merge these two sorted sublists of length two to obtain a sorted sublist of length four,

26   29   33   35.

second half   Now that the left half of the original list is sorted, we do the same steps on the right half. First, we chop it into the sublists

19   12   and   22.

The first of these is divided into two sublists of length one, which are merged to give 12 19. The second sublist, 22, has length one so needs no sorting. It is now merged with 12 19 to give the sorted list

12   19   22.

Finally, the sorted sublists of lengths four and three are merged to produce

12   19   22   26   29   33   35.

2. Quicksort Example

Let us again work through the same example, this time applying quicksort, and keeping careful account of the execution of steps from our outline of the method. To use quicksort, *choice of pivot*   we must first decide, in order to partition the list into two pieces, what key to choose as the pivot. We are free to choose any number we wish, but for consistency, we shall adopt a definite rule. Perhaps the simplest rule is to choose the first number on a list as the pivot, and we shall do so in this example. For practical applications, however, other choices are usually better.

partition   Our first pivot, then, is 26, and the list partitions into sublists

19   12   22   and   33   35   29

consisting, respectively, of the numbers less than and greater than the pivot. We have left the order of the items in the sublists unchanged from that in the original list, but this decision also is arbitrary. Some versions of quicksort put the pivot into one of the sublists, but we choose to place the pivot into neither sublist.

We now arrive at the next line of the outline, which tells us to sort the first sublist. We thus start the algorithm over again from the top, but this time applied to the shorter *lower half*   list

19   12   22.

The pivot of this list is 19, which partitions its list into two sublists of one number each, 12 in the first and 22 in the second. With only one entry each, these sublists do not need sorting, so we arrive at the last line of the outline, whereupon we combine the two sublists with the pivot between them to obtain the sorted list

12   19   22.

Now the call to the sort function is finished for this sublist, so it returns whence it was called. It was called from within the sort function for the full list of seven numbers, so we now go on to the next line of that function.

We have now used the function twice, with the second instance occurring within the first instance. Note carefully that the two instances of the function are working on different lists and are as different from each other as is executing the same code twice within a loop. It may help to think of the two instances as having different colors, so that the instructions in the second (inner) call could be written out in full in place of the call, but in a different color of ink, thereby clearly distinguishing them as a separate instance of the function. The steps of this process are illustrated in Figure 7.6.

Sort (26, 33, 35, 29, 19, 12, 22)

Partition into (19, 12, 22) and (33, 35, 29); pivot = 26

Sort (19, 12, 22)

Partition into (12) and (22); pivot = 19

Sort (12)

Sort (22)

Combine into (12, 19, 22)

Sort (33, 35, 29)

Partition into (29) and (35); pivot = 33

Sort (29)

Sort (35)

Combine into (29, 33, 35)

Combine into (12, 19, 22, 26, 29, 33, 35)

Figure 7.6. Execution trace of quicksort

upper half   Returning to our example, we find the next line of the first instance of the function to be another call to sort another list, this time the three numbers

$$33 \quad 35 \quad 29.$$

As in the previous (inner) call, the pivot 33 immediately partitions the list, giving sublists of length one that are then combined to produce the sorted list

$$29 \quad 33 \quad 35.$$

recombine   Finally, this call to sort returns, and we reach the last line of the (outer) instance that sorts the full list. At this point, the two sorted sublists of length three are combined with the original pivot of 26 to obtain the sorted list

$$12 \quad 19 \quad 22 \quad 26 \quad 29 \quad 33 \quad 35$$

and the process is complete.

7.6.3 Recursion

A function like divide and conquer, that calls itself (or calls one function that calls another and so on until the first is called again) is termed ***recursive***. Recursive functions are often the easiest and most natural way to solve a problem. At first, some people feel slightly uncomfortable with recursive functions. Recursion may perhaps appear at first to be an infinite process, but there is no more danger of writing infinite recursion than of writing an infinite iterative loop. In fact, the dangers are less, since an infinite recursion will soon run out of space and terminate the program, while infinite iteration *termination* may continue until manually terminated. In our function we have deliberately ensured that when the list has size 1 or less, there is no recursion. When the list is longer, each recursive call is with a list strictly smaller than before. The process will therefore terminate in a finite number of steps.

further study The importance of recursion makes it the major topic of Chapter 8, where we shall also explain some details of how a recursive function works on most computer systems. Appendix B, furthermore, describes methods for converting recursive functions into equivalent nonrecursive ones. These methods are useful if you must program in one of the older languages (such as FORTRAN, COBOL, or BASIC) that do not provide for recursion.

7.6.4 Tree of Subprogram Calls

With all the recursive calls through which we worked our way, the examples we have studied may lead you to liken recursion to the fable of the Sorcerer's Apprentice, who, when he had enchanted a broom to fetch water for him, did not know how to stop it and so chopped it in two, whereupon it started duplicating itself until there were so many brooms fetching water that disaster would have ensued had the master not returned.

The easy way to keep track of all the calls in our quicksort example is to draw a tree, as in Figure 7.7. The two calls to Sort at each level are shown as the children of the vertex. The sublists of size 1 or 0, which need no sorting, are drawn as the leaves. In the other vertices (to save space) we include only the pivot that is used for the call.

tree of subprogram Drawing a tree can prove a good way to study the structure of subprogram calls, even when recursion is not involved. The main program is shown as the root of the tree, *calls* and all the calls that the main program makes directly are shown as the vertices directly below the root. Each of these subprograms may, of course, call other subprograms, which are shown as further vertices on lower levels. In this way the tree grows into a

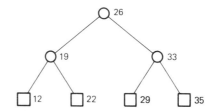

Figure 7.7. Recursion tree, quicksort of 7 numbers

recursion tree

form like the one in Figure 7.8. We shall call such a tree a ***tree of subprogram calls***. We are especially interested in recursion, so that often we draw only the part of the tree showing the recursive calls, and call it a ***recursion tree***.

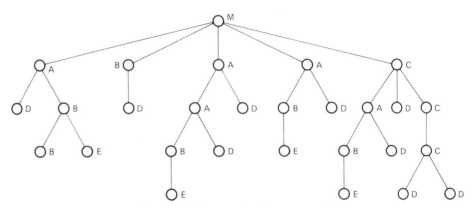

Figure 7.8. A tree of subprogram calls

execution trace

From the diagram, you should notice, first, that in drawing the tree recursion is in no way an exception: different recursive calls appear simply as different vertices that happen to have the same name of a subprogram. Second, note carefully that the tree shows the calls to subprograms, not the nesting of declarations of subprograms. Hence a subprogram called from only one place, but within a loop executed more than once, will appear several times in the tree, once for each execution of the loop. Similarly, if a subprogram is called from a conditional statement that is not executed, then the call will not appear in the tree.

stack frames

A closely related picture of recursion is that of ***stack frames***; refer for a moment to Figure 3.3. The stack frames show the nesting of recursive calls and also illustrate the storage requirements for recursion. If a function calls itself recursively several times, then separate copies of the variables declared in the function are created for each recursive call. In the usual implementation of recursion, these are kept on a stack. Note that the

space requirement

amount of space needed for this stack is proportional to the height of the recursion tree, not to the total number of nodes in the tree. That is, the amount of space needed to implement a recursive function depends on the *depth* of recursion, not on the *number* of times the function is invoked.

example

If you are still uneasy about the workings of recursion, then you will find it helpful to pause and work through sorting the list of 14 names introduced in previous sections, using both mergesort and quicksort. As a check, Figure 7.9 provides the tree of calls for quicksort in the same abbreviated form used for the previous example. This tree is given for two versions, one where the pivot is the first key in each sublist, and one where the central key (center left for even-sized lists) is the pivot.

Exercises
7.6

E1. Apply quicksort to the list of seven numbers considered in this section, where the pivot in each sublist is chosen to be **(a)** the last number in the sublist and **(b)** the center (or left-center) number in the sublist. In each case, draw the tree of recursive calls.

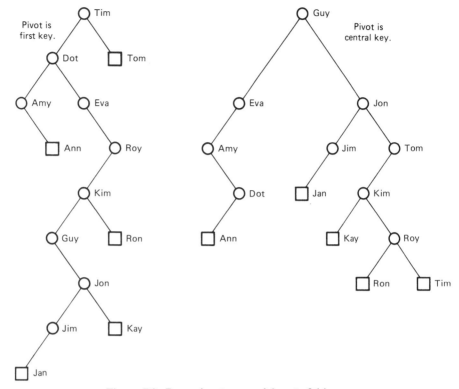

Figure 7.9. Recursion trees, quicksort of 14 names

E2. Apply mergesort to the list of 14 names considered for previous sorting methods:

Tim Dot Eva Roy Tom Kim Guy Amy Jon Ann Jim Kay Ron Jan.

E3. Apply quicksort to this list of 14 names, and thereby sort them by hand into alphabetical order. Take the pivot to be **(a)** the first key in each sublist and **(b)** the center (or left-center) key in each sublist. See Figure 7.9.

E4. In both divide-and-conquer methods we have attempted to divide the list into two sublists of approximately equal size, but the basic outline of sorting by divide-and-conquer remains valid without equal-sized halves. Consider dividing the list so that one sublist has size only 1. This leads to two methods, depending on whether the work is done in splitting one element from the list or in combining the sublists. Show that one of these methods is exactly the same method as insertion sort and the other is the same as selection sort.

    a. Split the list by finding the item with the largest key and making it the sublist of size 1. After sorting the remaining items, the sublists are combined easily by placing the item with largest key last.

    b. Split off the last item from the list. After sorting the remaining items, merge this item into the list.

7.7 MERGESORT FOR LINKED LISTS

Let us now turn to the writing of formal functions for each of our sorting methods. In the case of mergesort, we shall write a version for linked lists and leave the case of contiguous lists as an exercise. For quicksort, we shall do the reverse. Both of these methods, however, work well for both contiguous and linked lists.

7.7.1 The Functions

Our outline of the basic method for mergesort translates directly into the following function, which should be invoked from the calling program with its calling parameter being a pointer to the head of the list to be sorted. To establish parameter conventions the same as those for other sorting methods, this calling program should be a function with only one parameter, of type pointer to List_type, which is passed to the following function.

main function,
linked merge sort

```
/* MergeSort: use mergesort to sort a linked list */
List_type *MergeSort(List_type *p)
{
        List_type *q;
        List_type *head = p;

        if (p && p->next) {
                q = Divide(p);
                p = MergeSort(p);
                q = MergeSort(q);
                head = Merge(p, q);
        }
        return head;
}
```

The definition for List_type appears in list.h:

type item

```
typedef struct item_tag {
                Key_type key;
} Item_type;

typedef struct list_tag {
                Item_type info;
                struct list_tag *next;
} List_type;
```

The first subsidiary function, Divide, takes the list, divides it in half, and returns with a pointer to the start of the second half. The second function, Merge(p, q), merges the lists to which p and q point to, returning a pointer to the merged list. These subsidiary functions follow.

/ Divide: divide the list into two lists.* p *points to the first half of the list. The function returns a pointer to the second half of the list. */*

chop linked list in   List_type *Divide(List_type *p)
half   {

```
        List_type *q, *r;

        q = p;
        r = p->next->next;              /* There must be at least two nodes in the list. */
        while (r) {                         /* Move r two positions for each move of q. */
                r = r->next;
                q = q->next;
                if (r)
                        r = r->next;
        }
        r = q->next;                    /* Break the list after q.                         */
        q->next = NULL;
        return r;                       /* Return pointer to the second half.     */
}
```

/ Merge: merge two sorted lists into one and return a pointer to the resulting list. */*

merge two sorted   List_type *Merge(List_type *p, List_type *q)
linked lists   {

```
        List_type *head, *r;
        if (!p || !q)
                Error("Merge called with empty list(s).");
        if (LE(p->info.key, q->info.key)) {
                head = p;
                p = p->next;
        } else {
                head = q;
                q = q->next;
        }
        r = head;                       /* Point to first entry of merged list.     */
        while (p && q)                  /* Attach node with smaller key.            */
                if (LE(p->info.key, q->info.key)) {
                        r = r->next = p;
                        p = p->next;
                } else {
                        r = r->next = q;
                        q = q->next;
                }
        if (p)                          /* Attach remaining list to result.         */
                r->next = p;
        else
                r->next = q;
        return head;
}
```

7.7.2 Analysis of Mergesort

Now that we have a working function for mergesort, it is time to pause and determine its behavior, so that we can make reasonable comparisons with other sorting methods. As with other algorithms on linked lists, we need not be concerned with the time needed to move items. We concentrate instead on the number of comparisons of keys that the function will do.

1. Counting Comparisons

merge function

Comparison of keys is done at only one place in the complete mergesort function. This place is within the main loop of the merge (sub-)function. After each comparison one of the two nodes is sent to the output list. Hence the number of comparisons certainly cannot exceed the number of nodes being merged. To find the total lengths of these lists, let us again consider the recursion tree of the algorithm, which for simplicity we draw in Figure 7.10 for the case when $n = 2^m$ is a power of 2.

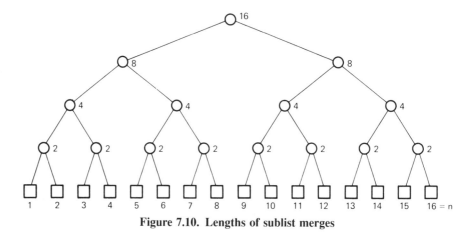

Figure 7.10. Lengths of sublist merges

It is clear from the tree of Figure 7.10 that the total length of the lists on each level is precisely n, the total number of items. In other words, every item is treated in precisely one merge on each level. Hence the total number of comparisons done on each level cannot exceed n. The number of levels, excluding the leaves (for which no merges are done), is $\lceil \lg n \rceil$. The number of comparisons of keys done by mergesort on a list of n items, therefore, is certainly no more than $n \lceil \lg n \rceil$.

2. Contrast with Insertion Sort

Recall (Section 7.2.3) that insertion sort does more than $\frac{1}{4}n^2$ comparisons of keys, on average, in sorting n items. As soon as n becomes greater than 16, $\lg n$ becomes less than $\frac{1}{4}n$, and when n is of practical size for sorting a list, $\lg n$ is far less than $\frac{1}{4}n$, and therefore the number of comparisons done by mergesort is far less than the number done by insertion sort. When $n = 1024$, for example, then $\lg n = 10$, so that the bound on comparisons for mergesort is 10,240, whereas the average number that insertion sort will do is more than 250,000. A problem requiring a half-hour of computer time using insertion sort will probably require hardly a minute using mergesort.

$n \lg n$

The appearance of the expression $n \lg n$ in the preceding calculation is by no means accidental, but relates closely to the lower bounds established in Section 7.5, where it was proved that any sorting method that uses comparisons of keys must do at least

$$\lg n! = n \lg n - 1.44n + O(\log n)$$

comparisons of keys. When n is large, the first term of this expression becomes more important than the others. We have now found, in mergesort, an algorithm that comes within reach of this lower bound.

3. Improving the Count

By being somewhat more careful we can, in fact, obtain a more accurate count of comparisons made by mergesort, that will show that its actual performance comes even closer to the best possible number of comparisons of keys allowed by the lower bound.

First, let us observe that merging two lists of total size k never requires k comparisons, but instead at most $k - 1$, since after the second largest key has been put out, there is nothing left to which to compare the largest key, so it goes out without another comparison. Hence we should reduce our total count of comparisons by 1 for each merge that is performed. The total number of merges is essentially

$$\frac{n}{2} + \frac{n}{4} + \frac{n}{8} + \cdots + 1 = n - 1.$$

(This calculation is exact when n is a power of 2 and is a good approximation otherwise.) The total number of key comparisons done by mergesort is therefore less than

$$n \lg n - n + 1.$$

Second, we should note that it is possible for one of the two lists being merged to be finished before the other, and then all items in the second list will go out with no further comparisons, so that the number of comparisons may well be less than we have calculated. Every element of one list, for example, might precede every element of the second list, so that all elements of the second list would come out using no comparisons.

improved count   The exercises outline a proof that the total count can be reduced, on average, to

$$n \lg n - 1.1583n + 1,$$

and the correct coefficient of n is likely close to -1.25. We thus see that, not only is the leading term as small as the lower bound permits, but the second term is also quite close. By refining the merge function even more, the method can be brought within a few percent of the theoretically optimal number of comparisons (see references).

4. Conclusions

advantages of linked
mergesort

From these remarks it may appear that mergesort is the ultimate sorting method, and, indeed, for linked lists in random order, it is difficult to surpass. We must remember, however, that considerations other than comparing keys are important. The program we have written spends significant time finding the center of the list, so that it can break it in half. The exercises discuss one method for saving some of this time. The linked version of mergesort uses space efficiently. It needs no large auxiliary arrays or other lists, and since the depth of recursion is only $\lg n$, the amount of space needed to keep track of the recursive calls is very small.

5. Contiguous Mergesort

three-way trade-off
for merging

For contiguous lists, unfortunately, mergesort is not such an unqualified success. The difficulty is in merging two contiguous lists without substantial expense in one of (1) space, (2) computer time, or (3) programming effort. The first and most straightforward way to merge two contiguous lists is to use an auxiliary array large enough to hold the combined list and copy the entries into the array as the lists are merged. This method requires extra space proportional to n. For a second method, we could put the sublists to be merged next to each other, forget the amount of order they already have, and use a method like insertion sort to put the combined list into order. This approach uses almost no extra space, but uses computer time proportional to n^2, compared to time proportional to n for a good merging algorithm. Finally (see references), algorithms have been invented that will merge two contiguous lists in time proportional to n while using only a small, fixed amount of extra space. These algorithms, however, are quite complicated.

Exercises
7.7

E1. An article in a 1984 professional journal stated, "This recursive process [merge-sort] takes time $O(n \log n)$, and so runs 64 times faster than the previous method [insertion sort] when sorting 256 numbers." Criticize this statement.

E2. The count of key comparisons in merging is usually too high, since it does not account for the fact that one list may be finished before the other. It might happen, for example, that all entries in the first list come before any in the second list, so that the number of comparisons is just the length of the first list. For this exercise, assume that all numbers in the two lists are different and that all possible arrangements of the numbers are equally likely.

   a. Show that the average number of comparisons performed by our algorithm to merge two ordered lists of length 2 is $8\!/\!3$. [*Hint*: Start with the ordered list 1, 2, 3, 4. Write down the six ways of putting these numbers into two ordered lists of length 2, and show that four of these ways will use 3 comparisons, and two will use 2 comparisons.]

   b. Show that the average number of comparisons done to merge two ordered lists of length 3 is 4.5.

   c. Show that the average number of comparisons done to merge two ordered lists of length 4 is 6.4.

   d. Use the foregoing results to obtain the improved total count of key comparisons for mergesort.

   e. Show that, as m tends to infinity, the average number of comparisons done to merge two ordered lists of length m approaches $2m - 2$.

fixed-space
linear-time merging

E3. [*Challenging*] The straightforward method for merging two contiguous lists, by building the merged list in a separate array, uses extra space proportional to the number of items in the two lists, but can be written to run efficiently, with time proportional to the number of items. Try to devise a merging method for contiguous lists that will require as little extra space as possible, but that will still run in time (linearly) proportional to the number of items in the lists. [There is a solution using only a small, constant amount of extra space. See references.]

Programming Projects 7.7

P1. Implement mergesort for linked lists on your computer. Use the same conventions and the same test data used for implementing and testing the linked version of insertion sort. Compare the performance of mergesort and insertion sort for short and long lists, as well as for lists nearly in correct order and in random order.

P2. Our mergesort program for linked lists spends significant time locating the center of each sublist, so that it can be broken in half. Implement the following modification that will save most of this time. First set up a structure to describe a linked list that will contain not only (a) a pointer to the head of the list, but also (b) a pointer to the center of the list and (c) the length of the list. At the beginning, the original list must be traversed once to determine this information. With this information, it becomes easy to break the list in half and obtain the lengths of the sublists. The center of a sublist can be found by traversing only half the sublist. Rewrite the mergesort function to pass the structures describing linked lists as calling parameters, and use them to speed up the subdivision of the lists.

P3. Our mergesort function pays little attention to whether or not the original list was partially in the correct order. In ***natural mergesort*** the list is broken into sublists at the end of an increasing sequence of keys, instead of arbitrarily at its halfway point. This exercise requests the implementation of two versions of natural mergesort.

natural mergesort

In the first version the original list is traversed only once, and only two sublists are used. As long as the order of the keys is correct, the nodes are placed in the first sublist. When a key is found out of order, the first sublist is ended and the second started. When another key is found out of order, the second sublist is ended, and the second sublist merged into the first. Then the second sublist is repeatedly built again and merged into the first. When the end of the original list is reached, the sort is finished. This first version is simple to program, but as it proceeds, the first sublist is likely to become much longer than the second, and the performance of the function will degenerate toward that of insertion sort.

one sorted list

The second version ensures that the lengths of sublists being merged are closer to being equal and, therefore, that the advantages of divide and conquer are fully used. This method keeps a (small) auxiliary array containing (a) the lengths and (b) pointers to the heads of the ordered sublists that are not yet merged. The entries in this array should be kept in order according to the length of sublist. As each (naturally ordered) sublist is split from the original list, it is put into the auxiliary array. If there is another list in the array whose length is between half and twice that of the new list, then the two are merged, and the process repeated. When the original list is exhausted, any remaining sublists in the array are merged (smaller lengths first) and the sort is finished.

several sorted lists

There is nothing sacred about the ratio of 2 in the criterion for merging sublists. Its choice merely ensures that the number of entries in the auxiliary array cannot exceed $\lg n$ (prove it!). A smaller ratio (required to be greater than 1) will make the auxiliary table larger, and a larger ratio will lessen the advantages of divide and conquer. Experiment with test data to find a good ratio to use.

contiguous mergesort

P4. Devise a version of mergesort for contiguous lists. The difficulty is to produce a function to merge two sorted lists in contiguous storage. It is necessary to use some additional space other than that needed by the two lists. The easiest solution is to use two arrays, each large enough to hold all the items in the two original lists. The two sorted sublists occupy different parts of the same array. As they are merged, the new list is built in the second array. After the merge is complete, the new list can, if desired, be copied back into the first array. Otherwise, the roles of the two arrays can be reversed for the next stage.

radix sort

P5. A formal sorting algorithm predating computers was first devised for use with punched cards, but can be developed into a very efficient sorting method for linked lists. The idea is to consider the key one character at a time and to divide the items, not into two sublists, but into as many sublists as there are possibilities for the given character from the key. If our keys, for example, are words or other alphabetic strings, then we divide the list into 26 sublists at each stage. Punched cards have 12 rows; hence mechanical card sorters work on only one column at a time and divide the cards into 12 piles.

method

A person sorting words by this method would first distribute the words into 26 lists according to the initial letter, then divide each of these sublists into further sublists according to the second letter, and so on. The following idea eliminates this multiplicity of sublists: Partition the items into sublists first by the least significant position, not the most significant. After this first partition, the sublists are put back together as a single list, in the order given by the character in the least significant position. The list is then partitioned according to the second least significant position and recombined as one list. When, after repetition of these steps, the list has been partitioned by the most significant place and recombined, it will be completely sorted.

program

Implement this method in C for linked lists, where the keys are strings of letters or blanks of fixed length. The sublists should be treated as linked queues, and you will need an array of 27 such queues, indexed by the letters and by the character blank (or some substitute character). Within a loop running from the least to most significant positions, you should traverse the linked list, and add each item to the end of the appropriate queue. After the list has been thus partitioned, recombine the queues into one list by linking the tail of each queue to the head of the next. At the end of the major loop on positions, the list will be completely sorted.

testing

Run radix sort on the same data used to check linked mergesort, and compare the results. Note that the time used by radix sort is proportional to nk, where n is the number of items being sorted and k is the number of characters in a key. The time for mergesort is proportional to $n \lg n$. The relative performance of the methods will therefore relate in some ways to the relative sizes of k and $\lg n$.

7.8 QUICKSORT FOR CONTIGUOUS LISTS

We now turn to the method of quicksort, in which the list is first partitioned into lower and upper sublists for which all keys are, respectively, less than some pivot key or greater than the pivot key. Quicksort can be developed for linked lists with little difficulty, and this project will be pursued in the exercises. The most important applications of quicksort, however, are to contiguous lists, where it can prove to be very fast, and where it has the advantage over contiguous mergesort of not requiring a choice between using substantial extra space for an auxiliary array or investing great programming effort in implementing a complicated and difficult merge algorithm.

7.8.1 The Main Function

Our task in developing contiguous quicksort consists essentially in writing an algorithm for partitioning items in an array by use of a pivot key, swapping the items within the array so that all those with keys before the pivot come first, then the item with the pivot key, and then the items with larger keys. We shall let pivotloc provide the index of the pivot in the partitioned list.

Since the partitioned sublists are kept in the same array, in the proper relative positions, the final step of combining sorted sublists is completely vacuous and thus is omitted from the function.

To apply the sorting function recursively to sublists, the bounds low and high of the sublists need to be parameters for the function. Our other sorting functions, however, had the list as the only parameter, so for consistency of notation we do the recursion in a function Sort that is invoked by the following function:

main function,
quicksort
```
/* QuickSort: use quicksort to sort a contiguous list. */
List_type *QuickSort(List_type *lp)
{
        Sort(lp, 0, lp->count − 1);
        return lp;
}
```

The actual quicksort function for contiguous lists is then

recursive function,
quicksort
```
/* Sort: sort the contiguous list between low and high. */
void Sort(List_type *lp, int low, int high)
{
        int pivotloc;

        if (low < high) {
                pivotloc = Partition(lp, low, high);
                Sort(lp, low, pivotloc − 1);
                Sort(lp, pivotloc + 1, high);
        }
}
```

7.8.2 Partitioning the List

Now we must construct the function Partition. There are several methods that we might use (one of which is suggested as an exercise), methods that sometimes are faster than the algorithm we develop but that are intricate and difficult to get correct. The algorithm we develop is much simpler and easier to understand, and it is certainly not slow; in fact, it does the smallest possible number of key comparisons of any partitioning algorithm.

1. Algorithm Development

Given a pivot value p, we must rearrange the entries of the array and compute the index pivotloc so that the pivot is at pivotloc, all entries to its left have keys less than p, and all entries to its right have larger keys. To allow for the possibility that more than one item has key equal to p, we insist that the items to the left of pivotloc have keys strictly less than p, and the items to its right have keys greater than or equal to p, as shown in the following diagram:

goal (postcondition)

To reorder the items this way, we must compare each key to the pivot. We shall use a for loop (running on a variable i) to do this. We shall use the variable pivotloc such that all items at or before location pivotloc have keys less than p. Suppose that the pivot p starts in the first position, and let us leave it there temporarily. Then in the middle of the loop the array has the following property:

loop invariant

When the function inspects entry i, there are two cases. If the entry is greater than or equal to p, then i can be increased and the array still has the required property. If the entry is less than p, then we restore the property by increasing pivotloc and swapping that entry (the first of those at least p) with entry i, as shown in the following diagrams:

restore the invariant

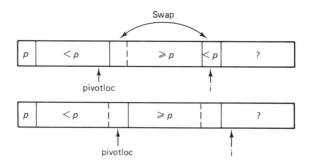

When the loop terminates, we have the situation:

final position

and we then need only swap the pivot from position low to position pivotloc to obtain the desired final arrangement.

2. Choice of Pivot

We are not bound to the choice of the first item in the list as the pivot; we can choose any item we wish and swap it with the first item before beginning the loop that partitions the list. In fact, the first item is often a poor choice for pivot, since if the list is already sorted, then the first key will have no others less than it, and so one of the sublists will *pivot from center*   be empty. Hence, let us instead choose a pivot near the center of the list, in the hope that our choice will partition the keys so that about half come on each side of the pivot.

3. Coding

With these decisions we obtain the following function, in which we use the swap function from Section 7.3. For convenience of reference we also include the property that holds during iteration of the loop as an assertion (loop invariant) in the function.

```
/* Partition: return the pivot location for a contiguous list. */
int Partition (List_type *lp, int low, int high)
{
        int i, pivotloc;
        Key_type pivotkey;
        Swap (low, (low + high) /2, lp);    /* Swap pivot into first position.      */
        pivotkey = lp->entry [low] .key;
        pivotloc = low;                      /* Remember its location.              */
        for (i = low + 1; i <= high; i++)
                if (LT (lp->entry [i] .key, pivotkey) )
                        Swap (++pivotloc, i, lp);    /* found smaller entry         */
        Swap (low, pivotloc, lp);
        return pivotloc;
}
```

7.8.3 Analysis of Quicksort

It is now time to examine the quicksort algorithm carefully, to determine when it works well and when not, and how much computation it performs.

1. Choice of Pivot

Our choice of a key at the center of the list to be the pivot is arbitrary. This choice may succeed in dividing the list nicely in half, or we may be unlucky and find that one sublist is much larger than the other. Some other methods for choosing the pivot are considered *worst case* in the exercises. An extreme case for our method occurs for the following list, where every one of the pivots selected turns out to be the largest key in its sublist:

$$2 \quad 4 \quad 6 \quad 7 \quad 3 \quad 1 \quad 5$$

Check it out, using the Partition function in the text. When quicksort is applied to this list, its label will appear to be quite a misnomer, since at the first recursion the nonempty sublist will have length 6, at the second 5, and so on.

If we were to choose the pivot as the first key or the last key in each sublist, then the extreme case would occur when the keys are in their natural order or in their reverse order. These orders, of course, are more likely to happen than some random order, and therefore choosing the first or last key as pivot is likely to cause problems.

2. Count of Comparisons and Swaps

Let us determine the number of comparisons and swaps that contiguous quicksort makes. Let $C(n)$ be the number of comparisons of keys made by quicksort when applied to a list of length n, and let $S(n)$ be the number of swaps of items. We have $C(1) = C(0) = 0$. The partition function compares the pivot with every other key in the list exactly once, and thus function Partition accounts for exactly $n - 1$ key comparisons. If one of the two sublists it creates has length r, then the other sublist will have length exactly $n - r - 1$. The number of comparisons done in the two recursive calls will then be $C(r)$ and $C(n - r - 1)$. Thus we have

total number of comparisons
$$C(n) = n - 1 + C(r) + C(n - r - 1).$$

To solve this equation we need to know r. In fact, our notation is somewhat deceptive, since the values of $C(\ )$ depend not only on the length of the list but also on the exact ordering of the items in it. Thus we shall obtain different answers in different cases, depending on the ordering.

3. Comparison Count, Worst Case

First, consider the worst case for comparisons. We have already seen that this occurs when the pivot fails to split the list at all, so that one sublist has $n - 1$ entries and the other is empty. In this case, since $C(0) = 0$, we obtain $C(n) = n - 1 + C(n - 1)$. An expression of this form is called a **recurrence relation** because it expresses its answer in terms of earlier cases of the same result. We wish to solve the recurrence, which means to find an equation for $C(n)$ that does not involve $C(\ )$ on the other side. Various (sometimes difficult) methods are needed to solve recurrence relations, but in this case we can do it easily by starting at the bottom instead of the top:

$$
\begin{aligned}
C(1) &= 0. \\
C(2) &= 1 + C(1) & &= 1. \\
C(3) &= 2 + C(2) & &= 2 + 1. \\
C(4) &= 3 + C(3) & &= 3 + 2 + 1. \\
& \qquad \cdots\cdots\cdots \\
C(n) &= n - 1 + C(n - 1) & &= (n - 1) + (n - 2) + \cdots + 3 + 1 \\
& & &= \tfrac{1}{2}(n - 1)n \\
& & &= (0.5)n^2 - (0.5)n.
\end{aligned}
$$

In this calculation we have applied Theorem A.1 to obtain the sum of the integers from 1 to $n - 1$.

Recall that selection sort makes about

$$(0.5)n^2 - (0.5)n$$

selection sort   key comparisons, and making too many comparisons was the weak point of selection sort (as compared with insertion). Hence in its worst case, quicksort is as bad as the worst case of selection sort.

4. Swap Count, Worst Case

Next let us determine how many times quicksort will swap items, again in its worst case. The partition function does one swap inside its loop for each key less than the pivot and two swaps outside its loop. In its worst case, the pivot is the largest key in the list, so the partition function will then make $n + 1$ swaps. With $S(n)$ the total number of swaps on a list of length n, we then have the recurrence

$$S(n) = n + 1 + S(n - 1)$$

in the worst case. The partition function is called only when $n \geq 2$, and $S(2) = 3$ in the worst case. Hence, as in counting comparisons, we can solve the recurrence by working downward, and we obtain

answer $$S(n) = (n + 1) + n + \cdots + 3 = \tfrac{1}{2}(n + 1)(n + 2) - 3 = 0.5n^2 + 1.5n - 1$$

swaps in the worst case.

5. Comparisons

In its worst case, contiguous insertion sort must make about twice as many comparisons and assignments of items as it does in its average case, giving a total of $0.5n^2 + O(n)$ for each operation. Each swap in quicksort requires three assignments of items, so quicksort in its worst case does $1.5n^2 + O(n)$ assignments, or, for large n, about three times as many as insertion sort. But moving items was the weak point of insertion sort in *poor worst-case* comparison to selection sort. Hence, in its worst case, quicksort (so-called) is worse *behavior* than the poor aspect of insertion sort, and, in regard to key comparisons, it is also as bad as the poor aspect of selection sort. Indeed, in the worst-case analysis, quicksort is a disaster, and its name is nothing less than false advertising.

It must be for some other reason that quicksort was not long ago consigned to the scrap heap of programs that never worked. The reason is the *average* behavior of *excellent* quicksort when applied to lists in random order, which turns out to be one of the best of *average-case* any sorting methods (using key comparisons and applied to contiguous lists) yet known! *behavior*

7.8.4 Average-Case Analysis of Quicksort

To do the average-case analysis, we shall assume that all possible orderings of the list are equally likely, and for simplicity, we take the keys to be just the integers from 1 to n. (In C, the index of an array always starts at zero. We are using 1 and n here so that we need to introduce only one complication at a time.)

1. Counting Swaps

When we select the pivot in the function Partition, it is equally likely to be any one of the keys. Denote by p whatever key is selected as pivot. Then after the partition, key p is guaranteed to be in index p, since the keys $1, \dots, p - 1$ are all to its left and $p + 1, \dots, n$ are to its right.

The number of swaps that will have been made in one call to Partition is $p + 1$, consisting of one swap in the loop for each of the $p - 1$ keys less than p and two swaps outside the loop. Let us denote by $S(n)$ the average number of swaps done by quicksort on a list of length n and by $S(n, p)$ the average number of swaps on a list of length n where the pivot for the first partition is p. We have now shown that, for $n \geq 2$,

$$S(n, p) = (p + 1) + S(p - 1) + S(n - p).$$

We must now take the average of these expressions, since p is random, by adding them from $p = 1$ to $p = n$ and dividing by n. The calculation uses the formula for the sum of the integers (Theorem A.1), and the result is

$$S(n) = \frac{n}{2} + \frac{3}{2} + \frac{2}{n}(S(0) + S(1) + \cdots + S(n - 1)).$$

2. Solving the Recurrence Relation

The first step toward solving this recurrence relation is to note that, if we were sorting a list of length $n - 1$, we would obtain the same expression with n replaced by $n - 1$, provided that $n \geq 2$:

$$S(n - 1) = \frac{n - 1}{2} + \frac{3}{2} + \frac{2}{n - 1}(S(0) + S(1) + \cdots + S(n - 2)).$$

Multiplying the first expression by n, the second by $n - 1$, and subtracting, we obtain

$$nS(n) - (n - 1)S(n - 1) = n + 1 + 2S(n - 1),$$

or

$$\frac{S(n)}{n + 1} = \frac{S(n - 1)}{n} + \frac{1}{n}.$$

We can solve this recurrence relation as we did a previous one by starting at the bottom. The result is

$$\frac{S(n)}{n + 1} = \frac{S(2)}{3} + \frac{1}{3} + \cdots + \frac{1}{n}.$$

The sum of the reciprocals of integers is studied in Appendix A.2.7, where it is shown that

$$1 + \frac{1}{2} + \cdots + \frac{1}{n} = \ln n + O(1).$$

The difference between this sum and the one we want is bounded by a constant, so we obtain $S(n)/(n + 1) = \ln n + O(1)$, or, finally,

$$S(n) = n \ln n + O(n).$$

To compare this result with those for other sorting methods, we note that

$$\ln n = (\ln 2)(\lg n)$$

and $\ln 2 \approx 0.69$, so that
$$S(n) \approx 0.69n \lg n + O(n).$$

3. Counting Comparisons

Since a call to the partition function for a list of length n makes exactly $n-1$ comparisons, the recurrence relation for the number of comparisons made in the average case will differ from that for swaps in only one way: Instead of $p+1$ swaps in the partition function, there are $n-1$ comparisons. Hence the first recurrence for the number $C(n,p)$ of comparisons for a list of length n with pivot p is

$$C(n,p) = n - 1 + C(p-1) + C(n-p).$$

When we average these expressions for $p=1$ to $p=n$, we obtain

$$C(n) = n - 1 + \frac{2}{n}(C(0) + C(1) + \cdots + C(n-1)).$$

Since this recurrence for the number $C(n)$ of key comparisons differs from that for $S(n)$ essentially only by the factor of $\frac{1}{2}$ in the latter, the same steps used to solve for $S(n)$ will yield

$$C(n) \approx 2n \ln n + O(n) \approx 1.39n \lg n + O(n).$$

7.8.5 Comparison with Mergesort

key comparisons

The calculation just completed shows that, on average, quicksort does about 39 percent more comparisons of keys than required by the lower bound and, therefore, also about 39 percent more than does mergesort. The reason, of course, is that mergesort is carefully designed to divide the list into halves of essentially equal size, whereas the sizes of the sublists for quicksort cannot be predicted in advance. Hence it is possible that quicksort's performance can be seriously degraded, but such an occurrence is unlikely in practice, so that averaging the times of poor performance with those of good performance yields the result just obtained.

data movement

Concerning data movement, we did not derive detailed information for mergesort, since we were primarily interested in the linked version. If, however, we consider the version of contiguous mergesort that builds the merged sublists in a second array, and reverses the use of arrays at each pass, then it is clear that, at each level of the recursion tree, all n items will be copied from one array to the other. The number of levels in the recursion tree is $\lg n$, and it therefore follows that the number of assignments of items in contiguous mergesort is $n \lg n$. For quicksort, on the other hand, we obtained a count of about $0.69n \lg n$ swaps, on average. A good (machine language) implementation should accomplish a swap of items in two assignments. Therefore, again, quicksort does about *optimization* 39 percent more assignments of items than does mergesort. The exercises, however, outline another partition function that does, on average, only about one-third as many swaps as the version we developed. With this refinement, therefore, contiguous quicksort may perform fewer than half as many assignments of data items as contiguous mergesort.

Exercises 7.8

E1. How will the quicksort function (as presented in the text) function if all the keys in the list are equal?

E2. [Due to HOARE] Suppose that, instead of sorting, we wish only to find the mth smallest key in a given list of size n. **(a)** Show how quicksort can be adapted to this problem, doing much less work than a complete sort. **(b)** Analyze your algorithm.

E3. Given an array of integers, develop a function, similar to the partition function, that will rearrange the integers so that either all the integers in even-numbered positions will be even or all the integers in odd-numbered positions will be odd. (Your function will provide a proof that one or the other of these goals can always be attained, although it may not be possible to establish both at once.)

E4. A different method for choosing the pivot in quicksort is to take the median of the first, last, and central keys of the list. Describe the modifications needed to the function QuickSort (contiguous version) to implement this choice. How much extra computation will be done? For $n = 7$, find an ordering of the keys

$$1, 2, \ldots, 7$$

that will force the algorithm into its worst case. How much better is this worst case than that of the original algorithm?

meansort **E5.** A different approach to the selection of pivot is to take the mean (average) of all the keys in the list as the pivot. The resulting algorithm is called **meansort**.

  a. Write a function to implement meansort. The partition function must be modified, since the mean of the keys is not necessarily one of the keys in the list. On the first pass, the pivot can be chosen any way you wish. As the keys are then partitioned, running sums and counts are kept for the two sublists, and thereby the means (which will be the new pivots) of the sublists can be calculated without making any extra passes through the list.

  b. In meansort, the relative *sizes* of the keys determine how nearly equal the sublists will be after partitioning; the initial *order* of the keys is of no importance, except for counting the number of swaps that will take place. How bad can the worst case for meansort be in terms of the relative sizes of the two sublists? Find a set of n integers that will produce the worst case for meansort.

E6. [Requires elementary probability theory] A good way to choose the pivot is to use a random-number generator to choose the index for the next pivot at each call to Sort. Using the fact that these choices are independent, find the probability that quicksort will happen upon its worst case. **(a)** Do the problem for $n = 7$. **(b)** Do the problem for general n.

optimize Partition

E7. At the cost of a few more comparisons of keys, the partition function can be rewritten so that the number of swaps is reduced by a factor of about 3, from $n/2$ to $n/6$ on average. The idea is to use two indices moving from the ends of the lists toward the center and to perform a swap only when a large key is found by the low index and a small key by the high index. This exercise outlines the development of such a function.

    a. Establish two indices i and j, and maintain the invariant property that all keys before position i are less than the pivot and all keys after position j are greater than or equal to the pivot. For simplicity, swap the pivot into the first position, and start the partition with the second element. Write a loop that will increase the index i as long as the invariant holds and another loop that will decrease j as long as the invariant holds. Your loops must also ensure that the indices do not go out of range, perhaps by checking that i ≤ j. When a pair of items, each on the wrong side, is found, then they should be swapped and the loops repeated. What is the termination condition of this outer loop? At the end, the pivot can be swapped into its proper place.

    b. Using the invariant property, verify that your function works properly.

    c. Show that each swap performed within the loop puts two items into their final position. From this, show that the function does at most $\frac{1}{2}n + O(1)$ swaps in its worst case for a list of length n.

    d. If, after partitioning, the pivot belongs in position p, then the number of swaps that the function does is approximately the number of items originally in one of the p positions at or before the pivot, but whose keys are greater than or equal to the pivot. If the keys are randomly distributed, then the probability that a particular key is greater than or equal to the pivot is $(n - p - 1)/n$. Show that the average number of such keys, and hence the average number of swaps, is approximately $p(n - p)/n$. By taking the average of these numbers from $p = 1$ to $p = n$, show that the number of swaps is approximately $n/6 + O(1)$.

    e. The need to check to make sure that the indices i and j in the partition function stay in bounds can be eliminated by using the pivot key as a sentinel to stop the loops. Implement this method in your function. Be sure to verify that your function works correctly in all cases.

Programming Projects 7.8

linked quicksort

P1. Implement quicksort (for contiguous lists) on your computer, and test it with the same data used with previous sorting algorithms. Compare the number of comparisons of keys, assignments of items, and total time required for sorting.

P2. Write a version of quicksort for linked lists, and run it on your computer for the same test data used for previous methods. The simplest choice for pivot is the first key in the list being sorted. You should find the partition function conceptually easier and more straightforward than the contiguous version, since items need not be swapped, but only links changed. You will, however, require a short additional function to recombine the sorted sublists into a single linked list.

P3. Because it may involve more overhead, quicksort may be inferior to simpler methods for short lists. Find experimentally a value where, on average, quicksort becomes more efficient than insertion sort. Write a hybrid sorting procedure that starts with quicksort and, when the sublists are sufficiently short, switches to insertion sort. Determine if it is better to do the switch-over within the recursive procedure or to terminate the recursive calls when the sublists are sufficiently short to change methods and then at the very end of the process run through insertion sort once on the whole list.

7.9 REVIEW: COMPARISON OF METHODS

In this chapter we have studied and carefully analyzed quite a variety of sorting methods. Perhaps the best way to summarize this work is to emphasize in turn each of the three important efficiency criteria:

- Use of storage space;
- Use of computer time;
- Programming effort.

1. Use of space

In regard to space, most of the algorithms we have discussed use little space other than that occupied by the original list, which is rearranged in its original place to be in order. The exceptions are quicksort and mergesort, where the recursion does require a small amount of extra storage to keep track of the sublists that have not yet been sorted. But in a well-written function, the amount of extra space used for recursion is $O(\log n)$ and will be trivial in comparison with that needed for other purposes.

Finally, we should recall that a major drawback of mergesort for contiguous lists is that the straightforward version requires extra space equal to that occupied by the original list.

In many applications the list to be sorted is much too large to be kept in high-speed memory, and when this is the case, other methods become necessary. A frequent approach is to divide the list into sublists that can be sorted internally within high-

external sorting and speed memory and then merge the sorted sublists externally. Hence much work has
merging been invested in developing merging algorithms, primarily when it is necessary to merge many sublists at once. We shall not discuss this topic further.

2. Computer Time

The second efficiency criterion is use of computer time, which we have already carefully analyzed for each of the methods we have developed.

3. Programming Effort

The third efficiency criterion is often the most important of all: this criterion is the efficient and fruitful use of the programmer's time.

If a list is small, the sophisticated sorting techniques designed to minimize computer time requirements are usually worse or only marginally better in achieving their goal than are the simpler methods. If a program is to be run only once or twice and there is enough machine time, then it would be foolish for a programmer to spend days or weeks investigating many sophisticated algorithms that might, in the end, only save a few seconds of computer time.

When programming in languages like FORTRAN, COBOL, or BASIC that do not support recursion, implementation of mergesort and quicksort becomes more complicated (see Appendix B). Shell sort comes not far behind mergesort and quicksort in performance, does not require recursion, and is easy to program. One should therefore never sell Shell sort short.

simplicity and correctness

The saving of programming time is an excellent reason for choosing a simple algorithm, even if it is inefficient, but two words of caution should always be remembered. First, saving programming time is never an excuse for writing an incorrect program, one that may usually work but can sometimes misbehave. Murphy's law will then inevitably come true. Second, simple programs, designed to be run only a few times and then discarded, often instead find their way into applications not imagined when they were first written. Lack of care in the early stages will then prove exceedingly costly later.

For many applications, insertion sort can prove to be the best choice. It is easy to write and maintain, and it runs efficiently for short lists. Even for long lists, if they are nearly in the correct order, insertion sort will be very efficient. If the list is completely in order, then insertion sort verifies this condition as quickly as can be done.

4. Statistical Analysis

mean

standard deviation

The final choice of algorithm will depend not only on the length of list, the size of structures, and their representation in storage, but very strongly on the way in which the structures can be expected to be ordered before sorting. The analysis of algorithms from the standpoint of probability and statistics is of great importance. For most algorithms, we have been able to obtain results on the mean (average) performance, but the experience of quicksort shows that the amount by which this performance changes from one possible ordering to another is also an important factor to consider. The ***standard deviation*** is a statistical measure of this variability. Quicksort has an excellent mean performance, and the standard deviation is small, which signifies that the performance is likely to differ little from the mean. For algorithms like selection sort and mergesort, the best-case and worst-case performances differ little, which means that the standard deviation is almost 0. Other algorithms, like insertion sort, will have a much larger standard deviation in their performance. The particular distribution of the orderings of the incoming lists is therefore an important consideration in choosing a sorting method. To enable intelligent decisions, the professional computer scientist needs to be knowledgeable about important aspects of mathematical statistics as they apply to algorithm analysis.

5. Empirical Testing

Finally, in all these decisions we must be careful to temper the theoretical analysis of algorithms with empirical testing. Different computers and compilers will produce different results. It is most instructive, therefore, to see by experiment how the different algorithms behave in different circumstances.

Exercises 7.9

E1. Classify the sorting methods we have studied into one of the following categories:
(a) the method does not require access to the items at one end of the list until the

items at the other end have been sorted; (b) the method does not require access to the items that have already been sorted; (c) the method requires access to all items in the list throughout the process.

E2. Some of the sorting methods we have studied are not suited for use with linked lists. Which ones, and why not?

E3. Rank the sorting methods we have studied (both for linked and contiguous lists) according to the amount of extra storage space that they require for indices or pointers, for recursion, and for copies of the items being sorted.

E4. Which of the methods we studied would be a good choice in each of the following applications? Why? If the representation of the list in contiguous or linked storage makes a difference in your choice, state how.

   a. You wish to write a general-purpose sorting program that will be used by many people in a variety of applications.
   b. You wish to sort 1000 numbers once. After you finish, you will not keep the program.
   c. You wish to sort 50 numbers once. After you finish, you will not keep the program.
   d. You need to sort 5 items in the middle of a long program. Your sort will be called hundreds of times by the long program.
   e. You have an array of 1000 keys to sort in high-speed memory, and key comparisons can be made quickly, but each time a key is moved a corresponding 500 block file on disk must also be moved, and doing so is a slow process.
   f. There is a twelve foot long shelf full of computer science books all catalogued by number. A few of these have been put back in the wrong places by readers, but rarely are they more than one foot from where they belong.
   g. You have a stack of 500 library index cards in random order to sort alphabetically.
   h. You are told that a list of 5000 words is already in order, but you wish to check it to make sure, and sort any words found out of order.

E5. Discuss the advantages and disadvantages of designing a general sorting function as a hybrid between quicksort and Shell sort. What criteria would you use to switch from one to the other? Which would be the better choice for what kinds of lists?

E6. Summarize the results of the test runs of the sorting methods of this chapter for your computer. Also include any variations of the methods that you have written as exercises. Make charts comparing **(a)** the number of key comparisons, **(b)** the number of assignments of items, **(c)** the total running time, **(d)** the working storage requirements of the program, **(e)** the length of the program, and **(f)** the amount of programming time required to write and debug the program.

E7. Write a one-page guide to help a user of your computer system select one of our sorting algorithms according to his needs.

E8. A sorting function is called **stable** if, whenever two items have equal keys, then on completion of the sorting function the two items will be in the same order in the list as before sorting. Stability is important if a list has already been sorted by one key and is now being sorted by another key, and it is desired to keep as much of the original ordering as the new one allows. Determine which of the sorting methods of this chapter are stable and which are not. For those that are not, produce a list (as short as possible) containing some items with equal keys whose orders are not preserved. In addition, see if you can discover simple modifications to the algorithm that will make it stable.

POINTERS AND PITFALLS

1. Many computer systems have a general-purpose sorting utility. If you can access this utility and it proves adequate for your application, then use it rather than writing a sorting program from scratch. ANSI C compilers, in particular, provide a general purpose sorting function qsort. The function qsort is usually a version of quicksort. See your compiler documentation.

2. In choosing a sorting method, take into account the ways in which the keys will usually be arranged before sorting, the size of the application, the amount of time available for programming, the need to save computer time and space, the way in which the data structures are implemented, the cost of moving data, and the cost of comparing keys.

3. For advice on programming and analyzing sorting algorithms, see the Pointers and Pitfalls at the end of Chapter 5.

REVIEW QUESTIONS

7.2   **1.** How many comparisons of keys are required to verify that a list of n items is in order?

2. Explain in twenty words or less how insertion sort works.

7.3   **3.** Explain in twenty words or less how selection sort works.

4. On average, about how many more comparisons does selection sort do than insertion sort on a list of 20 items?

5. What is the advantage of selection sort over all the other methods we studied?

7.4   **6.** What disadvantage of insertion sort does Shell sort overcome?

7.5   **7.** What is the lower bound on the number of key comparisons that any sorting method must make to put n keys into order, if the method uses key comparisons to make its decisions? Give both the average and worst-case bounds.

8. What is the lower bound if the requirement of using comparisons to make decisions is dropped?

7.6   **9.** Define the term *divide and conquer*.

10. Explain in twenty words or less how mergesort works.

11. Explain in twenty words or less how quicksort works.

12. What is a recursion tree?

7.7   **13.** Explain why mergesort is better for linked lists than for contiguous lists.

7.8 **14.** In quicksort, why did we choose the pivot from the center of the list rather than from one of the ends?

15. On average, about how many more comparisons of keys does quicksort make than the optimum? About how many comparisons does it make in the worst case?

7.9 **16.** Under what conditions are simple sorting algorithms better than sophisticated ones?

REFERENCES FOR FURTHER STUDY

The primary reference for this chapter is the comprehensive series by D. E. KNUTH (bibliographic details in Chapter 3). Internal sorting occupies Volume 3, pp. 73–180. KNUTH does algorithm analysis in considerably more detail than we have. He writes all algorithms in a pseudo-assembly language and does detailed operation counts there. He studies all the methods we have, several more, and many variations.

The original references to Shell sort and quicksort are, respectively,

> D. L. SHELL, "A high-speed sorting function," *Communications of the ACM* 2 (1959), 30–32.

> C. A. R. HOARE, "Quicksort," *Computer Journal* 5 (1962), 10–15.

The unified derivation of mergesort and quicksort, that can also be used to produce insertion sort and selection sort, is based on the work

> JOHN DARLINGTON, "A synthesis of several sorting algorithms," *Acta Informatica* 11 (1978), 1–30.

Mergesort can be refined to bring its performance very close to the optimal lower bound. One example of such an improved algorithm, whose performance is within 6 percent of the best possible, is

> R. MICHAEL TANNER, "Minimean merging and sorting: An algorithm," *SIAM J. Computing* 7 (1978), 18–38.

A relatively simple contiguous merge algorithm that operates in linear time with a small, constant amount of additional space appears in

> BING-CHAO HUANG and MICHAEL A. LANGSTON, "Practical in-place merging," *Communications of the ACM* 31 (1988), 348–352.

The algorithm for partitioning the list in quicksort was discovered by NICO LOMUTO and was published in

> JON BENTLEY, "Programming pearls: How to sort," *Communications of the ACM* 27 (1984), 287–291.

"Programming pearls" is a regular column that contains many elegant algorithms and helpful suggestions for programming. Collections of the "Programming pearls" columns appear in

> JON BENTLEY, *Programming Pearls*, Addison-Wesley, Reading, Mass., 1986, 195 pages.

and

> JON BENTLEY, *More Programming Pearls: Confessions of a coder*, Addison-Wesley, Reading, Mass., 1988, 207 pages.

An extensive analysis of the quicksort algorithm is given in

> ROBERT SEDGEWICK, "The analysis of quicksort programs," *Acta Informatica* 7 (1976/77), 327–355.

The exercise on meansort (taking the mean of the keys as pivot) comes from

DALIA MOTZKIN, "MEANSORT," *Communications of the ACM* 26 (1983), 250–251; 27 (1984), 719–722.

Expository surveys of various sorting methods are

W. A. MARTIN, "Sorting," *Computing Surveys* 3 (1971), 148–174.

H. LORIN, *Sorting and Sort Systems*, Addison-Wesley, Reading, Mass., 1975, 456 pages.

There is, of course, a vast literature in probability and statistics with potential applications to computers. A classic treatment of elementary probability and statistics is

W. FELLER, *An Introduction to Probability Theory and Its Applications*, Vol. 1, second edition, Wiley–Interscience, New York, 1957.

Recursion

As we have seen from studying sorting methods, recursion is a valuable programming tool. This chapter presents several applications of recursion that further illustrate its usefulness. Some of these applications are simple; others are quite sophisticated. Later in the chapter we analyze how recursion is usually implemented on a computer. In the process, we shall obtain guidelines regarding good and bad uses of recursion, when it is appropriate, and when it should best be avoided.

The first several sections of this chapter study various applications of recursion, in order to illustrate a range of possible uses. The programs we write are chosen to be especially simple, but to illustrate features that often appear in much more complicated applications.

8.1 DIVIDE AND CONQUER

The uses that we have made of recursion so far are of the form called *divide and conquer*, which can be defined generally as the method of solving a problem by dividing it into two or more subproblems, each of which is similar to the original problem in nature, but smaller in size. Solutions to the subproblems are then obtained separately, and combined to produce the solution of the original problem. Hence we can sort a list by dividing it into two sublists, sort them separately, and combine the results.

An even easier application of divide and conquer is the following recreational problem.

8.1.1 The Towers of Hanoi

In the nineteenth century a game called the *Towers of Hanoi* appeared in Europe, together with promotional material (undoubtedly apocryphal) explaining that the game represented a task underway in the Temple of Brahma. At the creation of the world, *the problem* the priests were given a brass platform on which were 3 diamond needles. On the first needle were stacked 64 golden disks, each one slightly smaller than the one under it. (The less exotic version sold in Europe had 8 cardboard disks and 3 wooden posts.) The priests were assigned the task of moving all the golden disks from the first needle to the third, subject to the conditions that only one disk can be moved at a time, and that no disk is ever allowed to be placed on top of a smaller disk. The priests were told that when they had finished moving the 64 disks, it would signify the end of the world. See Figure 8.1.

Our task, of course, is to write a computer program that will type out a list of instructions for the priests. We can summarize our task by the instruction

Move(64, 1, 3, 2);

which means

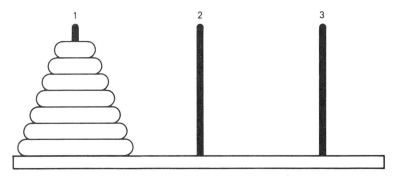

Figure 8.1. The Towers of Hanoi

Move 64 disks from needle 1 to needle 3 using needle 2 for intermediate storage.

8.1.2 The Solution

The idea that gives a solution is to concentrate our attention not on the first step (which must be to move the top disk somewhere), but rather on the hardest step: moving the bottom disk. There is no way to reach the bottom disk until the top 63 disks have been moved, and, furthermore, they must all be on needle 2 so that we can move the bottom disk from needle 1 to needle 3. This is because only one disk can be moved at a time and the bottom (largest) one can never be on top of any other, so that when we move the bottom one, there can be no other disks on needles 1 or 3. Thus we can summarize the steps of our algorithm as

```
Move(63, 1, 2, 3);
printf("Move a disk from needle 1 to needle 3.\n");
Move(63, 2, 3, 1);
```

We now have a small step toward the solution, only a very small one since we must still describe how to move the 63 disks two times, but a significant step nonetheless, since there is no reason why we cannot move the 63 remaining disks in the same way. (In fact, we must do so in the same way since there is again a largest disk that must be moved last.)

This is exactly the idea of recursion. We have described how to do the key step and asserted that the rest of the problem is done in essentially the same way.

8.1.3 Refinement

To write the algorithm formally we shall need to know at each step which needle may be used for temporary storage, and thus we will invoke the function in the form

```
Move(n, a, b, c);
```

which will mean

Move n disks from needle a to needle b using needle c as temporary storage.

Supposedly our task is to be finished in a finite number of steps (even if it does mark the end of the world!), and thus there must be some way that the recursion stops. The obvious stopping rule is that, when there are no disks to be moved, there is nothing to do. We can now write the complete program to embody these rules.

```
#define DISKS 64

/* Towers of Hanoi */
void main(void)
{
      Move(DISKS, 1, 3, 2);
}
```

recursive function
```
/* Move: moves n disks from a to b using c for temporary storage. */
void Move(int n, int a, int b, int c)
{
      if (n > 0) {
            Move(n−1, a, c, b);
            printf("Move a disk from %d to %d.\n", a, b);
            Move(n−1, c, b, a);
      }
}
```

8.1.4 Analysis

Note that this program not only produces a complete solution to the task, but it produces the best possible solution, and, in fact, the only solution that can be found except for the possible inclusion of redundant and useless sequences of instructions such as

Move a disk from needle 1 to needle 2.
Move a disk from needle 2 to needle 3.
Move a disk from needle 3 to needle 1.

To show the uniqueness of the irreducible solution, note that, at every stage, the task to be done can be summarized as to move a certain number of disks from one needle to another. There is no way to do this task except to move all the disks except the bottom one first, then perhaps make some redundant moves, then move the bottom one, possibly make more redundant moves, and finally move the upper disks again.

Next, let us find out how many times will the recursion proceed before starting to return and back out. The first time function Move is called, it is with $n = 64$, and each recursive call reduces the value of n by 1. Thus, if we exclude the calls with $n = 0$, which do nothing, we have a total depth of recursion of 64. That is, if we were to draw *depth of recursion* the tree of recursive calls for the program, it would have 64 levels above its leaves. Except for the leaves, each vertex results in two recursive calls (as well as in writing out one instruction), and so the number of vertices on each level is exactly double that of the level above. The recursion tree for the somewhat smaller task that moves 3 disks instead of 64 appears as Figure 8.2, and the progress of execution follows the path shown.

From the recursion tree we can easily calculate how many instructions are needed to move 64 disks. One instruction is printed for each vertex in the tree, except for the leaves (which are calls with $n = 0$). The number of non-leaves is

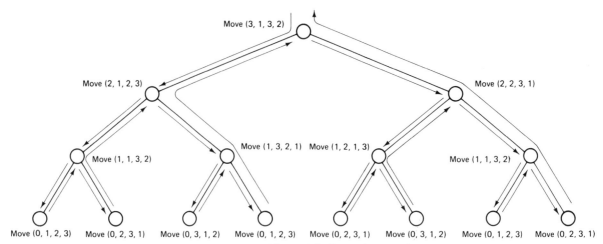

Figure 8.2. Recursion tree for 3 disks

total number of moves

$$1 + 2 + 4 + \cdots + 2^{63} = 2^{64} - 1,$$

and this is the number of moves required altogether.

We can estimate how large this number is by using the approximation

$$10^3 = 1000 < 1024 = 2^{10}.$$

There are about 3.2×10^7 seconds in one year. Suppose that the instructions could be carried out at the rather frenetic rate of one every second (the priests have plenty of practice). Since

$$2^{64} = 2^4 \times 2^{60} > 2^4 \times 10^{18} = 1.6 \times 10^{19},$$

the total task will then take about 5×10^{11} years. If astronomers estimate the age of the universe at about 10 billion (10^{10}) years, then according to this story the world will indeed endure a long time—50 times as long as it already has!

8.2 POSTPONING THE WORK

Divide and conquer, by definition, involves two or more recursive calls within the algorithm being written. In this section we illustrate two applications of recursion, each using only one recursive call. In these applications one case or one phase of the problem is solved without using recursion, and the work of the remainder of the problem is postponed to the recursive call.

8.2.1 Generating Permutations

Our first example is the problem of generating the $n!$ permutations of n objects as efficiently as possible. If we think of the number $n!$ as the product

$$n! = 1 \times 2 \times 3 \times \cdots \times n,$$

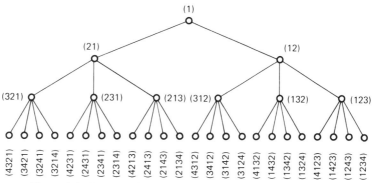

Figure 8.3. Permutation generation by multiplication, $n = 4$

then the process of multiplication can be pictured as the tree in Figure 8.3. (Ignore the labels for the moment.)

1. The Idea

We can identify permutations with the nodes as given by the labels in Figure 8.3. At the top is 1 by itself. We can obtain the two permutations of $\{1, 2\}$ by writing 2 first on the left, then on the right of 1. Similarly, the six permutations of $\{1, 2, 3\}$ can be obtained by starting with one of the permutations (2, 1) or (1, 2) and inserting 3 into one of the three possible positions (left, center, or right). The task of generating permutations of $\{1, 2, \ldots, k\}$ can now be summarized as

> *Take a given permutation of $\{1, 2, \ldots, k - 1\}$ and regard it as an ordered list. Insert k, in turn, into each of the k possible positions in this ordered list, thereby obtaining k distinct permutations of $\{1, 2, \ldots, k\}$.*

This algorithm illustrates the use of recursion to complete tasks that have been temporarily postponed. That is, we can write a function that will first insert 1 into an empty list, and then use a recursive call to insert the remaining numbers from 2 to n into the list. This first recursive call will insert 2 into the list containing only 1, and postpone further insertions to a recursive call. On the nth recursive call, finally, the integer n will be inserted. In this way, having begun with a tree structure as motivation, we have now developed an algorithm for which the given tree becomes the recursion tree.

2. Refinement

Let us restate the algorithm in slightly more formal terms. We shall invoke our function as

$$\text{Permute}(1, n);$$

which will mean to insert all integers from 1 to n to build all the $n!$ permutations. When it is time to insert the integer k, the remaining task is

```
/* Permute: build permutations. */
void Permute(int k, int n)
{
    for (each possible position in the list L) {
        Insert k into the given position;
        if (k == n)
            ProcessPermutation();
        else
            Permute(k + 1, n);
        Remove k from the given position;
    }
}
```

The function ProcessPermutation will make whatever disposition is desired of a complete permutation of $\{1, 2, \dots, n\}$. We might wish only to print it out, or we might wish to send it as input to some other task.

3. Data Structures

Let us now make some decisions regarding representation of the data. We use an ordered list to hold the numbers being permuted. This list is global to the recursive invocations of the function, that is, there is only the master copy of the list, and each recursive call updates the entries in this master list. Since we must continually insert and delete entries into and from the list, linked storage will be more flexible than keeping the entries in a contiguous list. But the total number of entries in the list never exceeds n, so we can (probably) improve efficiency by keeping the linked list within an array, rather than using dynamic

linked list in array   memory allocation. Our links are thus integer indices (cursors) relative to the start of the array. With an array, furthermore, the index of each entry, as it is assigned, will happen to be the same as the value of the number being inserted, so the need to keep this numerical value explicitly disappears, so that only the links need to be kept in the array.

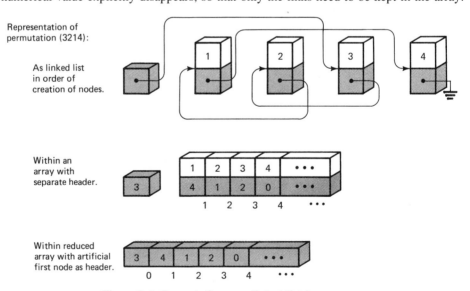

Figure 8.4. Permutation as a linked list in an array

artificial node   Insertions and deletions are further simplified if we put an artificial first node at the beginning of the list, so that insertions and deletions at the beginning of the (actual) list can be treated in the same way as those at other positions, always as insertions or deletions after a node.

This representation of a permutation as a linked list within an array is illustrated in Figure 8.4.

4. Final Program

With these decisions we can write our algorithm as a formal program.

```
#define MAX 20
int L[MAX + 1];                         /* holds the list of links              */

/* generate permutations */
int main(int argc, char *argv[])
{
        int n;
        if (argc != 2) {                                                          check usage
                fprintf(stderr, "Usage: permute < n > \n");
                exit(1);
        }
        n = atoi(argv[1]);
        if (n < 1 || n > MAX) {                                                   check range
                fprintf(stderr, "n must be between 1 and %d\n", MAX);
                exit(1);
        }
        L[0] = 0;                       /* Set the list to be initially empty.  */
        Permute(1, n);
        return 0;
}

/* Permute: generate permutations of n numbers */
void Permute(int k, int n)
{
        int p = 0;
        do {
                L[k] = L[p];            /* First insert k after entry p of the list.  */
                L[p] = k;
                if (k == n)
                        ProcessLinkedPerm();
                else
                        Permute(k + 1, n);
                L[p] = L[k];            /* Remove k from the list.              */
                p = L[p];               /* Advance p one position.              */
        } while (p != 0);
}
```

Recall that the array L describes a linked list of pointers and does not contain the objects being permuted. If, for example, it is desired to print the integers $1, ..., n$ being permuted, then the auxiliary function becomes

```
/* ProcessLinkedPerm: print permutation. */
void ProcessLinkedPerm (void)
{
    int q;
    for (q = 0; L[q] != 0; q = L[q])
        printf("%d ", L[q]);
    printf("\n");
}
```

5. Comparisons

It may be interesting to note that the simple algorithm developed here has execution time comparable with the fastest of all published algorithms for permutation generation. R. SEDGEWICK (reference at end of chapter) gives a survey of such algorithms and singles out the following algorithm, devised by B. R. HEAP, as especially efficient.

```
#define ODD(x) ((x)/2*2 != (x))

/* HeapPermute: generate permutations of n numbers. */
void HeapPermute (int n)
{
    int temp;                        /* used for swapping array elements      */
    int c = 1;
    if (n > 2)
        HeapPermute(n-1);
    else
        ProcessContPerm();
    while (c < n) {
        if (ODD(n)) {
            temp = L[n];
            L[n] = L[1];
            L[1] = temp;
        } else {
            temp = L[n];
            L[n] = L[c];
            L[c] = temp;
        }
        c++;
        if (n > 2)
            HeapPermute(n-1);
        else
            ProcessContPerm();
    }
}
```

timings   On one computer, this algorithm requires 930 milliseconds to generate the 40,320 permutations of 8 objects, whereas the linked-list algorithm accomplishes the task in 660 milliseconds, an improvement of about 30 percent. With other implementations these numbers will differ, of course, but it is safe to conclude that the linked-list algorithm is at least comparable in efficiency. The correctness of the linked-list method, moreover, is obvious, whereas a proof that this other method actually generates all $n!$ distinct permutations of n objects is much more involved.

8.2.2 Backtracking: Nonattacking Queens

For our second example of an algorithm where recursion allows the postponement of all but one case, let us consider the puzzle of how to place eight queens on a chessboard so that no queen can take another. Recall that a queen can take another piece that lies on the same row, the same column, or the same diagonal (either direction) as the queen. The chessboard has eight rows and columns.

It is by no means obvious how to solve this puzzle, and its complete solution defied even the great C. F. GAUSS, who attempted it in 1850. It is typical of puzzles that do not seem amenable to analytic solutions, but require either luck coupled with trial and error, or else much exhaustive (and exhausting) computation. To convince you that solutions to this problem really do exist, two of them are shown in Figure 8.5.

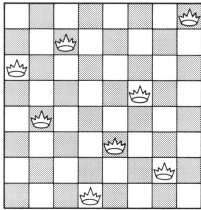

Figure 8.5. Two configurations showing eight nonattacking queens

1. Solving the Puzzle

A person attempting to solve the Eight Queens problem will usually soon abandon attempts to find all (or even one) of the solutions by being clever and will start to put queens on the board, perhaps randomly or perhaps in some logical order, but always making sure that no queen placed can take another already on the board. If the person is lucky enough to get eight queens on the board by proceeding in this way, then he has found a solution; if not, then one or more of the queens must be removed and placed elsewhere to continue the search for a solution. To start formulating a program let us sketch this method in algorithmic form. We denote by n the number of queens on the board; initially $n = 0$. The key step is described as follows.

outline

```
void AddQueen(void)
{
    for (every unguarded position p on the board) {
        Place a queen in position p;
        n++;
        if (n == 8)
            Print the configuration;
        else
            AddQueen( );
        Remove the queen from position p;
        n--;
    }
}
```

This sketch illustrates the use of recursion to mean "Continue to the next stage and repeat the task." Placing a queen in position p is only tentative; we leave it there only if we can continue adding queens until we have eight. Whether we reach eight or not, the function will return when it finds that it has finished or there are no further possibilities to investigate. After the inner call has returned, then, it is time to remove the queen from position p, because all possibilities with it there have been investigated.

2. Backtracking

This function is typical of a broad class called **backtracking algorithms** that attempt to complete a search for a solution to a problem by constructing partial solutions, always ensuring that the partial solutions remain consistent with the requirements of the problem. The algorithm then attempts to extend a partial solution toward completion, but when an inconsistency with the requirements of the problem occurs, the algorithm backs up (**backtracks**) by removing the most recently constructed part of the solution and trying another possibility.

Backtracking proves useful in situations where many possibilities may first appear, but few survive further tests. In scheduling problems, for example, it will likely be easy to assign the first few matches, but as further matches are made, the constraints drastically reduce the number of possibilities. Or consider the problem of designing a compiler. In some languages it is impossible to determine the meaning of a statement until almost all of it has been read. Consider, for example, the pair of FORTRAN statements

$$\text{DO 17 K = 1, 6}$$
$$\text{DO 17 K = 1. 6}$$

Both of these are legal: the first initiates a loop, and the second assigns the number 1.6 to *parsing*

the variable DO17K. In such cases where the meaning cannot be deduced immediately, backtracking is a useful method in *parsing* (that is, splitting apart to decipher) the text of a program.

3. Refinement: Choosing the Data Structures

To fill in the details of our algorithm for the Eight Queens problem, we must first decide how we will determine which positions are unguarded at each stage and how we will loop through the unguarded positions. This amounts to reaching some decisions about the representation of data in the program.

square Boolean array

A person working on the Eight Queens puzzle with an actual chessboard will probably proceed to put queens into the squares one at a time. We can do the same in a computer by introducing an 8×8 array with Boolean entries and by defining an entry to be true if a queen is there and false if not. To determine if a position is guarded, the person would scan the board to see if a queen is guarding the position, and we could do the same, but doing so would involve considerable searching.

A person working the puzzle on paper or on a blackboard often observes that when a queen is put on the board, time will be saved in the next stage if all the squares that the new queen guards are marked off, so that it is only necessary to look for an unmarked square to find an unguarded position for the next queen. Again, we could do the same by defining each entry of our array to be true if it is free and false if it is guarded. A problem now arises, however, when we wish to remove a queen. We should not necessarily change a position that she has guarded from false to true, since it may well be that some other queen still guards that position. We can solve this problem by making the entries of our array integers rather than Boolean, each entry denoting the number of queens guarding the position. Thus to add a queen we increase the count by 1 for each position on the same row, column, or diagonal as the queen, and to remove a queen we reduce the appropriate counts by 1. A position is unguarded if and only if it has a count of 0.

square integer array

In spite of its obvious advantages over the previous attempt, this method still involves some searching to find unguarded positions and some calculation to change all the counts at each stage. The algorithm will be adding and removing queens a great many times, so that this calculation and searching may prove expensive. A person working on this puzzle soon makes another observation that saves even more work.

pigeonhole principle

Once a queen has been put in the first row, no person would waste time searching to find a place to put another queen in the same row, since the row is fully guarded by the first queen. There can never be more than one queen in each row. But our goal is to put eight queens on the board, and there are only eight rows. It follows that there must be a queen, exactly one queen, in every one of the rows. (This is called the ***pigeonhole principle***: If you have n pigeons and n pigeonholes, and no more than one pigeon ever goes in the same hole, then there must be a pigeon in every hole.)

array of locations

Thus we can proceed by placing the queens on the board one row at a time, starting with the first row, and we can keep track of where they are with a single array

$$\text{int col[8]};$$

where col[i] gives the column containing the queen in row i. To make sure that no

two queens are on the same column or the same diagonal, we need not keep and search
through an 8×8 array, but we need only keep track of whether each column is free
guards   or guarded, and whether each diagonal is likewise. We can do this with three Boolean
arrays, colfree, upfree, and downfree, where diagonals from the lower left to the upper
right are considered upward and those from the upper left to lower right are considered
downward.

How do we identify the positions along a single diagonal? Along the main (downward) diagonal the entries are

$$[0,0], [1,1], \ldots, [7,7];$$

which have the property that the row and column indices are equal; that, is, their difference is 0. It turns out that along any downward diagonal the row and column indices
will have a constant difference. This difference is 0 for the main diagonal, and ranges
from $0 - 7 = -7$ for the downward diagonal of length 1 in the upper right corner, to
$7 - 0 = 7$ for the one in the lower left corner. Similarly, along upward diagonals the
sum of the row and column indices is constant, ranging from $0 + 0 = 0$ to $7 + 7 = 14$.

After making all these decisions, we can now define all our data structures formally,
and, at the same time, we can write the main program.

```
int col [8];                      /* column with the queen                   */
Boolean_type colfree [8];         /* Is the column free?                     */
Boolean_type upfree [15];         /* Is the upward diagonal free?            */
Boolean_type downfree [15];       /* Is the downward diagonal free?          */

int row = −1;                     /* row whose queen is currently placed     */
int sol = 0;                      /* number of solutions found               */
```

main program
```
/* Solve the Eight Queens problem. */
void main (void)
{
    int i;

    for (i = 0; i < 8; i++)
        colfree [i] = TRUE;
    for (i = 0; i < 15; i++) {
        upfree [i] = TRUE;
        downfree [i] = TRUE;
    }
    AddQueen ( );
}
```

Translation of the sketch of the function AddQueen into a program is straightforward,
given the use of the arrays that have now been defined.

recursive function

```
/* AddQueen: attempts to place queens, backtracking when needed */
void AddQueen (void)
{
        int c;                           /* column being tried for the queen      */

        row++;
        for (c = 0; c < 8; c++)
            if (colfree [c] && upfree [row + c] && downfree [row−c + 7]) {
                col [row] = c;         /* Put a queen in (row, c).              */
                colfree [c] = FALSE;
                upfree [row + c] = FALSE;
                downfree [row−c + 7] = FALSE;
                if (row == 7)          /* termination condition                 */
                    WriteBoard ( );
                else
                    AddQueen ( );  /* Proceed recursively.                  */
                colfree [c] = TRUE;    /* Now backtrack by removing the queen. */
                upfree [row + c] = TRUE;
                downfree [row−c + 7] = TRUE;
            }
        row−−;
}
```

4. Local and Global Variables

Note that in the Eight Queens program almost all the variables and arrays are declared globally, whereas in the Towers of Hanoi program the variables were declared in the recursive function. If variables are declared within a function, then they are local to the function and not available outside it. In particular, variables declared in a recursive function are local to a single occurrence of the function, so that if the function is called again recursively, the variables are new and different, and the original variables will be remembered after the function returns. The copies of variables set up in an outer call are not available to the function during an inner recursive call. In the Eight Queens program we wish the same information about guarded rows, columns, and diagonals to be available to all the recursive occurrences of the function, and to do this, the appropriate arrays are declared not in the function but in the main program. The only reason for the array col [ ] is to communicate the positions of the queens to the function WriteBoard. The information in this array is also preserved in the eight local copies of the variable c set up during the recursive calls, but only one of these local copies is available to the program at a given time.

5. Analysis of Backtracking

Finally, let us estimate the amount of work that our program will do. If we had taken the naive approach by writing a program that first placed all eight queens on the board and then rejected the illegal configurations, we would be investigating as many configurations as choosing eight places out of sixty-four, which is

$$\binom{64}{8} = 4{,}426{,}165{,}368.$$

The observation that there can be only one queen in each row immediately cuts this number to

$$8^8 = 16{,}777{,}216.$$

This number is still large, but our program will not investigate nearly this many positions. Instead, it rejects positions whose column or diagonals are guarded. The requirement that there be only one queen in each column reduces the number to

reduced count
$$8! = 40{,}320$$

which is quite manageable by computer, and the actual number of cases the program considers will be much less than this (see projects), since positions with guarded diagonals in the early rows will be rejected immediately, with no need to make the fruitless attempt to fill the later rows.

effectiveness of backtracking   This behavior summarizes the effectiveness of backtracking: positions that are early discovered to be impossible prevent the later investigation of many fruitless paths.

Another way to express this behavior of backtracking is to consider the tree of recursive calls to function AddQueen, part of which is shown in Figure 8.6. It appears formally that each vertex might have up to eight children corresponding to the recursive

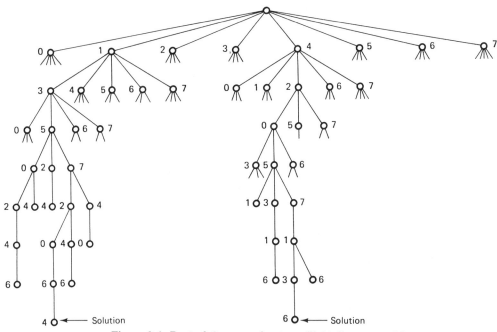

Figure 8.6. Part of the recursion tree, Eight Queens problem

calls to AddQueen for the eight iterations of the for loop. Even at levels near the root, however, most of these branches are found to be impossible, and the removal of one vertex on an upper level removes a multitude of its descendents. Backtracking is a most effective tool to prune a recursion tree to manageable size.

Exercises 8.2

E1. What is the maximum depth of recursion in the Eight Queens program?

E2. Starting with the following partial configuration of five queens on the board, construct the recursion tree of all situations that the Eight Queens program will consider in trying to add the remaining three queens. Stop drawing the tree at the point where the program will backtrack and remove one of the original five queens.

E3. Modify the linked-list algorithm for generating permutations so that the position occupied by each number does not change by more than one to the left or to the right from any permutation to the next one generated. [This is a simplified form of one rule for *campanology* (ringing changes on church bells).]

Programming Projects 8.2

P1. Run the Queen program on your computer. You will need to write function Write-Board to do the output. In addition, find out exactly how many positions are investigated by including a counter that is incremented every time function AddQueen is started. [Note that a method that placed all eight queens before checking for guarded squares would be equivalent to eight calls to AddQueen.]

P2. Write a program that will read a molecular formula such as H_2SO_4 and will write out the molecular weight of the compound that it represents. Your program should be able to handle bracketed radicals such as in $Al_2(SO_4)_3$. [*Hint*: Use recursion to find the molecular weight of a bracketed radical. *Simplifications:* You may find it helpful to enclose the whole formula in parentheses($\dots$). You will need to set up a table of atomic weights of elements, indexed by their abbreviations. For simplicity the table may be restricted to the more common elements. Some elements have one-letter abbreviations, and some two. For uniformity you may add blanks to the one-letter abbreviations.]

molecular weight

maze **P3.** Describe a rectangular maze by indicating its paths and walls within an array. Write a backtracking program to find a way through the maze.

knight's tour **P4.** Another chessboard puzzle (this one reputedly solved by GAUSS at the age of four) is to find a sequence of moves by a knight that will visit every square of the board exactly once. Recall that a knight's move is to jump two positions either vertically or horizontally and at the same time one position in the perpendicular direction. Such a move can be accomplished by setting x to either 1 or 2, setting y to $3 - x$, and then changing the first coordinate by $\pm x$ and the second by $\pm y$ (providing the resulting position is still on the board). Write a backtracking program that will input an initial position and search for a knight's tour starting at the given position and going to every square once and no square more than once. If you find that the program runs too slowly, a good method to help the knight find its way is to order the list of squares to which it can move from a given position so that it will first try to go to the squares with the least accessibility, that is, to the squares from which there are the fewest knight's moves to squares not yet visited.

8.3 TREE-STRUCTURED PROGRAMS: LOOK-AHEAD IN GAMES

In games of mental skill the person who can anticipate what will happen several moves in advance has a substantial advantage over a competitor who looks only for immediate gain. In this section we develop a computer algorithm to play games by looking at possible moves several steps in advance. This algorithm can be described most naturally in terms of a tree; afterward we show how recursion can be used to program this tree structure.

8.3.1 Game Trees

We can picture the sequences of possible moves by means of a ***game tree***, in which the root denotes the initial situation and the branches from the root denote the legal moves that the first player could make. At the next level down, the branches correspond to the legal moves by the second player in each situation, and so on, with branches from vertices at even levels denoting moves by the first player, and from vertices at odd levels denoting moves by the second player.

Eight The complete game tree for the trivial game of ***Eight*** is shown in Figure 8.7. In this game the first player chooses one of the numbers 1, 2, or 3. At each later turn the appropriate player chooses one of 1, 2, or 3, but the number previously chosen is not allowed. A running sum of the numbers chosen is kept, and if a player brings this sum to exactly eight, then the player wins. If the player takes the sum over eight, then the other player wins. No draws are possible. In the diagram, F denotes a win by the first player, and S a win by the second player.

Even a trivial game like Eight produces a good-sized tree. Games of real interest like Chess or Go have trees so huge that there is no hope of investigating all the branches, and a program that runs in reasonable time can examine only a few levels below the current vertex in the tree. People playing such games are also unable to see every possibility to the end of the game, but they can make intelligent choices, because, with experience, a person comes to recognize that some situations in a game are much better than others,

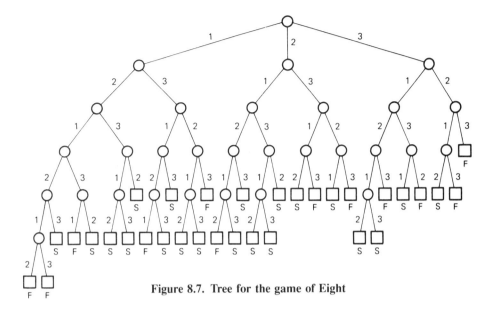

Figure 8.7. Tree for the game of Eight

even if they do not guarantee a win. Thus for any interesting game that we propose to play by computer, we shall need some kind of evaluation function that will examine the current situation and return a number assessing its benefits. To be definite we shall assume that large numbers reflect favorable situations for the first player, and therefore small (or more negative) numbers show an advantage for the second player.

8.3.2 The Minimax Method

Part of the tree for a fictitious game appears in Figure 8.8. Since we are looking ahead, we need the evaluation function only at the leaves of the tree (that is, the positions from which we shall not look further ahead in the game), and from this information we wish

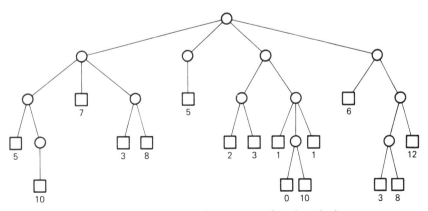

Figure 8.8. A game tree with values assigned at the leaves

to select a move. The move we eventually select is a branch coming from the root, and we take the evaluation function from the perspective of this player, which means that this player selects the maximum value possible. At the next level down the other player will select the smallest value possible, and so on. By working up from the bottom of the tree we can assign values to all the vertices. Since we alternately take minima and *minimax* maxima, this process is called a ***minimax*** function. The result is shown in Figure 8.9 (the dashed lines will be explained later, in one of the projects). The value of the current situation is 7, and the current (first) player should choose the leftmost branch.

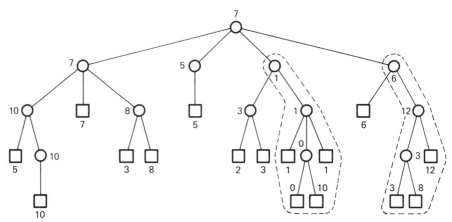

Figure 8.9. Minimax evaluation of a game tree

8.3.3 Algorithm Development

Next let us see how the minimax method can be embodied in a formal algorithm for looking ahead in a game-playing program. We wish to write a general-purpose algorithm that can be used with any two-player game; we shall therefore leave various types and data structures unspecified, since their choice will depend on the particular game being played. First, we shall need to use a function that we call

void Recommend(Player_type P, List_type *L, Value_type *v)

recommended moves that will return a list L of recommended moves for the player P, as well as a value that depends on the current situation in the game (but not yet on which of the recommended moves is eventually made). For the player we use the simple type declaration

typedef enum player_tag {FIRST, SECOND} Player_type;

and always take the first player as the one who wishes to maximize the value, while the second player wishes to minimize the value. The value will normally be a number.

list implementation How the list of recommended moves is to be implemented depends on the game. In some games the moves can be described concisely, and only a few different kinds of moves are appropriate; for such games a contiguous list may be best. In other games the number of recommended moves can change greatly from one turn to another, and a linked list may prove better. Hence we leave the type List_type unspecified, and use auxiliary functions FirstEntry and NextEntry to obtain the first and subsequent moves from the list, a Boolean function Finished to determine when traversing the list is complete, and an integer function Size to return the number of entries.

termination   Before writing the function that looks ahead in the tree, we should decide when the algorithm is to stop looking further. For a game of reasonable complexity, we must establish a number of levels MAXDEPTH beyond which the search will not go. But there are at least two other conditions under which exploring the tree is unnecessary. The first occurs when Recommend returns a list with only one recommended move, and the other occurs when the outcome of the game is already completely determined (it is a certain win, loss, or tie). We coalesce these two conditions by requiring Recommend to return only one move when the outcome of the game is certain. Thus, even if Recommend finds several winning moves, it must return only one of them.

The basic task of looking ahead in the tree can now be described with the following recursive algorithm.

```
/* LookAhead: searches up to depth levels through the game tree; returns the move m
      for player P, and the value v as an assessment of the situation */
void LookAhead(int depth, Player_type P, Value_type *v, Move_type *m)
{
    Recommend(P, &L, v);
    if (list L contains only one recommended move)
        Return the one move and associated value;
    else {
        for (each recommended move)
            Tentatively make the move and recursively LookAhead for the
            best move for the other player;
        Select the best value for P among the values returned in the loop above;
        Return the corresponding move and value as the result;
    }
}
```

outline

8.3.4 Refinement

To specify the details of this algorithm we must, finally, employ two more functions that depend on the game:

$$\text{void MakeMove(Player\_type P, Move\_type m)}$$

and

$$\text{void UndoMove(Player\_type P, Move\_type m)}$$

that make and undo tentative moves as indicated. In the formal function we also rearrange some of the steps from the outline.

```
/* LookAhead: searches up to depth levels through the game tree; returns the move m
      for player P and the value v as an assessment of the situation */
void LookAhead(int depth, Player_type P, Value_type *v, Move_type *m)
{
        Player_type opponent;          /* opponent of P                           */
        Move_type om;                  /* recommended move for opponent           */
        Value_type ov;                 /* value returned for opponent's move      */
        List_type L;                   /* list of recommended moves for P         */
        Move_type tm;                  /* tentative move being tried in tree       */

        Recommend(P, &L, v);
        if (Size(L) <= 0) {
                Forfeit();             /* cannot make any move                    */
        } else if (Size(L) == 1 || depth == 0) {
                /* Set the move; the value v has been set by Recommend. */
                *m = FirstEntry(L);
                return;
        } else {
            if (P == FIRST) {
                    opponent = SECOND;
                    *v = -INFINITY;    /* Set to a value less than any that occurs. */
            } else {
                    opponent = FIRST;
                    *v = INFINITY;
            }
            tm = FirstEntry(L);
            do {
                    MakeMove(P, tm);
                    LookAhead(depth - 1, opponent, &ov, &om);
                    UndoMove(P, tm);
                    if (P == FIRST && ov > *v) {
                            *v = ov;
                            *m = tm;
                    } else if (P == SECOND && ov < *v) {
                            *v = ov;
                            *m = tm;
                    }
                    tm = NextEntry(L);
            } while (!Finished(L));
        }
}
```

Exercises
8.3

E1. Assign values of +1 for a win by the first player, and −1 for a win by the second player in the game of Eight, and apply the minimax function to its tree as shown in Figure 8.7.

E2. A variation of the game of *Nim* begins with a pile of sticks, from which a player can remove 1, 2, or 3 sticks at each turn. The player must remove at least 1 (but no more than remain on the pile). The player who takes the last stick loses. Draw the complete game tree that begins with **(a)** 5 and **(b)** 6 sticks. Assign appropriate values for the leaves of the tree, and evaluate the other nodes by the minimax method.

E3. Draw the top three levels (showing the first two moves) of the game tree for the game of tic-tac-toe (Noughts and Crosses), and calculate the number of vertices that will appear on the fourth level. You may reduce the size of the tree by taking advantage of symmetries: At the first move, for example, show only three possibilities (the center square, a corner, or a side square) rather than all nine. Further symmetries near the root will reduce the size of the game tree.

E4. Write the auxiliary subprograms FirstEntry(L), NextEntry(L), and Size(L) for the case when the list is **(a)** contiguous and **(b)** linked.

Programming Projects 8.3

P1. Write a main program and the other functions needed to play Eight against a human opponent. Function Recommend can return all legal moves at each turn.

P2. Write a look-ahead program for playing tic-tac-toe. In the simplest version, function Recommend returns all empty positions as recommended moves. Approximately how many possibilities will then be investigated in a complete search of the game tree? Implement this simple method. Second, modify the function Recommend so that it searches for two marks in a row with the third empty, and thereby recommends moves more intelligently. Compare the running times of the two versions.

P3. Consider the following game played on an $n \times n$ board. Each player alternately puts a 1 or a 0 into an empty square (either player can use either number), and the game continues until the board is completely filled. The numbers along each row, column, and the two main diagonals are then added. If there are more odd sums than there are even sums, then the first player wins. If the number of even sums is greater, then the second player wins. Otherwise, the game is a tie. Write a look-ahead program to play this game against a human opponent, who chooses the value of n.

three-dimensional tic-tac-toe

P4. [*Major project*]   Write a look-ahead program that plays three dimensional tic-tac-toe. This game is played on a $4 \times 4 \times 4$ cube, with the usual rules. There are 76 possibly winning lines (rows, columns, stacks and diagonals) with four in a row.

Kalah

P5. [*Major project*]   Write a look-ahead program for the game of Kalah (See references at end of chapter for rules and strategy).

P6. If you have worked your way through the tree in Figure 8.9 in enough detail, you may have noticed that it is not necessary to obtain the values for all the vertices while doing the minimax process, for there are some parts of the tree in which the best strategy certainly cannot appear. Let us suppose that we work our way through the tree starting at the lower left, and filling in the value for a parent vertex as soon as we have the values for all its children. After we have done all the vertices in the two main branches on the left, we find values of 7 and 5, and therefore the maximum value will be at least 7. When we go to the next vertex on level 1 and its left child, we find that the value of this child is 3. At this stage we are taking minima, so the value to be assigned to the parent on level 1 cannot possibly be more than 3 (it is actually 1). Since 3 is less than 7, the first player will take the leftmost branch instead, *alpha-beta pruning*

and we can exclude the other branch. The vertices that, in this way, need never be evaluated, are shown within dotted lines in color in Figure 8.10. The process of eliminating vertices in this way is generally called ***alpha-beta pruning***. The letters α (alpha) and β (beta) are generally used to denote the cutoff points found.

Modify the function LookAhead so that it uses alpha-beta pruning to reduce the number of branches investigated. Compare the performance of the two versions in playing several games.

8.4 COMPILATION BY RECURSIVE DESCENT

Consider the problem of designing a compiler that translates a program written in C into machine language. As the compiler reads through the source program written in C, it must understand the syntax and translate each line into the equivalent instructions in machine language. C is more difficult to compile than some languages (such as Pascal) because it allows the programmer to split a program between different files and compile them separately. We need not be concerned with separate compilation for our brief discussion.

identifiers

The first part of a C program typically contains declarations of global types and variables. The compiler will use this information to allocate space for variables and at the same time remember the identifiers that have been declared as names of types, variables, and the like, so that these identifiers can be interpreted correctly when they appear later in the program. Hence the compiler sets up a ***symbol table*** to keep track of the identifiers. Some compilers use a binary tree to contain the symbol table; others use a hash table; still other compilers use some combination or some other data structure. Although many interesting ideas appear in the design and use of symbol tables, our goal here is only to obtain an overview of how a compiler can use recursion, so we shall not study symbol tables further.

When we come to the declarations of functions (or compound statements), we can see an application of recursion. C syntax allows for the declaration of local variables within functions. These local declarations can be parsed in the same manner as the global declarations so there is no need to write a separate section of the compiler to handle these.

tokens

Note that the compiler must continually check what is the next word or symbol in the program. Depending on what this word or symbol is, various actions will be taken. Such a word or symbol is called a ***token***, and for our purposes we take a token to be any one of a C reserved word, identifier, literal constant, operator, or punctuation mark. Note, furthermore, that the only way to tell that many constructions in C have terminated is when a token is found that is *not* part of the construction. Hence whenever we start to process part of the program, the variable nexttoken will be the token that initiates that part, and when the processing is complete, then nexttoken will be the first token not in the part just processed. The function GetToken will split out the next token.

parsing

The process of splitting a text or expression into pieces to determine its syntax is called ***parsing***. Parsing can proceed either by first examining the atomic (indivisible) building blocks and how they are put together (called ***bottom-up parsing***) or by splitting the text or expression into simpler components (called ***top-down parsing***). Hence comes *recursive descent*   the motivation for the term ***recursive descent***: the compiler parses large constructions by splitting them into smaller pieces and recursively parses each of the pieces. It thereby descends to simpler and smaller constructions, which are finally split apart into their atomic components, which can be evaluated directly.

Parsing the statements of a program can be done by recursive descent. The main part of a subprogram is a compound statement and is parsed by the function DoCompound-Statement. A compound statement is made up of zero or more declarations followed by zero or more statements, each of which will be parsed by DoStatement, which, in turn, invokes a different function for each possible kind of statement.

As an example, let us see how an if statement might be parsed and translated into an assembler language (that is, into a language that corresponds directly with machine-level instructions, but still allows symbolic names and statement labels). From its syntax diagram in Figure 8.10, we know that an if statement consists of the token if followed by a parenthesized Boolean expression followed by a statement, and finally optionally followed by the token else and another statement. See Figure 8.10.

The assembler-language equivalent of the if statement will first evaluate the expression, and then use conditional jumps (goto statements) to branch around the assembler code corresponding to the statements in the if or else clauses, as appropriate. The syntax diagram therefore translates into the following function.

```
/* DoIf: parse an if statement */
void DoIf(void)
{
    GetToken(nexttoken);              /* Skip if keyword.                          */
    if (nexttoken != '(')
        Error();
    GetToken(nexttoken);              /* Skip '('.                                */
    /* This writes the assembler code to evaluate the Boolean expression. */
    DoExpression();
    if (nexttoken != ')')
        Error();
    GetToken(nexttoken);              /* Skip ')'.                                */

    Generate a new assembler-language label x;
    Write assembler code that will cause a conditional jump
        to label x when the Boolean expression is false;
    DoStatement();                    /* statement in the first clause            */

    if (nexttoken != 'else') {
        Write the label x at this point in the assembler code;
    } else {                          /* case with no else clause                 */
        Generate a new assembler-language label y;
        Write an assembler unconditional jump to label y;
        Write the label x at this point in the assembler code;
        GetToken(nexttoken);          /* Skip else keyword.                       */
        DoStatement();                /* else clause                              */
        Write the label y at this point in the assembler code;
    }
}
```

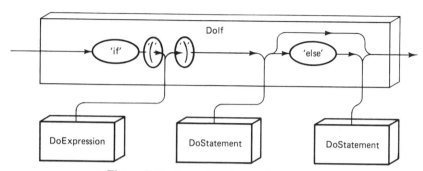

Figure 8.10. Parse tree for an if statement

exercise   Finally, as an exercise you should apply this algorithm to the statement

if (a > 0) b = 1; else if (a == 0) b = 2; else b = 3;

Since this line is made up of two if statements, the parsing function will call itself recursively and generate a total of four labels. The parse tree for this statement is shown in Figure 8.11.

In practice, an actual compiler may rearrange some of the jumps and thereby produce an answer superficially different from yours. The output of one such compiler (IBM C/2™ for an IBM PS/2™)[1] applied to the preceding statement is given in Figure 8.12, where

sample output

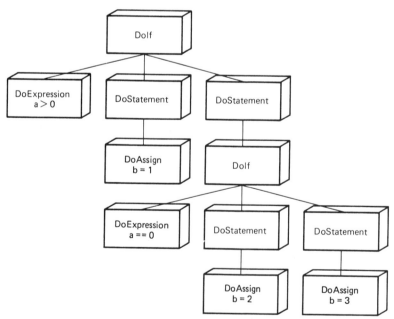

Figure 8.11. Parse tree for nested if statement

---

[1]   IBM C/2 and PS/2 are trademarks of the International Business Machines Corporation.

some changes were made to the actual output of the compiler to replace some numeric displacements calculated by the compiler by their symbolic forms and to simplify the labels. In the resulting assembly language, the instruction CMP tests the sign of an integer; JE branches if the integer is equal to 0, JG if it is greater than 0. JMP is an unconditional jump. MOV moves the second number given to the first location specified.

```
              CMP     A,0      ; if (a > 0)
              JG      L0
              JMP     L1
    L0:       MOV     B,1      ; b = 1;
              JMP     L2
    L1:       CMP     A,0      ; else if (a == 0)
              JE      L3
              JMP     L4
    L3:       MOV     B,2      ; b = 2;
              JMP     L5       ; else
    L4:       MOV     B,3      ; b = 3;
    L5:
    L2:
```

Figure 8.12. Output from a C compiler

compilers   As you can see from all this, the construction of a compiler is quite a complicated process. The present discussion has attempted only to give a broad overview of the way in which recursion proves useful in writing a compiler. If you take a more detailed view, you will find that we have not only omitted programming steps, but that it is necessary to address many problems that we have not considered at all (for example, error processing). Many interesting ideas arise in the consideration of these problems, so that compiler design and construction constitute a major subject within computer science, one worthy of extensive study in its own right.

Exercises 8.4

E1. For each of the following statements, draw a tree similar to Figure 8.11 showing the subprogram calls that will occur in parsing the statement. You may assume the existence of subprograms such as DoSwitch, DoWhile, and the like.

    a. while (x > 0) if (x > 10) x = −x; else x = y − x;

    b. if (a > b) if (c > d) x = 1; else if (e > f) x = 3;

E2. Draw parse trees and write outlines of functions for parsing the following kinds of statements.

    a. while (expression) statement

    b. Compound statement: { statement(s) }

    c. switch { ... }

8.5 PRINCIPLES OF RECURSION

8.5.1 Guidelines for Using Recursion

Recursion is a tool to allow the programmer to concentrate on the key step of an algorithm, without having initially to worry about coupling that step with all the others. As usual with problem solving, the first approach should usually be to consider several simple examples, and as these become better understood, to attempt to formulate a method that will work more generally. In regard to using recursion, you may begin by asking yourself, "How can this problem be divided into parts?" or "How will the key step in the middle be done?" Be sure to keep your answer simple but generally applicable. Do not come up with a multitude of special cases that work only for small problems or at the beginning and end of large ones. Once you have a simple, small step toward the solution, ask whether the remainder of the problem can be done in the same or a similar way, and modify your method if necessary so that it will be sufficiently general.

key step

stopping rule

Once the key step is determined, find a stopping rule that will indicate that the problem or a suitable part of it is done. Build this stopping rule into your key step. You should now be able to write the main program and a recursive function that will describe how to carry the step through.

termination

Next, and of great importance, is a verification that the recursion will always terminate. Start with a general situation and check that in a finite number of steps the stopping rule will be satisfied and the recursion terminate. Be sure also that your algorithm correctly handles extreme cases. When called on to do nothing, any algorithm should be able to return gracefully, but it is especially important that recursive algorithms do so, since a call to do nothing is often the stopping rule.

recursion tree

The key tool for the analysis of recursive algorithms is the recursion tree. As we shall see in the next section, the height of the tree is closely related to the amount of memory that the program will require, and the total size of the tree reflects the number of times the key step will be done, and hence the total time the program will use. It is usually highly instructive to draw the recursion tree for one or two simple examples appropriate to your problem.

8.5.2 How Recursion Works

design versus implementation

The question of how recursion is actually done in a computer should be carefully separated in our minds from the question of using recursion in designing algorithms. In the design phase, we should use all problem-solving methods that prove to be appropriate, and recursion is one of the most flexible and powerful of these tools. In the implementation phase, we may need to ask which of several methods is the best under the circumstances. There are at least two ways to accomplish recursion in computer systems. At present, the first of these is experimental and only starting to be available in commercial systems, but with changing costs and capabilities of computer equipment, it will probably soon be regarded as quite practical. Our major point in considering two different implementations is that, although restrictions in space and time do need to be considered, they should be considered separately from the process of algorithm design, since different kinds of computer equipment in the future may lead to different capabilities and restrictions.

1. Multiple Processors: Concurrency

Perhaps the most natural way to think of implementing recursion is to think of each subprogram not as occupying a different part of the same computer, but to think of each subprogram as running on a separate machine. In that way, when one subprogram invokes another, it starts the corresponding machine going, and when the other machine completes its work, it sends the answer back to the first machine, which can then continue its task. If a function makes two recursive calls to itself, then it will simply start two other processors working with the same instructions that it is using. When these processors complete their work, they will send the answers back to the processor that started them going. If they, in turn, make recursive calls, then they will simply start still more processors working.

costs

At one time, the central processor was the most expensive component of a computer system, and any thought of a system including more than one processor would have been considered extravagant. The price of processing power compared to other computing costs has now dropped radically, and in all likelihood we shall, before long, see large computer systems that will include hundreds, if not thousands, of identical microprocessors among their components. When this occurs, implementation of recursion via multiple processors may become commonplace if not inevitable.

With multiple processors, programmers no longer consider algorithms solely as a linear sequence of actions, but instead realize that some parts of the algorithm can be done at the same time as other parts. In divide-and-conquer algorithms such as quicksort, for example, the two halves into which the problem is divided often do not depend on each other and can be worked on simultaneously by multiple processors.

concurrency

Processes that take place simultaneously are called *concurrent*. The study of concurrent processes and the methods for communication between them is, at present, an active subject for research in computing science, one in which important developments will undoubtedly improve the ways in which algorithms will be described and implemented in coming years.

2. Single Processor Implementation: Storage Areas

In order to determine how recursion can be efficiently implemented in a system with only one processor, let us first for the moment leave recursion to consider the question of what steps are needed to call a subprogram, on the primitive level of machine-language instructions in a simple computer. The hardware of any computer has a limited range of instructions that includes (amongst other instructions) doing arithmetic on specified words of storage or on registers, moving data to and from the memory, and branching (jumping) to a specified address. When a calling program branches to the beginning of a subprogram, the address of the place whence the call was made must be stored in memory, or else the subprogram could not remember where to return. The addresses or

return address

values of the calling parameters must also be stored where the subprogram can find them, and where the answers can in turn be found by the calling program after the subprogram returns. When the subprogram starts, it will do various calculations on its local variables

local variables

and storage areas. Once the subprogram finishes, however, these local variables are lost, since they are not available outside the subprogram. The subprogram will of course have used the registers within the CPU for its calculations, so normally these would have different values after the subprogram finishes than before it is called. It is traditional, however, to expect that a subprogram will change nothing except its calling parameters or global variables (side effects). Thus it is customary that the subprogram will save all the registers it will use and restore their values before it returns.

storage area   In summary, when a subprogram is called, it must have a storage area (perhaps scattered as several areas); it must save the registers or whatever else it will change, using the storage area also for its return address, calling parameters, and local variables. As it returns, it will restore the registers and the other storage that it was expected to restore. After the return it no longer needs anything in its local storage area.

In this way we implement subprogram calls by changing storage areas, an action that takes the place of changing processors that we considered before. In these considerations it really makes no difference whether the subprogram is called recursively or not, providing that, in the recursive case, we are careful to regard two recursive calls as being different, so that we do not mix the storage areas for one call with those of another, any more than we would mix storage areas for different subprograms, one called from within the other. For a nonrecursive subprogram the storage area can be one fixed area, permanently reserved, since we know that one call to the subprogram will have returned before another one is made, and after the first one returns the information stored is no longer needed. For recursive subprograms, however, the information stored must be preserved until the outer call returns, so an inner call must use a different area for its temporary storage.

Note that the common practice of reserving a permanent storage area for a nonrecursive subprogram can in fact be quite wasteful, since a considerable amount of memory may be consumed in this way, memory that might be useful for other purposes while the subprogram is not active.

3. Re-Entrant Programs

Essentially the same problem of multiple storage areas arises in a quite different context, that of **re-entrant** programs. In a large time-sharing system there may be many users simultaneously using the C compiler or the text-editing system. These systems programs are quite large, and it would be very wasteful of high-speed memory to keep thirty or forty copies of exactly the same large set of instructions in memory at once, one for each user. What is generally done instead is to write large systems programs like the C compiler or the text editor with the instructions in one area, but the addresses of all variables or other data kept in a separate area. Then in the memory of the time-sharing system there will be only one copy of the instructions, but a separate data area for each user.

This situation is somewhat analogous to students writing a test in a room where the questions are written on the blackboard. There is then only one set of questions that all students can read, but each student separately writes answers on different pieces of paper. There is no difficulty for different students to be reading the same or different questions at the same time, and with different pieces of paper their answers will not be mixed with each other. See Figure 8.13.

4. Data Structures: Stacks and Trees

We have yet to specify the data structure that will keep track of all these storage areas for subprograms; to do so, let us look at the tree of subprogram calls. So that an inner subprogram can access variables declared in an outer block, and so that we can return

Instructions

Figure 8.13. Re-entrant processes

stacks

properly to the calling program, we must, at every point in the tree, remember all vertices on the path from the given point back to the root. As we move through the tree, vertices are added to and deleted from one end of this path; the other end (at the root) remains fixed. Hence the vertices on the path form a stack; the storage areas for subprograms likewise are to be kept as a stack. This process is illustrated in Figure 8.14.

time and space requirements

From Figure 8.14 and our discussion we can immediately conclude that the amount of space needed to implement recursion (which of course is related to the number of storage areas in current use) is directly proportional to the height of the recursion tree. Programmers who have not carefully studied recursion sometimes think mistakenly that the space requirement relates to the total number of vertices in the tree. The *time* requirement of the program is related to the number of times subprograms are done, and therefore to the total number of vertices in the tree, but the *space* requirement is only that of the storage areas on the path from a single vertex back to the root. Thus the space requirement is reflected in the height of the tree. A well-balanced, bushy recursion tree hence signifies a recursive process that can do much work with little need for extra space.

Figure 8.14 can, in fact, be interpreted in a broader context than as the process of invoking subprograms. It thereby elucidates an easy but important observation, providing an intimate connection between arbitrary trees and stacks:

THEOREM 8.1

During the traversal of any tree, vertices are added to or deleted from the path back to the root in the fashion of a stack. Given any stack, conversely, a tree can be drawn to portray the life history of the stack, as items are added to or deleted from it.

In most modern computers, efficient means are provided to allow the same instructions to refer to different storage areas as desired. In the IBM 370™ series, for example, every instruction that refers to memory calculates the address it uses by adding some value (displacement) to the contents of a specified register called the base register. If the value in the base register is set to the beginning of one storage area then all later

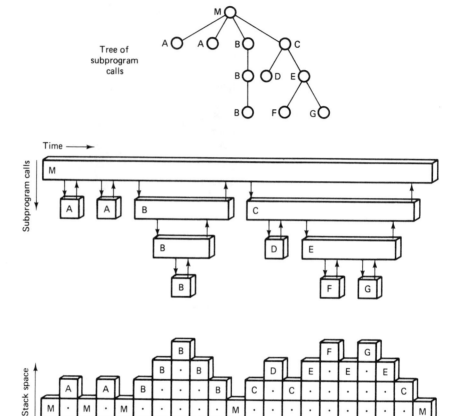

Figure 8.14. A tree of subprogram calls and the associated stack frames

instructions will refer to that area. Changing only the one value in the base register will make all the instructions refer to another storage area. A second example consists of most microcomputers. Most of the instructions on these machines can be made to push or pop a stack automatically as they refer to memory for their operands.

5. Conclusion

The moral of the story is that, when properly implemented, recursion is neither inefficient nor expensive, except perhaps on some machines of quite old design that are rapidly being retired. Some compilers, unfortunately, do make a mess out of recursive functions, but on a well-designed system there is essentially no additional time overhead for using recursion, and no reason to avoid it when it is the natural method.

8.5.3 Tail Recursion

Suppose that the very last action of a function is to make a recursive call to itself. In the stack implementation of recursion, as we have seen, the local variables of the function *discarding stack entries*

will be pushed onto the stack as the recursive call is initiated. When the recursive call terminates, these local variables will be popped from the stack and thereby restored to their former values. But doing so is pointless, because the recursive call was the last action of the function, so that the function now terminates and the just-restored local variables are immediately discarded.

When the very last action of a function is a recursive call to itself, it is thus pointless to use the stack, as we have seen, since no local variables need to be preserved. All that is needed is to set the dummy calling parameters to their new values and branch to the beginning of the function. We summarize this principle for future reference.

THEOREM 8.2

If the last executed statement of a function is a recursive call to itself, then this call can be eliminated by changing the values of the calling parameters to those specified in the recursive call, and repeating the whole function.

The process of this transformation is shown in Figure 8.15. Part (a) shows the storage areas used by the calling program M and several copies of the recursive function P. The colored arrows show the flow of control. Since each call by P to P is its last action, there is no need to maintain the storage areas after the call, as shown in part (b). Part (c), finally, shows these calls to P as repeated in iterative fashion on the same level.

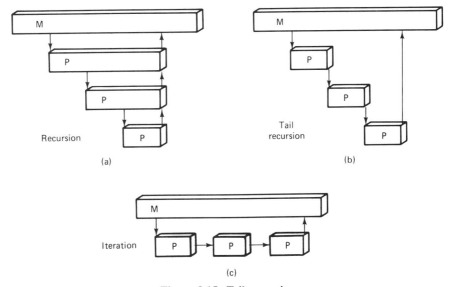

Figure 8.15. Tail recursion

tail recursion

This special case when a recursive call is the last executed statement of the function is especially important because it frequently occurs. It is called ***tail recursion***. You should carefully note that tail recursion means that the last executed statement is a recursive call, not necessarily that the recursive call is the last statement appearing in the function. Tail recursion may appear, for example, within one clause of a switch statement or an if statement where other program lines appear later.

time and space

With most modern compilers there will be little difference in execution *time* whether tail recursion is left in a program or is removed. If *space* considerations are important, however, then the principle of Theorem 8.2 should usually be followed if it is applicable, whether other recursion is being removed or not. By rearranging the termination condition if needed, it is usually possible to repeat the function using a do−while or a while statement.

Consider, for example, a divide-and-conquer algorithm like that devised for the Towers of Hanoi in Section 8.1. By removing tail recursion, function Move of the original recursive program can be expressed as

Hanoi without tail recursion

```
/* Move: move n disks from a to b using c for temporary storage. */
void Move(int n, int a, int b, int c)
{
    int t;

    while (n > 0) {
        Move(n−1, a, c, b);
        printf("Move a disk from %d to %d.\n", a, b);
        n−−;
        t = a;
        a = c;
        c = t;
    }
}
```

We should have been quite clever had we thought of this version of the function when we first looked at the problem, but now that we have discovered it via other considerations, we can give it a natural interpretation. Think of the two needles a and c as in the same class: we wish to use them for intermediate storage as we slowly move all the disks onto b. To move a stack of n disks onto b, then, we must move all except the bottom to the other one of a, c, then move the bottom one to b, and repeat after interchanging a and c, continuing to shuffle all except the bottom one between a and c, and at each pass getting a new bottom one onto b.

8.5.4 When Not to Use Recursion

1. Factorials

Many textbooks present the calculation of factorials as the first example of a recursive program:

```
/* Factorial: recursive version for n! */
int Factorial(int n)
{
    if (n <= 1)
        return 1;
    else
        return n * Factorial(n−1);
}
```

Although this program is simple and easy, there is an equally simple iterative program:

```
/* Factorial: iterative version for n! */
int Factorial (int n)
{
    int i, p;

    p = 1;
    for (i = 2; i <= n; i++)
         p *= i;
    return p;
}
```

Which of these programs uses less storage space? At first glance it might appear that the recursive one does, since it has no local variables, and the iterative program has two. But actually (see Figure 8.16) the recursive program will set up a stack and fill it with the $n - 1$ numbers

$$n, n - 1, n - 2, \ldots, 2$$

that are its calling parameters before each recursion and will then, as it works its way out of the recursion, multiply these numbers in the same order as does the second program. The progress of execution for the recursive function is as follows:

$$
\begin{aligned}
\text{Factorial(6)} \quad &= 6 * \text{Factorial(5)}\\
&= 6 * (5 * \text{Factorial(4)})\\
&= 6 * (5 * (4 * \text{Factorial(3)}))\\
&= 6 * (5 * (4 * (3 * \text{Factorial(2)})))\\
&= 6 * (5 * (4 * (3 * (2 * \text{Factorial(1)}))))\\
&= 6 * (5 * (4 * (3 * (2 * 1))))\\
&= 6 * (5 * (4 * (3 * 2)))\\
&= 6 * (5 * (4 * 6))\\
&= 6 * (5 * 24)\\
&= 6 * 120\\
&= 720.
\end{aligned}
$$

Thus the recursive program keeps considerably more storage, and will take more time as well, since it must store and retrieve all the numbers as well as multiply them.

Figure 8.16. Recursion tree for calculating factorials

2. Fibonacci Numbers

A far more wasteful example than factorials (that also appears as an apparently recommended program in some textbooks) is the computation of the **Fibonacci numbers**, which are defined by the recurrence relation

$$F_0 = 0, \quad F_1 = 1, \quad F_n = F_{n-1} + F_{n-2} \quad for \quad n \geq 2.$$

(If you are interested, consult Appendix A.4 for a discussion of the properties of these numbers.) The recursive program closely follows the definition:

```
/* Fib: recursive version to calculate Fibonacci numbers */
int Fib(int n)
{
        if (n <= 0)
                return 0;
        else if (n == 1)
                return 1;
        else
                return Fib(n-1) + Fib(n-2);
}
```

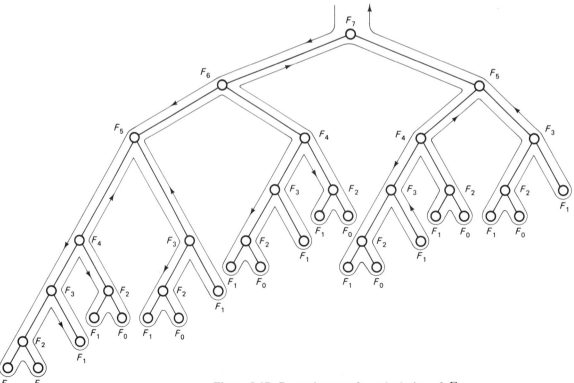

Figure 8.17. Recursion tree for calculation of F_7

In fact, this program is quite attractive, since it is of the divide-and-conquer form: The answer is obtained by calculating two simpler cases. As we shall see, however, in this example it is not "divide and conquer," but "divide and complicate."

To assess this algorithm, let us consider, as an example, the calculation of F_7, whose recursion tree is shown in Figure 8.17. The function will first have to obtain F_6 and F_5. To get F_6 requires F_5 and F_4, and so on. But after F_5 is calculated on the way to F_6, then it will be lost and unavailable when it is later needed to get F_7. Hence, as the recursion tree shows, the recursive program needlessly repeats the same calculations over and over. Further analysis appears as an exercise. It turns out that amount of time used by the recursive function to calculate F_n grows exponentially with n.

As with factorials, we can produce a simple iterative program by noting that we can start at 0 and keep only three variables, the current Fibonacci number and its two predecessors.

```
/* Fib: iterative version to calculate Fibonacci numbers */
int Fib(int n)
{
        int i;
        int twoback;                    /* second previous number, F_{i-2}    */
        int oneback;                    /* previous number, F_{i-1}           */
        int current;                    /* current number F_i                 */

        if (n <= 0)
                return 0;
        else if (n ==  1)
                return 1;
        else {
                twoback = 0;
                oneback = 1;
                for (i = 2; i <= n; i++) {
                        current = twoback + oneback;
                        twoback = oneback;
                        oneback = current;
                }
                return current;
        }
}
```

The iterative function obviously uses time that is $O(n)$, so that, as we saw in Section 5.6, the time difference between this function and the exponential time of the recursive function will be vast.

If you regard this nonrecursive program as too tricky, then you can write a straightforward iterative program that sets up a list of length n and calculates F_n simply by starting with F_0 and calculating and storing all the Fibonacci numbers up through F_n. Even this program will use only about n words of storage, which is less than the recursive program will use.

3. Comparisons Between Recursion and Iteration

What is fundamentally different between these two examples and the proper uses of recursion that were illustrated in the previous sections of this chapter? To answer this question we shall again turn to the examination of recursion trees. It should already be clear that a study of the recursion tree will provide much useful information to help us decide when recursion should or should not be used.

chain   If a function makes only one recursive call to itself, then its recursion tree has a very simple form: it is a chain; that is, each vertex has only one child. This child corresponds to the single recursive call that occurs. Such a simple tree is easy to comprehend. For the factorial function it is simply the list of requests to calculate the factorials from $(n-1)!$ down to 1!. By reading the recursion tree from bottom to top instead of top to bottom, we immediately obtain the iterative program from the recursive one. When the tree does reduce to a chain, then transformation from recursion to iteration is often easy, and will likely save both space and time.

Note that a function's making only one recursive call to itself is not at all the same as having the recursive call made only one place in the function, since this place might be inside a loop. It is also possible to have two places that issue a recursive call (such as both the then and else clauses of an if statement) where only one call can actually occur.

The recursion tree for calculating Fibonacci numbers is not a chain, but contains a great many vertices signifying duplicate tasks. When a recursive program is run, it *duplicate tasks* sets up a stack to use while traversing the tree, but if the results stored on the stack are discarded rather than kept in some other data structure for future use, then a great deal of duplication of work may occur, as in the recursive calculation of Fibonacci numbers.

change data   In such cases it is preferable to substitute another data structure for the stack, one *structures* that allows references to locations other than the top. The most obvious choice is that of an ordinary list holding all information calculated so far, and this in fact works nicely for the Fibonacci numbers. The iterative program that we wrote for the Fibonacci numbers, the one that uses only three temporary variables, is in one sense tricky, even though it is easy. The reason is that nothing similar is likely to be found for the numbers defined by the following recurrence relation, one that is similar in form to that for the Fibonacci numbers, and could likely not be separated from it by general programming methods:

$$G_0 = 0, \quad G_1 = 1, \quad G_n = G_{n-1} + G_k \quad \text{for } n \geq 2,$$

where $k = \lceil \ln n \rceil$.

After removal of tail recursion, most of the programs written earlier in this chapter each involve only one recursive call, but note carefully that this call is within a loop, and therefore their recursion trees will not reduce to chains. In some cases, nonetheless, *symmetrical trees* it is possible to predict what the parameters of each recursive call will be, and thereby to devise an equivalent nonrecursive program with no stacks. In Appendix B we exploit the complete symmetry of the recursion tree for mergesort, in order to derive an efficient nonrecursive version of this important sorting method.

recursion removal   Finally, by setting up an explicit stack, we can take any recursive program and rearrange it into nonrecursive form. Appendix B describes methods for doing so. The resulting program, however, is often more complicated and harder to understand than is the recursive version, and for many applications the saving of space and time is insignificant. On machines with hardware stack instructions, in fact, the nonrecursive form may actually require more running time than the equivalent recursive program. Appendix B develops a nonrecursive version of quicksort as an example.

8.5.5 Guidelines and Conclusions

In making a decision, then, about whether to write a particular algorithm in recursive or nonrecursive form, a good starting point is to consider the recursion tree. If it has a simple form, the iterative version may be better. If it involves duplicate tasks, then data structures other than stacks will be appropriate, and the need for recursion may disappear. If the recursion tree appears quite bushy, with little duplication of tasks, then recursion is likely the natural method.

The stack used to resolve recursion can be regarded as a list of postponed obligations for the program. If this list can be easily constructed in advance, then iteration is probably better; if not, recursion may be. Recursion is something of a top-down approach to problem solving; it divides the problem into pieces or selects out one key step, postponing the rest. Iteration is more of a bottom-up approach; it begins with what is known and from this constructs the solution step by step.

top-down design

It is always true that recursion can be replaced by iteration and stacks. It is also true, conversely (see references for the proof), that any (iterative) program that manipulates a stack can be replaced by a recursive program with no stack. Thus the careful programmer should not only ask whether recursion should be removed, but should also ask, when a program involves stacks, whether the introduction of recursion might produce a more natural and understandable program that could lead to improvements in the approach and in the results.

stacks or recursion

**Exercises
8.5**

E1. Determine which functions written in earlier sections of this chapter have tail recursion, and rewrite them to remove the tail recursion.

E2. In the recursive calculation of F_n, determine exactly how many times each smaller Fibonacci number will be calculated. From this, determine the order-of-magnitude time and space requirements of the recursive function. [You may find out either by setting up and solving a recurrence relation (top-down approach), or by finding the answer in simple cases and proving it more generally by mathematical induction (bottom-up approach). Consult Appendix A.4.]

E3. The **greatest common divisor** (GCD) of two positive integers is the largest integer that divides both of them. Thus the GCD of 8 and 12 is 4, the GCD of 9 and 18 is 9, and the GCD of 16 and 25 is 1. Write a recursive function int GCD (int x, int y) that implements the **division algorithm**: If y = 0, then the GCD of x and y is x; otherwise the GCD of x and y is the same as the GCD of y and x % y. Rewrite the function in iterative form.

E4. The binomial coefficients may be defined by the following recurrence relation, which is the idea of **Pascal's triangle**, the top of which is shown in Figure 8.18.

$$C(n,0) = 1 \quad \text{and} \quad C(n,n) = 1 \quad \text{for } n \geq 0.$$
$$C(n,k) = C(n-1,k) + C(n-1,k-1) \quad \text{for } n > k > 0.$$

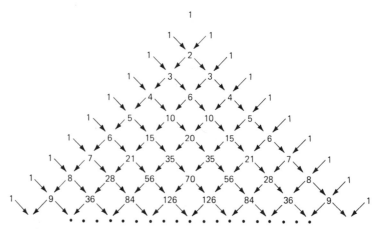

Figure 8.18. The top of Pascal's triangle of binomial coefficients

   a. Write a recursive function to generate $C(n, k)$ by the preceding formula.

   b. Draw the recursion tree for calculating $C(6, 4)$.

   c. Use a square array, and write a nonrecursive program to generate Pascal's triangle in the lower left half of the array.

   d. Write a nonrecursive program with neither array nor stack to calculate $C(n, k)$ for arbitrary $n \geq k \geq 0$.

   e. Determine the asymptotic space and time requirements for each of the algorithms devised in parts (a), (c), and (d).

E5. *Ackermann's function*, defined as follows, is a standard device to determine how well recursion is implemented on a computer.

$$
\begin{array}{ll}
A(0, n) = n + 1 & \text{for } n \geq 0. \\
A(m, 0) = A(m - 1, 1) & \text{for } m > 0. \\
A(m, n) = A(m - 1, A(m, n - 1)) & \text{for } m > 0 \text{ and } n > 0.
\end{array}
$$

   a. Write a recursive function to calculate Ackermann's Function.

   b. Calculate the following values:

$$
\begin{array}{lllll}
A(0, 0) & A(0, 9) & A(1, 8) & A(2, 2) & A(2, 0) \\
A(2, 3) & A(3, 2) & A(4, 2) & A(4, 3) & A(4, 0)
\end{array}
$$

   c. Write a nonrecursive function to calculate Ackermann's function.

POINTERS AND PITFALLS

   1. Recursion should be used freely in the initial design of algorithms. It is especially appropriate where the main step toward solution consists of reducing a problem to one or more smaller cases.

   2. Be very careful that your algorithm always terminates and handles trivial cases correctly.

3. Tail recursion should be removed if space considerations are important (Theorem 8.2).

4. The recursion tree should be studied to see whether the recursion is needlessly repeating work, or if the tree represents an efficient division of the work into pieces.

5. A tree that reduces to a chain implies that recursion can be replaced by iteration.

6. If the recursion tree shows complete regularity that can be determined in advance, then sometimes this regularity can be built into the algorithm in a way that will improve efficiency and perhaps remove the recursion.

7. Recursive functions and iterative functions using stacks can accomplish exactly the same tasks. Consider carefully whether recursion or iteration will lead to a clearer program and give more insight into the problem.

8. Recursion can always be translated into iteration, but the general rules (Appendix B) will often produce a result that greatly obscures the structure of the program. Such obfuscation should be tolerated only when the programming language makes it unavoidable, and even then it should be well documented.

REVIEW QUESTIONS

8.1 **1.** Define the term *divide and conquer*.

8.2 **2.** Describe *backtracking* as a problem-solving method.

   3. State the pigeonhole principle.

8.3 **4.** Determine the value of the following game tree by the *minimax* method.

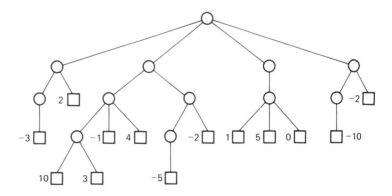

8.4 **5.** Draw a parse tree for the expression

   for (i = 0; i < 10; i++) if (array[i]) Process(i); else Redo(i);

8.5 **6.** Name two different ways to implement recursion.

   7. What is a *re-entrant* program?

8. How does the time requirement for a recursive function relate to its recursion tree?

9. How does the space requirement for a recursive function relate to its recursion tree?

10. What is *tail* recursion?

11. Rewrite the quicksort function Sort of Section 7.8.1 to remove tail recursion.

12. Describe the relationship between the shape of the recursion tree and the efficiency of the corresponding recursive algorithm.

REFERENCES FOR FURTHER STUDY

The examples and applications studied in this chapter come from a variety of sources. The Towers of Hanoi is quite well known, and appears in several textbooks. A survey of related papers is

D. Wood, "The Towers of Brahma and Hanoi revisited", *Journal of Recreational Mathematics* 14 (1981–82), 17–24.

Our treatment of the Eight Queens problem especially follows that given in

N. Wirth, *Algorithms + Data Structures = Programs*, Prentice Hall, Englewood Cliffs, N.J., 1976, pp. 143–147.

This book by Wirth also contains solutions of the Knight's Tour problem (pp. 137–142), as well as a chapter (pp. 280–349) on compiling and parsing.

The algorithm that generates permutations by insertion into a linked list was published in the ACM *SIGCSE Bulletin* 14 (February, 1982), 92–96. Useful surveys of many methods for generating permutations are

R. Sedgewick, "Permutation generation methods", *Computing Surveys* 9 (1977), 137–164; addenda, ibid., 314–317.

R. W. Topor, "Functional programs for generating permutations", *Computer Journal* 25 (1982), 257–263.

The original reference for the efficient algorithm by Heap is

B. R. Heap, "Permutations by Interchanges", *Computer Journal* 6 (1963), 293–294.

The applications of permutations to campanology (change ringing of bells) produce interesting problems amenable to computer study. An excellent source for further information is

F. J. Budden, *The Fascination of Groups*, Cambridge University Press, Cambridge, England, 1972, pp. 451–479.

Compilation by recursive descent is a standard topic in compiler design, a topic treated in detail in most newer textbooks in compiler design. Consult, for example,

Alfred V. Aho, Ravi Sethi, and Jeffrey D. Ullman, *Compilers: Principles, Techniques and Tools*, Addison-Wesley, Reading, Mass., 1988.

Many other applications of recursion appear in books such as

E. Horowitz and S. Sahni, *Fundamentals of Computer Algorithms*, Computer Science Press, 1978, 626 pages.

This book (pp. 290–302) contains more extensive discussion and analysis of game trees and look-ahead programs. An outline of a programming project for the game of Kalah appears in

CHARLES WETHERELL, *Etudes for Programmers*, Prentice Hall, Englewood Cliffs, N. J., 1978.

The general theory of recursion forms a topic of current research. A readable presentation from a theoretical approach is

R. S. BIRD, *Programs and Machines*, John Wiley, New York, 1976.

See also

R. S. BIRD, "Notes on recursion elimination", *Communications of the ACM* 20 (1977), 434–439.

R. S. BIRD, "Improving programs by the introduction of recursion", *Communications of the ACM* 20 (1977), 856–863.

A computer system made up from 64 small computers is described in

CHARLES L. SEITZ, "The Cosmic Cube," *Communications of the ACM* 28 (1985), 22–33.

The proof that stacks may be eliminated by the introduction of recursion appears in

S. BROWN, D. GRIES and T. SZYMANSKI, "Program schemes with pushdown stores," *SIAM Journal on Computing* 1 (1972), 242–268.

Binary Trees

Linked lists have great advantages of flexibility over the contiguous representation of data structures, but they have one weak feature. They are sequential lists; that is, they are arranged so that it is necessary to move through them only one position at a time. In this chapter we overcome these disadvantages by studying trees as data structures, using the methods of pointers and linked lists for their implementation. Data structures organized as trees will prove valuable for a range of applications, especially for problems of information retrieval.

Consider the problem of searching an ordinary linked list for some target key. There is no way to move through the list other than one node at a time, and hence searching through the list must always reduce to a sequential search. As you know, sequential search is usually very slow in comparison with binary search. The pivotal question for this chapter is,

> *Can we find a method for rearranging the nodes of a linked list so that we can search in time $O(\log n)$ instead of $O(n)$?*

If we consider applying binary search to the list of names in Figure 9.1, then the order in which comparisons will be made is shown in the accompanying comparison tree.

Amy Ann Dot Eva Guy Jan Jim Jon Kay Kim Ron Roy Tim Tom

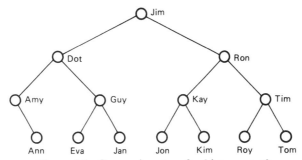

Figure 9.1. Comparison tree for binary search

From the diagram it may already be clear that the way in which we can keep the advantages of linked storage and obtain the speed of binary search is to store the nodes in the structure of the comparison tree itself, with links used to describe the relations of the tree.

9.1 DEFINITIONS

In binary search, when we make a comparison with a key, we then move either left or right depending on the outcome of the comparison. It is thus important to keep the relation of left and right in the structure we build. It is also possible that the part of the tree on one side or both below a given node is empty. In the example of Figure 9.1, the name Amy has an empty left subtree. For all the leaves, both subtrees are empty.

We can now give the formal definition of a new data structure.

DEFINITION   A *binary tree* is either empty, or it consists of a node called the *root* together with two binary trees called the *left subtree* and the *right subtree* of the root.

ADT   Note that this definition is that of a mathematical structure. To specify binary trees as an abstract data type, we must state what operations can be performed on binary trees. Rather than doing so at once, we shall develop the operations while the chapter progresses.

Note also that this definition makes no reference to the way in which binary trees will be implemented in memory. As we shall presently see, a linked representation is natural and easy to use, but other methods are possible as well. Note finally that this definition makes no reference to keys or the way in which they are ordered. Binary trees are used for many purposes other than searching; hence we have kept the definition general. Information retrieval is, nonetheless, one of the most important uses for binary trees, and therefore we use a special term for binary trees in which there are keys with a special order:

DEFINITION

A binary *search tree* is a binary tree that is either empty or in which each node contains a key that satisfies the conditions:

1. All keys (if any) in the left subtree of the root precede the key in the root.

2. The key in the root precedes all keys (if any) in its right subtree.

3. The left and right subtrees of the root are again search trees.

Before we consider search trees further, let us return to the general definition of binary trees and see how the recursive nature of the definition works out in the construction of small binary trees.

The first case, which involves no recursion, is that of an empty binary tree. For ordinary trees we would never think of allowing an empty one, but for binary trees it is convenient, not only in the definition, but in algorithms, since the empty binary tree will be naturally represented by a NULL pointer.

small binary trees   The only way to construct a binary tree with one node is to make that node its root, and to make both the left and right subtrees empty. Thus a single node with no branches is a binary tree.

With two nodes in the tree, one of them will be the root and the other will be in a subtree. Thus either the left or right subtree must be empty, and the other will contain exactly one node. Hence there are two different binary trees with two nodes.

At this point you should note that the concept of a binary tree differs from that of an ordinary tree, in that left and right are important. The two binary trees with two nodes can be drawn as

left and right

and

which are different from each other, but neither can be distinguished from

as ordinary trees.

2-trees   Binary trees, moreover, are not the same class as the 2-trees studied in the analysis of algorithms. Each node in a 2-tree has either 0 or 2 children, never 1 as can happen with a binary tree. Left and right are not important for 2-trees, but they are crucial in working with binary trees.

For the case of a binary tree with three nodes, one of these will be the root, and the others will be partitioned between the left and right subtrees in one of the ways

$$2 + 0 \qquad 1 + 1 \qquad 0 + 2.$$

Since there are two binary trees with two nodes and only one empty tree, the first case gives two binary trees. The third case does similarly. In the second case the left and right subtrees both have one node, and there is only one binary tree with one node, so there is one binary tree in the second case. Altogether, then, there are five binary trees with three nodes.

These binary trees are all drawn in Figure 9.2. Before proceeding, you should pause to construct all fourteen binary trees with four nodes. This exercise will further help you establish the ideas behind the definition of binary trees.

Figure 9.2. The binary trees with three nodes

linked
implementation   A binary tree has a natural implementation in linked storage. As usual, we shall wish all the nodes to be acquired as dynamic storage, so we shall need a separate pointer variable to enable us to find the tree. Our usual name for this pointer variable will be **root**, since it will point to the root of the tree. With this pointer variable, it is easy to recognize an empty binary tree as precisely the condition

root == NULL

Each node of a binary tree (as the root of some subtree) has both a left and a right
C declaration of   subtree, which we can reach with pointers by declaring
binary tree

```
typedef struct node_tag {
    /* information fields with the node go here */
    struct node_tag *left;
    struct node_tag *right;
} Node_type;
```

These declarations turn the comparison tree for the 14 names from Figure 9.1 into the linked binary tree of Figure 9.3. As you can see, the only difference between the comparison tree and the linked binary tree is that we have explicitly shown the NULL links in the latter, whereas it is customary in drawing trees to omit all empty subtrees and the branches going to them. The tree of Figure 9.3, furthermore, is automatically a binary search tree, since the decision to move left or right at each node is based on the same comparisons of keys used in the definition of a search tree.

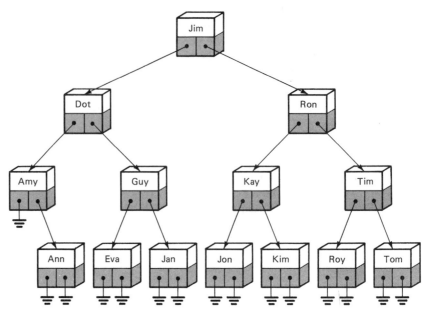

Figure 9.3. A linked binary tree

9.2 TREESEARCH

At this point we should tie down some of the major ideas by writing a short function to search through a linked binary tree for the item with a particular key. First, let us write some declarations that would appear in the main program, in a form similar to those introduced for searching in Chapter 5. Recall that we used Item_type as the name for the structures in the list, each of which contained a key field. You can change the definition of Key_type to suit your own applications.

In this chapter, we always assume that no two items have the same key.

C declaration of binary search tree

The items are placed in nodes that embody the tree structure, as follows.

```
typedef struct item_tag {
        Key_type key;
} Item_type;

typedef struct node_tag {
        Item_type info;
        struct node_tag *left;
        struct node_tag *right;
} Node_type;

Node_type *root;              /* pointer to the root of binary tree    */
Node_type *p;                 /* temporary pointer for the tree        */
Key_type target;             /* key for which we search               */
```

To search for the target we first compare it with the key at the root of the tree. If it is not the same, we go to the left subtree or right subtree as appropriate and repeat the search in that subtree. What event will be the termination condition? Clearly if we find the key, the function succeeds. If not, then we continue searching until we hit an empty subtree. By using a pointer p to move through the tree, we can use p also to send the results of the search back to the calling program. Thus,

precondition and postcondition

> *Function* TreeSearch *receives a pointer* p *as one of its calling parameters. This pointer must be the root of a binary search tree. The function returns a pointer to the node containing the target if the search was successful, and* NULL *if it was unsuccessful.*

Perhaps the simplest way to write the function is to use recursion:

recursive search

```
/* TreeSearch: search for target starting at node p. */
Node_type *TreeSearch(Node_type *p, Key_type target)
{
    if (p)
        if (LT(target, p->info.key))
            p = TreeSearch(p->left, target);
        else if (GT(target, p->info.key))
            p = TreeSearch(p->right, target);
    return p;
}
```

The recursion in this function can easily be removed, since it is tail recursion, essentially by writing a loop in place of the nested if statements. The function then becomes

nonrecursive search

```
/* TreeSearch: nonrecursive search for target starting at p. */
Node_type *TreeSearch(Node_type *p, Key_type target)
{
    while (p && NE(target, p->info.key))
        if (LT(target, p->info.key))
            p = p->left;
        else
            p = p->right;
    return p;
}
```

9.3 TRAVERSAL OF BINARY TREES

In many applications it is necessary, not only to find a node within a binary tree, but to be able to move through all the nodes of the binary tree, visiting each one in turn. If there are n nodes in the binary tree, then there are $n!$ different orders in which they could be visited, but most of these have little regularity or pattern. When we write an algorithm to traverse a binary tree we shall almost always wish to proceed so that the same rules are applied at each node. At a given node, then, there are three tasks we shall wish to do in some order: We shall visit the node itself; we shall traverse its left subtree; and we shall traverse its right subtree. If we name these three tasks V, L, and R, respectively, then there are six ways to arrange them:

$$V\,L\,R \qquad L\,V\,R \qquad L\,R\,V \qquad V\,R\,L \qquad R\,V\,L \qquad R\,L\,V.$$

By standard convention these six are reduced to three by considering only the ways in which the left subtree is traversed before the right. The other three are clearly similar. These three remaining ways are given names:

$$
\begin{array}{ccc}
V\,L\,R & L\,V\,R & L\,R\,V \\
\textit{Preorder} & \textit{Inorder} & \textit{Postorder}
\end{array}
$$

preorder, inorder,
and postorder

These three names are chosen according to the step at which the given node is visited. With **preorder traversal** the node is visited before the subtrees, with **inorder traversal** it is visited between them, and with **postorder traversal** the root is visited after both of the subtrees.

Inorder traversal is also sometimes called **symmetric order**, and postorder traversal was once called **endorder**.

The translation from the definitions to formal functions to traverse a linked binary tree in these ways is especially easy. As usual, we take root to be a pointer to the root of the tree, and we assume the existence of another function Visit that does the desired task for each node.

```
/* Preorder: visit each node of the tree in preorder. */
void Preorder(Node_type *root)
{
    if (root) {
        Visit(root);
        Preorder(root->left);
        Preorder(root->right);
    }
}


/* Inorder: visit each node of the tree in inorder. */
void Inorder(Node_type *root)
{
    if (root) {
        Inorder(root->left);
        Visit(root);
        Inorder(root->right);
    }
}
```

```
/* Postorder: visit each node of the tree in postorder. */
void Postorder(Node_type *root)
{
    if (root) {
        Postorder(root->left);
        Postorder(root->right);
        Visit(root);
    }
}
```

expression tree

The choice of the names *preorder*, *inorder* and *postorder* is not accidental, but relates closely to a motivating example of considerable interest, that of expression trees. An **expression tree** is built up from the simple operands and operators of an (arithmetical or logical) expression by placing the simple operands as the leaves of a binary tree, and the operators as the interior nodes. For each binary operator, the left subtree contains all the simple operands and operators in the left operand of the given operator, and the right subtree contains everything in the right operand. For a unary operator, one subtree will be empty.

operators

We traditionally write some unary operators to the left of their operands, such as $'-'$ (unary negation) or the standard functions like log( ), and cos( ). Others are written on the right, such as the factorial function ( )!, or the function that takes the square of a number, $(\ )^2$. Sometimes either side is permissible, such as the derivative operator, which can be written as d/dx on the left, or as $(\ )'$ on the right, or the incrementing operator $++$ in the C. If the operator is written on the left, then in the expression tree we take its left subtree as empty. If it appears on the right, then its right subtree will be empty.

The expression trees of a few simple expressions are shown in Figure 9.4, together with the slightly more complicated example of the quadratic formula in Figure 9.5, where we denote exponentiation by ↑.

Figure 9.4. Expression trees

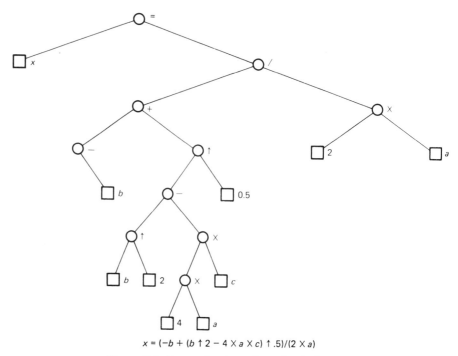

$$x = (-b + (b \uparrow 2 - 4 \times a \times c) \uparrow .5)/(2 \times a)$$

Figure 9.5. Expression tree of quadratic formula

Polish notation   If you apply the traversal algorithms to these trees, you will immediately see how their names are related to the well-known **Polish forms** of expressions: Traversal of an expression tree in preorder yields the **prefix form** of the expression, in which every operator is written before its operand(s); Inorder traversal gives the **infix form** (the customary way to write the expression); and postorder traversal gives the **postfix form,** in which all operators appear after their operand(s). A moment's consideration will convince you of the reason: The left and right subtrees of each node are its operands, and the relative position of an operator to its operands in the three Polish forms is the same as the relative order of visiting the components in each of the three traversal methods. The Polish notation is the major topic of Chapter 11.

9.4 TREESORT

examples of search   As a further example, let us take the binary tree of 14 names from Figure 9.1 or Figure
tree traversal   9.3, and write them in the order given by each traversal method:

preorder:
Jim Dot Amy Ann Guy Eva Jan Ron Kay Jon Kim Tim Roy Tom

inorder:
Amy Ann Dot Eva Guy Jan Jim Jon Kay Kim Ron Roy Tim Tom

postorder:
Ann Amy Eva Jan Guy Dot Jon Kim Kay Roy Tom Tim Ron Jim

It is no accident that inorder traversal produces the names in alphabetical order. A search tree is set up so that all the nodes in the left subtree of a given node come before it in the ordering, and all the nodes in its right subtree come after it. Hence inorder traversal produces all the nodes before a given one first, then the given one, and then all the later nodes.

treesort   We now have the idea for an interesting sorting method, called **treesort**. We simply take the items to be sorted, build them into a binary search tree, and use inorder traversal to put them out in order. This method has the great advantage, as we shall see, that it is easy to make changes in the list of items considered. Adding and deleting items in a sorted contiguous list is oppressively slow and painful; searching for an item in a sequential linked list is equally inefficient.

Treesort has the considerable advantages that it is almost as easy to make changes as in a linked list, the sort is as fast as quicksort, and searches can be made with the efficiency of binary search.

9.4.1 Insertion into a Search Tree

The first part of treesort is to build a sequence of nodes into a binary search tree. We can do so by starting with an empty binary tree and inserting one node at a time into the tree, always making sure that the properties of a search tree are preserved. The first case, inserting a node into an empty tree, is easy. We need only make root point to the new node. If the tree is not empty, then we must compare the key with the one in the root. If it is less, then the new node must be inserted into the left subtree; if it is more, then it must be inserted into the right subtree. If the keys are equal, then our assumption that no two nodes have the same key is violated.

From this outline we can now write our function.

recursive insertion
```
/* Insert: insert newnode in tree starting at root. */
Node_type *Insert(Node_type *root, Node_type *newnode)
{
      if (root == NULL) {
            root = newnode;
            root->left = root->right = NULL;
      } else if (LT(newnode->info.key, root->info.key))
            root->left = Insert(root->left, newnode);
      else if (GT(newnode->info.key, root->info.key))
            root->right = Insert(root->right, newnode);
      else
            Error("Duplicate key in binary tree");
      return root;
}
```

The use of recursion in this function is not essential, since it is tail recursion. To replace recursion with iteration we must introduce a local pointer p that will move to the left or right subtree. We use the condition p == NULL to terminate the loop.

nonrecursive insertion

```
/* Insert: nonrecursive insertion of newnode in tree. */
Node_type *Insert(Node_type *root, Node_type *newnode)
{
    Node_type *p = root;

    while (p != NULL) {
        if (LT(newnode->info.key, p->info.key))
            if (p->left)
                p = p->left;
            else {
                p->left = newnode;
                break;
            }
        else if (GT(newnode->info.key, p->info.key))
            if (p->right)
                p = p->right;
            else {
                p->right = newnode;
                break;
            }
        else
            Error("Duplicate key in binary tree");
    }
    newnode->left = newnode->right = NULL;
    if (root == NULL)
        root = newnode;
    return root;
}
```

9.4.2 The Treesort Algorithm

Now that we can insert new nodes into the search tree, we can build it up and thus devise the new sorting method. In the resulting function, we assume the existence of a function GetNode that will provide a pointer to the next node to be sorted. GetNode returns NULL when there are no more nodes to be inserted. The function will return a pointer to the root of the search tree it builds.

sorting

```
/* TreeSort: make a search tree and return its root. */
Node_type *TreeSort(Node_type *root)
{
    Node_type *p;

    root = NULL;
    while ((p = GetNode()) != NULL)
        root = Insert(root, p);
    Inorder(root);
    return root;
}
```

Note carefully that, if the same set of nodes is presented to TreeSort in a different order, then the search tree that is built may have a different shape. When it is traversed in inorder, the keys will still be properly sorted, but the particular location of nodes within the tree depends on the way in which they were initially presented to Treesort. If the 14 names of Figure 9.1, for example, are presented in the order

Tim Dot Eva Roy Tom Kim Guy Amy Jon Ann Jim Kay Ron Jan

then the resulting search tree will be the one in Figure 9.6. If the names are presented sorted in their alphabetical order, then the search tree will degenerate into a chain.

As an example, let us write a function GetNode that allocates space for a node, puts a random number in it, and returns a pointer to the node.

get a new node

```
/* GetNode: get a new node with data for a binary tree. */
Node_type *GetNode(void)
{
       Node_type *p = NULL;
       extern int howmany;
       if (howmany −−) {                    /* Any more nodes to build ?             */
             if ((p = (Node_type *) malloc(sizeof(Node_type))) == NULL)
                   Error("Cannot allocate node.");
             p−>info.key = rand();
             p−>left = p−>right = NULL;
       }
       return p;
}
```

The integer variable howmany is an external variable defined and initialized elsewhere. The declaration

extern int howmany;

allows us to access that variable.

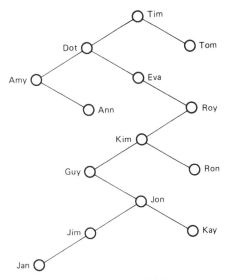

Figure 9.6. Search tree of 14 names.

key comparisons   Let us briefly study what comparisons of keys are done by treesort. The first node goes directly into the root of the search tree, with no key comparisons. As each succeeding node comes in, its key is first compared to the key in the root and then it goes either into the left subtree or the right subtree. Notice the similarity with quicksort, where, at the first stage, every key is compared with the first pivot key, and then put into the left or the right sublist. In treesort, however, as each node comes in it goes into its final position in the linked structure. The second node becomes the root of either the left or right subtree (depending on the comparison of its key with the root key). From then on, all keys going into the same subtree are compared to this second one. Similarly in quicksort all keys in one sublist are compared to the second pivot, the one for that sublist. Continuing in this way, we can make the following observation.

THEOREM 9.1   *Treesort makes exactly the same comparisons of keys as does quicksort when the pivot for each sublist is chosen to be the first key in the sublist.*

As we know, quicksort is usually an excellent method. On average, only mergesort among the methods we studied makes fewer key comparisons. Hence, on average, we *advantages*   can expect treesort also to be an excellent sorting method in terms of key comparisons. Quicksort, however, needs to have access to all the items to be sorted throughout the process. With treesort, the nodes need not all be available at the start of the process, but are built into the tree one by one as they become available. Hence treesort is preferable for applications where the nodes are received one at a time. The major advantage of treesort is that its search tree remains available for later insertions and deletions, and that the tree can subsequently be searched in logarithmic time, whereas all our previous sorting methods either required contiguous lists, for which insertions and deletions are difficult, or produced simply linked lists for which only sequential search is available.

drawbacks   The major drawback of treesort is already implicit in Theorem 9.1. Quicksort has a very poor performance in its worst case, and, although a careful choice of pivots makes this case extremely unlikely, the choice of pivot to be the first key in each sublist makes the worst case appear whenever the keys are already sorted. If the keys are presented to treesort already sorted, then treesort too will be a disaster—the search tree it builds will reduce to a chain. Treesort should never be used if the keys are already sorted, or are nearly so. There are few other reservations about treesort that are not equally applicable to all linked structures. For small problems with small items, contiguous storage is usually the better choice, but for large problems and bulky structures, linked storage comes into its own.

9.4.3 Deletion from a Search Tree

At the beginning of the discussion of treesort, the ability to make changes in the search tree was mentioned as an advantage. We have already obtained an algorithm that adds a new node to the search tree, and it can be used to update the tree as easily as to build it from scratch. But we have not yet considered how to delete a node from the tree. If *method*   the node to be deleted is a leaf, then the process is easy: We need only replace the link to the deleted node by NULL. The process remains easy if the deleted node has only one subtree: We adjust the link from the parent of the deleted node to point to its subtree.

When the item to be deleted has both left and right subtrees nonempty, however, the problem is more complicated. To which of the subtrees should the parent of the deleted node now point? What is to be done with the other subtree? This problem is illustrated in Figure 9.7, together with one possible solution. (An exercise outlines another, sometimes better solution.) What we do is to attach the right subtree in place of the deleted node, and then hang the left subtree onto an appropriate node of the right subtree.

To which node of the right subtree should the former left subtree be attached? Since every key in the left subtree precedes every key of the right subtree, it must be as far to the left as possible, and this point can be found by taking left branches until an empty left subtree is found.

requirements   We can now write a function to implement this plan. As a calling parameter it will use the address of the pointer to the node to be deleted. Since the object is to update the search tree, we must assume that the corresponding actual parameter is the address of one of the links of the tree, and not just a copy, or else the tree structure itself will not be changed as it should. In other words, if the node at the left of the node x is to be deleted, the call should be

Delete (&x->left);

and if the root is to be deleted the call should be

Delete (&root);

On the other hand, the following call will not work properly:

y = x->left;
Delete (&y);

Case: deletion of a leaf   Case: empty right subtree

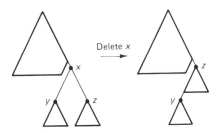

Case: neither subtree is empty

Figure 9.7. Deletion of a node from a search tree

deletion

```
/* Delete: delete node p, reattach left and right subtrees. */
void Delete(Node_type **p)
{
    Node_type *q;                   /* used to find place for left subtree   */
    if (*p == NULL)
        Error("Cannot delete empty node");
    else if ((*p)->right == NULL) {
        q = *p;
        *p = (*p)->left;            /* Reattach left subtree.                */
        free(q);                    /* Release node space.                   */
    } else if ((*p)->left == NULL) {
        q = *p;
        *p = (*p)->right;           /* Reattach right subtree.               */
        free(q);
    } else {                        /* Neither subtree is empty.             */
        for (q = (*p)->right; q->left; q = q->left)
            ;                       /* right, then to the left               */
        q->left = (*p)->left;       /* Reattach left subtree.                */
        q = *p;
        *p = (*p)->right;           /* Reattach right subtree.               */
        free(q);
    }
}
```

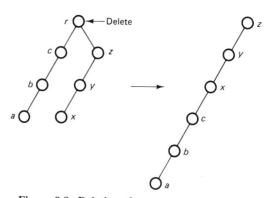

Figure 9.8. Deletions from two search trees

You should trace through this function to check that all pointers are updated properly, especially in the case when neither subtree is empty. Note the steps needed to make the loop stop at a node with an empty left subtree, but not to end at the empty subtree itself.

This function is far from optimal, in that it can greatly increase the height of the tree. Two examples are shown in Figure 9.9. When the roots are deleted from these two trees, the one on the top reduces its height, but the one below increases its height. Thus the time required for a later search can substantially increase, even though the total size of the tree has decreased. There is, moreover, often some tendency for insertions and deletions to be made in sorted order, that will further elongate the search tree. Hence, to optimize the use of search trees, we need methods to make the left and *balancing*   right subtrees more nearly balanced. We shall consider this important topic later in this chapter.

Exercises 9.4

E1. Construct the 14 binary trees with four nodes.

E2. Write a function that will count all the nodes of a linked binary tree.

E3. Determine the order in which the vertices of the following binary trees will be visited under **(a)** preorder, **(b)** inorder, and **(c)** postorder traversal.

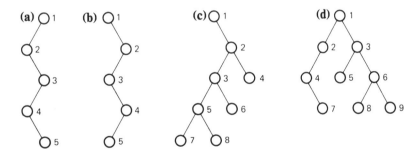

E4. Draw the expression trees for each of the following expressions, and show the order of visiting the vertices in **(1)** preorder, **(2)** inorder, and **(3)** postorder.

    a. $\log n!$ **c.** $a - (b - c)$
    b. $(a - b) - c$ **d.** $(a < b)$ and $(b < c)$ and $(c < d)$

E5. Write a function that will count the leaves (i.e., the nodes with both subtrees empty) of a linked binary tree.

E6. Write a function that will find the height of a linked binary tree.

double-order   **E7.** Write a function to perform a ***double-order traversal*** of a binary tree, meaning that *traversal*   at each node of the tree, the function first visits the node, then traverses its left subtree (in double order), then visits the node again, then traverses its right subtree (in double order).

E8. For each of the binary trees in Exercise E3, determine the order in which the nodes will be visited in the mixed order given by invoking function A:

```
void A(Node_type *p)                    void B(Node_type *p)
{                                       {
   if (p) {                                if (p) {
      Visit(p);                               A(p->left);
      B(p->left);                             Visit(p);
      B(p->right);                            A(p->right);
   }                                       }
}                                       }
```

E9. Write a function that will make a copy of a linked binary tree. The function should obtain the necessary new nodes from the system and copy the information fields from the nodes of the old tree to the new one.

E10. Write a function that will print the keys from a binary tree in the **bracketed form**

$$(\text{key} : \text{LT, RT})$$

printing a binary tree   where key is the key in the root, LT denotes the left subtree of the root printed in bracketed form, and RT denotes the right subtree in bracketed form. *Optional part*: Modify the function so that it prints nothing instead of (:,) for an empty tree, and x instead of (x:,) for a tree consisting of only one node with key x.

E11. Write a function that will interchange all left and right subtrees in a linked binary tree. (See the example in Figure 9.9.)

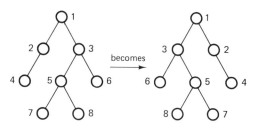

Figure 9.9. Reversal of a binary tree.

E12. Draw the search trees that function TreeSort will construct for the list of 14 names presented in each of the following orders.

   a. Jan Guy Jon Ann Jim Eva Amy Tim Ron Kim Tom Roy Kay Dot
   b. Amy Tom Tim Ann Roy Dot Eva Ron Kim Kay Guy Jon Jan Jim
   c. Jan Jon Tim Ron Guy Ann Jim Tom Amy Eva Roy Kim Dot Kay
   d. Jon Roy Tom Eva Tim Kim Ann Ron Jan Amy Dot Guy Jim Kay

deletion   **E13.** Write a function that will delete a node from a linked binary tree, using the following method in the case when the node to be deleted has both subtrees nonempty. First, find the immediate predecessor of the node under inorder traversal (the immediate successor would work just as well), by moving to its left child and then as far right as possible. This immediate predecessor is guaranteed to have at most one child (why?), so it can be deleted from its current position without difficulty. It can then be placed into the tree in the position formerly occupied by the node that was supposed to be deleted, and the properties of a search tree will still be satisfied (why?).

level-by-level
traversal
E14. Write a function that will traverse a binary tree level by level. That is, the root is visited first, then the immediate children of the root, then the grandchildren of the root, and so on. [*Hint*: Use a queue.]

E15. Write a function that will return the width of a linked binary tree, that is, the maximum number of nodes on the same level.

doubly linked list
E16. Write a function that converts a binary tree into a doubly linked list, in which the nodes have the order of inorder traversal of the tree. The function returns a pointer to the leftmost node of the doubly linked list, and the links right and left should be used to move through the list, and be NULL at the two ends of the list.

traversal sequences
For the following exercises, it is assumed that the keys stored in the nodes of the binary trees are all distinct, but it is not assumed that the trees are search trees. That is, there is no necessary connection between the ordering of the keys and their location in the trees. If a tree is traversed in a particular order, and each key printed when its node is visited, the resulting sequence is called the sequence corresponding to that traversal.

E17. Suppose that you are given two sequences that supposedly correspond to the preorder and inorder traversals of a binary tree. Prove that it is possible to reconstruct the binary tree uniquely.

E18. Either prove or disprove (by finding a counter example) the analogous result for inorder and postorder traversal.

E19. Either prove or disprove the analogous result for preorder and postorder traversal.

E20. Find a pair of (short) sequences of the same keys that could not possibly correspond to the preorder and inorder traversals of the same binary tree.

Programming
Project 9.4
P1. Write a function for searching, using a binary search tree with sentinel as follows. Introduce a new sentinel node, and keep a pointer to it. Replace all the NULL links within the search tree with links to the sentinel (see Figure 9.10). Then, for each search, first store the target into the sentinel. Run both this function and the original function TreeSearch to compare the time needed both for successful and unsuccessful search.

9.5 BUILDING A BINARY SEARCH TREE

Suppose that we have a list of nodes that is already in order, or perhaps a file of structures, with keys already sorted alphabetically. If we wish to use these nodes to look up information, add additional nodes, or make other changes, then we would like to take the list or file of nodes and make it into a binary search tree.

We could, of course, start out with an empty binary tree and simply use the tree insertion algorithm to insert each node into it. But the nodes were given already in order, so the resulting search tree will become one long chain, and using it will be too slow—with the speed of sequential search rather than binary search. We wish instead,

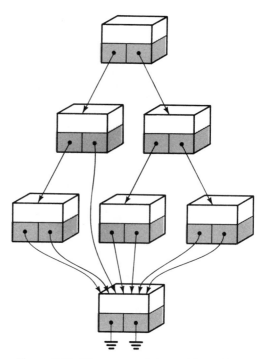

Figure 9.10. Binary search tree with sentinel

goal   therefore, to take the nodes and build them into a tree that will be as bushy as possible, so as to reduce both the time to build the tree and all subsequent search time. When the number of nodes, n, is 31, for example, we wish to build the tree of Figure 9.11.

In Figure 9.11 the nodes are numbered in their natural order, that is, in inorder sequence, which is the order in which they will be received and built into the tree. If you examine the diagram for a moment, you may notice an important property of the labels. The labels of the leaves are all odd numbers; that is, they are not divisible by 2. The labels of the nodes one level above the leaves are 2, 6, 10, 14, 18, 22, 26, and 30. These numbers are all double an odd number; that is, they are all even, but are not divisible by 4. On the next level up, the labels are 4, 12, 20, and 28, numbers that are

Figure 9.11. Complete binary tree with 31 nodes

divisible by 4, but not by 8. Finally, the nodes just below the root are labeled 8 and 24, and the root itself is 16. The key observation is

> *If the nodes of a complete binary tree are labeled in inorder sequence, then each node is exactly as many levels above the leaves as the highest power of 2 that divides its label.*

Let us now put one more constraint on our problem: Let us suppose that we do not know in advance how many nodes will be built into the tree. If the nodes are coming from a file or a linked list, then this assumption is quite reasonable, since we may not have any convenient way to count the nodes before receiving them.

This assumption also has the advantage that it will stop us from worrying about the fact that, when the number of nodes is not exactly one less than a power of 2, then the resulting tree will not be complete and cannot be as symmetric as the one in Figure 9.11. Instead, we shall design our algorithm as though it were completely symmetric, and after receiving all nodes we shall determine how to tidy up the tree.

9.5.1 Getting Started

There is no doubt what to do with node number 1 when it arrives. It will be a leaf, and therefore its left and right pointers should both be set to NULL. Node number 2 goes above node 1, as shown in Figure 9.12. Since node 2 links to node 1, we obviously must keep some way to remember where node 1 is. Node 3 is again a leaf, but it is in the right subtree of node 2, so we must remember a pointer to node 2.

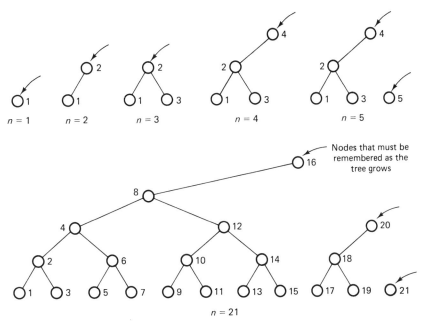

Figure 9.12. Building the first nodes into a tree

Does this mean that we must keep a list of pointers to all nodes previously processed, to determine how to link in the next one? The answer is no, since when node 3 is received, all connections for node 1 are complete. Node 2 must be remembered until node 4 is received, to establish the left link from node 4, but then a pointer to node 2 is no longer needed. Similarly, node 4 must be remembered until node 8 has been processed. In Figure 9.12, arrows point to each node that must be remembered as the tree grows.

It should now be clear that to establish future links, we need only remember pointers to one node on each level, the last node processed on that level. We keep these pointers in an array called lastnode that will be quite small. For example, a tree with 20 levels can accommodate

$$2^{20} - 1 > 1,000,000$$

nodes.

As each new node arrives, it is clearly the last one received in the order, so we can set its right pointer to NULL (at least temporarily). The left pointer of the new node is NULL if it is a leaf, and otherwise is the entry in lastnode one level lower than the new node. So that we can treat the leaves in the same way as other nodes, we consider the leaves to be on level 1, index the array lastnode from 0 to the maximum height allowed, and ensure that lastnode[0] == NULL.

9.5.2 Declarations and the Main Program

We can now write down declarations of the variables needed for our task, and, while we are at it, we can outline the main routine. The first step will be to receive all the nodes and insert them into the tree. To obtain each new node, we assume the existence of an auxiliary function GetNode that returns a pointer to the new node, or NULL when all nodes have been delivered. After all the nodes have been inserted, we must find the root of the tree and then connect any right subtrees that may be dangling. (See Figure 9.12 in the case of 5 or 21 nodes.)

The main routine thus becomes

main function

```
/* BuildTree: build nodes from GetNode into a binary tree. */
Node_type *BuildTree(void)
{
       Node_type *p;                      /* pointer to current node                 */
       int count = 0;                     /* number of nodes so far                  */
       int level;                         /* level for current node                  */
       Node_type *lastnode[MAXHEIGHT];    /* pointers to last node on each level     */

       for (level = 0; level < MAXHEIGHT; level++)
              lastnode[level] = NULL;
       while ((p = GetNode()) != NULL)
              Insert(p, ++count, lastnode);
       p = FindRoot(lastnode);
       ConnectSubtrees(lastnode);
       return p;                          /* Return root of the tree.                */
}
```

9.5.3 Inserting a Node

The discussion in the previous section shows how to set up the left links of each node correctly, but for some of the nodes the right link should not permanently have the value NULL. When a new node arrives, it cannot yet have a proper right subtree, since it is the latest node (under the ordering) so far received. The node, however, may be the right child of some previous node. On the other hand, it may instead be a left child, in which case its parent node has not yet arrived. We can tell which case occurs by looking in the array lastnode. If level denotes the level of the new node, then its parent has level level + 1. We look at lastnode [level + 1]. If its right link is still NULL, then its right child must be the new node; if not, then its right child has already arrived, and the new node must be the left child of some future node.

We can now formally describe how to insert a new node into the tree.

insertion
```
/* Insert: insert p as the rightmost node of a partial tree. */
void Insert(Node_type *p, int count, Node_type *lastnode[])
{
        int level = Power2(count) + 1;

        p->right = NULL;
        p->left = lastnode[level − 1];
        lastnode[level] = p;
        if (lastnode[level + 1] && !lastnode[level + 1]->right)
                lastnode[level + 1]->right = p;
}
```

This function uses another function to find the level of the node that p points to:

```
#define ODD(x) ((x)/2*2 != (x))
```

finding the level
```
/* Power2: find the highest power of 2 that divides count. */
int Power2(int count)
{
        int level;

        for (level = 0; !ODD(count); level++)
                count /= 2;
        return level;
}
```

9.5.4 Finishing the Task

Finding the root of the tree is easy: the root is the highest node in the tree; hence its pointer is the highest entry not equal to NULL in the array lastnode. We therefore have *finding the root*

```
/* FindRoot: find root of tree (highest entry in lastnode). */
Node_type *FindRoot (Node_type *lastnode [ ] )
{
        int level;

        for (level = MAXHEIGHT−1; level > 0 && !lastnode [level]; level − − )
                ;
        if (level <= 0)
                return NULL;
        else
                return lastnode [level] ;
}
```

Finally, we must determine how to tie in any subtrees that may not yet be connected properly after all the nodes have been received. The difficulty is that some nodes in the upper part of the tree may still have their right links set to NULL, even though further nodes have come in that belong in their right subtrees.

Any node for which the right child is still NULL will be one of the nodes in lastnode. Its right child should be set to the highest node in lastnode that is not already in its left subtree. We thus arrive at the following algorithm.

tying subtrees
together

```
/* ConnectSubtrees: connect free subtrees from lastnode [ ] . */
void ConnectSubtrees (Node_type *lastnode [ ] )
{
        Node_type *p;
        int level, templevel;

        for (level = MAXHEIGHT − 1; level > 2 && !lastnode [level]; level − − )
                ;                                   /* Levels 1 and 2 are already OK.          */
        while (level > 2) {
                if (lastnode [level] −>right)
                        level − − ;                 /* Search for highest dangling node.      */
                else {                              /* Right subtree is undefined.            */
                        p = lastnode [level] −>left;
                        templevel = level − 1;
                        do {                        /* Find highest entry not in left subtree.  */
                                p = p−>right;
                        } while (p && p == lastnode [ − −templevel] );
                        lastnode [level] −>right = lastnode [templevel] ;
                        level = templevel;
                }
        }
}
```

9.5.5 Evaluation

The algorithm of this section produces a binary search tree that is not always completely balanced. If 32 nodes come in, for example, then node 32 will become the root of the tree, and all 31 remaining nodes will be in its left subtree. Thus the leaves are five steps removed from the root. If the root were chosen optimally, then most of the leaves would be four steps from it, and only one would be five steps. Hence one comparison more than necessary will usually be done.

One extra comparison in a binary search is not really a very high price, and it is easy to see that a tree produced by our method is never more than one level away from optimality. There are sophisticated methods for building a binary search tree that is as balanced as possible, but much remains to recommend a simpler method, one that does not need to know in advance how many nodes are in the tree.

The exercises outline ways in which our algorithm can be used to take an arbitrary binary search tree and rearrange the nodes to bring it into better balance, so as to improve search times. Again, there are more sophisticated methods (which, however will likely be slower) for rebalancing a tree. In Section 9.6 we shall study AVL trees, in which we perform insertions and deletions in such a way as always to maintain the tree in a state of near balance. For many practical purposes, however, the simpler algorithm described in this section should prove sufficient.

9.5.6 Random Search Trees and Optimality

To conclude this section, let us ask whether it is worthwhile on average to keep a binary search tree balanced or to rebalance it. If we assume that the keys have arrived in random order, then, on average, how many more comparisons are needed in a search of the resulting tree than would be needed in a completely balanced tree?

extended binary tree   In answering the question we first convert the binary search tree into a 2-tree, as follows. Think of all the vertices of the binary tree as drawn as circles, and add on new, square vertices replacing all the empty subtrees (NULL links). This process is shown in Figure 9.13. All the vertices of the original binary tree become internal vertices of the 2-tree, and the new vertices are all external (leaves). A successful search terminates at an interior vertex of the 2-tree, and an unsuccessful search at a leaf. Hence the internal path length gives us the number of comparisons for a successful search, and the external path length gives the number for an unsuccessful search.

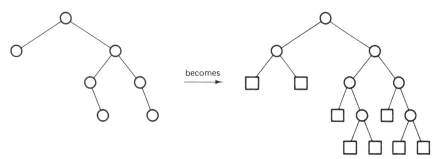

Figure 9.13. Extension of a binary tree into a 2-tree

We shall assume that the $n!$ possible orderings of keys are equally likely in building the tree. When there are n nodes in the tree, we denote by $S(n)$ the number of comparisons done in the average successful search and by $U(n)$ the number in the average unsuccessful search.

counting
comparisons   The number of comparisons needed to find any key in the tree is exactly one more than the number of comparisons that were needed to insert it in the first place, and inserting it required the same comparisons as the unsuccessful search showing that it was not yet in the tree. We therefore have the relationship

$$S(n) = 1 + \frac{U(0) + U(1) + \cdots + U(n-1)}{n}.$$

The relation between internal and external path length, as presented in Theorem 5.4, states that

$$S(n) = \left(1 + \frac{1}{n}\right) U(n) - 1.$$

recurrence relation   The last two equations together give

$$(n+1)U(n) = 2n + U(0) + U(1) + \cdots + U(n-1).$$

We solve this recurrence by writing the equation for $n-1$ instead of n:

$$nU(n-1) = 2(n-1) + U(0) + U(1) + \cdots + U(n-2),$$

and subtracting, to obtain

$$U(n) = U(n-1) + \frac{2}{n+1}.$$

The sum

$$H_n = 1 + \frac{1}{2} + \frac{1}{3} + \cdots + \frac{1}{n}$$

harmonic number   is called the nth **harmonic number**, and it is shown in Appendix A.2.7 that this number is approximately the natural logarithm $\ln n$. Since $U(0) = 0$, we can now evaluate $U(n)$ by starting at the bottom and adding:

$$U(n) = 2 \left[\frac{1}{1} + \frac{1}{2} + \cdots + \frac{1}{n+1} \right] = 2H_{n+1} - 2 \approx 2 \ln n.$$

By Theorem 5.4 the number of comparisons for a successful search is also approximately $2 \ln n$. By Theorem 5.6, the optimal number of comparisons in a search of n items is the base 2 logarithm, $\lg n$. But (see Appendix A.2.5)

$$\ln n = (\ln 2)(\lg n).$$

Finally, therefore, we have

THEOREM 9.2   *The average number of comparisons needed in the average binary search tree with*
n nodes is approximately $2 \ln n = (2 \ln 2)(\lg n)$.

COROLLARY 9.3   *The average binary search tree requires approximately* $2 \ln 2 \approx 1.39$ *times as many*
comparisons as a completely balanced tree.

cost of not balancing   In other words, the average cost of not balancing a binary search tree is approximately 39 percent more comparisons. In applications where optimality is important, this cost must be weighed against the extra cost of balancing the tree, or of maintaining it in balance. Note especially that these latter tasks involve not only the cost of computer time, but the cost of the extra programming effort that will be required.

Exercises   **E1.** Draw the sequence of partial search trees (like Figure 9.12) that the method in this
9.5   section will construct for $n = 6$ through $n = 8$.

E2. Write a function GetNode that will traverse a linked list and get each node from the list in turn. Assume that the list is simply linked with the links in the right field of each node.

E3. Write a version of function GetNode that traverses a binary tree in inorder without first converting it into a linked sequential list. Make sure that the algorithm of this section will not change any links in the tree until your traversal algorithm no longer needs them. Thereby obtain a self-contained function for putting a binary search tree into better balance with only one pass through its nodes.

E4. Suppose that the number of nodes in the tree is known in advance. Modify the algorithm of this section to take advantage of this knowledge, and produce a tree in which any imbalance is of at most one level, and occurs at the leaves rather than near the root.

E5. There are $3! = 6$ possible orderings of three keys, but only 5 distinct binary trees with three nodes. Therefore these binary trees are not equally likely to occur as search trees. Find which search tree corresponds to each possible order, and thereby find the probability for building each of the binary search trees from randomly ordered input.

E6. Repeat Exercise E5, with the $4! = 24$ orderings of four keys and the 14 binary trees with four nodes.

9.6 HEIGHT BALANCE: AVL TREES

The algorithm of Section 9.5 can be used to build a nearly balanced binary search tree, or to restore balance when it is feasible to restructure the tree completely. In many applications, however, insertions and deletions occur continually, with no predictable order. In some of these applications, it is important to optimize search times by keeping the tree very nearly balanced at all times. The method of this section for achieving this goal was described in 1962 by two Russian mathematicians, G. M. ADEL'SON-VEL'SKIĬ and E. M. LANDIS, and the resulting binary search trees are called *AVL trees* in their honor.

AVL trees achieve the goal that searches, insertions, and deletions in a tree with n nodes can all be achieved in time that is $O(\log n)$, even in the worst case. The height of an AVL tree with n nodes, as we shall establish, can never exceed $1.44 \lg n$, and thus even in the worst case, the behavior of an AVL tree could not be much below that of a random binary search tree. In almost all cases, however, the actual length of a search is very nearly $\lg n$, and thus the behavior of AVL trees closely approximates that of the ideal, completely balanced binary search tree.

9.6.1 Definition

In a completely balanced tree, the left and right subtrees of any node would have the same height. Although we cannot always achieve this goal, by building a search tree carefully we can always ensure that the heights of every left and right subtree never differ by more than 1. We accordingly make the following:

DEFINITION   An *AVL tree* is a binary search tree in which the heights of the left and right subtrees of the root differ by at most 1 and in which the left and right subtrees are again AVL trees.

With each node of an AVL tree is associated a *balance factor* that is *left high*, *equal*, or *right high* according, respectively, as the left subtree has height greater than, equal to, or less than that of the right subtree.

In drawing diagrams, we shall show a left-high node by '/', a node whose balance factor is equal by '−', and a right-high node by '\'. Figure 9.14 shows several small AVL trees, as well as some binary trees that fail to satisfy the definition.

Note that the definition does not require that all leaves be on the same or adjacent levels. Figure 9.15 shows several AVL trees that are quite skewed, with right subtrees having greater height than left subtrees.

9.6.2 Insertion of a Node

1. Introduction

We can insert a new node into an AVL tree by first using the usual binary tree insertion algorithm, comparing the key of the new node with that in the root, and inserting the new

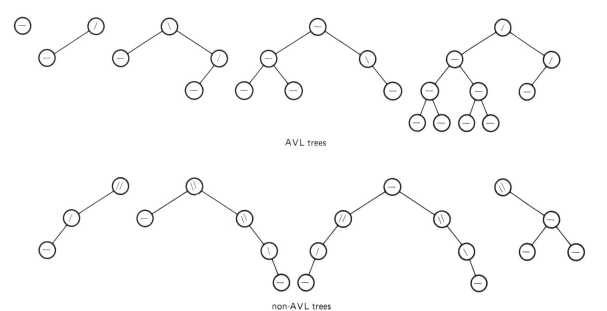

AVL trees

non-AVL trees

Figure 9.14. Examples of AVL trees and other binary trees

node into the left or right subtree as appropriate. It often turns out that the new node can be inserted without changing the height of the subtree, in which case neither the height nor the balance of the root will be changed. Even when the height of a subtree does increase, it may be the shorter subtree that has grown, so that only the balance factor of the root will change. The only case that can cause difficulty occurs when the new *problem* node is added to a subtree of the root that is strictly taller than the other subtree, and the height is increased. This would cause one subtree to have height 2 more than the other, whereas the AVL condition is that the height difference is never more than 1. Before we

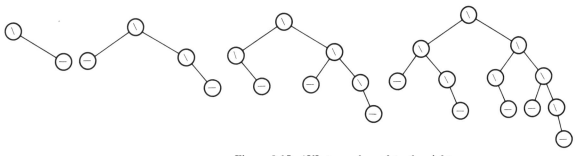

Figure 9.15. AVL trees skewed to the right

consider this situation more carefully, let us illustrate in Figure 9.16 the growth of an AVL tree through several insertions, and then we shall tie down the ideas by outlining our algorithm in C.

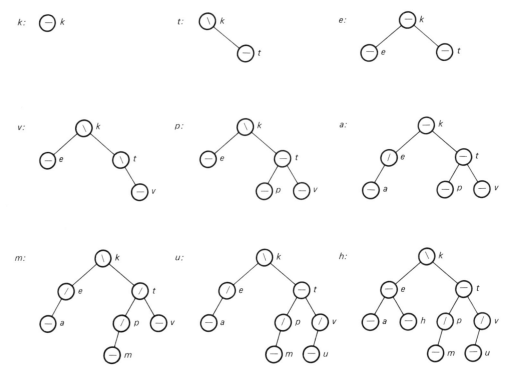

Figure 9.16. Simple insertions of nodes into an AVL tree

2. C Conventions

The basic structure of our algorithm will be the same as the ordinary binary tree insertion algorithm of Section 9.4.1, but with certain additions to accommodate the structure of AVL trees. First, each structure corresponding to a node will have an additional field (along with its information field and left and right pointers), defined as

> BalanceFactor_type bf;

where we employ the enumerated type

> typedef enum balancefactor_tag { LH, EH, RH } BalanceFactor_type;

which symbols denote *left high, equal height,* and *right high,* respectively. Second, we must keep track of whether an insertion has increased the height or not, so that the balance factors can be changed appropriately. This we do by including an additional calling parameter taller of Boolean_type. The task of restoring balance when required will be done in the subsidiary functions LeftBalance and RightBalance.

```
                    /* Insert: insert newnode in AVL tree starting at the root. */
AVL tree insertion  Node_type *Insert(Node_type *root, Node_type *newnode, Boolean_type *taller)
                    {
                         if (!root) {
                              root = newnode;
                              root->bf = EH;
                              root->left = root->right = NULL;
                              *taller = TRUE;
                         } else if (EQ(newnode->info.key, root->info.key)) {
                              Error("Duplicate key in binary tree");
                         } else if (LT(newnode->info.key, root->info.key)) {
                              root->left = Insert(root->left, newnode, taller);
                              if (*taller)                /* Left subtree is taller.            */
                                   switch(root->bf) {
                                   case LH:               /* Node was left high.                */
                                        root = LeftBalance(root, taller);
                                        break;
                                   case EH:
                                        root->bf = LH;    /* Node is now left high.             */
                                        break;
                                   case RH:
                                        root->bf = EH;    /* Node now has balanced height.      */
                                        *taller = FALSE;
                                        break;
                                   }
                         } else {
                              root->right = Insert(root->right, newnode, taller);
                              if (*taller)                /* Right subtree is taller.           */
                                   switch(root->bf) {
                                   case LH:
                                        root->bf = EH;    /* Node now has balanced height.      */
                                        *taller = FALSE;
                                        break;
                                   case EH:
                                        root->bf = RH;    /* Node is right high.                */
                                        break;
                                   case RH:               /* Node was right high.               */
                                        root = RightBalance(root, taller);
                                        break;
                                   }
                         }
                         return root;
                    }
```

3. Rotations

Let us now consider the case when a new node has been inserted into the taller subtree
of the root and its height has increased, so that now one subtree has height 2 more than

the other, and the tree no longer satisfies the AVL requirements. We must now rebuild part of the tree to restore its balance. To be definite, let us assume that we have inserted the new node into the right subtree, its height has increased, and the original tree was right high. That is, we wish to consider the case covered by the function BalanceRight. Let r be the root of the tree and x the root of its right subtree.

There are three cases to consider, depending on the balance factor of x.

4. Case 1: Right High

left rotation

The first case, when x is right high, is illustrated in Figure 9.17. The action needed in this case is called a ***left rotation***; we have rotated the node x upward to the root, dropping r down into the left subtree of x; the subtree T_2 of nodes with keys between those of r and x now becomes the right subtree of r rather than the left subtree of x. A left rotation is succinctly described in the following C function. Note especially that, when done in the appropriate order, the steps constitute a rotation of the values in three pointer variables. Note also that, after the rotation, the height of the rotated tree has decreased by 1; it had previously increased because of the insertion; hence the height finishes where it began.

```
/* RotateLeft: rotate a binary tree to the left. */
Node_type *RotateLeft(Node_type *p)
{
        Node_type *temp = p;

        if (p == NULL)
                Error("Cannot rotate an empty tree");
        else if (p->right == NULL)
                Error("Cannot rotate left");
        else {
                temp = p->right;
                p->right = temp->left;
                temp->left = p;
        }
        return temp;
}
```

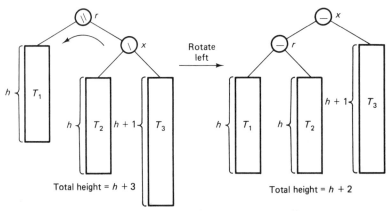

Figure 9.17. First case: Restoring balance by a left rotation

5. Case 2: Left High

double rotation

The second case, when the balance factor of x is left high, is slightly more complicated. It is necessary to move two levels, to the node w that roots the left subtree of x, to find the new root. This process is shown in Figure 9.18 and is called a ***double rotation***, because the transformation can be obtained in two steps by first rotating the subtree with root x to the right (so that w becomes its root), and then rotating the tree with root r to the left (moving w up to become the new root).

In this second case, the new balance factors for r and x depend on the previous balance factor for w. The diagram shows the subtrees of w as having equal heights, but it is possible that w may be either left or right high. The resulting balance factors are

old w	*new r*	*new x*
—	—	—
/	—	\
\	/	—

6. Case 3: Equal Height

It would appear, finally, that we must consider a third case, when the two subtrees of x have equal heights, but this case, in fact, can never happen. To see why, let us recall that we have just inserted a new node into the subtree rooted at x, and this subtree now has height 2 more than the left subtree of the root. The new node went either into the left or right subtree of x. Hence its insertion increased the height of only one subtree of x. If these subtrees had equal heights after the insertion, then the height of the full subtree rooted at x was not changed by the insertion, contrary to what we already know.

7. C Routine for Balancing

It is now straightforward to incorporate these transformations into a C function. The forms of functions RotateRight and LeftBalance are clearly similar to those of RotateLeft and RightBalance, respectively, and are left as exercises.

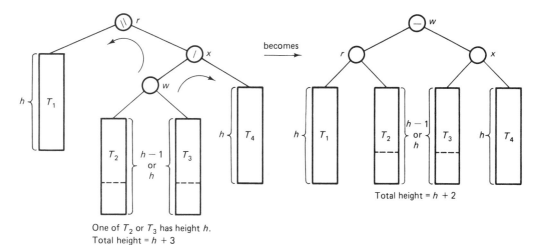

One of T_2 or T_3 has height h.
Total height = $h + 3$

Figure 9.18. Second case: Restoring balance by double rotation

restoring balance

```
/* RightBalance: right balance a binary tree. */
Node_type *RightBalance (Node_type *root, Boolean_type *taller)
{
        Node_type *rs = root->right;      /* right subtree of root              */
        Node_type *ls;                     /* left subtree of right subtree     */

        switch (rs->bf) {
        case RH:
                root->bf = rs->bf = EH;
                root = RotateLeft (root);   /* single rotation left              */
                *taller = FALSE;
                break;
        case EH:
                Error ("Tree is already balanced");
                break;
        case LH:                           /* double rotation left              */
                ls = rs->left;
                switch (ls->bf) {
                case RH:
                        root->bf = LH;
                        rs->bf = EH;
                        break;
                case EH:
                        root->bf = rs->bf = EH;
                        break;
                case LH:
                        root->bf = EH;
                        rs->bf = RH;
                        break;
                }
                ls->bf = EH;
                root->right = RotateRight (rs);
                root = RotateLeft (root);
                *taller = FALSE;
        }
        return root;
}
```

Examples of insertions requiring single and double rotations are shown in Figure 9.19.

8. Behavior of the Algorithm

The number of times that function Insert calls itself recursively to insert a new node can be as large as the height of the tree. At first glance it may appear that each one of these calls might induce either a single or double rotation of the appropriate subtree, but, in fact, at most only one (single or double) rotation will ever be done. To see this, let us recall that rotations are done only in functions RightBalance and LeftBalance and that

counting rotations

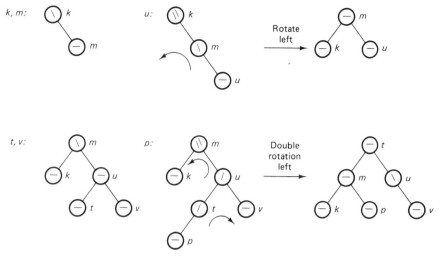

Figure 9.19. AVL insertions requiring rotations

these functions are called only when the height of a subtree has increased. When these functions return, however, the rotations have removed the increase in height, so, for the remaining (outer) recursive calls, the height has not increased, so no further rotations or changes of balance factors are done.

Most of the insertions into an AVL tree will induce no rotations. Even when rotations are needed, they will usually occur near the leaf that has just been inserted. Even though the algorithm to insert into an AVL tree is complicated, it is reasonable to expect that its running time will differ little from insertion into an ordinary search tree of the same height. Later we shall see that we can expect the height of AVL trees to be much less than that of random search trees, and therefore both insertion and retrieval will be significantly more efficient in AVL trees than in random binary search trees.

9.6.3 Deletion of a Node

Deletion of a node x from an AVL tree requires the same basic ideas, including single and double rotations, that are used for insertion. We shall give only the steps of an informal outline of the method, leaving the writing of complete algorithms as a programming project.

method   1. Reduce the problem to the case when the node x to be deleted has at most one child. For suppose that x has two children. Find the immediate predecessor y of x under inorder traversal (the immediate successor would be just as good), by first taking the left child of x, and then moving right as far as possible to obtain y. The node y is guaranteed to have no right child, because of the way it was found. Place y (or a copy of y) into the position in the tree occupied by x (with the same parent, left and right children, and balance factor that x had). Now delete y from its former position, by proceeding as follows, using y in place of x in each of the following steps.

2. Delete the node x from the tree. Since we know (by step 1) that x has at most one child, we delete x simply by linking the parent of x to the single child of x (or to NULL, if no child). The height of the subtree formerly rooted at x has been reduced by 1, and we must now trace the effects of this change on height through all the nodes on the path from x back to the root of the tree. We use a Boolean variable shorter to show if the height of a subtree has been shortened. The action to be taken at each node depends on the value of shorter, on the balance factor of the node, and sometimes on the balance factor of a child of the node.

3. The Boolean variable shorter is initially TRUE. The following steps are to be done for each node p on the path from the parent of x to the root of the tree, provided shorter remains TRUE. When shorter becomes FALSE, then no further changes are needed, and the algorithm terminates.

4. *Case 1*: The current node p has balance factor equal. The balance factor of p is changed according as its left or right subtree has been shortened, and shorter becomes FALSE.

5. *Case 2*: The balance factor of p is not equal, and the taller subtree was shortened. Change the balance factor of p to equal, and leave shorter as TRUE.

6. *Case 3*: The balance factor of p is not equal, and the shorter subtree was shortened. The height requirement for an AVL tree is now violated at p, so we apply a rotation as follows to restore balance. Let q be the root of the taller subtree of p (the one not shortened). We have three cases according to the balance factor of q.

7. *Case 3a*: The balance factor of q is equal. A single rotation (with changes to the balance factors of p and q) restores balance, and shorter becomes FALSE.

8. *Case 3b*: The balance factor of q is the same as that of p. Apply a single rotation, set the balance factors of p and q to equal, and leave shorter as TRUE.

9. *Case 3c*: The balance factors of p and q are opposite. Apply a double rotation (first around q, then around p), set the balance factor of the new root to equal and the other balance factors as appropriate, and leave shorter as TRUE.

In cases 3a, b, c, the direction of the rotations depends on whether a left or right subtree was shortened. Some of the possibilities are illustrated in Figure 9.20, and an example of deletion of a node appears in Figure 9.21.

9.6.4 The Height of an AVL Tree

It turns out to be very difficult to find the height of the average AVL tree, and thereby to determine how many steps are done, on average, by the algorithms of this section. It is much easier, however, to find what happens in the worst case, and these results show that the worst-case behavior of AVL trees is essentially no worse than the behavior of random trees. Empirical evidence suggests that the average behavior of AVL trees is much better than that of random trees, almost as good as that which could be obtained from a perfectly balanced tree.

worst-case analysis   To determine the maximum height that an AVL tree with n nodes can have, we can instead ask what is the minimum number of nodes that an AVL tree of height h can have. If F_h is such a tree, and the left and right subtrees of its root are F_l and F_r,

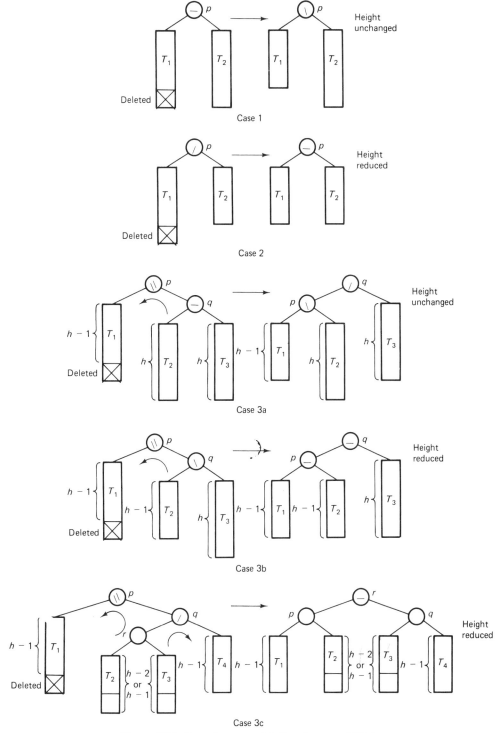

Figure 9.20. Sample cases, deletion from an AVL tree

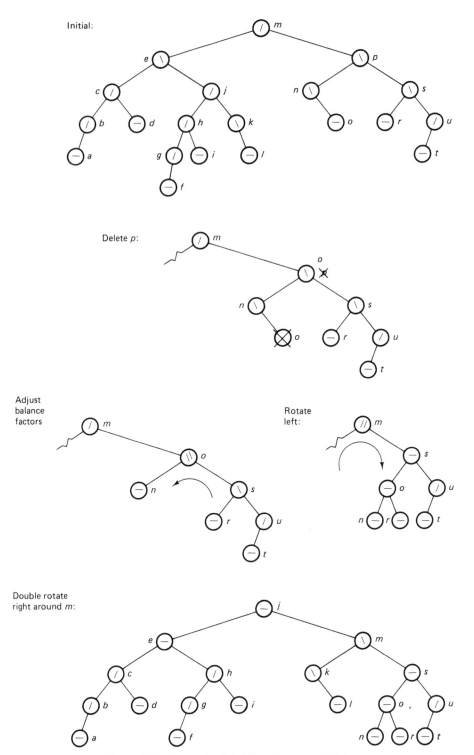

Figure 9.21. Example of deletion from an AVL tree

then one of F_l and F_r must have height $h - 1$, say, F_l, and the other has height either $h - 1$ or $h - 2$. Since F_h has the minimum number of nodes among AVL trees of height h, it follows that F_l must have the minimum number of nodes among AVL trees of height $h - 1$ (that is, F_l is of the form F_{h-1}), and F_r must have height $h - 2$ with minimum number of nodes (so that F_r is of the form F_{h-2}).

Fibonacci trees   The trees built by the above rule, which are therefore as sparse as possible for AVL trees, are called ***Fibonacci trees***. The first few are shown in Figure 9.22.

counting nodes of a   If we write $|T|$ for the number of nodes in a tree T, we then have (counting the
Fibonacci tree   root as well as the subtrees) the recurrence relation

$$|F_h| = |F_{h-1}| + |F_{h-2}| + 1,$$

where $|F_0| = 1$ and $|F_1| = 2$. By adding 1 to both sides, we see that the numbers $|F_h| + 1$ satisfy the definition of the Fibonacci numbers (see Appendix A.4), with the subscripts changed by 3. By the evaluation of Fibonacci numbers in Appendix A.4, we therefore see that

$$|F_h| + 1 \approx \frac{1}{\sqrt{5}} \left[\frac{1 + \sqrt{5}}{2} \right]^{h+2}$$

Next, we solve this relation for h by taking the logarithms of both sides, and discarding

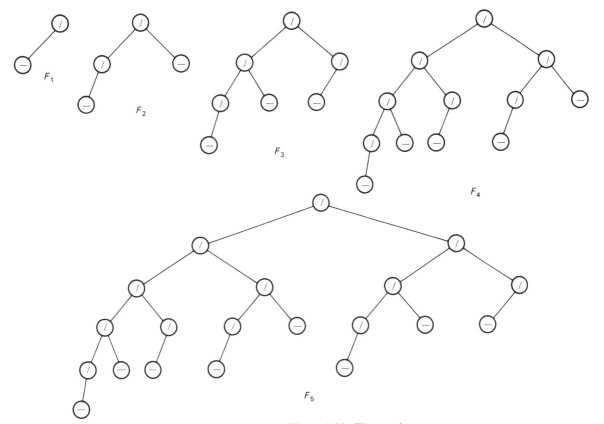

Figure 9.22. Fibonacci trees

height of a all except the largest terms. The approximate result is that
Fibonacci tree

$$h \approx 1.44 \lg |F_h|.$$

worst-case bound This means that the sparsest possible AVL tree with n nodes has height approximately $1.44 \lg n$. A perfectly balanced binary tree with n nodes has height about $\lg n$, and a degenerate tree has height as large as n. Hence the algorithms for manipulating AVL trees are guaranteed to take no more than about 44 percent more time than the optimum. In practice, AVL trees do much better than this. It can be shown that, even for Fibonacci trees, which are the worst case for AVL trees, the average search time is only 4 percent more than the optimum. Most AVL trees are not nearly as sparse as Fibonacci trees, and therefore it is reasonable to expect that average search times for average AVL trees are very close indeed to the optimum. Empirical studies, in fact, show that the

average-case average number of comparisons seems to be about
observation

$$\lg n + 0.25$$

when n is large.

Exercises 9.6

E1. Determine which of the following binary search trees are AVL trees. For those that are not, find all nodes at which the requirements are violated.

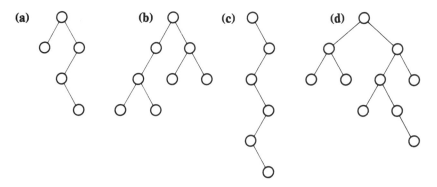

E2. In each of the following, insert the keys, in the order shown, to build them into an AVL tree.

(a) A, Z, B, Y, C, X.
(b) A, B, C, D, E, F.
(c) M, T, E, A, Z, G, P.

(d) A, Z, B, Y, C, X, D, W, E, V, F.
(e) A, B, C, D, E, F, G, H, I, J, K, L.
(f) A, V, L, T, R, E, I, S, O, K.

E3. Delete each of the keys inserted in Exercise E2 from the AVL tree, in LIFO order (last key inserted is first deleted).

E4. Delete each of the keys inserted in Exercise E2 from the AVL tree, in FIFO order (first key inserted is first deleted).

E5. Prove that the number of (single or double) rotations done in deleting a key from an AVL tree cannot exceed half the height of the tree.

**Programming
Projects
9.6**

P1. Write a C program that will accept keys from the user one at a time, build them into an AVL tree, and write out the tree at each stage. You will need a function to print a tree, perhaps in the bracketed form defined in Exercise E10 of Section 9.4.

P2. Write C functions to delete a node from an AVL tree, following the steps in the text.

P3. [*Major project*] Conduct empirical studies to estimate, on average, how many rotations are needed to insert an item and to delete an item from an AVL tree.

9.7 CONTIGUOUS REPRESENTATION OF BINARY TREES: HEAPS

There are several ways other than the usual linked structures to implement binary trees, and some of these ways lead to interesting applications. This section presents one such example: a contiguous implementation of binary trees that is employed in a sorting algorithm for contiguous lists called ***heapsort***. This algorithm sorts a contiguous list of length n with $O(n \log n)$ comparisons and movements of items, even in the worst case. Hence it achieves worst-case bounds better than those of quicksort, and for contiguous lists is better than mergesort, since it needs only a small and constant amount of space apart from the array being sorted.

9.7.1 Binary Trees in Contiguous Storage

Let us begin with a complete binary tree such as the one shown in Figure 9.23, and number the vertices, beginning with the root, from left to right on each level.

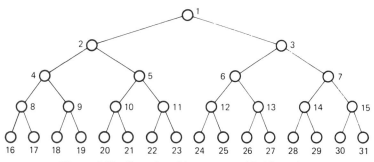

Figure 9.23. Complete binary tree with 31 vertices

We can now put the binary tree into a contiguous array by storing each node in the position shown by its label. We conclude that

finding the children

The left and right children of the node with index k are in positions $2k$ and $2k+1$, respectively, under the assumption that k starts at 1. If these positions are beyond the bounds of the array, then these children do not exist.

This contiguous implementation can, in fact, be extended to arbitrary binary trees, provided that we can flag locations in the array to show that the corresponding nodes do not exist. The results for several binary trees are shown in Figure 9.24.

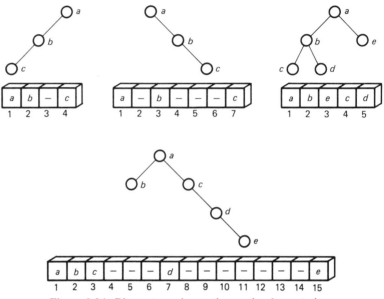

Figure 9.24. Binary trees in contiguous implementation

It is clear from the diagram that, if a binary tree is far from a complete tree, then the contiguous representation wastes a great deal of space. Under other conditions, however, no space at all is wasted. It is this case that we shall now apply.

9.7.2 Heaps and Heapsort

1. Definition

DEFINITION

A **heap** is defined to be a binary tree with a key in each node, such that

1. All the leaves of the tree are on two adjacent levels.
2. All leaves on the lowest level occur to the left and all levels, except possibly the lowest, are filled.
3. The key in the root is at least as large as the keys in its children (if any), and the left and right subtrees (if they exist) are again heaps.

The first two conditions ensure that the contiguous representation of the tree will be space efficient. The third condition determines the ordering. Note that a heap is definitely *not*

not search trees   a search tree. The root, in fact, must have the largest key in the heap. Figure 9.25 shows four trees, the first of which is a heap, with the others violating one of the three properties.

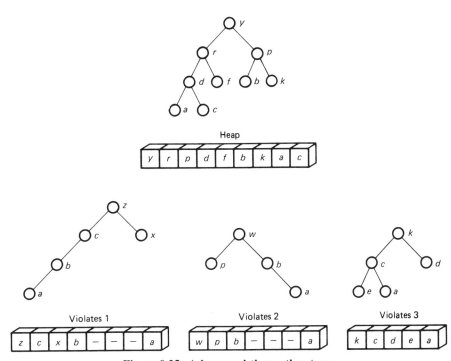

Figure 9.25. A heap and three other trees

REMARK   Some implementations of C refer to the area used for dynamic memory as the "heap"; this use of the word "heap" has nothing to do with the present definition.

2. Outline of Heapsort

two-phase function   Heapsort proceeds in two phases. The entries in the array being sorted are interpreted as a binary tree in contiguous implementation. The first two properties of a heap are automatically satisfied, but the keys will not generally satisfy the third property. Hence the first phase of heapsort is to convert the tree into a heap.

For the second phase, we recall that the root (which is the first entry of the array as well as the top of the heap) has the largest key. This key belongs at the end of the list. We therefore move the first entry to the last position, replacing an entry x. We then decrease a counter i that keeps track of the size of the list, thereby excluding the largest entry from further sorting. The entry x that has been moved from the last position, however, may not belong on the top of the heap, and therefore we must insert x into the proper position to restore the heap property before continuing to loop in the same way.

Let us summarize this outline by rewriting it in C. We use the same notation and conventions used for all the contiguous sorting algorithms of Chapter 7.

main routine

```
/* HeapSort: Sort a contiguous list beginning at index 1 of the array. */
void HeapSort (List_type *lp)
{                               /* The array indices used start at 1; entry 0 is ignored. */
    int i;
    Item_type item;                    /* temporary storage                            */

    BuildHeap (lp);
    for (i = lp->count; i >= 2; i--) {
        item = lp->entry [i];          /* Extract the last element from the list.    */
        lp->entry [i] = lp->entry [1];
                                       /* Move top of the heap to end of the list. */
        InsertHeap (lp, item, 1, i-1); /* Restore the heap properties.            */
    }
}
```

3. An Example

Before we begin work on the two functions BuildHeap and InsertHeap, let us see what happens in the first few stages of sorting the heap shown as the first diagram in Figure 9.25. These stages are shown in Figure 9.26. In the first step, the largest key, *y*, is moved from the first to the last entry of the list. The first diagram shows the resulting tree, with *y* removed from further consideration, and the last entry, *c*, put aside as the temporary variable *x*.

To find how to rearrange the heap and insert *c*, we look at the two children of the root. Each of these is guaranteed to have a larger key than any other entry in its subtree, and hence the largest of these two entries or the new entry *x* = *c* belongs in the root. We therefore promote *r* to the top of the heap, and repeat the process on the subtree whose root has just been removed. Hence the largest of *d*, *f* and *c* is now inserted where *r* was formerly. At the next step, we would compare *c* with the two children of *f*, but these do not exist, so the promotion of entries through the tree ceases, and *c* is inserted in the empty position formerly occupied by *f*.

At this point we are ready to repeat the algorithm, again moving the top of the heap to the end of the list and restoring the heap property. The sequence of actions that occurs in the complete sort of the list is shown in Figure 9.27.

4. The Function InsertHeap

It is only a short step from this example to a formal function for inserting the entry item into the heap.

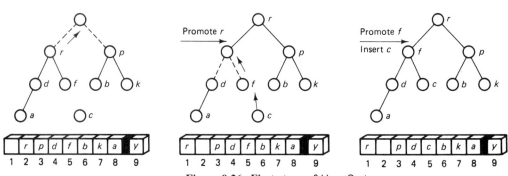

Figure 9.26. First stage of HeapSort

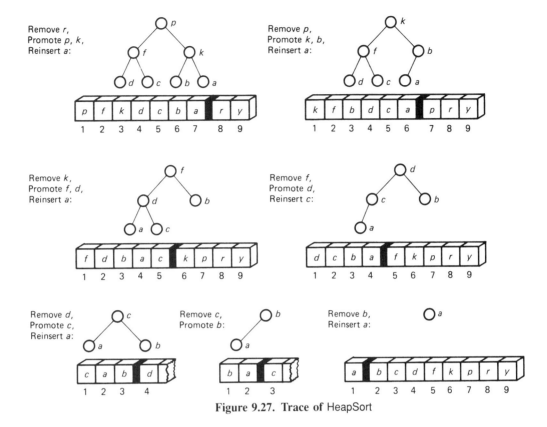

Figure 9.27. Trace of HeapSort

/* *InsertHeap: insert item in partial heap with empty root at* start. *The heap is between* start *and* maxheap *in the list.* */

heap insertion
```
void InsertHeap(List_type *lp, Item_type item, int start, int maxheap)
{
        int m;                                  /* child of start with larger key          */

        m = 2 * start;
                                                /* When start is 0, child is at 1.         */
        while (m <= maxheap) {
                if (m < maxheap && lp->entry[m].key < lp->entry[m + 1].key)
                        m++;                    /* m contains index of larger key.         */
                if (item.key >= lp->entry[m].key)
                        break;                  /* item belongs in position start.         */
                else {
                        lp->entry[start] = lp->entry[m];
                        start = m;
                        m = 2 * start;
                }
        }
        lp->entry[start] = item;
}
```

5. Building the Initial Heap

initialization

The remaining task that we must specify is to build the initial heap from a list in arbitrary order. To do so, we first note that a binary tree with only one node automatically satisfies the properties of a heap, and therefore we need not worry about any of the leaves of the tree, that is, about any of the entries in the second half of the list. If we begin at the midpoint of the list and work our way back toward the start, we can use the function InsertHeap to insert each entry into the partial heap consisting of all later entries, and thereby build the complete heap. The desired function is therefore simply

```
/* BuildHeap: build a heap from a contiguous list. */
void BuildHeap (List_type *lp)
{
        int i;
        for (i = lp->count/2; i >= 1; i−− )
                InsertHeap (lp, lp->entry [i] , i, lp->count 1 );
}
```

9.7.3 Analysis of Heapsort

From the example we have worked it is not at all clear that heapsort is efficient, and in fact heapsort is not a good choice for short lists. It seems quite strange that we can sort by moving large keys slowly toward the beginning of the list before finally putting them away at the end. When n becomes large, however, such small quirks become unimportant, and heapsort proves its worth as one of very few sorting algorithms for contiguous lists that is guaranteed to finish in time $O(n \log n)$ with minimal space requirements.

worst-case insertion

First, let us determine how much work InsertHeap does in its worst case. At each pass through the loop, the index start is doubled; hence the number of passes cannot exceed lg(maxheap/start); this is also the height of the subtree rooted at lp->entry [start]. Each pass through the loop does two comparisons of keys (usually) and one assignment of items. Therefore, the number of comparisons done in InsertHeap is at most 2 lg(maxheap/start) and the number of assignments lg(maxheap/start).

first phase

Let $m = \lfloor \frac{1}{2}n \rfloor$. In BuildHeap we make m calls to InsertHeap, for values of i ranging from lp->count/2 down to 1. Hence the total number of comparisons is about

$$2 \sum_{i=1}^{m} \lg(n/i) = 2(m \lg n - \lg m!) \approx 5m \approx 2.5n,$$

since, by Stirling's approximation (Corollary A.6) and $\lg m = \lg n - 1$, we have

$$\lg m! \approx m \lg m - 1.5m \approx m \lg n - 2.5m.$$

second phase

Similarly, in the sorting and insertion phase, we have about

$$2 \sum_{i=1}^{n} \lg i = 2 \lg n! \approx 2n \lg n - 3n$$

total worst-case counts

comparisons. This term dominates that of the initial phase, and hence we conclude that the number of comparisons is $2n \lg n + O(n)$.

One assignment of items is done in InsertHeap for each two comparisons (approximately). Therefore the total number of assignments is $n \lg n + O(n)$.

comparison with quicksort

From Section 7.8.4 we can see that the corresponding numbers for quicksort in the average case are $1.39n \lg n + O(n)$ comparisons and $0.69n \lg n + O(n)$ swaps, which can be reduced to $0.23n \lg n + O(n)$ swaps. Hence the worst case for heapsort is somewhat poorer than is the average case for quicksort. Quicksort's worst case, however, is $O(n^2)$, which is far worse than the worst case of heapsort for large n. An average-case analysis of heapsort appears to be very complicated, but empirical studies show that (as for selection sort) there is relatively little difference between the average and worst cases, and heapsort usually takes about twice as long as quicksort. Heapsort, therefore, should be regarded as something of an insurance policy: On average, heapsort costs about twice as much as quicksort, but heapsort avoids the slight possibility of a catastrophic degradation of performance.

9.7.4 Priority Queues

To conclude this section we briefly mention another application of heaps. A *priority queue* is a data structure with only two operations:

1. Insert an item.

2. Remove the item having the largest (or smallest) key.

If items have equal keys, then the usual rule is that the first item inserted should be removed first.

applications

In a time-sharing computer system, for example, a large number of tasks may be waiting for the CPU. Some of these tasks have higher priority than others. Hence the set of tasks waiting for the CPU forms a priority queue. Other applications of priority queues include simulations of time-dependent events (like the airport simulation in Chapter 3) and solution of sparse systems of linear equations by row reduction.

implementations

We could represent a priority queue as a sorted contiguous list, in which case removal of an item is immediate, but insertion would take time proportional to n, the number of items in the queue. Or we could represent it as an unsorted list, in which case insertion is rapid but removal is slow. If we used an ordinary binary search tree (sorted by the size of the key) then, on average, insertion and removal could both be done in time $O(\log n)$, but the tree could degenerate and require time $O(n)$. Extra time and space may be needed, as well, to accommodate the linked representation of the binary search tree.

Now consider the properties of a heap. The item with largest key is on the top and can be removed immediately. It will, however, take time $O(\log n)$ to restore the heap property for the remaining keys. If, however, another item is to be inserted immediately, then some of this time may be combined with the $O(\log n)$ time needed to insert the new item. Thus the representation of a priority queue as a heap proves advantageous for large n, since it is represented efficiently in contiguous storage and is guaranteed to require only logarithmic time for both insertions and deletions.

Exercises   **E1.** Determine the contiguous representation of each of the following binary trees.
9.7   Which of these trees are heaps? For those that are not, state which rule(s) is
                  (are) violated at which node(s).

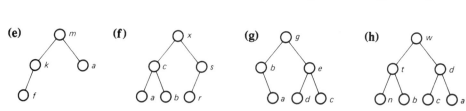

E2. By hand, trace the action of HeapSort on each of the following lists. Draw the
initial tree to which the list corresponds, show how it is converted into a heap, and
show the resulting heap as each item is removed from the top and the new item
inserted.

a. The list of five playing cards used in Chapter 7:

$$S\,Q \qquad S\,A \qquad C\,7 \qquad H\,8 \qquad D\,K$$

b. The list of seven numbers:

$$26 \quad 33 \quad 35 \quad 29 \quad 19 \quad 12 \quad 22$$

c. The list of 14 names:

Tim Dot Eva Roy Tom Kim Guy Amy Jon Ann Jim Kay Ron Jan

E3. **(a)** Design a function that will insert a new item into a heap, obtaining a new heap.
(The function InsertHeap in the text requires that the root be unoccupied, whereas
for this exercise the root will already contain the item with largest key, which must
remain in the heap. Your function will increase the count of items in the list.)
(b) Analyze the time and space requirements of your function.

E4. **(a)** Design a function that will delete the item with largest key (the root) from the top
of the heap and restore the heap properties of the resulting, smaller list. **(b)** Analyze
the time and space requirements of your function.

E5. **(a)** Design a function that will delete the item with index pos from a heap, and
restore the heap properties of the resulting, smaller list. **(b)** Analyze the time and
space requirements of your function.

E6. Consider a heap of n keys, with x_k being the key in position k (in the contiguous
representation) for $1 \le k \le n$. Prove that the height of the subtree rooted at x_k is
$\lfloor \lg(n/k) \rfloor$, for $1 \le k \le n$. [*Hint:* Use "backward" induction on k, starting with
the leaves and working back toward the root, which is x_1.]

E7. Define the notion of a *ternary heap*, analogous to an ordinary heap except that each node of the tree except the leaves has three children. Devise a sorting method based on ternary heaps, and analyze the properties of the sorting method.

**Programming
Project 9.7**

P1. Conduct empirical studies to compare the performance of HeapSort with QuickSort.

POINTERS AND PITFALLS

1. Consider binary search trees as an alternative to lists (indeed, as a way of implementing the abstract data type *list*). At the cost of an extra pointer field in each node, binary search trees allow random access (with $O(\log n)$ key comparisons) to all nodes while maintaining the flexibility of linked lists for insertions, deletions, and rearrangement.

2. Consider binary search trees as an alternative to tables (indeed, as a way of implementing the abstract data type *table*). At the cost of access time that is $O(\log n)$ instead of $O(1)$, binary search trees allow traversal of the data structure in the order specified by the keys while maintaining the advantage of random access provided by tables.

3. In choosing your data structures, always consider carefully what operations will be required. Binary trees are especially appropriate when random access, traversal in a predetermined order, and flexibility in making insertions and deletions are all required.

4. While choosing data structures and algorithms, remain alert to the possibility of highly unbalanced binary trees. If the incoming data are likely to be in random order, then an ordinary binary search tree should prove entirely adequate. If the data may come in a sorted or nearly sorted order, then the algorithms should take appropriate action. If there is only a slight possibility of serious imbalance, it might be ignored. If, in a large project, there is greater likelihood of serious imbalance, then there may still be appropriate places in the software where the trees can be checked for balance and rebuilt if necessary. For applications in which it is essential to maintain logarithmic access time at all times, AVL trees provide nearly perfect balance at a slight cost in computer time and space, but with considerable programming cost.

5. Binary trees are defined recursively; algorithms for manipulating binary trees are usually best written recursively. In programming with binary trees, be aware of the problems generally associated with recursive algorithms. Be sure that your algorithm terminates under any condition and that it correctly treats the trivial case of an empty tree.

6. Although binary trees are usually implemented as linked structures, remain aware of the possibility of other implementations. In programming with linked binary trees, keep in mind the pitfalls attendant on all programming with linked lists.

7. Priority queues are important for many applications, and heaps provide an excellent implementation of priority queues.

8. Heapsort is like an insurance policy: It is usually slower than quicksort, but it guarantees that sorting will be completed in $O(n \log n)$ comparisons of keys, as quicksort cannot always do.

REVIEW QUESTIONS

9.1 **1.** Define the term *binary tree*.

2. Define the term *binary search tree*.

3. What is the difference between a binary tree and an ordinary tree in which each vertex has at most two branches?

9.2 **4.** If a binary search tree with *n* nodes is well balanced, what is the approximate number of comparisons of keys needed to find a target? What is the number if the tree degenerates to a chain?

9.3 **5.** Give the order of visiting the vertices of each of the following binary trees under **(1)** preorder, **(2)** inorder, and **(3)** postorder traversal.

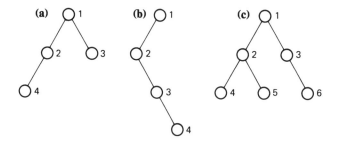

6. Draw the expression trees for each of the following expressions, and show the result of traversing the tree in **(1)** preorder, **(2)** inorder, and **(3)** postorder.

    a. $a - b$.
    b. $n/m!$.
    c. $\log m!$.
    d. $(\log x) + (\log y)$.
    e. $x \times y \le x + y$.
    f. $a > b \;\|\; b \ge a$.

9.4 **7.** In twenty words or less explain how treesort works.

8. What is the relationship between treesort and quicksort?

9. What causes deletion from a search tree to be more difficult than insertion into a search tree?

9.5 **10.** When is the algorithm for building a binary search tree developed in Section 9.5 useful, and why is it preferable to simply using the function for inserting an item into a search tree for each item in the input?

11. How much slower, on average, is searching a random binary search tree than is searching a completely balanced binary search tree?

9.6   **12.** What is the purpose for AVL trees?

13. What condition defines an AVL tree among all binary search trees?

14. Draw a picture explaining how balance is restored when an insertion into an AVL tree puts a node out of balance.

15. How does the worst-case performance of an AVL tree compare with the worst-case performance of a random binary search tree? with its average-case performance? How does the average-case performance of an AVL tree compare with that of a random binary search tree?

9.7   **16.** What is a heap?

17. How does heapsort work?

18. Compare the worst-case performance of heapsort with the worst-case performance of quicksort, and compare it also with the average-case performance of quicksort.

19. What is a priority queue?

20. Give three possible implementations of priority queues, and give the approximate number of key comparisons needed, on average, for insertion and deletion in each implementation.

REFERENCES FOR FURTHER STUDY

The most comprehensive source of information on binary trees is the series of books by KNUTH. The properties of binary trees, other classes of trees, traversal, path length, and history, altogether occupy pp. 305–405 of Volume 1. Volume 3, pp. 422–480, discusses binary search trees, AVL trees, and related topics. Heapsort is discussed in pp. 145–149 of Volume 3. The proof of Theorem 9.2 is from Volume 3, p. 427.

A mathematical analysis of the behavior of AVL trees appears in

E. M. REINGOLD, J. NIEVERGELT, N. DEO, *Combinatorial Algorithms: Theory and Practice*, Prentice Hall, Englewood Cliffs, N. J., 1977.

The original reference for AVL trees is

G. M. ADEL'SON-VEL'SKIĬ and E. M. LANDIS, *Dokl. Akad. Nauk SSSR* 146 (1962), 263–266; English translation: *Soviet Math. (Dokl.)* 3 (1962), 1259–1263.

Heapsort was discovered and so named by

J. W. J. WILLIAMS, *Communications of the ACM* 7 (1964), 347–348.

Several algorithms for constructing a balanced binary search tree are discussed in

HSI CHANG and S. S. IYENGAR, "Efficient algorithms to globally balance a binary search tree," *Communications of the ACM* 27 (1984), 695–702.

A simple but complete development of algorithms for heaps and priority queues appears in

JON BENTLEY, "Programming pearls: Thanks, heaps," *Communications of the ACM* 28 (1985), 245–250.

Collections of the "Programming pearls" column appear in

JON L. BENTLEY, *Programming Pearls*, Addison-Wesley, Reading, Mass., 1986, 195 pages.

This book contains (pp. 125–137) more details for heaps and priority queues.

Trees and Graphs

This chapter continues the study of trees as data structures, now concentrating on trees with more than two branches at each node. We then turn to algorithms for graphs, which are more general structures that include trees as a special case. Each of the major sections of this chapter is independent of the others and can be studied separately.

10.1 ORCHARDS, TREES, AND BINARY TREES

Binary trees, as we have seen, are a powerful and elegant form of data structures. Even so, the restriction to no more than two children at each node is severe, and there are many possible applications for trees as data structures where the number of children of a node can be arbitrary. This section elucidates a pleasant and helpful surprise: Binary trees provide a convenient way to represent what first appears to be a far broader class of trees.

10.1.1 On the Classification of Species

Since we have already sighted several kinds of trees in the applications we have studied, we should, before exploring further, put our gear in order by settling the definitions. In mathematics, the term **tree** has a quite broad meaning: It is any set of points (called vertices) and any set of pairs of distinct vertices (called edges or branches) such that (1) there is a sequence of edges (a path) from any vertex to any other, and (2) there are no circuits, that is, no paths starting from a vertex and returning to the same vertex.

free tree   In computer applications we usually do not need to study trees in such generality, and when we do, for emphasis we call them **free trees**. Our trees are almost always tied down by having one particular vertex singled out as the **root**, and for emphasis we call
rooted tree   such a tree a **rooted tree**.

A rooted tree can be drawn in our usual way by picking it up by its root and shaking it so that all the branches and other vertices hang downward, with the leaves at the bottom. Even so, rooted trees still do not have all the structure that we usually use. In a rooted tree there is still no way to tell left from right, or, when one vertex has several children, to tell which is first, second, and so on. If for no other reason, the restraint of sequential execution of instructions (not to mention sequential organization of storage) usually imposes an order on the children of each vertex. Hence we define
ordered tree   an **ordered tree** to be a rooted tree in which the children of each vertex are assigned an order.

Note that ordered trees for which no vertex has more than two children are still not the same class as binary trees. If a vertex in a binary tree has only one child, then it could be either on the left side or on the right side, and the two resulting binary trees are different, but both would be the same as ordered trees.

2-tree   As a final remark related to the definitions, let us note that the 2-trees that we studied as part of algorithm analysis are rooted trees (but not necessarily ordered trees) with the property that every vertex has either 0 or 2 children. Thus 2-trees do not coincide with any of the other classes we have introduced.

Figure 10.1 shows what happens for the various kinds of trees with a small number of vertices. Note that each class of trees after the first can be obtained by taking the trees from the previous class and distinguishing those that differ under the new criterion. Compare the list of five ordered trees with four vertices with the list of fourteen binary trees with four vertices constructed as an exercise in Section 9.4. You will find that, again, the binary trees can be obtained from the appropriate ordered trees by distinguishing a left branch from a right branch.

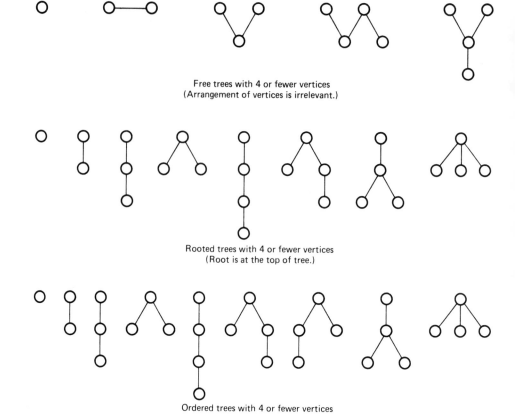

Free trees with 4 or fewer vertices
(Arrangement of vertices is irrelevant.)

Rooted trees with 4 or fewer vertices
(Root is at the top of tree.)

Ordered trees with 4 or fewer vertices

Figure 10.1. Various kinds of trees

10.1.2 Ordered Trees

1. Computer Implementation

If we wish to use an ordered tree as a data structure, the obvious way to implement it in computer memory would be to extend the standard way to implement a binary tree, keeping as many fields in each node as there may be subtrees, in place of the two links needed for binary trees. Thus in a tree where some nodes have as many as ten subtrees, we would keep ten link fields in each node. But this will result in a great many of the *multiple links* link fields being NULL. In fact, we can easily determine exactly how many. If the tree has n nodes and each node has k link fields, then there are $n \times k$ links altogether. There is exactly one link that points to each of the $n - 1$ nodes other than the root, so the proportion of NULL links must be

$$\frac{(n \times k) - (n - 1)}{n \times k} > 1 - \frac{1}{k}.$$

Hence if a vertex might have ten subtrees, then more than ninety percent of the links will be NULL. Clearly this method of representing ordered trees is very wasteful of space.

The reason is that, for each node, we are maintaining a contiguous list of links to all its children, and these contiguous lists reserve much unused space. We now investigate a way that replaces these contiguous lists with linked lists and leads to an elegant connection with binary trees.

2. Linked Implementation

To keep the children of each node in a linked list, we shall need two kinds of links. First comes the header for each such list; this will be a link from each node to its leftmost child, which we may call firstchild. Second, each node except the root will appear in one of these lists, and hence requires a link to the next node on the list, that is, to the next child of the parent. We may call this second link nextchild. This implementation is illustrated in Figure 10.2.

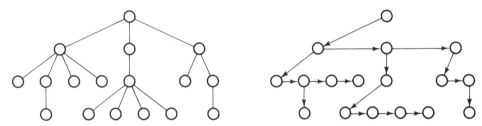

Figure 10.2. Linked implementation of an ordered tree

3. The Natural Correspondence

For each node of the ordered tree we have defined two links (that will be NULL if not otherwise defined), firstchild and nextchild. By using these two links we now have the structure of a binary tree; that is, the linked implementation of an ordered tree is a linked binary tree. If we wish, we can even form a better picture of a binary tree by taking the linked representation of the ordered tree and rotating it a few degrees clockwise, so that downward (firstchild) links point leftward and the horizontal (nextchild) links point downward and to the right.

4. Inverse Correspondence

Suppose that we reverse the steps of the foregoing process, beginning with a binary tree and trying to recover an ordered tree. The first observation that we must make is that not every binary tree is obtained from a rooted tree by the above process: Since the nextchild link of the root is always NULL, the root of the corresponding binary tree will always have an empty right subtree. To study the inverse correspondence more carefully, we must consider another class of data structures.

10.1.3 Forests and Orchards

In our work so far with binary trees we have profited from using recursion, and for other classes of trees we shall continue to do so. Employing recursion means reducing a problem to a smaller one. Hence we should see what happens if we take a rooted tree or an ordered tree and strip off the root. What is then left is (if not empty) a set of rooted trees or an ordered set of ordered trees, respectively.

forest

The standard term for an arbitrary set of trees is *forest*, but when we use this term, we generally assume that the trees are rooted. The phrase *ordered forest* is sometimes used for an ordered set of ordered trees, but we shall adopt the equally descriptive (and more colorful) term *orchard* for this book. (Although this term is not yet in common use, perhaps it will soon become standard.)

orchard

Note that not only can we obtain a forest or an orchard by removing the root from a rooted tree or an ordered tree, respectively, but we can build a rooted or an ordered tree by starting with a forest or an orchard, attaching a new vertex at the top, and adding branches from the new vertex (which will be the root) to the roots of all trees in the forest or the orchard.

recursive definitions

We shall use this observation to give a new, recursive definition of ordered trees and orchards, one that yields a formal proof of the connection with binary trees. First, let us consider how to start. Recall that it is possible that a binary tree be empty; that is, it may have no vertices. It is also possible that a forest or an orchard be empty; that is, that it contain no trees. It is, however, not possible that a rooted or an ordered tree be empty, since it is guaranteed to contain a root, at least. If we wish to start building trees and forests, we can note that the tree with only one vertex is obtained by attaching a new root to an empty forest. Once we have this tree, we can make a forest consisting of as many one-vertex trees as we wish and attach a new root to build all rooted trees of height 1. In this way we can continue to construct all the rooted trees in turn in accordance with the following mutually recursive definitions.

DEFINITION   A *rooted tree* consists of a single vertex v, called the *root* of the tree, together with a forest F, whose trees are called the *subtrees* of the root.

DEFINITION   A *forest* F is a (possibly empty) set of rooted trees.

A similar construction works for ordered trees and orchards.

DEFINITION   An *ordered tree* T consists of a single vertex v, called the *root* of the tree, together with an orchard O, whose trees are called the *subtrees* of the root v. We may denote the ordered tree with the ordered pair

$$T = \{v, O\}.$$

An *orchard* O is either the empty set $\emptyset$, or consists of an ordered tree T, called the *first tree* of the orchard, together with another orchard O' (which contains the remaining trees of the orchard). We may denote the orchard with the ordered pair

$$O = (T, O').$$

Notice how the ordering of trees is implicit in the definition of orchard. A nonempty orchard contains a first tree, and the remaining trees form another orchard, which again has a first tree that is the second tree of the original orchard. Continuing to examine the remaining orchard yields the third tree, and so on, until the remaining orchard is the empty one.

10.1.4 The Formal Correspondence

We can now obtain the principal result of this section.

THEOREM 10.1   *Let S be any finite set of vertices. There is a one-to-one correspondence f from the set of orchards whose set of vertices is S to the set of binary trees whose set of vertices is S.*

Proof   Let us use the notation introduced in the definitions to prove the theorem. First, we need a similar notation for binary trees: A binary tree B is either the empty set $\emptyset$ or consists of a root vertex v with two binary trees B_1 and B_2. We may thus denote a binary tree with the ordered triple

$$B = [v, B_1, B_2].$$

We shall prove the theorem by mathematical induction on the number of vertices in S. The first case to consider is the empty orchard $\emptyset$, which will correspond to the empty binary tree:

$$f(\emptyset) = \emptyset.$$

If the orchard O is not empty, then it is denoted by the ordered pair

$$O = (T, O_2)$$

where T is an ordered tree and O_2 another orchard. The ordered tree T is denoted as the pair

$$T = \{v, O_1\}$$

where v is a vertex and O_1 is another orchard. We substitute this expression for T in the first expression, obtaining

$$O = (\{v, O_1\}, O_2).$$

By the induction hypothesis f provides a one-to-one correspondence from orchards with fewer vertices than in S to binary trees, and O_1 and O_2 are smaller than O, so the binary trees $f(O_1)$ and $f(O_2)$ are determined by the induction hypothesis. We define the correspondence f from the orchard to a binary tree by

$$f(\{v, O_1\}, O_2) = [v, f(O_1), f(O_2)].$$

It is now obvious that the function f is a one-to-one correspondence between orchards and binary trees with the same vertices. For any way to fill in the symbols v, O_1, and O_2 on the left side, there is exactly one way to fill in the same symbols on the right, and vice versa.

end of proof

10.1.5 Rotations

We can also use this notational form of the correspondence to help us form the picture of the transformation from orchard to binary tree. In the binary tree $[v, f(O_1), f(O_2)]$ the left link from v goes to the root of the binary tree $f(O_1)$, which in fact was the first child of v in the ordered tree $\{v, O_1\}$. The right link from v goes to the vertex that was formerly the root of the next ordered tree to the right. That is, "left link" in the binary tree corresponds to "first child" in an ordered tree, and "right link" corresponds to "next sibling." In geometrical terms the transformation reduces to the rules:

1. Draw the orchard so that the first child of each vertex is immediately below the vertex, rather than centering the children below the vertex.

2. Draw a vertical link from each vertex to its first child, and draw a horizontal link from each vertex to its next sibling.

3. Remove the remaining original links.

4. Rotate the diagram 45 degrees clockwise, so that the vertical links appear as left links and the horizontal links as right links.

This process is illustrated in Figure 10.3.

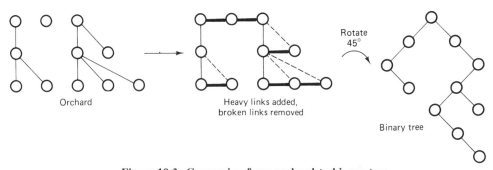

Figure 10.3. Conversion from orchard to binary tree

10.1.6 Summary

We have seen three ways to describe the correspondence between orchards and binary trees:

- firstchild and nextchild links,
- rotations of diagrams,
- formal notational equivalence.

Most people find the second way, rotation of diagrams, the easiest to remember and to picture. It is the first way, setting up links to give the correspondence, that is usually needed in actually writing computer programs. The third way, the formal correspondence, finally, is the one that proves most useful in constructing proofs of various properties of binary trees and orchards.

Exercises 10.1

E1. Convert each of the following orchards into a binary tree.

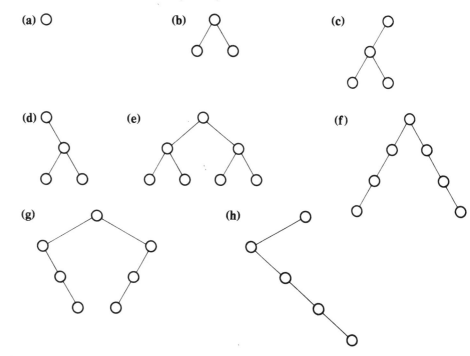

E2. Convert each of the following binary trees into an orchard.

E3. Draw all the **(a)** free trees, **(b)** rooted trees, and **(c)** ordered trees with five vertices.

E4. We can define the ***preorder traversal*** of an orchard as follows. If the orchard is empty, do nothing. Otherwise, first visit the root of the first tree, then traverse the orchard of subtrees of the first tree in preorder, and then traverse the orchard of remaining trees in preorder. Prove that preorder traversal of an orchard and preorder traversal of the corresponding binary tree will visit the vertices in the same order.

E5. We can define the ***inorder traversal*** of an orchard as follows. If the orchard is empty, do nothing. Otherwise, first traverse the orchard of subtrees of the first tree's root in inorder, then visit the root of the first tree, and then traverse the orchard of remaining subtrees in inorder. Prove that inorder traversal of an orchard and inorder traversal of the corresponding binary tree will visit the vertices in the same order.

E6. Describe a way of traversing an orchard that will visit the vertices in the same order as postorder traversal of the corresponding binary tree. Prove that your traversal method visits the vertices in the correct order.

10.2 LEXICOGRAPHIC SEARCH TREES: TRIES

multiway branching

Several times in previous chapters we have contrasted searching a list with looking up an entry in a table. We can apply the idea of table lookup to information retrieval from a tree by using a key or part of a key to make a *multiway branch*.

Instead of searching by comparison of entire keys, we can consider a key as a sequence of characters (letters or digits, for example), and use these characters to determine a multiway branch at each step. If our keys are alphabetic names, then we make a 26-way branch according to the first letter of the name, followed by another branch according to the second letter, and so on. This multiway branching is the idea of a thumb index in a dictionary. A thumb index, however, is generally used only to find the words with a given initial letter; some other search method is then used to continue. In a computer we can proceed two or three levels by multiway branching, but then the tree will become too large, and we shall need to resort to some other device to continue.

10.2.1 Tries

One method is to prune from the tree all the branches that do not lead to any key. In English, for example, there are no words that begin with the letters 'bb', 'bc', 'bf', 'bg', ..., but there are words beginning with 'ba', 'bd', or 'be'. Hence all the corresponding branches and nodes can be removed from the tree. The resulting tree is called a ***trie***. (This term originated as letters extracted from the word *retrieval*, but it is usually pronounced like the word "try.")

A trie of order m can be defined formally as being either empty or consisting of an ordered sequence of exactly m tries of order m.

10.2.2 Searching for a Key

A trie describing the words (as listed in the *Oxford English Dictionary*) made up only from the letters *a*, *b*, and *c* is shown in Figure 10.4. Along with the branches to the next level of the trie, each node contains a pointer to a structure of information about the key, if any, that has been found when the node is reached. The search for a particular key begins at the root. The first letter of the key is used as an index to determine which branch to take. An empty branch means that the key being sought is not in the tree. Otherwise, we use the second letter of the key to determine the branch at the next level, and so continue. When we reach the end of the word, the information pointer directs us to the desired information. A NULL information pointer shows that the string is not a word in the trie. Note, therefore, that the word *a* is a prefix of the word *aba*, which is a prefix of the word *abaca*. On the other hand, the string *abac* is not an English word, and therefore has a NULL information pointer.

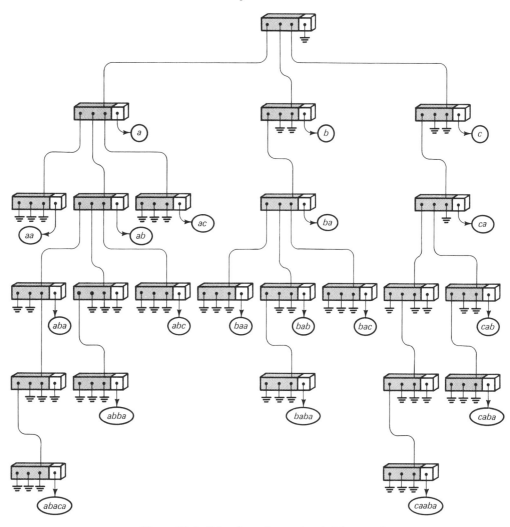

Figure 10.4. Trie of words constructed from *a*, *b*, *c*

10.2.3 C Algorithm

trie declaration

The search process described above translates easily into a function. First we need some declarations, which we put in the file trie.h.

```
#define MAXLENGTH 10
#define LETTERS 26                    /* number of letters in the alphabet    */

typedef char Key_type [MAXLENGTH];    /* contains only 'a' – 'z'              */

typedef struct keyinfo_type {
        int info;
        Key_type k;
} Keyinfo_type;

typedef struct node_type {
        struct node_type *branch [LETTERS];
        Keyinfo_type *info;
} Node_type;
```

Keyinfo_type may be bound to some other type that contains the desired information for each key. We shall assume that all keys contain only lowercase letters and that a key is terminated by the null character '\0'. The searching method then becomes the following function.

trie retrieval

```
/* TrieSearch: root is the root of a trie; the return value will be a pointer to the trie
    structure that points to the information for the target if the search is successful, NULL
    if the search is unsuccessful. */
Node_type *TrieSearch (Node_type *root, Key_type target)
{
        int i = 0;

        while (i < MAXLENGTH && root)
                if (target [i] == '\0')
                        i = MAXLENGTH;          /* terminates search                   */
                /* root is left pointing to node with information for target. */
                else {
                        root = root->branch [target [i] – 'a'];
                                        /* Move down appropriate branch.       */
                        i++;                    /* Move to the next character of the target. */
                }
        if (root && ! root->info)
                        return NULL;
        return root;
}
```

The termination condition for the loop is made more complicated to avoid an index error after an iteration with i = MAXLENGTH. At the conclusion, the return value (if not NULL) points to the node in the trie corresponding to the target.

10.2.4 Insertion into a Trie

Adding a new key to a trie is quite similar to searching for the key: we must trace our way down the trie to the appropriate point and set the info pointer to the information structure for the new key. If, on the way, we hit a NULL branch in the trie, we must now not terminate the search, but instead we must add new nodes to the trie so as to complete the path corresponding to the new key. We thereby obtain the following function.

trie insertion

```
/* InsertTrie: insert a new key into a trie. */
Node_type *InsertTrie(Node_type *root, Key_type k, Keyinfo_type *info)
{
    int i = 0;
    int ch;

    if (!root) {                              /* Create a new trie with all empty subtries. */
        root = (Node_type *)malloc(sizeof(Node_type));
        for (ch = 0; ch < LETTERS; ch++)
            root->branch[ch] = NULL;
        root->info = NULL;
    }
    while (i < MAXLENGTH)
        if (k[i] == '\0')                     /* Terminate the search.                      */
            i = MAXLENGTH;
        else {
            if (root->branch[k[i]])           /* Move down the appropriate branch.      */
                root = root->branch[k[i]];
            else {                            /* Make a new node on the route for key k. */
                root->branch[k[i]] = (Node_type *)malloc(sizeof(Node_type));
                root = root->branch[k[i]];
                for (ch = 0; ch < LETTERS; ch++)
                    root->branch[ch] = NULL;
                root->info = NULL;
            }
            i++;                              /* Continue to the next character in k.    */
        }                     /* At this point, we have tested for all characters of k. */
    if (root->info != NULL)
        Error("Tried to insert a duplicate key.");
    else
        root->info = info;
    return root;
}
```

10.2.5 Deletion from a Trie

The same general plan used for searching and insertion also works for deletion from a trie. We trace down the path corresponding to the key being deleted, and when we reach the appropriate node, we set the corresponding info field to NULL. If now, however, this node has all its fields NULL (all branches and the info field), then we should dispose of this node. To do so, we can set up a stack of pointers to the nodes on the path from the root to the last node reached. Alternatively, we can use recursion in the deletion algorithm and avoid the need for an explicit stack. In either case, we shall leave the programming as an exercise.

10.2.6 Assessment of Tries

The number of steps required to search a trie (or insert into it) is proportional to the number of characters making up a key, not to a logarithm of the number of keys, as in other tree-based searches. If this number of characters is small relative to the (base 2) logarithm of the number of keys, then a trie may prove superior to a binary tree. If, for example, the keys consist of all possible sequences of five letters, then the trie can locate any of $n = 26^5 = 11,881,376$ keys in 5 iterations, whereas the best that binary search

comparison with
binary search

can do is $\lg n \approx 23.5$ key comparisons.

In many applications, however, the number of characters in a key is larger, and the set of keys that actually occurs is sparse in the set of all possible keys. In these applications the number of iterations required to search a trie may very well exceed the number of key comparisons needed for a binary search.

The best solution, finally, may be to combine the methods. A trie can be used for the first few characters of the key, and then another method can be employed for the remainder of the key. If we return to the example of the thumb index in a dictionary, we see that, in fact, we use a multiway tree to locate the first letter of the word, but we then use some other search method to locate the desired word among those with the same first letter.

Exercises
10.2

E1. Draw the tries constructed from each of the following sets of keys.

    a. All three-digit integers containing only 1, 2, 3 (in decimal representation).

    b. All three-letter sequences built from *a, b, c, d* where the first letter is *a*.

    c. All four-digit binary integers (built from 0 and 1).

    d. The words

pal   lap   a   papa   al   papal   all   ball   lab

built from the letters *a, b, l, p.*

E2. Write a function that will traverse a trie and print out all its words in alphabetical order.

E3. Write a function that will traverse a trie and print out all its words, with the order determined first by the length of the word, with shorter words first, and, second, by alphabetical order for words of the same length.

E4. Write a function that will delete a word from a trie.

Programming
Project 10.2

P1. Run the insertion, search, and deletion functions for appropriate test data, and compare the results with similar experiments for binary search trees.

10.3 EXTERNAL SEARCHING: B-TREES

In our work throughout this book we have assumed that all our data structures are kept in high-speed memory; that is, we have considered only *internal* information retrieval. For many applications, this assumption is reasonable, but for many other important applications, it is not. Let us now turn briefly to the problem of *external* information retrieval, where we wish to locate and retrieve records stored in a disk file.

10.3.1 Access Time

The time required to access and retrieve a word from high-speed memory is a few microseconds at most. The time required to locate a particular record on a disk is measured in milliseconds, and for floppy disks can exceed a second. Hence the time required for a single access is thousands of times greater for external retrieval than for internal retrieval. On the other hand, when a record is located on a disk, the normal practice is not to read only one word, but to read in a large *page* or *block* of information at once. Typical sizes for blocks range from 256 to 1024 characters or words.

Our goal in external searching must be to minimize the number of disk accesses, since each access takes so long compared to internal computation. With each access, however, we obtain a block that may have room for several records. Using these records we may be able to make a multiway decision concerning which block to access next. Hence multiway trees are especially appropriate for external searching.

10.3.2 Multiway Search Trees

Binary search trees generalize directly to multiway search trees in which, for some integer m called the *order* of the tree, each node has at most m children. If $k \leq m$ is the number of children, then the node contains exactly $k - 1$ keys, which partition all the keys into k subsets. If some of these subsets are empty, then the corresponding children in the tree are empty. Figure 10.5 shows a 5-way search tree in which some of the children of some nodes are empty.

10.3.3 Balanced Multiway Trees

Our goal is to devise a multiway search tree that will minimize file accesses; hence we wish to make the height of the tree as small as possible. We can accomplish this by insisting, first, that no empty subtrees appear above the leaves (so that the division of keys into subsets is as efficient as possible); second, that all leaves be on the same level (so that searches will all be guaranteed to terminate with about the same number of accesses); and, third, that every node (except the leaves) have at least some minimal number of children. We shall require that each node (except the leaves) have at least half as many children as the maximum possible. These conditions lead to the following formal definition.

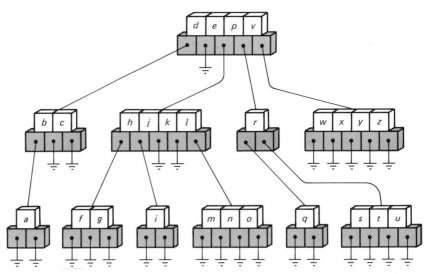

Figure 10.5. A 5-way search tree

DEFINITION

A ***B-tree of order*** m is an m-way tree in which

1. All leaves are on the same level.

2. All internal nodes except the root have at most m (nonempty) children, and at least $\lceil m/2 \rceil$ (nonempty) children.

3. The number of keys in each internal node is one less than the number of its children, and these keys partition the keys in the children in the fashion of a search tree.

4. The root has at most m children, but may have as few as 2 if it is not a leaf, or none if the tree consists of the root alone.

The tree in Figure 10.5 is not a B-tree, since some nodes have empty children, and the leaves are not all on the same level. Figure 10.6 shows a B-tree of order 5 whose keys are the 26 letters of the alphabet.

10.3.4 Insertion into a B-tree

method

The condition that all leaves be on the same level forces a characteristic behavior of B-trees: In contrast to binary search trees, B-trees are not allowed to grow at their leaves; instead, they are forced to grow at the root. The general method of insertion is as follows. First, a search is made to see if the new key is in the tree. This search (if the key is truly new) will terminate in failure at a leaf. The new key is then added to the leaf node. If the node was not previously full, then the insertion is finished. When a key is added to a full node, then the node splits into two nodes on the same level, except that the median key is not put into either of the two new nodes, but is instead sent up the tree to be inserted into the parent node. When a search is later made through the

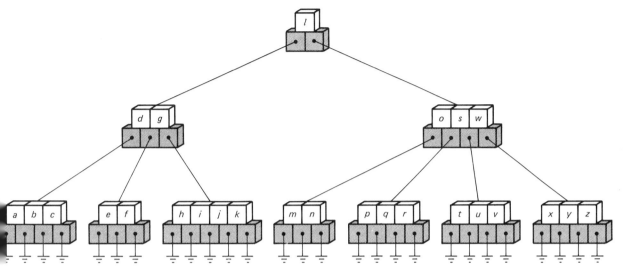

Figure 10.6. A B-tree of order 5

tree, therefore, a comparison with the median key will serve to direct the search into the proper subtree. When a key is added to a full root, then the root splits in two and the median key sent upward becomes a new root.

This process is greatly elucidated by studying an example such as the growth of the B-tree of order 5 shown in Figure 10.7. We shall insert the keys

a g f b k d h m j e s i r x c l n t u p

into an initially empty tree, in the order given.

The first four keys will be inserted into one node, as shown in the first diagram of Figure 10.7. They are sorted into the proper order as they are inserted. There is no room, however, for the fifth key, *k*, so its insertion causes the node to split into two, and the median key, *f*, moves up to enter a new node, which is a new root. Since the split nodes are now only half full, the next three keys can be inserted without difficulty. Note, however, that these simple insertions can require rearrangement of the keys within a node. The next insertion, *j*, again splits a node, and this time it is *j* itself that is the median key, and therefore moves up to join *f* in the root.

node splitting

upward propagation

The next several insertions proceed similarly. The final insertion, that of *p*, is more interesting. This insertion first splits the node originally containing *k l m n*, sending the median key *m* upward into the node containing *c f j r*, which is, however, already full. Hence this node in turn splits, and a new root containing *j* is created.

improving balance

Two comments regarding the growth of B-trees are in order. First, when a node splits, it produces two nodes that are now only half full. Later insertions, therefore, can more likely be made without need to split nodes again. Hence one splitting prepares the way for several simple insertions. Second, it is always a median key that is sent upward, not necessarily the key being inserted. Hence repeated insertions tend to improve the balance of the tree, no matter in what order the keys happen to arrive.

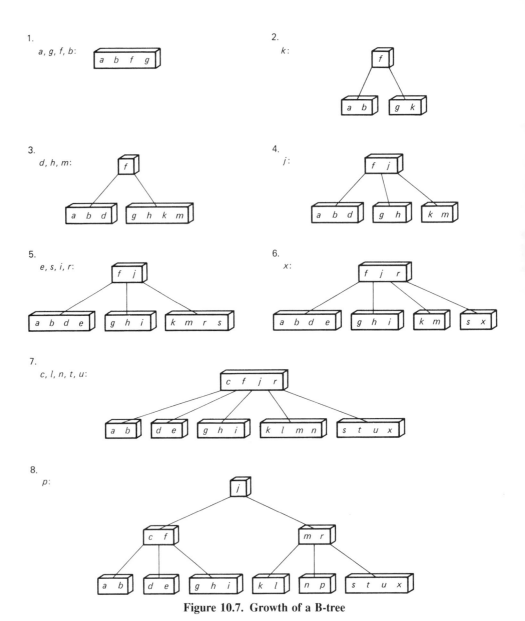

Figure 10.7. Growth of a B-tree

10.3.5 C Algorithms: Searching and Insertion

To develop C algorithms for searching and insertion in a B-tree, let us begin with the declarations needed to set up a B-tree. For simplicity we shall construct our B-tree entirely in high-speed memory, using pointers to describe its structure. In most applications, these pointers would be replaced by the addresses of various blocks or pages on a disk, and taking a pointer reference would become making a disk access. We shall also construct our tree from keys alone; in any practical application each key would be associated with other information.

1. Declarations

We assume that Key_type is defined already. Within one node there will be a list of keys and a list of pointers to the children of the node. Since these lists are short, we shall, for simplicity, use contiguous arrays and a separate variable count for their representation. This yields btree.h:

```
#define MAX 4               /* maximum number of keys in node; MAX = m − 1 */
#define MIN 2               /* minimum number of keys in node; MIN = ⌈m/2⌉ − 1 */

typedef int Key_type;

typedef struct node_tag {
        int count;                  /* Except for the root, the lower limit is MIN */
        Key_type key[MAX + 1];
     struct node_tag *branch[MAX + 1];
} Node_type;
```

The way in which the indices are arranged implies that in some of our algorithms we shall need to investigate branch[0] separately, and then consider each key in association with the branch on its right.

2. Searching

As a simple first example we write a function to search through a B-tree for a target key. The input parameters for the function are the target key and a pointer to the root of the B-tree. The function value is a pointer to the node where the target was found, or NULL if it was not found. The last parameter is the position of the target within that node. The general method of searching by working our way down through the tree is similar to a search through a binary search tree. In a multiway tree, however, we must examine each node more extensively to find which branch to take at the next step. This examination is done by the auxiliary function SearchNode that returns a Boolean value indicating if the search was successful and targetpos, which is the position of the target if found, and otherwise is the number of the branch on which to continue the search.

B-tree retrieval
```
/* Search: traverse B-tree looking for target. */
Node_type *Search(Key_type target, Node_type *root, int *targetpos)
{
        if (root == NULL)
                return NULL;
        else if (SearchNode(target, root, targetpos))
                return root;
        else
                return Search(target, root->branch[*targetpos], targetpos);
}
```

This function has been written recursively to exhibit the similarity of its structure to that of the insertion function to be developed shortly. The recursion is tail recursion, however, and can easily be replaced by iteration if desired.

3. Searching a Node

This function determines if the target is in the current node, and, if not, finds which of the count + 1 branches will contain the target key. For convenience, the possibility of taking branch 0 is considered separately, and then a sequential search is made through the remaining possibilities.

sequential search

```
/* SearchNode: searches keys in node p for target; returns location k of target, or
    branch on which to continue search */
Boolean_type SearchNode(Key_type target, Node_type *p, int *k)
{
    if (LT(target, p->key[1])) {        /* Take the leftmost branch.            */
        *k = 0;
        return FALSE;
    } else {                            /* Start a sequential search through the keys. */
        *k = p->count;
        while (LT(target, p->key[*k]) && *k > 1)
            (*k) --;
        return EQ(target, p->key[*k]);
    }
}
```

For B-trees of large order, this function should be modified to use binary search.

4. Insertion: The Main Function

Insertion can be most naturally formulated as a recursive function, since after insertion in a subtree has been completed, a (median) key may remain that must be reinserted higher in the tree. Recursion allows us to keep track of the position within the tree and work our way back up the tree without need for an explicit auxiliary stack.

parameters

We shall assume that the key being inserted is not already in the tree. The insertion function then needs only two parameters: newkey, the key being inserted, and root, the root of the B-tree. The function value is a pointer to the root of the tree after insertion. For the recursion, however, we need three additional output parameters. The first of these is the function value which indicates whether the root of the subtree has split into two, also producing a (median) key to be reinserted higher in the tree. When this happens, we shall adopt the convention that the old root node contains the left half of the keys and a new node contains the right half of the keys. When a split occurs, the second output parameter x is the median key, and the third parameter xr is a pointer to the new node, the right half of the former root *p of the subtree.

To keep all these parameters straight, we shall do the recursion in a function called PushDown. This situation is illustrated in Figure 10.8.

The recursion is started by the main function Insert. If the outermost call to function PushDown should return with the value TRUE, then there is a key to be placed in a new root, and the height of the entire tree will increase. The main function follows.

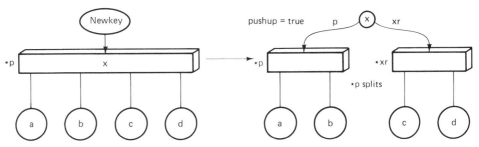

Figure 10.8. Action of PushDown **function**

/* Insert: inserts newkey into the B-tree with the given root; requires that newkey is not already present in the tree */

B-tree insertion: Node_type *Insert(Key_type newkey, Node_type *root)
main function {

```
        Key_type x;                      /* node to be reinserted as new root    */
        Node_type *xr;                   /* subtree on right of x                */
        Node_type *p;                    /* pointer for temporary use            */
        Boolean_type pushup;             /* Has the height of the tree increased? */

        pushup = PushDown(newkey, root, &x, &xr);
        if (pushup) {                    /* Tree grows in height.                */
            p = (Node_type *)malloc(sizeof(Node_type));  /* Make a new root. */
            p->count = 1;
            p->key[1] = x;
            p->branch[0] = root;
            p->branch[1] = xr;
            return p;
        }
        return root;
}
```

5. Recursive Insertion into a Subtree

Next we turn to the recursive function PushDown. In a B-tree, a new key is first inserted into a leaf. We shall thus use the condition p == NULL to terminate the recursion; that is, we shall continue to move down the tree searching for newkey until we hit an empty subtree. Since the B-tree does not grow by adding new leaves, we do not then immediately insert target, but instead send the key back up (now called x) for insertion.

When a recursive call returns TRUE, then we attempt to insert the key x in the current node. If there is room, then we are finished. Otherwise, the current node *p splits into *p and *xr and a (possibly different) median key x is sent up the tree. The function uses three auxiliary functions: SearchNode (same as before); PushIn puts the key x into node *p provided that there is room; and Split chops a full node *p into two.

```
                    /* PushDown: recursively move down tree searching for newkey. */
                    Boolean_type PushDown (Key_type newkey, Node_type *p, Key_type *x,
                                          Node_type **xr)
                    {
                        int k;                          /* branch on which to continue the search */
                        if (p == NULL) {                /* cannot insert into empty tree; terminates */
found the leaf where         *x = newkey;
key goes                     *xr = NULL;
                             return TRUE;
                        } else {                        /* Search the current node.             */
                             if (SearchNode (newkey, p, &k))
                                 Error ("inserting duplicate key");
return from                  if (PushDown (newkey, p->branch [k], x, xr))
recursion                                               /* Reinsert median key.                */
                                 if (p->count < MAX) {
insert into node                     PushIn (*x, *xr, p, k);
                                     return FALSE;
                                 } else {
split node                           Split (*x, *xr, p, k, x, xr);
                                     return TRUE;
                                 }
                             return FALSE;
                        }
                    }
```

6. Insert a Key into a Node

The next function inserts the key x and its right-hand pointer xr into the node *p. The function is called only when there is room for the insertion.

```
/* PushIn: inserts key x and pointer xr into node p at position k; requires that the node
   was not previously full. */
void PushIn (Key_type x, Node_type *xr, Node_type *p, int k)
{
    int i;                                  /* index to move keys to make room for x */
    for (i = p->count; i > k; i--) {
    /* Shift all the keys and branches to the right. */
        p->key [i + 1] = p->key [i];
        p->branch [i + 1] = p->branch [i];
    }
    p->key [k + 1] = x;
    p->branch [k + 1] = xr;
    p->count++;
}
```

7. Splitting a Full Node

The next function inserts the key x with subtree pointer xr into the full node *p; splits the right half off as new node *yr; and sends the median key y upward for reinsertion later. It is, of course, not possible to insert key x directly into the full node: we must instead first determine whether x will go into the left or right half, divide the node (at position median) accordingly, and then insert x into the appropriate half. While this work proceeds, we shall leave the median key y in the left half.

```
/* Split: splits node *p with key x and pointer xr at position k into nodes *p and *yr
     with median key y */
void Split (Key_type x, Node_type *xr, Node_type *p, int k,
            Key_type *y, Node_type **yr)
{
        int i;                              /* used for copying from *p to new node  */
        int median;
```

find splitting point
```
        if (k <= MIN)                   /* Determine if new key x goes to left or right half. */
                median = MIN;
        else
                median = MIN + 1;
        /* Get a new node and put it on the right. */
        *yr = (Node_type *) malloc (sizeof (Node_type));
        for (i = median + 1; i <= MAX; i++) {  /* Move half the keys.        */
```
move keys to right
node
```
                (*yr)->key [i − median] = p->key [i];
                (*yr)->branch [i − median] = p->branch [i];
        }
        (*yr)->count = MAX − median;
        p->count = median;
```
insert new key
```
        if (k <= MIN)                            /* Push in the new key.              */
                PushIn (x, xr, p, k);
        else
                PushIn (x, xr, *yr, k − median);
        *y = p->key [p->count];
        (*yr)->branch [0] = p->branch [p->count];
        p->count −−;
}
```

10.3.6 Deletion from a B-tree

1. Method

During insertion, the new key always goes first into a leaf. For deletion we shall also wish to remove a key from a leaf. If the key that is to be deleted is not in a leaf, then its immediate predecessor (or successor) under the natural order of keys is guaranteed to be in a leaf (prove it!). Hence we can promote the immediate predecessor (or successor) into the position occupied by the deleted key, and delete the key from the leaf.

If the leaf contains more than the minimum number of keys, then one can be deleted with no further action. If the leaf contains the minimum number, then we first look at the two leaves (or, in the case of a node on the outside, one leaf) that are immediately adjacent and children of the same node. If one of these has more than the minimum number of keys, then one of them can be moved into the parent node, and the key from the parent moved into the leaf where the deletion is occurring. If, finally, the adjacent leaf has only the minimum number of keys, then the two leaves and the median key from the parent can all be combined as one new leaf, which will contain no more than the maximum number of keys allowed. If this step leaves the parent node with too few keys, then the process propagates upward. In the limiting case, the last key is removed from the root, and then the height of the tree decreases.

2. Example

The process of deletion in our previous B-tree of order 5 is shown in Figure 10.9. The first deletion, *h*, is from a leaf with more than the minimum number of keys, and hence causes no problem. The second deletion, *r*, is not from a leaf, and therefore the immediate successor of *r*, which is *s*, is promoted into the position of *r*, and then *s* is deleted from its leaf. The third deletion, *p*, leaves its node with too few keys. The key *s* from the parent node is therefore brought down and replaced by the key *t*.

Deletion of *d* has more extensive consequences. This deletion leaves the node with too few keys, and neither of its sibling nodes can spare a key. The node is therefore combined with one of the siblings and with the median key from the parent node, as shown by the dotted line in the first diagram and the combined node *a b c e* in the second diagram. This process, however, leaves the parent node with only the one key *f*. The top three nodes of the tree must therefore be combined, yielding the tree shown in the final diagram of Figure 10.9.

3. C Functions

We can write a deletion algorithm with overall structure similar to that used for insertion. Again we shall use recursion, with a separate main function to start the recursion. Rather than attempting to pull a key down from a parent node during an inner recursive call, we shall allow the recursive function to return even though there are too few keys in its root node. The outer function will then detect this occurrence and move keys as required.

The main function is as follows.

B-tree deletion

```
/* Delete: deletes the key target from the B-tree with the given root */
Node_type *Delete(Key_type target, Node_type *root)
{
    Node_type *p;                    /* used to dispose of an empty root    */
    if (!RecDelete(target, root))
        Error("Target was not in the B-tree.");
    else if (root->count == 0) {     /* Root is empty.                      */
        p = root;
        root = root->branch[0];
        free(p);
    }
    return root;
}
```

4. Recursive Deletion

Most of the work is done in the recursive function. It first searches the current node for the target. If it is found and the node is not a leaf, then the immediate successor of the key is found and is placed in the current node, and the successor is deleted. Deletion from a leaf

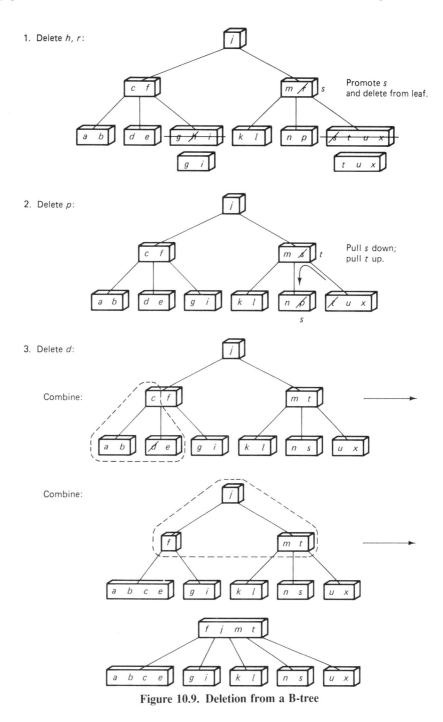

Figure 10.9. Deletion from a B-tree

is straightforward, and otherwise the process continues by recursion. When a recursive call returns, the function checks to see if enough keys remain in the appropriate node, and, if not, moves keys as required. Auxiliary functions are used in several of these steps.

```
/* RecDelete: look for target to delete. */
Boolean_type RecDelete (Key_type target, Node_type *p)
{
        int k;                          /* location of target or of branch on which to search */
        Boolean_type found;

        if (p == NULL)
                return FALSE;                   /* Hitting an empty tree is an error.      */
        else {
            if ((found = SearchNode (target, p, &k)))
                    if (p->branch [k−1]) {
                            Successor (p, k);  /* replaces key [k] by its successor    */
                            if (!(found = RecDelete (p->key [k], p->branch [k])))
                                    /* We know that the new key [k] is in the leaf. */
                                    Error ("Key not found.");
                    } else
                            Remove (p, k);  /* removes key from position k of *p      */
            else                                    /* Target was not found in the current node. */
                    found = RecDelete (target, p->branch [k]);
            /* At this point, the function has returned from a recursive call. */
            if (p->branch [k] != NULL)
                    if (p->branch [k] ->count < MIN)
                            Restore (p, k);
            return found;
        }
}
```

found node with target — annotation for the `if (p->branch [k−1])` block

search a subtree — annotation for the `found = RecDelete (target, p->branch [k]);` line

5. Auxiliary Functions

```
/* Remove: removes key [k] and branch [k] from *p */
void Remove (Node_type *p, int k)
{
        int i;                                  /* index to move entries                   */
        for (i = k + 1; i <= p->count; i++) {
                p->key [i−1] = p->key [i];
                p->branch [i−1] = p->branch [i];
        }
        p->count−−;
}
```

remove key from a leaf — annotation for the Remove function

```
/* Successor: replaces p->key [k] by its immediate successor under natural order */
void Successor (Node_type *p, int k)
{
        Node_type *q;                           /* used to move down the tree to a leaf    */
        for (q = p->branch [k]; q->branch [0]; q = q->branch [0])
                ;
        p->key [k] = q->key [1];
}
```

copy successor of key — annotation for the Successor function

Finally, we must show how to restore p->branch[k] to the minimum number of keys if a recursive call has reduced its count below the minimum. The function we write is somewhat biased to the left; that is, it looks first to the sibling on the left, and uses the right sibling only when necessary. The steps that are needed are illustrated in Figure 10.10.

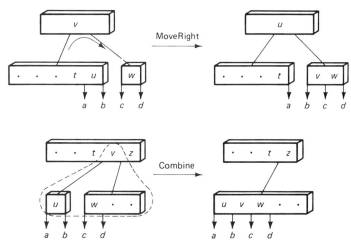

Figure 10.10. Restoration of the minimum number of keys.

```
/* Restore: finds a key and inserts it into p->branch[k] */
void Restore (Node_type *p, int k)
{
        if (k == 0)                          /* case: leftmost key          */
            if (p->branch[1]->count > MIN)
                MoveLeft(p, 1);
            else
                Combine(p, 1);
        else if (k == p->count)        /* case: rightmost key         */
            if (p->branch[k-1]->count > MIN)
                MoveRight(p, k);
            else
                Combine(p, k);
        else if (p->branch[k-1]->count > MIN)  /* remaining cases      */
            MoveRight(p, k);
        else if (p->branch[k + 1]->count > MIN)
            MoveLeft(p, k + 1);
        else
            Combine(p, k);
}
```

The actions of the remaining three functions MoveRight, MoveLeft, and Combine are clear from Figure 10.10, but for completeness, they are written in full below.

move a key to the right

```
/* MoveRight: move a key to the right. */
void MoveRight(Node_type *p, int k)
{
    int c;
    Node_type *t;

    t = p->branch[k];
    for (c = t->count; c > 0; c--) {
    /* Shift all keys in the right node one position. */
        t->key[c + 1] = t->key[c];
        t->branch[c + 1] = t->branch[c];
    }
    t->branch[1] = t->branch[0];       /* Move key from parent to right node.   */
    t->count++;
    t->key[1] = p->key[k];

    t = p->branch[k-1];                /* Move last key of left node into parent.  */
    p->key[k] = t->key[t->count];
    p->branch[k]->branch[0] = t->branch[t->count];
    t->count--;
}
```

move a key to the left

```
/* MoveLeft: move a key to the left. */
void MoveLeft(Node_type *p, int k)
{
    int c;
    Node_type *t;

    /* Move key from parent into left node. */
    t = p->branch[k-1];
    t->count++;
    t->key[t->count] = p->key[k];
    t->branch[t->count] = p->branch[k]->branch[0];

    /* Move key from right node into parent. */
    t = p->branch[k];
    p->key[k] = t->key[1];
    t->branch[0] = t->branch[1];
    t->count--;
    for (c = 1; c <= t->count; c++) {
        /* Shift all keys in right node one position leftward. */
        t->key[c] = t->key[c + 1];
        t->branch[c] = t->branch[c + 1];
    }
}
```

combine adjacent nodes

```
/* Combine: combine adjacent nodes. */
void Combine (Node_type *p, int k)
{
    int c;
    Node_type *q;
                    /* points to the right node, which will be emptied and deleted */
    Node_type *l;

    q = p->branch [k];
    l = p->branch [k-1];                /* Work with the left node.            */
    l->count++;                         /* Insert the key from the parent.     */
    l->key [l->count] = p->key [k];
    l->branch [l->count] = q->branch [0];
    for (c = 1; c <= q->count; c++) {   /* Insert all keys from right node.    */
        l->count++;
        l->key [l->count] = q->key [c];
        l->branch [l->count] = q->branch [c];
    }
    for (c = k; c < p->count; c++) {    /* Delete key from parent node.        */
        p->key [c] = p->key [c + 1];
        p->branch [c] = p->branch [c + 1];
    }
    p->count--;
    free (q);                           /* Dispose of the empty right node.    */
}
```

Exercises 10.3

E1. Insert the six remaining letters of the alphabet in the order

$$z, \ v, \ o, \ q, \ w, \ y$$

into the final B-tree of Figure 10.7.

E2. Insert the keys below, in the order stated, into an initially empty B-tree of order (**a**) 3, (**b**) 4, (**c**) 7.

$$a \ g \ f \ b \ k \ d \ h \ m \ j \ e \ s \ i \ r \ x \ c \ l \ n \ t \ u \ p$$

E3. What is the smallest number of keys that, when inserted in an appropriate order, will force a B-tree of order 5 to have height 2 (that is, 3 levels)?

E4. If a key in a B-tree is not in a leaf, prove that both its immediate predecessor and immediate successor (under the natural order) are in leaves.

E5. Remove the tail recursion from the function Search.

E6. Rewrite the function SearchNode to use binary search.

E7. A **B*-tree** is a B-tree in which every node, except possibly the root, is at least two-thirds full, rather than half full. Insertion into a B*-tree moves keys between sibling nodes (as done during deletion) as needed, thereby delaying splitting a node until two sibling nodes are completely full. These two nodes can then be split into three, each of which will be at least two-thirds full.

 a. Specify the changes needed to the insertion algorithm so that it will maintain the properties of a B*-tree.
 b. Specify the changes needed to the deletion algorithm so that it will maintain the properties of a B*-tree.
 c. Discuss the relative advantages and disadvantages of B*-trees compared to ordinary B-trees.

Programming Project 10.3   **P1.** Combine all the functions of this section into a complete program for manipulating B-trees. You will need to add functions to input keys to be inserted or deleted, to traverse a B-tree, and to print its keys.

10.4 GRAPHS

This section introduces an important mathematical structure that has applications in subjects as diverse as sociology, chemistry, geography, and electrical engineering.

10.4.1 Mathematical Background

1. Definitions and Examples

A **graph** G consists of a set V, whose members are called the **vertices** of G, together with a set E of pairs of distinct vertices from V. These pairs are called the **edges** of G. If $e = (v, w)$ is an edge with vertices v and w, then v and w are said to *lie on* e, and e is said to be **incident** with v and w. If the pairs are unordered, then G is called an **undirected graph**; if the pairs are ordered, then G is called a **directed graph**.

graphs and directed graphs
The term *directed graph* is often shortened to **digraph**, and the unqualified term *graph* usually means *undirected graph*.

drawings
The natural way to picture a graph is to represent vertices as points or circles and edges as line segments or arcs connecting the vertices. If the graph is directed, then the line segments or arcs have arrowheads indicating the direction. Figure 10.11 shows several examples of graphs.

applications
Graphs find their importance as models for many kinds of processes or structures. Cities and the highways connecting them form a graph, as do the components on a circuit board with the connections among them. An organic chemical compound can be considered a graph with the atoms as the vertices and the bonds between them as edges. The people living in a city can be regarded as the vertices of a graph with the relationship *is acquainted with* describing the edges. People working in a corporation form a directed graph with the relation "supervises" describing the edges.

2. Undirected Graphs

Several kinds of undirected graphs are shown in Figure 10.12. Two vertices in an undirected graph are called **adjacent** if there is an edge from the first to the second.

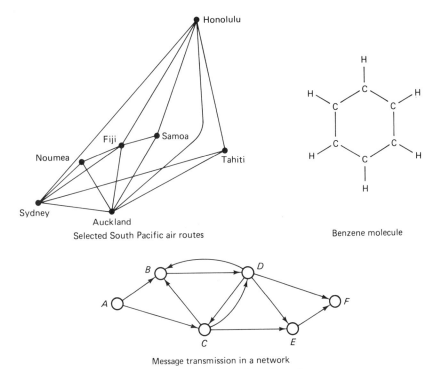

Selected South Pacific air routes

Benzene molecule

Message transmission in a network

Figure 10.11. Examples of graphs

Hence, in the undirected graph of panel (a), vertices 1 and 2 are adjacent, as are 3 and 4, but 1 and 4 are not adjacent. A *path* is a sequence of distinct vertices, each adjacent to the next. Panel (b) shows a path. A *cycle* is a path containing at least three vertices such that the last vertex on the path is adjacent to the first. Panel (c) shows a cycle. A graph is called *connected* if there is a path from any vertex to any other vertex; panels (a), (b), and (c) show connected graphs, and panel (d) shows a disconnected graph.

paths, cycles, connected

Panel (e) of Figure 10.12 shows a connected graph with no cycles. You will notice that this graph is, in fact, a tree, and we take this property as the definition: A *free tree* is defined as a connected undirected graph with no cycles.

free tree

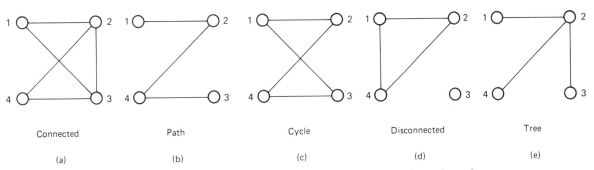

Connected	Path	Cycle	Disconnected	Tree
(a)	(b)	(c)	(d)	(e)

Figure 10.12. Various kinds of undirected graphs

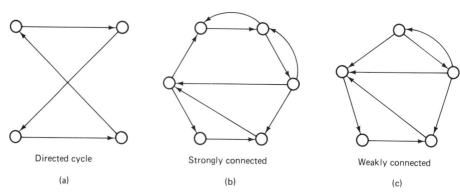

Figure 10.13. Examples of directed graphs.

3. Directed Graphs

directed paths and cycles

For directed graphs we can make similar definitions. We require all edges in a path or a cycle to have the same direction, so that following a path or a cycle means always moving in the direction indicated by the arrows. Such a path (cycle) is called a ***directed*** path (cycle). A directed graph is called ***strongly connected*** if there is a directed path from any vertex to any other vertex. If we suppress the direction of the edges and the resulting undirected graph is connected, we call the directed graph ***weakly connected***. Figure 10.13 illustrates directed cycles, strongly connected directed graphs, and weakly connected directed graphs.

multiple edges

The directed graphs in panels (b) and (c) of Figure 10.13 show pairs of vertices with directed edges going both ways between them. Since directed edges are ordered pairs and the ordered pairs (v, w) and (w, v) are distinct if $v \neq w$, such pairs of edges are permissible in directed graphs. Since the corresponding unordered pairs are not distinct, however, in an undirected graph there can be at most one edge connecting a pair of vertices. Similarly, since the vertices on an edge are required to be distinct, there can

self-loops

be no edge from a vertex to itself. We should remark, however, that (although we shall not do so) sometimes these requirements are relaxed to allow multiple edges connecting a pair of vertices and self-loops connecting a vertex to itself.

10.4.2 Computer Representation

If we are to write programs for solving problems concerning graphs, then we must first find ways to represent the mathematical structure of a graph as some kind of data structure. There are two methods in common use, which differ fundamentally in the choice of abstract data type used, and there are several variations depending on the implementation of the abstract data type.

1. The Set Representation

Graphs are defined in terms of sets, and it is natural to look first to sets to determine their representation as data. First, we have a set of vertices and, second, we have the edges as a set of pairs of vertices. Rather than attempting to represent this set of pairs directly, we divide it into pieces by considering the set of edges attached to each vertex separately. In other words, we can keep track of all the edges in the graph by keeping, for all vertices v in the graph, the set E_v of edges containing v, or, equivalently, the set A_v of all vertices adjacent to v. In fact, we can use this idea to produce a new, equivalent definition of a graph:

DEFINITION

A **graph** G consists of a set V, called the **vertices** of G, and, for all $v \in V$, a subset A_v of V, called the set of vertices **adjacent** to v.

From the subsets A_v we can reconstruct the edges as ordered pairs by the rule: The pair (v, w) is an edge if and only if $w \in A_v$. It is easier, however, to work with sets of vertices than with pairs. This new definition, moreover, works for both directed and undirected graphs; the graph is undirected means that it satisfies the following symmetry property: $w \in A_v$ implies $v \in A_w$ for all $v, w \in V$.

2. Implementation of Sets

sets as bit strings

There are two general ways for us to implement sets of vertices in data structures and algorithms. One way is to represent the set as a *list* of its elements; this method we shall study presently. The other implementation, often called a **bit string**, keeps a Boolean value for each possible member of the set to indicate whether or not it is in the set. Some languages, such as Pascal, provide these sets as part of the language. Other programming languages, such as C, however, do not provide sets as part of the language. We can overcome this difficulty, nonetheless, and at the same time we obtain a better representation of graphs.

3. Adjacency Tables

One way to implement a graph in C is with a two-dimensional array of Boolean values. For simplicity, we shall consider that these vertices are indexed with the integers from 0 to $n - 1$, where n denotes the number of vertices. Since we shall wish n to be variable, we shall also introduce a constant MAX bounding the number of vertices, with which we can fully specify the first representation of a graph:

first implementation: adjacency table

```
typedef Boolean_type AdjacencyTable_type [MAX] [MAX];

typedef struct graph_tag {
    int n;                          /* number of vertices in the graph      */
    AdjacencyTable_type A;
} Graph_type;
```

meaning

The adjacency table A has a natural interpretation: A[v][w] is TRUE if and only if vertex v is adjacent to vertex w. If the graph is directed, we interpret A[v][w] as indicating whether or not the edge from v to w is in the graph. If the graph is undirected, then the adjacency table is symmetric, that is, A[v][w] == A[w][v] for all v and w. The representation of a graph by adjacency sets and by an adjacency table is illustrated in Figure 10.14.

4. Adjacency Lists

Another way to represent a set is as a *list* of its elements. For representing a graph we shall then have both a list of vertices and, for each vertex, a list of adjacent vertices.

Figure 10.14. Adjacency set and an adjacency table

We shall consider implementation of graphs by using both contiguous lists and simply linked lists. For more advanced applications, however, it is often useful to employ more sophisticated implementations of lists as binary or multiway search trees or as heaps.

Note that by identifying vertices with their indices in the previous representations we have *ipso facto* implemented the vertex set as a contiguous list, but now we should make a deliberate choice concerning the use of contiguous or linked lists.

5. Linked Implementation

Greatest flexibility is obtained by using linked lists for both the vertices and the adjacency lists. This implementation is illustrated in panel (a) of Figure 10.15 and results in a declaration such as the following:

second implementation: linked lists

```
typedef struct vertex_tag Vertex_type;
typedef struct edge_tag Edge_type;

struct vertex_tag {
      Edge_type *firstedge;              /* start of the adjacency list          */
      Vertex_type *nextvertex;           /* next vertex on the linked list       */
};

struct edge_tag {
      Vertex_type *endpoint;             /* vertex to which the edge points      */
      Edge_type *nextedge;               /* next edge on the adjacency list      */
};

typedef Vertex_type *Graph_type;         /* header for the list of vertices      */
```

6. Contiguous Implementation

Although this linked implementation is very flexible, it is sometimes awkward to navigate through the linked lists, and many algorithms require random access to vertices. Therefore the following contiguous implementation is often better. For a contiguous adjacency list we must keep a counter, and for this we use standard notation from graph theory: the **valence** of a vertex is the number of edges on which it lies, hence also the number of vertices adjacent to it. This contiguous implementation is illustrated in panel (b) of Figure 10.15.

(a) Linked lists

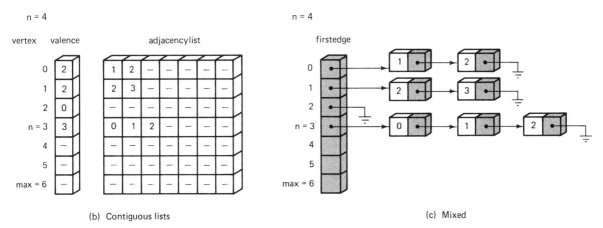

(b) Contiguous lists

(c) Mixed

Figure 10.15. Implementations of a graph with lists

third
implementation:
contiguous lists

```
typedef int AdjacencyList_type [MAX];

typedef struct graph_tag {
        int n;                                /* number of vertices in the graph        */
        int valence [MAX];
        AdjacencyList_type A [MAX];
} Graph_type;
```

7. Mixed Implementation

The final implementation uses a contiguous list for the vertices and linked storage for the adjacency lists. This mixed implementation is illustrated in panel (c) of Figure 10.15.

fourth
implementation:
mixed lists

```
typedef struct edge_tag {
        int endpoint;
        struct edge_tag *next;
} Edge_type;

typedef struct graph_tag {
        int n;                          /* number of vertices in the graph          */
        Edge_type *firstedge [MAX] ;
} Graph_type;
```

8. Information Fields

Many applications of graphs require not only the adjacency information specified in the various representations but also further information specific to each vertex or each edge. In the linked representations, this information can be included as additional fields within appropriate structures, and in the contiguous representations it can be included by making array entries into structures.

networks, weights   An especially important case is that of a ***network***, which is defined as a graph in which a numerical ***weight*** is attached to each edge. For many algorithms on networks, the best representation is an adjacency table where the entries are the weights rather than Boolean values.

10.4.3 Graph Traversal

1. Methods

In many problems we wish to investigate all the vertices in a graph in some systematic order, just as with binary trees we developed several systematic traversal methods. In tree traversal, we had a root vertex with which we generally started; in graphs we often do not have any one vertex singled out as special, and therefore the traversal may start at an arbitrary vertex. Although there are many possible orders for visiting the vertices of the graph, two methods are of particular importance.

depth-first   ***Depth-first traversal*** of a graph is roughly analogous to preorder traversal of an ordered tree. Suppose that the traversal has just visited a vertex v, and let $w_0, w_1, \ldots, w_k$ be the vertices adjacent to v. Then we shall next visit w_0 and keep $w_1, \ldots, w_k$ waiting. After visiting w_0 we traverse all the vertices to which it is adjacent before returning to traverse $w_1, \ldots, w_k$.

breadth-first   ***Breadth-first traversal*** of a graph is roughly analogous to level-by-level traversal of an ordered tree. If the traversal has just visited a vertex v, then it next visits *all* the vertices adjacent to v, putting the vertices adjacent to these in a waiting list to be traversed after all vertices adjacent to v have been visited. Figure 10.16 shows the order of visiting the vertices of one graph under both depth-first and breadth-first traversal.

2. Depth-First Algorithm

Depth-first traversal is naturally formulated as a recursive algorithm. Its action, when it reaches a vertex v, is

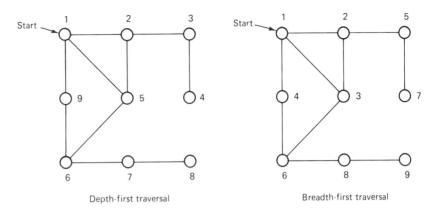

Depth-first traversal   Breadth-first traversal

Note: The vertices adjacent to a given one are considered as arranged in clockwise order.

Figure 10.16. Graph traversal

```
Visit(v);
for (all vertices w adjacent to v)
        Traverse(w);
```

complications In graph traversal, however, two difficulties arise that cannot appear for tree traversal. First, the graph may contain cycles, so our traversal algorithm may reach the same vertex a second time. To prevent infinite recursion, we therefore introduce a Boolean-valued array visited, set visited[v] to TRUE before starting the recursion, and check the value of visited[w] before processing w. Second, the graph may not be connected, so the traversal algorithm may fail to reach all vertices from a single starting point. Hence we enclose the action in a loop that runs through all vertices.

With these refinements we obtain the following outline of depth-first traversal. Further details depend on the choice of implementation of graphs, and we postpone them to application programs.

main function
```
/* DepthFirst: depth-first traversal of a graph */
void DepthFirst(Graph_type G)
{
        Boolean_type visited[MAX];
        int v;

        for (all v in G)
                visited[v] = FALSE;
        for (all v in G)
                if (!visited[v])
                        Traverse(v);
}
```

The recursion is performed in the following function, to be declared along with the previous one.

recursive traversal

```
/* Traverse: recursive traversal of a graph */
void Traverse (int v)
{
        int w;

        visited [v] = TRUE;
        Visit (v);
        for (all w adjacent to v)
                if ( ! visited [w] )
                        Traverse (w);
}
```

3. Breadth-First Algorithm

stacks and queues

Since using recursion and programming with stacks are essentially equivalent, we could formulate depth-first traversal with a stack, pushing all unvisited vertices adjacent to the one being visited onto the stack and popping the stack to find the next vertex to visit. The algorithm for breadth-first traversal is quite similar to the resulting algorithm for depth-first traversal, except that a queue is needed instead of a stack. Its outline follows.

breadth-first traversal

```
/* BreadthFirst: perform breadth-first traversal of a graph. */
void BreadthFirst (Graph_type G)
{
        Vertexqueue_type Q;
        Boolean_type visited [MAX];
        int v, w;

        for (all v in G)
                visited [v] = FALSE;
        Initialize (Q);                    /* Set the queue to be empty.        */
        for (all v in G)
                if ( ! visited [v] ) {
                        AddQueue (v, Q);
                        do {
                                DeleteQueue (v, Q);
                                visited [v] = TRUE;
                                Visit (v);
                                for (all w adjacent to v)
                                        if ( ! visited [w] )
                                                AddQueue (w);
                        } while ( ! Empty (Q) );
                }
}
```

10.4.4 Topological Sorting

1. The Problem

topological order

If G is a directed graph with no directed cycles, then a ***topological order*** for G is a sequential listing of all the vertices in G such that, for all vertices $v, w \in G$, if there is an edge from v to w, then v precedes w in the sequential listing. Throughout this section we shall consider only directed graphs that have no directed cycles.

applications

As a first application of topological order, consider the courses available at a university as the vertices of a directed graph, where there is an edge from one course to another if the first is a prerequisite for the second. A topological order is then a listing of all the courses such that all prerequisites for a course appear before it does. A second example is a glossary of technical terms that is ordered so that no term is used in a definition before it is itself defined. Similarly, the author of a textbook uses a topological order for the topics in the book. An example of two different topological orders of a directed graph is shown in Figure 10.17.

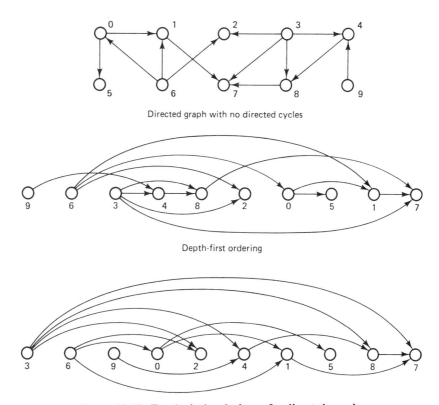

Directed graph with no directed cycles

Depth-first ordering

Figure 10.17. Topological orderings of a directed graph

graph representation

As an example of algorithms for graph traversal, we shall develop functions that produce a topological ordering of the vertices of a directed graph that has no cycles. We shall develop two functions, first for depth-first traversal and then for breadth-first traversal. Both the functions will operate on a graph G given in the mixed implementation (with a contiguous list of vertices and linked adjacency lists), and both functions will produce an array of type

int Toporder [MAX] ;

that will specify the order in which the vertices should be listed to obtain a topological order.

2. Depth-First Algorithm

method

In a topological order each vertex must appear before all the vertices that are its successors in the directed graph. For a depth-first topological ordering, we therefore start by finding a vertex that has no successors and place it last in the order. After we have, by recursion, placed all the successors of a vertex into the topological order, then we can place the vertex itself in a position before any of its successors. The variable place indicates the position in the topological order where the next vertex to be ordered will be placed. Since we first order the last vertices, we begin with place equal to the number of vertices in the graph. The main function is a direct implementation of the general algorithm developed in the last section.

```
#include "top.h"

/* TopSort: G is a directed graph with no cycles implemented with a contiguous list of
      vertices and linked adjacency lists. */
void TopSort (Graph_type *G)
{
        Boolean_type visited [MAX] ;        /* checks that G contains no cycles      */
        int v;                      /* next vertex whose successors are to be ordered */
        int place;                  /* next position in the topological order to be filled */

        for (v = 0; v < G->n; v++)
             visited [v] = FALSE;
        place = G->n;
        for (v = 0; v < G->n; v++)
             if ( !visited [v] )
                  Sort (G, v, &place) ;
}
```

depth-first topological sorting

The include file **top.h** contains the appropriate declarations.

```
typedef struct edge_tag {
        int endpoint;
        struct edge_tag *next;
} Edge_type;

typedef struct graph_tag {
        int n;                              /* number of vertices in the graph        */
        Edge_type *firstedge [MAX] ;
} Graph_type;
```

typedef int Toporder_type[MAX];

Boolean_type visited[MAX];

Toporder_type T;

The function Sort that performs the recursion, based on the outline for the general function Traverse, first places all the successors of v into their positions in the topological order and then places v into the order.

/ Sort: puts all the successors of* v *and finally* v *itself into the topological order, begin-*
      ning at position place *and working down.* */*

recursive traversal   void Sort(Graph_type *G, int v, int *place)
                          {
                              int w;   /* *one of the vertices that immediately succeed* v */*
                              Edge_type *p;   /* *traverses adjacency list of vertices succeeding* v */*

                              visited[v] = TRUE;
                              p = G->firstedge[v];   /* *Find the first vertex succeeding* v.   */*
                              while (p) {
                                  w = p->endpoint;   /* *w is an immediate successor of* v.   */*
                                  if (!visited[w])
                                      Sort(G, w, place);   /* *Order the successors of* w *and* w *itself.* */*
                                  p = p->next;   /* *Go on to the next immediate successor of* v.* */*
                              }
                              (*place)--;   /* *Put* v *itself into the topological order.*   */*
                              T[*place] = v;
                          }

performance   Since this algorithm visits each node of the graph exactly once and follows each edge once, doing no searching, its running time is $O(n + e)$ where n is the number of nodes and e is the number of edges in the graph.

3. Breadth-First Algorithm

method   In a breadth-first topological ordering of a directed graph with no cycles, we start by finding the vertices that should be first in the topological order and then apply the fact that every vertex must come before its successors in the topological order. The vertices that come first are those that are not successors of any other vertex. To find these we set up an array predecessorcount such that predecessorcount[v] will be the number of immediate predecessors of each vertex v. The vertices that are not successors are those with no predecessors. We therefore initialize the breadth-first traversal by placing these vertices into the queue of vertices to be visited. As each vertex is visited, it is removed from the queue, assigned the next available position in the topological order (starting at the beginning of the order), and then removed from further consideration by reducing the predecessor count for each of its immediate successors by one. When one of these counts reaches zero, all predecessors of the corresponding vertex have been visited, and the vertex itself is then ready to be processed, so it is added to the queue. We therefore obtain the following function.

```
#include "top.h"

typedef int Queue_type [MAX];
```

/* *TopSort:* G is a directed graph with no cycles implemented with a contiguous list of
vertices and linked adjacency lists; the function makes a breadth-first traversal of G
and generates the resulting topological order in T. */

breadth-first   `void TopSort (Graph_type *G)`
topological order   `{`

```
    int predecessorcount [MAX];
                                /* number of immediate predecessors of each vertex */
    Queue_type Q;               /* vertices ready to be placed into the order */
    int v;                      /* vertex currently being visited              */
    int w;                      /* one of the immediate successors of v   */
    Edge_type *p;               /* traverses the adjacency list of v      */
    int place;                  /* next position in topological order      */

    /* Initialize all the predecessor counts to 0. */
    for (v = 0; v < G->n; v++)
        predecessorcount [v] = 0;
    /* Increase the predecessor count for each vertex that is a successor. */
    for (v = 0; v < G->n; v++) {
        for (p = G->firstedge [v]; p; p = p->next)
            predecessorcount [p->endpoint] ++;
    }
    Initialize (Q);
    /* Place all vertices with no predecessors into the queue. */
    for (v = 0; v < G->n; v++)
        if (predecessorcount [v] == 0)
            AddQueue (v, Q);
    /* Start the breadth-first traversal. */
    place = 0;
    while (!Empty (Q)) {
        /* Visit v by placing it into the topological order. */
        DeleteQueue (v, Q);
        T [place++] = v;
        /* Traverse the list of immediate successors of v. */
        for (p = G->firstedge [v]; p; p = p->next) {
        /* Reduce the predecessor count for each immediate successor. */
            w = p->endpoint;
            predecessorcount [w] --;
            if (predecessorcount [w] == 0)
            /* w has no further predecessors, so it is ready to process. */
                AddQueue (w, Q);
        }
    }
}
```

This algorithm requires auxiliary functions for processing the queue. The entries in the queue are to be vertices, and the queue can be implemented in any of the ways described in Chapters 3 and 4; the details are left as an exercise.

As with depth-first traversal, the time required by the breadth-first function is also *performance* $O(n + e)$, where n is the number of vertices and e is the number of edges in the directed graph.

10.4.5 A Greedy Algorithm: Shortest Paths

1. The Problem

As a final application of graphs, one requiring somewhat more sophisticated reasoning, we consider the following problem. We are given a directed graph G in which every edge has a nonnegative *weight* attached, and our problem is to find a path from one vertex v to another w such that the sum of the weights on the path is as small as possible. We *shortest path* call such a path a **shortest path**, even though the weights may represent costs, time, or some quantity other than distance. We can think of G as a map of airline routes, for example, with each vertex representing a city and the weight on each edge the cost of flying from one city to the second. Our problem is then to find a routing from city v to city w such that the total cost is a minimum. Consider the directed graph shown in Figure 10.18. The shortest path from vertex 0 to vertex 1 goes via vertex 2 and has a total cost of 4, compared to the cost of 5 for the edge directly from 0 to 1 and the cost of 8 for the path via vertex 4.

It turns out that it is just as easy to solve the more general problem of starting at *source* one vertex, called the **source**, and finding the shortest path to every other vertex, instead of to just one destination vertex. For simplicity, we take the source to be vertex 0, and our problem then consists of finding the shortest path from vertex 0 to every vertex in the graph. We require that the weights are all nonnegative.

2. Method

The algorithm operates by keeping a set S of those vertices whose shortest distance from 0 is known. Initially, 0 is the only vertex in S. At each step we add to S a

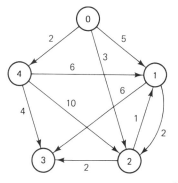

Figure 10.18. A directed graph with weights

distance table

remaining vertex for which the shortest path from 0 has been determined. The problem is to determine which vertex to add to S at each step. Let us think of the vertices already in S as having been labeled with heavy lines, and think of the edges making up the shortest paths from the source 0 to these vertices as also marked.

We shall maintain a table D that gives, for each vertex v, the distance from 0 to v along a path all of whose edges are marked, except possibly the last one. That is, if v is in S, then $D[v]$ gives the shortest distance to v and all edges along the corresponding path are marked. If v is not in S, then $D[v]$ gives the length of the path from 0 to some vertex w in S plus the weight of the edge from w to v, and all the edges of this path except the last one are marked. The table D is initialized by setting $D[v]$ to the weight of the edge from 0 to v if it exists and to ∞ if not.

greedy algorithm

To determine what vertex to add to S at each step, we apply the *greedy* criterion of choosing the vertex v with the smallest distance recorded in the table D, such that v is not already in S.

verification

We must prove that for this vertex v the distance recorded in D really is the length of the shortest path from 0 to v. For suppose that there were a shorter path from 0 to v, such as shown in Figure 10.19. This path first leaves S to go to some vertex x, then goes on to v (possibly even reentering S along the way). But if this path is shorter than the marked path to v, then its initial segment from 0 to x is also shorter, so that the greedy criterion would have chosen x rather than v as the next vertex to add to S,

end of proof

since we would have had $D[x] < D[v]$. When we add v to S we think of v as now marked and also mark the shortest path from 0 to v (every edge of which except the last was actually already marked). Next, we must update the entries of D by checking,

maintain the invariant

for each vertex w not in S, whether a path through v and then directly to w is shorter than the previously recorded distance to w. That is, we replace $D[w]$ by $D[v]$ plus the weight of the edge from v to w if the latter quantity is smaller.

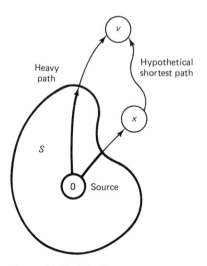

Figure 10.19. Finding a shortest path

3. Example

Before writing a formal function incorporating this method, let us work through the example shown in Figure 10.20. For the directed graph shown in panel (a), the initial situation is shown in panel (b): The set S (marked vertices) consists of 0 alone, and the entries of the distance table D are shown beside the other vertices. The distance to vertex 4 is shortest, so 4 is added to S in panel (c), and the distance $D[4]$ is updated to the value 6. Since the distances to vertices 1 and 2 via vertex 4 are greater than those already recorded in T, their entries remain unchanged. The next closest vertex to

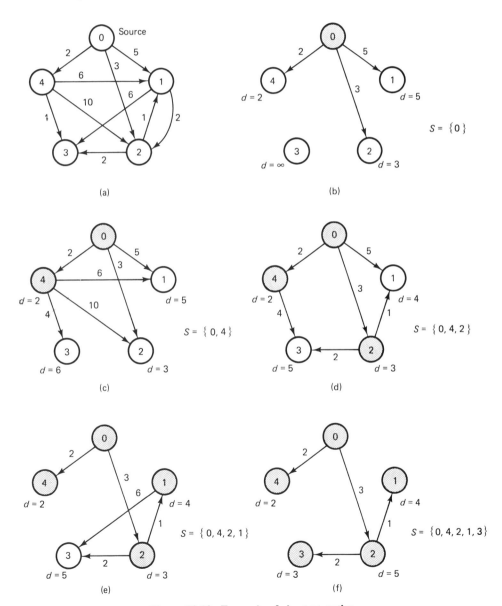

Figure 10.20. Example of shortest paths

0 is vertex 2, and it is added in panel (d), which also shows the effect of updating the distances to vertices 1 and 3, whose paths via vertex 2 are shorter than those previously recorded. The final two steps, shown in panels (e) and (f), add vertices 1 and 3 to S and yield the paths and distances shown in the final diagram.

4. Implementation

For the sake of writing a function to embody this algorithm for finding shortest distances, we must choose an implementation of the directed graph. Use of the adjacency-table implementation facilitates random access to all the vertices of the graph, as we need for this problem. Moreover, by storing the weights in the table we can use the table to give weights as well as adjacencies. We shall place a special large value ∞ in any position of the table for which the corresponding edge does not exist. These decisions are incorporated in the following C declarations, short.h, to be included in the calling program.

graph representation

```
#include <limits.h>

#define INFINITY INT_MAX                    /* value for ∞                                */

typedef int AdjacencyTable_type [MAX] [MAX] ;
typedef int DistanceTable_type [MAX] ;

int n;                                      /* number of vertices in the graph           */
AdjacencyTable_type cost;                   /* describes the graph                       */
DistanceTable_type D;                       /* shortest distances from vertex 1          */
```

The function that we write will accept the adjacency table and the count of vertices in the graph as its input parameters and will produce the table of closest distances as its output parameter.

```
#include "short.h"

/* Distance: calculates the cost of the shortest path from vertex 0 to each vertex of the
     graph. */
```

shortest-distance function

```
void Distance (int n, AdjacencyTable_type cost, DistanceTable_type D)
{
     Boolean_type final [MAX] ;         /* Has the distance from 0 to v been found? */
                                        /* final [v] is true iff v is in the set S. */
     int i;                             /* repetition count for the main loop        */
     /* One distance is finalized on each pass through the loop. */
     int w;                             /* a vertex not yet added to the set S        */
     int v;                             /* vertex with minimum tentative distance in D [ ] */
     int min;                           /* distance of v, equals D [v]                */

     final [0] = TRUE;                  /* Initialize with vertex 0 alone in the set S. */
     D [0] = 0;
     for (v = 1; v < n; v++) {
          final [v] = FALSE;
          D [v] = cost [0] [v] ;
     }
```

```
/* Start the main loop; add one vertex v to S on each pass. */
for (i = 1; i < n; i++) {
        min = INFINITY;                    /* Find the closest vertex v to vertex 0.    */
        for (w = 1; w < n; w++)
            if (!final[w])
                    if (D[w] < min) {
                            v = w;
                            min = D[w];
                    }
        final[v] = TRUE;                   /* Add v to the set S.                       */
        for (w = 1; w < n; w++)            /* Update the remaining distances in D.      */
            if (!final[w])
                    if (min + cost[v][w] < D[w])
                            D[w] = min + cost[v][w];
    }
}
```

performance   To estimate the running time of this function, we note that the main loop is executed
$n - 1$ times, and within it are two other loops, each executed $n - 1$ times, so these
loops contribute a multiple of $(n - 1)^2$ operations. Statements done outside the loops
contribute only $O(n)$, so the running time of the algorithm is $O(n^2)$.

10.4.6 Graphs as Data Structures

In this section we have studied a few applications of graphs, but we have hardly begun
to scratch the surface of the broad and deep subject of graph algorithms. In many of
these algorithms, graphs appear, as they have in this section, as mathematical structures
capturing the essential description of a problem rather than as computational tools for its
solution.

mathematical   Note that in this section we have spoken of graphs as mathematical structures, and
structures and data not as data structures, for we have used graphs to formulate mathematical problems,
structures   and to write algorithms we have then implemented the graphs within data structures like
tables and lists. Graphs, however, can certainly be regarded as data structures themselves,
data structures that embody relationships among the data more complicated than those
describing a list or a tree.

Because of their generality and flexibility, graphs are powerful data structures that
flexibility and power prove valuable in more advanced applications such as the design of data base management
systems. Such powerful tools are meant to be used, of course, whenever necessary, but
they must always be used with care so that their power is not turned to confusion.
Perhaps the best safeguard in the use of powerful tools is to insist on regularity, that is,
to use the powerful tools only in carefully defined and well understood ways. Because
of the generality of graphs, it is not always easy to impose this discipline on their use.

irregularity   In this world, nonetheless, irregularities will always creep in, no matter how hard we
try to avoid them. It is the bane of the systems analyst and programmer to accommodate
these irregularities while trying to maintain the integrity of the underlying system design.
Irregularity even occurs in the very systems that we use as models for the data structures
we devise, models such as the family trees whose terminology we have always used.

An excellent illustration of what can happen is the following classic story, quoted by N. WIRTH from a Zurich newspaper of July 1922.

> I married a widow who had a grown-up daughter. My father, who visited us quite often, fell in love with my step-daughter and married her. Hence, my father became my son-in-law, and my step-daughter became my mother. Some months later, my wife gave birth to a son, who became the brother-in-law of my father as well as my uncle. The wife of my father, that is my step-daughter, also had a son. Thereby, I got a brother and at the same time a grandson. My wife is my grandmother, since she is my mother's mother. Hence, I am my wife's husband and at the same time her step-grandson; in other words, I am my own grandfather.

Exercises   **E1.** **(a)** Find all the cycles in each of the following graphs. **(b)** Which of these graphs
10.4   are connected? **(c)** Which of these graphs are free trees?

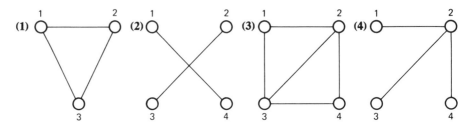

E2. For each of the graphs shown in Exercise E1, give the implementation of the graph as **(a)** an adjacency table, **(b)** a linked vertex list with linked adjacency lists, **(c)** a contiguous vertex list of contiguous adjacency lists.

E3. A graph is *regular* if every vertex has the same valence (that is, if it is adjacent to the same number of other vertices). For a regular graph, a good implementation is to keep the vertices in a linked list and the adjacency lists contiguous. The length of all the adjacency lists is called the *degree* of the graph. Write C declarations for this implementation of regular graphs.

E4. The topological sorting functions as presented in the text are deficient in error checking. Modify the **(a)** depth-first and **(b)** breadth-first functions so that they will detect any (directed) cycles in the graph and indicate what vertices cannot be placed in any topological order because they lie on a cycle.

Programming   **P1.** Write C functions called ReadGraph that will read from the terminal the number
Projects   of vertices in an undirected graph and lists of adjacent vertices. Be sure to include
10.4   error checking. The graph is to be implemented as **(a)** an adjacency table, **(b)** a
                         linked vertex list with linked adjacency lists, **(c)** a contiguous vertex list of linked
                         adjacency lists.

P2. Write C functions called WriteGraph that will write pertinent information specifying a graph to the terminal. The graph is to be implemented as **(a)** an adjacency table,

(b) a linked vertex list with linked adjacency lists, **(c)** a contiguous vertex list of linked adjacency lists.

P3. [Requires graphics capability] Rewrite the functions WriteGraph to use a graphics-capable terminal and draw the graph.

P4. Use the functions ReadGraph and WriteGraph to implement and test the topological sorting functions developed in this section for **(a)** depth-first order and **(b)** breadth-first order. In part (b) you will also need to use functions for processing the queue.

P5. Implement and test the function for determining shortest distances in directed graphs with weights.

POINTERS AND PITFALLS

1. Trees are flexible and powerful structures both for modeling problems and for organizing data. In using trees in problem solving and in algorithm design, first decide on the kind of tree needed (ordered, rooted, free, or binary) before considering implementation details.

2. Most trees can be described easily by using recursion; their associated algorithms are often best formulated recursively.

3. For problems of information retrieval, consider the size, number, and location of the records along with the type and structure of the keys while choosing the data structures to be used. For small records or small numbers of keys, high-speed internal memory will be used, and binary search trees will likely prove adequate. For information retrieval from disk files, methods employing multiway branching, such as tries, B-trees, and hash tables, will usually be superior. Tries are particularly suited to applications where the keys are structured as a sequence of symbols and where the set of keys is relatively dense in the set of all possible keys. For other applications, methods that treat the key as a single unit will often prove superior. B-trees, together with various generalizations and extensions, can be usefully applied to many problems concerned with external information retrieval.

4. Graphs provide an excellent way to describe the essential features of many applications, thereby facilitating specification of the underlying problems and formulation of algorithms for their solution. Graphs sometimes appear as data structures but more often as mathematical abstractions useful for problem solving.

5. Graphs may be implemented in many ways by the use of different kinds of data structures. Postpone implementation decisions until the applications of graphs in the problem-solving and algorithm-development phases are well understood.

6. Many applications require graph traversal. Let the application determine the traversal method: depth first, breadth first, or some other order. Depth-first traversal is naturally recursive (or can use a stack). Breadth-first traversal normally uses a queue.

7. Greedy algorithms represent only a sample of the many paradigms useful in developing graph algorithms. For further methods and examples, consult the references.

REVIEW QUESTIONS

10.1   **1.** Define the terms **(a)** *free tree*, **(b)** *rooted tree*, and **(c)** *ordered tree*.

2. Draw all the different **(a)** free trees, **(b)** rooted trees, and **(c)** ordered trees with three vertices.

3. Name three ways describing the correspondence between orchards and binary trees, and indicate the primary purpose for each of these ways.

10.2   **4.** What is a trie?

5. How may a trie with six levels and a five-way branch in each node differ from the rooted tree with six levels and five children for every node except the leaves? Will the trie or the tree likely have fewer nodes, and why?

6. Discuss the relative advantages in speed of retrieval of a trie and a binary search tree.

10.3   **7.** How does a multiway search tree differ from a trie?

8. What is a B-tree?

9. What happens when an attempt is made to insert a new key into a full node of a B-tree?

10. Does a B-tree grow at its leaves or at its root? Why?

11. In deleting a key from a B-tree, when is it necessary to combine nodes?

12. For what purposes are B-trees especially appropriate?

10.4   **13.** In the sense of this chapter, what is a graph?

14. What does it mean for a directed graph to be strongly connected? weakly connected?

15. Describe three ways to implement graphs in computer memory.

16. Explain the difference between *depth-first* and *breadth-first* traversal of a graph.

17. What data structures are needed to keep the waiting vertices during **(a)** depth-first and **(b)** breadth-first traversal?

18. For what kind of graphs is *topological sorting* defined?

19. What is a topological order for such a graph?

20. Why is the algorithm for finding shortest distances called *greedy*?

REFERENCES FOR FURTHER STUDY

One of the most thorough available studies of trees is in the series of books by KNUTH. The correspondence from ordered trees to binary trees appears in Volume 1, pp. 332–347. Volume 3, pp. 471–505, discusses multiway trees, B-trees, and tries. Mathematical results concerning trees and graphs are in Volume 1, pp. 362–385. Topological sorting (with the breadth-first algorithm) appears in Volume 1, pp. 258–268.

Tries were first studied in

EDWARD FREDKIN, "Trie memory," *Communications of the ACM* 3 (1960), 490–499.

The original reference for B-trees is

R. Bayer and E. McCreight, "Organization and maintenance of large ordered indexes," *Acta Informatica* 1 (1972), 173–189.

An interesting survey of applications and variations of B-trees is

D. Comer, "The ubiquitous B-tree," *Computing Surveys* 11 (1979), 121–137.

The quotation at the end of the chapter is taken from

N. Wirth, *Algorithms + Data Structures = Programs*, Prentice Hall, Englewood Cliffs, N. J., 1976, p. 170.

This book also contains (pp. 242–264) an exposition of B-trees with Pascal algorithms for insertion and deletion.

The study of graphs and algorithms for their processing is a large subject and one that involves both mathematics and computing science. Three books, each of which contains many interesting algorithms, are

R. E. Tarjan, *Data Structures and Network Algorithms*, Society for Industrial and Applied Mathematics, Philadelphia, 1983, 131 pages.

Shimon Even, *Graph Algorithms*, Computer Science Press, Rockville, Md., 1979, 249 pages.

E. M. Reingold, J. Nievergelt, N. Deo, *Combinatorial Algorithms: Theory and Practice*, Prentice Hall, Englewood Cliffs, N. J., 1977, 433 pages.

The original reference for the greedy algorithm determining the shortest paths in a graph is

E. W. Dijkstra, "A note on two problems in connexion with graphs," *Numerische Mathematik* 1 (1959), 269–271.

Case Study: The Polish Notation

This chapter studies the Polish notation for arithmetic or logical expressions, first in terms of problem solving, and then as applied to a program that interactively accepts an expression, compiles it, and evaluates it. This chapter illustrates uses of recursion, stacks, and trees, as well as their interplay in problem solving and algorithm design.

11.1 THE PROBLEM

One of the most important accomplishments of the early designers of computer languages was allowing a programmer to write arithmetic expressions in something close to their usual mathematical form. It was a real triumph to design a compiler that understood expressions such as

$$(x + y) * \exp(x - z) - 4.0$$
$$a * b + c/d - c * (x + y)$$
$$(p \,\&\&\, q) \,||\, (x <= 7.0)$$

etymology: FORTRAN   and produced machine-language output. In fact, the name FORTRAN stands for

FORmula TRANslator

in recognition of this very accomplishment. It often takes only one simple idea that, when fully understood, will provide the key to an elegant solution of a difficult problem, in this case the translation of expressions into sequences of machine-language instructions.

The triumph of the method to be developed in this chapter is that, in contrast to the first approach a person might take, it is not necessary to make repeated scans through the expression to decipher it, and, after a preliminary translation, neither parentheses nor priorities of operators need be taken into account, so that evaluation of the expression can be achieved with great efficiency.

11.1.1 The Quadratic Formula

Before we discuss this idea, let us briefly imagine the problems an early compiler designer might have faced when confronted with a fairly complicated expression. Even the quadratic formula produces problems:

$$x = (-b + (b \uparrow 2 - (4 \times a) \times c) \uparrow \tfrac{1}{2})/(2 \times a)$$

(Here, and throughout this chapter, we denote exponentiation by $\uparrow$. We limit our attention to one of the two roots.) Which operations must be done before others? What are the effects of parentheses? When can they be omitted? As you answer these questions for this example, you will probably look back and forth through the expression several times.

In considering how to translate such expressions, the compiler designers soon settled on the conventions that are familiar now: operations are ordinarily done left to right, subject to the priorities assigned to operators, with exponentiation highest, then multiplication and division, then addition and subtraction. This order can be altered by parentheses. For the quadratic formula, the order of operations is

$$x = (-b + (b \uparrow 2 - (4 \times a) \times c) \uparrow \tfrac{1}{2}) / (2 \times a)$$
$$\begin{array}{ccccccccccc} & \uparrow & \uparrow & \uparrow & \uparrow & \uparrow & \uparrow & \uparrow & \uparrow & \uparrow & \uparrow \\ & 10 & 1 & 7 & 2 & 5 & 3 & 4 & 6 & 9 & 8 \end{array}$$

Note that assignment ' $=$ ' really is an operator that takes the value of its right operand and assigns it to the left operand. The priority of ' $=$ ' will be the lowest of any operator, since it cannot be done until the expression is fully evaluated.

11.1.2 Unary Operators and Priorities

With one exception, all the operators in the quadratic equation are **binary**, that is, they have two operands. The one exception is the leading minus sign in $-b$. This is a **unary** operator, and unary operators provide a slight complication in determining priorities. Normally we interpret -2^2 as -4, which means that negation is done after exponentiation, but we interpret 2^{-2} as $1/4$ and not as -4, so that here negation is done first. It is reasonable to assign unary operators the same priority as exponentiation and, in order to preserve the usual algebraic conventions, to evaluate operators of this priority from right to left. Doing this, moreover, also gives the ordinary interpretation of $2 \uparrow 3 \uparrow 2$ as

$$2^{(3^2)} = 512 \quad \text{and not as} \quad (2^3)^2 = 64.$$

There are unary operators other than negation. These include such operations as taking the factorial of x, denoted $x!$, the derivative of a function f, denoted f', as well as all functions of a single variable, such as the trigonometric, exponential, and logarithmic functions.

Several binary operators produce Boolean (true/false) results: the operators && and || as well as the comparison operators ==, !=, <, <=, >, and >=. These comparisons are normally done after the arithmetic operators, but before && || and assignment.

priority list   We thus obtain the following list of priorities to reflect our usual customs in evaluating operators:

Operators	Priority
$\uparrow$, all unary operators	6
$\times$ / %	5
+ − (binary)	4
== !=	3
< <= > >=	2
&& ||	1
=	0

Note that these priorities are similar but not the same as those used in C, where && has higher priority than ||. As long as we are designing our own system, however, we are free to set our own conventions, provided that they are consistent, reasonable, and appropriate.

11.2 THE IDEA

11.2.1 Expression Trees

Drawing a picture is often an excellent way to gain insight into a problem. For our current problem, the appropriate picture is the **expression tree**, as first introduced in section 9.3. Recall that an expression tree is a binary tree in which the leaves are the simple operands and the interior vertices are the operators. If an operator is binary, then it has two nonempty subtrees, that are its left and right operands (either simple operands or subexpressions). If an operator is unary, then only one of its subtrees is nonempty, the one on the left or right according as the operator is written on the right or left of its operand. You should review Figure 9.4 for several simple expression trees, as well as Figure 9.5 for the expression tree of the quadratic formula.

Let us determine how to evaluate an expression tree such as, for example, the one shown in panel (a) of Figure 11.1. It is clear that we must begin with one of the leaves,

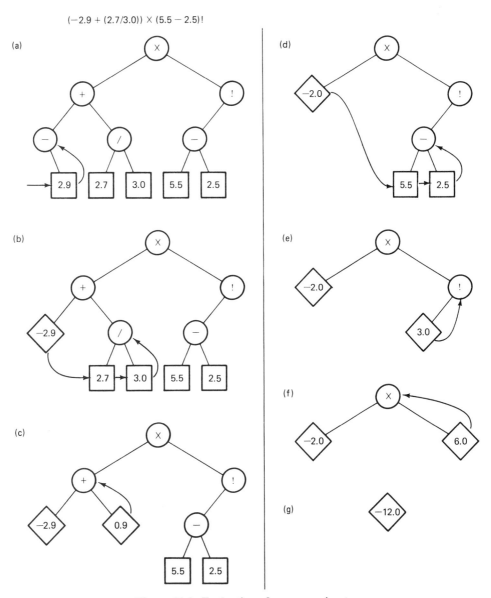

Figure 11.1. Evaluation of an expression tree

since it is only the simple operands for which we know the values when starting. To be consistent, let us start with the leftmost leaf, whose value is 2.9. Since, in our example, the operator immediately above this leaf is unary negation, we can apply it immediately and replace both the operator and its operand by the result, −2.9. This step results in the diamond-shaped node in panel (b) of the diagram.

The parent of the diamond-shaped node in panel (b) is a binary operator, and its second operand has not yet been evaluated. We cannot, therefore, apply this operator yet, but must instead consider the next two leaves, as shown by the colored path. After moving past these two leaves, the path moves to their parent operator, which can now be evaluated, and the result placed in the second diamond-shaped node, as shown in panel (c).

At this stage, both operands of the (first) addition are available, so we can perform it, obtaining the simplified tree in panel (d). And so we continue, until the tree has been reduced to a single node, which is the final result. In summary, we have processed the nodes of the tree in the order

$$2.9 \quad - \quad 2.7 \quad 3.0 \quad / \quad + \quad 5.5 \quad 2.5 \quad - \quad ! \quad \times$$

postorder traversal   The general observation is that we should process the subtree rooted at any given operator in the order: "Evaluate its left subtree; Evaluate its right subtree; Perform the operator." (If the operator is unary, then one of these steps is vacuous.) This order is precisely a postorder traversal of the expression tree. We have already observed in Section 9.3 that the postorder traversal of an expression tree yields the postfix form of the expression, in which each operator is written after its operands, instead of between them.

This simple idea is the key to efficient calculation of expressions by computer.

As a matter of fact, our customary way to write arithmetic or logical expressions with the operator between its operands is slightly illogical. The instruction

"Take the number 12 and multiply by . . . ."

is incomplete until the second factor is given. In the meantime it is necessary to remember both a number and an operation. From the viewpoint of establishing uniform rules it makes more sense either to write

"Take the numbers 12 and 3; then multiply."

or to write

"Do a multiplication. The numbers are 12 and 3."

11.2.2 Polish Notation

This method of writing all operators either before their operands, or after them, is called **Polish notation**, in honor of its discoverer, the Polish mathematician JAN ŁUKASIEWICZ.

When the operators are written before their operands, it is called the **prefix form**. When the operators come after their operands, it is called the **postfix form**, or, sometimes, **reverse Polish form** or **suffix form**. Finally, in this context, it is customary to use the coined phrase **infix form** to denote the usual custom of writing binary operators between their operands.

The expression $a \times b$ becomes $\times ab$ in prefix form and $ab\times$ in postfix form. In the expression $a + b \times c$, the multiplication is done first, so we convert it first, obtaining first $a + (bc\times)$ and then $abc \times +$ in postfix form. The prefix form of this expression is $+a \times bc$. Note that prefix and postfix forms are not related by taking mirror images or other such simple transformation. Note also that all parentheses have been omitted in the Polish forms. We shall justify this omission later.

As a more complicated example we can write down the prefix and postfix forms of the quadratic formula, starting from its expression tree, as shown in Figure 9.5.

preorder traversal

First, let us traverse the tree in preorder. The operator in the root is the assignment '=', after which we move to the left subtree, which consists only of the operand x. The right subtree begins with the division '/', and then moves leftward to '+' and to the unary negation '$-$'.

We now have an ambiguity that will haunt us later if we do not correct it. The first '$-$' (minus) in the expression is unary negation, and the second is binary subtraction. In Polish form it is not obvious which is which. When we go to evaluate the prefix string we will not know whether to take one operand for '$-$' or two, and the results will be quite different. To avoid this ambiguity we shall reserve '$-$' to denote binary subtraction, and use the special symbol '$\doteq$' for unary negation. (This terminology is certainly not standard. There are other ways to resolve the problem.)

The preorder traversal up to this point has yielded

$$=\quad x \quad / \quad + \quad \doteq \quad b$$

and the next step is to traverse the right subtree of the operator '+'. The result is the sequence

$$\uparrow \quad - \quad \uparrow \quad b \quad 2 \quad \times \quad \times \quad 4 \quad a \quad c \quad \tfrac{1}{2}$$

Finally, we traverse the right subtree of the division '/', obtaining

$$\times \quad 2 \quad a$$

Hence the complete prefix form for the quadratic formula is

$$=\quad x \quad / \quad + \quad \doteq \quad b \quad \uparrow \quad - \quad \uparrow \quad b \quad 2 \quad \times \quad \times \quad 4 \quad a \quad c \quad \tfrac{1}{2} \quad \times \quad 2 \quad a$$

You should verify yourself that the postfix form is

$$x \quad b \quad \doteq \quad b \quad 2 \quad \uparrow \quad 4 \quad a \quad \times \quad c \quad \times \quad - \quad \tfrac{1}{2} \quad \uparrow \quad + \quad 2 \quad a \quad \times \quad / \quad =$$

11.2.3 C Method

Before concluding this section, we should remark that most C compilers do not use Polish forms in translating expressions into machine language (although many other languages do). Some C compilers, instead, use the method of recursive descent as introduced in Section 8.4. In this method, each priority of operator requires a separate function for its compilation.

parsing
Translation of an expression by recursive descent is called **top-down parsing**, whereas this chapter's method of translating an expression by looking at each of its components in turn is an example of **bottom-up parsing**.

Exercises 11.2

(a) Draw the expression tree for each of the following expressions. Using the tree, convert the expression into (b) prefix and (c) postfix form. Use the table of priorities developed in this section, not those in C.

E1. $a + b < c$

E2. $a < b + c$

E3. $a - b < c - d \ || \ e < f$

E4. $n! / (k! \times (n - k)!)$ (Formula for binomial coefficients.)

E5. $s = (n/2) \times (2 \times a + (n - 1) \times d)$ (This is the sum of the first n terms of an arithmetic progression.)

E6. $g = a \times (1 - r^n)/(1 - r)$ (Sum of first n terms of a geometric progression.)

E7. $a \ == \ 1 \ || \ b \times c \ == \ 2 \ || \ (a > 1 \ \&\& \ b < 3)$

11.3 EVALUATION OF POLISH EXPRESSIONS

We first introduced the postfix form as a natural order of traversing an expression tree in order to evaluate the corresponding expression. Later in this section we shall formulate an algorithm for evaluating an expression directly from the postfix form, but first (since it is even simpler) we consider the prefix form.

11.3.1 Evaluation of an Expression in Prefix Form

Preorder traversal of a binary tree works from the top down. The root is visited first, and the remainder of the traversal then divided into two parts. The natural way to organize the process is as a recursive, divide-and-conquer algorithm. The same situation holds for an expression in prefix form. The first symbol (if there is more than one) is an operator (the one that will actually be done last), and the remainder of the expression comprises the operand(s) of this operator (one for a unary operator, two for a binary operator). Our function for evaluating the prefix form should hence begin with this first symbol.

If it is a unary operator, then the function should invoke itself recursively to determine the value of the operand. If the first symbol is a binary operator, then it should make two recursive calls for its two operands. The recursion terminates in the remaining case: When the first symbol is a simple operand, it is its own prefix form and the function should only return its value.

The following outline thus summarizes the evaluation of an expression in prefix form:

outline
```
/* Evaluate: evaluate an expression in prefix form. */
Value Evaluate(expression)
{
    Value x, y;

    Let token be the first symbol in the expression,
    and remove token from the expression

    if (token is a unary operator) {
        x = Evaluate(expression);
        return result of applying operator token to x;
    } else if (token is a binary operator) {
        x = Evaluate(expression);
        y = Evaluate(expression);
        return result of applying operator token to x and y;
    } else {
        return token;
    }
}
```

11.3.2 C Conventions

To tie down the details in the above outline, let us establish some conventions and rewrite the algorithm in C. The operators and operands in our expression may well have names that are more than one character long; hence we do not scan the expression one character at a time. Instead we define a token to be a single operator or operand from the expression. To emphasize that the function scans through the expression only once, we shall employ an auxiliary function

```
void GetToken(Token_type token);
```

that will move through the expression and return one token at a time in token. We need to know whether the token is a unary operator, a binary operator, or an operand, so we assume the existence of a function Kind that will return one of the enumeration constants

```
UNARYOP,   BINARYOP,   OPERAND.
```

For simplicity we shall assume that all the operands and the results of evaluating the operators are of the same type, which we leave unspecified and call Value_type. In many applications, this type would be one of integer or double.

Finally, we must assume the existence of three auxiliary functions that return a result of type Value_type.

Value_type DoUnary(Token_type token, Value_type x);

Value_type DoBinary(Token_type token, Value_type x, Value_type y);

actually perform the given operation on their operand(s). They need to recognize the symbols used for the operation token and the operands x and y, and invoke the necessary machine-language instructions. Similarly,

Value_type GetValue(Token_type token);

returns the actual value of a simple operand token, and might need, for example, to convert a constant from decimal to binary form, or look up the value of a variable. The actual form of these functions will depend very much on the application. We cannot settle all these questions here, but want only to concentrate on designing one important part of a compiler or expression evaluator.

11.3.3 C Function for Prefix Evaluation

With these preliminaries we can now translate our outline into a C program to evaluate prefix expressions.

```
/* EvaluatePrefix: evaluate an expression in prefix form. */
Value_type EvaluatePrefix(void)
{
    Token_type token;
    Value_type x, y;

    GetToken(token);
    switch(Kind(token)) {
    case UNARYOP:
        x = EvaluatePrefix( );
        return DoUnary(token, x);
    case BINARYOP:
        x = EvaluatePrefix( );
        y = EvaluatePrefix( );
        return DoBinary(token, x, y);
    case OPERAND:
        return GetValue(token);
    }
}
```

Our include file expr.h contains the definitions:

```
#define MAXTOKEN 10                    /* Change as appropriate.          */

typedef double Value_type;

typedef char Token_type [MAXTOKEN];

typedef enum kind_tag { UNARYOP, BINARYOP, OPERAND } Kind_type;
```

11.3.4 Evaluation of Postfix Expressions

It is almost inevitable that the prefix form so naturally calls for a recursive function for its evaluation, since the prefix form is really a "top-down" formulation of the algebraic expression: the outer, overall actions are specified first, then later in the expression the component parts are spelled out. On the other hand, in the postfix form the operands appear first, and the whole expression is slowly built up from its simple operands and the inner operators, in a "bottom-up" fashion. Therefore, iterative programs using stacks appear more natural for the postfix form. (It is of course possible to write either recursive or nonrecursive programs for either form. We are here discussing only the motivation, or what first appears more natural.)

stacks　To evaluate an expression in postfix form, it is necessary to remember the operands until their operator is eventually found some time later. The natural way to remember them is to put them on a stack. Then when the first operator to be done is encountered, it will find its operands on the top of the stack. If it puts its result back on the stack, then its result will be in the right place to be an operand for a later operator. When the evaluation is complete, the final result will be the only value on the stack. In this way, we obtain a function to evaluate a postfix expression.

At this time we should note a significant difference between postfix and prefix expressions. There was no need, in the prefix function, to check explicitly that the end of the expression had been reached, since the entire expression automatically constituted the operand(s) for the first operator. Reading a postfix expression from left to right, however, we can encounter sub-expressions that are, by themselves, legitimate postfix expressions. For example, if we stop reading

$$b \quad 2 \quad \uparrow \quad 4 \quad a \quad \times \quad c \quad \times \quad -$$

after the '$\uparrow$', we find that it is a legal postfix expression. To remedy this problem we shall suppose that the expression ends with a special sentinel, and for this sentinel token the function Kind returns the special value

ENDEXPR.

The remaining defined types in C, as well as the other auxiliary functions are the same as for the prefix evaluation. The function EvaluatePostfix follows.

```
/* EvaluatePostfix: evaluate expression in postfix form. */
Value_type EvaluatePostfix (void)
{
        Kind_type type;
        Token_type token;
        Value_type x, y;
        Stack_type stack;

        Initialize ( &stack);
        do {
                GetToken (token);
                switch (type = Kind(token)) {
                case OPERAND:
                        Push(GetValue(token), &stack);
                        break;
                case UNARYOP:
                        Pop( &x, &stack);
                        Push(DoUnary(token, x), &stack);
                        break;
                case BINARYOP:
                        Pop( &y, &stack);
                        Pop( &x, &stack);
                        Push(DoBinary(token, x, y), &stack);
                        break;
                case ENDEXPR:
                        Pop( &x, &stack);
                        if (!Empty( &stack))
                                Error("Incorrect expression");
                        break;
                }
        } while (type != ENDEXPR);
        return x;
}
```

At the end there is an error if there is more than one result or no result on the stack.

11.3.5 Proof of the Program: Counting Stack Entries

So far we have given only an informal motivation for the above program, and it may not be clear that it will produce the correct result in every case. Fortunately it is not difficult to give a formal justification of the program and, at the same time, to discover a useful criterion as to whether an expression is properly written in postfix form or not.

The method we shall use is to keep track of the number of entries in the stack. When each operand is obtained, it is immediately pushed onto the stack. A unary operator first *running-sum* pops, then pushes the stack, and thus makes no change in the number of entries. A *condition* binary operator pops the stack twice and pushes it once, giving a net decrease of one entry in the stack. More formally, we have

For a sequence E of operands, unary operators, and binary operators, form a running sum by starting at the left end of E and counting +1 for each operand, 0 for each unary operator, and −1 for each binary operator. E satisfies the **running-sum condition** *provided that this running sum never falls below 1, and is exactly 1 at the right-hand end of E.*

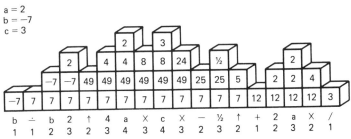

Figure 11.2. Stack frames and running sums, quadratic formula

THEOREM 11.1

If E is a properly formed expression in postfix form, then E must satisfy the running-sum condition.

THEOREM 11.2

A properly formed expression in postfix form will be correctly evaluated by function EvaluatePostfix.

Proof

induction proof

We shall prove the theorems together by using mathematical induction on the length of the expression E being evaluated.

The starting point for the induction is the case that E is a single operand alone, with length 1. This operand contributes +1, and the running-sum condition is satisfied. The function, when applied to a simple operand alone, gets its value, pushes it on the stack (which was previously empty) and at the end pops it as the final value of the function, thereby evaluating it correctly.

For the induction hypothesis we now assume that E is a proper postfix expression of length more than 1, that the program correctly evaluates all postfix expressions of length less than that of E, and that all such shorter expressions satisfy the running-sum condition. Since the length of E is more than 1, E is constructed at its last step either as F op, where op is a unary operator and F a postfix expression, or as F G op, where op is a binary operator and F and G are postfix expressions.

In either case the lengths of F and G are less than that of E, so by induction hypothesis both of them satisfy the running-sum condition, and the function would evaluate either of them separately and would obtain the correct result.

unary operator

First, take the case when op is a unary operator. Since F satisfies the running-sum condition, the sum at its end is exactly +1. As a unary operator, op contributes 0 to the sum, so the full expression E satisfies the running-sum condition. When the function reaches the end of F, similarly, it will, by induction hypothesis, have evaluated *binary operator*

F correctly and left its value as the unique stack entry. The unary operator *op* is then finally applied to this value, which is popped as the final result.

Finally take the case when *op* is binary. When the function reaches the last token of F, then the value of F will be the unique entry on the stack. Similarly, the running sum will be 1. At the next token the program starts to evaluate G. By the induction hypothesis the evaluation of G will also be correct and its running sum alone never falls below 1, and ends at exactly 1. Since the running sum at the end of F is 1, the combined running sum never falls below 2, and ends at exactly 2 at the end of G. Thus the evaluation of G will proceed and never disturb the single entry on the bottom of the stack, which is the result of F. When the evaluation reaches the final binary operator *op*, the running sum is correctly reduced from 2 to 1, and the operator finds precisely its two operands on the stack, where after evaluation it leaves its unique result. This completes the proof of Theorems 11.1 and 11.2.

end of proof

This error checking by keeping a running count of the number of entries on the stack provides a handy way to verify that a sequence of tokens is in fact a properly formed postfix expression, and is especially useful because its converse is also true:

THEOREM 11.3

If E is any sequence of operands and operators that satisfies the condition on running sums, then E is a properly formed expression in postfix form.

Proof

We shall again use mathematical induction to prove Theorem 11.3. The starting point is an expression containing only one token. Since the running sum (same as final sum) for a sequence of length 1 will be 1, this one token must be a simple operand. One simple operand alone is indeed a syntactically correct expression.

induction proof

Now for the inductive step, suppose that the theorem has been verified for all expressions strictly shorter than E, and E has length greater than 1. If the last token of E were an operand, then it would contribute +1 to the sum, and since the final sum is 1, the running sum would have been 0 one step before the end, contrary to the assumption that the running-sum condition is satisfied. Thus the final token of E must be an operator.

If the operator is unary, then it can be omitted and the remaining sequence still satisfies the condition on running sums, so by induction hypothesis is a syntactically correct expression, and all of E then also is.

Finally suppose that the last token is a binary operator *op*. To show that E is syntactically correct, we must find where in the sequence the first operand of *op* ends and the second one starts, by using the running sum. Since the operator *op* contributes -1 to the sum, it was 2 one step before the end. This 2 means that there were two items on the stack, the first and second operands of *op*. As we step backward through the sequence E, eventually we will reach a place where there is only one entry on the stack (running sum 1), and this one entry will be the first operand of *op*. Thus the place to break the sequence is at the last position before the end where the running sum is exactly 1. Such a position must exist, since at the far left end of E (if not before) we will find a running sum of 1. When we break E at its last 1, then it takes the form F G *op*. The subsequence F satisfies the condition on running sums, and ends with a sum of 1, so by induction hypothesis it is a correctly formed postfix expression. Since the running sums during G of F G *op* never again fall to 1, and end at 2 just before *op*, we may subtract 1 from each of them and conclude that the running sums for G alone satisfy the condition. Thus by induction hypothesis G is also a correctly formed postfix expression. Thus both F and G are correct expressions, and can be combined by the binary operator *op* into a correct expression E. Thus the proof of the theorem is complete.

end of proof

We can take the proof one more step, to show that the last position where a sum of 1 occurs is the *only* place where the sequence E can be split into syntactically correct subsequences F and G. For suppose it was split elsewhere. If at the end of F the running sum is not 1, then F is not a syntactically correct expression. If the running sum is 1 at the end of F, but reaches 1 again during the G part of F G *op*, then the sums for G alone would reach 0 at that point, so G is not correct. We have now shown that there is only one way to recover the two operands of a binary operator. Clearly there is only one way to recover the single operand for a unary operator. Hence we can recover the infix form of an expression from its postfix form, together with the order in which the operations are done, which we can denote by bracketing the result of every operation in the infix form with another pair of parentheses. We have therefore proved

THEOREM 11.4

An expression in postfix form that satisfies the running-sum condition corresponds to exactly one fully bracketed expression in infix form. Hence no parentheses are needed to achieve the unique representation of an expression in postfix form.

Similar theorems hold for the prefix form; their proofs are left as exercises. The above theorems provide both a theoretical justification of the use of Polish notation and a convenient way to check an expression for correct syntax.

11.3.6 Recursive Evaluation of Postfix Expressions

Most people find that the recursive function for evaluating prefix expressions is easier to understand than the stack-based (nonrecursive) function for evaluating postfix expressions. In this (optional) section we show how the stack can be eliminated in favor of recursion for postfix evaluation.

First, however, let us see why the natural approach leads to a recursive function for prefix evaluation but not for postfix. We can describe both prefix and postfix expressions by the syntax diagrams of Figure 11.3. In both cases there are three possibilities: the expression consists of only a single operand or the outermost operator is unary or is binary.

prefix evaluation

In tracing through the diagram for prefix form, the first token we encounter in the expression determines which of the three branches we take, and there are then no further choices to make (except within recursive calls, which need not be considered just now). Hence the structure of the recursive function for prefix evaluation closely resembles the syntax diagram.

postfix evaluation

With the postfix diagram, however, there is no way to tell from the first token (which will always be an operand) which of the three branches to take. It is only when the last token is encountered that the branch is determined. This fact does, however, lead to one easy recursive solution: Read the expression from right to left, reverse all the arrows on the syntax diagram, and use the same function as for prefix evaluation!

If we wish, however, to read the expression in the usual way from left to right, then we must work harder. Let us consider separately each of the three kinds of tokens in a postfix form. We have already observed that the first token in the expression must be an operand; this follows directly from the fact that the running sum after the first token

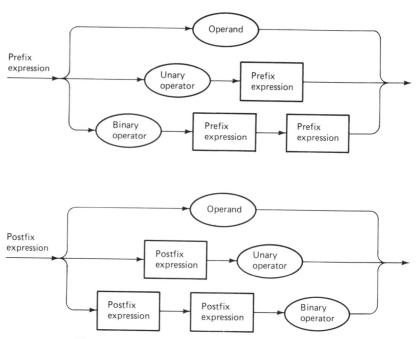

Figure 11.3. Syntax diagrams of Polish expressions

is (at least) 1. Since unary operators do not change the running sum, unary operators can be inserted anywhere after the initial operand. It is the third case, binary operators, whose study leads to the solution.

running sum   Consider the sequence of running sums, and the place(s) in the sequence where the sum drops from 2 to 1. Since binary operators contribute -1 to the sum, such places must exist if the postfix expression contains any binary operators, and correspond to the places in the expression where the two operands of the binary operator constitute the whole expression to the left. Such situations are illustrated in the stack frames of Figure 11.2. The entry on the bottom of the stack is the first operand; a sequence of positions where the height is at least 2, starting and ending at exactly two, make up the calculation of the second operand, and, taken in isolation, this sequence is itself a properly formed postfix expression. A drop in height from 2 to 1 marks one of the binary operators in which we are interested.

After the binary operator more unary operators may appear, and then the process may repeat itself (if the running sums again increase) with more sequences that are self-contained postfix expressions followed by binary and unary operators. In summary, we have shown that postfix expressions are described by the syntax diagram of Figure 11.4, which translates easily into the recursive function that follows. The C conventions are the same as in the previous functions.

left recursion   The situation appearing in the postfix diagram of Figure 11.3 is called ***left recursion***, and the steps we have taken in the transition to the diagram in Figure 11.4 are typical of those needed to remove left recursion.

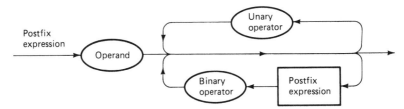

Figure 11.4. Alternative syntax diagram, postfix expression

```
Token_type token;

/* EvaluatePostfix: evaluate expression in postfix form. */
Value_type EvaluatePostfix(void)
{
     Value_type result;

     GetToken(token);
     if (Kind(token) != OPERAND)
          Error("Postfix expression does not start with operand");
     else
          result = Parse();
     if (Kind(token) != ENDEXPR)
          Error("Missing end expression");
     else
          return result;

}
/* Parse: parse and evaluate expression in postfix form. */
Value_type Parse(void)
{
     Kind_type type;
     Value_type x;
     Value_type result;

     result = GetValue(token);
     for (GetToken(token); (type = Kind(token)) == UNARYOP ||
                              type == OPERAND; GetToken(token)) {
          if (type == UNARYOP)
                result = DoUnary(token, result);
          else {
                x = Parse();
                if (Kind(token) == BINARYOP)
                     result = DoBinary(token, result, x);
                else
                     Error("Expecting binary operator");
          }
     }
     return result;
}
```

Exercises 11.3

E1. Trace the action on each of the following expressions by the function EvaluatePostfix in (1) nonrecursive and (2) recursive versions. For the recursive function, draw the tree of recursive calls, indicating at each node which tokens are being processed. For the nonrecursive function, draw a sequence of stack frames showing which tokens are processed at each stage.

a. $a \quad b \quad + \quad c \quad \times$
b. $a \quad b \quad c \quad + \quad \times$
c. $a \quad ! \quad b \quad ! \quad / \quad c \quad d \quad - \quad a \quad ! \quad - \quad \times$
d. $a \quad b \quad < \quad c \quad d \quad \times \quad < \quad e \quad \|$

E2. Trace the action of the function EvaluatePrefix on each of the following expressions, by drawing a tree of recursive calls showing which tokens are processed at each stage.

a. $/ \quad + \quad x \quad y \quad ! \quad n.$
b. $/ \quad + \quad ! \quad x \quad y \quad n.$
c. $\&\& \quad < \quad x \quad y \quad \| \quad == \quad + \quad x \quad y \quad z \quad > \quad x \quad 0$

E3. Which of the following are syntactically correct postfix expressions? Show the error in each incorrect expression. Translate each correct expression into infix form, using parentheses as necessary to avoid ambiguities.

a. $a \quad b \quad c \quad + \quad \times \quad a \quad / \quad c \quad b \quad + \quad d \quad / \quad -$
b. $a \quad b \quad + \quad c \quad a \quad \times \quad b \quad c \quad / \quad d \quad -$
c. $a \quad b \quad + \quad c \quad a \quad \times \quad - \quad c \quad \times \quad + \quad b \quad c \quad -$
d. $a \quad \dot{-} \quad b \quad \times$
e. $a \quad \times \quad b \quad \dot{-}$
f. $a \quad b \quad \times \quad \dot{-}$
g. $a \quad b \quad \dot{-} \quad \times$

E4. Translate each of the following expressions from prefix form into postfix form.

a. $/ \quad + \quad x \quad y \quad ! \quad n$
b. $/ \quad + \quad ! \quad x \quad y \quad n$
c. $\&\& \quad < \quad x \quad y \quad \| \quad == \quad + \quad x \quad y \quad z \quad > \quad x \quad 0$

E5. Write a C program to translate an expression from prefix form into postfix form. Use the C conventions of this chapter.

E6. Translate each of the following expressions from postfix form into prefix form.

a. $a \quad b \quad + \quad c \quad \times$
b. $a \quad b \quad c \quad + \quad \times$
c. $a \quad ! \quad b \quad ! \quad / \quad c \quad d \quad - \quad a \quad ! \quad - \quad \times$
d. $a \quad b \quad < \quad c \quad d \quad \times \quad < \quad e \quad \|$

E7. Write a C program to translate an expression from postfix form into prefix form. Use the C conventions of this chapter.

E8. A *fully bracketed* expression is one of the following forms:

1. a simple operand;

2. $(op \; E)$ where op is a unary operator and E is a fully bracketed expression;

3. $(E \; op \; F)$ where op is a binary operator and E and F are fully bracketed expressions.

Hence, in a fully bracketed expression, the results of every operation are enclosed in parentheses. Examples of fully bracketed expressions are $((a + b) - c)$, $(-a)$, $(a + b)$, $(a + (b + c))$. Write C programs that will translate expressions from **(a)** prefix and **(b)** postfix form into fully bracketed form.

E9. Formulate and prove theorems analogous to Theorems **(a)** 11.1, **(b)** 11.3 and **(c)** 11.4 for the prefix form of expressions.

11.4 TRANSLATION FROM INFIX FORM TO POLISH FORM

Very few (if any) programmers habitually write algebraic or logical expressions in Polish form, or even in fully bracketed form. To make convenient use of the algorithms we have developed, we must have an efficient method to translate arbitrary expressions from infix form into Polish notation. As a first simplification, we shall consider only the postfix form. Secondly, we shall exclude unary operators that are placed to the right of their operands. Such operators cause no conceptual difficulty, but would make the algorithms more complicated.

One method that we could use would be to build the expression tree from the infix form and traverse the tree to obtain the postfix form, but, as it turns out, constructing the tree is actually more complicated than constructing the postfix form directly. Since, in postfix form, all operators come after their operands, the task of translation from infix to postfix form is simply

delaying operators

> *Delay each operator until its right-hand operand has been translated. Pass each simple operand through without delay.*

This action is illustrated in Figure 11.5.

The major problem we must resolve is to find what token will terminate the right-hand operand of a given operator. We must take both parentheses and priorities of operators into account. The first problem is easy. If a left parenthesis is in the operand, then everything through the matching right parenthesis must also be. For the second problem, that of priorities of operators, we consider binary operators separately from those of priority 6, namely, unary operators and exponentiation.

Figure 11.5. Delaying operators in postfix form

*finding the end of
the right operand*

Most binary operators are evaluated from left to right. Let op_1 be such a binary operator, and let op_2 be the first nonbracketed operator to the right of op_1. If the priority of op_2 is less than or equal to that of op_1, then op_2 will not be part of the right operand of op_1, and its appearance will terminate the right operand of op_1. If the priority of op_2 is greater than that of op_1, then op_2 is part of the right operand of op_1, and we can continue through the expression until we find an operator of priority less than or equal to that of op_1; this operator will then terminate the right operand of op_1.

*right-to-left
evaluation*

Next, suppose that op_1 has priority 6 (it is unary or exponentiation), and recall that operators of this priority are to be evaluated from right to left. If the first operand op_2 to the right of op_1 has equal priority, it therefore will be part of the right operand of op_1, and the right operand is terminated only by an operator of strictly smaller priority.

There are two more ways in which the right operand can terminate: the expression can end, or the given operator may itself be within a bracketed subexpression, in which case its right operand will end when an unmatched right parenthesis ')' is encountered. In summary, we have the rules:

> *If op is an operator in an infix expression, then its right-hand operand contains all tokens on its right until one of the following is encountered:*
>
> *1. the end of the expression;*
>
> *2. an unmatched right parenthesis ')';*
>
> *3. an operator of priority less than or equal to that of op, and not within a bracketed sub-expression, if op has priority less than 6;*
>
> *4. an operator of priority strictly less than that of op, and not within a bracketed subexpression, if op has priority 6.*

stack of operators

From these rules, we can see that the appropriate way to remember the operators being delayed is to keep them on a stack. If operator op_2 comes on the right of operator op_1 but has higher priority, then op_2 will be output before op_1 is. Thus the operators are output in the order last in, first out.

The key to writing an algorithm for the translation is to make a slight change in our point of view by asking, as each token appears in the input, which of the operators previously delayed (that is, on the stack) now have their right operands terminated because of the new token, so that it is time to move them into the output. The preceding conditions then become

popping the stack

> *1. At the end of the expression, all operators are output.*
>
> *2. A right parenthesis causes all operators found since the corresponding left parenthesis to be output.*
>
> *3. An operator of priority not 6 causes all other operators of greater or equal priority to be output.*
>
> *4. An operator of priority 6 causes all other operators of strictly greater priority to be output, if such operators exist.*

To implement the second rule, we shall put each left parenthesis on the stack when it is encountered. Then, when the matching right parenthesis appears and the operators have been popped from the stack, the pair can both be discarded.

We can now incorporate these rules into a function. To do so, we shall use the same auxiliary types and functions as in the last section, except that now the function Kind can return two additional values:

LEFTPAREN   RIGHTPAREN.

These two values denote, respectively, left and right parentheses. The functions Push and Pop will now process tokens (operators) rather than values. In addition to the function GetToken that obtains the next token from the input (infix expression), we use an auxiliary function

PutToken(Token_type token);

that puts the given token into the postfix expression. Thus these two functions might read and write with files or might only refer to arrays already set up, depending on the desired application. Finally, we shall use a function Priority(op) that will return the priority of an operator op.

With these conventions we can write the function.

translation into postfix

```
/* Translate: translate from infix to postfix form. */
void Translate(void)
{
      Stack_type stack;
      Token_type token;
      Kind_type type;
      Boolean_type endright;

      Initialize( &stack);

      do {
      GetToken(token);
      switch (type = Kind(token)) {
      case OPERAND:
         PutToken(token);
         break;

      case LEFTPAREN:
         Push(token, &stack);
         break;

      case RIGHTPAREN:
         for (Pop(token, &stack); Kind(token) != LEFTPAREN;
                                   Pop(token, &stack))
            PutToken(token);
         break;
```

```
        case UNARYOP:                        /* Treat both kinds together.            */
        case BINARYOP:
            do {
                if (stack.top <= 0)
                    endright = TRUE;
                else if (Kind(stack.entry[stack.top-1]) == LEFTPAREN)
                    endright = TRUE;
                else if (Priority(stack.entry[stack.top-1]) < Priority(token))
                    endright = TRUE;
                else if (Priority(stack.entry[stack.top-1]) == Priority(token)
                        && Priority(token) == MAXPRIORITY)
                    endright = TRUE;
                else {
                    endright = FALSE;
                    Pop(token, &stack);
                    PutToken(token);
                }
            } while (!endright);
            Push(token, &stack);
            break;
        case ENDEXPR:
            while(stack.top > 0) {
                Pop(token, &stack);
                PutToken(token);
            }
            break;
        }
    } while (type != ENDEXPR);
    PutToken("\n");                          /* end of expression                     */
}
```

Figure 11.6 shows the steps performed to translate the quadratic formula

$$x = (\dot{-} b + (b^2 - 4 \times a \times c)^{\frac{1}{2}})/(2 \times a)$$

into postfix form, as an illustration of this algorithm. (Recall that we are using ' $\dot{-}$ ' to denote unary negation.)

This completes the discussion of translation into postfix form. There will clearly be similarities in describing the translation into prefix form, but some difficulties arise because of the seemingly irrelevant fact that, in European languages, we read from left to right. If we were to translate an expression into prefix form working from left to right, then not only would the operators need to be rearranged but operands would need to be delayed until after their operators were output. But the relative order of operands is not changed in the translation, so the appropriate data structure to keep the operands would not be a stack (it would in fact be a queue). Since stacks would not do the job, neither would recursive programs with no explicit arrays, since these two kinds of programs

Input Token	Contents of Stack (rightmost token is on top)						Output Token(s)	
x							x	
$=$	$=$							
(	$=$	(						
$\div$	$=$	(	$\div$					
b	$=$	(	$\div$				b	
$+$	$=$	(	$+$				$\div$	
(	$=$	(	$+$	(				
b	$=$	(	$+$	(			b	
↑	$=$	(	$+$	(	↑			
2	$=$	(	$+$	(	↑		2	
$-$	$=$	(	$+$	(	$-$		↑	
4	$=$	(	$+$	(	$-$		4	
$\times$	$=$	(	$+$	(	$-$	$\times$		
a	$=$	(	$+$	(	$-$	$\times$	a	
$\times$	$=$	(	$+$	(	$-$	$\times$	$\times$	
c	$=$	(	$+$	(	$-$	$\times$	c	
)	$=$	(	$+$				$\times$	$-$
↑	$=$	(	$+$	↑				
½	$=$	(	$+$	↑			½	
)	$=$						↑	$+$
/	$=$	/						
(	$=$	/	(					
2	$=$	/	(				2	
$\times$	$=$	/	(	$\times$				
a	$=$	/	(	$\times$			a	
)	$=$	/					$\times$	
ENDEXPR							/	$=$

Figure 11.6. Translation of the quadratic formula into postfix form

can do equivalent tasks. Thus a left-to-right translation into prefix form would need a different approach. The trick is to translate into prefix form by working from right to left through the expression, using methods quite similar to the left-to-right postfix translation that we have developed. The details are left as an exercise.

Exercises 11.4

E1. Note that in function Translate the action taken at the end of the input is much the same as when a right parenthesis is encountered. Suppose that the entire expression is enclosed in a pair of parentheses to serve as sentinels for the beginning and end. Write a simplified version of function Translate that no longer needs to check explicitly for the end of input.

E2. Function Translate is sadly deficient in error checking. Unmatched parentheses, for example, may send it off into a nonexistent part of the expression. Add error checking to the function so that it will detect syntax errors in its input (infix) expression.

E3. Modify the function Translate so that it will accommodate unary operators that are written to the right of their operands. You should assume that the function Kind returns rightunary when such an operator appears.

11.5 AN INTERACTIVE EXPRESSION EVALUATOR

There are many applications for a program that can evaluate a function that is typed in interactively while the program is running. One such application is a program that will draw the graph of a mathematical function (either on a plotter or on a graphics video terminal). Suppose that you are writing such a program to be used to help first-year calculus students graph functions. Most of these students will not know how to write or compile programs, so you wish to include in your program some way that the user can put in an expression for a function such as

$$x \times \log(x) - x^{1.25}$$

while the program is running, which the program can then graph for appropriate values of x.

goal   The goal of this section is to describe such a program, and especially to complete the writing of two subprograms to help with this problem. The first subprogram will take as input an expression involving constants, variable(s), arithmetic operators, and standard functions, with bracketing allowed, as typed in from the terminal. It will then translate the expression into postfix form and keep it in an appropriate array. The second subprogram will evaluate the expression for values of the variable(s) given as its calling parameter(s) and return the answer.

purpose   We undertake this project for several reasons. It shows how to take the ideas already developed for working with Polish notation and build these ideas into a complete, concrete, and functioning program. In this way, the project illustrates a problem-solving approach to program design, in which we begin with solutions to the key questions and complete the structure with auxiliary functions as needed. Finally, since this project is intended for use by people with little computer experience, it provides opportunity to test **robustness**, that is, the ability of the program to withstand unexpected or incorrect input without catastrophic failure.

11.5.1 The Main Program

The main program outlines how the work is divided into routines; hence we look at it first.

```
Token_type lexicon [MAXTOKEN];
int hashtable [MAXTOKEN];              /* indices for lexicon table            */
int infix [MAXTOKEN];                  /* indices of tokens in infix form      */
int postfix [MAXTOKEN];                /* indices of tokens in postfix form    */
int parameter [MAXTOKEN];

int exprlength;                        /* length of the infix expression       */
int nparameter;                        /* number of parameters in expression   */
int parencount;                        /* parenthesis count for expression     */
int tokencount;                        /* number of tokens in lexicon [ ]      */

/* Read infix expression, change it to postfix, and graph it. */
void main (void)
{
      double x, y;
      double incr, xlow, xhigh;

      printf ("Welcome to the function-graphing program.\n");
      printf ("Do you need instructions?");
      if (Enquire ( ))
            Instruct ( );
      DefineTokens ( );                /* Initialize tokens.                   */
      do {
            Expression ( );            /* Get expression and convert.          */
            do {
                  ReadGraphLimits ( &xlow, &xhigh, &incr);
                  ReadParameters ( );
                  for (x = xlow; x <= xhigh; x += incr) {
                        lexicon [FIRSTOPERAND].info.val = x;
                        y = EvaluatePostfix ( );
                        Graph (x, y);
                  }
                  printf ("Repeat for new graphing limits?");
            } while (Enquire ( ));
            printf ("Repeat for a new expression?");
      } while (Enquire ( ));
}
```

1. Instructions

As with most programs written for casual users, the first step is to determine if instructions should be given. To save space, however, we shall not include a text for the function Instruct here. The response to questions to the user is obtained through the function Enquire that we used in Chapter 1.

2. Error Processing

In several routines we shall use a function

```
void Error (char *msg);
```

that will print a message and terminate the program. That is, for simplicity, we shall make all errors that the program detects be fatal to its execution.

3. Further Routines

The second task of the main program is to establish the definitions of the predefined tokens (such as the operators +, −, * amongst others, the operand x that will be used in the graphing, and perhaps some constants). We shall write function DefineTokens after we have decided on the data structures.

Function Expression reads in an expression, splits it into tokens, and translates it into postfix form. Here arise several design problems, and the greatest need to check the input for possible errors that the user might make.

graphing The function ReadGraphLimits sets up any initialization required to draw the graph, obtains the bounds and scale for drawing, and determines the range of values for x and the increment to be used. These requirements, unfortunately, differ greatly from one system to another, so that we cannot hope to write a function that is widely applicable. For testing the program, therefore, we must be content with a small stub that only obtains the bounds and increment for x. Similarly, function Graph(x, y) that actually graphs the point (x,y) is also system dependent, and so is not included here. For testing our program, a stub that writes out the values of x and y will suffice.

expression parameters It may be that the expression as typed in contains variables other than x, the one used for graphing. If so, our program will treat these other variables as parameters that will keep the same value while one graph is drawn, but whose values can be changed from one graph to the next, without other change in the expression. Function ReadParameters obtains values for these variables.

The innermost loop of the main program moves through the range of values for x, sets them into the place where they can be found by function EvaluatePostfix, and graphs the results.

11.5.2 Representation of the Data

Our data-structure decisions concern how to store and retrieve the tokens used in Polish expressions and their evaluation. For each different token we must remember (1) its name (as a string of characters), so that we can recognize it in the input expression; (2) its kind (UNARYOP, BINARYOP, OPERAND, LEFTPAREN, RIGHTPAREN, or ENDEXPR); (3) for operators, its priority; for operands, its value. It is reasonable to think of representing each token as a structure containing this information. One small difficulty arises: The same token may appear several times in an expression. If it is an operand, then we must be certain that it is given the same value each time. If we put the structures themselves into the expressions, then when a value is assigned to an operand we must be sure that it is updated in all the structures corresponding to that operand. We can avoid having to keep chains of references to a given variable by associating an integer code with each token, and placing this code in the expression, rather than the full structure. We shall *lexicon* then set up a *lexicon* for the tokens, which will be an array indexed by the integer codes, and which will hold the full structures for the tokens. In this way, if k is the code for a variable, then every appearance of k in the expression will cause us to look in position k of the lexicon for the corresponding value, and we are automatically assured of getting the same value each time.

Placing integer codes rather than structures in the expressions also has the advantage of saving some space, but space for tokens is unlikely to be a critical constraint for this project. The time required to evaluate the postfix expression at many different values of the argument x is more likely to prove expensive.

As the input expression is decoded, the program may find constants and new variables (parameters), which it will then add to the lexicon. These will all be classed as operands, but recall that, in the case of parameters, the user will be asked to give values before the expression is evaluated. Hence it is necessary to keep one more list, a list of the codes that correspond to parameters.

All these data structures are illustrated in Figure 11.7, along with some of the data structures used in the principal functions.

Let us summarize the types and symbolic constants by showing expr.h:

```
#define MAXVARS 50              /* maximum number of variables    */
#define MAXPRIORITY 6           /* largest operator priority      */
#define MAXSTACK 100            /* stack size                     */
#define MAXSTRING 101           /* maximum tokens in expression   */
#define MAXTOKEN 101            /* maximum distinct tokens        */
#define MAXNAME 7               /* number of characters in identifier  */

#define FIRSTUNARY 3            /* index of first unary operator  */
#define LASTUNARY 11            /* index of last unary operator   */
#define FIRSTBINARY 12          /* index of first binary operator */
#define LASTBINARY 17           /* index of last binary operator  */
#define FIRSTOPERAND 18         /* index of first operand         */
#define LASTOPERAND 20          /* index of last predefined operand  */

#define HASHSIZE 101

typedef double Value_type;

typedef enum kind_tag { UNARYOP, BINARYOP, OPERAND,
                        LEFTPAREN, RIGHTPAREN, ENDEXPR } Kind_type;

union info_tag {
        int pri;
        Value_type val;
};

typedef struct token_tag {
        char name[MAXNAME];
        int kind;
        union info_tag info;
} Token_type;
```

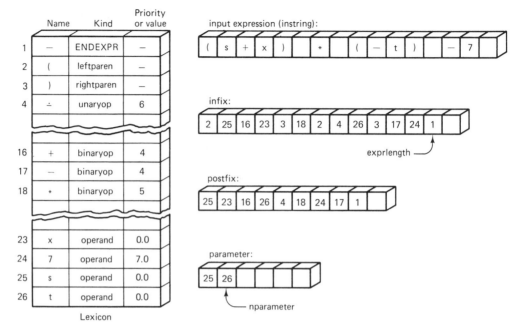

Figure 11.7. Data structures for program GraphFunction

11.5.3 Predefined Tokens

The only task to be done by DefineTokens is to place the names, kinds, priorities (for operators), and values (for operands) of all the predefined tokens into the lexicon. Hence the function consists only of a long series of assignment statements, which we omit to save space.

The complete list of predefined tokens used in this implementation is shown in Figure 11.8. Note that we can add operators that are not part of the C language (such as exponentiation) and constants such as e and π. The expressions in which we are interested in this section begin and end with real numbers.

11.5.4 Translation of the Expression

In this section of the program, we must read an expression in ordinary (infix) form, check that it is syntactically correct, split it apart into tokens, and find their codes. As a sequence of tokens, the expression can then be converted to postfix form by the function written in Section 11.4.

1. Finding the Definitions of Tokens

As each token is split from the input string, we must find its code. This is an information retrieval problem: The name of the token is the key, and the integer code must be retrieved. In the expression there will usually be no more than a few dozen tokens, and it is quite arguable that the best way to retrieve the code is by sequential search through the lexicon. Sequential search would be easy to program, would require no further data

Token	Name	Kind	Priority/Value	
0		ENDEXPR		
1	(	LEFTPAREN		
2	)	RIGHTPAREN		
3	$\doteq$	UNARYOP	6	*negation*
4	abs	UNARYOP	6	
5	sqrt	UNARYOP	6	
6	exp	UNARYOP	6	
7	ln	UNARYOP	6	*natural log*
8	log10	UNARYOP	6	*base 10 log*
9	sin	UNARYOP	6	
10	cos	UNARYOP	6	
11	tanh	UNARYOP	6	
12	+	BINARYOP	4	
13	−	BINARYOP	4	
14	*	BINARYOP	5	
15	/	BINARYOP	5	
16	%	BINARYOP	5	
17	↑	BINARYOP	6	
18	x	OPERAND	0.00000	
19	pi	OPERAND	3.14159	
20	e	OPERAND	2.71828	

Figure 11.8. Predefined tokens for GraphFunction

structures, and the cost in time over more sophisticated methods would be negligible. One of the objects of this project, however, is to illustrate larger applications, where the expense of sequential search may no longer be negligible. In a compiler, for example, there may be many hundreds of distinct symbols that must be recognized, and more sophisticated symbol tables must be used. A good choice is to use a hash table together with the lexicon. In the hash table we shall store only codes, and use these to look in the lexicon to locate the token with a given name.

In this way, we obtain the following functions.

2. The Main Program

```
/* Expression: get and evaluate an infix expression. */
void Expression(void)
{
    MakeHashTable();            /* Set up initial values for hash table.    */
    ReadExpression();
    Translate();                /* from infix to postfix expression         */
}
```

3. Processing the Hash Table

```
/* Hash: find hash entry for name in hashtable[]. */
int Hash(char *name)
{
    int h = name[0] % HASHSIZE;
    while (1) {
        if (hashtable[h] == −1)
            break;                    /* Entry is empty.                      */
        else if (strcmp(lexicon[hashtable[h]].name, name) == 0)
            break;                    /* name in the hash table               */
        else {
            if (name[1] == '\0')
                h += 31;
            else
                h += name[1];
            h %= HASHSIZE;            /* Find another position.               */
        }
    }
    return abs(h);
}
```

Since many of the tokens have names only one character long, we have written the hash function to give special emphasis to this possibility. The spread achieved by this function appears fairly good, although other functions may do better.

It is also necessary to initialize the hash table with entries corresponding to the predefined tokens. The first such token, however, is ENDEXPR, which is determined by reaching the end of the input, and not by looking in the hash table. Hence token 0 is not placed in hashtable.

```
/* MakeHashTable: make hash table for the lexicon. */
void MakeHashTable(void)
{
    int i;
    for (i = 0; i < HASHSIZE; i++)
        hashtable[i] = −1;
    for (i = 1; i <= LASTOPERAND; i++)
        hashtable[Hash(lexicon[i].name)] = i;
}
```

4. Decoding the Expression

Figure 11.8 includes both some tokens whose names are single special characters and some tokens whose names are words beginning with a letter. These latter may be any of unary or binary operators or operands. It is also possible to have tokens that are numbers, that is, which are made up of digits (and possibly a decimal point). Hence in splitting the input expression into tokens, we shall consider three cases, using three functions in the main loop, FindWord, FindNumber, and FindSymbol, that will determine the name of the token and put its code into the output expression (still in infix at this stage).

input format   We must now establish conventions regarding the input format. Let us assume that the input expression is typed as one line, so that when we reach the end of the line, we have also reached the end of the input string. Let us use the conventions of C concerning spaces: blanks are ignored between tokens, but the occurrence of a blank terminates a token. If a token is a word, then it begins with a letter, which can be followed by letters or digits. Let us translate all uppercase letters to lowercase, and use only lowercase in comparisons. (Be sure that the predefined tokens are hashed as lowercase only.) Let us truncate names to MAXNAME characters, where the symbolic constant MAXNAME is defined in expr.h.

error checking   It is in reading the input string that the greatest amount of error checking is needed to make sure that the syntax of the input expression is correct, and to make our program as robust as possible. Most of this error checking will be done in the subsidiary functions, but in the main program, we keep a counter to make sure that parentheses are nested correctly, that is, that more right than left parentheses never appear and at the end the parentheses are balanced.

With these provisions, we obtain the following function:

```
/* ReadExpression: read an expression in infix form. */
void ReadExpression(void)
{
    int len, pos;
    char instring[MAXSTRING];

    exprlength = -1;                    /* Initialize global variables.       */
    nparameter = -1;
    parencount = 0;
    tokencount = LASTOPERAND;

    printf("Please type the expression to graph:\n");
    fgets(instring, MAXSTRING, stdin);
    len = strlen(instring);
    instring[len-1] = ' ';              /* sentinel for searches              */
    for (pos = 0; pos < len; ) {
        if (instring[pos] == ' ')
            pos++;
        else if (isalpha(instring[pos]))
            pos = FindWord(instring, pos);
        else if (isdigit(instring[pos]) || instring[pos] == '.')
            pos = FindNumber(instring, pos);
        else
            pos = FindSymbol(instring, pos);
    }
    if (parencount)
        Error("Number of left and right parentheses incorrect");
    if (Leading())
        Error("Input expression is incomplete");
    PutToken(0);                        /* Put out end of expression.         */
}
```

5. Error Checking for Correct Syntax

The most important aspect of error checking that makes its first appearance in the above function is the function **Leading**. To motivate the inclusion of this function, let us first consider a special case. Suppose that an expression is made up only from simple operands and binary operators, with no parentheses or unary operators. Then the only syntactically correct expressions are of the form

$$operand \quad binaryop \quad operand \quad binaryop \ldots operand$$

leading positions

where the first and last tokens are operands, and the two kinds of tokens alternate. It is illegal for two operands to be adjacent, or for two binary operators to be adjacent. In the leading position there must be an operand, as there must be after each operator, so we can consider these positions also as "leading," since the preceding operator must lead to an operand.

Now suppose that unary operators are to be inserted into the above expression. Any number of unary operators can be placed before any operand (recall that we are allowing only unary operators that go to the left of their operands), but it is illegal to place a unary operator immediately before a binary operator. That is, unary operators can appear exactly where operands are allowed, in leading positions but only there. On the other hand, the appearance of a unary operator leaves the position still as a "leading" position, since an operand must still appear before a binary operator becomes legal.

Let us now, finally, also allow parentheses in the expression. A bracketed sub-expression is treated as an operand and, therefore, can appear exactly where operands are legal. Hence left parentheses can appear exactly in leading positions, and leave the position as leading, and right parentheses can appear only in nonleading positions, and leave the position as nonleading.

All the possibilities are summarized in Figure 11.9.

	Previous token any one of:	*Legal tokens any one of:*
Leading position:		
	start of expression	operand
	binary operator	unary operator
	unary operator	left parenthesis
	left parenthesis	
Nonleading position:		
	operand	binary operator
	right parenthesis	right parenthesis
		end of expression

Figure 11.9. Tokens legal in leading and nonleading positions

These requirements are built into the following function that will be used in the subsidiary functions to check the syntax of the input.

```
/* Leading: TRUE if start, left parenthesis, unary or binary operator. */
Boolean_type Leading(void)
{
        int k;

        if (exprlength <= -1)
                return TRUE;
        else
                return (k = Kind(infix[exprlength])) == LEFTPAREN ||
                                k == UNARYOP || k == BINARYOP;
}
```

6. Auxiliary Subprograms

Amongst the other auxiliary subprograms needed are the function

void PutToken(Token_type token);

that adds a token to the list in the array infix, and the function

Kind_type Kind(Token_type token);

that returns the kind of a token. PutToken is straightforward, and we leave it as an exercise. Kind could just as easily be written in line each time it is used, since we employ a structure for tokens, but to remain consistent with earlier sections of this chapter (where Kind was used but not yet programmed), we instead use a separate function whose body consists of the single statement

return lexicon[token].kind;

7. Case: Token is a Word

We now turn to the three subsidiary functions for processing words, numbers, and special symbols. The first of these must implement the decisions about the structure of words that we made in part 4 of this section. From Figure 11.8 we see that a word token can be any one of an operand, unary operator, or binary operator. The error checking must be adjusted accordingly. Or it may be that the word token does not yet appear in the lexicon, in which case it represents the first appearance of a new parameter, which must be entered accordingly into the lexicon and into the list of parameters. These requirements translate into the following functions, the first of which extracts a word from the input string, and the second processes a word.

```
/* ExtractWord: extract word from str[] starting at pos. */
int ExtractWord(char str[], int pos, char *word)
{
        int i;
        char *pw = word;
```

```
        for (i = pos; isalpha(str[i]) || isdigit(str[i]); i++)
                *word++ = tolower(str[i]);
        *word = '\0';
        if (i - pos > MAXNAME) {
                printf("Word %s was truncated.\n", pw);
                pw[MAXNAME] = '\0';
        }
        return i;                          /* Return next position in str[].        */
}


/* FindWord: find word in str[] starting at pos. */
int FindWord(char str[], int pos)
{
        int h;
        char word[MAXTOKEN];

        pos = ExtractWord(str, pos, word);
        h = hashtable[Hash(word)];
        if (h != -1) {                     /* Token is already defined.            */
                if (Leading())
                        if (Kind(h) == BINARYOP)
                                Error("Binary operator in illegal position");
                        else
                                PutToken(h);
                else
                        if (Kind(h) != BINARYOP)
                                Error("Binary operator expected");
                        else
                                PutToken(h);
        } else {                           /* New name: Set up definition.         */
                if (tokencount >= MAXTOKEN)
                        Error("Too many variables and constants");
                else if (!Leading())
                        Error("Operand follows ) or another operand");
                else {
                        hashtable[h] = ++tokencount;
                        lexicon[tokencount].kind = OPERAND;
                        strcpy(lexicon[tokencount].name, word);
                        if (nparameter >= MAXVARS)
                                Error("Expression has too many parameters");
                        else {
                                parameter[++nparameter] = tokencount;
                                PutToken(tokencount);
                        }
                }
        }
        return pos;
}
```

8. Case: Token is a Number

The treatment of numbers is generally similar to that of variables, but with two differences. One is that we must convert the number to binary so that we can use its value
directly from the lexicon, rather than reading its value into a list of parameters. In converting the number from a character string into binary we use the function atof available
in the C compiler library. The other difference is that there is not necessarily a unique
name for a number. If MAXNAME is large enough so that a string can hold as many digits
as the precision of the machine, then unique names can be assigned, but if not, two
different numbers might get the same name. To guard against this possibility, we shall
regard every occurrence of a number as a newly defined token, and act accordingly. We
do assign the number a name, but only for debugging purposes, and we do not even
enter the name into the hash table.

```
/* FindNumber: find number in str[] starting at pos. */
int FindNumber(char str[], int pos)
{
      if (!Leading())
            Error("Constant in illegal position");

      else if (tokencount >= MAXTOKEN)
            Error("Too many constants and variables");

      else {
            lexicon[++tokencount].kind = OPERAND;
            lexicon[tokencount].info.val = atof(&str[pos]);
            strcpy(lexicon[tokencount].name, "number");
            PutToken(tokencount);
            for (; isdigit(str[pos]) || str[pos] == '.'; pos++)
                  ;
            return pos;
      }
}
```

9. Case: Token is a Special Symbol

The third subsidiary function treats the special symbols. Most of its work is simpler than
the previous cases; it need create no new tokens: If it fails to recognize a symbol then
an error occurs.

The only complication concerns the two symbols '+' and '−', which can be either
unary or binary operators. Fortunately, the function Leading will tell us which case
occurs, since only a unary operator is legal in a leading position. We shall take no
action for a unary '+', since it has no effect, and we replace a unary '−' by our private
notation '@'. Note, however, that this change is local to our program. The user is not
required—or even allowed—to use the symbol '@' or '±' for unary negation.

```
/* FindSymbol: find symbol in str[] starting at pos. */
int FindSymbol(char str[], int pos)
{
      int h, i, k;
      char word[MAXTOKEN];

      for (i = 0; str[pos] != ' '; i++, pos++)
            word[i] = str[pos];
      word[i] = '\0';
      if ((h = hashtable[Hash(word)]) == -1)
            Error("Unrecognized symbol in expression");
      else if (Leading()) {
            if (Kind(h) == RIGHTPAREN)
                  Error("Unexpected right parenthesis");
            else if (Kind(h) != BINARYOP)
                  PutToken(h);
            else {                              /* Handle leading binary operator.    */
                  if (strcmp(word, "+") == 0)
                        ;                       /* Do nothing with unary plus.        */
                  else if (strcmp(word, "-") == 0)
                        PutToken(hashtable[Hash("@")]);
                  else
                        Error("Unexpected binary operator");
            }
      } else {                                  /* not leading position               */
            if (Kind(h) == BINARYOP || Kind(h) == RIGHTPAREN)
                  PutToken(h);
            else
                  Error("Expecting binary operator or )");
      }
      if ((k = Kind(h)) == LEFTPAREN)
            parencount++;
      else if (k == RIGHTPAREN)
            if (--parencount < 0)
                  Error("Too many right parentheses");
      return pos;
}
```

10. Translation into Postfix Form

At the conclusion of function ReadExpression, the input expression has been converted into an infix sequence of tokens, in exactly the form needed by function Translate as derived in Section 11.4. In fact, we now arrive at the key step of our algorithm and can apply the previous work without essential change; the only modifications needed in function Translate are the addition of two variables used to index the input and output expressions, and even this indexing is done only in the straightforward subsidiary functions GetToken and PutToken, which we leave as exercises.

We also omit the auxiliary subprograms Push, Pop, and Priority, since they involve no new problems or ideas.

When function Translate has finished, the expression is a sequence of tokens in postfix form, and can be evaluated efficiently in the next stage. This efficiency, in fact, is important so that a graph can be drawn without undue delay, even though it requires evaluation of the expression for a great many different values.

11.5.5 Evaluating the Expression

1. Reading the Parameters

The first step in evaluating the expression is to establish values for the parameters, if any. This is done only once for each graph, in the straightforward function below.

```
/* ReadParameters: read values for each parameter in the expression. */
void ReadParameters(void)
{
    int i;

    for (i = 0; i <= nparameter; i++) {
        printf("Value for %s? ", lexicon[parameter[i]].name);
        scanf("%lf", &lexicon[parameter[i]].info.val);
    }
}
```

2. Postfix Evaluation

To evaluate the postfix expression, we again use a function developed in the first part of this chapter. Either the recursive or the nonrecursive version of function EvaluatePostfix can be used, again with no significant change (the nonrecursive version requires Push and Pop functions for values). There will likely be no significant difference in running time between the two versions, so it is a matter of taste which to use. Both versions, however, require subsidiary functions GetValue, DoUnary, and DoBinary, to which we now turn.

3. Evaluation of Operands

The first function need only look in the lexicon:

```
/* GetValue: get a value from lexicon[] for token. */
Value_type GetValue(int token)
{
    if (Kind(token) != OPERAND)
        Error("Cannot get value for nonoperand");
    else
        return lexicon[token].info.val;
}
```

4. Operators

Since we have integer codes for all the tokens, the application of operators can be done within a simple switch statement. We leave the one for unary operators as an exercise. For binary operators, we have the function below.

```
/* DoBinary: apply binary operator on x and y; return the result. */
Value_type DoBinary(int token, Value_type x, Value_type y)
{
        switch(token) {
        case 12:                        /* binary plus            */
            return x + y;
        case 13:                        /* binary minus           */
            return x - y;
        case 14:                        /* times                  */
            return x * y;
        case 15:                        /* divide                 */
            if (y != (Value_type) 0)
                return x/y;
            else
                Error("Zero divisor");
        case 16:                        /* modulus operator       */
            if (y != (Value_type) 0)
                return fmod(x, y);
            else
                Error("Zero divisor");
        case 17:                        /* x to the power y       */
            return pow(x, y);
        default:
            printf("%d, invalid Binary token\n", token);
            break;
        }
}
```

Note that we can easily use the structure of this function to improve the error checking usually provided to the user by the operating system. The messages given for division by 0 will likely prove more helpful than something like

> Floating point error,

which may be all that the system normally provides.

11.5.6 Summary

At this point, we have surveyed the entire project. Figure 11.10 lists all the subprograms required for this project, arranged in their proper hierarchy of declaration. Most of these appear in the text, but several have been left as exercises for the programmer to supply. These are marked with a dagger (†) in the right margin.

```
void main(void)
    int Kind(Token_type token)
    Boolean_type Enquire(void)
    void Error(char *msg)                                              /* † */
    void Instruct(void)                                                /* † */
    void DefineTokens(void)                                            /* † */

    void Expression(void)
        int Hash(char *name)
        void MakeHashTable(void)

        void ReadExpression(void)
            void PutToken(Token_type token)        /* into infix expression   † */
            int Leading(void)
            int ExtractWord(char *str, int pos, char *word)
            int FindWord(char *str, int pos)
            int FindNumber(char *str, int pos)
            int FindSymbol(char *str, int pos)

        void Translate(void)
            void Push(int token)                                       /* † */
            void Pop(int *token)                                       /* † */
            void GetToken(int *token)              /* from infix expression   † */
            void PutPostfix(int token)             /* into postfix expression † */
            int Priority(int token)                                    /* † */

    void ReadParameters(void)

    void ReadGraphLimits(Value_type *xlow, Value_type *xhigh,
                         Value_type *incr)

    void Graph(Value_type x, Value_type y)                            /* † */

    Value_type EvaluatePostfix(void)                 /* either recursive or not */
        void EPush(Value_type val)           /* value, for nonrecursive version † */
        void EPop(Value_type *val)           /* value, for nonrecursive version † */
        Value_type Parse(void)                        /* for recursive version */
        void GetPostfix(int *token)            /* from postfix expression † */
        Value_type GetValue(int token)
        Value_type DoUnary(int token, Value_type x)                  /* † */
        Value_type DoBinary(int token, Value_type x, Value_type y)
```

Figure 11.10. Summary of subprograms for GraphFunction

Exercises 11.5

E1. State precisely what changes in the program are needed to add the base 2 logarithm function as an additional unary operator.

E2. Naive users of this program might (if graphing a function involving money) write a dollar sign '$' within the expression. What will the present program do if this happens? What changes are needed so that the program will ignore a '$'?

E3. C or Pascal programmers might accidentally type a semicolon ';' at the end of the expression. What changes are needed so that a semicolon will be ignored at the end of the expression, but will be an error elsewhere?

E4. Explain what changes are needed to allow the program to accept either square brackets [. . .] or curly brackets { . . . } as well as round brackets (. . .). The nesting must be done with the same kind of brackets; that is, an expression of the form (. . . [. . .) . . .] is illegal, but forms like [. . . (. . .) . . . { . . . } . . .] are permissible.

Programming Projects 11.5

P1. Provide the missing subprograms (marked with daggers in Figure 11.10) and implement Program GraphFunction on your computer. Most of the subprograms are straightforward, although several involve graphics and will be system dependent.

P2. Modify the error checking so that several severities of errors are detected and appropriate actions are taken for each. Error severities might include (a) Warning: Continue execution; (b) Bad value: Repeat with new bounds; (c) Bad Expression: Ask user to re-enter the expression; (d) Limit: found an internal limit—Ask the user to try a simpler expression; and (e) Fatal: The program is internally inconsistent.

REFERENCES FOR FURTHER STUDY

The Polish notation is so natural and useful that one might expect its discovery to be hundreds of years ago. It may be surprising to note that it is a discovery of this century:

JAN ŁUKASIEWICZ, *Elementy Logiki Matematyczny*, Warsaw, 1929; English translation: *Elements of Mathematical Logic*, Pergamon Press, 1963.

The development of iterative algorithms to form and evaluate Polish expressions (usually postfix form) can be found in several data structures books, as well as more advanced books on compiler theory. The iterative algorithm for translating an expression from infix to postfix form appears to be due independently to E. W. DIJKSTRA and to C. L. HAMBLIN, and appears in

E. W. DIJKSTRA, "Making a Translator for ALGOL 60", *Automatic Programming Information* number 7 (May 1961); reprinted in *Annual Revue of Automatic Programming* 3 (1963), 347–356.

C. L. HAMBLIN, "Translation to and from Polish notation", *Computer Journal* 5 (1962), 210–213.

The recursive algorithm (section 11.3.6) for evaluation of postfix expressions is derived, albeit from a rather different point of view, and for binary operators only, in

EDWARD M. REINGOLD, "A comment on the evaluation of Polish postfix expressions", *Computer Journal* 24 (1981), 288.

Mathematical Methods

The first part of this appendix supplies several mathematical results used in algorithm analysis. The final two sections (Fibonacci and Catalan numbers) are optional topics for the mathematically inclined reader.

A.1 SUMS OF POWERS OF INTEGERS

The following two formulas are useful in counting the steps executed by an algorithm.

THEOREM A.1

$$1 + 2 + \cdots + n = \frac{n(n+1)}{2}.$$

$$1^2 + 2^2 + \cdots + n^2 = \frac{n(n+1)(2n+1)}{6}.$$

Proof   The first identity has a simple and elegant proof. We let S equal the sum on the left side, write it down twice (once in each direction), and add vertically:

$$
\begin{array}{ccccccccccc}
1 & + & 2 & + & 3 & + & \cdots & + & n-1 & + & n & = & S \\
n & + & n-1 & + & n-2 & + & \cdots & + & 2 & + & 1 & = & S \\
\hline
n+1 & + & n+1 & + & n+1 & + & \cdots & + & n+1 & + & n+1 & = & 2S
\end{array}
$$

There are n columns on the left; hence $n(n + 1) = 2S$ and the identity follows.

The first identity also has the proof without words shown in Figure A.1.

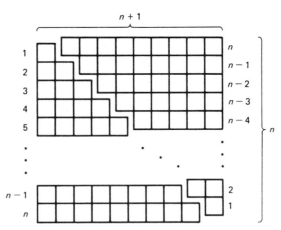

Figure A.1. Geometrical proof for sum of integers

proof by induction   We shall use the method of **mathematical induction** to prove the second identity. This method requires that we start by establishing an initial case, called the **induction base**, which for our formula is the case $n = 1$. In this case the formula becomes

$$1^2 = \frac{1(1+1)(2+1)}{6},$$

which is true, so the induction base is established. Next, using the formula for the case $n - 1$, we must establish it for case n. For case $n - 1$ we thus shall assume

$$1^2 + 2^2 + \cdots + (n-1)^2 = \frac{(n-1)n(2(n-1)+1)}{6}$$

It follows that

$$
\begin{aligned}
1^2 + 2^2 + \cdots + (n-1)^2 + n^2 &= \frac{(n-1)n(2(n-1)+1)}{6} + n^2 \\
&= \frac{2n^3 - 3n^2 + n + 6n^2}{6} \\
&= \frac{n(n+1)(2n+1)}{6},
\end{aligned}
$$

which is the desired result, and the proof by induction is complete.

A convenient shorthand for a sum of the sort appearing in these identities is to use the capital Greek letter sigma

$$\sum$$

summation notation   in front of the typical summand, with the initial value of the index controlling the summation written below the sign, and the final value above. Thus the identities in Theorem A.1 can be written as

$$\sum_{k=1}^{n} k = \frac{n(n+1)}{2}$$

and

$$\sum_{k=1}^{n} k^2 = \frac{n(n+1)(2n+1)}{6}.$$

Two other formulas are also useful, particularly in working with trees.

THEOREM A.2

$$1 + 2 + 4 + \cdots + 2^{m-1} = 2^m - 1.$$

$$1 \times 1 + 2 \times 2 + 3 \times 4 + \cdots + m \times 2^{m-1} = (m-1) \times 2^m + 1.$$

In summation notation these equations are

$$\sum_{k=0}^{m-1} 2^k = 2^m - 1.$$

$$\sum_{k=1}^{m} k \times 2^{k-1} = (m-1) \times 2^m + 1.$$

Proof   The first formula will be proved in a more general form. We start with the following identity, which, for any value of $x \neq 1$, can be verified simply by multiplying both sides by $x - 1$:

$$\frac{x^m - 1}{x - 1} = 1 + x + x^2 + \cdots + x^{m-1}$$

for any $x \neq 1$. With $x = 2$ this expression becomes the first formula.

To establish the second formula we take the same expression in the case of $m + 1$ instead of m :

$$\frac{x^{m+1} - 1}{x - 1} = 1 + x + x^2 + \cdots + x^m$$

for any $x \neq 1$, and differentiate with respect to x:

$$\frac{(x-1)(m+1)x^m - (x^{m+1} - 1)}{(x-1)^2} = 1 + 2x + 3x^2 + \cdots + mx^{m-1}$$

end of proof   for any $x \neq 1$. Setting $x = 2$ now gives the second formula.

Suppose that $|x| < 1$ in the above formulas. As m becomes large, it follows that x^m becomes small, that is

$$\lim_{m \to \infty} x^m = 0.$$

Taking the limit as $m \to \infty$ in the preceding equations gives

THEOREM A.3

If $|x| < 1$ then

infinite series

$$\sum_{k=0}^{\infty} x^k = \frac{1}{1-x}.$$

$$\sum_{k=1}^{\infty} kx^{k-1} = \frac{1}{(1-x)^2}.$$

A.2 LOGARITHMS

The primary reason for using logarithms is to turn multiplication and division into addition and subtraction, and exponentiation into multiplication. Before the advent of pocket calculators, logarithms were an indispensable tool for hand calculation: witness the large tables of logarithms and the once ubiquitous slide rule. Even though we now have other methods for numerical calculation, the fundamental properties of logarithms give them importance that extends far beyond their use as computational tools.

The behavior of many phenomena, first of all, reflects an intrinsically logarithmic structure; that is, by using logarithms we find important relationships that are not oth-

physical measurements

erwise obvious. Measuring the loudness of sound, for example, is logarithmic: if one sound is 10 db (decibels) louder than another, then the actual acoustic energy is 10 times as much. If the sound level in one room is 40 db and it is 60 db in another, then the human perception may be that the second room is half again as noisy as the first, but there is actually 100 times more sound energy in the second room. This phenomenon is why a single violin soloist can be heard above a full orchestra (when playing a different line), and yet the orchestra requires so many violins to maintain a proper balance of sound.

large numbers

Logarithms, secondly, provide a convenient way to handle very large numbers. The scientific notation, where a number is written as a small real number (often in the range from 1 to 10) times a power of 10, is really based on logarithms, since the power of 10 is essentially the logarithm of the number. Scientists who need to use very large numbers (like astronomers, nuclear physicists, and geologists) frequently speak of orders of magnitude, and thereby concentrate on the logarithm of the number.

A logarithmic graph, thirdly, is a very useful device for displaying the properties of a function over a much broader range than a linear graph. With a logarithmic graph, we can arrange to display detailed information on the function for small values of the argument and at the same time give an overall view for much larger values. Logarithmic graphs are especially appropriate when we wish to show percentage changes in a function.

A.2.1 Definition of Logarithms

base

Logarithms are defined in terms of a real number $a > 1$, which is called the **base** of the logarithms. (It is also possible to define logarithms with base a in the range $0 < a < 1$, but doing so would introduce needless complications into our discussion.) For any number $x > 0$, we define $\log_a x = y$ where y is the real number such that $a^y = x$. The logarithm of a negative number, and the logarithm of 0, are not defined.

A.2.2 Simple Properties

From the definition and from the properties of exponents we obtain

$$\log_a 1 = 0,$$
$$\log_a a = 1,$$
$$\log_a x < 0 \quad \text{for all } x \text{ such that } 0 < x < 1.$$
$$0 < \log_a x < 1 \quad \text{for all } x \text{ such that } 1 < x < a.$$
$$\log_a x > 1 \quad \text{for all } x \text{ such that } a < x.$$

The logarithm function has a graph like the one in Figure A.2.

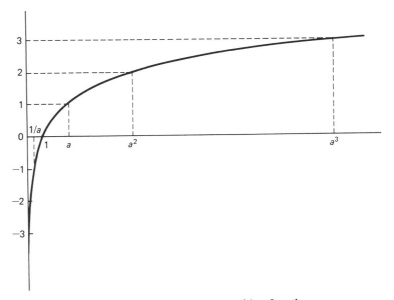

Figure A.2. Graph of the logarithm function

We also obtain the identities

$$\log_a(xy) = (\log_a x) + (\log_a y)$$
$$\log_a(x/y) = (\log_a x) - (\log_a y)$$
$$\log_a x^z = z \log_a x$$
$$\log_a a^z = z$$
$$a^{\log_a x} = x$$

that hold for any positive real numbers x and y, and for any real number z.

From the graph in Figure A.3 you will observe that the logarithm grows more and more slowly as x increases. The graphs of positive powers of x less than 1, such as the square root of x or the cube root of x, also grow progressively more slowly, but never become as flat as the graph of the logarithm. In fact,

As x grows large, $\log x$ grows more slowly than x^c, for any $c > 0$.

A.2.3 Choice of Base

common logarithms

Any real number $a > 1$ can be chosen as the base of logarithms, but certain special choices appear much more frequently than others. For computation and for graphing, the base $a = 10$ is often used, and logarithms with base 10 are called **common** logarithms. In studying computer algorithms, however, base 10 appears infrequently, and we do not often use common logarithms. Instead, logarithms with base 2 appear the most frequently, and we therefore reserve the special symbol

$$\lg x$$

to denote a logarithm with base 2.

A.2.4 Natural Logarithms

In studying mathematical properties of logarithms, and in many problems where logarithms appear as part of the answer, the number that appears as the base is

$$e = 2.718281828459\ldots.$$

Logarithms with base e are called **natural** logarithms. In this book we always denote the natural logarithm of x by

$$\ln x.$$

In many mathematics books, however, other bases than e are rarely used, in which case the unqualified symbol $\log x$ usually denotes a natural logarithm. Figure A.2 shows the graph of logarithms with respect to the three bases 2, e, and 10.

The notation just used for logarithms with different bases is our standard. We thus summarize:

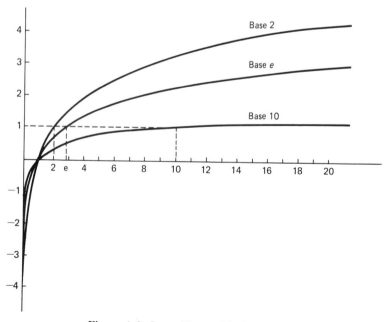

Figure A.3. Logarithms with three bases

> **Convention**
>
> Unless stated otherwise, all logarithms are taken with base 2.
> The symbol lg denotes a logarithm with base 2,
> and the symbol ln denotes a natural logarithm.
> If the base for logarithms is not specified or makes no difference,
> then the symbol log will be used.

The properties of logarithms that make e the natural choice for the base are thoroughly developed as part of the calculus, but we can mention a few of these properties without proof. First, the graph of $\ln x$ has the property that its slope at each point x is $1/x$; that is, the derivative of $\ln x$ is $1/x$ for all real numbers $x > 0$. Second, the natural logarithm satisfies the infinite series

$$\ln(x+1) = x - \frac{x^2}{2} + \frac{x^3}{3} - \frac{x^4}{4} + \cdots$$

for $-1 < x < 1$, but this series requires many terms to give a good approximation and therefore, is not useful directly for computation. It is much better to consider instead the

exponential function   exponential function that "undoes" the logarithm, and that satisfies the series

$$e^x = 1 + x + \frac{x^2}{2!} + \frac{x^3}{3!} + \cdots$$

for all real numbers x. This exponential function e^x also has the important property that it is its own derivative.

A.2.5 Change of Base

Logarithms with respect to one base are closely related to logarithms with respect to any other base. To find this relation, we start with the following relation that is essentially the definition

$$x = a^{\log_a x}$$

for any $x > 0$. Then

$$\log_b x = \log_b a^{\log_a x} = (\log_a x)(\log_b a).$$

The factor $\log_b a$ does not depend on x, but only on the two bases. Therefore:

> *Logarithms can be converted from one base to another simply by multiplying by a constant factor, the logarithm of the first base with respect to the second.*

conversion factors   The most useful numbers for us in this connection are

$$\lg e \approx 1.442695041,$$
$$\ln 2 \approx 0.693147181,$$
$$\ln 10 \approx 2.302585093.$$

A.2.6 Logarithmic Graphs

In a logarithmic scale the numbers are arranged as on a slide rule, with larger numbers closer together than smaller numbers. In this way, equal distances along the scale represent equal *ratios* rather than the equal *differences* represented on an ordinary linear scale. A logarithmic scale should be used when percentage change is important to measure, or when perception is logarithmic. Human perception of time, for example, would seem to be nearly linear in the short term—what happened two days ago is twice as distant as what happened yesterday—but is more nearly logarithmic in the long term: we draw less distinction between one million years ago and two million years ago than we do between ten years ago and one hundred years ago.

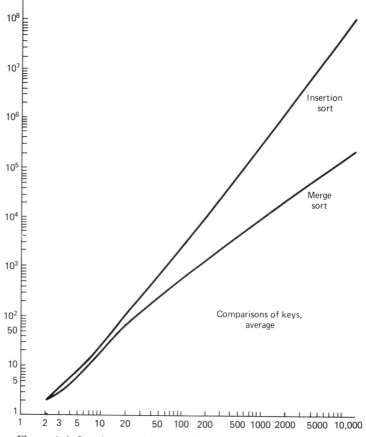

Figure A.4. Log-log graph, comparisons, insertion and merge sorts

log-log graphs   Graphs in which both the vertical and horizontal scales are logarithmic are called ***log-log graphs***. In addition to phenomena where the perception is naturally logarithmic in both scales, log-log graphs are useful to display the behavior of a function over a very wide range. For small values the graph records a detailed view of the function, and for large values a broad view of the function appears on the same graph. For searching and sorting algorithms, we wish to compare methods both for small problems and large problems; hence log-log graphs are appropriate. See Figure A.4.

One observation is worth noting: Any power of x graphs as a straight line with a log-log scale. To prove this, we start with an arbitrary power function $y = x^n$, and take logarithms on both sides, obtaining

$$\log y = n \log x.$$

A log-log graph in x and y becomes a linear graph in $u = \log x$ and $v = \log y$, and the equation becomes $v = nu$ in terms of u and v, which indeed graphs as a straight line.

A.2.7 Harmonic Numbers

As a final application of logarithms, we obtain an approximation to a sum that appears frequently in the analysis of algorithms, especially that of sorting methods. The nth ***harmonic number*** is defined to be the sum

$$H_n = 1 + \frac{1}{2} + \frac{1}{3} + \cdots + \frac{1}{n}$$

of the reciprocals of the integers from 1 to n.

To evaluate H_n we consider the function $1/x$, and the relationship shown in Figure A.5. The area under the step function is clearly H_n, since the width of each step

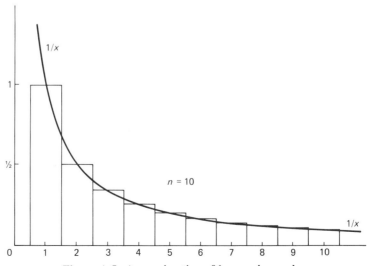

Figure A.5. Approximation of harmonic numbers

is 1, and the height of step k is $1/k$, for each integer k from 1 to n. This area is approximated by the area under the curve $1/x$ from $\frac{1}{2}$ to $n + \frac{1}{2}$. The area under the curve is

$$\int_{\frac{1}{2}}^{n+\frac{1}{2}} \frac{1}{x} dx = \ln(n + \tfrac{1}{2}) - \ln(\tfrac{1}{2}) \approx \ln n + 0.7.$$

When n is large, the fractional term 0.7 is insignificant, and we obtain $\ln n$ as a good approximation to H_n.

By refining this method of approximation by an integral, it is possible to obtain a very much closer approximation to H_n, if such is desired. Specifically,

THEOREM A.4

The harmonic number H_n, $n \geq 1$, satisfies

$$H_n = \ln n + \gamma + \frac{1}{2n} - \frac{1}{12n^2} + \frac{1}{120n^4} - \epsilon,$$

*where $0 < \epsilon < 1/(252n^6)$, and $\gamma \approx 0.577215665$ is known as **Euler's constant**.*

A.3 PERMUTATIONS, COMBINATIONS, FACTORIALS

A.3.1 Permutations

A ***permutation*** of objects is an ordering or arrangement of the objects in a row. If we begin with n different objects, then we can choose any of the n objects to be the first one in the arrangement. There are then $n - 1$ choices for the second object, and since these choices can be combined in all possible ways, the number of choices multiplies. Hence the first two objects may be chosen in $n(n - 1)$ ways. There remain $n - 2$ objects, any one of which may be chosen as the third in the arrangement. Continuing in this way, we see that the number of permutations of n distinct objects is

count of
permutations

$$n! = n \times (n - 1) \times (n - 2) \times \ldots \times 2 \times 1.$$

Objects to permute:	a b c d					
Choose a first:	a b c d	a b d c	a c b d	a c d b	a d b c	a d c b
Choose b first:	b a c d	b a d c	b c a d	b c d a	b d a c	b d c a
Choose c first:	c a b d	c a d b	c b a d	c b d a	c d a b	c d b a
Choose d first:	d a b c	d a c b	d b a c	d b c a	d c a b	d c b a

Figure A.6. Constructing permutations

Note that we have assumed that the objects are all distinct, that is, that we can tell each object from every other one. It is often easier to count configurations of distinct objects than when some are indistinguishable. The latter problem can sometimes be solved by temporarily labeling the objects so they are all distinct, then counting the configurations, and finally dividing by the number of ways in which the labeling could have been done. The special case in the next section is especially important.

A.3.2 Combinations

A **combination** of n objects taken k at a time is a choice of k objects out of the n, without regard for the order of selection. The number of such combinations is denoted either by

$$C(n, k) \text{ or by } \binom{n}{k}.$$

We can calculate $C(n, k)$ by starting with the $n!$ permutations of n objects and form a combination simply by selecting the first k objects in the permutation. The order, however, in which these k objects appear is ignored in determining a combination, so we must divide by the number $k!$ of ways to order the k objects chosen. The order of the $n - k$ objects not chosen is also ignored, so we must also divide by $(n - k)!$. Hence:

count of combinations

$$C(n, k) = \frac{n!}{k!(n-k)!}$$

Objects from which to choose:		a b c d e f		
a b c	a c d	a d f	b c f	c d e
a b d	a c e	a e f	b d e	c d f
a b e	a c f	b c d	b d f	c e f
a b f	a d e	b c e	b e f	d e f

Figure A.7. Combinations of 6 objects, taken 3 at a time

binomial coefficients

The number of combinations $C(n, k)$ is called a **binomial coefficient**, since it appears as the coefficient of $x^k y^{n-k}$ in the expansion of $(x + y)^n$. There are hundreds of different relationships and identities about various sums and products of binomial coefficients. The most important of these can be found in textbooks on elementary algebra and on combinatorics.

A.3.3 Factorials

We frequently use permutations and combinations in analyzing algorithms, and for these applications we must estimate the size of $n!$ for various values of n. An excellent approximation to $n!$ was obtained by JAMES STIRLING in the eighteenth century:

THEOREM A.5

$$n! = \sqrt{2\pi n} \left(\frac{n}{e}\right)^n \left[1 + \frac{1}{12n} + O\left(\frac{1}{n^2}\right)\right].$$

We usually use this approximation in logarithmic form instead:

COROLLARY A.6

$$\ln n! = \left(n + \tfrac{1}{2}\right)\ln n - n + \tfrac{1}{2}\ln(2\pi) + \frac{1}{12n} + O\left(\frac{1}{n^2}\right).$$

Note that, as n increases, the approximation to the logarithm becomes more and more accurate; that is, the difference approaches 0. The difference between the direct approximation to the factorial and $n!$ itself will not necessarily become small (that is, the difference need not go to 0), but the percentage error becomes arbitrarily small (the ratio goes to 1). KNUTH (Volume 1, page 111) gives refinements of Stirling's approximation that are even closer.

The complete proof of Stirling's approximation requires techniques from advanced calculus that would take us too far afield here. We can, however, use a bit of elementary calculus to illustrate the first step of the approximation. First, we take the natural logarithm of a factorial, noting that the logarithm of a product is the sum of the logarithms:

$$\ln n! = \ln(n \times (n-1) \times \cdots \times 1)$$
$$= \ln n + \ln(n-1) + \cdots + \ln 1$$
$$= \sum_{x=1}^{n} \ln x.$$

Next, we approximate the sum by an integral, as shown in Figure A.8.

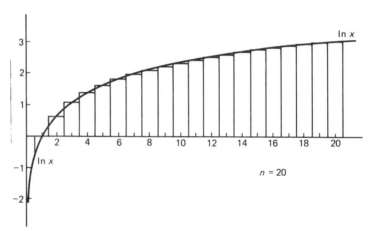

Figure A.8. Approximation of $\ln n!$ by an integral

It is clear from the diagram that the area under the step function, which is exactly $\ln n!$, is approximately the same as the area under the curve, which is

$$\int_{\frac{1}{2}}^{n+\frac{1}{2}} \ln x \, dx = (x \ln x - x) \Big|_{\frac{1}{2}}^{n+\frac{1}{2}}$$
$$= \left(n + \tfrac{1}{2}\right)\ln\left(n + \tfrac{1}{2}\right) - n + \tfrac{1}{2}\ln 2.$$

For large values of n, the difference between $\ln n$ and $\ln(n + \frac{1}{2})$ is insignificant, and hence this approximation differs from Stirling's only by the constant difference between $\frac{1}{2} \ln 2$ (about 0.35) and $\frac{1}{2} \ln(2\pi)$ (about 0.919).

A.4 FIBONACCI NUMBERS

The Fibonacci numbers originated as an exercise in arithmetic proposed by Leonardo Fibonacci in 1202:

rabbits

> *How many pairs of rabbits can be produced from a single pair in a year? We start with a single newly born pair; it takes one month for a pair to mature, after which they produce a new pair each month, and the rabbits never die.*

In month 1, we have only one pair. In month 2, we still have only one pair, but they are now mature. In month 3, they have reproduced, so we now have two pairs. And so it goes. The number F_n of pairs of rabbits that we have in month n satisfies

recurrence relation
$$F_0 = 0, \quad F_1 = 1, \quad \text{and} \quad F_n = F_n - 1 + F_{n-2} \quad \text{for} \quad n \geq 2.$$

This same sequence of numbers, called the **Fibonacci sequence**, appears in many other problems. In Section 9.6.4, for example, F_n appears as the minimum number of nodes in an AVL tree of height n. Our object in this section is to find a formula for F_n.

generating function
We shall use the method of **generating functions**, which is important for many other applications. The generating function is a formal infinite series in a symbol x, with the Fibonacci numbers as coefficients:

$$F(x) = F_0 + F_1 x + F_2 x^2 + \cdots + F_n x^n + \cdots.$$

We do not worry about whether this series converges, or what the value of x might be, since we are not going to set x to any particular value. Instead, we shall only perform formal algebraic manipulations on the generating function.

Next, we multiply by powers of x:

$$\begin{aligned} F(x) &= F_0 + F_1 x + F_2 x^2 + \cdots + F_n x^n + \cdots \\ x F(x) &= \quad\quad F_0 x + F_1 x^2 + \cdots + F_{n-1} x^n + \cdots \\ x^2 F(x) &= \quad\quad\quad\quad F_0 x^2 + \cdots + F_{n-2} x^n + \cdots \end{aligned}$$

and subtract the second two equations from the first:

$$(1 - x - x^2) F(x) = F_0 + (F_1 - F_0)x = x,$$

since $F_0 = 0, F_1 = 1$, and $F_n = F_{n-1} + F_{n-2}$ for all $n \geq 2$. We therefore obtain

$$F(x) = \frac{x}{1 - x - x^2}.$$

The roots of $1 - x - x^2$ are $\frac{1}{2}(-1 \pm \sqrt{5})$. By the method of partial fractions we can thus rearrange the formula for $F(x)$ as:

closed form

$$F(x) = \frac{1}{\sqrt{5}} \left(\frac{1}{1 - \phi x} - \frac{1}{1 - \psi x} \right)$$

where

$$\phi = \tfrac{1}{2}(1 + \sqrt{5}) \text{ and } \psi = 1 - \phi = \tfrac{1}{2}(1 - \sqrt{5}).$$

(Check this equation for $F(x)$ by putting the two fractions on the right over a common denominator.) The next step is to expand the fractions on the right side by dividing their denominators into 1:

$$F(x) = \frac{1}{\sqrt{5}}(1 + \phi x + \phi^2 x^2 + \cdots - 1 - \psi x - \psi^2 x^2 - \cdots).$$

The final step is to recall that the coefficients of $F(x)$ are the Fibonacci numbers, and therefore to equate the coefficients of each power of x on both sides of this equation. We thus obtain

solution

$$F_n = \frac{1}{\sqrt{5}}(\phi^n - \psi^n).$$

Approximate values for ϕ and ψ are

$$\phi \approx 1.618034 \quad \text{and} \quad \psi \approx -0.618034.$$

This surprisingly simple answer to the values of the Fibonacci numbers is interesting in several ways. It is, first, not even immediately obvious why the right side should always be an integer. Second, ψ is a negative number of sufficiently small absolute value that we always have $F_n = \phi^n/\sqrt{5}$ rounded to the nearest integer. Third, the number *golden mean* ϕ is itself interesting. It has been studied since the times of the ancient Greeks—it is often called the **golden mean**—and the ratio of ϕ to 1 is said to give the most pleasing shape of a rectangle.

A.5 CATALAN NUMBERS

The purpose of this section is to count the binary trees with n vertices. We shall accomplish this result via a slightly circuitous route, discovering along the way several other problems that have the same answer. The resulting numbers, called the **Catalan numbers**, are of considerable interest in that they appear in the answers to many apparently unrelated problems.

A.5.1 The Main Result

DEFINITION

For $n \geq 0$, the nth **Catalan number** is defined to be

$$\text{Cat}(n) = \frac{C(2n, n)}{n + 1} = \frac{(2n)!}{(n + 1)!n!}.$$

THEOREM A.7   *The number of distinct binary trees with n vertices, $n \geq 0$, is the nth Catalan number $Cat(n)$.*

A.5.2 The Proof by One-to-One Correspondences

1. Orchards

Let us first recall the one-to-one correspondence (Theorem 10.1) between the binary trees with n vertices and the orchards with n vertices. Hence to count binary trees, we may just as well count orchards.

2. Well-Formed Sequences of Parentheses

Second, let us consider the set of all well-formed sequences of n left parentheses '(' and n right parentheses ')'. A sequence is **well formed** means that, when scanned from left to right, the number of right parentheses encountered never exceeds the number of left parentheses. Thus '((()))' and '()()()' are well formed, but '())(()' is not, nor is '(()', since the total numbers of left and right parentheses in the expression must be equal.

LEMMA A.8   *There is a one-to-one correspondence between the orchards with n vertices and the well-formed sequences of n left parentheses and n right parentheses, $n \geq 0$.*

To define this correspondence, we first recall that an orchard is either empty or is an ordered sequence of ordered trees. We define the **bracketed form** of an orchard to be the sequence of bracketed forms of its trees, written one after the next in the same order as the trees in the orchard. The bracketed form of the empty orchard is empty. We recall also that an ordered tree is defined to consist of its root vertex, together with an orchard of subtrees. We thus define the **bracketed form** of an ordered tree to consist of a left parenthesis '(' followed by the (name of the) root, followed by the bracketed form of the orchard of subtrees, and finally a right parenthesis ')'.

The bracketed forms of several ordered trees and orchards appear in Figure A.9. It should be clear that the mutually recursive definitions above produce a unique bracketed form for any orchard and that the resulting sequence of parentheses is well formed. If, on the other hand, we begin with a well-formed sequence of parentheses, then the outermost pair(s) of parentheses correspond to the tree(s) of an orchard, and within such a pair of parentheses is the description of the corresponding tree in terms of its root and

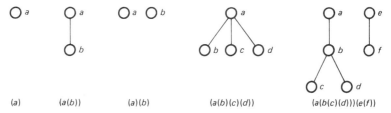

Figure A.9. Bracketed form of orchards

its orchard of subtrees. In this way, we have now obtained a one-to-one correspondence between the orchards with n vertices and the well-formed sequences of n left and n right parentheses.

In counting orchards we are not concerned with the labels attached to the vertices, and hence we shall omit the labels and, with the correspondence outlined above, shall now count well-formed sequences of n left and n right parentheses, with nothing else inside the parentheses.

3. Stack Permutations

Let us note that, by replacing each left parenthesis by $+1$ and each right parenthesis by -1, the well-formed sequences of parentheses correspond to sequences of $+1$ and -1 such that the partial sums from the left are always nonnegative, and the total sum is 0. If we think of each $+1$ as pushing an item onto a stack, and -1 as popping the stack, then the partial sums count the items on the stack at a given time. From this it can be shown that the number of stack permutations of n objects (see the exercises in Section 4.2) is yet another problem for which the Catalan numbers provide the answer. Even more, if we start with an orchard and perform a complete traversal (walking around each branch and vertex in the orchard as though it were a decorative wall), counting $+1$ each time we go down a branch, and -1 each time we go up a branch (with $+1 \ -1$ for each leaf), then we thereby essentially obtain the correspondence with well-formed sequences over again.

4. Arbitrary Sequences of Parentheses

Our final step is to count well-formed sequences of parentheses, but to do this we shall instead count the sequences that are *not* well formed, and subtract from the number of all possible sequences. We need a final one-to-one correspondence:

LEMMA A.9   *The sequences of n left and n right parentheses that are not well formed corre-spond exactly to all sequences of $n-1$ left parentheses and $n+1$ right parentheses (in all possible orders).*

To prove this correspondence, let us start with a sequence of n left and n right parentheses that is not well formed. Let k be the first position in which the sequence goes wrong, so the entry at position k is a right parenthesis, and there is one more right parenthesis than left up through this position. Hence strictly to the right of position k there is one fewer right parenthesis than left. Strictly to the right of position k, then, let us replace all left parentheses by right and all right parentheses by left. The resulting sequence will have $n-1$ left parentheses and $n+1$ right parentheses altogether.

Conversely, let us start with a sequence of $n-1$ left parentheses and $n+1$ right parentheses, and let k be the first position where the number of right parentheses exceeds the number of left (such a position must exist, since there are more right than left parentheses altogether). Again let us exchange left for right and right for left parentheses in the remainder of the sequence (positions after k). We thereby obtain a sequence of n left and n right parentheses that is not well formed and have constructed the one-to-one correspondence as desired.

5. End of the Proof

With all these preliminary correspondences, our counting problem reduces to simple combinations. The number of sequences of $n - 1$ left and $n + 1$ right parentheses is the number of ways to choose the $n - 1$ positions occupied by left parentheses from the $2n$ positions in the sequence, that is, the number is $C(2n, n - 1)$. By Lemma A.9, this number is also the number of sequences of n left and n right parentheses that are not well formed. The number of all sequences of n left and n right parentheses is similarly $C(2n, n)$, so the number of well-formed sequences is

$$C(2n, n) - C(2n, n - 1)$$

which is precisely the nth Catalan number.

Because of all the one-to-one correspondences, we also have:

COROLLARY A.10   *The number of well-formed sequences of n left and n right parentheses, the number of permutations of n objects obtainable by a stack, the number of orchards with n vertices, and the number of binary trees with n vertices are all equal to the nth Catalan number* Cat(n).

A.5.3 History

It is, surprisingly, for none of the above questions that Catalan numbers were first discovered, but rather for questions in geometry. Specifically, Cat(n) provides the number of ways to divide a convex polygon with $n + 2$ sides into triangles by drawing $n - 1$ non-intersecting diagonals. See Figure A.10. This problem seems to have been proposed by L. EULER and solved by J. A. V. SEGNER in 1759. It was then solved again by E. CATALAN in 1838. Sometimes, therefore, the resulting numbers are called the *Segner numbers*, but more often they are called *Catalan numbers*.

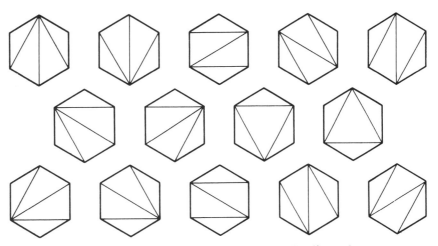

Figure A.10. Triangulations of a hexagon by diagonals

A.5.4 Numerical Results

We conclude this section with some indications of the sizes of Catalan numbers. The first twenty values are given in Figure A.11.

n	$\text{Cat}(n)$	n	$\text{Cat}(n)$
0	1	10	16,796
1	1	11	58,786
2	2	12	208,012
3	5	13	742,900
4	14	14	2,674,440
5	42	15	9,694,845
6	132	16	35,357,670
7	429	17	129,644,790
8	1,430	18	477,638,700
9	4,862	19	1,767,263,190

Figure A.11. The first 20 Catalan numbers

For larger values of n, we can obtain an estimate on the size of the Catalan numbers by using Stirling's approximation. When it is applied to each of the three factorials, and the result is simplified, we obtain

$$\text{Cat}(n) \quad \approx \quad \frac{4^n}{(n+1)\sqrt{\pi n}}$$

When compared with the exact values in Figure A.11, this estimate gives a good idea of the accuracy of Stirling's approximation. When $n = 10$, for example, the estimated value for the Catalan number is 17,007, compared to the exact value of 16,796.

REFERENCES FOR FURTHER STUDY

More extensive discussions of proof by induction, the summation notation, sums of powers of integers, and logarithms appear in many algebra textbooks. These books will also provide examples and exercises on these topics. An excellent discussion of the importance of logarithms and of the subtle art of approximate calculation is

logarithms   N. DAVID MERMIN, "Logarithms!", *American Mathematical Monthly* 87 (1980), 1–7.

Several interesting examples of estimating large numbers and thinking of them logarithmically are discussed in

DOUGLAS R. HOFSTADTER, "Metamagical themas" (regular column), *Scientific American* 246, no. 5 (May 1982), 20–34.

harmonic numbers   Several surprising and amusing applications of harmonic numbers are given in the non-technical article

> RALPH BOAS, "Snowfalls and elephants, pop bottles and π", *Two–Year College Math. Journal* 11 (1980), 82–89.

The detailed estimates for both harmonic numbers and factorials (Stirling's approximation) are quoted from KNUTH, Volume 1, pp. 108–111, where detailed proofs may be found. KNUTH, Volume 1, is also an excellent source for further information regarding permutations, combinations, and related topics. The original reference for Stirling's approximation is

factorials   JAMES STIRLING, *Methodus Differentialis* (1730), p. 137.

combinatorics   The branch of mathematics concerned with the enumeration of various sets or classes of objects is called ***combinatorics***. This science of counting can be introduced on a very simple level, or studied with great sophistication. Two elementary textbooks containing many further developments of the ideas introduced here are

> GERALD BERMAN and K. D. FRYER, *Introduction to Combinatorics*, Academic Press, 1972.

> ALAN TUCKER, *Applied Combinatorics*, John Wiley, New York, 1980.

Fibonacci numbers   The derivation of the Fibonacci numbers will appear in almost any book on combinatorics, as well as in KNUTH, Volume 1, pp. 78–86, who includes some interesting history as well as many related exercises. The appearance of Fibonacci numbers in nature is illustrated in

> PETER STEVENS, *Patterns in Nature*, Little, Brown, Boston, 1974.

Many hundreds of other properties of Fibonacci numbers have been and continue to be found; these are often published in the research journal *Fibonacci Quarterly*.

Catalan numbers   A derivation of the Catalan numbers (applied to triangulations of convex polygons) appears in the first of the above books on combinatorics (pp. 230–232). KNUTH, Volume 1, pp. 385–406, enumerates several classes of trees, including the Catalan numbers applied to binary trees. A list of 46 references providing both history and applications of the Catalan numbers appears in

> W. G. BROWN, "Historical note on a recurrent combinatorial problem", *American Mathematical Monthly* 72 (1965), 973–977.

The following article expounds many other applications of Catalan numbers:

> MARTIN GARDNER, "Mathematical games" (regular column), *Scientific American* 234, no. 6 (June, 1976), 120–125.

The original references for the derivation of the Catalan numbers are:

> J. A. V. SEGNER, "Enumeratio modorum, quibus figuræ planæ rectilinæ per diagonales dividuntur in triangula", *Novi Commentarii Academiæ Scientiarum Imperialis Petropolitanæ* 7 (1758–1759), 203–209.

> E. CATALAN, "Solution nouvelle de cette question: un polygone étant donné, de combien de manieres peut-on le partager en triangles au moyen de diagonales?", *Journal de Mathématiques Pures et Appliquées* 4 (1839), 91–94.

Removal of Recursion

In some contexts (like FORTRAN 77 and COBOL) it is not possible to use recursion. This appendix discusses methods for reformulating algorithms to remove recursion. First comes a general method that can always be used, but is quite complicated and yields a program whose structure may be obscure. Next is a simpler transformation that, although not universally applicable, covers many important applications. This transformation yields, as an example, an efficient nonrecursive version of quicksort. A nonrecursive version of mergesort is also developed to illustrate other techniques for recursion removal. Finally this appendix studies threaded binary trees, which provide all the capabilities of ordinary binary trees without reference to recursion or stacks.

Although the methods developed in this appendix can be used with any higher-level algorithmic language, they are most appropriate in contexts that do not allow recursion. When recursion is available, the techniques described here are unlikely to save enough computer time or space to prove worthwhile or to compensate for the additional programming effort that they demand. Although, for the sake of clarity, the sample programs are written in C, they are designed to facilitate translation into languages not allowing recursion.

prerequisite   Section 8.5 (Principles of Recursion) should be studied before this appendix.

B.1 GENERAL METHODS FOR REMOVING RECURSION

Recall from Section 8.5.2 that each call to a subprogram (recursive or not) requires that the subprogram have a storage area where it can keep its local variables, its calling parameters, and its return address (that is, the location of the statement following the one that made the call). In a recursive implementation, the storage areas for subprograms are kept in a stack. Without recursion, one permanent storage area is often reserved for each subprogram, so that an attempt to make a recursive call would change the values in the storage area, thereby destroying the ability of the outer call to complete its work and return properly.

To simulate recursion we must therefore eschew use of the local storage area reserved for the subprogram, and instead set up a stack, in which we shall keep all the local variables, calling parameters, and the return address for the function.

B.1.1 Preliminary Assumptions

It is frequently true that stating a set of rules in the most general possible form requires so many complicated special cases that it obscures the principle ideas. Such is indeed true for recursion removal, so we shall instead develop the methods only for a special case and separately explain how the methods can be applied to all other categories of subprograms.

direct and indirect recursion
Recursion is said to be ***direct*** if a subprogram calls itself; it is ***indirect*** if there is a sequence of more than one subprogram call that eventually calls the first subprogram, such as when function A calls function B, which in turn calls A. We shall first assume that the recursion is direct, that is, we deal only with a single subprogram that calls itself.

For simplicity we shall, second, assume that we are dealing with a function with no return value (void). This is no real restriction, since any function can be turned into a void function by including one extra calling parameter that will be used to hold the output value. This output parameter is then used instead of the function value in the calling program.

parameters
We have used two kinds of parameters for functions: those called by value and those called by address (reference). Parameters called by value are copied into local variables within the function that are discarded when the function returns; parameters called by address exist in the calling program, so that the function refers to them there. The same observations are true of all other variables used by the function: they are either declared locally within the function or exist outside, globally to the function. Parameters and variables in the first category are created anew every time the function is started; hence, before recursion they must be pushed onto a stack so that they can be restored after the function returns. Parameters and variables of the second category must not be stacked, since every time the function changes them it is assumed that the global variables have been changed, and if they were restored to previous values the work of the function would be undone.

If the function has parameters called by address (arrays in C), then we shall assume that the actual parameters are exactly the same in every call to the function. This is again no real restriction, since we can introduce an additional global variable, say, t, and instead of writing P(x) and P(y) for two different calls to the function (where x, y, and t are called by address), we can write

$$copy \text{ x } to \text{ t;}\quad \text{P(t)};\quad copy \text{ t } to \text{ x;}$$

for one and

$$copy \text{ y } to \text{ t;}\quad \text{P(t)};\quad copy \text{ t } to \text{ y;}$$

for the other.

B.1.2 General Rules

We now take P to satisfy these assumptions; that is, P is a directly recursive function for which the actual parameters called by address in P are the same in every call to

P. We can translate P into a nonrecursive function by including instructions in P to accomplish the following tasks. These steps involve insertion of statement labels and goto statements as well as other constructions that will make the result appear messy. At the moment, however, we are proceeding mechanically, essentially playing compiler, and doing these steps is the easiest way to go, given that the original function works properly. Afterward, we can clean and polish the function, making it into a form that will be easier to follow and be more efficient.

initialization

1. Declare a stack (or stacks) that will hold all local variables, parameters called by value, and flags to specify whence P was called (if it calls itself from several places). As the first executed statement of P, initialize the stack(s) to be empty by setting the counter to 0. The stack(s) and the counter are to be treated as global variables, even though they are declared in P.

2. To enable each recursive call to start at the beginning of the original function P, the first executable statement of the original P should have a label attached to it.

recursive call

The following steps should be done at each place inside P where P calls itself.

3. Make a new statement label L_i (if this is the ith place where P is called recursively) and attach the label to the first statement after the call to P (so that a return can be made to this label).

4. Push the integer i onto the stack. (This will convey on return that P was called from the ith place.)

5. Push all local variables and parameters called by value onto the stack.

6. Set the dummy parameters called by value to the values given in the new call to P.

7. Replace the call to P with a goto to the statement label at the start of P.

At the end of P (or wherever P returns to its calling program), the following steps should be done.

return

8. If the stack is empty then the recursion has finished; make a normal return.

9. Otherwise, pop the stack to restore the values of all local variables and parameters called by value.

10. Pop an integer i from the stack and use this to go to the statement labeled L_i. In FORTRAN this can be done with a *computed goto* statement, in BASIC with an on … goto, and in C with a switch statement.

By mechanically following the preceding steps we can remove direct recursion from any function.

B.1.3 Indirect Recursion

The case of indirect recursion requires slightly more work, but follows the same idea. Perhaps the conceptually simplest way (which avoids goto's from one function to another) is first to rename variables as needed to ensure that there are no conflicts of names of local variables or parameters between any of the mutually recursive functions, and then write them one after another, not as separate functions, but as sections of a longer one. The foregoing steps can then be carried through for each of the former functions, and the goto's used according to which function is calling which. Separate stacks can be used for different functions, or all the data can be kept on one stack, whichever is more convenient.

B.1.4 Towers of Hanoi

As an illustration of the above method, let us write out a nonrecursive version of the program for the Towers of Hanoi, as it was developed in Section 8.1, to which you should compare the following program. This program is obtained as a straightforward application of the rules just formulated. You should compare the result with the original version.

```
/* Move: moves n disks from a to b using c for temporary storage */
/* nonrecursive version */
void Move(int n, int a, int b, int c)
{
        Stack_type stack;
        int return_address;              /* selects place to return after recursion  */
        stack.count = 0;                 /* Initialize the stack.                     */
L0:                                      /* marks the start of the original recursive function */
        if (n > 0) {
                Push(n, a, b, c, 1, &stack);
                n--;
                Swap(&b, &c);
                goto L0;
L1:                                      /* marks the return from the first recursive call */
                printf("Move a disk from %2d to %2d\n", a, b);
                Push(n, a, b, c, 2, &stack);
                n--;
                Swap(&a, &c);
                goto L0;
        }
L2:                                      /* marks the return from the second recursive call */
        if (stack.count > 0) {
                Pop(&n, &a, &b, &c, &return_address, &stack);
                switch (return_address) {
                case 1 :
                        goto L1;
                        break;
                case 2 :
                        goto L2;
                        break;
                }
        }
}
```

first recursive call

second recursive call

This version of function Move uses several auxiliary functions, as follows:

```
void Push (int n, int a, int b, int c, int address, Stack_type *stack)
{
      int i = stack->count;

      stack->entry [i] .n = n;
      stack->entry [i] .a = a;
      stack->entry [i] .b = b;
      stack->entry [i] .c = c;
      stack->entry [i] .address = address;
      stack->count++;
}
void Pop (int *n, int *a, int *b, int *c, int *address, Stack_type *stack)
{
      int i = --stack->count;

      *n = stack->entry [i] .n;
      *a = stack->entry [i] .a;
      *b = stack->entry [i] .b;
      *c = stack->entry [i] .c;
      *address = stack->entry [i] .address;
}
void Swap (int *x, int *y)
{
      int tmp;

      tmp = *x;
      *x = *y;
      *y = tmp;
}
```

As you can see, a short and easy recursive function has turned into a complicated mess. The function even contains branches that jump from outside into the middle of the block controlled by an if statement, an occurrence that should always be regarded as very poor style, if not an actual error. Fortunately, much of the complication results only from the mechanical way in which the translation was done. We can now make several simplifications.

Note what happens when the function recursively returns from a call at the second place (return_address = 2). After the stack is popped it branches to statement L2, which does nothing except run down to pop the stack again. Thus what was popped off the stack the first time is lost, so that there was no need to push it on in the first place. In the original recursive function, the second recursive call to Move occurs at the end of the function. At the end of any function its local variables are discarded; thus there was no need to preserve all the local variables before the second recursive call to Move, since they will be discarded when it returns in any case.

tail recursion   This situation is ***tail recursion***, and from this example we see graphically the unnecessary work that tail recursion can induce. Before translating any program to nonrecursive form, we should be careful to apply Theorem 8.2 and remove the tail recursion.

B.1.5 Further Simplifications

While we are considering simplifications, we can make a more general observation about local variables and parameters called by value. In a function being transformed to nonrecursive form, these will need to be pushed onto the stack before a recursive call only when they have both been set up before the call and will be used again after the call, with the assumption that they have unchanged values. Some variables may have been used only in sections of the function not involving recursive calls, so there is no need to preserve their values across a recursive call. For example, the index variable of a for loop might be used to control loops either before or after a recursive call or even both before and after, but if the index variable is initialized when a loop starts after the call, there is no need to preserve it on the stack. On the other hand, if the recursive call is in the middle of a for loop, then the index variable must be stacked. By applying these principles we can simplify the resulting program and conserve stack space, and thereby perform optimizations of the program that a recursive compiler would likely not do, since it would probably preserve all local variables on the stack.

B.2 RECURSION REMOVAL BY FOLDING

B.2.1 Program Schemata

We can now further simplify our method for removing recursion: a function that includes a recursive call from only one place will not need to include flags to show where to return, since there is only one possibility. In many cases, we can also rearrange parts of the program to clarify it by removing goto statements.

    After removal of the tail recursion, the second recursive version of the function Move for the Towers of Hanoi, as given in Section 8.5.3, is a program of the general schema:

recursive schema
```
void P (/* parameters */)              /* recursive version              */
{
    /* local declarations to be inserted here */

    while ( ! termination) {
        Block A;                       /* first part of program; empty for example */
        P;                             /* only recursive call to function itself    */
        Block B;                       /* next part of program            */
    }
    Block C;                           /* final part of program; empty for our example */
}
```

Our general rules presented in the last section will translate this schema into the nonrecursive form:

first nonrecursive schema

```
void P (/* parameters */)              /* preliminary nonrecursive version      */
{
    /* local declarations to be inserted here */
    /* Declaration of stack goes here. */

    Set stack to be empty;
L0:
    while (!termination) {
        Block A;                       /* first part of program                 */
        Push data onto stack and change parameters;
        goto L0;
L1:
        Block B;                       /* next part of program                  */
    }
    Block C;                           /* final part of program                 */
    if (stack not empty) {
        Pop data from stack;
        goto L1;
    }
}
```

If we terminate the while loop after the line changing the parameters, then we can eliminate the goto L0. Doing this will require that when Block B is complete, we go back to the while statement. By moving the part of the schema that pops the stack to the front of Block B, we no longer need the other goto. On the first time through, the stack will be empty, so the popping section will be skipped. These steps can all be accomplished by enclosing the function in a statement

$$\text{do \{ ... \} while (stack not empty);}$$

We thus obtain:

folded nonrecursive schema

```
void P (/* parameters */)              /* nonrecursive version                  */
{
    /* local declarations to be inserted here */
    /* Declaration of stack goes here. */

    Set stack to be empty;
    do {
        if (stack not empty) {
            Pop data from stack;
            Block B;                   /* next part of program                  */
        }
        while (!termination) {
            Block A;                   /* first part of program                 */
            Push data onto stack and change parameters;
        }
        Block C;                       /* final part of program                 */
    } while (stack not empty);
}
```

This rearrangement is essentially "folding" the loop around the recursive call. Thus the part coming after the recursive call now appears at the top of the program instead of the bottom.

B.2.2 Proof of the Transformation

Since deriving the above rearrangement has required several steps, let us now pause to provide a formal verification that the changes we have made are correct.

THEOREM B.1   *The recursive function P of the form given previously and the folded, nonrecursive version of P both accomplish exactly the same steps.*

To prove the theorem, we shall trace through the recursive and the folded nonrecursive versions of P and show that they perform exactly the same sequence of blocks A, B, and C. The remaining parts of both versions do only bookkeeping, so that if the same sequence of the blocks is done, then the same task will be accomplished. In tracing through the programs, it will help to note that there are two ways to call a recursive function: either from outside, or from within itself. We refer to these as ***external*** *external and* and ***internal*** calls, respectively. These two forms of call are indistinguishable for the *internal calls* recursive version, but are quite different for the nonrecursive form. An external call starts at the beginning of the function and finishes at the end. An internal call starts after the data are pushed onto the stack and the parameters are changed and finishes when the line is reached that pops the stack.

proof by induction: We shall prove the theorem by using mathematical induction on the height of the *initial case* recursion tree corresponding to a given call to P. The starting point is the case when P is called with the termination condition already true, so that no recursion takes place (the height of the tree is 0). In this case the recursive version performs Block C once, and nothing else is done. For the nonrecursive version we consider the two kinds of calls separately. If the call is external, then the stack is empty, so that the if statement does nothing, and the while statement also does nothing since the termination condition is assumed to be true. Thus only Block C is done, and since the stack is empty, the function terminates. Now suppose that the call to P is internal. Then P has arrived at the line that pushes the stack (so it is not empty). Since the termination condition is true, the while loop now terminates, and Block C is done. Since the stack is not empty, the do ... while loop next proceeds to the line that pops the stack, and this line corresponds to returning from the internal call. Thus in every case when the recursion tree has height 0, only Block C is done once.

induction step For the induction step we consider a call to P where the recursion tree has height $k > 0$, and by induction we assume that all calls whose trees have height less than k will translate correctly into nonrecursive form. Let r be the number of times that the while loop iterates in the call to P under consideration.

This situation is illustrated in the sample recursion tree shown in Figure B.1. Each node in this tree should be considered as expanded to show the sequence of blocks being performed at each stage. The tree also, of course, shows when the stack will be pushed and popped: Consider traversing the tree by walking around it in a counterclockwise direction following each edge both down and up and going around each node. It is

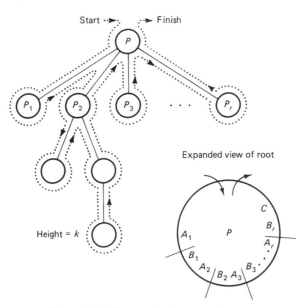

Figure B.1. Traversal of a recursion tree

precisely as a branch is traversed going downward that the stack is pushed, and as we return up a branch the stack is popped.

The recursive version thus performs a sequence of blocks and calls:

$$A_1 \quad P_1 \quad B_1 \qquad A_2 \quad P_2 \quad B_2 \quad \ldots \quad A_r \quad P_r \quad B_r \quad C$$

where the subscripts specify only the iteration at which the block or call is done. The calls to P denoted $P_1, P_2, \ldots, P_r$ all have recursion trees of heights strictly less than k (at least one has height exactly $k - 1$), so by induction hypothesis the sequence of blocks embedded in these calls will be the same for the recursive and nonrecursive versions (provided that we can show that the sequence of outer blocks is the same, so that the calling parameters will be the same). In tracing through the nonrecursive function, we again consider the two kinds of calls separately.

external call   If the call is external, then the stack is initially empty, so the while loop begins iterating. First Block A is done, and then an internal call to P is started by pushing the stack. The corresponding return occurs when the stack is eventually popped and becomes empty again. The sequence of blocks and calls occurring in the meantime all correspond to the recursive call P_1, and by induction hypothesis correspond correctly to the recursive version. When the stack is popped and empty, then Block B is done and we reach the while statement to begin the second iteration. The program thus continues, with each iteration starting with Block A, then an internal call, then Block B. After r iterations the total sequence of blocks will have been the same as in the recursive version, and therefore the termination condition will become true for the first time, and so the while loop will be skipped. Block C is then done, and since the stack is empty, the function terminates. Hence the total sequence of blocks is the same as in the recursive version.

internal call   Finally consider that the call (with tree of height k) is internal. The call then begins where the stack is pushed, so it then has $s > 0$ sets of data. Next Block A is done, and another internal call instituted, that includes all steps until the stack is popped and again has exactly s sets of data. Next Block B is done, and the iterations continue as in the previous case, except that now the returns from internal calls that interest us are those leaving s sets of data on the stack. After r iterations the termination condition becomes true, so the while loop terminates, and Block C is done. The stack has $s > 0$ entries, so the function now moves to the line that pops the stack, which constitutes the return from the internal call that we have been tracing. Thus in every case the sequence

end of proof   of blocks done is the same, and the proof of the theorem is complete.

B.2.3 Towers of Hanoi: The Final Version

With the method of folding that we have now developed, we can now write our final nonrecursive version of the program for the Towers of Hanoi, a version that is much clearer than the first nonrecursive one, although still not as natural as the recursive program.

```c
/* Move: moves n disks from a to b using c for temporary storage */
/* folded nonrecursive version */
void Move (int n, int a, int b, int c)
{
        Stack_type stack;
        stack.count = 0;
        do {
            if (stack.count != 0) {
                    Pop( &n, &a, &b, &c, &stack);
                    printf("Move a disk from %2d to %2d\n", a, b);
                    n−−;
                    Swap( &a, &c);
            }
            while (n > 0) {
                    Push(n, a, b, c, &stack);
                    n−−;
                    Swap( &b, &c);
            }
        } while (stack.count > 0);
}
```

Exercises   **E1.** Remove the tail recursion from the algorithm for preorder traversal of a linked binary
B.2   tree (Section 9.3). Show that the resulting program fits the schema of Theorem B.1, and thereby devise a nonrecursive algorithm, using a stack, that will traverse a binary tree in preorder.

E2. Repeat Exercise E1 for inorder traversal.

E3. Devise a nonrecursive algorithm, using one or more stacks, that will traverse a linked binary tree in postorder. Why is this project more complicated than the preceding two exercises?

E4. Consider a pair of mutually recursive functions P and Q that have the following schemata.

```
void P(void)                                      void Q(void)
{ /* local declarations for P       */            { /* local declarations for Q       */
    while (!termP) {                                  while (!termQ) {
        Block A;                                          Block X;
        Q();                                              P();
        Block B;                                          Block Y;
    }                                                 }
    Block C;                                          Block Z;
}                                                 }
```

Assume that there are no conflicts of names between local variables or dummy parameters in P and in Q.

a. Write a nonrecursive function made up from the blocks in P and Q that will perform the same action as a call to P.

b. Prove your translation correct in a way similar to the proof of Theorem B.1.

Programming Project B.2

P1. Show that the program Queen from Section 8.2.2 has the schema needed for Theorem B.1, and apply folding to remove the recursion. Run both the recursive and nonrecursive versions to see which is faster.

B.3 NONRECURSIVE QUICKSORT

Because of its importance as an efficient sorting algorithm for contiguous lists, we shall devise a nonrecursive version of quicksort, as an application of the methods of the last section. Before proceeding, you should briefly review Section 7.8, from which we take all the notation.

The first observation to make about the original recursive function Sort written for quicksort is that its second call is tail recursion, which can easily be removed. We thus obtain the following intermediate form.

tail recursion removed

```
void Sort(List_type *list, int low, int high)  /* Sort: removed tail recursion       */
{
    int pivotloc;

    while (low < high) {
        pivotloc = Partition(list, low, high);
        Sort(list, low, pivotloc - 1);
        low = pivotloc + 1;
    }
}
```

This function is in precisely the form covered by Theorem B.1, so it can be folded to remove the recursive call. The only variables needed after the recursive call are low and pivotloc, so only these two variables need to be stacked.

Before we proceed with the program transformation, let us note that, in doing the sorting, it really makes no difference which half of the list is sorted first. The calling parameters to be stacked mark the bounds of sublists yet to be sorted. It turns out that it is better to put the longer sublist on the stack and immediately sort the shorter one. The *stack space*

longer sublist along with the pivot will account for at least half of the items. Hence at each level of recursion, the number of items remaining to be sorted is reduced by half or more, and therefore the number of items on the stack is guaranteed to be no more than $\lg n$. In this way, even though quicksort has a worst-case running time that is $O(n^2)$, the extra space needed for its stack can be guaranteed not to exceed $O(\log n)$.

This decision to stack the larger sublist at each stage does not affect the application of folding, but only introduces an if statement at the appropriate point. We thus arrive at the following nonrecursive version of quicksort:

```
#define MAXSTACK 20                   /* allows sorting up to 1,000,000 items   */

void NRQuickSort (List_type *list)    /* NRQuickSort: nonrecursive quicksort    */
{
      int low, high;                  /* bounds of list being sorted            */
      int pivotloc;
      int lowstack [MAXSTACK];        /* Declare two arrays for the stack.      */
      int highstack [MAXSTACK];
      int nstack = 0;

      low = 1;
      high = list->count;
      do {
            if (nstack > 0) {          /* Pop the stack.                        */
                  nstack--;
                  low = lowstack [nstack];
                  high = highstack [nstack];
            }
            while (low < high) {
                  pivotloc = Partition (list, low, high);
                  /* Push larger sublist onto stack, and do smaller. */
                  if (pivotloc - low < high - pivotloc) {
                  /* Stack right sublist and do left. */
                        if (nstack >= MAXSTACK)
                              Error ("overflow");
                        lowstack [nstack] = pivotloc + 1;
                        highstack [nstack] = high;
                        nstack++;
                        high = pivotloc - 1;
                  } else {             /* Stack left sublist and do right.      */
                        if (nstack >= MAXSTACK)
                              Error ("overflow");
                        lowstack [nstack] = low;
                        highstack [nstack] = pivotloc - 1;
                        nstack++;
                        low = pivotloc + 1;
                  }
            }
      } while (nstack != 0);
}
```

B.4 STACKLESS RECURSION REMOVAL: MERGESORT

This section discusses point 5 of the guidelines for using recursion in Section 8.5.5; that is, the translation of a program into nonrecursive form by exploiting the regularity of its recursion tree, thereby avoiding the need to use a stack. The program we develop in this section is not likely to prove a great improvement over the recursive version, since the stack space saved is only $O(\lg n)$. It is primarily a matter of taste which version to use.

Mergesort is one of the most efficient sorting methods we have studied; it and heapsort are the only ones we considered for which the number of comparisons in the worst case, as well as in the average case, is $O(n \log n)$. Mergesort is therefore a good choice for large sorting problems when time constraints are critical. The recursion used in mergesort, however, may entail some overhead costs that can be avoided by rewriting mergesort in nonrecursive form.

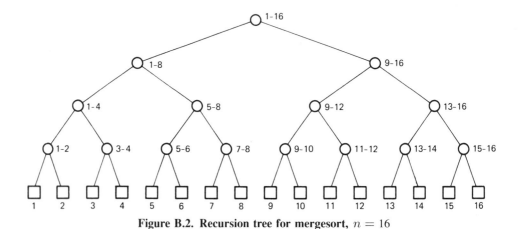

Figure B.2. Recursion tree for mergesort, $n = 16$

Let us begin by considering the tree of recursive calls that mergesort will make in sorting a list; this tree for $n = 16$ is drawn in Figure B.2. In the recursive formulation of mergesort, we begin at the root of the tree and divide the list in half. We then look at the left list (move to the left subtree) and repeat the division. Afterward, we look at the right sublist and move to the right subtree. In other words,

Recursion in mergesort performs a preorder traversal of the tree.

Now let us determine the order in which the merges are actually done. No sublists are actually merged until the list has been divided all the way down to sublists of one element each. The first two one-element sublists, represented as the leftmost two leaves in the tree, are then merged. Then the next two one-element sublists are merged, and afterward the resulting two-element sublists are merged into a four-element sublist. In this way the process continues building small sublists into larger ones. In fact,

> *The order in which the merges are actually done constitutes a postorder traversal of the tree.*

traversal orders   Translating mergesort into nonrecursive form amounts to rewriting the algorithm to perform a postorder traversal of the tree instead of a preorder traversal. We could, of course, use a stack to assist with the postorder traversal, but instead we shall take advantage of the fact that, when n is a power of 2, the tree has a completely symmetric structure. Using this structure we can obtain a nonrecursive traversal algorithm with no need for a stack. The idea that we shall employ is the same as that used in Section 9.5, where we developed an algorithm for building elements from an ordered list into a balanced binary search tree. In fact, the algorithm we now need differs from that of Section 9.5 only in that we now wish to make a postorder traversal of the tree, whereas in Section 9.5 we did an inorder traversal.

We shall also find that, when n is not a power of 2 (as in Section 9.5), few further difficulties arise. The present algorithm will also have the advantage over the recursive form, that it is not necessary to know or calculate in advance how many items are in the list being sorted. (Recall that our original recursive version of mergesort spent significant time finding the center of a linked list.)

To design our algorithm, let us imagine receiving the elements of the unsorted list one at a time, and as each element arrives, let us continue the postorder traversal of the tree by doing as many merges as possible with the elements that we have available. When only the first element has arrived, no merge can be done; when the second one comes, the first two sublists of size 1 will be merged. Element 3 does not induce any merges, but element 4 is first compared with element 3, and the resulting two-element sublist is then merged with the first two-element sublist. Continuing in this way, we see that element 5 does not induce any merge, element 6 induces only 1, element 7 none, and element 8 induces 3 merges. Further study of the tree will convince you that:

> *When mergesort processes the item in position c of its input, then the number of times that sublists are merged before proceeding to the next element is exactly the highest power of 2 that divides c.*

In writing our algorithm we shall, as in Section 7.7, consider only a version sorting linked lists. In this way, we can use the same function presented in Section 7.7 to merge two sorted sublists, and we need not consider the auxiliary space or complicated algorithms needed to accomplish merging in contiguous lists.

As we progress through the tree, we shall find that at various stages several sublists will have been constructed that have not yet been merged with each other. We shall keep track of these sublists by using an auxiliary array of pointers. At any point in the process, there can be at most one such sublist corresponding to each level in the tree; hence the size of this array grows only logarithmically with the length of the list being sorted, and the amount of additional memory that it requires is inconsequential.

The main part of our algorithm can now be described completely: we shall traverse the linked list of input and use the function Power2(c) (taken from Section 9.5) to determine the number mergecount of times that sublists will be merged. We do these merges using the sublists whose headers are in the auxiliary array. After the appropriate merges are made, a pointer to the resulting sorted sublist is placed in location mergecount of the auxiliary array.

It now remains only for us to describe what must be done to complete the sort after the end of the input list is reached. If n is an exact power of 2, then the list will be completely sorted at this point. Otherwise, it turns out that

> *At the end of receiving input, the sorted sublists that must still be merged will occupy precisely the same relative positions in the auxiliary array as those occupied by the nonzero digits in the representation of the counter c as a binary integer.*

proof by induction   We can prove this observation by mathematical induction.

When $n = 1$ it is certainly true. In fact, when n is any exact power of 2, $n = 2^k$, the first part of the algorithm will have merged all the items as received into a single sorted sublist, and the integer n when written in binary has a single 1 in the digit position k corresponding to the power of 2, and 0's elsewhere.

Now consider the algorithm for an arbitrary value of n, and let 2^k be the largest power of 2 such that $2^k \leq n$. The binary representation of n contains a 1 in position k (the count of digits starts at 0), which is its largest nonzero digit. The remaining digits form the binary representation of $m = n - 2^k$. When the first 2^k items have been received, the algorithm will have merged them into a single sublist, a pointer to which is in position k of the auxiliary array, corresponding properly to the digit 1 in position k of the binary representation of n. As the remaining m items are processed, they will, by induction hypothesis, produce sublists with pointers in positions corresponding to 1's in the binary representation of m, which, as we have observed, is the same as the remaining positions in the binary representation of n. Hence the proof
end of proof   is complete.

With this background we can now produce a formal description of the algorithm. The notational conventions are those of Section 7.7.

```
#define MAXLOG 20                          /* allows over 1,000,000 entries in list    */

/* NRMergeSort: nonrecursive mergesort */
List_type *NRMergeSort(List_type *head)
{
        List_type *sublist[MAXLOG + 1];
        List_type *p;                      /* first unsorted item from list            */
        List_type *q;                      /* head of a (partial) merged list          */
        int i;
        int c = 0;                         /* counter (index) of current item          */
        int mergecount;                    /* largest power of 2 dividing c             */
        int d;                             /* a digit in binary representation of c     */

        p = head;
        while (p) {                        /* Traverse the unsorted list.              */
                c++;
                mergecount = Power2(c);
                q = p;
                p = p->next;
                q->next = NULL;            /* Split off q as a sublist of size 1.      */
                for (i = 0; i < mergecount; i++)
                        q = Merge(q, sublist[i]);
                sublist[mergecount] = q;
        }

/* At this point, the list has been traversed. The unmerged sublists correspond
   to the 1's in the binary representation of the counter c. Note that p == NULL at
   this point. */

        mergecount = -1;
        while (c != 0) {
                d = c % 2;                 /* d is a binary digit in c.                */
                c /= 2;
                mergecount++;
                if (d != 0)
                        if (p == NULL)     /* This only occurs for first nonzero d.    */
                                p = sublist[mergecount];
                        else
                                p = Merge(p, sublist[mergecount]);
        }
        return p;
}
```

Exercise B.4

E1. The algorithm for the Towers of Hanoi has a completely symmetric recursion tree. Design a nonrecursive program for this problem that uses no stacks, lists, or arrays.

Programming   **P1.** Run the nonrecursive mergesort of this section, and compare timings with those of
Project B.4   the recursive version of Section 7.7.

B.5 THREADED BINARY TREES

Because of the importance of linked binary trees, it is worthwhile to develop nonrecursive
algorithms to manipulate them, and to study the time and space requirements of these
algorithms. We shall find that, by changing the NULL links in a binary tree to special
links called *threads*, it is possible to perform traversals, insertions, and deletions without
using either a stack or recursion.

B.5.1 Introduction

First, let us note that the second recursive call in the ordinary recursive versions of both
preorder and inorder traversal of a linked binary tree is tail recursion, and so can be
removed easily, with no need to set up a stack. From now on we shall assume that this
has been done, so that preorder and inorder traversal each involve only one recursive
call. The situation with postorder traversal is more complicated, so we shall postpone
its study to the end of the section.

use of stack   Removal of the remaining recursive call in preorder or inorder traversal does at
first appear to require a stack. Let us see how many entries can possibly be on the
stack. Since the functions use no local variables, the only value to be stacked is the
calling parameter, which is a (simple, one-word) pointer variable, a pointer to the current
position in the tree. After the pointer has been stacked, the algorithm moves to the left
subtree as it calls itself. (Note that when the algorithm later moves to the right subtree it
need only change the pointer, not push it onto the stack, since the tail recursion has been
removed.) The pointers stop being stacked and the recursion terminates when a leaf is
reached. Thus the total number of pointers that may appear on the stack is the number
of left branches taken in a path from the root to a leaf of the tree, plus one more since
a pointer to the leaf itself is stacked. The algorithms could easily be rewritten to avoid
stacking this last pointer.

Since most binary trees are fairly bushy, the number of pointers on the stack is likely
to be $O(\log n)$ if the tree has n nodes. Since $\lg n$ is generally small in comparison to
n, the space taken by the stack is usually small in comparison to the space needed for
the nodes themselves. Thus if it is reasonable to assume that the tree is quite bushy, then
it is probably not worth the effort to pursue sophisticated methods to save space, and
either the recursive algorithms or their straightforward translation to nonrecursive form
with a stack will likely be satisfactory.

It is, on the other hand, certainly possible that a binary tree will have few right
branches and many left branches. In fact, the tree that is a chain moving to the left will
put pointers to every one of its nodes onto the stack before working out of the recursion.
stack space   Hence, if we wish to ensure that the traversal algorithms will never fail for want of space,
we must be careful to reserve stack space for $n + 1$ pointers if there are n nodes in the
binary tree. (Keeping the recursion for the system to handle will, of course, not help at
all, since the system must still find space for the stack, and will likely also use space for
stacking return addresses, etc., and so will need more than $n + 1$ words of memory.) If

we are working with a large binary tree that takes almost all the memory, then finding extra stack space can be a problem.

Whenever you run out of some resource, a good question to ask yourself is whether some of that same resource is being left unused elsewhere. In the current problem, the answer is *yes*. For all the leaves of any binary tree, both the left and right pointers are NULL, and often for some of the other nodes one of the pointers is NULL. In fact, the following easy observation shows that there are exactly enough NULL pointers in the tree to take care of the stack.

LEMMA B.2   *A linked binary tree with n nodes, $n \geq 0$, has exactly $n + 1$ NULL links.*

Proof   We first note that each node of the tree contains two pointers, so there are $2n$ pointers altogether in a tree with n nodes, plus one more in the header. There is exactly one pointer to each of the n nodes of the tree (coming from the parent of each node except the root, and from the header to the root). Thus the number of NULL pointers is exactly

$$(2n + 1) - n = n + 1.$$

With this result, we could devise an algorithm to use the space occupied by NULL pointers and traverse the tree with no need for auxiliary space for a stack.

We shall not solve the problem this way, however, because of one danger in such a method. If the program should happen to crash in the middle of traversing the binary tree, having changed various pointers within the tree to reflect a (now-forgotten) current situation, it may later be difficult or impossible to recover the structure of the original tree. We might thereby lose all our data, with far more serious consequences than the original crash.

goal   What we want, then, is a way to set up the pointers within the binary tree permanently so that the NULL pointers will be replaced with information that will make it easy to traverse the tree (in either preorder or inorder) without setting up a stack or using recursion.

Let us see how far ordinary inorder traversal can go before it must pop the stack. It begins by moving left as many times as it can, while the left subtree is not empty. Then it visits the node and moves to the right subtree (if nonempty) and repeats the process, moving to the left again. Only when it has just visited a node and finds that its right subtree is empty must it pop the stack to see where to go next. In C we could write

```
p = root;                         /* pointer that moves through the tree      */
while (p) {
    while (p->left)
        p = p->left;
    Visit(p);
    p = p->right;
}
```

When this sequence of instructions is complete, we have p = NULL, and we must find some way to locate the next node under inorder traversal.

B.5.2 Threads

In a ***right-threaded binary tree*** each NULL right link is replaced by a special link to the successor of that node under inorder traversal, called a ***right thread***. Using right threads we shall find it easy to do an inorder traversal of the tree, since we need only follow either an ordinary link or a thread to find the next node to visit. For later applications, we shall also find it useful to put ***left threads*** into the tree, which means to replace each NULL left link by a special link to the predecessor of the node under inorder traversal. The result is called a ***fully threaded binary tree***. The word *fully* is omitted if there is no danger of confusion. Figure B.3 shows a threaded binary tree, where the threads are shown as dotted lines.

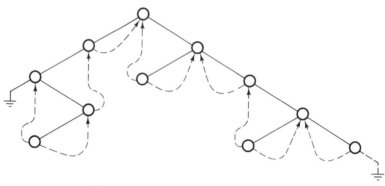

Figure B.3. A fully threaded binary tree

Note that two threads have been left as NULL in the diagram, the left thread from the first node under inorder traversal, and the right thread from the last node. We shall leave these two pointers as NULL. Another convention that is sometimes useful is to let these two nodes have threads pointing back to the root of the tree. This convention sometimes makes termination conditions slightly more complicated, but sometimes allows easier repetition of the full traversal of the tree, if that is desired.

implementation   In implementing threads in a programming language, we must have some way to determine whether each link is a true pointer to a nonempty subtree, or a thread to some node higher in the tree. With C structures, the usual way to do this would be to attach to each pointer a Boolean variable (that need only take one bit) that specifies if the pointer is a link or a thread.

In some environments, however, we can represent threads even more compactly. Nonrecursive traversal is most commonly used in nonrecursive languages, and in this case the nodes are usually represented as entries of arrays, and the pointers are indices (cursors) within the arrays. Thus true links are represented as positive integers, and the NULL link is usually represented as 0. We can then easily represent threads as negative integers, so that if a pointer variable p is less than 0, then it is a thread to the node at $-p$.

For the remainder of this section we shall adopt this positive-negative convention, and use the implementation of linked lists with cursors in a workspace array that was developed in Section 4.5. This decision is implemented in the following declarations (tree.h), for which the constant MAX gives the size (in nodes) of the workspace ws.

```
typedef int Key_type;

typedef struct node_tag {
        Key_type key;
        /* Other information fields go here. */
        int left, right;
} Node_type;

Node_type ws [MAX + 1];          /* workspace for linked trees           */
int root;                        /* root of the threaded binary search tree */

typedef enum action_tag {GOLEFT, GORIGHT, VISITNODE} Action_type;
```

B.5.3 Inorder and Preorder Traversal

First, let us see how easy it now is to traverse a threaded binary tree in inorder.

```
/* Inorder: inorder traversal of a threaded binary tree */
void Inorder (int p)
{
        if (p > 0)                      /* Find the first (leftmost) node for inorder traversal. */
                while (ws [p] .left > 0)
                        p = ws [p] .left;
        while (p) {                     /* Now visit the node, and go to its successor. */
                Visit (p);
                p = ws [p] .right;
                if (p < 0)              /* If this is a thread link, it gives the successor. */
                        p = -p;
                else if (p > 0)         /* Otherwise, move as far left as possible. */
                        while (ws [p] .left > 0)
                                p = ws [p] .left;
                /* If neither section is done, p = 0 and the traversal is done. */
        }
}
```

As you can see, this algorithm is somewhat longer than the original algorithm for inorder traversal. A direct translation of the original algorithm into nonrecursive form would be of comparable length and would, of course, require additional space for a stack that is not needed when we use threaded trees.

It is a surprising fact that preorder traversal of an inorder threaded tree is just as easy to write:

```
/* Preorder: preorder traversal of a threaded binary tree */
void Preorder(int p)
{
    while (p > 0) {
        Visit(p);
        if (ws[p].left > 0)
            p = ws[p].left;
        else if (ws[p].right > 0)
            p = ws[p].right;
/* Otherwise, p is a leaf. We take its right thread, which will return to a node
    already visited, and move to the right again. */
        else {
            while (ws[p].right < 0)
                p = -ws[p].right;
            p = ws[p].right;
        }
    }
}
```

B.5.4 Insertion in a Threaded Tree

To use threaded trees, we must be able to set them up. Thus we need an algorithm to add a node to the tree. We first consider the case where a node is added to the left of a node that previously had an empty left subtree. The other side is similar. Since the node we are considering has empty left subtree, its left link is a thread to its predecessor under inorder traversal, which will now become the predecessor of the new node being added. The successor of the new node will, of course, be the node to which it is attached on the left. This situation is illustrated in Figure B.4 and implemented in the following function.

```
/* LeftInsert: inserts the node at q as the left subtree of the node at p */
void LeftInsert(int q, int p)
{
    if (ws[p].left > 0) {
        Error("non-empty left subtree");
    } else {
        ws[q].left = ws[p].left;
        ws[q].right = -p;
        ws[p].left = q;
    }
}
```

The general insertion algorithm for a threaded binary search tree can now be formulated like the nonrecursive insertion function developed in Section 9.4.1.

```
/* Insert: inserts the node at q into a threaded tree given by root */
int Insert(int q, int root)
{
    int k;

    if (root == 0) {                    /* Insert into an empty tree.           */
        ws[q].left = 0;
        ws[q].right = 0;
        return q;
    } else {                /* Look for the place for the new key, starting at the root. */
        k = root;
        do {
            if (ws[q].key < ws[k].key) {
                if (ws[k].left <= 0) {
                    /* We have an empty left subtree, insert the node. */
                    LeftInsert(q, k);
                    break;
                } else          /* Move to left subtree and continue search. */
                    k = ws[k].left;
            } else if (ws[q].key > ws[k].key) {
                if (ws[k].right <= 0) {
                    /* We have an empty right subtree, insert the node. */
                    RightInsert(q, k);
                    break;
                } else          /* Move to right subtree and continue search. */
                    k = ws[k].right;
            } else {                    /* We have found a duplicate of the new key. */
                printf("Duplicate key: %d at positions %d and %d\n",
                    ws[q].key, q, k);
                break;
            }
        } while (1);
        return root;
    }
}
```

As you can see, this algorithm is only a little more complicated than that required to add a node to an unthreaded tree. Similarly, an algorithm to delete a node (which is left as an exercise) is not much more difficult than before. It is only in the traversal algorithms where the additional cases lengthen the programs. Whether the saving of stack space is worth the programming time needed to use threads depends, as usual, on the circumstances. The differences in running time will usually be insignificant; it is only the saving in stack space that need be considered. Even this is lessened if the device of using negative indices to represent threads is not available.

Finally, we should mention the possibility of shared subtrees. In some applications a subtree of a binary tree is sometimes processed separately from other actions taken on

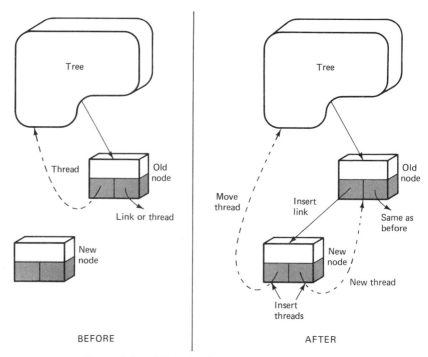

Figure B.4. Adding a node to a threaded binary tree

the entire tree. With ordinary binary trees this can be done easily by setting the root of the subtree to the appropriate node of the larger tree. With threads, however, traversal of the smaller tree will fail to terminate properly, since after all nodes of the subtree have been traversed, there may still be a thread pointing to some successor node in the larger tree. Hence threads are often better avoided when processing complicated data structures with shared substructures.

B.5.5 Postorder Traversal

Traversal of a threaded binary tree in postorder, using neither recursion nor stacks, is somewhat more complicated than the other traversal orders. The reason is that postorder traversal investigates each node several times. When a node is first reached, its left subtree is traversed. The traversal then returns to the node in order to traverse its right subtree. Only when it returns to the node the third time does it actually visit the node. Finally it must find the parent of the node to continue the traversal.

We can obtain an initial outline of an algorithm by following these steps. We shall use the enumerated type

```
typedef enum action_tag {GOLEFT, GORIGHT, VISITNODE} Action_type;
```

to indicate the stage of processing the node in the following outline.

outline   void PostOrder(void)

```
{
    while (not all nodes have been visited)
        switch (nextaction) {
        case GOLEFT:
            Traverse the left subtree;
            Return to the node;
            nextaction = GORIGHT;
            break;
        case GORIGHT:
            Traverse the right subtree;
            Return to the node;
            nextaction = VISITNODE;
            break;
        case VISITNODE:
            Visit the node;
            Find the parent of the node;
            Set nextaction appropriately for the parent;
            break;
        }
}
```

Note that this algorithm is written so that it performs three iterations for each node. In this way, at every point we need only know the value of nextaction to determine at what stage of the traversal we are. Had we written the three stages sequentially within a single iteration of the loop, then we would need to use recursion or a stack to determine our status after completing the traversal of a subtree.

Closer consideration, however, will show that even this outline does not yet succeed in avoiding the need for a stack. As we traverse a subtree, we shall continually change nextaction as we process each node of the subtree. Hence we must use some method to determine the previous value as we return to the original node. We shall first postpone this problem, however, by assuming the existence of an auxiliary function Parent that will determine the parent of a node and the new value of nextaction.

With these assumptions we arrive at the following function.

```
/* PostOrder: postorder traversal of binary tree with (inorder) threads */
void PostOrder(int p)
{
    Action_type nextaction;

    nextaction = GOLEFT;
    while (p)
        switch (nextaction) {
        case GOLEFT:                        /* Traverse the left subtree if it is nonempty. */
            if (ws[p].left > 0)
                p = ws[p].left;
            else
                nextaction = GORIGHT;
            break;
```

```
case GORIGHT:                    /* Traverse the right subtree if it is nonempty. */
    if (ws [p] .right > 0) {
        p = ws [p] .right;
        nextaction = GOLEFT;
    } else
        nextaction = VISITNODE;
    break;

case VISITNODE:                  /* Visit the node and find its parent.        */
    Visit (p) ;
    Parent (p, &p, &nextaction) ;
    break;
    }
}
```

Finally, we must solve the problem of locating the parent of a node and determining the proper value of the code, without resorting to stacks or recursion. The solution to this problem, fortunately, already appears in the outline obtained earlier. If we have *finding the parent* just finished traversing a left subtree, then we should now set nextaction to GORIGHT; if we have traversed a right subtree, then nextaction becomes VISITNODE. We can determine which of these cases has occurred by using the threads, and at the same time we can find the node that is the parent node of the last one visited. If we are in a left subtree, then we find the parent by moving right as far as possible in the subtree, then take a right thread. If the left child of this node is the original one, then we know that we have found the parent and are in a left subtree. Otherwise, we must do the similar steps through left branches to find the parent. This process is illustrated in Figure B.5.

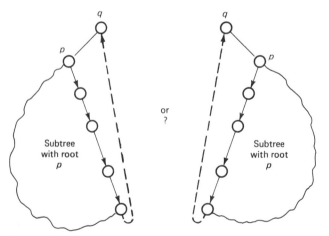

Figure B.5. Finding the parent of a node in a threaded tree

The translation of this method into a formal function is straightforward.

```
/* Parent:  Finds the parent of node p, and sets q to the parent.  Returns nextac-
   tion = GORIGHT if p is the left child of q, and nextaction = VISITNODE if p is the right
   child of q.  If p is the root, returns q = 0. */
void Parent(int p, int *q, Action_type *nextaction)
{
        *q = p;                         /* Locate the inorder successor of p; set it to q. */
        while (*q > 0)
                *q = ws[*q].right;
        if (*q == 0)                    /* No successor: p cannot be a left child. */
                *nextaction = VISITNODE;
        else if (ws[−*q].left == p) {   /* p is left child of −q.                   */
                *nextaction = GORIGHT;
                *q = −*q;
        } else
                *nextaction = VISITNODE;
/* If nextaction = GORIGHT, then we are finished.  If nextaction = VISITNODE, find the
   parent as the inorder predecessor of subtree of p. */
        if (*nextaction == VISITNODE) {
                *q = p;
                while (*q > 0)
                        *q = ws[*q].left;
                *q = −*q;
        }
}
```

Exercises
B.5

E1. Write the threaded-tree algorithms in C for **(a)** insertion of a new node on the left, **(b)** inorder traversal, and **(c)** preorder traversal, using dynamic memory and Boolean flags to determine whether links are threads or real branches.

E2. What changes must be made in the algorithm of Section 9.2 in order to search for a key in a threaded binary search tree?

E3. Write a function to insert a new node on the right of one in a threaded binary tree.

E4. Write a function to delete a node from a threaded binary tree.

E5. Write a function that will insert threads into an unthreaded binary tree, by traversing it once in inorder, using a stack.

E6. Modify the function of Exercise E5 so that it uses no extra space for a stack, but the unused link space and threads already constructed instead.

E7. Write a function to insert a new node between two others in a threaded binary tree. That is, if p is a link to a node in the threaded tree, and p has nonempty left subtree, insert the new node (with q the pointer to it) as the left subtree of the one at p, with the left subtree of q being the former left subtree of p, and the right subtree of q being empty. Be sure to adjust all threads properly.

REFERENCES FOR FURTHER STUDY

Some good ideas about techniques and procedures for the removal of recursion appear in

D. E. KNUTH, "Structured programming with goto statements", *Computing Surveys* 6 (1974), 261–302.

R. S. BIRD, "Notes on recursion elimination", *Communications of the ACM* 20 (1977), 434–439.

R. S. BIRD, "Improving programs by the introduction of recursion", *Communications of the ACM* 20 (1977), 856–863.

KNUTH (*op. cit.*, page 281) writes

There has been a good deal published about recursion elimination ... ; but I'm amazed that very little of this is about "down to earth" problems. I have always felt that the transformation from recursion to iteration is one of the most fundamental concepts of computer science, and that a student should learn it at about the same time he is studying data structures.

A nonrecursive program using no stack is developed for the Towers of Hanoi in the paper

HELMUT PARTSCH and PETER PEPPER, "A family of rules for recursion removal," *Information Processing Letters 5* (1976), 174–177.

Further papers on the Towers of Hanoi appear sporadically in the *SIGPLAN Notices* published by the A.C.M.

Presentation of nonrecursive versions of quicksort is a common topic, but so many slight variations are possible that few of the resulting programs are exactly the same. More extensive analysis is given in:

ROBERT SEDGEWICK, "The analysis of quicksort programs", *Acta Informatica 7* (1976/77), 327–355.

Threaded binary trees constitute a standard topic in data structures, and will appear in most textbooks on data structures. Many of these books, however, leave the more complicated algorithms (such as postorder traversal) as exercises. The original reference for right-threaded binary trees is

A. J. PERLIS and C. THORNTON, "Symbol manipulation by threaded lists", *Communications of the ACM 3* (1960), 195–204.

Fully threaded trees were independently discovered by

A. W. HOLT, "A mathematical and applied investigation of tree structures for syntactic analysis", Ph.D. dissertation (mathematics), University of Pennsylvania, 1963.

APPENDIX C

An Introduction to C

C.1 INTRODUCTION

The following sections will give the reader a brief introduction to the C programming language. We have adhered to the American National Standards Institute (ANSI) standard definition of C (hereafter referred to as the ANSI C standard or just ANSI C). For those readers who are not familiar with C, we assume some previous experience with a similar high level language such as Pascal and some rudimentary programming skills. Finally, readers are advised to consult a textbook on C for a thorough treatment of the language. Several such books are listed in the references at the end of this appendix.

C.1.1 Overview of a C Program

A typical C program is made up of several functions which may be contained in one or more source files. Every C program must have a function named main which is where program execution always begins. Each source file is compiled separately, and then all are linked together to form the executable program. Quite often declarations or functions in one source file are referenced in another source file. In order for the compiler to be aware of the external references, "include" files are usually used. These will be covered in a later section.

C.2 C ELEMENTS

C.2.1 Reserved Words

The following are *reserved words* in C:

auto	double	int	struct
break	else	long	switch
case	enum	register	typedef
char	extern	return	union
const	float	short	unsigned
continue	for	signed	void
default	goto	sizeof	volatile
do	if	static	while

These words serve a special purpose and may not be used as program identifiers. Two former reserved words, asm and fortran, may still be found in older programs but are now rarely used.

C.2.2 Constants

Constants are program elements that do not change their value during the course of program execution. C has several different types of constants.

Integer constants are assumed to be decimal unless prefixed with a 0 (zero) to signify octal or 0X or 0x to signify hexadecimal. An integer constant may also be suffixed by u or U to specify that it is unsigned or l or L to specify that it is long.

Character constants are delimited by single quotes such as $'x'$. There are several character constants that are used to specify certain special characters.

newline	\n	backslash	\\
horizontal tab	\t	single quote	\'
vertical tab	\v	double quote	\"
backspace	\b	audible alert	\a
carriage return	\r	octal number	\ooo
formfeed	\f	hex number	\xhh

The octal and hex number escapes are used to specify the code of the desired character. For example, $'\007'$ or $'\x7'$ may be used to specify the ASCII bell character.

Floating point constants are decimal numbers with an optional signed integer exponent specified with either e or E. The number may also be suffixed by f, F, l or L to specify float or long double. If no suffix is given, the default is double.

String constants are a sequence of characters delimited by double quotes, for example, "this is a string". The double quotes are not part of the string itself. A string constant is actually represented internally as an array of characters terminated by the null character $'\0'$. String handling functions expect the null character to be present, signifying the end of the string.

Enumeration constants are those declared when defining an enumeration. For example, one that will be used throughout the book is

enum boolean_tag { FALSE, TRUE };

This statement defines FALSE and TRUE to be enumeration constants with the values 0 and 1 respectively. Enumerations will be covered in more detail in a later section.

Symbolic constants are handled by the C preprocessor and are defined using the #define construct. It is a good programming practice to use symbolic constants where possible. This enables certain changes to be made with a minimal amount of effort. For instance,

#define MAXSIZE 20

defines the symbolic constant MAXSIZE to represent the value 20. MAXSIZE may now be used to define arrays, loop bounds, and such within the program. Now suppose the programmer decides to change this value to 100. Only one change is necessary; yet the change will be reflected throughout the program.

Finally, there is also the const qualifier that may be applied to any variable declaration to signify that its value cannot be modified. Hence, the following declares the floating point variable pi to be constant.

const float pi = 3.1416;

C.3 TYPES AND DECLARATIONS

C provides several built-in data types as well as the facilities for the programmer to define further types. Variables are declared using the following syntax:

type identifier_list;

where type is one of the types discussed below and the identifier_list contains one or more comma separated identifiers.

C.3.1 Basic Types

The basic types are char, int, float and double. A char is a single byte, which is capable of holding a single character. The character type may also be qualified with either signed or unsigned. The int type specifies an integer whose size depends on the particular machine. In addition to the signed and unsigned qualifiers, an int may also be short or long. The types float and double specify single-precision and double-precision floating point numbers respectively. The type qualifier long may be applied to double to specify extended-precision floating point. As with integers, the size of these numbers is also machine dependent. There is also a special type called void. It is usually used to declare a function that has no return value or takes no arguments.

C.3.2 Arrays

C allows the declaration of multidimensional arrays using the following form:

type name [constant_expression] . . .

where type is the data type of the array elements, name is the array being declared and constant_expression is the size of the array. All arrays in C are indexed from 0 to constant_expression − 1. The bracketed expression may be repeated to declare arrays with more than one dimension. For example, to declare a 5 by 5 integer matrix named Matrix_A one would use:

int Matrix_A [5] [5] ;

Arrays will be discussed again when pointers are introduced.

C.3.3 Enumerations

Enumerations provide a method of associating a constant set of values to a set of identifiers. Suppose a program was working with the days of the week. Rather than using the numbers 0 through 6 to represent Sunday through Saturday, the following could be used.

enum day_tag {SUNDAY, MONDAY, TUESDAY, WEDNESDAY,
THURSDAY, FRIDAY, SATURDAY};

enum day_tag day_of_week;

The variable day_of_week may take on the values SUNDAY, MONDAY, and so on, which have more intuitive meanings than 0, 1, etc. The advantage of using enumerations over #define is that the values are generated automatically and the declarations of variables contain a little more information as to what values might be assigned. For instance, if the day of the week example had been done using:

```
#define SUNDAY 0
#define MONDAY 1
#define TUESDAY 2
#define WEDNESDAY 3
#define THURSDAY 4
#define FRIDAY 5
#define SATURDAY 6
```

The variable day_of_week would be declared as type int, imposing no restrictions on the integer values it could be assigned. (Note: most compilers do not restrict integer valued assignments to variables declared as enum.)

C.3.4 Structures

The type declaration

struct *tag* { . . . }

in C establishes a type consisting of several ***members*** (also called ***components***), each of which is itself of some (arbitrarily defined) type. The *tag* is optional and is called a *structure tag*. The use of a *tag* gives a name to the structure which can then be used in a subsequent declaration with the bracketed declaration list omitted. For example, we may define a type for a list of integers with the following declaration:

```
                 #define MAXLIST 200                    /* maximum size of lists              */
declaration of list    struct list_tag {
                     int count;                         /* how many elements are in the list  */
                     int entry [MAXLIST] ;              /* the actual list of integers        */
                 };
```

Now when we want a list of integers we can use the following:

struct list_tag list;

which declares list to be our desired list.

1. Accessing Structures

Individual parts of a C structure variable are referenced by giving first the name of the variable, then a period (.), then the member name as declared in the structure. Another method of access involves the arrow (->) operator. This is used when dereferencing a pointer to a structure. (We will discuss pointers in Section C.6.)

C.3.5 Unions

Depending on the particular information stored in a structure, some of the members may sometimes not be used. If the data are of one kind, then one member may be required, but if they are of another kind, a second member will be needed. Suppose, for example, *example* that structures represent geometrical figures. If the figure is a circle, then we wish a member giving the *radius* of the circle. If it is a rectangle, then we wish the *height* and the *width* of the rectangle and whether or not it is a *square*. If it is a triangle, we wish the three *sides* and whether it is *equilateral*, *isosceles*, or *scalene*. For any of the figures we wish to have the *area* and the *circumference*. One way to set up the structure type for all these geometrical figures would be to have separate members for each of the desired attributes, but then, if the figure is a rectangle, the members giving the radius, sides of a square, and kind of triangle would all be meaningless. Similarly, if the figure is a circle or a triangle, several of the members would be undefined.

To avoid this difficulty, C provides **variant structures**, called **unions**, in which certain members are used only when the information in the structure is of a particular kind. Unions are similar to structures except that only one member is active at a time. It is up to the programmer to keep track of which member is currently being used. Thus, a union is a means to store any one of several types using a single variable. Unions are often combined with structures where one member in the structure is a union and another is used as a *tag* to determine which member of the union is in use.

All this will be clarified by returning to our geometrical example. The type specifying the kind of information in the structure is the enumerated type

enum shape_tag { CIRCLE, RECTANGLE, TRIANGLE };

and the type specifying the kind of triangle is

enum triangle_tag { EQUILATERAL, ISOSCELES, SCALENE };

The structure can then be declared as follows:

geometry example

```
struct figure_tag {
        float area;                    /* This is the fixed part of the structure.  */
        float circumference;
        enum shape_tag shape;          /* This is the tag.                          */
        union {
                float radius;          /* first variant for CIRCLE                  */
                struct {               /* second variant for RECTANGLE              */
                        float height;
                        float width;
                        enum boolean_tag square;
                } rectangle;
                struct {               /* third variant for TRIANGLE                */
                        float side1;
                        float side2;
                        float side3;
                        enum triangle_tag kind;
                } triangle;
        } u;
}
```

advantages of unions

The first advantage of unions is that they clarify the logic of the program by showing exactly what information is required in each case. A second advantage is that they allow the system to save space when the program is compiled. Since only one of the union members is usable at any time for a particular union, the others members can be assigned to the same space by the compiler, and hence the total amount of space that needs to be set aside for the union is just the amount needed if the largest member is the one that occurs. This situation is illustrated in Figure C.1 for the example of structures describing geometrical shapes.

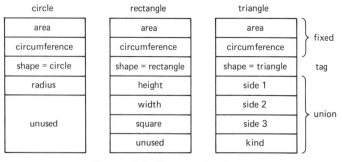

Figure C.1. Storage of unions

C.3.6 typedef

C provides a way of declaring new type names using the typedef construct. The basic syntax is

```
typedef data_type new_name;
```

where new_name is the new name given to the type data_type. (This is a simplified view of typedef, but it is sufficient for our purposes. A C textbook should be consulted for a complete explanation.) For instance, an earlier example declared a structure for a list of integers struct list_tag. If we wanted to give a name to this, such as List_type, we could do so in the following manner

typedef struct list_tag List_type;

To declare a structure for a list of integers we may now use

List_type list;

instead of

struct list_tag list;

(although both are equivalent).

We could also have defined the structure and the type at the same time by using

```
typedef struct list_tag {
    int count;                      /* how many elements are in the list      */
    int entry [MAXLIST];            /* the actual list of integers            */
} List_type;
```

C.4 OPERATORS

C has a large set of operators, and no attempt will be made to explain all of them here. The following chart lists the operators from highest to lowest precedence along with their associativity.

Operators	Associativity
( ) [ ] -> .	*left to right*
! ~ ++ -- + — * & (*type*) sizeof	*right to left*
* / %	*left to right*
+ -	*left to right*
« »	*left to right*
< <= > >=	*left to right*
== !=	*left to right*
&	*left to right*
^	*left to right*
|	*left to right*
&&	*left to right*
||	*left to right*
? :	*right to left*
= += —= *= /= %= &= ^= |= »= «=	*right to left*
,	*left to right*

A few of the operators seem to have two different precedences. This is not the case. The & operator on the second line refers to the address of an object whereas the & operator on the eighth line is the bitwise AND. The $*$ on the second line is the dereferencing operator and the $*$ on the third line is multiplication. The $+$ and $-$ operators on the second line refer to the unary plus and minus as opposed to the binary plus and minus on the fourth line.

The $++$ and $--$ operators are increment and decrement respectively. The $\ll$ and $\gg$ perform left shift and right shift operations. All the operators of the form *op* = are called assignment operators and provide a sort of shorthand. Expressions of the form

variable = variable op value;

may be replaced by

variable op = value;

The ternary operator ? : provides a conditional expression of the form

expression1 ? expression2 : expression3

where expression1 is evaluated first followed by expression2 or expression3 depending on whether expression1 evaluates to *true* (nonzero) or *false*. A C text should be consulted for a full treatment of all the operators.

C.5 CONTROL FLOW STATEMENTS

In C, the semicolon is used as a statement terminator, not a separator as in Pascal. A *null* statement is signified by an isolated semicolon. For example, the following while loop reads characters until a newline is read. All the action is performed in the while expression so a loop body is not needed.

```
while ((ch = getchar()) != '\n')
    /* null statement */;
```

A compound statement, or block, is a series of statements enclosed by braces, i.e.,

```
{
    statement1;
    statement2;
}
```

and is allowed wherever a single statement is valid. Variables may also be declared at the beginning of a block.

C.5.1 If-Else

The if statement has the following syntax,

```
if (expression)
        statement
else
        statement
```

with the else part being optional. If there are several nested if statements without a matching number of else clauses, each else is associated with the most recent previous if statement not containing an else.

C.5.2 Switch

The switch statement is a multiway branch based on a single expression.

```
switch (expression) {
case constant_expression: statements
case constant_expression: statements
/* as many cases as needed... */
default: statements
}
```

If none of the cases satisfy the expression, the default part of the switch is executed. The default clause is optional and the switch statement will do nothing if none of the cases match (any side effects caused by the evaluation of the expression will still occur). The case and default clauses may be in any order.

One very important characteristic of the switch is that the cases *fall through*, that is, execution will continue to the following case unless explicit action is taken to leave the switch. That explicit action comes in the form of the break statement. When used anywhere in a switch statement (usually at the end of a case), the break will cause execution to continue after the switch.

C.5.3 Loops

C provides several loops constructs, two of which test for loop termination at the top of the loop and one that tests at the bottom.

1. While

The while loop has the form:

```
while (expression)
     statement
```

where statement will be executed as long as expression evaluates to a nonzero value.

2. For

The for statement has the following syntax:

```
for (expression1; expression2; expression3)
     statement
```

All three expressions are optional; however, the semicolons are not. The for statement is equivalent to the following while loop:

```
expression1;
while (expression2) {
     statement
     expression3;
}
```

It is not uncommon for the comma operator to be used in expression1 and expression3 to allow multiple initializations and updates.

3. Do-while

The do−while loop in C provides a loop that tests for loop termination at the end of the loop. Its syntax is

do
    statement
while (expression);

where statement will be executed at least once and then as long as expression remains *nonzero* thereafter.

C.5.4 Break and Continue

The break statement will cause program execution to continue after the enclosing for, while, do or switch statement. The continue statement will result in the next iteration of the enclosing for, while or do loop to execute.

C.5.5 Goto

C does contain the goto statement but since its use is not looked upon with favor, it will not be discussed here.

C.6 POINTERS

A pointer is a variable that may contain the address of another variable. All variables in C, except variables of type register, have an address. The address is the location where the variable exists in memory. We use a ∗ in front of a variable to declare the variable to be a pointer.

C.6.1 Pointer to a Simple Variable

We can declare a variable of type char by

char c = 'a';

and we can declare a pointer to something of type char by

char ∗p;

where p is the pointer. The ∗ in front of p identifies it as a pointer, that is, a variable that may contain the address of another variable. In this case, p is a pointer to something of type char so p may contain the address of a variable of type char.

The pointer p has not been initialized yet so its current value is undefined—its value is whatever existed in the space reserved for p. To initialize the pointer we need to assign it an address. We can obtain the address of a simple variable by using the unary operator &:

p = &c;

Now p contains the address of the variable c. It is important that the type of the variable and the type of the pointer match. We will explain why when we discuss pointers to arrays.

To refer to a value that a pointer points to we need to *dereference* the pointer. In effect, we take the value in p, an address, and we go to that address to get the final value. Thus the following two statements print the same value:

```
printf("c is %c\n", c);
printf("c is %c\n", *p);
```

We can refer to the variable c by using its name or by using the pointer p that points to c. Consequently, we can change the value of c to be the representation for 'b' by using an assignment to c or indirectly (dereferencing) by using the pointer p:

```
p = &c;        /* initialize p          */
c = 'b';       /* assigns 'b' to c      */
*p = 'b';      /* assigns 'b' to c      */
```

C.6.2 Pointer to an Array

We can declare an array of characters and a pointer to character. For example,

```
char line[100], *p;
```

We may refer to the first two elements of line using

```
line[0] = 'a';
line[1] = 'b';
```

For each assignment the compiler will have to calculate the address: line plus offset zero, and line plus offset one. Another way to perform the above assignments is to use a pointer. First, we need to initialize the pointer p to point to the beginning of the array line:

```
p = &line[0];
```

Since an array name is a synonym for the array's starting address we can use

```
p = line;
```

Now we can perform the assignments

```
*p = 'a';
```

and

```
*(p + 1) = 'b';
```

The pointer p continues to point to the beginning of the array line. As an alternative, we could increment the pointer after each assignment

$$*p++ = 'a';$$
$$*p++ = 'b';$$

and the pointer p will be pointing to line [2] after the assignments.

When we use + 1 or the ++ operator with a pointer we are referring to the next element after the current element. If p points to the beginning of the array line (line [0]), then p++ moves the pointer to line [1]. Notice that when we increment the pointer we point to the next element of the array. In this case the pointer is of type char so when we increment it we point to the next byte which is the next character.

If we have a pointer to an int,

> int numbers [10], *q = numbers;

then q points to numbers [0]. When we increment q we point to numbers [1] which could be two or four bytes away—depending on the hardware you are using an int could be two bytes or four bytes long.

We can add an integer expression to a pointer or we can subtract an integer expression from a pointer. We can also compare two pointers if they point to the same array, otherwise the comparison is not meaningful.

C.6.3 Array of Pointers

In C we can create arrays of variables of any type. Since a pointer is a variable that may contain the address of another variable it is feasible to create an array of pointers. Each element of the array is a pointer. For example, the declaration

> char *ap [3];

declares ap as an array of pointers to char. Each element of ap may point to the beginning of a character string. If we use malloc to allocate space for each string then each element of ap may point to some area in memory that contains the string. On the other hand, the strings could be in some array line with each element of ap pointing to different parts of the array.

C.6.4 Pointer to Structures

We can declare an array of structures and then use a pointer to point to the first element of the array. This is similar to the pointer to arrays we discussed above. For example,

```
struct example_tag {
        char c;
        int i;
};
struct example_tag ae [10], *p;
p = ae;
p->c = 'a';              /* character in the first structure        */
p->i = 0;               /* integer in the first structure          */
p++;                    /* make p point to ae [1]                  */
p->c = 'b';             /* character in the second structure       */
```

The -> operator is used to dereference a pointer to a structure and access a member of that structure. The construction p->c is therefore equivalent to (*p).c.

An element of a structure can be a pointer to another structure of the same type. This is called a *self-referential* structure. For example,

```
struct selfref_tag {
        char c;
        struct selfref_tag *next;
};
struct selfref_tag *p;
```

declares p as a pointer to a structure of type struct selfref_tag. This could be a linked list (see Chapter 4) and p points to a structure in the list. To access the next element in the list we use

```
p = p->next;
```

since the structure contains the address of the next structure in the pointer next.

C.7 FUNCTIONS

In programming we normally break a task into separate functions because it is easier to deal with smaller tasks that may be independent of other parts of the program. A C program is normally a collection of functions. The main program, called main, is a function that may invoke other functions. The information we pass to a function is called an *argument*. The information the function receives is called a *parameter*.

The ANSI C standard allows the programmer to declare a *function prototype*, which is a concise way of describing the number and type of arguments a function expects and what the function returns. Take for example, the following code:

```
void f(int);

int main(void)
{
    int i = 3;

    f(i);
    return 0;
}
```

The main program is a function main that does not expect any arguments and returns an integer to the calling environment. The function f expects one argument of type integer and does not return anything to its calling function.

The function prototype informs the compiler of the number and type of arguments it expects. If the function does not expect any arguments then we use void, in parentheses, to indicate that fact. The type in front of the function name indicates the type of the expression returned. If the function does not return anything we use void as the return type.

C.7.1 Arguments to Functions: Call by Value

C passes arguments to functions by value. That is, C makes a copy of the argument and passes the copy to the function: in effect it passes the value of the argument to the function. If the function modifies a parameter, the function is modifying only a copy of the original argument. Consider the function

```
void f(int j)
{
    j——;
    printf("j is %d\n", j);
}
```

f receives an integer, decrements it, prints its new value, and returns. If we invoke f with the argument i,

```
int i = 3;
```

```
f(i);
```

the function receives a copy of i. When f decrements j it decrements a copy of the argument but not the argument itself. When the function returns, the value of i has not changed.

C.7.2 Arguments to Functions: Call by Reference

Often we want the function to have access to the original argument in the invoking function instead of its copy. In this case we pass the argument by reference; that is, we pass the address of the argument as a parameter for the function. Since the function has the address of the actual argument (not just a copy), it can change the value of this argument. For example, the function

```
void g(int *k)
{
    *k = 2;
}
```

expects a pointer to an integer variable and assigns 2 to the integer variable that k points to. As an example of invoking this function, consider the following code

```
void g(int *);
```

```
int main(void)
{
    int i;

    g(&i);
    printf("i = %d\n", i);
    return 0;
}
```

This program passes the address of the variable i to g, the function receives a pointer to a variable in the invoking function (the address of i), and it modifies i. When the function g terminates the main program has a modified variable i.

Arrays provide an exception to the rule of pass by value in C. Arrays are always passed by reference.

```
int getline (char *, int);
...
int n;
char line [100];
n = getline (line, 100);
```

The above code fragment invokes a function getline that expects a pointer to a character and an integer. Since an array name is like an address we pass the array name, line, and an integer that indicates the size of the array. If the function modifies the first parameter it modifies the array in the invoking function.

C.7.3 Function Prototypes and Include Files

A *function prototype* is a declaration of a function type (what it returns) and the number and type of arguments, if any, that the function expects. Our earlier example,

```
void f (int);
```

is the function prototype for the function f. The function expects one argument of type int and it does not return anything as the function value; consequently it has the type void.

Standard library functions have their prototypes in the *.h files (where * denotes any name) available with your C compiler. Check your documentation to find out which *.h file applies to the library functions you are going to use. For example, the function strcpy has its prototype in string.h, so in order to let the compiler know what arguments strcpy expects and what it returns we include string.h in our program:

```
#include <string.h>

...
char buffer [100], line [100];
...
strcpy (line, buffer);
```

Standard *.h file names are enclosed in angle brackets < ... > . Other *.h files that we create are in the current directory and their names are enclosed in double quotes. If we put the prototype for the function getline in a file called calls.h then the code fragment we used earlier could change to

```
#include "calls.h"

...
int n;
char line [100];
n = getline (line, 100);
```

C.8 POINTERS AND FUNCTIONS

We now discuss some common operations using pointers and functions.

C.8.1 Pointer to a Function

In C we can get the address of a function as well as that of variables. This allows us to pass a pointer to a function as an argument to another function. For example, we can write a function sort that invokes another function to perform the comparison of the elements being sorted. We can pass to sort the address of the function that will perform the comparisons. If we are sorting character strings we can use the standard library function strcmp and if we are sorting integers we can write our own numcmp function. The code fragment could look like

```
int strcmp (char *, char *);
int numcmp (char *, char *);

void sort (int (*fnc_ptr) (char *, char *));

void main (void)
{
    . . .
    sort (strcmp);                    /* Sort character strings.      */
    . . .
    sort (numcmp);                    /* Sort integers.               */
}
```

The function sort expects one argument: a pointer to a function that expects two pointers to characters and returns an integer. Normally the integer returned is < 0 when the first argument is less than the second, 0 when the arguments are equal, and > 0 when the first argument is greater than the second. The definition for less than, equal, and greater than depends on the application. The function sort will eventually invoke the function whose address we passed:

```
void sort (int (*f) (char *, char *))
{
    int condition;
    char *p, *q;
        /* p and q are initialized. */

        . . .
    condition = (*f) (p, q);
        . . .
        /* Take an action based on the condition. */
}
```

C.8.2 Functions that Return a Pointer

There are some standard library functions that return a pointer, such as strcpy (char *to, char *from), which copies the string from to the string to and returns a pointer to the beginning of the string to. The function prototype for strcpy appears in the standard include file string.h and looks like

```
char *strcpy(char *, char *);
```

The type char * in front of the function name indicates the type returned: strcpy returns a pointer to a character.

We can write our own functions that return pointers. In Chapter 4 we wrote a function MakeNode that allocates space for a node and returns a pointer to the allocated space. Each node is a structure defined as

```
typedef char Item_type;
```

```
typedef struct node_tag {
        Item_type item;
        struct node_tag *next;
} Node_type;
```

MakeNode expects an argument, invokes the standard library function malloc to allocate enough space for a node, copies the argument into the node, and returns a pointer to the node. The function looks like

```
/* MakeNode: make a new node and insert item. */
Node_type *MakeNode(Item_type item)
{
    Node_type *p;
    if ((p = (Node_type *)malloc(sizeof(Node_type))) != NULL)
        p->info = item;
    return p;
}
```

C.8.3 Pointer to a Pointer as an Argument

Whenever we want to modify an argument we pass it by reference. For example, we invoke a function f that modifies whatever the pointer p points to:

```
void f(char *);
```

```
void main(void)
{
    char c;
    f( &c);
}
void f(char *p)
{
    *p = 'a';
}
```

What if we want to modify the pointer itself, instead of what it points to? Then we have to pass the pointer by reference. We do that by passing the address of the pointer. What should the function expect? The function should expect the address of a variable that in this case is a pointer—a pointer to a pointer. The code fragment could look like

```
void g (char **);
void main (void)
{
    char line [100];
    char *p = line;              /* p points to line [0]           */

    g ( &p);                     /* p points to line [1]           */
}
void g (char **p)
{
    (*p)++;                      /* Increment the pointer.         */
}
```

As you may suspect, there is a lot more about functions, about pointers, about C. This has been an introduction to some aspects of the language that we use in this book. As you write programs in C these constructs become familiar and you become proficient in the language and in data structures.

REFERENCES FOR FURTHER STUDY

The programming language C was devised by DENNIS M. RITCHIE. The standard reference is

> BRIAN W. KERNIGHAN and DENNIS M. RITCHIE, *The C Programming Language*, second edition, Prentice Hall, Englewood Cliffs, N.J., 1988, 272 pages.

This book contains many examples and exercises. For the solutions to the exercises in KERNIGHAN and RITCHIE, together with a chance to study C code, see

> CLOVIS L. TONDO and SCOTT E. GIMPEL, *The C Answer Book*, second edition, Prentice Hall, Englewood Cliffs, N.J., 1989, 208 pages.

Two more references are

> SAMUEL P. HARBISON and GUY L. STEELE JR., *C: A Reference Manual*, second edition, Prentice Hall, Englewood Cliffs, N.J., 1987, 404 pages.

> NARAIN GEHANI, *C: An Advanced Introduction*, Computer Science Press, Rockville, Maryland, 1985, 332 pages.

Beginning and intermediate-level programmers may find the following books to be more readable.

> THOMAS PLUM, *Learning to Program in C*, Prentice Hall, Englewood Cliffs, N.J., 1983.

> ALLEN I. HOLUB, *The C Companion*, Prentice Hall, Englewood Cliffs, N.J., 1987, 284 pages.

Index

M

N

O